Also by Jimmy Carter

We Can Have Peace in the Holy Land: A Plan That Will Work
A Remarkable Mother
Beyond the White House: Waging Peace, Fighting Disease, Building Hope
Palestine Peace Not Apartheid
Our Endangered Values: America's Moral Crisis
Sharing Good Times
The Hornet's Nest: A Novel of the Revolutionary War
The Nobel Peace Prize Lecture
Christmas in Plains: Memories (illustrated by Amy Carter)
An Hour Before Daylight: Memories of a Rural Boyhood
The Virtues of Aging
Sources of Strength: Meditations on Scripture for a Living Faith
Living Faith
The Little Baby Snoogle-Fleejer (illustrated by Amy Carter)
Always a Reckoning, and Other Poems (illustrated by
Sarah Elizabeth Chuldenko)
Talking Peace: A Vision for the Next Generation
Turning Point: A Candidate, a State, and a Nation Come of Age
An Outdoor Journal: Adventures and Reflections
Everything to Gain: Making the Most of the Rest of Your Life
(with Rosalynn Carter)
The Blood of Abraham: Insights into the Middle East
Negotiation: The Alternative to Hostility
Keeping Faith: Memoirs of a President
A Government as Good as Its People
Why Not the Best?

WHITE HOUSE DIARY

WHITE HOUSE DIARY

JIMMY CARTER

FARRAR, STRAUS AND GIROUX   NEW YORK

FARRAR, STRAUS AND GIROUX
18 West 18th Street, New York 10011

Unless otherwise noted, all photos in the insert following page 302 are courtesy
of the Jimmy Carter Presidential Library and Museum.

Library of Congress Cataloging-in-Publication Data
Carter, Jimmy, 1924–
     White House diary / Jimmy Carter. — 1st ed.
          p.   cm.
     Includes index.
     ISBN 978-0-374-28099-4 (alk. paper)
     1. Carter, Jimmy, 1924—Diaries.   2. Presidents—United States—Diaries.
     3. United States—Politics and government—1977–1981.   I. Title.

E873.A3 2010
973.926092—dc22

                                                                    2010015544

Designed by Abby Kagan

www.fsgbooks.com

1   3   5   7   9   10   8   6   4   2

To the memory

of my chief of staff,

Hamilton Jordan,

and my press secretary,

Jody Powell

Contents

A Chronology of My White House Years
ix
Senior Officials in My Administration
xi
Preface
xiii

Prelude: The Campaign
3

1977
7

1978
157

1979
269

1980
385

1981
501

Aftermath
519

Afterword
525

Acknowledgments
539

Index
541

A Chronology of My White House Years

1977

JANUARY 20	Inaugurated as thirty-ninth president
APRIL 4	First meeting with Anwar Sadat
APRIL 18	Address to nation on energy
MAY 7–8	London Economic Summit
JUNE 30	Announcement of end of B-1 bomber production
JULY 19	First meeting with Menachem Begin
AUGUST 4	Establishment of Department of Energy
SEPTEMBER 7	Signing ceremony for Panama Canal treaties
SEPTEMBER 21	Bert Lance resigns
OCTOBER 5	Signing of international covenants on human rights
DECEMBER 29–	Visits to Poland, Iran, India, Saudi Arabia,
JANUARY 6	France, Belgium, and Egypt

1978

MARCH 16	Senate ratifies first Panama Canal Treaty
APRIL 3	Visits to Venezuela, Brazil, Nigeria, and Liberia
APRIL 18	Senate ratifies second Panama Canal Treaty
JUNE 7	Speech on U.S.-Soviet relations at Annapolis
SEPTEMBER 5	Camp David Middle East peace talks begin
SEPTEMBER 17	Camp David Accords signed
OCTOBER 13	Signing of Civil Service Reform Act
OCTOBER 15	Congress passes energy package
DECEMBER 15	Announcement of normalization of relations with People's Republic of China

1979

JANUARY 16	Shah leaves Iran
JANUARY 29–31	Meetings with Deng Xiaoping
FEBRUARY 1	Ayatollah Khomeini returns to Iran
MARCH 8–14	Peace mission to Egypt and Israel
MARCH 26	Egypt-Israel peace treaty signed
MARCH 28	Nuclear accident at Three Mile Island
JUNE 12	National health proposal sent to Congress

JUNE 18	Signing of SALT II treaty with Soviet Union
JULY 5–13	Camp David meetings to reassess administration
JULY 15	Address on national goals and energy
JULY 17–20	Announcements of cabinet and senior staff changes
AUGUST 15	Andrew Young resigns
OCTOBER 17	Department of Education established
OCTOBER 20	Decision to admit shah to U.S. for medical treatment
NOVEMBER 4	U.S. embassy in Iran overrun by militants, who seize American hostages
NOVEMBER 14	Freezing of all Iranian assets
DECEMBER 4	Announcement of decision to seek reelection
DECEMBER 27	Soviets invade Afghanistan

1980

JANUARY 4	Announcement of severe sanctions against Soviets
JANUARY 23	Announcement of "Carter Doctrine" to Congress
FEBRUARY 20	Recommendation of U.S. withdrawal from Moscow Olympics
APRIL 2	Approval of windfall profits tax on oil
APRIL 7	Breaking off of diplomatic relations with Iran
APRIL 21	Cyrus Vance submits resignation
APRIL 24	Unsuccessful hostage rescue attempt
JUNE 30	Signing of Energy Security Act
JULY 16	Republicans nominate Ronald Reagan
AUGUST 4	News conference about Billy Carter and Libya
AUGUST 13	Nomination for a second term
SEPTEMBER 22	Iraq invades Iran
OCTOBER 28	Presidential campaign debate with Reagan
NOVEMBER 4	Anniversary of hostages' capture; Reagan wins election
DECEMBER 2	Signing of Alaska lands legislation
DECEMBER 11	Signing of Superfund Act to control toxic wastes

1981

JANUARY 16	Negotiation of final terms for hostage release
JANUARY 20	Reagan inaugurated; hostages released; departure from Washington for Plains
JANUARY 21	Meeting with hostages in Wiesbaden, Germany

Senior Officials in My Administration

PRESIDENT   Jimmy Carter, 1977–81
VICE PRESIDENT   Walter F. (Fritz) Mondale, 1977–81

Department Secretaries
STATE   Cyrus R. Vance, 1977–80
                    Edmund S. Muskie, 1980–81
TREASURY   W. Michael Blumenthal, 1977–79
                    G. William Miller, 1979–81
DEFENSE   Harold Brown, 1977–81
JUSTICE   Griffin B. Bell, 1977–79
                    Benjamin R. Civiletti, 1979–81
INTERIOR   Cecil D. Andrus, 1977–81
COMMERCE   Juanita M. Kreps, 1977–79
                    Philip M. Klutznick, 1980–81
LABOR   F. Ray Marshall, 1977–81
AGRICULTURE   Bob S. Bergland, 1977–81
HEALTH, EDUCATION, AND WELFARE
                    Joseph A. Califano, Jr., 1977–79
HEALTH AND HUMAN SERVICES
                    Patricia R. Harris, 1979–81
EDUCATION   Shirley M. Hufstedler, 1979–81
HOUSING AND URBAN DEVELOPMENT
                    Patricia R. Harris, 1977–79
                    Maurice E. (Moon) Landrieu, 1979–81
TRANSPORTATION   Brock Adams, 1977–79
                    Neil E. Goldschmidt, 1979–81
ENERGY   James R. Schlesinger, 1977–79
                    Charles W. Duncan, Jr., 1979–81

Other Senior Officials
WHITE HOUSE CHIEF OF STAFF
                    Hamilton Jordan, 1979–80
                    Jack H. Watson, Jr., 1980–81

NATIONAL SECURITY ADVISOR
Zbigniew Brzezinski, 1977–81

DOMESTIC POLICY ADVISOR
Stuart E. Eizenstat, 1977–81

DIRECTOR OF THE OFFICE OF MANAGEMENT AND BUDGET
Thomas Bertram (Bert) Lance, 1977
James T. McIntyre, Jr., 1977–81

PRESS SECRETARY   Joseph L. (Jody) Powell, 1977–81

COUNSEL TO THE PRESIDENT
Robert J. Lipshutz, 1977–79
Lloyd N. Cutler, 1979–81

ASSISTANT TO THE PRESIDENT FOR CONGRESSIONAL LIAISON
Frank B. Moore, 1977–81

DIRECTOR OF CENTRAL INTELLIGENCE
Stansfield Turner, 1977–81

CHAIRMAN OF THE COUNCIL OF ECONOMIC ADVISORS
Charles L. Schultze, 1977–81

UNITED STATES AMBASSADOR TO THE UNITED NATIONS
Andrew Young, 1977–79
Donald McHenry, 1979–81

UNITED STATES TRADE REPRESENTATIVE
Robert S. Strauss, 1977–79
Reubin O'Donovan Askew, 1979–81

Preface

During my four years in the White House, I kept a personal diary by dictating my thoughts and observations several times each day. Some days I kept notes and dictated later. When time permitted, my secretary, Susan Clough, would type the notes and file the pages in large binders.

Each week, a record of every public statement or activity of the president of the United States is published, including documents signed, visits to any site, speeches made, and even answers to shouted questions from news reporters. When dictating entries to my diary, I tended to ignore this public record and interwined my personal opinions and activities with a brief description of the official duties I performed. Readers should remember that I seldom exercised any restraint on what I dictated, because I did not contemplate the more personal entries ever being made public. When my opinions of people changed, for instance, I did not go back and amend the entries.

Except for a few entries, I never examined these typed notes until February 1981, when Rosalynn and I unpacked our belongings after returning to our home in Plains, Georgia. I was surprised to find twenty-one large volumes of double-spaced text—a total of more than five thousand pages! I still have the original document in my home, and one copy has been sequestered in the Carter Presidential Library and Museum in Atlanta. Until

now, none of the diary entries have been revealed except when snippets
have been used in museum exhibits or when I have quoted brief excerpts
in some of the books I've written about official matters.

Despite a temptation to conceal my errors, misjudgments of people, or
lack of foresight, I decided when preparing this book not to revise the original transcript, but just to use the unchanged excerpts from the diaries that
I consider to be most revealing and interesting. Admittedly, it was somewhat painful for me to omit about three-fourths of the diary, but for the
sake of compression I concentrated on a few general themes that are still
pertinent—especially Middle East peace negotiations, nuclear weaponry,
U.S.-China relations, energy policy, anti-inflation efforts, health policy,
and my relationships with Congress. I also included some elements of my
personal life that illustrate how it feels and what it means to be president.
At times, I abbreviated or omitted a sentence in a particular entry, but I
was careful not to change the entry's original meaning. For the sake of
readability, I did not include ellipses to indicate deletions, and I occasionally changed a word or two where the original text was confusing. Further,
I sometimes used phrases within brackets to identify people and organizations. And to help orient the reader, when the date of an entry fell on a
Monday, I noted that.

I also decided to make the entire diary (including my detailed handwritten notes) available at the Carter Presidential Library in the near future for scholars, journalists, historians, or others who might wish to explore
more deeply some events of those four years. As anyone who reviews the
complete diary will see, in only a very few cases did I delete an entry to
protect the privacy of members of my own family or people still active in
public life. To supplement this diary, of course, all my official and public
activities are available from the U.S. Government Printing Office in nine
volumes titled *Public Papers of the Presidents of the United States: Jimmy
Carter, 1977–81.*

While working on this abbreviated version of my White House diary, I
was surprised by the number of subjects that were of common interest to
me and other presidents. Throughout this book, I wrote explanatory notes
to help the reader understand the context of the entries, bring to life the
duties of a president, offer insights into a number of the people I worked
with, and point out how many of the important challenges remain the
same. At times we presidents have reacted to similar events in much the
same way; at other times we've responded quite differently. In presenting

this annotated diary, my intention is not to defend or excuse my own actions or to criticize others, but simply to provide, based on current knowledge, an objective analysis of differences. Whenever possible, I attempt to articulate what lessons I learned and offer my own frank assessment of what I or others might have done differently.

WHITE HOUSE DIARY

Prelude: The Campaign

About the time I announced my candidacy for president in December 1974, Gallup published a poll that included the question "Among Democrats, whom do you prefer as the next nominee?" There were thirty-two names on Gallup's list of potential candidates, including George Wallace, Hubert Humphrey, Henry (Scoop) Jackson, Walter Mondale, John Glenn, and even the Georgia legislator Julian Bond. My name was not mentioned.

Our campaign's original presumption was that the major Democratic contenders would be Edward Kennedy on the left and Wallace on the right, and that I could occupy the middle of the political spectrum and prevail with persistence, hard work, and a bit of good luck. I was very disappointed when Kennedy announced his decision to end his campaign in September 1974; his unfortunate experience a few years earlier at Chappaquiddick was frequently mentioned in the news media as the primary reason for his withdrawal. Almost immediately, a number of new candidates announced; the most prominent were Kennedy's brother-in-law, Sargent Shriver; Senators Fred Harris, Birch Bayh, Henry Jackson, and Lloyd Bentsen; Governors Milton Shapp and Terry Sanford; Congressman Morris Udall; and of course George Wallace. Later, Governor Jerry Brown and Senator Frank Church entered the race, as did Adlai Stevenson III, who was a favorite son in Illinois. Almost without exception, they were better known and financed than I.

It was obvious to me and my advisors that many Americans were deeply concerned about the competence and integrity of our government. Still fresh in memory were the assassinations of John Kennedy, Robert Kennedy, and Martin Luther King, Jr.; the disgrace of Watergate; the failure in Vietnam and the misleading statements about the war from top civilian and military leaders; and the revelation that emerged from the Frank Church Senate committee that our government's intelligence services had condoned assassination plots against foreign leaders. After much thought and discussion, I chose to focus my campaign on three basic themes: truthfulness, management competence, and distance from the unattractive aspects of Washington politics.

To every audience, large or small, I swore "never to tell a lie or to make a misleading statement." I was able to point to my success, as governor of Georgia, in completely reorganizing the state government and instituting an innovative technique that made annual comparisons possible between old and new programs. My campaign literature emphasized my roots as a peanut farmer from the tiny village of Plains, Georgia. The support of Andrew Young, the King family, and other civil rights heroes helped me overcome the potential racist stigma of coming from the Deep South; I was well aware that if I won, I would be the first successful candidate from this region since Zachary Taylor in 1848.

I had very little money, but I began campaigning as soon as I left the Georgia governor's office in January 1975. My former press secretary, Jody Powell, was my traveling companion. In Atlanta, we had a superb team of issue analysts working under the direction of Stuart Eizenstat, who had performed the same service for Hubert Humphrey in 1968. During the succeeding months, our campaign team put together two groups of surrogates that supplemented my full-time effort, an unusual technique that ultimately prevailed. One was a large group of my fellow Georgians, known as the "Peanut Brigade." At their own expense, they traveled to New Hampshire, Wisconsin, Pennsylvania, Florida, and other key states. They walked door-to-door handing out my campaign literature and extolling my record and my views to every citizen they encountered.

Even more effective were the members of my own family. As directed by my campaign manager, Hamilton Jordan, six teams campaigned separately, led by my wife, Rosalynn; my sons, Jack, Chip, and Jeff, and their wives; my mother, Lillian; and her youngest sister, Emily. When we got together, we shared experiences, discussed subjects that seemed most important to prospective voters, and made sure that we would be "preaching the same sermon" during the week ahead. All of us understood that it was critical that we speak with one voice regarding abortion, education, farm policy, Israel, nuclear weaponry, and other important and sensitive issues. To save money, we spent nights with families supportive of (or at least interested in) our campaign.

During most of 1975, the other candidates were campaigning part-time, and they never realized the effectiveness of what we were doing—until it was too late. Rosalynn, for instance, visited 115 towns and cities in Iowa and spent seventy-five days in Florida. We concentrated on the key states with the earliest returns, and in the winter of 1976 I came in first in Iowa, New Hampshire, and Florida. After that, my opponents cooperated in what became known as ABC—Anybody But Carter. They would choose the most popular person for a particular state and give that candidate their concerted support. This tactic sometimes succeeded, but by the end of the primary season I had a clear majority of delegates to the Democratic National Convention.

My first decision after being assured of victory was to choose my running mate. I decided that I needed to compensate for my lack of experience in Washington, and seriously considered Senators John Glenn, Frank Church, Scoop Jackson, Ed Muskie, and Walter Mondale. After long meetings and interviews, I found that Mondale was personally most compatible with me, and we shared similar ideas on how he and I could work together as a team.

For me, the general election was much more difficult than the Democratic primaries. I had been running as a somewhat lonely and independent candidate—a peanut farmer and former governor who was quite removed from the Washington scene. Now I inherited the leadership mantle of the Democratic Party, including all its negative and burdensome trappings. My opponent, Gerald Ford, was a fine man who had survived a brutal primary challenge from California governor Ronald Reagan. Many Americans felt indebted to President Ford for having salvaged the integrity of the White House after Richard Nixon resigned in political disgrace.

Despite these handicaps, Fritz Mondale and I won a narrow victory. The day after the election, I began to prepare for my inauguration and the responsibility of serving as president of the United States.

1977

I began keeping this diary in part due to an offhand comment by Richard Nixon. Rosalynn and I first met Nixon when we attended the National Governors' Conference in 1971. The president walked up to us at a White House reception, turned to Rosalynn, and asked, "Young lady, do you keep a diary?" Rosalynn replied, "No, sir." Nixon then said, "You'll be sorry!" Since this was our first conversation with a president, it made a lasting impact.

Within a day or two of my inauguration, I began making written notes of my thoughts and activities on the pages of a legal pad, and on February 26 I began dictating into a small tape recorder more frequently and currently.

JANUARY 20   A couple months before the inauguration, I got a letter from Senator [William] Proxmire, who is very interested in physical fitness. He suggested that I walk from the Capitol to the White House on Inauguration Day. I responded without making any promise, and about three weeks before the inauguration I informed the Secret Service that I would do so. I later told my wife, my son Chip, and no one else until the night before inauguration, at which time I told Vice President Mondale and a couple of staff members, including Jody Powell.

I thought it would be a good demonstration of confidence by the new president in the people of our country as far as security was concerned, and also would be a tangible indication of some reduction in the imperial status of the president and his family. We were gratified at the response. Many people along the parade route, when they saw that we were walking, began to weep, and it was an emotional experience for us as well. I was surprised at the enormous attention this act received from the news media and believe it was a good decision.

I think the inauguration speech itself, perhaps one of the briefest on record for the first inauguration of a president, was quite compatible with my announcement speech in December 1974, and also with my acceptance speech at the Democratic convention. It accurately expressed some of the major themes of my administration. Even though I had been preparing to be president, I was genuinely surprised when in the benediction by the bishop from Minnesota, he referred to "blessings on President Carter"; just the phrase "President Carter" was startling to me.

I would say that the quarters at the White House are quite similar to those we enjoyed as the governor's family in Georgia, but I have been constantly impressed—I almost said overwhelmed—at the historical nature of the White House, occupied for the first time by our second president, John Adams. When I see a desk or a writing cabinet or a book or a sideboard or a bed that was used by Thomas Jefferson or Abraham Lincoln, Franklin Roosevelt or Truman or Kennedy, I have a feeling of almost unreality about my being president, but also a feeling of both adequacy and determination that I might live up to the historical precedents established by my predecessors.

That night we had our first of what has been a very relaxed and informal series of meals with our family. Early on, when Rosalynn was visiting the White House, some of our staff asked the chef and cooks if they thought they could prepare the kind of meals which we enjoyed in the South, and the cook said, "Yes, ma'am, we've been fixing that kind of food for the servants for a long time." The meals in general have been superb. The only shock was that for the first ten days our food bill in the White House was six hundred dollars! Part of this was carelessness because we didn't let the cooks know when some of our family members would not be present; part of it was because of the excessive amount of company that we had the first few days. We quickly discovered that the president himself pays for all personal meals, gifts, and travel—for himself and for other family members as well. All official expenses are, of course, paid by the government.

JANUARY 21   We had a series of receptions for people that we cared about, the first one of which was for seven or eight hundred Americans with whom we had spent the night during the long campaign. In some instances this was an emotional meeting because they had meant so much to us when no one knew or cared who I was, and we had formed such close personal friendships with them and had not had a chance to thank them adequately. I was genuinely surprised at how deeply moved I was to see these people. We gave each one of the families a small brass plaque stating that a member of my family had stayed with them during the campaign.

The first couple days we shook hands with literally thousands of people in receiving lines. Quite important to do this—to thank people who had helped us, to cement ties with the members of Congress, the diplomatic officials, and also with the members of the Armed Forces. I was particularly impressed as the leaders of the military branches came by and shook hands with me and Rosalynn to find the extraordinary number who made some reference to their prayers for us or "God be with you"—statements of that kind—much more than had been the case with others during those two days.

My normal, almost unvarying routine is to get up at 6:30, sometimes earlier if I have special work to do, get to the office at about 7:00. Most mornings I spend an hour to an hour and a half by myself reading the paper, writing memoranda to my staff members, and then I have a security briefing by Dr. [Zbigniew] Brzezinski [my national security advisor], read the CIA's "Intelligence Report to the President," meet with Hamilton Jordan and Frank Moore [my liaison officer with the Congress] to go over the day's business with the Congress or other matters, and then I start my regular appointments.

For the first couple of weeks I did all this work out in the Oval Office, but later moved into a more private small office on the west side of the West Wing. The Oval Office is quite impressive, and I've noticed that many of my long-standing friends, quite self-assured and sometimes cosmopolitan, are not urbane when they come into the Oval Office; they become almost completely inarticulate, get nervous and unsure of themselves, impressed greatly by the fact that this is the center of our government. One of the almost routine problems I have is to put them at ease so we can continue with the conversation that brought them there.

JANUARY 22   We continued our series of receptions but had our first National Security Council meeting to get organized. This was an organization that in the past had consisted of, I think, seven different committees, and we cut this down to two different committees.

I've been determined to have Dr. Brzezinski be a constant source of stimulation for the Departments of Defense and State, but always work in the role of a staff person to me. In fact, I've pledged that none of the members of my staff would dominate members of the cabinet. Zbig agrees completely with this, and because of his constant access to me several times each day, perhaps second only to Hamilton Jordan in frequency, his influence over my own thinking and judgment, ultimate decisions, is certainly adequate.

As a college student, Hamilton had volunteered to help me in my campaign for governor in 1966; four years later, after serving in Vietnam, he became my top political leader. He was my executive secretary in the governor's office and the primary strategist in planning and conducting our presidential campaign. In the White House, he continued to be one of my key advisors; although he did not want any title, he effectively served as my chief of staff. Everyone in my administration—and in Congress—recognized Hamilton as the most influential of my advisors in Washington.

In the inner White House office we established a high-fidelity sound system, and for eight or ten hours every day I listen to classical music. Records are changed by Susan Clough, my secretary.

In the evening we watched our first movie in a long time, *All the President's Men*. I was impressed with the insistence of the press in uncovering information about Watergate and also felt strange occupying the same living quarters and position of responsibility as Richard Nixon, who had brought such disgrace on the White House and the presidency itself. And of course I was determined all anew not ever to let the same thing happen while I was president.

JANUARY 23   We had an early send-off for Vice President Mondale, who was asked by me to visit our major democratic allies and friends in Europe and Japan. I particularly wanted an early demonstration of our friendship for them. I believe the best way to deal with problems in the world is to have a sound basis of consultation and mutual trust among the developed democracies, and also, of course, I was glad to show that Vice President Mondale will be carrying out important missions for me—both domestic and foreign. He was received well by the leaders of other nations, and I think the substance of his discussions with them was equivalent to what it would have been had I been there myself.

Even before my inauguration, Brzezinski, Mondale, Cyrus Vance (my secretary of state), and I decided to launch a program to visit as many key nations as possible. We agreed, in very general terms, that my personal focus would be on western Europe and the Middle East, while Cy would concentrate on Russia and Japan. Andrew Young, the congressman and civil rights hero who became my ambassador to the United Nations, played a key role in maintaining and improving relations with African nations and other countries that were susceptible to Soviet enticement. Later, Rosalynn assumed a major role in Latin America, and Zbig developed a valuable rapport with the Chinese. These visits permitted intimate, detailed conversations that led to personal relationships with leaders, ascertained their primary goals and problems, and helped us learn how the United States could be of help. Our inherent advantage wherever we competed with the Soviet Union was our strong emphasis on peace and human rights.

We decided to join the First Baptist Church, primarily because [my son] Chip and [his wife] Caron, during the pre-inauguration days, had attended several of the churches and found this one to be both warm and friendly, even when the people there didn't know who our children were. Also, Amy decided to become a member of the church and to be baptized there.

My daughter, Amy, who was born fifteen years after her youngest brother, Jeff, was three years old when I became governor and nine when we moved into the White House. She had attended a racially integrated school in Plains, and we enrolled her in a similar public school in Washington. Thoroughly engaged in politics, she joined in our often heated family discussions during mealtimes. Amy was naturally shy and always wanted to avoid the limelight.

MONDAY, JANUARY 24   I instructed the director of the Secret Service to limit their coverage of me and my family within the White House. When we got there we found that all the doors and stairwells going from the first, second, and the third floor were locked permanently, and that we could only move vertically by the elevator. Also, as soon as I came out of the mansion part of the White House, I was surrounded by Secret Service agents. I told them to stay discreetly distant from me. They unlocked all the doors except just during public visiting hours, and the White House is much more an informal living quarters now than it was before.

I found out quickly that the animosities and distrust that had been prevalent during the eight years of Republican administration between the White House and Congress were still present, and I've decided to stay as close to the key members as I can, with a breakfast every week or two weeks on Tuesday morning, and with frequent visits to me by the key chairmen of committees when we deal with welfare or health or the budget or with economics, defense, or foreign affairs.

JANUARY 26 The oath of office [for Attorney General Griffin Bell] was administered at the Department of Justice, and my intention is to visit all the major departments of the federal government, not only to shake hands and let them know I'm interested, but also to speak and answer questions from them.

Griffin Bell had served for fourteen years on the Fifth Circuit Court before becoming my attorney general. He carried out my orders to professionalize the FBI and create an independent Justice Department, which created some conflicts with the White House staff. He made public all contacts he or his top assistants had with any third parties that might affect judicial decisions.

JANUARY 27 I participated in the annual Prayer Breakfast and intend to pursue as much as possible a normal religious schedule.

I was determined to have a complete separation of church and state, compatible with my personal beliefs. This included a departure from the custom of some other presidents, who invited Billy Graham and other Christian leaders to hold services in the East Room of the White House. I still had strong ties in those days to the Southern Baptist Convention, and on occasion I worked with SBC president Jimmy Allen and other leaders on some denominational affairs, either in our private living quarters or in a room at First Baptist Church.

The last thing Rosalynn and I do every day is read a chapter in the Bible in Spanish, and we'll have prayer at all our meals and attend regular church services wherever we are. When we had the first meeting with congressional leaders for breakfast, afterward [House Speaker] Tip O'Neill and [Senate Majority Leader] Bob Byrd both told me that was the first time they'd ever had prayer at such a meeting and they hoped that I would continue it.

We have tried to hold down drastically the ceremonial events that presidents ordinarily attend and to let my sons and their wives and Rosalynn and Amy and others substitute for me. The time pressures are so tremendous that every minute is valuable and it's hard to draw the line once this habit is established.

In the past, two formal dinners were held during each visit of a head of state, one in the White House and one in the foreign embassy. I ended the visits to the dignitary's embassy and had a difficult time explaining to my first few visitors that it was not a slight.

JANUARY 28   I decided to set up the Diplomatic Selection Commission and called Reubin Askew [governor of Florida] to see if he would be the chairman of it. He agreed to do so.

During the election, I had made no promises to anyone about specific appointments, so I was free to select judges, ambassadors, and other top appointees strictly on a merit basis. Before I filled each ambassadorial vacancy, a blue ribbon commission of about twenty members gave me a list of the best five people for the post, from which I made my choice. I maintained a high proportion of professional diplomats but also chose distinguished Americans from business, professional, and academic life when it was more appropriate. I initiated the same screening process in choosing more than two hundred federal judges.

FEBRUARY 1   Had my first meeting with [Soviet ambassador Anatoly] Dobrynin for about an hour. He was remarkably frank and unstructured and covered a wide range of interests, and I was favorably impressed with him. He seems to have direct communication with the Politburo, and he's a member of the Central Committee.

Charles Kirbo was up and looked over the operation of the White House staff. His basic opinion is that Hamilton Jordan is overworked, bogged down with the dozens of personnel appointments, and that he needs some help returning his calls. We agreed to let Chip go by several hours a day and return some of the calls for Hamilton. It always is a great help to me to talk to Kirbo and listen to him. He has a way of absorbing complicated questions, and although he seems to talk about unimportant issues at times, the cumulative summary of his conversations is always one of guidance toward the right strategic objectives. He and I agreed before the inauguration not to talk about any business matters that relate to my own affairs, and, of course, we will adhere to that restriction.

Kirbo had been my friend and advisor when I was elected to the Georgia Senate and served as governor. With the exception of Rosalynn, he was my most trusted advisor throughout my presidency. He refused an appointment by me as U.S. senator when Richard Russell died, in January 1971, and always preferred to maintain his unofficial status. He was the final person with whom I consulted before choosing my vice president or any members of my cabinet. When he came to Washington, my top advisors and all members of Congress considered him to be the ultimate link to me. He was also the trustee of my private affairs concerning our family farms and warehouse business. Everyone who knew him respected his quiet, unobtrusive manner and his sound judgment. Although a partner in one of Atlanta's largest and most prestigious firms, he retained such genuinely folksy ways that we all considered him to be a country lawyer. Before and after I was president, Kirbo and I spent many days together hunting, fishing, or just visiting on our respective farms.

FEBRUARY 2   When I woke up I thought immediately about naming Admiral Stansfield Turner to be director of [the] Central Intelligence [Agency], and Secretary of Defense Harold Brown agreed that he would be an outstanding person. I asked him to bring Stan Turner back to the United States from Naples.

Harold Brown had been secretary of the Air Force and president of Caltech, and was a noted physicist. I wanted him to bring scientific and technical innovations to the military forces. Stan Turner, my U.S. Naval Academy classmate, had been commander of the midshipman brigade, a famous football player, and later a Rhodes Scholar. I always knew he was destined for a top leadership position in the military service.

FEBRUARY 3   Although Stan was not enthusiastic about it at first, he said he would be glad to do anything I wanted him to, and I decided right then that he would be the best director.

We began a detailed study of the SALT issues both quickly for SALT II and ultimately for SALT III. This is being done by the National Security Council Special Coordination Committee.

SALT—which stands for Strategic Arms Limitation Talks—established some limits on nuclear armaments; they were negotiated between President Gerald Ford and Soviet president Leonid Brezhnev in 1974. My agreement with Brezhnev to limit warheads was called SALT II, and we also contemplated a third treaty, called SALT III, which would have mandated a much greater reduction.

I talked to Chancellor Helmut Schmidt about holding down the sale of reprocessing equipment for plutonium to Brazil and also asked him to stimulate the West German economy more than he had planned. He was quite reluctant to agree to either one of these proposals.

Germany was supplying Brazil's nuclear program with fuel and technology, and Switzerland was providing the same to Argentina. I wanted both Latin American nations to comply with the Treaty of Tlatelolco, which was designed to keep the region free of nuclear weapons.

We've had a hard time getting enough women and minority groups in the various departments. [Secretary of Commerce] Juanita Kreps told me today that of the ten top people in the Department of Commerce, half of them would be women.

MONDAY, FEBRUARY 7   One of the biggest headaches I have ever run across is personnel appointments that the president has to make. Hamilton does a good job in screening these appointments, but all the controversial cases eventually get to me and there's no way to win.

FEBRUARY 8   I had my first press conference. I felt completely at ease and leveled with the press as best I could, describing frankly some of the crucial issues that face our country. The major emphasis was on SALT talks and human rights. I spelled out in general terms our positions on these issues and intend to keep the press conferences on schedule and not evade issues any more than necessary for national security.

FEBRUARY 9   Later I asked Dr. Frank Press to be scientific advisor to the president. In the past most of them have been physicists—in fact, the first six recommendations that I got were for physics majors—but I wanted to get an earth science professor to help me in a more general way to assess some of the questions raised by the first report of the Club of Rome [regarding the fragility of the environment]. I believe Dr. Press will be a good man.

Began my first visits to the different departments today with the Labor Department. They tell me that since the Department of Labor was founded, fifty years ago, no president had ever been there. I generally make a short speech, then answer questions from the workers. Then we went to the Commerce Department, where we did the same thing.

FEBRUARY 10   Also went to the Departments of Treasury and Housing and Urban Development. While I was there [at HUD] I was asked a question, "What are you going to do about the families?" And I said, humorously— half-humorously—that I think everyone who's living in sin ought to get married, that all the husbands that left their wives ought to go home, and all the parents who didn't remember their children's names ought to get reacquainted with their children.

FEBRUARY 11   The president of India died, and I called Mama to ask her to leave that afternoon for India to represent me there. Chip decided to go with her. When she answered the phone I asked her what she was doing. She said she was sitting around the house looking for something to do, and I said, "How would you like to go to India?" She said, "Love to go someday. Why?" And I said, "How about this afternoon?" She said, "Okay, I'll be ready."

My mother had a special affection for India: in 1966, at the age of sixty-eight, she went there as a Peace Corps volunteer. A registered nurse, she had worked quietly and without notice among the "untouchables" in Vikhroli, a small village near Mumbai (Bombay). Before traveling to India, she had been deeply involved in local politics, serving as county chair of Lyndon Johnson's campaign in 1964 and as a delegate that year to the Democratic

National Convention. While Rosalynn's mother cared for Amy, Mama cam-
paigned almost full-time for me in 1976 and 1980, and never hesitated to let
me have her advice, especially with respect to the interests of poor or ne-
glected people. Mother became quite well-known when I was governor and
then president, and took full advantage of her fame to become friends with
notable people, enjoy worldwide travel, appear as a frequent guest of Johnny
Carson on The Tonight Show *and on other TV talk shows, and attend as*
many major sports events as possible.

We went home in the afternoon for the first time since we came to
Washington. When we arrived in Warner Robins Air Force Base, there was
a large crowd, and I had instructed the Secret Service that we would go by
motorcade to save money instead of a helicopter. But I discovered that because of the tremendous amount of effort that has to go into traffic control
for intersections, it's much less expensive to go by helicopter, which we will
do in the future. Saturday morning I went down to the warehouse early
and took an almost two-hour stroll down the Plains main street, stopping to
talk to the storekeepers. The press stayed very close and could overhear
everything I said, but I enjoyed the walk and the talks very much.

There is no way to describe the relationship that Rosalynn and I have with
the small town of Plains. Both our families have lived in the community for
five generations, and when I was four years old and she was a baby we were
next-door neighbors. Plains has been a haven for us, drawing us back when
I left the navy, the governor's office, and the White House. This is where our
families have worked, worshipped, been educated, intermarried, and are
buried. Whenever we are away, there is always a quiet yearning to come
back home. Returning here while president was like taking a vacation—
except when we walked or drove along the only downtown street, which was
always packed with tourists when we came to visit.

FEBRUARY 13   After arriving back in Washington I met with Vance, Brzezinski, and Andy Young, since Andy had just returned from a trip to the
southern African region and he wanted to make a report. The South African situation is very confused, of course, but I think there is some possibility if we are forceful enough to bring about some sort of solution; we've
got to put a lot of pressure on [Rhodesian president] Ian Smith and [South
African] prime minister [John] Vorster to accept the proposition of major-

ity rule. The British have practically no remaining influence, but my inclination is to keep them in the forefront for a while and to give them strong backing. We have had indications from Vorster that Ian Smith is ready to accept the majority rule concept, but I still have my doubts until we exert more pressure.

We were all determined to bring an end to apartheid in Africa, and I was destined to spend as much time on this issue as bringing peace to Israel and its neighbors. For tactical reasons, we decided to start with Rhodesia, and making any significant progress required cooperation with black African leaders, positive influence from South Africa, and a clear procedure. The country was to be a constantly festering sore until 1980, when it became the Republic of Zimbabwe and a reasonably honest election was held, with fair treatment for the minority white citizens. (Within fifteen years, however, Zimbabwe's president, Robert Mugabe, degenerated into an abusive and corrupt leader.) At the time, it was clear to everyone that the end of apartheid in Rhodesia would set an example for future action in South Africa. The first free election in South Africa came in 1994, with the election of Nelson Mandela as president.

MONDAY, FEBRUARY 14   I was able to send my second letter to Secretary General Brezhnev, much more substantive than the first one. I hope and believe that this exchange of confidential messages will lead to a better understanding between the Soviets and us. It's important that he understand the commitment I have to human rights preservation first of all, and secondly that he understand I'm sincere about my desire to reduce nuclear armaments. If he's willing to cooperate, we'll get something done before four years goes by.

FEBRUARY 15   I met with Clark Clifford, who is preparing to go to the Mediterranean area to meet with the Greeks, the Turks, and also to visit Cyprus in hopes that he might bring back some prospect for a settlement of that very difficult question.

Clifford was an influential Washington lawyer and lobbyist who had served as secretary of defense under President Johnson and advised my Democratic predecessors and me. We labored for my entire tenure to end the conflict between Greece and Turkey over Cyprus, and to improve relations between the two countries. Thirty-three years later, however, the division in Cyrus is unresolved. In 2008, after several nations and the United Nations had failed to make progress, I joined a group of "elders" in a continuing effort to reduce tensions in a divided Cyprus.

Cy Vance left last night on a trip to the Middle East to meet with the leaders of Israel, Egypt, Jordan, Saudi Arabia, Syria, and Iran on a fact-finding trip just to see if there was some common ground on which we might predicate a meeting in Geneva the second half of this year to help solve the Mideast problem.

Seeking peace between Israel and its neighbors had become a major interest of mine long before I became president. Beginning in 1973 with an extended visit to the Holy Land as a personal guest of General Yitzhak Rabin and Prime Minister Golda Meir, I made an intensive and ongoing study of the area. One of the commitments I made during my campaign was to meet with all the leaders mentioned above as soon as possible, and this trip by the secretary of state was designed to prepare for this effort.

I was informed that *The Washington Post* had information that over a period of twenty years our country had had an agreement with Jordan's King Hussein, to pay him a certain amount of money each year for intelligence information and to induce his tribal chieftains to be loyal to our country. This was initiated in the early stages of King Hussein's reign when Jordan was just an embryonic nation, and it was very doubtful if it would survive. They called Jody to ask if we would confirm the story, and, of course, we would not.

Everyone understood that in this and all other issues, foreign or domestic, Jody Powell could speak with my full confidence and complete understanding of my position. Jody had been my constant traveling companion and, except for Rosalynn, the closest person to me for many years. He was never excluded even from the most sensitive discussions, and his judgment about how much could be revealed was impeccable.

FEBRUARY 16   [Executive Editor] Ben Bradlee and his reporter [Bob Woodward] came by to talk to me about it. I told them, without confirming or denying the story, I wanted to let them know how sensitive the negotiations were in the Middle East at this point and asked that they put themselves in my position, think about what was best for the country, and if possible refrain from publishing the story until Cy Vance can return from the Middle East. They did agree to give me a notice ahead of time before the story was published, and that night they called and said they would publish it the following day. We immediately notified Cy Vance and King Hussein of this development. I did not ask the editor not to publish this story. I think this is something that the news media should always decide themselves. But I thought it was quite irresponsible, at least before Cy Vance could return to our country from the Middle East.

FEBRUARY 17   Mama returned from India, and I had a brief meeting with her early this morning. I think the trip was a superb diplomatic effort, and the State Department later said that we have the best relationship since 1960, to a large degree because of Mother's visit there and her obvious concern about the Indian people. She got along well with Mrs. Indira Gandhi, by the way, whom she formerly had not liked or admired as a political figure.

Got my first haircut up in Rosalynn's little beauty parlor next to the dining room. The barber is from Puerto Rico, and he and I spoke Spanish during the haircut. I think he might take over the regular barbershop in the West Wing shortly since the present barber is a strong Nixonite.

Amy and I went swimming for the first time. The temperature was freezing, and the outdoor pool had been slightly heated. We enjoyed it, though, and I'm going to try to do as many things as possible with Amy. I see her at least for supper every night, and quite often, I'd say two or three times a week after supper, we have some time together, either bowling or going to a movie or going swimming; and then the weekends we have always several hours together. She seems to like her school fine, but she still prefers Plains, which she has known all her life.

Since I first entered politics as a member of our county board of education, one of my interests was in the public school system. At least in the South, a number of competitive "segregation academies" had sprung up after the public schools were racially integrated, so this was a factor in our decision to enroll Amy in a public school. Most of her classmates were children of janitors and other workers in foreign embassies, so she had friends from many different countries. They visited often for weekends in the White House and enjoyed the movie theater, swimming pool, and a bowling alley that Harry Truman had installed in the basement.

FEBRUARY 18   Had a brief meeting with [U.S. diplomat and defense expert] Paul Warnke to give him some advice on how to appear before the Senate Armed Services Committee, most of whose members consider him too much of a dove to be a good arms negotiator, but I think we'll get some votes on the committee, at least for his serving as ACDA [Arms Control and Disarmament Agency] director and a fewer number for him to serve as the actual arms negotiator. I've been calling a number of senators to ask them to vote for Warnke and believe we now have his confirmation assured. The attacks on him, which have been fairly rough, are primarily from those who don't want to see substantive reductions in nuclear weapons achieved on a mutually advantageous basis with the Soviet Union. They distrust any move by the Soviets, and I hope they're not right.

We began to notify members of Congress that I was deleting nineteen water resources projects that had previously been approved by Congress, the Corps of Engineers, and the Department of Interior. I know this is going to create a political furor, but it's something that I am committed to accomplish. These projects ultimately would cost at least $5.1 billion, and the country would be better off if none of them were built. It's going to be a pretty touchy legislative fight to get these projects removed permanently.

This would evolve into the most long-lasting and bitter dispute that I would have with the Congress. The main problem was that many members would identify a site in their district for a dam and lake that would be politically attractive and put it on the long list of pending Corps of Engineers projects. With highly distorted estimates of costs and benefits, the project would slowly but inexorably rise to the top, so that those eventually approved would belong to the most senior legislators—often committee chairmen—and would be slated to be fully financed by the federal treasury. Ultimately, I was able to block many ill-advised projects, as well as bring significant reforms to the system.

Dr. Brzezinski has, I think, fit in well with Cy Vance and with me and Harold Brown. He's inquisitive and innovative, and I think has not been a problem in attempting to repeat what [Henry] Kissinger did, and that was to run the major departments from the position of advisor to the National Security Council.

Zbig had been my primary foreign affairs advisor during my presidential campaign and continued in this role as national security advisor. He and I were in close contact throughout each day and had an excellent personal relationship.

Tim Kraft, Rick Hutcheson, and Susan Clough have been doing a good job in analyzing how we might cut down on paperwork. I would say now I get sixty or seventy different papers coming onto my desk every day which I have to handle before and in between my other meetings and appointments. This is excessive, and there's a constant inclination to circumvent the obstacles we place in the path of this stream of memoranda coming to me.

I like both the domestic and foreign aspects of the job so far. The working conditions here, my own family's life, have been pleasant. The personnel assignments and paperwork are the most disagreeable parts of the presidency. I enjoy the studying. Rosalynn's taking Spanish lessons. Most of my family members and I have begun a speed-reading course. When these have been completed maybe I can cut down on the amount of time I have to spend each day reading newspapers, magazines, and reports on weapons systems, foreign affairs, relationships, proposed legislation, and so forth.

My staff estimated that I was having to read about three hundred pages of official documents every day. Evelyn Wood offered us a series of free weekly instructions (with no advertising benefits), and about thirty of us derived great benefit from them.

I think I can sense a general alleviation of tension around the nation—a more positive attitude among American people toward government and business and labor. My sense is that most people wish me well, and so far the news coverage has been fairly objective. But, as always, the reporters are searching for some signs of discontent or disharmony, and when a slight incident does occur and is quickly resolved, it's greatly exaggerated in the news media.

I very seldom watch television, but read a news summary late each night of all the television news programs, and then early in the morning read two or three newspapers (*The Washington Post, The New York Times* always, *The Washington Star,* sometimes *The Wall Street Journal,* most of the time *The Atlanta Constitution* and/or *The Atlanta Journal*) and news-magazines (mostly *Newsweek, Time,* and *U.S. News & World Report*).

I would guess that the energy policy that we will pursue this year—the creation of a new department and a comprehensive energy program—will perhaps be the most important domestic challenge and, I hope, accomplishment. I intend to make my first appearance before a joint session of Congress to describe the new proposals by the twentieth of April.

FEBRUARY 20   Amy's been much happier since Mary Fitzpatrick got out of prison and came up to be with us at the White House. She likes her school, has fit in well, and after a few days of sorrow about leaving Plains I think now she's become happy again.

In 1970, while visiting some friends in Lumpkin, Georgia, Mary Fitzpatrick, a young African American, had been falsely accused of a murder, indicted, and sentenced to life imprisonment. She never saw her court-appointed attorney until they were entering the courtroom, and he told her just to plead guilty and he could get her off with a light sentence. Instead, she was sent to prison for life. As a prison trustee, she served our family in the governor's mansion, beginning when Amy was three years old. Convinced of Mary's innocence, I had myself designated as her parole officer, and she moved into the White House with us. Later, the trial judge in her case (who by then was chief justice of Georgia's supreme court) ordered a new examination of her case, and she was found completely innocent and granted a full pardon. For all practical purposes, she is still a member of our family.

Rosalynn is overworked, has too small a staff, and is called on to do an enormous amount of entertaining for official visits. She's also formed the Commission on Mental Health, is taking Spanish lessons three hours a day, the speed-reading course, and has an almost unbelievable amount of press coverage and requirements for her appearances at special events. A lot of that work would be on my shoulders if she were not willing and confident to take it.

MONDAY, FEBRUARY 21   One of the most difficult problems we face is maintaining the confidentiality of memoranda and other discussions within the White House office structure, and at the same time having key staff members conversant with what issues are being assessed. So far we've not been able to resolve this question. Everyone wants to be considered a member of the top staff. I think frequent meetings of the staff themselves when appropriate matters can be discussed, the weekly cabinet meeting where discussion is unrestrained, and my press conference every couple of weeks all help to present accurate assessments of issues. The more secrecy that surrounds important matters, the more distortion is likely to be engendered.

Constant leaks of sensitive information—much of which was often distorted—were to plague us during the entire term. Government officials with special interests—the awarding of defense contracts or the political status of Taiwan, to name just two examples—were eager to use their knowledge of inside information to further their causes.

Rosalynn has been extremely successful so far even in the most formal circumstances to make people feel at home, and I think both the president of Mexico and the prime minister of Canada have enjoyed having Amy, for instance, at the ceremonies, although Amy proceeded with her Carter family habit of reading at the table during the banquets.

FEBRUARY 22   I've enjoyed the advantage of having selection commissions choose a small group of highly qualified people for controversial appointments. This will include federal court judges, ultimately Supreme Court justices, the director of the FBI, major diplomatic appointees. It gives the accurate image of merit selection, and it also removes from us part of the onerous task of personnel selection.

In the first budget message I have sent to Congress, signed today, we made some fairly substantial changes and initiated programs or policies that will be of significance in the future: a much more careful assessment of long-range commitments on expensive projects, including military weapons, new social programs, the construction of dams and other water projects, and so forth. I may not win on all these deletions and revisions from the budget this first time around, but I intend to be persistent about them. Many people who want to see the budget balanced before I go out of office don't want to have their own pet projects removed. I'm determined to go to the public with these issues if necessary in order to prevail.

I worked assiduously throughout my tenure to control the national debt, with some success. The best yardstick for measuring the debt is to calculate the total national debt as a percentage of gross domestic product. The year I left office, this debt-to-GDP ratio was 32.5 percent, the lowest it has been at any time since World War II. Under Ronald Reagan it increased to 53.1 percent; after the end of George W. Bush's term, the ratio was 83.4 percent. The accumulated debt for fiscal year 2009 is thirteen times greater than in 1980 and is projected to be 100 percent of GDP in 2011.

FEBRUARY 23   My inclination is to alleviate tension around the world, including disharmonies between our country and those with whom we have no official diplomatic relationships, like China, North Korea, Vietnam, Cambodia, Laos, Cuba, and I'll be moving in this direction. I think the country's ready for it, although in some instances like Cuba it's going to be quite controversial to do so. If I get an equivalent response from these countries, then I would be glad to meet them more than halfway.

I eased travel restraints to Cuba and ultimately established diplomatic offices in Havana and Washington, but Castro's decision to send troops to Africa in 1977 and his promotion of illegal emigration to the United States prevented further progress.

We still continue to get some criticism in the press and from other sources about our emphasis on human rights. I think it's beginning to have some impact, though, in most countries around the world. A special emissary from Romania came by today to let me know they had approved 5,200 exit visas for those who want to leave Romania, and in the past they've been quite reluctant to take actions like this. The significant thing is not the 5,200 people but the fact that they are joining in an effort even among the Communist countries to prepare for the Belgrade conference where the Helsinki Agreements on human rights will be assessed. I'm determined to continue with this policy, in spite of complaints from some of the countries involved.

FEBRUARY 24   Senator Sam Nunn came by. I asked him to help me with the Paul Warnke appointment and also expressed my admiration for him. He's one of the outstanding young members of the Senate. I think he's destined for great things there. I also advised him to keep his interests as broad as possible and not to get boxed into a narrow viewpoint.

FEBRUARY 25   Admiral Rickover came by to give me an old workbook, dating back to 1953, which I used at Knolls Atomic Power Laboratory, and he also gave Amy a photograph of an atomic submarine surfacing at the North Pole with a sample of water obtained when they melted the snow there. Rickover seems to be very proud of the fact that I'm president. He gives me frequent memoranda concerning ways to make the government more effective, and although he's highly opinionated and is sometimes perhaps in error, his suggestions have been very helpful.

In 1952, I was one of two young submarine officers chosen to lead the pre-commissioning crews of the original nuclear submarines, Nautilus *and* Sea Wolf, *and Hyman Rickover was in charge of everything that related to the peaceful use of atomic energy and therefore my commanding officer. Known as "the Father of the Atomic Navy," Rickover is widely considered to be the greatest engineer of all time. Other than my father, he shaped my life more than any other man. He always demanded perfection, never admitted satisfaction with any level of my performance, and worked harder and more hours than anyone I ever knew. Not surprisingly, he and I had a completely different relationship after I became president.*

Later on in the afternoon, about 4:00, [Chip's wife] Caron went to the hospital after her labor pains began. Later in the evening, at 8:41 to be exact, the baby boy was born. We flew back to Bethesda to see the baby, and less than an hour after it was born we were on the way back to Camp David. We really liked the camp, and I think we'll use it every now and then. It's secluded and is one of the perquisites of the White House that I intend to retain. I've asked [Office of Management and Budget director] Bert Lance not even to let me know how much it costs to maintain Camp David during the year. I also instructed Bert not to let any more construction be initiated at Camp David.

Idi Amin [military dictator and president of Uganda] announced that no Americans could leave or enter the country, and that he was demanding that they all report personally to Entebbe to meet with him. We were quite concerned about this threatening attitude, and often during the weekend at Camp David I was communicating back and forth with the secretary of state and Dr. Brzezinski. The primary question was whether or not to move the aircraft carrier *Enterprise*, the cruiser *Long Beach*, and another cruiser to the eastern coast of Africa. We're also recruiting help from countries with some influence on Amin to induce him to protect the American people. We were very cautious not to aggravate him because he's obviously crazy and we didn't want to have any murders of Americans result from any comment that I might make criticizing him. Ultimately the question was resolved.

Furious at my comments about human rights abuse, Amin was threatening more than one hundred missionaries serving in Uganda. Primarily under pressure from Saudi Arabia, Amin finally agreed to let them leave Uganda. They all refused the offer and dispersed into the villages to continue their Christian work.

MONDAY, FEBRUARY 28   In the afternoon John Denver came by to let me know that he had no obligations during 1977 and was available to help me with any major programs that we had to put over to the American people, including environmental quality or the reduction of expenditures for un-necessary dams, energy policy, particularly with emphasis on conserva-tion and so forth. He and Robert Redford and others I think can be used with effectiveness, and we intend to do so.

MARCH 1   Jim Schlesinger [secretary of defense under Presidents Nixon and Ford, and my choice to head my planned Department of Energy] has completed presenting to the Congress today proposals for creation of the Department of Energy. This is a first step toward implementation of a comprehensive energy policy. Because the time is right and because we've laid very careful groundwork with the members of Congress, even begin-ning before I was elected, and because of the esteem with which the Con-gress regards Schlesinger, I think we'll get the Department of Energy created without too much delay. We have also had remarkable coopera-tion among the seven cabinet members who are giving up parts of their departments that would go into the new Department of Energy.

MARCH 2   Got a not very encouraging report from Ellsworth Bunker and Sol Linowitz on the Panama Canal Treaty. I told them to hang tough on the post-2000 period because we've got to have some way to guarantee unilaterally if necessary that the canal will stay open and protected.

These two diplomats were the chief negotiators working full-time with Pana-manian president Omar Torrijos and his associates to reach a full agree-ment regarding the canal. The key was giving Panama ownership and control of the canal but retaining the United States' right to defend it as well as guaranteeing our country priority in its use in an emergency. The canal had been a lightning rod for years: in January 1964, for example, an American flag was raised in a disputed place, thus violating some commitments Presi-dent Eisenhower had made to the Panamanians. A violent confrontation resulted in the loss of several lives; soon thereafter Panama broke diplomatic relations with the United States, and almost all Latin American nations and the entire community of developing countries demanded that corrective action be taken. Johnson, Nixon, and Ford all promised to negotiate a new and more balanced canal treaty, but public and congressional opposition had been too intense and powerful to confront.

During my presidential campaign in 1975, thirty-eight U.S. senators sponsored a resolution pledging never to change the treaty, and this prompted me to study the terms and history of the original agreement, which had been in effect since 1903. It was obviously unfair, and I learned that it was hastily signed in the middle of the night before any Panamanian official could read its terms. My commitment to furthering justice and human rights made me determined to negotiate a new treaty; it was also important to ensure the long-term safety of the canal. Securing the Senate ratification of this agree-ment was to become the most difficult task of my political life.

When dictating these entries, I used "treaty" and "treaties" interchange-ably. There were actually two Panama Canal treaties: one applicable until the end of the year 2000 and the other covering the years thereafter.

MARCH 3 Met to discuss the question of Africa, the interrelationship between South Africa, its government leaders, the UN involvement in Namibia, and how we ought to work with the British on the Rhodesian change toward majority government. It's a little frustrating to be dealing with Ian Smith through Vorster, and to be deferring to the British, who've shown a remarkable incapacity to put the thing together so we know which way to exert our influence. We'll let the British try a little longer, then my own inclination is to move.

MARCH 5 Had a two-hour call-in show, with Walter Cronkite moderat-ing, during the afternoon. I think it went over well. I will probably do this twice, maybe three times each year, just to stay in touch with the American people. I think it's crucial that I keep in touch with the people of the country and let them know I'm interested in their viewpoint. The Congress has got to know that I can go directly over their heads when necessary. And, of course, I wouldn't hesitate to do it. So far I don't feel isolated from the rest of the country since I've been in the White House. Reverend James Baker from South Carolina, immediately after he talked to me, called his sister-in-law and was so excited that he died, unfortunately. I called his wife to express my regrets.

MONDAY, MARCH 7   Prime Minister Rabin came over from Israel. I've put in an awful lot of time studying the Middle Eastern question and was hoping that Rabin would give me some outline of what Israel ultimately hopes to see achieved in a permanent peace settlement, and found him very timid, stubborn, and also somewhat ill at ease. When he went upstairs with me, just the two of us, I asked him to tell me what Israel wanted me to do when I met with the Arab leaders and if there were something specific that I could get [Egyptian president Anwar] Sadat to do. He didn't unbend at all, nor did he respond. It seems to me the Israelis, at least Rabin, don't trust our government or any of their neighbors. I guess there's some justification for this distrust.

I had decided before my inauguration to meet all the key players in the region and make a full-court press for a peace agreement. It was necessary to meet first with the Israelis. When Rabin visited us in March 1977 he was under great stress and feeling some embarrassment, since he knew it would soon be revealed that he and his wife had some improper U.S. bank accounts. In his autobiography, Rabin said I was putting too much pressure on him to make concessions, especially given that there was an impending election.

MARCH 8   We had our regular meeting with the congressional leadership. So far all our legislation's making good progress. The water resources or dam projects have caused some consternation in the Congress and I don't know if I'll win on this subject or not, but I am going to pursue it for four years until we cut out some of the unnecessary projects. Met with General [John] Morris, chief of the Corps of Engineers. He's very eager to see us eliminate some of the pork barrel projects, but I doubt that he's going to advocate this with the Congress. I guess that would be expecting too much.

MARCH 9   Went to the CIA headquarters to get a briefing on the interrelationship among the different intelligence agencies. I think they're going to resent Stan Turner's strength and also my own inclination that Stan be the boss of the nine different agencies that comprise the intelligence community. One of the top leaders, Lieutenant General Sam Wilson, for instance, said they were glad to welcome the titular head of the community, which was a new job. And I pointed out before the whole group that my intention was not to see Stan Turner be a titular head.

One of my early goals was to reorganize completely the confused intelligence community. Responsibilities were fragmented among many agencies, each one jealously guarding its independence and prerogatives. The situation in Congress—which had multiple committees correlating with the agencies— was no better. I used my executive authority to put Stan in ultimate control of all the agencies and to merge many of them, but congressional action was needed to consummate the process.

We were able to accomplish this goal, but the previous fragmentation returned under Reagan and other succeeding presidents. Years later, after George W. Bush's botched intelligence regarding Iraq, a similar but partial consolidation effort was made. After the attempted airplane bombing on Christmas Day, 2009, it became evident that responsibility for gathering, assessing, and acting on intelligence was still fragmented.

MARCH 11   Had breakfast with John Shanklin, who was the first person I ever asked to vote for me, when I had a meeting with the Godfrey Sperling breakfast group on December 12, 1974. He was a building engineer for the Sheraton Carlton Hotel. I shook hands with him and said, "I'm Jimmy Carter from Georgia, running for president. I'd like to have your vote." He looked at me, thought for a long time, and said, "I'll vote for you." I saw him once after that and asked, "If I get to be president, will you have breakfast with me in the White House?" And he promised to do so. I think had Mr. Shanklin turned me down that first morning when I was quite unsure of myself, it would have made a difference in my whole attitude. Later in that same day back in 1974, I spoke to the Washington press corps and that night announced as a candidate in Atlanta.

We showed Rosalynn the tree house that Amy and I had designed and the White House carpenters built.

Just about forgot how to play tennis but am going to try. In more than two years I've just played twice. I've been getting a good bit of exercise with the bowling alley in the basement and the swimming pool with Amy. I always feel so much better when I have some exercise.

MARCH 12   I met with the delegation going to Vietnam and Laos to get an accounting for servicemen who are missing in action. The Vietnamese leaders have been very receptive to this, and I hope this is a preview of the possibility of normalizing relationships with Vietnam. If they don't insist on reparations and don't castigate us publicly, I think we can accept some reasonable accounting for the MIAs.

MONDAY, MARCH 14   Every Monday morning we have cabinet meetings, and they have been very productive. We've tried to hold them to a couple of hours, but I believe all the cabinet officers have a chance to participate adequately. It's to clear the air and let them understand what my policies are on various controversial issues.

MARCH 15   I got up early again and worked on the trip [to Clinton, Massachusetts] and the UN speech. I've not been able to have a speech prepared that I liked very much, so I've done a great deal of rewriting.

Stan Turner gives me a briefing a couple of times a week, along with Brzezinski and Fritz Mondale. These briefings are getting increasingly comprehensive and worthwhile. I think Turner's going to do an excellent job as director of the CIA and also the entire intelligence community.

MARCH 16   I went to Clinton, Massachusetts. It's been well reported in the papers; there's no need for me to go into it.

While in Clinton, I held a town hall meeting and later spent the night in a private home. These sorts of visits became a regular custom during my tenure. The trip to Clinton turned out to be quite significant because my answers to questions about the Middle East peace process were the most definitive I had given. It was the first time I called for "a homeland for Palestinian refugees."

Earlier today I called Cher Allman [at the time married to Gregg Allman, leader of the Allman Brothers Band] to ask her on some future [TV] program to brag on Washington, D.C. The last time she had a program she said it was the crime center of the nation, and they've really done a lot to correct their problems. She promised she would.

MARCH 18   Signed the bill repealing the Byrd Amendment concerning Rhodesian chrome. I believe this will be of help to us in southern Africa. I have the authority to reestablish the purchase of Rhodesian chrome whenever I choose, so this would give us some leverage perhaps over the Rhodesians and complete the long struggle for majority rule. I'm considering moving more forcefully rather than continuing to play a dormant role. I told Cy Vance today to have Ambassador P. W. Botha from South Africa come by to see me next week. He will be foreign minister when he returns to Africa and eventually may replace Vorster as prime minister. I'm not sure about that.

I told Bill Scranton [former governor of Pennsylvania and ambassador to the United Nations] if we could have the Chinese agree not to solve the Taiwan question with force that we would try to bring about normal relationships with the People's Republic.

Henry and Nancy Kissinger came by for supper, with Cy Vance, [his wife] Gay, and Dr. Brzezinski. We had a delightful and interesting three-hour discussion with Kissinger about foreign affairs. In general he thought we'd done an extremely good job. The only thing he questioned was the timing on the Middle East proposal. He thought the proposals themselves were good, but said he thought he would have waited a little later to put them forward.

My proposal was to consult as early as possible with the leaders of Israel, Jordan, Syria, Egypt, and Saudi Arabia and put together a framework for comprehensive peace between Israel and all its neighbors. At that time, the presumption under UN Security Resolution 338 was that the United States and the Soviet Union would convene an international conference to seek acceptance from key players and the world community.

Henry was open and constructive in recommendations concerning China and Cyprus, southern Africa, and the SALT talks. He thought the deep-cut proposal that we had put together on SALT had a good chance to be accepted by the Soviets if they are sincere and want to make progress on disarmament. It was a good way for all of us to exchange ideas, and I think it'll also prevent or reduce the chance that Kissinger will publicly criticize our foreign affairs positions in the future. I've always liked Kissinger and appreciated the constructive attitude he assumed in the transition period when he gave frank and good advice to both me and Cy Vance.

MARCH 19   We spent several hours this morning going over the details of the SALT negotiations. Our basic thrust will be to present the Soviets with a substantial and well-balanced mutual reduction in the number and complexity of weapons and a freeze on enhancement, or as an alternative just a ratification of the Vladivostok Agreement, which prescribes rules under which the expensive competition continues. We don't know what the Soviets' attitude will be until Cy gets back from Moscow, but we're hoping they will meet us halfway and negotiate in good faith.

MARCH 20   I taught Sunday school and broached the idea to the Sunday school class, from which no action is to be expected, that Baptists and other evangelical groups ought to adopt the same policy that the Mormon Church has: to send large numbers of young men and women volunteers around the world for a year or two of service to the church, working with missionaries. I have an inclination to pursue this more in the future when I have time to put my thoughts together.

This proposal for volunteer missionaries was supported by President Jimmy Allen and adopted by the Southern Baptist Convention, but the commitment was largely abandoned after more fundamentalist leaders gained control in 1979.

MONDAY, MARCH 21   Had lunch with Fritz and five representative farmers from around the country. So far we're in fairly good shape with the agricultural representatives, but I'm going to be much more conservative on farm price supports than they anticipate. This is something I'll have to work out with [Agriculture] Secretary [Bob] Bergland.

   I'm trying to keep the Jewish leaders with us as we explore ways for progress on the Middle Eastern question. Bob Lipshutz and Stu Eizenstat are a great help, and I think some of the liberal leaders in the Congress, particularly Senator Humphrey and others, are trying to hold public support with me on this effort. Nineteen seventy-seven might very well be our best opportunity in all these areas, but I can't afford to back down or be reticent about the controversies.

I remained surrounded by key officials who were strong advisors and trusted by the American Jewish community: White House legal advisor Lipshutz; domestic policy advisor Eizenstat; Treasury Secretary Mike Blumenthal; media advisor Jerry Rafshoon; later Commerce Secretary Phil Klutznick; his deputy Sidney Harman and Harman's wife, Jane. Bob Strauss, Sol Linowitz, and Arthur Goldberg served as special Middle East advisors. In addition, Ed Sanders and Al Moses were White House staff members whose primary duty was dealing with the Jewish community.

MARCH 23 Ambassador Botha from South Africa came by. We had a thorough discussion about how to put together a comprehensive package in southern Africa. My own thought is that we might get ourselves, Great Britain, South Africa, and some of the frontline presidents—maybe [Samora] Machel (Mozambique), [Kenneth] Kaunda (Zambia), and [Olusegun] Obasanjo (Nigeria)—to agree on an overall approach to Rhodesia and Namibia, and then just ram it through and in the process get a commitment from South Africa to meet certain deadline dates for liberalizing attitudes toward blacks, moving toward ultimate full participation by black citizens of South Africa. If we don't do something like this in a very forceful way, my belief is that this situation will deteriorate. Things that are acceptable now to the radical elements will not be acceptable a year or more hence. Fritz Mondale will take this responsibility and will do background study in the history and possibilities of southern Africa, and perhaps later I'll ask him to go to that region to work out a final position for our country to take.

MARCH 24 It's been difficult for the Democratic Congress to learn to work with a Democratic president. First of all they expect too much, and secondly they still have a combative attitude carried over from the Nixon-Ford years, but I intend to step up considerably my relationships with the congressional leaders that I never get to see, except during a time of crisis.

President Ford came, and our scheduled thirty-minute meeting lasted for about an hour and fifteen minutes. He's extremely interested in what is going on in our diplomatic relationships and in my dealings with the Congress. He was quite complimentary about what we had done so far, except he was concerned about spending getting out of hand and the budget becoming more deeply unbalanced. I have the same concern, and I think our meeting was productive. He arranged with Brzezinski for continuing briefings concerning international affairs. I asked him if he would be willing to help me on a special mission in the future or special assignment if it was necessary, and he said he would be honored if I would ask him.

I kept both Ford and Nixon thoroughly informed, until Nixon sent me word that he was getting too many briefings. After I left the White House I rarely had any such briefings, except under George H. W. Bush. When I told Reagan that I planned to inform the media that neither he nor his staff had kept their obligation to brief me, he sent his national security advisor to Plains, but the briefing was pointless. All he gave me were a few items of information that had already been published in the news media.

MARCH 25   Senator [Howard] Metzenbaum [Democrat from Ohio] yesterday gathered fifty-seven senators' names on a letter supporting my stand on human rights. The response was very good, and that relatively small number was because he didn't have time to contact more people. The one disconcerting aspect of the human rights effort has been the weak-kneed approach of columnists who would be willing to abandon the concept of human rights in order to appease dictators and totalitarian government leaders in South America and in the Soviet Union. I don't intend to modify my position. I think it has strong support among the American people.

MARCH 27   I'm planning to ask Nelson Rockefeller [former governor of New York and vice president under Gerald Ford] to go down to a few of our doubtful countries in South America — Brazil and some others — to try to shore up relations that have been damaged by my nonproliferation and human rights statements. The primary concern, however, has been with the Soviet Union. We've had about ten proposals that we've put to them in addition to the SALT negotiations, and perhaps we can make some progress there.

MARCH 29   I'm beginning to get concerned about the coordination of a balanced budget, the cost of welfare reform, the cost of tax reform, and the energy policy consequences. [Economic advisor] Charlie Schultze and

[Treasury Secretary] Mike Blumenthal and the vice president and others have begun to draw all this together with Jim Schlesinger.

Harold Brown came by this afternoon to talk about our future relationship with China. He feels that we ought to move as rapidly as we can to normalize relations and is going to talk to the Joint Chiefs about their beginning to assess the military defense consequences of such a move.

I had been fascinated with China since visiting there in April 1949 as a young submarine officer. Just a few months later, the Nationalist forces abandoned the mainland and moved to Taiwan, and the People's Republic of China was formed on October 1 (my birthday). Although President Nixon visited mainland China and declared that there was only one China, he refrained from saying which one because of the tremendous influence of the pro-Taiwan lobby and the Republican Party derogation of "Red China." The strategic advantages of diplomatic relations with the People's Republic of China seemed obvious, as a means to enhance peace and stability in the region, a further weakening of Soviet influence, and future benefits from trade and commerce.

Went swimming with Amy in the afternoon and have a good feeling about my relationship with her, perhaps closer now than ever. She's become remarkably well adjusted to our Washington life, and we have an opportunity at Camp David and with the swimming pool here to stay fairly close to one another. She's beginning to feel free to invite in more young people her age, and we've encouraged cabinet officers and staff members to let their children come whenever it's convenient to be with Amy. She's beginning to get invited to some of the parties for congressional leaders' children. I'm very proud of the way she's become acclimated to the White House.

APRIL 1   Began to discuss the prospect of Chip going to China and the public relations connotation of this visit. It sounds like a good idea to me.

MONDAY, APRIL 4   Welcomed President and Mrs. Anwar Sadat this morning and had my first meeting with him. At first he was a little shy, or ill at ease, perhaps because he was sick, but it soon became obvious to me that he was a charming and frank and also very strong and courageous leader who has never shrunk from making difficult public decisions. If he should become a personal ally, I think that would be significant to him and me. I believe he'll be a great aid if we get down to the final discussions on the Middle East.

He gave us fairly good news from [PLO leader Yasir] Arafat's private conversations with Sadat concerning the PLO's desire for peace. He modified his position considerably on what the nature of permanent peace might be and how soon open borders and diplomatic relationships might be established between the Arab countries and Israel. These may be simply optimistic assessments, but my judgment is that he will deliver on a lot of these promises.

Met with Andy Young and the vice president to discuss the possibilities in southern Africa. I've been getting very impatient having to wait for the British to timidly negotiate and the reluctance of frontline black presidents to cooperate with one another or with us and the timidity of the South Africans to expose themselves to public scrutiny or involvement. The best thing we can do is put together a clear concept of what we want, get as many people to join us as possible, ram it through, and then just take the consequences. Continued timidity and hesitation is working against us and for the Soviet Union and Cuba.

APRIL 5   I liked Sadat very much, and his request for military weapons was very modest. He said he would rather do without items that he needed like the F-5A fighter plane in order not to endanger the possibilities of a Middle Eastern settlement. There was a good personal friendship formed, I think, between me and Sadat.

We wound up our speed-reading course tonight. My own reading speed, maintaining I think a fairly constant level of comprehension, has been increased fourfold.

APRIL 6   Began to call and talk to senators about their voting for the fifty-dollar tax refund bill. I have mixed emotions about whether it's actually needed, but it's kind of a test now about whether we can hold together our stimulus package. I'm becoming more concerned about inflation than I am about stimulation, but our economists are almost universally committed to the proposition that this is needed.

With unemployment at almost 7 percent and slow economic growth, I decided to allot about $30 billion to stimulate the economy, focusing on funds for local governments, federal work programs, and tax reductions.

APRIL 7   Had a meeting with about fifty members of the Congress. I intend to do this about once a week, just to make a brief statement, introduce them to my staff, and then answer questions. This was a productive meeting, and it's encouraging to know that we'll have this in the future.

APRIL 8   Got a thorough briefing on zero-base budgeting, and we decided to go ahead 100 percent using this system for the fiscal year 1979 budget preparation.

I used this incisive budgeting technique for four years as governor; when I became president, I had to make some adjustments to the technique so it could be used to prepare the more complex federal budget. It requires all existing programs and proposed new ones to be compared each year, and gives the president maximum control over all items in each department's proposals. The secretary of defense objected strenuously, but he and all other cabinet leaders had to comply.

Admiral Rickover came by to talk to me about unwarranted naval contract claims and the need to strengthen the renegotiation board. He said if I would stick to principle as I had so far on things like water projects and human rights, I would come out all right. He commented that I may not win reelection in 1980, but I could come back in 1984 and win, he was sure.

APRIL 14   Later in the day a group of governors, county and city officials came to meet with me and Dr. Schlesinger about our energy policy and to present the problem they have with reduced highway maintenance and construction revenues as gasoline consumption drops.

Met with Harold Brown, Cy, and Brzezinski to prepare for SALT discussions between Vance and Dobrynin. The Soviets have proposed that Brezhnev and I work out the general terms through Dobrynin and Vance, and then let the agreement be negotiated in detail by Paul Warnke.

APRIL 15   Marty Schram gave me a copy of his new book on the election campaign. I was sitting on the Truman Balcony at lunchtime, reading it, and thought I had an appointment at 1:30, which turned out to be 1:00. That's one of the few times I've been late for a meeting.

We're trying to decide how much control there should be over warrants to tap the phones or eavesdrop on American citizens overseas and on foreign citizens who are visiting our own country or living here. My own decision is to require warrants in every doubtful case and to set up a panel of judges, one of whom would have to back up the attorney general to issue the warrant after an adequate show of cause.

This was a brief outline of the legislation that we would pass in 1978 called the Foreign Intelligence Surveillance Act (FISA). It worked well and remained in effect until the Bush administration decided to ignore or circumvent its restraints after the 9/11 attack in 2001.

APRIL 16   We [my top advisors and I] met to discuss air pollution and decided to take a strong and tough stand, which is going to be opposed by the automobile manufacturers and the UAW [United Auto Workers]. Trade-offs will be necessary, but my inclination when there's a direct conflict is to stick with environmental quality.

APRIL 17   After Sunday school and church I talked to President [Marion G.] Romney of the Mormon Church in Salt Lake City and then met with our regular Sunday school teacher, Fred Gregg, to explore the possibility for a more substantial effort in volunteer mission work for our church. The total Protestant denominations' missionary effort consists of about twenty-five thousand people. The Mormon Church alone, their volunteer short-term effort, recruits about twenty-six thousand. I'd like to see the Baptist Church take this on as a major undertaking if we can work it out, and Fred Gregg's going to Nashville to talk to the Southern Baptist Convention leaders this week.

MONDAY, APRIL 18   I gave the energy message on television and think it came out all right. Immediately began to work on the speech to the Congress for Wednesday night and to put the final touches on legislative details.

This address to the nation was to be one of the most important of my presidency. I began by saying, "Tonight I want to have an unpleasant talk with you about a problem that is unprecedented in our history. With the excep-

tion of preventing war, this is the greatest challenge that our country will face during our lifetime. The energy crisis has not yet overwhelmed us, but it will if we do not act quickly. It's a problem that we will not be able to solve in the next few years, and is likely to get progressively worse through the rest of this century . . . This difficult effort will be the 'moral equivalent of war,' except that we will be uniting our efforts to build and not to destroy."

Two nights later, I presented the details of my proposals to a joint session of Congress, and I spent the rest of my term working to pass the needed legislation.

APRIL 19   Met with the Democratic congressional leaders. We do this every two weeks, and I've always come out of these sessions with an appreciation for what they accomplish. There are so many opportunities to get divided from Congress, to inadvertently hurt someone's feelings, or to ignore their interests, and I believe these sessions are valuable on both sides.

I also met with Republican leaders. This paid rich dividends. Despite the controversial and often unpopular nature of my proposals to the Congress, I had remarkably good success in congressional approval of bills I supported. The Congressional Quarterly reported that since 1953 Lyndon Johnson, John Kennedy, and I ranked in that order in obtaining approval of legislation proposed to Congress. The Miller Center reported that my record exceeded Kennedy's.

Representative John Dingell [Democrat from Michigan] is furious about our proposals on automobile emissions. I invited him to come over to talk it over with me. He blames my staff for being incompetent, rude.

APRIL 20   Made some last-minute adjustments on the energy speech, then met with Pope Shenouda, head of the Coptic Church in Egypt. I enjoyed his visit very much. We talked about Saint Mark, the patron saint and first pope, about the places in Egypt where the Holy Family is supposed to have visited or lived while they were escaping threats against the baby Jesus from King Herod. The pope maintains that he has all the records from about 170 predecessors between him and Mark.

APRIL 21   We've begun making plans for Rosalynn to take a trip to South America. I'm concerned about our relationship with Brazil, and while she's on the trip I want her to go through Jamaica and perhaps to Peru,

Ecuador, Venezuela, and possibly Colombia. It's a rare thing for a member of the First Family to travel in Latin America, and I believe her trip can be beneficial. She's coming along well with her Spanish lessons and might take [former missionary] Wayne Smith to help her out in Brazil, where they speak Portuguese.

I talked to Senator Long again about holding the tax bill firm and asked him to come up and meet me later on in the day, which he did. Senator Long is one of the shrewdest legislative tacticians that ever lived. He always takes the attitude that he's innocent, doesn't quite know what's going on, and that other senators put things over on him, but that he'll do the best he can. He's a shrewd negotiator, and I like him.

Russell Long of Louisiana had been a senator since 1948 and was chairman of the Finance Committee, an expert on all aspects of tax law, and well-known to be dedicated to protecting oil and sugar interests.

APRIL 24   Since Fred Gregg was in Nashville, I taught Sunday school. I've done this every month, really enjoy it, and look forward to the preparation of the lesson. It's time-consuming, but it's something of a religious discipline that I need.

I had been teaching Bible lessons all my adult life, beginning as a midshipman at the U.S. Naval Academy. After leaving the White House, I continued this practice in my hometown church in Plains, Georgia.

MONDAY, APRIL 25   King Hussein from Jordan came. We all really liked him and got along well. Enjoyed his visit and believe he'll be a strong and staunch friend for us as we approach the time for a Mideast conference later this year. Although he and I both expressed public doubt about how easy a solution would be in order not to unnecessarily raise expectation for the fall, he said that for the first time in twenty-five or thirty years he felt hopeful that this year we could reach some agreements. I feel the same way.

During our meeting, King Hussein burst into tears as he was telling me about the recent death of his first wife. I arranged for him to go to the Georgia coast, where my young friends Carlton Hicks and Jimmy Bishop entertained him for about a week as he fished, swam, and flew U.S. helicopters.

Later, Hussein was a bitter disappointment, proving to be reticent and even obstructive during crucial negotiating times. He was too financially dependent on rich Arab nations to act independently. I considered him, however, to be an honest and decent man.

My basic plan is to meet with the leaders of the nations involved, completing this round in May, and then put together our own concept of what should be done in the Middle East; let Cy Vance make a trip around the area to consult with leaders, listening more than he talks—and then perhaps put as much pressure as we can on the different parties to accept the solution that we think is fair.

My own judgment at this time is that the Arab leaders want to settle it and the Israelis don't. The Israeli government has been pretty much in limbo for the last few years. I don't know if the elections in May will help or not, but we are thinking about having someone meet with the representatives of the PLO after the Israeli elections and my final meeting with other Middle East leaders.

The new prime minister of Israel should be invited to come over here, even before the government is put together, if that's possible.

APRIL 27   Stu Eizenstat came in early in the morning to tell me that they had worked out a compromise solution on the antiboycott legislation that apparently satisfies the Jewish citizens, the business leaders, and the Congress. If true, this is a remarkable achievement.

Before I was elected, the League of Arab States had a long-standing embargo of trade with Israel and a secondary boycott of U.S. corporations that did business with Israel. My proposal was to make it a crime for any corporation to comply with the boycott. It was difficult to meet the demands of the Jewish community regarding our response to the boycott and at the same time overcome strong opposition to antiboycott legislation by the business executives who had been yielding to this blackmail. In June, we finally passed legislation based on an agreement among the groups mentioned above.

I've decided to send Fritz to meet with Vorster in South Africa and also want him to visit Portugal and Spain just to show our appreciation for their move toward democracy.

Met with the leaders of the NEA [National Education Association]. They are quite interested in having a separate education department formed. If we can work out some independent agency just for education where the teachers don't dominate it, then I would favor the idea.

APRIL 28 [White House physician] Dr. [William] Lukash called to tell me that the little lump in Rosalynn's breast had been examined and the mammogram had shown that it was benign, but they were going to operate if I had no objection because there was still a doubt. We all agreed that the operation should be conducted as early as possible, and they did it right after I talked to him. The tumor when removed proved to be all right. We had been worried about this for two or three days. Because of the rain and heavy traffic she was late getting home from the hospital. I sat on the balcony waiting for her. She seemed to be feeling well with not much pain from the operation.

APRIL 29 The National Security Council staff has prepared for me what we call our international goals. This is a good framework around which to build our day-to-day decisions. I think a growing consciousness of these tangible goals will be good to bind us all together in a common effort.

I had launched this effort immediately after being elected, under the direction of Brzezinski, Cy Vance, Harold Brown, Andy Young, and some of their assistants. Our early priorities were a Panama treaty, peace for Israel and its neighbors, normal relations with China, nuclear arms control with the Soviets, the end of racial supremacy in Rhodesia and South Africa, better relations with less-developed countries, a strengthened NATO, reform of intelligence agencies, reduction in U.S. arms sales, and nuclear nonproliferation. I met with a bipartisan group of congressional leaders at the Smithsonian Institution on January 12, before my inauguration, and described these plans to them. I ordered Presidential Review Memoranda on all these goals, and the last one was completed on this date. (Brzezinski describes this process in detail in his book Power and Principle.)

MAY 3 The congressional leadership breakfast was devoted almost entirely to expressions on the part of the liberal members (Tip O'Neill, Shirley Chisholm, and John Brademas) that we were neglecting social programs in order to try to balance the budget in four years. I took very strong exception to this and asked the vice president to delineate in a memorandum all the things that we are doing far beyond what anyone has ever attempted, including Lyndon Johnson, in my opinion. But because the Congress doesn't oppose what we put forward, there's been very little acknowledgment of the progress that we're trying to make. In my opinion there's no way to have available financial resources in two or three years for better health care or welfare reform if we don't put some tight constraints on unnecessary spending quite early.

MAY 4   Met with Congressman Steve Solarz, who is primarily interested in the Syrian Jews being able to leave and in particular five hundred young women who are unmarried. Some of the young men have been permitted to immigrate to this country, but they can't find wives, and the women who are still in Syria can't find husbands. I'll discuss this with President Assad when I get to Geneva.

Amazingly, we were successful. The young women came to New York, young men made their choices, a large number of marriages were performed, and the remaining unmarried women returned to Syria. In later years, Hafez al-Assad teased me about some of the Jews preferring Syria to America.

MAY 6   Departed on Air Force One for the northeastern part of England in the Newcastle area, Tyne and Wear County, which was coincidentally the only county that the Labour Party didn't lose in the elections yesterday.

This was a state visit prior to the G7 meeting involving Great Britain, France, Germany, the United States, Canada, Japan, and Italy. I had wanted to visit the Welsh home of my favorite poet, Dylan Thomas, but British prime minister Jim Callaghan asked me to make an appearance here to help Labour candidates. Coached by Jim, I shouted their local slogan, "Ha'way the Lads," and the crowd of thirty thousand responded enthusiastically. They made me an honorary citizen, with lifetime grazing rights on the common pasture.

I'm at somewhat of a disadvantage in discussing the finance matters because [Jim] Callaghan, [Yasuo] Fukuda [Japan], [Valéry] Giscard [D'Estaing, France], and [Helmut] Schmidt [Germany] have all been finance ministers and have economics as a background. I've already begun to see the need for me to travel more and learn more about other leaders and countries. There's a great desire in the Western world for a restoration of confidence, and I believe that unless that confidence is derived from the strength of our country it won't be coming from any other source. There doesn't seem to be any jealousy of the strength of the United States, only an eagerness to see their own nations consulted on matters and an assurance that we won't make peremptory decisions that might be embarrassing to them at home. Every one of the other leaders is very weak politically, and they recognize that at least for the moment I'm quite strong politically. They also see that to show a friendly relationship with me but to retain their own independence and prerogatives is a good combination for them politically. And, of course, I'm eager to accommodate that desire on their part.

I was surprised at the strength of Pierre Trudeau [prime minister of Canada], who seems to be at ease with all the others, quite uninhibited in his expressions of opinion, and they seemed to listen to him quite closely.

The Germans have some concern about our human rights position because they feel that in a quiet, unpublicized way they've extracted many East European citizens into the western European area.

Callaghan showed us the room at 10 Downing Street where we will be meeting. It's so small that only twenty-two people can get in it, but it's been set up in a wonderful way, I think, for free discussions where there will be a disinclination to make speeches. Obviously there's a tremendous struggle among staff members and others to get inside the room, but I think Callaghan did wisely to hold the room so there's no way to stretch the limit.

MAY 7   Had a very productive breakfast with Helmut Schmidt. We worked out all our differences, I think, on assistance to Portugal, the MBFR [mutual and balanced force reductions] data revelations on both sides, nonproliferation, and the German-Brazilian nuclear reprocessing problem. The chancellor is concerned about overemphasis on Germany's leadership position in Europe. He said it arouses competition among the other European countries, particularly France, revives the old concern about Nazism, and also overemphasizes Soviet concern about German military strength.

We spent this morning getting acquainted with President Giscard, [Giulio] Andreotti [prime minister of Italy], and the other leaders and discussing the world economic situation. The Germans, we, and the Japanese are the strong countries now. There was a general feeling put forward by Schmidt and me and Trudeau that the major outcome of our meeting ought to be a genuine expression of confidence in the future without misleading the people about the problems that we face. It's obvious to me that together we can meet the present economic difficulties, and my own hope is that we might begin to bring into our councils OPEC nations like the Saudi Arabians who have shown every inclination to cooperate and be a part of the political decision-making body of national leaders.

During the afternoon we addressed two questions that had not been confronted before because of their divisive nature. One was nuclear energy and particularly nonproliferation. The other was the question of human rights. The Canadians have become extremely strict in their sale of natural uranium, and we are becoming increasingly strict about the sale of our enriched uranium to nations that don't agree to adequate international safeguards. This has really upset the other countries who attended the conference. We debated for three hours about the subject. Some of the nations have signed a nonproliferation treaty and agreed not to produce weapons, like Germany and Japan. Others have signed the NPT and are producing weapons like us. Others are producing weapons and haven't signed the NPT, like France. Some are heavily dependent on imports of nuclear fuel. And some, like the United States and Canada, are heavy exporters of nuclear fuels.

There's a general feeling that we ought to have adequate fuel supplies to generate electric power, but we ought to have some constraints so the fuel we sell can't be changed into weapons. But the national pride of nations like France, Germany, Japan, Great Britain, and Italy prevent their acceptance of intrusion into their right to reprocess and do as they please with the reprocessed fuel, which does contain plutonium suitable for bombs.

We alleviated a great deal of misunderstanding. For instance, the Germans were quite shocked when I told Helmut Schmidt that we would not permit other nations to export their nuclear wastes to be stored in North America. He had a genuine feeling or belief that because of our broad areas of land we and the Canadians would be glad to accept nuclear wastes from the European countries. I pointed out to him that you could store all the nuclear waste there was on one square mile if you were willing to accept its presence; the size of the country was not particularly significant.

The other point was human rights. The Canadians and French agreed with me that the free world ought to take the initiative in espousing human rights and not let that initiative remain erroneously with the Communist countries. The British and Germans were quite concerned that we might upset the sensitivities of the Soviet Union and we ought to stay quiet. The Italian and the Japanese leaders had very little to say about it.

Tonight I went to Buckingham Palace for the first time, and it is absolutely beautiful. The royal family was there, and I let the queen know how grateful we were last year when she came to visit our country on the bicentennial of our independence. Although she has to be very cautious about what she says, she's apparently very well informed about British politics and world affairs.

She pointed out that her waist had to be watched very closely because she had seven different tunics, her uniforms to wear for the seven different guard troops, and that she couldn't afford to change the costumes and had to wear the same size for a number of years. Just jokingly we decided that when we shift to the metric system we'll measure waist dimensions in inches and everything else in centimeters. And that seemed to suit her well.

MAY 8   Went to Westminster Abbey early this morning. Bishop Fisher welcomed us and after the communion service took us on a tour of Westminster, which was very exciting. We visited the room where thirty-two scholars translated the King James Bible, finishing work in 1601. We also visited the Poets' Corner, where they've honored people like Dryden, Poe, Longfellow, Shakespeare, and others. I suggested to Bishop Fisher it was time for them to do the same thing for Dylan Thomas.

The bishop condemned Dylan as a drunkard, and I pointed out the personal fallibilities of Poe, Lord Byron, and others. Prime Minister Callaghan later warned me that the selection committee was a distinguished group and impervious to outside influence. Despite this, I persisted, and early in 1981 Dylan Thomas was given equal honors. A special message from me was played at the ceremony, and the people of Wales presented me with a duplicate of Dylan's marble slab in Westminster.

We finished our summit talks today. They were very productive, far beyond anything I had anticipated — in the outcome and also in the freedom and openness of the debate. I've gotten to know the other leaders, and I think we have a good relationship. I was particularly impressed with Valéry Giscard d'Estaing from France. Of course, along with him in intellect and strength would be Helmut Schmidt.

MONDAY, MAY 9   Had breakfast with Giscard, who seems to be a brilliant and strong man. He doesn't waste words and seems to have a very analytical mind. Certain autocratic demeanor, but perhaps that's what France needs now in a time of economic crisis and prospective takeover by the leftists in the 1978 election. He seemed to be quite convinced that Israelis are international outlaws and that the Arab position is proper.

We then went to a four-power conference which ostensibly was to discuss Berlin, but it was a two-and-a-half-hour private talk with us, British, German, and French leaders only. Most of their interest was in our relationship with the Soviets, SALT, comprehensive test ban, progress we had made with Israeli and Arab leaders. This was a good chance for the British, French, and Germans to relieve some of the small dissensions that inevitably arise over a year's time.

I then went to Geneva for a three-and-a-half-hour session with President Assad from Syria. It was a very interesting and enjoyable experience. He and I hit it off well. We had a lot of humor between us, and I found him to be constructive toward the need for a Middle Eastern settlement and somewhat flexible in dealing with the more crucial items involving peace, the Palestinians, the refugee problem, and borders—plus international supervision of borders once they are established later this year. He seemed to be eager that this be accomplished and said that a year or two ago it would have been almost suicidal in his own country to talk about peace with the Israelis. They've come a long way and were willing to cooperate. I'm beginning to feel a little hope for the first time about a Middle East settlement or at least major progress this year. The biggest unknown factor is of course the Israeli attitude because they are so fearful about their permanent security and perhaps more inclined to be distrustful about us and others. This is a question I'll have to address when I get back home.

When I arrived back at Heathrow Airport, Clark Clifford met me to give me a report on the Greek-Turkish interrelationship—one of distrust, animosity, but reluctance to become involved in war over the Aegean Sea. They relegate the Cyprus question, which is important in the United States, to a position of secondary importance between them.

MAY 10   I had a meeting with the Greeks early. [Prime Minister Konstantinos] Karamanlis is completely convinced that the Greeks are angels, the Turks are devils, and in giving me his completely objective analysis, he tried to prove this point. He claimed great reticence in not responding to the constant Turkish provocations, and still claimed a willingness to meet on a continuing basis with the Turks to resolve the Aegean Sea dispute over the continental shelf oil exploration, airplane overflights, and the illegal fortification by the Greeks of some of their islands. He admitted the latter but said it was a result of Turkish provocation.

Then I met with [Prime Minister Süleyman] Demirel of Turkey, who was pouting about our failures to approve the military assistance treaty. I pointed out to him that there was no hope for the Congress to approve this agreement unless the Turks showed some constructive progress on Cyprus. He relegated that to a position of inconsequence and said he didn't want to equate the two. I told him that he should take a positive attitude—take credit among his own people for the increase in the allotment of military purchases from $127 to $175 million in public, deplore lack of progress on Cyprus and the military assistance treaty, but not constantly complain about our lack of progress, which hurts U.S.-Turkish relationships and also makes him look as though he is an ineffective leader. I think he understood our position, but of course he didn't agree with it.

We went to a NATO meeting, and I gave the keynote address. The basic thrust was that the U.S. had overcome the problem of a lack of commitment to NATO. I believe that the overall result of these discussions (I had to listen to fourteen speeches after I got through) was that there was a renewed commitment to NATO, although some of the countries are very weak economically and can't do very much. But there's a new spirit and a sense of confidence that didn't exist before. In all on this trip I had private bilateral meetings with sixteen or seventeen leaders of the Western democracies and accomplished all our purposes. We arrived back home late that evening.

Rosalynn and Fritz met me at the airport and reported that response in our own country to our tremendous reception had been very favorable. It was a good trip. I enjoyed it, learned a lot, established a position of leadership, and look forward to building on this to meet our purposes in the future.

MAY 11   Played tennis with Bert Lance, and it was one of the few times that I've ever beat him, pretty badly. He's a much better tennis player than I am.

In the evening Rosalynn and I went to the Kennedy Center to the opera *The Barber of Seville*. When we saw the performers after the opera was over, they were quite surprised that we stayed to the end. I really enjoyed it. One of the most remarkable sets I've ever seen. It was beautiful, with innovative costumes, and the acting was perhaps better than the music.

MAY 12   Had my seventh press conference, which I enjoy and believe they give me the opportunity to both educate the American people and give them a sense of participation in government. Sometimes it seems that twice a month is too frequent, but I intend to maintain this pace throughout my service as president.

After a couple of years, we reduced the frequency. There were only the three major television networks then, and they would grant full coverage in the evening for major news stories. Increasingly the afternoon sessions were not live, and only snippets of the news conference would be shown later, often heavily edited.

Brzezinski and I went over the list of twenty-five to thirty nations that had reported to us improvements in the field of human rights, and he made a list of those for me. In general, the leaders of the world are constantly preoccupied with the human rights issue, and this is a good pressure for us to maintain through public statements and through preparation for the Belgrade conference.

MAY 13   Signed the public works job bill and the appropriations bill for the economic stimulus package. About $4 billion for public works and about $20 billion in all for economic stimulus. In my opinion this will be adequate as a program for this year.

I then had a meeting with Robert Goheen, who's going to be ambassador to India. The biggest immediate problem is whether or not we should provide atomic fuel for India's power plants, absent their willingness to comply with international safeguards on reprocessing. We may make a temporary delivery, but I'm going to be firm with India if they want to get fuel from us.

Then met with the Brotherhood Commission of the Southern Baptist Convention and made a short talk with them. I felt at home and have a sense that there is strong support among them and millions of Baptists for me. I think they recognize the special problems of the president, and they all talk about praying for me to do a good job.

Had lunch with Rosalynn. We intend to do this every week so that we can actually discuss official business that exists between the East Wing and the West Wing. This has tended to be delayed too long.

MAY 15   We spent Sunday at Camp David. This is a perfect place to actually rest. It's about the only place I've found where our family can be alone and where I can get private work done and do some thinking on long-range subjects. Also we're close enough to Washington so I can be in charge of any emergency that arises in just a few minutes. The communications setup is almost as good as at the White House. I expect that in the future we will restrict our vacation time to Camp David, after I make the planned trip down to Saint Simons Island [in Georgia].

MAY 17   Took a long, all-day trip out to Los Angeles to speak to the United Auto Workers convention. The response was very good. I outlined the administration's policies on basic domestic issues and announced that Leonard Woodcock would be my representative to the People's Republic of China.

Although not familiar with foreign affairs, as head of the UAW Woodcock was a superb negotiator. This is what I wanted, since I was ready to begin serious talks with China, largely bypassing the State Department except for Cy Vance. To preserve absolute secrecy, all messages concerning the talks with China would be sent directly from the White House.

MAY 18   I briefed key senators on our SALT negotiation positions that would be put forward by Cy Vance to [Foreign Minister Andrei] Gromyko in Geneva. We hope they will be successful, but the Soviets have been adamant about not cutting back on their very large missiles. We've been equally adamant about not cutting back on our freedom to evolve cruise missiles in the future. The senators were supportive, but I doubt that their support will last if we start compromising on an equal basis with the Soviets' compromises.

Had our first meeting with Mike Blumenthal and his people on tax reform. My feeling is that they have not gone nearly far enough in getting to a basic reform effort but were somewhat superficial in their proposals. I told them what I wanted, and maybe in the next meeting we'll make some progress. I don't believe we'll ever get tax reform through the Congress unless it is bold, drastically simplifies the system, and provides for better equity. Just amending what we have now will make us subject to successful competition from the special interest groups because the public can't understand the complexities.

MAY 19 We met with some of the congressional campaign committee concerning the voter registration law. This is going to be a hard one to pass, but I'm going to put a lot of time in on it, and so is Fritz. Maybe we can get it through.

I found even the most liberal members averse to any new openings for voter registration, because they wanted to retain the same constituencies that had elected them. As governor, I had deputized all high school principals as voter registrars and set aside a week every May to register all students approaching the age of eighteen. The quiet but all-pervasive opposition to national reform finally prevailed, although some individual states made progress.

Later met with Kingman Brewster, who is leaving for Great Britain to be our ambassador there. He seems to be more British than American in his demeanor and somewhat pompous attitude, but he gets very high marks from those who know him better than I do.

Billy and I had a long talk. I think his interest in being a public figure has probably interfered with his interest in Carter's Warehouse, which is of some concern to me.

My brother Billy, who was thirteen years younger than I, had become a partner in our family business when he returned home from service in the U.S. Marine Corps. Until I became president, I had made all the major decisions involving the business, but now Billy had to accommodate the advice of my trustee, Charles Kirbo. Billy's relationship with Kirbo was somewhat strained; in addition, Billy had become quite famous and was spending a lot of his time traveling to several countries and earning substantial fees for some of his appearances. With the lease of our warehouse to a large cooperative, this problem was eventually resolved.

MAY 20   President Ford came to spend almost an hour with me. He's very eager to learn about some of the projects that are going on in his absence, and when he's with me he's very congenial, constructive, helpful, and complimentary. I notice that when he's away speaking to Republican groups he can be quite critical, but in general I've been pleased with my relationship with him since he's been out of office. I've been completely frank with him in discussing some of our foreign affairs and feel better knowing that he and I are congenial about these matters.

I continued to keep Ford and Nixon well informed, and they gave me invaluable support among Republican legislators and the general public in controversial decisions involving the Middle East, Panama, China, and our energy proposals. Later, as ex-presidents, Jerry Ford and I formed a close personal friendship, as did our wives, Rosalynn and Betty.

MAY 21   During the afternoon I met with Major General [John] Singlaub about his statement that if we withdrew troops from South Korea a war would result. He denied making the statement. He said he was just quoting from Korean officials. Then he said that the reporter was not given authority to quote him. I don't think he was telling the truth, but I felt sorry for him. He emphasized over and over that he was not disloyal, that he'd meant no insubordination. So instead of reprimanding him I just told him that we would transfer him out of Korea.

MAY 22   I went to Sunday school and then to Notre Dame, where I received an honorary degree. Had I known ahead of time they planned to do this, I would have not let them. My own intentions were to receive an honorary degree only from Georgia Tech.

Subsequently I have received several dozen honorary doctorates, ranging from William Jewell College in Missouri (which has about one thousand students) to Oxford University in England. In many cases, of course, the university offering the degree is interested in obtaining a free speaker for graduation exercises.

MONDAY, MAY 23   I watched a replay of an *Issues and Answers* interview with Menachem Begin, chairman of the Likud Party and prospective prime minister of Israel. It was frightening to watch his adamant position on issues that must be resolved if a Middle Eastern peace settlement is going to be realized.

We had our first session on the budget preparation for fiscal year 1979. It's going to be difficult to balance the budget if the Congress continues to spend money like it was going out of style.

MAY 24   Called Harold Brown and [Secretary of Interior] Cecil Andrus and told them to expedite the sale of the USS *Sequoia*, which was costing about $250,000 a year to maintain and which I would never use. This was completed, and the purchaser agreed to treat it as though it was a national monument.

I was quite surprised when this sale aroused public and media criticism that persisted long after I left office. Some historians, political writers, and political opponents claimed that I was failing to honor the history and legacy of the U.S. presidency, but the Sequoia's *historical significance was scanty. The yacht was named by the CEO of Sequoia Oil Company before being acquired by the U.S. government in 1931 as a patrol boat. Herbert Hoover borrowed it during his presidency; later, the vessel was used by various cabinet officers and presidents before I sold it. Under pressure from its protectors, the ship was designated a National Historic Landmark in 1987 and is now in private ownership.*

Fritz reported that we were doing well with Spain and Portugal, that he and Vorster [of South Africa] had had a very clear understanding of one another's position. He thought there was some help that Vorster might give us with Namibia and that he has agreed that in Zimbabwe the government would be based on majority rule. However, on change in South Africa itself, Vorster retained his own long-standing commitment to apartheid, insisted that the blacks were a different kind of human beings, and was recalcitrant about changing the attitude or structure of the government. My own guess, however, is that our quiet but persistent pressure along with other nations might force evolutionary changes in South Africa. They are not going to give up the white-controlled government, however.

Crown Prince Fahd arrived, along with Prince Saud, representing Saudi Arabia. As has been the case with other Arab leaders, we got along well. They're very frank, speak easily, want friendship with us, are heavily dependent upon us for their military security, look on war in the Mideast with abhorrence, know that disruptions might endanger their great wealth and precarious position, are deeply religious, despise communism, and are fearful of Israel. Fahd was very friendly, certified that there was no problem with a possible embargo, attributed to us the authority which we don't have to require a settlement from Israel, was insistent that occupied territory be relinquished by Israel, seemed more interested in the Palestinian question than all the other problems that are faced in the Middle East. He was quite disturbed about Begin's election in Israel and felt that this was quite a setback, but he still retained an outward display of confidence that we could make progress during 1977.

I had not dreamed that Menachem Begin, once declared by Great Britain to be a foremost terrorist leader in the region, would win the election that May and become Israel's leader. Before Israel gained independence in 1948, Begin had headed an extremist group known as the Irgun; later, he became leader of the conservative political party, the Likud.

MAY 25   I've let the Saudis know that any meetings with the PLO would have to be combined with the PLO endorsement of UN Resolution 242 with minor adjustments involving the identification of the Palestinians other than as refugees.

In the evening I went to the annual Senate and House Democratic fund-raising dinner and made a so-called humorous address to them. These have been the major kinds of speeches that I have to perform since I've been president. They would be better off electing Bob Hope president as far as public statements are concerned, since that seems to be the heaviest demand on a president's speaking time. The banquet was very successful, the best one ever, raising about $1.2 million in gross receipts.

MAY 26   I signed Protocol I of the Treaty of Tlatelolco, which joins us with Latin American nations in prohibiting the deployment of atomic weapons in that region.

Following that we went to Saint Simons. Musgrove Plantation is a fine place to go, but the movement of the entourage and the heavy publicity makes it not nearly so pleasant as going, for instance, to Camp David. Of course, there's the advantage of being near the sea, on the marshland, and the possibility of seeing some of our Georgia friends as a compensating factor. I think trips other than to Camp David might be much fewer than we thought before inauguration.

MAY 27   Rosalynn and I flew down to Cape Canaveral to spend the day with Admiral Rickover—about nine hours on the nuclear attack submarine USS *Los Angeles*. It was one of the most interesting days I've ever spent, both being with Rickover and also seeing the developments in the submarine force since I left, twenty-four years ago. Some of the things we had put on USS *K-1* are being used, but of course a nuclear sub is completely different. It's about three times as large as a fleet-type submarine. Probably the finest military weapon ever devised. Rickover has approached perfection in the design, construction, training, and operation of these nuclear ships, and at a very low relative price to our country. As a matter of fact, all the nuclear ships that he's built, as he says, stretched end to end would be over ten miles long. They've never had a nuclear mishap or accident of any kind. They have never released radioactive materials into the ocean, and the total cost of all these ships is less than sending the first man into a space flight.

Rosalynn and I were given a thorough briefing on the characteristics of the ship—to see it dive and surface, to steer it and control the depth, see it engaged in violent maneuvers, watch the reactors in emergency shutdown—and spent hours listening to Rickover with his experts talk about the tactics of using the ships to escort surface ships like carriers, and also to attack other ships.

I was surprised when I asked Rickover how he would react to a total elimination of all nuclear weapons from the earth. He said it would be one of the greatest things that could happen and he would also be pleased to see the removal of all nuclear power plants. He wished atomic power had never been discovered. I didn't tell him, but I've decided to ask Rickover to stay on duty for another two years, although he's seventy-seven years old. I've never been more weary than I was when I arrived back in Brunswick, but Rickover didn't seem to be fatigued at all, even though he stayed with us throughout the whole day—up and down ladders to the bridge, standing for hours discussing the ship's characteristics, and he gave most of the lectures while we just listened in the wardroom. He corrected the enlisted men and officers as they discussed their own battle stations and made a few mistakes.

MAY 28   We went fishing on Blackbeard Island, leaving about 6:00 a.m. and getting over there about 9:00 a.m. We fished for bluegill bream, and Charlie and I caught the largest bream I've ever seen. I enjoyed talking with Kirbo about the problems that I face as president, with big business, who are a greedy bunch; or the special interest groups; Congress; some of the foreign leaders. Quite often when I talk to him this in itself is helpful, but in addition he's sometimes able to solve my problems. He has unique interrelationships both inside and outside of government, and he's close enough to understand me well, and very discreet. He's able to separate his law practice from his relationship with me, which is also reassuring.

MAY 29   After fishing in the Gulf Stream, Rosalynn spent the rest of the day studying for her trip to South America, and after supper I spent several hours answering questions that she had listed from her twenty-five or thirty hours of briefings by the National Security Council and the State Department. With her normal White House duties, running the house, taking care of all our books, working on problems of the aged, mental health hearings around the country, and this trip, she's had too much to do, and she's planning not to schedule any specific responsibilities during July.

MONDAY, MAY 30   Rosalynn left this morning, going to Jamaica and then to Costa Rica, Ecuador, Peru, Brazil, Colombia, and Venezuela. My hope and expectation are that her conversations will both convince the people of these countries of our interest and friendship and also provide the leaders with an avenue directly to me for their problems, opportunities, and requests from our own government. My guess is that she'll more than live up to expectations.

MAY 31   Back in Plains, I went to the warehouse and then walked down Main Street and visited all the stores. In spite of hundreds of tourists crowding in, I enjoyed it very much. Amy and I ate lunch at the Pond House with Mother, who is in better physical and mental condition than I've seen her in years. We put fish in her pond, which I think is going to help even more. Amy would rather be in Plains than anywhere else. We came back to Washington to a lonely White House without Rosalynn.

After eating home cooking for a week, I found that I weighed 162 pounds, and I resolved to lose 6 pounds. When I started running regularly, I main-

tained my weight at about 145 and my pulse at 40. I am now eighty-five years old, and they're about 150 and 60.

JUNE 1   The backlog of paperwork was mountainous. This is my biggest headache, trying to keep current with routine work and still have time for long-range strategic decisions. It doesn't stop when I'm not here; just piles up deeper.

I was a fast reader and wanted to know as much as possible about the issues I had to decide, but still had to chastise my staff on occasion when I was overloaded with paperwork.

Tip O'Neill came over for supper, and we had a long talk. He thought that relations between the Congress and me were very good, that we were too much involved in details of legislation, and we ought to deal just with the major items. This is not something that I could accept, but it was interesting to have his advice. He is determined to help me all he can, I believe. He is quite impressed with a poll in Massachusetts showing I had a 20 percent higher rating than Senator Kennedy or any other political leader in the state.

JUNE 2   Rosalynn calls each day and feels that her trip is extremely successful. The private communiqués from State and NSC confirm this, and in addition there is superb editorial comment from the Latin American countries about her visits. I was sure that she would be underestimated even by herself, but I've had complete confidence in her ability to carry out her successful mission.

Cy Vance made a report to me about his European trips, particularly [his] meeting with the less-developed countries. This is one area where we have no adequate policy, and I believe that we are just postponing from one meeting to another an ultimate showdown. There's just no public support in any of the developed nations for a massive aid program for the LDCs.

I had my first budget hearing today—about three hours on defense. No president has ever done this before, but it's a preliminary review of the major options that we have through the year 1981–82. It will help prevent a lot of unnecessary work on the part of the departments and OMB [Office of Management and Budget], and assure that the differences between me and my cabinet members are revealed early.

JUNE 3   The Mormon Church leaders presented me a fairly complete genealogical record of my father's family, back, I think, twelve generations, to about 1600. I appreciated it and of course wrote thank-you notes.

Since returning home, I have been the Carter family's genealogist, keeping records on a computer program called Family Tree Maker. Others have produced research that shows I'm kin to six other presidents.

Rosalynn called from Ecuador this morning. They're concerned about an attack from Peru and are proud that they will have democratic elections soon. She got along well with the three-man military junta members. I told her to pursue Ecuadorian concerns with the Peruvians when she arrives there next.

JUNE 4   I've had my leg taped up now for about three weeks because of a severe sprain, but it's almost healed.

Rosalynn called twice today and is almost euphoric about her reception and the cohesive nature of her traveling delegation. She feels that the Peruvian visit has been the best.

MONDAY, JUNE 6   I began working today on the B-1 bomber—whether to commit ourselves to a massive construction program on it. I'll have to make this decision during this month.

JUNE 7   Rosalynn was concerned about her conversations with the foreign minister of Brazil, [Antonio] Silveira. She felt they wanted to be friendly but were trying to prove that Brazil is equal with us and will not be dominated, which of course suits me fine. [President Ernesto] Geisel is personally upset about our moves toward a SALT agreement with the Soviets and more normal relations with Cuba. They strongly oppose the Convention on Human Rights. She seems much more sure of herself than at the beginning of the trip.

I had my meeting today with the proponents of the B-1 bomber, who pointed out all the advantages of it, conveniently forgetting that there is such a thing as a cruise missile and insinuating that all B-52s are ancient and decrepit, whereas the cruise missile is a viable attack weapon and Air Force officials unanimously believe the B-52 will be effective through the 1990s.

[Maryland senator Charles] Mathias gave me a report on his opinions about Israel, which confirms what we've always said: the Israelis for a number of years have never intended to withdraw from the West Bank, and their major commitment, regardless of party, is to maintain the status quo and basically let us pay for it.

JUNE 8   We are preparing for votes on deregulation of natural gas and on tax measures to implement the energy policy. I'm quite concerned about lobbying efforts on the Hill by the oil industry and automobile companies. I think progress on the Department of Energy is quite good.

I briefed key members of Congress for about an hour and a half on our basic foreign policy proposals. It's part of a periodic effort, commenced before inauguration, to let them know what we hope to achieve because of the need for the Senate and the House to concur.

John Brademas [Democratic congressman from Indiana], Claiborne Pell [Democratic senator from Rhode Island], and I discussed what ought to be done about the Endowment for the Humanities. I've not found anyone who could explain what it's for or why it shouldn't be combined with the Endowment for the Arts. My time in choosing a director for the Endowment [of the Arts] has been about equal to the time I've spent on solving the Middle East problem.

Paul Austin [CEO of Coca-Cola Company] came by to report on his personal visit with Castro. He is eager to go into Cuba with Coca-Cola and was favorably impressed with Castro's attitude toward me and eventual lifting of the trade embargo and normalizing relationships with Cuba. Unless Castro's willing to release political prisoners and start withdrawing from Africa, this prospect is still quite distant.

Rosalynn was quite exhausted and pointed out that five countries on one trip was enough; her studies and the demanding schedule had just about worn her out. She's got Colombia and Venezuela still to go, but I think their natural friendship toward us will make it the easiest part of her trip.

JUNE 9   Met with congressional leaders for breakfast, and their primary concern was the excessive agenda we had put on them. We had a fairly good analysis of where we are going this year and how much has already been achieved. The major challenges are excessive appropriations and implementation of an adequate energy policy. The influence of the special interest lobbies is almost unbelievable, particularly from the automobile and oil industries.

I met with Senator Humphrey about the Middle East. He is supportive and will make a public statement confirming my commitment to Israel and the general framework of my proposals on the Middle East. He specifically suggested I meet with Arthur Goldberg, author of UN Resolution 242, which is a basis for agreement in general terms.

We continued our budget meetings. It's obvious that the space shuttle is just a contrivance to keep NASA alive, and that no real need for the space shuttle was determined before the massive construction program was initiated.

We had a meeting in the afternoon with top advisors about how we should move on the Middle East, with the shock of the Begin election and the pressure we've been applying to bring the different parties together. There's beginning to evolve an adverse reaction within the American Jewish community. We want to stop this and cement our own efforts with support from the Senate and other congressional leaders.

The Senate voted a very good automobile and air pollution control measure. If we can hold this intact, it will be adequate. When I called [Tennessee senator] Howard Baker, he said he had never been called before by a president as a result of his action in the Senate.

JUNE 10   I had a meeting with the anti–B-1 bomber group, which presented a very good and comprehensive analysis of why the B-1 should not be built. I will undoubtedly devote a good bit more time to it than I have already.

JUNE 11   Met for about an hour with Arthur Goldberg to get his historical background on UN Resolutions 242 and 338, to discuss his thought about what should be the outlines of the final settlement, and to explore the possibility that he might help us. I found him to be extremely knowledgeable, even about the most minute detail—and that his concepts were very compatible with my own.

As a U.S. Supreme Court justice, Goldberg had been a strong opponent of the death penalty. He was induced by President Johnson to resign and become ambassador to the United Nations, where he was one of those who drafted Resolution 242 as a basis for a peace settlement in the Middle East. He was also president of the American Jewish Committee. I decided to recruit him as an official advisor on Middle East affairs and later as chairman of our delegation to the Belgrade conference on human rights.

JUNE 12   Rosalynn was very satisfied with the results of her visits with the foreign leaders. This may be the longest that we have been apart since I left the navy, and twelve days is just too long.

MONDAY, JUNE 13   Had the cabinet meeting, which was pleasant and relaxed, perhaps because Cy Vance and I were glad to have our wives home. [Gay Vance had just returned from a trip of her own.]

JUNE 15   Had a morning meeting with ten Democratic senators, and I'll continue these meetings until I have a chance to talk to all of them. They are eager to be involved in the early stages of [some of my] major decisions, and I encourage them to call me directly in case of need—which they are reluctant to do.

JUNE 16   I started the day in a private meeting with the vice president, Dr. Brzezinski, [and Senators] Abe Ribicoff, Ed Muskie, Hubert Humphrey, and Scoop Jackson. I think I convinced them that concerns within the Jewish community could only be alleviated if they took a role as leaders in supporting what I have proposed. Also, when Begin comes there must be an effort to convince him that with a definition of peace, which is a major concession on the part of the Arabs, and with a Palestinian state tied to Jordan, the Israelis must relinquish occupied territories as part of the overall peace settlement. If I and the Senate are not in harmony, it would be very bad. I think the meeting was constructive, and I was pleased with it.

Senator Ribicoff, from Connecticut, Muskie, Humphrey, and Jackson were very influential with Jewish citizens. This dialogue between the American Jewish community and me would continue during the next thirty years, with the key issue being my belief that peace could come to Israel and its neighbors only with withdrawal of Israeli military and political forces from occupied territories, as defined by UN resolutions, international law, and official U.S. policy. It was and is my view that borders between Israel and its neigh-

bors should approximate the pre-1967 "green line," modified by some swaps of territory as decided in peace talks.

We've a problem because of my income tax return where we owe no tax for 1976. We're trying to decide what to do about it. My inclination is to go ahead and announce the return to the public. Jody and Lipshutz feel that we should put some of the book royalties in 1976 so I can pay some taxes. We have paid taxes every year before, and I've paid corporate taxes on the farm for 1976.

JUNE 19   We had religious services at Camp David. Colonel [Cecil] Reed came over from a nearby military base. It's more convenient for us, and a good many of the marines and other military personnel come to worship with us.

It was our custom while at Camp David on Sundays to have services in a small movie theater. Later, George H. W. Bush had a lovely little chapel built at Camp David, using privately contributed funds.

MONDAY, JUNE 20   We had a meeting on airline deregulation, which will be the first test case. Later I hope to move on to deregulation of other industries. It's not going to be easy.

JUNE 21   Had a private meeting with Bob Byrd and Tip O'Neill to work out priorities on sixty or seventy bills in the Congress that we support, and I believe the Congress is making good progress on them. My reports are that the Congress in both houses is working harder than ever before for a sustained period of time.

Received a message from Prime Minister Begin accepting our invitation for a visit July the nineteenth. He was eager to do this, and I think he believes he can change my mind on the need for comprehensive decisions on Middle Eastern questions—specifically the withdrawal from the West Bank.

I signed the antiboycott legislation and included in the statement another strong profession of commitment to Israel.

JUNE 23   Had a meeting with eight or ten senators, and each one had a chance to express advice or concern about what we were doing. I learned a lot and from now on will be sure in this series of meetings to give each one a chance to speak.

JUNE 25   We had our first foreign policy breakfast with me, the vice president, Cy Vance, and Brzezinski. This will be a regular thing from now on, and I think we covered points that had been neglected because of an absence of consultation with Cy Vance. Fritz, Brzezinski, and I talk to one another daily, but Vance has traveled a lot and we've never had any routine time to meet.

Later I scheduled these breakfast meetings on Fridays and expanded them to include Harold Brown, Hamilton Jordan, and others as appropriate. I wanted to minimize any misunderstandings among the cabinet officers and ensure that everyone understood the decisions I made.

MONDAY, JUNE 27   Following the cabinet meeting I told Harold Brown that my inclination was not to build the B-1 at all. He seemed to be relieved and somewhat pleased. I asked him to give me an analysis of what this decision would mean, and obviously keep it in close confidence.

[Transportation Secretary] Brock Adams informed me that he will let the seat belt or air bag requirement go into effect in 1982 for the large automobiles and in the next two years for medium- and small-size automobiles. It's a difficult decision, but I think it's right.

JUNE 29   Harold Brown went over with me how to announce the decision not to continue with the B-1 bomber. He's been very supportive and courageous, in my opinion, to recommend that this be done. It was an easy and logical decision for me, but difficult for the Air Force. This is a turning point from manned bombers to unmanned cruise missiles and aircraft.

Secretary Kissinger came to let me know, despite reports to the contrary, that he had been very supportive as he met with foreign ambassadors around Washington and New York. I told him that reports *had* been to the contrary but I would take him at his word.

I have always had great respect for Kissinger's incisive analyses of international affairs. He supported many of my key proposals but could not resist the temptation to snipe at my administration's policies when on the lecture circuit, especially to Republican and foreign audiences. My secretary of state and other officials spent a lot of time dealing with Kissinger's criticisms.

JULY 1   Met with Gerard Smith [nominee for special representative for nonproliferation matters] and talked to him about my commitment to nuclear nonproliferation. I think we've turned the general opinion of world leaders around in the last six months. This is tied to the comprehensive test ban we've been discussing with the Soviets.

The overall reaction to the B-1 decision has been good. Both Tip O'Neill and Bob Byrd have committed to go all out in assuring that Congress accepts my position, and Harold Brown will be a staunch ally. The adverse reaction was predictable, but less than I anticipated.

Under pressure from lobbyists and the defense establishment, President Reagan later reversed my decision to cancel the B-1 bomber. The older B-52s with air-launched cruise missiles could perform the same mission at one-twentieth the cost, and our secret B-2 with "stealth" technology (invisible to radar) was in the planning stage. The B-1s were not necessary, and $10 billion was wasted on one hundred of them.

I discussed with Charlie Schultze our adverse trade balance of about $25 billion this year. Our exports have held steady and imports have increased because of a growing economy compared to the rest of the world.

For comparison, our 2008 adverse trade balance was $696 billion.

Met with [Congressman] Mike McCormack, a strong proponent of the breeder reactor and the atomic power industry. He is a nuclear physicist, has worked at the Hanford Works in Richland, Washington, and is stubborn, dedicated, and knowledgeable. His time schedule on the need for the breeder reactor is probably ten years ahead of my own.

JULY 6   I met with about fifty leaders in the American Jewish community, the presidents of organizations. We approached this with trepidation, but the meeting came out well. I reassured them that our basic commitment was the preservation of Israel as a secure and peaceful and sovereign nation. We were insisting that the Arabs commit themselves to implementing peace in its fullest sense, that my own preference was that the Palestinian state or entity should not be independent but part of Jordan. We maintained our position that Israel would have to withdraw from a substantial portion of the occupied territories.

JULY 7　Helmut Schmidt has indicated that he's quite disturbed by our nonproliferation attitudes and also by the potential disturbance of eastern Europe because of our human rights stand. He seems to be quite volatile—goes up and down in his attitude toward us—but is a good and strong and able leader.

Had lunch with Rosalynn, our thirty-first wedding anniversary, and she stayed to listen to [Ambassador and Soviet scholar] Marshall Shulman describe his impressions of the Soviet Union and give his recommendation on some things that could stabilize our relationship with them. He emphasized the age of the Soviet leadership, their relative inflexibility, concern about being treated as equals, and additional worry when we adopt a competitive position in public.

Leonard Woodcock came by to talk about the potential for normalizing relationships with China. I told him I thought normal relations were advisable, I believed I could sell it to the American people, and I would be willing to take on the political responsibility of doing so. The only remaining obstacle is our commitment not to abandon the peaceful existence of the Chinese who live on Taiwan.

We decided to get Arthur Goldberg to work with Cy as an ambassador at large, specializing in the Middle East question. I'll give Cy specific directions that can be read by Goldberg, assuring that Cy is his boss, and his responsibility would be predicated on his compatibility with the rest of our foreign policy team.

I used ambassadors at large very sparingly; in most cases, I appointed them when I felt it would be helpful to engage prominent Jewish citizens as specialists in the Middle East peace process. Even then, conflicts sometimes arose between my ambassadors at large and the secretary of state when I did not establish a clear chain of command.

JULY 8　Roberta Peters came by to speak to me. She's one of my favorite opera performers, and I enjoyed meeting her. She's just as beautiful close up as on the stage.

MONDAY, JULY 11   Discussed with Paul Warnke demilitarization of the Indian Ocean area and the test ban proposals. He's going back to Geneva to meet with the Soviets. Even if we accepted the present Soviet proposal without further negotiations, it would be a good step in the right direction, but we have hopes to abolish nuclear explosives altogether for a limited period of time—maybe three years.

JULY 12   Reports from the Middle East are slightly encouraging, with the Egyptians, Jordanians, Israelis making friendly gestures to one another.

Talked to Turner today and Brzezinski about the [former CIA director] Richard Helms case, where he's accused of perjury. He's likely to be indicted and tried, and highly sensitive data would have to be released to the public. I will discuss this with Griffin Bell before I make a decision.

Lunch with Morris Dees [head of the Southern Poverty Law Center], a superb young man very interested in doing something to constrain the death penalty. He feels that under the present Supreme Court ruling we will have maybe ten or twelve executions per month. He feels that primarily the murderers of white people are convicted, and there's still a great deal of economic and racial discrimination in the judicial system.

An unofficial moratorium on executions began in 1967, and the Supreme Court stopped them in 1972. They were reauthorized five years later; hundreds of people have been put to death since then. (In 2009 alone, fifty-two people were executed.) There is no evidence that the death penalty deters murder or other serious crimes.

JULY 13   I liked Helmut Schmidt and got along with him well when we were together in London, but reports from Europe indicate there's a difference between him and me concerning our human rights effort and the control of atomic fuel. These differences need not cause a problem, and his visit is very important.

Schmidt was a strong-willed and competent chancellor of Germany who seemed to believe that he knew more about each of the other G-7 nations than did their elected leaders. To his own and international news media he expressed his critical views frequently, as will be seen throughout my diary.

His wife [Loki] turned out to be the favorite first lady who has been here. The overall visit was almost perfect. I was particularly pleased to have Richard Rodgers, the music composer, for the entertainment tonight—a presentation by the Metropolitan Opera of excerpts from *Carousel*. This was the first stage play I ever saw, and it's always been one of my favorites.

JULY 14   Had a meeting with Hugh Carter and other members of the staff to discuss how we would react to an imminent nuclear attack. My intention is to stay here at the White House as long as I live to administer the affairs of government, and to get Fritz Mondale into a safe place, underground or in a command airplane.

JULY 15   I told Tim Kraft and Fran Voorde that I was going to change my appointments staff if I ever had another two days like yesterday and today, and was not going to warn them again.

The complete diary entries for these two days suggest that I had at least twenty-eight separate appointments during that forty-eight-hour period.

Bill Gunter outlined his program for settling the Indian claims question in the state of Maine. He acted not as an intermediary but as a judge and did a superb job.

This intriguing case addressed violations of Indian rights during the eighteenth and nineteenth centuries. The Passamaquoddy and Penobscot Indians were now claiming 60 percent of the state of Maine, an area with a population of 350,000 people. I asked Bill Gunter, a personal friend and the former Supreme Court justice of Georgia, to negotiate a settlement, which he ultimately did. The tribes received $81.4 million and special rights in the disputed area, while other citizens retained their property.

JULY 16   Spending the weekend at Camp David studying for the Begin visit, and making some notes on a speech to be made in Charleston. Got a call from Joe Califano [secretary of Health, Education, and Welfare (HEW)] expressing his strong support of my expressed opinion that the federal government should not finance abortions.

Because of my religious beliefs I have never supported abortions, except to protect the life and health of the mother or in cases where pregnancies resulted from rape or incest. But as president I had to comply with Roe v. Wade. I studied the causes of abortions carefully, and to minimize them I promoted sex education among teenagers, put forward laws that encouraged and facilitated adoptions, and established the Women and Infant Children (WIC) support program to provide guaranteed financial and medical care, among other measures.

MONDAY, JULY 18   I discovered that Prime Minister Begin wants a fully kosher meal in the White House Tuesday night, and I authorized it to be prepared.

JULY 19   We welcomed Prime Minister and Mrs. Begin from Israel. There have been dire predictions that he and I would not get along, but I found him to be quite congenial, dedicated, sincere, and deeply religious. Although it will be difficult for him to change his position, opinion polls from Israel show that the people there are quite flexible toward the West Bank, Palestinians, PLO, negotiations with the Arabs, and genuinely want peace. My guess is that if we give Begin support, he is a strong leader, quite different from Rabin, who is one of the most ineffective persons I've ever met.

In his second term, in the 1990s, Rabin proved to be a strong and courageous prime minister.

We outlined our own principles to Begin: comprehensive peace, based on UN Resolutions 242 and 338; the definition of peace would be fairly extensive; it would involve withdrawal from territory to secure boundaries in stages as the parties demonstrated their good faith; and a Palestinian entity should be created. He agreed with all the principles except the Palestinian entity. I can see some compromise positions probably acceptable to the Arabs and Israelis in arranging for a Geneva peace conference.

He agreed to keep an open mind as much as possible, pointed out that he was making tentative plans to meet directly with Sadat, and that he would use his influence in the ultimate negotiations for peace. I found him to be eager to work with me, compatible with what he considers to be the best interest of Israel.

JULY 21   Jim Schlesinger has been successful in opening up the first storage facility for oil reserves, in Louisiana. Also, we are on the verge of getting final approval on the new Department of Energy, having gotten most of what we want, not everything.

As part of our overall energy policy we began to store oil in the huge underground caves in Louisiana, which reduced the threat of another oil embargo. Now, thirty years later, the policy is to retain enough oil to supply our nation's needs for about ninety days.

JULY 22   We went to New Orleans and then out to the *Zapata Yorktown* oil rig on a helicopter. Its electronic and engineering features were very impressive. It can anchor in up to 1,000 feet of water, and the day before we got there they drilled 1,100 feet deeper into a 9,000-foot test well. This technology has good safety features and controls to prevent a major oil spill.

JULY 23   Met with British foreign minister David Owen and others on the Rhodesian question. The British have been reluctant to move on a Commonwealth peacekeeping force to permit elections. They also have a heavy financial involvement with South Africa and are cautious about aggravating Vorster. We will never get unanimity among the frontline presidents, Ian Smith, Vorster, us, and the British—and I asked Vance to prepare a comprehensive proposal to be presented to the public and to the UN. After consulting with the African parties involved, we would call for fair treatment for the black majority and the whites; early elections based on one-man/one-vote principle; a free entry into the electoral process; a small peacekeeping force; a constitution to be provided by the British, who have legal authority in Rhodesia; and a Zimbabwe development fund guaranteeing the rights of the whites. This won't be approved by everyone, but at least it will get the specific issues out in public for debate.

MONDAY, JULY 25   Admiral Rickover came to support a testing program for schoolchildren similar to the one we have in Georgia, an all-out effort on organized-crime control, and an end to the giveaway of patents taken out by contractors whose new discoveries were developed using federal money. He disagreed with me on the abortion issue but agreed the federal government should not finance them—which is basically my position.

JULY 27   Secretary Patricia Harris gave me a superb report on progress in the Housing and Urban Development Department. She's one of my stronger cabinet members, all of them being good, and really has firm control over that department for the first time in its history.

JULY 28   Rosalynn brought instructors to report on Amy and her tests in the advanced reading course at George Washington University. In spite of her low-quality schools in Plains and here at Stevens, she is in the top one-tenth of 1 percent of the young people of her age. They recommended special attention be given to her reading programs, and they'll possibly have a small class at Stevens with her and several other students to try this out.

We had our third and last congressional picnic on the South Lawn — one of the most successful things Rosalynn has done. All members of Congress — House and Senate — with all family members, children particularly, have come. Had calliopes, clowns, entertainment, free popcorn, ice cream, hamburgers, hot dogs, and Rosalynn and Amy and I spent at least two hours just shaking hands with children and having our photographs taken. The response from the members of Congress has been great.

JULY 29   I met with our own Panama Canal negotiators — [Ellsworth] Bunker and [Sol] Linowitz — and the negotiators from Panama were also present. I wrote a letter to General Torrijos stating that I thought the talks had made good progress finally after thirteen years, that we were determined to have a treaty, and that our financial payments would be limited compared to what he wanted. It's difficult to evolve a treaty that's acceptable to Panama and also to the American public and Congress, since we have to get a two-thirds vote in the Senate. There's a lot of natural opposition to this treaty. The only possibility I see is to marshal tremendous support for the treaty among our Latin American friends and for me to make an all-out public relations effort among American citizens.

I received the credentials of four nations' new ambassadors this morning: Afghanistan, Zambia, Britain, Canada. I invite the families for photographs and spend about five minutes or so discussing general interrelationships. Make them feel welcome, and on occasion discuss a specific item like heroin production in Afghanistan.

I met with about forty news editors from around the country. We give them a couple of days' free access to the news before it goes on the wire services. By the time this year's over, I will have met with more than four hundred editors and TV and radio executives.

[Dr.] Peter Bourne came by to go over the final drug message and to talk about his role in the White House. I want him to be in charge of drugs, world hunger, world health, and so forth, and to work directly with me.

Bourne was responsible for reducing the supply of illegal drugs and improving the treatment of addicts. The most newsworthy aspect of the message we discussed that day was my call for the decriminalization (not legalization) of possessing less than one ounce of marijuana. My most quoted comment from the message was: "Penalties against possession of a drug should not be more damaging to an individual than the use of the drug itself; and where they are, they should be changed." We strongly urged a full program for treatment of addicts, which would help to address the problem of consumption as well as production of narcotics. We cautioned against filling up our prisons with young people who were no threat to society. These proposals were accepted quite well at the time, but after Reagan's election, the emphasis shifted almost exclusively toward controlling production in foreign countries, with severe criminal penalties instead of treatment for consumers. Unfair laws evolved that prescribed the same punishment for one gram of crack cocaine (used mostly by poor people of color) as for one hundred grams of white cocaine powder (used mostly by rich white people).

In April 2009, President Barack Obama stated that Congress "should completely eliminate the disparity" between the two forms of cocaine. Congress has yet to take up the issue.

Editors and key reporters of *Time* magazine came to do a cover story on our foreign policy, and we had a very surprising argument. They wanted to paraphrase my replies to their questions, shift my reply to a different question, and still put quotation marks on them as though they came directly from me. They refused to back down until we threatened to release the entire transcript of the interview to the wire services.

JULY 30   The shah of Iran sent an angry message to me that because of our one-month delay in presenting the AWACS [airborne warning and control system] proposal to the Congress, he was thinking about withdrawing his letter of intent to purchase these planes from the United States. I don't care whether he buys them from us or not.

MONDAY, AUGUST 1   Talked to Claiborne Pell about testing of educational achievement around the country. We would like to make it all-inclusive and mandatory, but there's opposition from two sources: teachers and minority groups. I called Califano, and he's going to get together with Claiborne to see what is the maximum we might achieve.

AUGUST 2   Pennsylvania congressmen sent a message that they were going to vote against all my bills unless we appointed their choice for U.S. attorney in Philadelphia. I told them in a nice way to go to hell.

Harold Brown reported from Korea concerning the withdrawal of our atomic weapons. We have been very firm with Korea and Taiwan that they should not get into the atomic production business themselves.

The question of lost uranium in the 1960s that may or may not have gone to Israel is a matter we've been discussing. It's going to be a public issue shortly when ERDA [Energy Research and Development Administration] makes its report.

AUGUST 3   The newspapers had verbatim quotes from a secret discussion of the Soviet strategic strength compared to our own [PRM-10, now declassified]. We will have to do something about the number of people who attend those meetings and the notes taken, and how highly sensitive documents are handled.

Spent a good bit of the day working on welfare reform. It will have to encompass reducing the welfare rolls, giving fiscal relief for local and state governments, cutting out fraud, simplifying the system, having a work incentive aspect, and something to hold families together. It's so complicated that it's going to take at least a year to get the proposal through Congress, and two or three more years to put it into effect. Senators Long and [Al] Ullman, chairmen of the two committees, are much more conservative than the people at HEW, and I tend to agree with them more than I do with my own staff on many of the key items.

Had a signing ceremony for the strip mining control bill, which was the culmination of many years of work by Congress, environmental groups, coal miners, local and state officials.

AUGUST 4   We are rolling well these last two days on conference committee reports and on floor votes. We've gotten little coordinated support from
Republicans, and in the future I need to consult more closely with Howard Baker, for instance, on foreign affairs, to see if it does any good. If not,
we'll just have to fight them. My preference is cooperation.

*The relationship I formed with House Republicans and with Senator Baker
proved to be extremely valuable, especially later in my tenure when Senator
Kennedy decided to run for president and I lost much of the support I had
previously counted on from him and many of the more liberal Democratic
members of Congress.*

I signed legislation creating a Department of Energy, and I immediately announced that Jim Schlesinger would be the head of it, and I think
the Senate committee will act on this today.

President Julius Nyerere of Tanzania came, and we had a productive
meeting, discussing almost exclusively the problem in Rhodesia. I was
expecting a considerable amount of disagreement from Nyerere, but he
agreed with every point.

I revealed a statement on undocumented aliens which will go to the
House and Senate. [Peter] Rodino will sponsor the legislation in the House.
We have a wide range of support in the Senate, with the two main spon-
sors being Kennedy and Eastland.

This was a balanced proposal, described on pages 1416–1421 of Public Papers of the Presidents: Jimmy Carter, 1977. *Although not implemented, its
terms are quite applicable to the much more serious challenges of 2010.*

Met with the Committee on Present Danger, Paul Nitze, Gene Rostow, and others. It was an unpleasant meeting where they insinuated that
we were on the verge of catastrophe, inferior to the Soviets, and I and
previous presidents had betrayed the nation's interests. I told them I'd like
to have constructive advice, balancing all factors with at least the possibility considered that the Soviets did want a permanent peace and not suicidal nuclear war. I don't know if they'll be helpful or not.

*As it turned out, this group and their associates created serious problems for me
whenever we attempted to do anything that related even remotely to a weapons*

*system, the Soviet Union, Cuba, China, or Israel. They had close ties to high-
level staff members in the defense and intelligence services and were privy to
confidential material—sometimes even before information reached me. True to
their name, they were inclined to overemphasize dangers from the Soviets, Cubans, North Koreans, and others. Also, they worked closely with key members
of Congress, especially Senator Scoop Jackson and his staff. Much later, I
learned that Nitze deeply resented my decision not to offer him a top position
in my administration, but to his credit he was an expert on nuclear weapons
and worked closely with Reagan in arms control talks with the Soviet Union.*

This last week in the Congress has been like a madhouse with everybody threatening filibusters and constant squabbles within conference
committees—almost like the last week of the Georgia legislature.

During the evening meal with Nyerere, he was asked two basic questions. First, why the newly emerging nations of Africa accepted help from
Communist countries. He replied verbosely that Russia was the only
source of weapons, that the Democratic nations would not provide them,
but that this had never resulted in Communist takeover once independence was achieved.

The other question was about South Africa supporting racism in Namibia and in Rhodesia. He thinks the South Africans will back down on
those two countries if they're given some time. But all he wants out of
South Africa is a statement that they accept a multiracial society, but need
time to implement it.

On Rhodesia, he agreed to convene a meeting of the frontline presidents and pursue what he and I had decided earlier. These are major
concessions on his part, compared to his desire in the past, based primarily on continued wars for liberation.

AUGUST 5   This is the last day before the Congress recesses for the summer. I've been very pleased at the accomplishments of the Congress and
the relationships I have with the leaders and the members. The House will
complete all its work on the energy package, leaving almost intact what
we proposed. It's going to be more difficult in the Senate, with Russell
Long being a spokesman for the oil companies, but maybe with public
opinion marshaled we can prevail on most points.

I signed the youth employment bill and swore in Jim Schlesinger today as secretary of energy. This rounds out the formation of the new de-

partment and completion of the stimulus package that we proposed. The beneficial impact of the $21 billion in public service jobs, public works, youth employment, tax reduction, should be felt the rest of this year, and should prevent a further decrease in the nation's growth rate, and maybe we can hold unemployment figures at around 7 percent.

We designed our stimulus legislation so that it would lead to the rapid creation of jobs, and the tax reductions were focused on businesses that increased employment. Unemployment during my tenure reached a maximum of 7.8 percent in July 1980.

Monitoring the Vance trip to the Middle East, it's becoming more and more obvious that the Arab leaders want a settlement, want peace—and that the Israelis don't want a settlement. They're going to be adamant against any sort of progress and probably will stir up trouble in Lebanon, with the Palestinians, Syrians, with Arabs in general. The difficulty will be in keeping public opinion in this country and around the world focused on the prospects for peace, in which case we might make some progress.

Had lunch with the Joint Chiefs of Staff to let them know that I needed their advice re normalizing relationship with China. They all agreed, provided we could continue to trade and supply arms to Taiwan. They were unanimously in favor of a Panama Canal treaty provided the land and waters issue could be resolved, which it can. They favored negotiations on the Indian Ocean provided we didn't have to give up our base on Diego Garcia. They're not enthusiastic about the comprehensive test ban but will go along with it. They thought we ought to continue with both air-launched cruise missiles until one shows a definite superiority. They felt that a simple extension of the SALT agreement passed in October was preferable, and we ought not sign a treaty with the Soviets that might give away some of our bargaining strength. General [David] Jones of the Air Force wanted us to stop all production or experimenting with the B-1 bomber and shift to a stretched FB-111, using the B-1 bomber engines. It was a good meeting and helped clear the air and let them know they are an integral part of the process.

We came down to Plains for a few days, and we were again pleasantly surprised at the quality of the town, attitude of the people. The biggest division is in the Baptist Church, where twenty-five or thirty of the former members have formed a new church—Maranatha. These are the leaders of the group that supported my position [approving black members]. We'll try to stay neutral as long as possible between the churches.

While I'm in Plains I have a fairly large staff. I get a briefing each morning from the State Department, a separate one from the CIA, dispatches fairly frequently from the National Security Council, telephone communications with my staff in the White House, and call key members of Congress when appropriate as has been the case on this trip, with the Panama Canal Treaty negotiations.

I spent time visiting Mother, walking in the woods behind our house, hunting arrowheads, visiting the farm, playing softball, reading. On this trip we looked at all our old home movies and color slides. We had all our family here on this visit.

Each August, while Congress was on its summer recess, we took the opportunity to enjoy a complete change of scenery, either in Plains or on one of Georgia's coastal islands. During these vacations, I limited the time spent on government affairs and relaxed with relatives and longtime friends. I was an avid reader, a farmer and an outdoorsman, so we were never lacking for a way to enjoy the relatively simple life of my prepolitical years. I also used these breaks as opportunities to make more in-depth studies of complex issues I would be facing back in Washington.

AUGUST 6   I revealed our welfare reform proposal, and it received surprisingly unanimous approval around the country. A few partisan jibes from people like Senator [Carl] Curtis and others, but I think it'll be approved by the Congress substantially in its introduced form. It's the result of a tremendous amount of work, and I'm proud of the departments and what they've contributed to it.

We went fishing in our Webster County pond and caught enough bream for supper Saturday night for our family.

MONDAY, AUGUST 8   Rosalynn and I went arrowhead hunting, and the ground was just right. In all, we found twenty complete arrowheads.

I have a collection of about fifteen hundred points, all found on fields near our home where we knew Indian villages had been located. Each time the ground is deeply cultivated a new portion of soil is exposed, and heavy rains leave the flint pieces on the surface.

AUGUST 9 I spent some time on the Panama Canal Treaty terms and in the evening talked to Senator Baker, President Ford, and Secretary Kissinger. It's important that I have Republican support, and that the terms we've reached are compatible with what they attempted to do while Ford was president.

We played softball again [Billy and I were opposing pitchers], and we finally won, I think 19–17 [after two losses]. The tourists really flock in, and two hours before the game starts the bleachers at the Plains High School are already filled. There's an intense competitive attitude among all the players; generally the team that makes the fewest errors wins.

Ate lunch at Joe Bacon's place, where they have good barbeque. I've tried to act as much like a resident as possible; it helps me restore a rural perspective to my own concept of the nation. The image of a president at home is a good one, politically speaking.

The crops are in bad shape. Corn is 95 percent destroyed by drought, and peanuts are off at least 30 percent. Army worms are taking over patches of peanuts, soybeans, even any grass that they ordinarily wouldn't eat because they don't have any cornfields to go into. Insecticides are scarce, and the soybean crop is off to a shaky start. So this is not going to be a good farming year at all.

Three of the four years I was president, our farm and many others were stricken by drought, which caused heavy financial losses for our family and created a sense of despair and anger among farmers throughout the nation. During my term, we were as generous as possible to the agricultural community, but enormous protests against government policy were organized, with thousands of tractors assembling in Washington and also in Plains.

Ford, Kissinger, and Baker all gave me encouraging reports on attitudes concerning the Panama Canal Treaty, and unless the public pressure is too heavy on them I think they can help me a great deal to have the treaty ratified. As soon as we get some assurance from our negotiators that a treaty's imminent, I'll begin to call senators and commit them at least to neutrality for the time being. This past Saturday I sent all senators a telegram urging them not to speak out against the treaty until they know details of the agreement. It worked with most of them except a few nuts like Strom Thurmond and Jesse Helms.

In general our progress on foreign affairs has been minimal, but we're moving with a well-planned effort on a broad basis, and I intend to be quite persistent in pursuing our goals.

AUGUST 10   We are returning to Washington, and we're ready to go back. The children have scattered. It's difficult to hold a presidential family together, particularly when the children are adults, but in balance it's not been harmful to us.

The Panama Canal Treaty principles have been approved, and I called fifteen or twenty members of the House and Senate. The response from these particular ones was good, including Senator [John] Sparkman, Senator [Barry] Goldwater, and others. It's going to be a difficult problem to get a two-thirds vote, however, unless we do a lot of public relations work, which we are prepared to do.

We approached this legislative battle with trepidation, but still underestimated the difficulty we would experience. Rallying support for the treaty would evolve into a highly partisan political test for me, while Reagan and others would be able to demagogue the issue among Americans who were convinced we were "giving away our canal." Opponents portrayed the Panamanians as subhumans who were dedicated to the narcotics trade, incompetent to operate the canal, and led by a drunken dictator. In the months ahead, we mounted an unprecedented personal effort among senators and their constituents. Getting the treaty passed was worth the effort, but there was nothing pleasant about it.

The day-by-day drama of this effort is spelled out more completely in my presidential memoir, Keeping Faith.

Vance['s] reports from the Mideast [are] still discouraging, with Israel intransigent on almost every issue.

Had a TV interview with Harry Reasoner and Sam Donaldson concerning Harry's poll, pretty well confirmed by Caddell's, that my personal popularity is as high as ever, but on specific issues the American people disagree with me or think we're not moving fast enough. Although we've done a lot of things, we're not moving fast enough to suit me either. It would be easier if I was a dictator and didn't have to worry about the Congress or other foreign leaders who don't agree with us. But we have a well-coordinated effort, fairly clear goals, and will be persistent.

AUGUST 11   Arthur Goldberg recommended that we proceed aggressively and without being discouraged to bring the Middle East leaders together at Geneva for long and extended negotiations, and that Brezhnev and I preside over the first session.

Ambassadors Bunker and Linowitz gave me a more complete report on the Panama Canal principles. The Joint Chiefs were there and unanimously expressed their support of the treaty terms.

We have evidence that the South Africans are preparing to test a nuclear device, as has been reported by the Soviets. Vance will meet tomorrow with Foreign Minister Botha of South Africa and will bring this matter up with him.

AUGUST 12   Still concerned about South Africa's testing a nuclear explosive. Photography shows that such a site may be in preparation.

AUGUST 13   Talked to Ronald Reagan about the Panama Canal. He said he was basically opposed but would reserve judgment pending a study and would consult with me before he made a public statement against it.

AUGUST 14   At Sunday school Ambassador [Francis] Dennis from Liberia taught the lesson. Clennon King showed up for publicity and tried to interrupt him all during the lesson period—without success.

King was pastor of a church in Albany, Georgia, who had disrupted our worship services in Plains during 1976 by demanding membership in our Plains Baptist Church. (King was African American, and because our church—despite my family's long-standing objection—did not admit blacks, his request to become a member was refused.) This effort almost cost me my victory in 1976. On the last Sunday before Election Day, the Gallup poll showed President Ford one percentage point ahead of me. King came to Plains Baptist Church with two women and a child, and found that services had been canceled. Ford's campaign manager, James Baker, sent telegrams to four hundred black ministers condemning me as an ineffective Christian, and therefore unqualified to be president. I was questioned about this during a campaign stop in Fort Worth and stated, "My own deep belief is that anyone who lives in our community and wants to be a member of our church, re-

gardless of race, ought to be admitted." My black supporters remained loyal, and two days later I won a narrow victory.

When King came to Washington on this occasion to embarrass me at First Baptist Church, he was surprised that a black ambassador was teaching, but created as much disharmony as possible nevertheless.

Spent several hours with Brzezinski and Vance. His report on the Mideast was encouraging, with almost a consensus among Arab countries. The Israelis are going to be typically recalcitrant, but the more we go public with a reasonable proposition the more difficult it will be for them not to make an effort. We've asked all of them to submit to us their own draft of the eventual peace treaty to be signed.

Cy's meeting with David Owen, Nyerere, and Botha was encouraging, although we can't predict what the South Africans might do. We are prepared to move strongly to implement our position, which is a fair one, including the use of sanctions against South Africa and encouraging Iran to cut off oil supplies if they don't cooperate. This applies primarily to Rhodesia, but also Namibia. We don't have any intention to push South Africa around on their own racial and political characteristics, except over a long period of time. Still, they believe we're trying to destroy them, and this is an obstacle.

MONDAY, AUGUST 15   I talked to President Ford about the Panama agreement, and he is going to make a public announcement strongly supporting the treaty. We'll send one of our negotiators and one of the Joint Chiefs out tomorrow to brief him, then he'll make his statement with maximum news coverage.

Had an enjoyable lunch with Henry Kissinger and talked about the Panama Canal, mostly about the Middle East, some about southern Africa. He offered to help with the Panama Canal Treaty with the same format as Ford, and made a supportive statement to the news media as he was leaving.

Botha called from South Africa to tell me the reaction in their government was "green light" and that Vorster would like to meet with me personally. I agreed with this.

AUGUST 16   President Ford called to let me know he had endorsed the Panama Canal Treaty, and he suggested that we have as large a ceremony as possible to publicize the interests of other Latin American countries in the treaty.

AUGUST 19   We were riding our bikes around Camp David, and when I turned the corner at moderate speed the left pedal hit the ground, the bike slid, and so did I for about five feet on the asphalt. I skinned my left shoulder, left toes, leg, arm, side—nothing serious except a lot of abrasions. Dr. Lukash sprayed some New-Skin on me.

AUGUST 21   I received South Africa's commitment not to have a nuclear explosive test.

MONDAY, AUGUST 22   Talked to Howard Baker, who still has not decided what position to take on the Panama Canal Treaty, but will wait until a text is evolved. Had the same conversation with Barry Goldwater, who's supportive but will be affected by the treaty's final terms and also by Republican-Democratic prospects at the time of the treaty vote.

Partisan advantage, the issue raised in my conversation with Goldwater, now gets far more attention than it did when I was president. Opposition to the treaty was largely based on what individual senators believed was best for them in their home states, not on what was good for their political party. However, partisan advantage became a major factor during subsequent elections, in 1978 and 1980. Ronald Reagan, for instance, made condemnation of the treaty a major factor in his presidential campaign.

AUGUST 23   Got a report from Cy Vance in China. The talks are slow moving, not very highly publicized in China, apparently.

Afterward, we gave a briefing on the Panama Canal Treaty to twenty-five or thirty people from Kentucky and the same number from Mississippi, selected by their senators. We'll do this with ten or twelve key states, working with doubtful senators who need some awareness of the treaty among leaders in their own states.

We later expanded this briefing to many more states and much larger audiences, sometimes two hundred people at a time. The idea was to demonstrate local support to senators who might be willing to cast an unpopular vote for the treaty.

Senator Bob Byrd and his wife, Erma, had supper with us and stayed about three hours. I enjoyed talking to the senator more than before. We went over the agenda for this congressional season, which he anticipates will be concluded before the end of October. He seemed preoccupied with the Panama Canal Treaty, and unless we can come up with an assured two-thirds vote beforehand, his inclination is to delay the vote until next February. We're going to go all out to get the votes earlier. We cannot afford a filibuster, as much as we have on the schedule for this year already. The more I discuss my programs with him, the better off we'll be. He has been somewhat disconcerted because he's worked very hard and received very little recognition, but it's because most of the action so far has been in the House. This will shift to the Senate inevitably. I like Senator Byrd very much, and he's a good ally to have.

My harmonious relationship with Byrd was to continue until Ted Kennedy mounted his campaign for president, at which point he seemed to develop dual and conflicting loyalties. My personal respect for him as majority leader never wavered.

AUGUST 24   I talked to General Torrijos in Panama about plans for a signing ceremony on the seventh of September. We decided to invite as many of the members of the OAS [Organization of American States] as will come.

We are trying to decide if we can help King Juan Carlos of Spain with his upcoming election. They've not had much experience with democratic processes. We may send someone over to give him private advice on how an election should be conducted, how to use television, to get-out-the-vote processes, and so forth.

Report from Cy Vance was mildly encouraging. He met with the vice chairman [and supreme leader] Teng Hsiao-ping [later spelled Deng Xiaoping], and tomorrow he'll meet with Premier Hua [Guofeng]. We're not particularly eager to proceed now with this complex negotiation on a public basis because the Panama Canal question needs to be resolved before we inject another major foreign policy altercation.

AUGUST 25   Bob Strauss called to say that [business and political leaders] were talking to Ronald Reagan and there's a two-to-one chance that he will not say anything about the Panama Canal for the next two weeks. My guess is that he will come out against the treaty.

AUGUST 26   I met with another twenty-five to thirty editors and broadcast-ers from around the country. It always surprises me how much more rea-sonable and substantive their questions are than the ones I get from the White House press corps. Many of the regular news conference questions are superficial and relate to transient, cute political questions.

More than fifteen hundred reporters were accredited to cover the White House, and they were intensely competitive. The more prominent ones were present at my regular press conferences, and they were all eager to ask one of the few questions possible during the relatively brief television coverage. Most of them were more interested in their own questions than my answers.

Rosalynn returned from the Vancouver mental health meeting. The international mental health officials are apparently looking to the com-mission reports under Rosalynn for guidance on how to act in the future in several countries around the world.

Since 1971, Rosalynn had been a champion of mental health issues, and her leadership in this cause continues even now. She mounted a worldwide crusade to reduce the stigma associated with mental illness and helped per-suade the World Health Organization and Centers for Disease Control to include mental health on their agendas. In 2008, she was instrumental in the effort to induce the U.S. Congress to extend insurance coverage equally to cover mental and physical ailments.

Zbig called to tell me that the American embassy in Moscow was burn-ing and that the top three floors contain highly sensitive cryptographic machines, ciphers, and documents. I told him to let it burn in that area rather than permit Soviet firefighters to compromise our ciphers, but try to restrict the flames to the floors where people don't live and where the con-fidential material is isolated.

AUGUST 27   Spent a lot of the time swimming, playing tennis with Rosa-lynn, and reading the book *The Path Between the Seas: The Creation of the Panama Canal* [by David McCullough]. It's obvious that we cheated the Panamanians out of their canal. As a matter of fact, no Panamanian ever saw the treaty at all before it was signed.

MONDAY, AUGUST 29   Assad in an interview in *The New York Times* proposed that the PLO not participate in the Geneva conference, but that the Arab League might substitute for them. We'll pursue this idea.

Had a regular lunch with Fritz. We have an easy relationship and discuss matters of the most personal and national importance without constraint. Today we talked about Lance, southern Africa, China, Israel, the American Jewish community, the Panama Canal vote, and individual senators' attitudes and interests.

Andy Young called from South Africa, saying that the talks with Vorster had been encouraging but nothing definite was committed regarding the proposed Rhodesian settlement. They go now to Rhodesia to meet with Ian Smith, and I think they'll stop on the way to see Nyerere again.

AUGUST 30   Admiral Turner reported that the assessment of all CIA operations has been completed and there are no illegal or improper actions now being conducted, although some very embarrassing things in the past.

I called President Ford to ask him if he would participate in the Panama Canal Treaty signing ceremonies and spend the night with us at the White House, and he accepted with pleasure.

Now that we had finally negotiated the text, I felt that a large ceremony would be helpful in the next, much more difficult step: to induce two-thirds of the U.S. senators to ratify it.

SEPTEMBER 1   Late last night I told Jody that I'd been feeling kind of discouraged all day but I felt much better when I talked to him. He replied that the days were always worse than the nights. Apparently *The Washington Post* is conducting a vendetta against Bert and have ordered two front-page stories about him each day. This morning, for instance, they had nine separate stories about Lance—headline stories—throughout the paper. In contrast, *The New York Times* didn't mention him.

Bert Lance had been one of my most intimate friends for many years. He was an expert on finance and budgeting and had been a natural leader among all my gubernatorial cabinet officers. As Office of Management and Budget director in Washington, he was also my primary contact with the business community. Suddenly, however, he became engulfed in controversy when it was revealed that while he had been president of a country bank largely owned by his wife's family, the bank had permitted them to make personal overdrafts. All of this had happened before he came to Washington with me.

This vendetta against Bert took a lot of our time and ultimately resulted in his resigning. This was a difficult emotional experience for all of us who trusted and cared for Bert. The investigation continued for months after his resignation, and all the allegations were either withdrawn or disproved.

Griffin Bell came to report to me on the *Bakke* decision. The basic thrust of it is that we support the concept of affirmative action but not quotas. This decision was worked up by the solicitor and the head of the Civil Rights Section, both of whom happen to be black. The decision will be revealed early next week.

This would prove to be a landmark Supreme Court case, involving a white applicant, Allan Bakke, who was denied admission to medical school while minority students with weaker academic records were accepted. Our position was that Bakke should be admitted to the med school, but we did not want to reverse our commitment to the right of minority groups to be protected by affirmative action programs, or to the principle that race could be one of the factors assessed. In June 1978, by a 5–4 vote, the Court agreed with our position.

We had another good Panama Canal briefing, for Arkansas and West Virginia. A Gallup poll shows 39 percent of Americans in favor of our canal treaty [proposal] and 46 percent against it—which is a dramatic improvement in the last few weeks.

SEPTEMBER 2   Senator Byrd came to discuss the Lance matter and how it was going to be extremely difficult for the Senate to deal with it. He indicated that [he preferred that] we move away from it and the Panama Canal Treaty for the time being and concentrate on getting our energy package through the Senate.

Before leaving for Camp David I received voluminous briefings on about twenty-five Latin American countries and the different leaders with whom I'll meet next week.

After we got to Camp David, Kirbo called and we had a long discussion about Bert Lance. I stayed up late Friday night, and then early Saturday morning I called Bert and told him that I thought it would be better for him not to step down as OMB director but to take a leave of absence so that he could spend full-time preparing his case and also get me and others in the White House out of being his spokesmen.

MONDAY, SEPTEMBER 5 (LABOR DAY)   Met with Ribicoff and [Charles] Percy, and told them I preferred an expeditious hearing to let all the facts come out and let Bert have a chance to refute the allegations against him. They agreed with that.

I spent the evening preparing our SALT negotiation position and studying for bilateral meetings with six heads of state for Tuesday.

SEPTEMBER 6   We have a fairly good consensus on SALT among State, NSC, Defense, Joint Chiefs, and myself, and I believe it's a reasonable proposal for the Soviets to accept.

At lunch, Fritz Mondale and I discussed key issues, and Fritz gave me an analysis of his first months in office and how he thought he could perform better.

Mondale was a protégé of Hubert Humphrey and was known as a liberal senator from Minnesota. Both geographically and politically, his knowledge and interests correlated with and supplemented mine. He was closely allied to the major labor unions and other politically important groups with whom I had minimal contacts. When Rosalynn and I met with all the potential running mates, we felt an almost instantaneous affinity for Fritz and his wife, Joan. Before meeting with me, he had consulted closely with former vice presidents Humphrey and Nelson Rockefeller and was extremely well prepared. Later, when I asked him to prepare a definitive list of everything he hoped for after our election, I approved all his requests. He was, for instance, the first vice president whose office was in the White House, adjacent to mine.

Mondale was kept thoroughly informed about the most sensitive and difficult subjects, and I trusted his judgment, honesty, and frankness. He never deviated from my policies in his actions or statements, he was careful not to usurp my authority as president, and I never failed to honor his suggestions on how his partnership with me could be enhanced. Although Mondale was habitually more cautious than I when we faced controversies, he and I maintained a superb relationship.

Before lunch, I met with General Torrijos to discuss the signing ceremonies, implementation of the treaties, the time of his plebiscite, and I outlined to him the problems if there was any implied threat against our nation, since this would prevent senators from being able to vote for ratification. He was quite emotional about what this meant to Panama and outlined the embarrassment they had felt for decades about this colonial intrusion into their country. He is a military dictator, but my sense is that he genuinely cares for the poor—a sincere populist.

This was the first of a remarkable series of meetings between me and Latin American leaders. My administration concentrated a tremendous portion of our attention on this region, becoming intimately involved in an ongoing effort to help solve their problems, elevating the stature and influence of the Organization of American States, promoting the Treaty of Tlatelolco, which prohibited nuclear weapons, and—above all—promoting respect for human rights and democratization of the numerous military dictatorships. The abbreviated accounts that follow will give the reader an insight into the diversity of issues and the importance of our bilateral relations, including regimes with which we had important differences.

I met with Morales Bermúdez, president of Peru. He reconfirmed his commitment to have elections in 1980, promised that their arms purchases program was completed, authorized me to tell Chile and Ecuador this news, and claimed they would help Bolivia with access to the sea. He impressed us as a very strong and good leader.

I then met with General [Alfredo] Stroessner, president of Paraguay. They have a repressive government, fairly poor. He's caught between two powerful nations, Argentina and Brazil. Quite friendly to the United States, he doesn't understand our condemnation because of the prisoners they have incarcerated. He said he would receive the Human Rights Commission investigating team, and claimed he was eager to step down from office and go fishing, but I'm sure he's been saying this for the last twenty years.

Stroessner later released eight hundred political prisoners and announced that he did so to honor my human rights policy.

I met with President López Michelsen of Colombia. It's hard to size him up. I think he's probably weak, somewhat insecure, a little autocratic. His major problem is corruption within his government caused by narcotics. It's hard for him to stamp it out when some of the top members of his own government are involved and the local police stay bribed.

During her recent visit, Rosalynn had informed him about one of his top cabinet officers who was colluding with the cocaine drug cartel.

Colombia has signed the Human Rights Convention and the Treaty of Tlatelolco. He feels that we ought not be the singular proponent for human rights but it should be internationalized as much as possible. I agree with this.

I then met with the most highly publicized leader, General [Augusto] Pinochet of Chile. I informed him about the serious problem with Chile because of human rights deprivation. Eventually he agreed to let a couple of observers come in from the United Nations, but not an entire committee or commission. He was concerned about Peru's buildup of weapons. I told him about Peru's commitment that new weapons purchases were over. They have ratified the Treaty of Tlatelolco, and he said they would put it into effect as soon as Argentina signed. He was apparently willing to give Bolivia access to the sea but insisted that equal territory be exchanged from Bolivia to them in return. All of his problems were derived from Cuba and Russia, according to him. He seems to be a very strong leader, sure of himself, beginning to be more worried about outside condemnation on human rights issues, and defensive of their attitudes because of instability in Chile.

When he appeared at the reception this evening, according to Rosalynn and the news media, he was the center of attention and the women particularly seemed to be his admirers, although it's hard to look at him and tell why.

Pinochet was arrested in 1998 in Great Britain on a Spanish warrant for human rights violations in Chile against Spanish citizens. This was the first time a former president was arrested in a foreign country on the basis of "universal jurisdiction," and it remains a warning to others who have violated international law. He was allowed to return to Chile on medical grounds in 2000 and, at the time of his death, faced charges of numerous human rights crimes.

Countries like Panama, Paraguay, Uruguay, Argentina, Chile are really feeling the pressure on human rights and want to do something to repair their damaged public image because they see it hurting them economically. Human rights and nuclear nonproliferation are the two major issues, but throughout Latin America there's a general economic problem, high unemployment, low standards of living, difficult trade matters because their raw material prices fluctuate so widely.

SEPTEMBER 7   I had an early morning meeting with the Black Caucus, which I dreaded, but I had done a lot of homework and took the initiative. I believe we have a new and better understanding and relationship for the future. The agreement was that within ten days or so we would move on the Humphrey-Hawkins bill by bringing their differences to me for final resolution. The major issue is extremely high unemployment among blacks. In the last ten years employment has gone up about 20 percent for blacks and the same for whites, but the black addition to the workforce has doubled compared to whites.

The Humphrey-Hawkins Full Employment Act established as national policy the right to a job for every American who is willing, able, and seeking to work. It directs the nation to seek four goals: full employment, growth in production, price stability, and balance of trade and budget. The act is much stronger than its 1946 predecessor and was a test case for minority groups. I signed it into law in October 1978.

We had a breakfast for about sixty-five of the top business, professional, and educational leaders in the nation on the Panama Canal, and I guess 80 percent of them expressed support for the treaty. They might help with some of the moderate to conservative senators who are now inclined to vote against the treaty.

Met with General [Kjell] Laugerud from Guatemala. He's Norwegian, whose father came to Guatemala as a sailor, got drunk, the ship left him, he married Laugerud's mother and is still living there. He's a fairly impressive man whose primary concern is to acquire at least part of the country of Belize. The Guatemala constitution says that Belize is a part of Guatemala. They've moved fairly well on the issue of human rights, are very poor, and will have an election in March of 1978.

Then I met with President [Carlos] Pérez of Venezuela. He'd like to have more Pan-American unity and has been helping us relieve tensions concerning Caribbean development, Andean disputes on weapons, borders, access to the Amazon, access to the sea, international nuclear nonproliferation, and he can—if he will—hold down OPEC price increases. In fact, OPEC meets in Venezuela this December.

President Ford came by, and we discussed the latest developments on different international questions. He and Lady Bird [Johnson] will spend the night with us to demonstrate their support for the Panama Canal Treaty. The four of us went to the Pan-American Union building for a reception, for signing ceremonies and a state dinner afterward. I was disappointed with the signing ceremony because individual Latin American leaders were not adequately recognized. This is an argument with my staff that I lost, unfortunately. We had twenty-six or twenty-seven nations represented, with twenty heads of state present. Although some senators have resented this as unwarranted pressure on them, I think the outcome will be beneficial.

SEPTEMBER 8   I met with Pierre Trudeau to discuss the natural gas pipeline. We've reached agreement with them to use the so-called Alcan Route, and all other elements have been resolved. We announced that an agreement had been reached and Jim Schlesinger and his Canadian counterpart will reveal the details. We discussed the possibility of Canada becoming part of the OAS, and if other members of the OAS desire it, Trudeau might go along. Pierre and I have a very easy personal relationship. I like him very much.

Canada became a member of the OAS in 1990.

Met with Admiral [Alfredo] Poveda from Ecuador. He was highly complimentary about Rosalynn's visit there earlier this year. I informed him that Peru had committed to me not to buy any more weapons. We also discussed Ecuador's access to the Amazon River, and he's to follow up this with Morales Bermúdez from Peru. They are planning elections in 1978, and this is one of the emerging democracies in Latin America of which we are very proud.

Most South American nations had military governments when I became president, and we actively encouraged movements to democracy, using our aggressive human rights policy as a lever. Most of the governments began changing before I left office, and all nations in Latin America ultimately developed democracies, except Cuba, which has clung to a dictatorship.

Met with President [Hugo] Banzer of Bolivia, who repeated that they are moving toward civilian rule in 1980. We discussed the possibility of a corridor from Bolivia to the sea. Both Peru and Chile have said they would like this to be done, but each one has technical objections which have so far blocked any progress. They hope to arrange a meeting before all three presidents leave Washington.

Despite our best efforts, Bolivia has still not acquired access to the sea through a proposed corridor just south of the Chile-Peru border.

Next was President [Joachín] Balaguer of the Dominican Republic. They have elections scheduled next year, have signed the Convention on Human Rights, are very cooperative with us on the International Sugar Agreement, and were profoundly affected by Andy Young's recent visit.

President [Carlos] Romero of El Salvador. My major purpose was to get El Salvador to agree to a mediation formula for the border dispute with Honduras. He agreed to move on this, which has kept the Pan-American Highway closed for a long time and resulted in severing of relationships altogether between Honduras and El Salvador. Before they left Washington, this was done.

I then met with General [Juan] Melgar [Castro] from Honduras. He discussed primarily the border dispute with El Salvador, and they have ratified today the Pan-American Convention on Human Rights, which is quite a step forward for Honduras. They will have elections in 1980.

SEPTEMBER 9   My first meeting was with President [Jorge] Videla from Argentina. He was calm, strong, competent, sure of himself enough to admit Argentina does have problems in the eyes of the world. He promised me that before the end of this year Argentina would sign the Treaty of Tlatelolco. We then discussed human rights. Terrorism has been replaced under Videla and the military junta with political repression. They have about a thousand political prisoners incarcerated and three thousand names listed who are missing. I pointed out the need for an accounting for Jacobo Timerman, former editor of *La Opinion,* and the Deutsch family, who have relatives in Los Angeles. He admitted that these people were being held. He promised that by the end of this year all pending cases will be resolved. [They released only Timerman and a few others.] Videla knows that their access to nuclear fuel and heavy water and the approbation or condemnation of the rest of the world depends upon his actions on human rights and nonproliferation.

I then met with Uruguay president [Aparicio] Méndez: not nearly so impressive, highly defensive, denied there were any political prisoners in Uruguay. Our information is that they have between two thousand and five thousand. I asked if they would permit the UN Human Rights Commission to visit. He replied no, but they would let people from the United States come in to observe what goes on. Although he's a professor with a good legal and scholarly background and apparently a good administrator, he was highly evasive, more so than any other Latin head of state.

As this next entry illustrates, the president of the United States has a wide gamut of responsibilities and concerns!

I met with Rex Scouten and superintendents from the General Services Administration to complain about the numerous mice in my office. For two or three months now I've been telling them to get rid of the mice. They still seem to be growing in numbers, and I am determined either to fire somebody or get the mice cleared out—or both.

In the afternoon I met with Prime Minister [Eric] Gairy of Grenada. Grenada is the smallest country in our hemisphere, and Gairy was primarily concerned with mysticism, the definition of God, and a resolution that he sponsored for years before the United Nations to investigate unidentified flying objects.

I remember with particular clarity that when he opened the wrong briefcase to give me some papers, his dirty laundry fell out on the conference room table.

My next meeting was with Prime Minister [Lynden] Pindling from the Bahamas. A very impressive man. We had several questions to discuss with him that, because of the newness of the nation, they've not been ready to negotiate: four small U.S. military installations, the fishery and maritime boundary problem because we both have two-hundred-mile claims and we're only about eighty miles apart. Pindling also requested increased air service to the Bahamas, claiming that the one airline, Delta, was not handling all the traffic that wanted to come to the Bahamas from New York [City].

The last meeting of the day was with President [Daniel] Oduber of Costa Rica, one of the finest little countries in the world—innovator in human rights, no army or air force, zero illiteracy, heavily dependent on exports, and of course we're their biggest customer. At the press conference outside he was complimentary about the fact that the entire hemispheric interrelationship had been changed by my pursuit of human rights and by the symbolism of the Panama treaty.

During the day we worked out the thrust of the attorney's general brief in the *Bakke* case.

SEPTEMBER 10–11   I went to New Jersey to campaign for Brendan Byrne, although he's ten points behind in the polls. I think my visit helped to restore some of the spirit to his campaign. He's a good, decent, courageous, plodding sort of governor, but I believe he's got New Jersey coming around, much of an improvement over what it was four years ago. The crowds were large—*The New York Times* said fifteen thousand at Newark and thirty thousand at Trenton. General friendship toward me, and some organized demonstration against him on the income tax issue, which we met head-on.

I was tired when I got back home and didn't feel too well. [My sister] Ruth came to Washington for a forum on stress, which was attended by several thousand people. She spent the night with us, and we enjoyed being with her.

MONDAY, SEPTEMBER 12   We've been doing a great deal of preparation for Gromyko's upcoming visit to Washington, and French prime minister [Raymond] Barre is coming this week.

Gallup polls show that I still have the same approval rating as last February—66 percent.

At the same moment in their terms, the two Democratic presidents who fol-
lowed me, Bill Clinton and Barack Obama, had approval ratings of about
44 percent and 52 percent, respectively. In retrospect, it is surprising that my
poll ratings were so high, given the controversial nature of many of our pro-
posals. One explanation by experts is that we hadn't backed down on any of
the hotly disputed issues. The good thing was that high popularity strength-
ened my influence with the Congress and with foreign leaders.

I met with Archbishop [Joseph] Bernardin, president of the National
Conference of Catholic Bishops, and he expressed his support for me on
the issue of abortion and gave his commitment on behalf of the bishops to
our human rights stand.

I met with [Budget Director] Jim McIntyre and urged him to restrict
supplementary budget requests to rare occasions rather than making them
routine and frequent. He's doing a good job running the Office of Management and Budget since Bert's fooling around with the investigation.

SEPTEMBER 13   We had adverse reaction from the Israelis, as expected,
from our release concerning the need for Palestinians to participate in any
future Geneva conference. We have to continue to lay out specific negotiating issues.

Later met with Margaret Thatcher, leader of the Conservative Party in
Britain. She's obviously an overbearing, not unattractive woman. Thinks
she can win easily if there is an election to be held.

Bob Bowie from CIA gave us an assessment of the British/French/
Italian/German/Spanish economic situations and the European Commu-
nity as a whole. Their growth rates are lower than ours. The EU [European
Union] is doing a good job for its members, and in all likelihood Spain,
Greece, and Portugal will become members.

I met with Bert. He's determined to stay on, thinks he and Clark Clifford
have worked out a complete answer to every allegation, and will answer
them this week.

Russell and Carolyn Long ate supper with us, and as usual I enjoyed
being with them. We had a long talk about energy taxes, tax reform, welfare reform, and Social Security. Although no decisions were made, I think
Russell and I understanding one another will help in the future. There are
some items on which he feels very strong, and others on which I feel very

strong, but most of the differences between us can be reconciled. He agreed that it might be good to send groups of senators down to Panama to see firsthand the circumstances there. He thought this would give the ones leaning in my direction, like himself, a chance to go home and say, "Well, I've been there and I've talked to General So-and-so, and I think I ought to support this treaty."

We adopted this policy, and ultimately about half the senators traveled to Panama and were favorably impressed.

Senator [James] Eastland this morning said I had an 81 percent favorable rating in Mississippi, which is a pleasant surprise. I doubt if it would be that much in Louisiana, where the oil industry has been working against me.

SEPTEMBER 14   Met with Governor Wendell Anderson [of Minnesota], [Arkansas senator] Dale Bumpers, and Secretary Andrus about the prospective sale of surface rights over federally owned coal deposits in the western states. We'll try to announce that these areas will not be leased for mining until we can get legislation to remove the possibility of financial abuse.

Met with DNC [Democratic National Committee] chairman Ken Curtis and his staff. Apparently some of the American Jews are thinking about boycotting our Los Angeles fund-raiser as a pressure tactic to modify our Mideast position.

SEPTEMBER 15   Bert came by at 6:30 for a brief prayer session before his testimony. He had selected three Bible passages. One was Joshua 1:5–7. One was Ecclesiastes 3:1–8. The other was 1 Peter 2:17–25. He's feeling quite sure of himself and thinks the statement is going to put his point across and also put the senators on the defensive. Also the press that have distorted the facts about him.

Rosalynn presented her interim report on the mental health commission, modest but clear. I think most of the recommendations will be carried out.

Prime Minister Barre from France came and mentioned privately the Concorde issue, and their sale of nuclear reprocessing equipment to Pakistan. [The rights of the Concorde to land in U.S. airports were threatened because of its high noise level.] We discussed the Middle East at great length. They are strongly inclined to support the Arab position and believe they've made a contribution just by keeping quiet about it. Barre also discussed the need to continue nuclear power production, including their fast breeder reactor.

I watched some of the live testimony at the Lance hearing and thought Bert did very well. He has difficulty answering why he had overdrafts so numerous and large, but perhaps he can clarify that point tomorrow. The news reports were fairly favorable about his appearance.

Had an evening meeting with Prime Minister Barre, and the violinist who entertained us was both beautiful and superb. She played two selections, the last one of which was extraordinary. [It was Elisabeth Matesky, playing the Sonata no. 3 for Violin in D Minor, "Ballade," by Eugène Ysaÿe.]

SEPTEMBER 16   At our foreign policy breakfast we spent most of the morning talking about the Middle East. Our assessment is that the Israelis are deliberately trying to block an agreement by creating disturbances in Lebanon, being adamant on Palestinian representation, and supporting their settlements. We outlined our policy toward Israel, and Cy will present it to [Moshe] Dayan while he's here later this week.

I called Helmut Schmidt to give him support in his problem with terrorists. They are negotiating through Switzerland but will not release any terrorists already in prison. I think he appreciated my calling him.

I told Prime Minister Barre that I would come to Paris late in November and would have to meet [Jacques] Chirac and [François] Mitterrand while I was there. He seemed eager for me to come, and to know about our SALT negotiations. As an economist and finance minister, he was very boring if he was ever asked a question related to economics, but we got along well with each other.

Had a thirty-minute interview with [columnist] Jack Anderson. He was primarily interested in what kind of person I was and how my religious life was affected by the campaign and my being president. Talked about the family—how we raised our children. I think this is going to be in *Parade* magazine.

We took off for Camp David. Amy came later with Frank Moore's daughter, Elizabeth. I told Amy I'd give her a present to wear on one condition: that if she liked it, she'd wear it to school. She promised she would do so, but after she got her swim flippers she talked me into letting her back out of the deal.

SEPTEMBER 18 Most of the morning newspapers were fairly reasonable about Bert Lance. We feel that Bert has won a great victory and now is the best time for him to step down. After returning to Washington I called Bert and asked him to talk to me early Monday morning. I didn't sleep much Sunday night.

One other person I called was Senator Byrd, who said he'd like a few days to think it over, but he doubted that some of his answers were adequate in the long run. He said I could be charged with a double standard if I had a doubtful employee in the future; if I kept him on or discharged him, it would be compared with Bert. People expected different standards from me than previous presidents, the press and the Senate committee members were not going to let the issue rest, and he didn't think any Democratic senators would be particularly disappointed if Bert resigned. He'd like to get back in touch after he reads the testimony—both with me and with Lance.

MONDAY, SEPTEMBER 19 Bert came at 6:15, and I got over here almost an hour earlier. I told him he was vindicated for now, but the Senate and press were not going to let up on his net worth analysis, the airplane use, a possible SEC [Securities and Exchange Commission] investigation, whether or not his acting for [his wife] LaBelle's family was going to be an embarrassment. We had a two- or three-day opening now where we could decide what to do without seeing a substantial lessening of his esteem throughout the country. He agreed to talk to Clark Clifford, LaBelle, and a few other people, and let me know what he decided. I felt better after this conversation than I had in a long time. When Bert left I didn't have any doubt that he would do what was right for him and for me.

I met with a group of senators who favored natural gas deregulation.

A major facet of my comprehensive energy package was to permit regulated oil and gas prices to rise in a free market, and to capture the increased prices in a windfall profits tax; those funds would then be used to help poorer families afford home heating fuel and to finance alternative energy sources. This initiative was opposed by liberals who feared price increases and by representatives of petroleum-producing states who wanted increased profits to flow to oil and gas companies. We persevered, however, and it became law in 1980.

Had lunch with the vice president. We talked about Israel and of course Lance. I have kept my conversations with Bert confidential, except for Rosalynn.

Met Moshe Dayan and discussed privately with him and Fritz the fact that I thought the Israelis were deliberately blocking the peace treaty and were being remarkably inflexible. I told him that in spite of this we would see the negotiations through to a successful conclusion if it was within my ability. He was a little taken aback, but he said that I was wrong; they were willing to accommodate our concerns on the settlements as best they could. No more civilians would go into the settlements, but only people to existing military settlements who were in uniform. On Lebanon, they thought the six tanks they had sent in over the weekend would be the limit of their involvement. That was his hope. I asked him about Israel's relationship to South Africa. He responded that he could not answer my question before the new government took office, but if I would propose a question to Begin they could give me a satisfactory answer.

He showed some flexibility on Palestinian representation, agreeing on a joint Arab delegation at the opening and then Palestinians could be represented in the Jordanian delegation. If they were not well-known PLO members, they would not examine their credentials. He was insistent that in negotiations on territory they only deal with one nation at a time: the Syrians for the Golan Heights, the Egyptians for the Sinai, and the Jordanians with some Palestinians for the West Bank.

He said that a multinational group might be formed separate from the peace treaty talks to handle the Palestinian refugee question because they lived in Lebanon, Syria, Jordan, Egypt, Kuwait, even Iraq, and that that would be suitable to the Israeli government. I thought the meeting was productive and might give us enough opening to bring the Arabs around.

On many of these key issues, Dayan's positions were later refuted by Begin — and by his successors as prime minister of Israel. The most important was his opinion that only military personnel should be added to the settlements.

Senator Byrd came by, completely convinced that Bert should resign. He said he would talk to Bert the following day.

SEPTEMBER 20   I discussed with the attorney general and a few others removing the congressional one-house veto, which we think is unconstitutional. We'll do the best we can to preserve the constitutional prerogatives of the president against the encroachment of Congress—even taking the test case to the Supreme Court if necessary.

I met with Stan Turner, the vice president, and Zbig to discuss the strategic importance of Berlin—our monitoring of potential preparations for an armed attack by the Russians into West Germany and how important Berlin is to give us this early warning. We also assessed the possibility of other nuclear test sites in South Africa; evidence is that there are no others except the one at Kalahari.

I played tennis with Bert, who indicated that he wanted to resign. I didn't argue with him. He's going to go home and talk to LaBelle.

SEPTEMBER 21   Probably one of the worst days I've ever spent. Bert came almost an hour late, which is not like him, to inform me that LaBelle objected so strongly to his resigning that he didn't know what he was going to do, and asked what I thought. I told him I believed his decision to resign was best. He decided to talk to LaBelle again and to call Clark Clifford. I told him I would have a hard time at the press conference in the afternoon without having the matter decided one way or the other, and Bert agreed.

Frank Moore came by to report we were in bad shape on energy tax measures in the Senate, and he's to talk to Russell Long to see if we can adopt a modified proposal that doesn't hurt our energy conservation measures.

Had lunch with Senator Ted Kennedy, who has a 100 percent voting record as far as our program is concerned. He's the only member of Congress that does, so far as I know. We discussed primarily the upcoming tax reform proposal, and he'll give me his analysis of the different controversial issues. He gave me a copy of a letter that Brezhnev had written him, which repeated the Soviet positions on SALT.

I really appreciated Kennedy's early support as a leader of the liberals in Congress. It was obvious that he had a powerful influence in the Capitol, throughout the nation, and especially with the news media. As later entries will show, he played a complex and important role while I was president.

Bert called and asked if I would talk to LaBelle on the phone, and I suggested they come by to see me, which they did. LaBelle is adamantly opposed to Bert's resigning. She said she knew the decision had already been made by me and Bert, but she disagreed with both of us. I could see that LaBelle was creating a very serious problem for Bert, and of course he was trying to accommodate her as I would Rosalynn. Clark Clifford came shortly afterward and pointed out that they decided even before the Senate hearings last week that Bert should resign. He was going to leave here and meet with Bert to prepare the resignation letter. I decided to postpone the news conference from 3:00 to 5:00 to give him a chance to do so.

I went to a Panama Canal briefing for Tennessee and North Carolina. These briefings have been very successful, and perhaps this one most of all because of my strong political support base in the two states. Tennessee is important because Howard Baker, a Republican leader, needs to have his home people at least willing to accept his decision to support the canal treaty if he should be inclined to do so.

As I was preparing to go to the press conference, LaBelle called and in bitter terms said I had destroyed Bert and betrayed my friend. [We were soon reconciled and remained close friends.] The press conference went well. For the first time the AP reporter did not say "Thank you, Mr. President." I had to end the press conference myself, about five minutes late. Afterward I had a rash of calls [from senators], and there was a general feeling that the episode had been concluded as best we could.

Went to see *The Longest Yard*, a movie, so that we could forget about the day's events.

Afterward I had a call from Chief Justice Warren Burger, who said he had watched a replay of the press conference, that he was overwhelmed with emotion and gratitude that the Bert Lance thing had been handled in such a way as to point out the extreme dangers from the press in subverting justice. He thought there might be a beneficial result from this conclusion.

SEPTEMBER 22   I came over early to prepare for the meeting with Gromyko, which I consider to be one of the most important I've had this year.

Put the final touches on the announcement of the eight-nation trip for the end of November and met with Senator Jennings Randolph. I urged him to run for reelection next year, or there's a good likelihood that Arch Moore, former Republican governor, will be elected. Also talked to Randolph about his support for the Panama Canal Treaty. He promised me his vote if it was needed.

Senator Randolph, a Democrat from West Virginia, kept this promise until the last minute, when I obtained the requisite number of votes without calling on him to take this politically damaging step.

Henry Kissinger called to say he knew how character assassinations could take place in the press and to express his appreciation for the way the Lance matter had been handled by the White House.

I had lunch with Mike Blumenthal to discuss tax reform and the relationship between our administration and the business community now that Bert has gone.

Hugh Carter came to discuss proposed change in funding for the Nixon and Ford staffs. Apparently Ford had asked the Speaker for an increase in funding for him, but to exclude Nixon. I told Hugh I did not like this approach and to leave me out of it but to work with the vice president.

We lost a deregulation vote in the Senate after we came from about thirty-three votes up to forty-six. We've shown enough strength so we might come out with a reasonable compromise in a conference committee. I will veto it if necessary.

I spent hours preparing for the Gromyko talks, looking over the past history of the SALT negotiations, and getting my own thoughts clearly in mind. It's time for some progress in our relationship with the Soviet Union, and I guess the major responsibility is on me — if the Soviets want progress and peace.

SEPTEMBER 23   Met with Frank Moore and Jim Schlesinger to clarify my determination to veto the natural gas deregulation bill if necessary and also the wellhead tax legislation.

With enormous amounts of money at stake, every interest group had their lobbyists working full-time to add special benefits within the primary legislation I was proposing. This was something I could not accept, and would veto.

Spent about three hours with Gromyko and went over the issues between us and the Soviet Union, pointing out that this was the most important international relationship that we have, that most of the threat to world peace and the prospects for improvement throughout the world were re-

lated to how well our countries got along with each other. We would compete when we were able to do it. Both nations would maintain a strong
defense. Our country has superb technology and the ability to produce
food, and international trade capabilities. We would like to improve trade
with the Soviet Union, but the human rights question stands in the way:
the imprisoned Russian Jews, the Sharansky case. We discussed southern
Africa, the Middle East, Korea. We are willing to cooperate with the Soviets on the Middle East as long as they are not an obstacle to peace.

I pointed out that the China-U.S. relationship would never be used
against the Soviets, and we would keep the Soviets informed about our
relationship with China. We welcomed Soviet improvements in relations
with our NATO allies. At the same time we were determined to improve
our own relations with countries in the Warsaw Pact.

I outlined our hope that [a] comprehensive test ban [treaty] could be
consummated without delay, including the peaceful nuclear explosive
question and adequate verification. I then outlined in detail our SALT
proposal.

Gromyko responded that they'd been concerned about some of the
criticism from me of the Soviets, that my attitudes had varied. I pointed
out that this was not the case, that we reserve the right to criticize when it
was important. He wanted to know how I saw prospects for the Soviet-U.S.
relationship in the future. I told him I thought the prospects for improvement were good. He said that improved trade relationships would lead to
improved political relationships.

He said that Sharansky was a microscopic dot who was of no consequence to anyone. I responded that Sharansky was an important person in
our own country because he was a test case of fair treatment of those accused of political crimes, and that in the past the Soviets had been free to
criticize us when they saw fit.

*Natan Sharansky, a Soviet dissident, had been arrested and was later con-
victed by the Soviets of treason and spying for the United States. I never met
with any Soviet leader without emphasizing the importance of Sharansky's
freedom. In 1986 he was freed and went to Israel, where in the 1990s he
became involved in politics and government. Israeli peace and human rights
advocates believe he abandoned his principles when he emerged as an im-
placable opponent of compromise with the Palestinians.*

He [Gromyko] said if we would just establish a miniature state for the Palestinians "as big as a pencil eraser," that would lead to a resolution of the PLO problem for the Geneva conference. I pointed out the difficulty of this tiny state being formed. Gromyko said that peace was more than the end of war in the Middle East. They agreed with us that the ultimate goal was normal relationships between the Arab and Israeli governments and people. They were determined to cooperate with us on reconvening the Geneva conference, that the Mideast was casting a shadow on the whole world, certainly including the U.S. and the Soviet Union, that they would like to see no further arms sales in the Middle East in the future, and they would cooperate with us on reductions of arms sales throughout the world.

He said when we established our base in Diego Garcia that we tread on Soviet toes. I told him that I did not know the Soviet Union foot was underneath the "little tiny rock," as he had referred to it.

He said our positions on nonproliferation are identical. I think they are. They were eager to cooperate with us on arms sales. He thought the Senate should ratify the Limited Test Ban Treaty, which would help to consummate a comprehensive test ban treaty. SALT was the question of questions. They were approaching the air-launched cruise missile (ALCM) and the modern large ballistic missile (MLBM) questions as the Soviets had done at Stalingrad, saying, "Seeing beyond the Volga there is nothing." They had gone as far as they were going to go. They had made concessions on lower ceilings, counting in the total of all missiles which had any portion of them MIRVed. I quickly pointed out that an adamant position on ALCMs and MLBMs was a mistake. This was no time for adamant positions on anything, and the concessions that he pointed out were mutually advantageous and were certainly not to be interpreted as a concession by the Soviet Union for our benefit.

A MIRVed missile has multiple warheads, each of which is independently aimed. I have included most of this entry about the discussion between Gromyko and me since many of the same bilateral issues are still of crucial importance. The Soviets depended on very large silo-based missiles and smaller ones that could be moved around on rails. We had medium-sized missiles on land and in our submarines, and small but accurate cruise missiles that could be launched from the ground or from aircraft.

He pointed out that they had offered to forgo the use of atomic weapons altogether if other nations would agree, and then he closed his comments by saying that President Brezhnev certainly had no opposition to meeting me and they insisted that the meeting would result in a major agreement of some kind.

I closed the meeting by pointing out that the American and Soviet people wanted peace, I hoped that Brezhnev and I would not be obstacles to that peace, and he had more experience than I did in diplomatic affairs—maybe five hundred months' more experience. We did not want any advantage in the SALT talks, but we had different concerns; the heavy missiles were important to them, and the cruise missiles were important to us. I pointed out that I hoped in the future to have no nuclear weapons throughout the world. After we concluded SALT II, I would consider favorably a recommendation from them that SALT III limits would be cut in half.

SEPTEMBER 24   Last night we sent a very strong message to Begin that unless they withdraw troops and weapons they acquired from us immediately from Lebanon, then we will go to the Congress and demand that all shipment of military supplies cease. This accords with U.S. law.

We got a message back from Israel that they were withdrawing their troops immediately from Lebanon. We are notifying the Syrians and the Lebanese and demanding that they mutually participate in a cease-fire and withdrawal of the Palestinians back ten kilometers from the Israeli borders.

There were a few times when I confronted Israel quite forcefully, despite Israel's relative immunity from restraints by the U.S. Congress. Inevitably, these were difficult moments. Since Israel's founding in 1948, every U.S. president—myself included—has been a staunch supporter of the country. We have protected Israel from critical UN resolutions, using our influence and Security Council vetoes. We have always been generous with financial aid, although President George H. W. Bush withheld a substantial amount of funds when Prime Minister Yitzhak Shamir insisted on building a large settlement between Jerusalem and Bethlehem. (Construction was stopped, but then resumed when President Clinton took office.) In addition, we have for many years sent the Israel Defense Forces some of our latest and most destructive weapons, including cluster bombs. Our laws prohibit use of these weapons for offensive purposes, and these were the laws I enforced in September 1977. Since then, however, Israel has ignored these restraints when attacking Lebanon and during the sustained assault on Gaza in January 2009.

SEPTEMBER 25 I slept until almost 7:00—latest in months. Taught Sunday school at First Baptist Church, then we went to the Zion Baptist Church, where I introduced Dr. Martin Luther King, Sr., who gave the sermon. The program lasted two and a half hours, but we really enjoyed it and I think once a year it's a good thing to do.

The evening news showed almost unanimous improvement in the international affairs picture, although all of this could go back again quite rapidly. With the Middle East, Rhodesia, the Soviets on SALT, European acceptance of the neutron bomb, and the general reaction to my late November trip, all seem to be good.

MONDAY, SEPTEMBER 26 At the cabinet meeting we discussed a wide range of issues, including the fact that Canada with its public health program had 7 percent of its GNP spent on health—our figure is 10 percent.

U.S. spending on health care was more than 17 percent of our GNP (gross national product) in 2009.

I talked to Mother in New York. She was given an award as the Outstanding Humanitarian of the Year with an eighteen-thousand-dollar stipend, which she's given to charity. It was by the United Jewish Appeal, and after they gave her "This Is My Life" presentation she stood up and said, "I've never been with so many Jews before in my life"—and got a standing ovation.

We went over the NASA program with Robert Frosch, administrator, and decided that we didn't need any major innovations but to use the space shuttle and other existing technology more effectively.

It's an unbelievable relief to all of us not to have the Bert Lance thing hanging over us. Even adverse votes in the Congress are much easier to accept, and a lot of the tension is gone.

SEPTEMBER 27 Ed Koch [soon to be elected mayor of New York City] came by, and Bess Myerson was with him. They make an excellent team and were in good spirits. I told him I wanted to see what his spirits were six months after he took over as mayor.

Gromyko, [Deputy Foreign Minister Georgi] Kornienko, and Dobrynin gave a very positive response to proposals for SALT. It was obvious to me they want an agreement. There's a new tone of cooperation that has not existed since I first came in office. He [Gromyko] talked about concession so much that I finally told him I had a dual responsibility: to protect the interest of the American people and secondly to protect the interests of the Soviet people that he might not adequately protect. He laughed and realized he had made too much of the Soviet concessions. I gave him a little model of all the Soviet missiles and the U.S. missiles—which show the enormous size of the Soviets' and the tiny size of American missiles. He was taken aback and intrigued that I would give him this summary in visual form.

SEPTEMBER 28   During the morning I met with Prime Minister [Abd al-Halim] Khaddam of Syria. I pointed out that they had not been helpful in getting the PLO to accept UN Resolution 242. I told him we would accept the United Arab delegation at Geneva with Palestinians being represented who were not well-known members of the PLO. Then we'd break into separate meetings between Israel and Egypt, Israel and Syria, Israel and Lebanon, and Israel and Jordan. Plus another meeting between Israel and a combined Jordan-Palestinian delegation. Khaddam and Assad are very tough and extremely suspicious—not quite as bad as the Israelis but worst of the Arabs.

Jody and Hamilton discovered a sweeping news media premise claiming that Vice President Mondale had lost influence within the White House. It was ridiculous, so I called Jack Nelson with the *Los Angeles Times* and Hedrick Smith with *The New York Times*, and succeeded beyond my expectations. The following day superb articles came out telling how influential the vice president was. I think Fritz appreciated this more than anything that's ever happened between me and him.

The most competent and balanced news reporter I ever knew was Jack Nelson, who had won a Pulitzer Prize in Atlanta before heading the Los Angeles Times *bureau in Washington. He also had great influence among other journalists.*

SEPTEMBER 29   Brzezinski reported long and productive discussions with Callaghan, Giscard, and Schmidt. In general, they are relieved about our basic foreign policy, our relationship with them, prospective progress being made with the Soviets. We discussed with them the non-first-use question and deployment of the neutron bomb.

The deployment of neutron bombs in western Europe became a contentious issue. The enhanced-radiation weapon was designed to kill people while doing less structural damage. Later, I was unable to persuade key nations to deploy it, and I finally canceled its production. The bombs were later produced by Reagan and then retired by George H. W. Bush.

Senate is still deadlocked on the energy package. The influence of the oil and gas industry is unbelievable, and it's impossible to arouse the public to protect themselves. The leadership is not well coordinated. Scoop Jackson and Bob Byrd are doing the best they can, but Russell Long and others plus the lobbyists are prevailing.

Had a meeting with the last group of House Republican members of Congress. They've helped me a great deal on some of the crucial items—reorganization, AWACS sale, questions concerning the prerogatives of the president—and I expressed my appreciation.

The strict partisan alignment and animosity that now prevails in the Congress did not exist twenty-five years ago. On many issues regarding defense or controlling deficits, I received more support from Republicans than from Democrats.

I signed the agriculture bill, about $600 million more than I had wanted but the best we could get. It's far-reaching and has some very good features in it. This has been a tough one, and I'm glad we don't have to do this every year.

Met with [Federal Reserve chairman] Arthur Burns and economic advisors for lunch. Dr. Burns is quite concerned about some of the reported changes in income tax law. Of course, he's almost 100 percent attuned to the business community.

Stopped to see chief executives of the major motion picture companies. They are concerned about the pirating of films and also about import quotas and tariffs. They can reach public consciousness on Panama and other controversial questions, and I'd like to stay close to them.

Kirbo spent the night and outlined special problems with Billy and the warehouse. Since the warehouse is now under the management of Gold Kist, there's no conflict of interest for me to discuss these matters, which are very serious. Kirbo is willing to keep the responsibility.

Gold Kist was the nation's largest agricultural cooperative. It leased Carter's Warehouse, our family business, for the four years I was president.

SEPTEMBER 30   I met with farm editors of the nation. Luckily I had just studied to sign the agriculture bill, so I was able to answer their questions in some detail.

Chief Justice Burger came to give me a report on his confrontation with Brezhnev, where Brezhnev berated Burger for forty minutes about our obstinate position on SALT and other items. Burger said that he responded in kind, and he was quite excited about this encounter. Following that, all members of the Supreme Court paid their respects as they prepared to begin the fall session.

Immediately afterward, we left by helicopter to go to Camp David. All the staff assembled on the lawn to wish me a Happy Birthday [the next day].

OCTOBER 1–2   I spent a good part of the weekend on my UN speech. Read a book, worked on the tax reform options, held church at Camp David chapel, and we returned to the mansion. I finished the final draft of the UN speech before I went to bed.

MONDAY, OCTOBER 3   I read about the American Jewish uproar because the Soviets and I had spelled out general principles of the Mideast Geneva conference agenda, all compatible with what we had said publicly before and also what we had discussed with the foreign ministers of the Arab states and Israel. When it's confronted frankly, the screams arise immediately.

Bergland reported agricultural exports last year were $24 billion — the highest in history.

I met with Livingston Biddle, who is being considered for the Endowment for the Arts. I decided without enthusiasm to choose him.

My lack of enthusiasm was not for the appointee but for the extremely dense political thicket surrounding the Endowment.

OCTOBER 4 Went to New York for a two-day visit, primarily to the United Nations. When we arrived at the Wall Street helipad, I was met by Democratic officials, and Ed Koch in a prepublicized but friendly way handed me a letter about the Mideast, which I accepted and gave to Jody. The news media, as is often the custom, completely distorted this incident, which was very friendly.

At the UN I delivered the speech on peace, disarmament, nonproliferation, nuclear weapons, and some other trouble points in the world. There was a heavy attendance, and I think the speech was well received. Rosalynn had come down from Boston to meet me, and this was her first visit to the UN. There's a different attitude among the nations of the world toward us, brought about by our own new policies and by the influence of Andrew Young.

I then walked over to the Plaza Hotel for a meeting with [Egyptian] foreign minister [Ismail] Fahmy. He agreed with our joint statement with the Soviets, reported that the Jordanians and Syrians had some problems with it, brought me a letter from Sadat urging that nothing be done to prevent Israel and Egypt from negotiating directly with our serving as an intermediary either before or after the Geneva conference. Egypt is the most forthcoming and cooperative nation in the Middle East in working toward a peace settlement.

We had a luncheon for forty-five or fifty African nations—about the same number of countries as we have states, and about the same population—around 220 million. Many of these countries would not permit Kissinger to visit them and would not attend any events sponsored by the United States a year ago. Now they are very warm in their friendship, and the acrimony that existed throughout the General Assembly against our country has been eliminated almost completely. Most of what remains is because of our support for Israel.

I had a productive meeting with Dayan. He was quite nervous and deeply concerned about the Soviet-American statement. I told him that our commitments to Israel still stood, we were not trying to impose a settlement from outside, we had no intentions of withholding military or economic aid that we thought necessary to Israel because of their recalcitrance on certain issues, and they were to go to Geneva on the basis of UN Resolutions 242, 338, and our commitments to them.

The Israelis agreed to consider the refugee problem on a multinational basis for the first time as part of the peace talks themselves, to consider the question of the West Bank and the Gaza Strip jointly with Palestinians, the Jordanians, and the Egyptians. They talked freely about partition of the West Bank area between themselves and Jordan, and were adamant against any prospect of an independent Palestinian state. They were not ready to face up to the ultimate question of the Golan Heights, but Dayan pointed out that he had always been against the Israelis occupying the Golan Heights on a permanent basis with settlements.

I pointed out the damaging effect on Israel of their public attacks on me and our good faith efforts in the negotiations. Israel was going to find itself isolated, and if I had to defend my position publicly, which I had refrained from doing, it would cause a cleavage that might be serious. I told the group that there was no doubt that, of all the nations with whom we had negotiated on the Middle East, Israel was by far the most obstinate and difficult. This seemed to cause them genuine concern and they kept coming back to the point, but of course Cy and Zbig and all of us know that it's absolutely a fact. I would say that Egypt's been the best, Jordan next, Syria far back, and Israel worse than Syria. In the last few days they have been a little more flexible on settlements, Palestinian representation, joint Arab delegations, and so forth. This session lasted until about 2:00 a.m., following which Dayan and Jody made a statement to the press. I went to bed a little after midnight.

At the working dinner with western and eastern European leaders, Dayan was something of an outcast. The animosity toward Israel is always a surprise to me. The people sitting at the table with Dayan and the secretary of state refused to speak to him.

OCTOBER 5   I met with [outgoing New York City] mayor [Abraham] Beame and asked him to be chairman of the Intergovernmental Advisory Commission, a nonpaid job but one that could be very important. Then I toured the South Bronx area with him and Pat Harris. It was a shocking, devastated area, and it's going to take a lot of work and effort to turn it around — if it can be done. There are about 1,200 abandoned buildings, there had been 2,000 fires, almost all of which had been deliberately set in the last two years, and the government housing projects were standing almost like oases. The spirit of the people seemed to be quite good. It's obvious that it will have to be an effort by Interior, Commerce, Labor, and HUD, along with state and local governments, banks, and private owners of those buildings before it can be improved. It was a sobering visit, but exciting for me.

Some real progress has been made since those days of arson and general dilapidation, but the South Bronx still has a long way to go. It is in the poorest congressional district in the country, and more than half the children live below the poverty line.

I met privately with [UN secretary-general Kurt] Waldheim [and] signed the Human Rights Covenants, then had a reception with the specialized agency heads, a very good group who do tremendous work around the world but are often not recognized as being part of the UN. They help with health, refugees, civilian air safety, atomic energy supervision, and so forth. We probably waste a lot of money and effort in our own government by not coordinating better with these standing groups, where more than 85 percent of the UN budget goes. The only part we hear about are crazy resolutions pushed through the General Assembly.

I emphasized that an analysis of their organizational structure, obsolescence of some of their programs, and tightening of their budget was crucial, and I will let some of our OMB officials give me an assessment of what they ought to do.

Although I proudly signed the covenants on this date, the one on civil and political rights was not ratified by the United States until 1992, and then with so many exceptions and caveats that this ratification was meaningless. The U.S. Senate has still not considered the Covenant on Economic, Social, and Cultural Rights.

Then I met with President [Spyros] Kyprianou of Cyprus, and of course he presented the Greek Cypriot point of view, claiming to be quite flexible — that [Rauf] Denktash representing the Turks is the only recalcitrant one. The solution to the Cyprus situation obviously is not on Cyprus itself but in Greece and Turkey. We have pressure on the Turks in that we're holding up their general security agreement if they don't do something on Cyprus.

I met with Imelda Marcos, who had brought me a letter from President [Ferdinand] Marcos. She's very attractive, very strong-willed, very competent. She also brought very expensive gifts to me and Rosalynn, which we'll turn over to the state.

Her husband, a serious human rights oppressor, was not welcome in the White House, so Imelda served as his surrogate. I decided to turn the responsibility for these bilateral discussions over to Fritz Mondale.

I had a reception for all Latin American/Caribbean officials. I felt more at home with them than any others since the Panama signings. I pointed out that the Tlatelolco treaty was a very good example for the rest of the world to follow, and we dealt with them now as equals and hope that the tensions of the past were being alleviated.

The Treaty of Tlatelolco was fully implemented, and Latin America remains a nuclear-weapons-free zone.

The two days in New York were very successful. We made good progress on the Middle East and Cyprus, met officials from almost every country in the world, had a dozen or so bilateral meetings, signed the Human Rights Covenants, and delivered a speech that I think will be constructive in the months ahead. And the news reports from the South Bronx area have been very good.

OCTOBER 6   This was a busy day, putting out fires. Met early this morning with thirty or forty western senators who had been irate about our national water policy. I described the need for comprehensive planning, involvement of state and local officials and the private interests, their need to learn different viewpoints on water around the country, [the need for] my administration to learn about specific regional problems, and the need to establish orders of priority in the allocation of federal funding. These recommendations will come to me at the end of this year, and beginning in February we'll probably be able to promulgate some of the decisions. I think they went away assuaged.

Then I met with the House Jewish Caucus, explained the difficulty of dealing with a complex Middle East question, the fact that my decisions were being trusted by all the Arab nations, the Soviets, and the Israelis, and asked the same degree of trust from the Congress. I pointed out the damage to Israel if it was isolated from us and from all the other nations where the isolation already exists. I believe their concerns were reduced substantially, and their statements afterward to the press were helpful.

I met with Secretary Brown and all five Joint Chiefs to explain our SALT position in detail, getting very technical on occasion, and believe I convinced them it was a good and equitable proposal. [General] George Brown said that although he wouldn't acknowledge it was enhancing our national security, it certainly did not hurt it. My impression was they just wanted to go on the record as being cautious, which is understandable.

Played tennis with Hamilton and did okay using my new topspin stroke, but still not easy with it.

After this, we left for Camp David, and this is one weekend I won't even pick up a tennis racquet, but we have bikes to ride and the swimming pool to use. I needed to rest.

OCTOBER 7   I called Senator Byrd, and he said he was doing a poll among the Democratic senators to see how many would support the comprehensive energy package, including a wellhead tax. He still had hope. He thinks he did the right thing along with Fritz to stamp out the filibuster, but I believe they used the wrong tactics; a little too abrasive. The Senate's not accustomed to that.

I went to the Democratic National Committee meeting at a downtown hotel. I spelled out my program for them and described the complexity of it, how difficult and controversial the individual major items were, and asked for their support. I told them I did not intend to back down, which I won't.

OCTOBER 8   I worked on tax reform, read a book by [Chinua] Achebe, a Nigerian, called *Things Fall Apart*, before I meet with the leaders this coming week, and also read *The Village Beyond* by Livingston Biddle, my choice for director of the Endowment for the Arts. I thought it was a good book.

Camp David is a beautiful place to stay. The children had contests to see who got the most different kinds of leaves and identified them. Amy and her friend tied with Jeff and [his wife] Annette in getting fifty different species.

OCTOBER 9   We went all around the periphery of Camp David on bikes, and I made it without stopping, which is quite an achievement on those hills.

MONDAY, OCTOBER 10   Came back to the White House, and Rosalynn left for Puerto Rico. I spent about four hours with Mike Blumenthal, Stu, [Assistant Treasury Secretary] Larry Woodworth, Jim McIntyre, Charlie Schultze—going over tax reform measures. In order to preserve confidentiality, I told them I would not let them know my choice on the options until shortly before it was time to submit our plan to the public and the Congress.

OCTOBER 11   Senator Long called me to suggest that the Senate Finance Committee do very little and wait for floor action approving a skeleton bill—then going into conference with the House. He suggested, strangely enough, that I then put a five-dollar import fee on oil and let Congress vote for the equalization tax as a better alternative than the five-dollar fee. I have some doubt about the course of action he advocates, but of course I listened with care.

I met with a group of senators concerning Panama Canal ambiguities, and all of us approved a clarification statement that might be signed by me and Torrijos. I don't think there's any possibility of having the treaty ratified unless the question of our right to protect the canal after the year 2000 is clarified and also the right of expeditious passage in case of a national emergency.

Then the Nigerian delegation and I met for about two and a half hours—an hour more than we had anticipated. I was really impressed with the structure of their government, their own leadership capabilities, the relative unselfishness of the Nigerians, and the tremendous and growing influence they have in Africa. Although a year ago they would not permit Kissinger to come into their country, because of Andy Young's efforts and our own new administration policy, they are now becoming close and good friends of ours. They can be extremely valuable in helping us with African affairs, because they are too strong to be ignored by the other African leaders.

Tragically, Nigeria is now afflicted with terrible corruption in the national and state governments, and had completely fraudulent presidential elections in 1999, 2003, and 2007. Reform efforts seem to be faltering as preparations are made for 2011.

Congressman Ullman gave me a typical report of his, saying that he hoped we would not offer a quickie tax reduction without comprehensive reforms—with which I agreed. Then he added that the comprehensive reform we've proposed shouldn't involve controversial matters!

OCTOBER 12   At our congressional leadership breakfast this morning, the overriding question is on the energy policy. I expressed concern about wasting $1.4 billion in trying to build more B-1s that we don't need. I guess this is typical, but the whole congressional process seems to be bogged down, and of course, the president gets blamed for lack of leadership capability—an accusation that may be justified.

I signed the 1977 bill on housing and community development, which is a major step forward. We've tried to renovate the decrepit housing program in the country and so far had very good success.

Fritz and I discussed the problem with public perception of our commitment—the multiple efforts we are making that fragment public attention and give an appearance of confusion and incapacity. Had an analysis from Pat Caddell and Jerry Rafshoon showing a devastating reduction in public opinion of me. Still favorable—around 60 percent—but specifics and achievement, leadership and so forth, very low.

I considered polling results carefully and tried to overcome revealed problems. In this case, I agreed that we had too many public proposals being considered and too few successes. The obvious solution was not to be more timid with our agenda but to strive for better results.

We went to the Kennedy Center to hear a Rostropovich–Leonard Bernstein concert. It was an all-Bernstein concert, and I was very disappointed. The second half especially dragged, and I had a real hunger for some Brahms, Sibelius, Bach, Beethoven, Rachmaninoff—even Prokofiev or Shostakovich before it was over.

OCTOBER 13   I called [columnist] Jack Germond. His daughter, Mandy, had leukemia and died last night. I discovered [that she was ill] when I was making my first campaign trip in January 1975, and I sent her a couple of arrowheads and felt very close to her.

It's become obvious to me that we've had too much of my own involvement in different matters simultaneously. I need to concentrate on energy and fight for passage of an acceptable plan. We've not been able to do it in a quiet, unobtrusive, and private way with the members of the Senate. The oil lobbies are too strong.

I needed to confront the lobbyists for the oil industry more strongly on this key issue and attempt to recruit the public to our side. Members of Congress were heavily influenced by campaign contributions, and pressure from their own constituents was the only antidote. I also knew that the collective voices of my cabinet officers could be a great help in the effort to advance our cause, especially outside Washington in the individual states and districts.

Since Rosalynn had gotten angry last night when we didn't go backstage after the Bernstein concert [to thank the performers], I called both him and Rostropovich and believe they appreciated the calls.

Tip O'Neill reported that Ed Koch was seriously hurt by the allegation that he had insulted the president. I told him this was not true. Koch wants me to come to New York, which I won't do, but he can come by and see me.

I spoke to the Young Presidents Organization, told them I thought I was a young president till I saw them, and said I'm sure they wanted to meet the most famous young president in the nation and tomorrow they'd have their chance when Bert Lance spoke to them. [By this point, Bert had become quite famous.]

Bob Byrd called to tell me that Russell Long is coming out of the Finance Committee with an energy bill of some sort, and requested that neither I nor Schlesinger attack the bill as inadequate until they have a chance to let it go through the Senate floor debate, go to conference, and then they are determined to come out with a better one.

OCTOBER 14   I met with General Torrijos, just back from a trip through the Mideast and Europe. He and I finally agreed on the two issues of most concern on the Panama Canal: our right to defend the canal after the year 2000 without intervening in the internal affairs of Panama; and the right of our ships to have expeditious passage in time of need or emergency.

Met with western state members of Congress to get their support for the evolution of a comprehensive national policy on water.

I told Brzezinski I wanted South Africa invited to the International Fuel Cycle Study meeting. There's opposition among members of my administration, and they are putting up every obstacle they can.

Bob Strauss came to say we had another two or three months during which we could recruit support from the business community. If we don't move, we're going to lose that support, maybe permanently. I told him and Hamilton to start working on meetings between me and maybe three or four hundred leaders around the country who will come in groups to be briefed, and be reassured about my ability and attitude.

Strauss's comments corroborated the earlier polling data, and I began working much more closely with leaders of the Business Roundtable, National Association of Manufacturers, and chambers of commerce. They were glad to accept my invitation to come to the White House for personal briefings by me and cabinet officers.

OCTOBER 15   The [Rowland] Evans and [Robert] Novak article this morning was deliberately false, stating that Hamilton had met with Senate staff members and said we only had two competent cabinet officers. Hamilton hasn't met with any Senate staff members or said anything about cabinet officers. There ought to be a law against liars like these two reporters and just a few others in the country.

OCTOBER 16   I'm beginning to feel better narrowing down my public involvement to just two or three issues at any one time. I can still work behind the scenes on a wide range of programs and foreign policy matters.

MONDAY, OCTOBER 17   I talked to the cabinet about a team effort on the energy legislation passage, and we all will spend this week in schooling to learn the issues. Unless we get a responsible energy package through the Congress, the sense of weakness of our administration will endanger our programs in the future.

Had lunch with Fritz, who is too sensitive about newspaper criticism, particularly from his former liberal friends who've turned on him to some degree.

Met with President [Omar] Bongo of Gabon, who's president of the Organization of African Unity. He stayed about forty-five minutes too long, in spite of all we could do to end the meeting.

OCTOBER 18   We've been very pleased at the German success in releasing their hostages, and we provided them a great deal of intelligence information during the long ordeal. [German commandos had liberated eighty-six hostages in Mogadishu, Somalia, who were held by hijackers.] We have similar capability, but our people are not as highly trained as they should be. I directed Zbig and Harold to get our units a thorough briefing by the Israelis, Germans, and perhaps the Dutch on how they've dealt with terrorism.

Several factors may have reduced the risk of terrorist attacks against the United States during my presidency; among other things, we were attempting to protect the rights of Palestinians, we had no major military bases in Saudi Arabia or other sensitive Islamic states, and NATO forces were not dispatched to fight in Arab countries. Also, the G7 leaders decided to get tough with Libya and other nations that cooperated with terrorists.

With Rosalynn, we worked out a genuine role for her to play on foreign trips, decided to increase her public involvement with the antidrug program as part of mental health, and use her in times of local disaster as my representative. Then we discussed planting trees dug up in Georgia on the White House grounds and decided on a Georgia dogwood, red maple, sycamore, and a loblolly pine.

Met with a young man named Amory Lovins who's written a book called *Soft Energy Paths.* He has some intriguing ideas about avoiding "hard technology" atomic power plants, et cetera. Jim Schlesinger was there, and we will be pursuing these issues as much as we can without creating an excessive shock to our nation's political and economic structure. I think in the long run Lovins's ideas are going to prove correct.

Lovins's proposals were compatible with many of ours, including those dealing with energy efficiency, the use of renewable energy, and the generation of energy by windmills, solar panels, and from small local hydroelectric projects feeding into power grids. Three decades later, many of these ideas are being pursued once again.

OCTOBER 19   John Gardner [head of Common Cause] came by to congratulate us on what we had done so far, and to promise an effort to get the Panama treaties ratified and that Common Cause would help me with the energy package. He said the most important thing in the long run was to get public financing of congressional elections, since so many of the congressman were still being bought.

OCTOBER 20   I met with the leaders of the consumer groups on energy. They are intense in their feeling that we can't go further in concessions to the oil companies at the expense of consumers, and I agree with them. They've not been supportive, but I think they now see that an energy bill is necessary.

OCTOBER 21   The British have finally decided to hold firm on the Rhodesian proposal. I told Cy we absolutely had to hold down arms sales around the world, including the Middle East–Persian Gulf area.

Our policy of severely restricting arms sales was abandoned by all my successors. U.S. sales are now about $38 billion annually, equal to the combined sales of all other weapons-producing nations. Sales in 2009 reflected a 465 percent growth just in the last ten years.

OCTOBER 22   We flew to Omaha, Nebraska—Offutt Field—to meet with the Strategic Air Command leaders and see how we planned our Strategic Force utilization in an emergency and how we assess target areas for our nuclear weapons. It was very informative, and I had a chance to speak to our Strategic Forces all over the world on the intercommunication system. It helped relieve some of the problems that had arisen with my veto of the B-1 bomber.

Then we flew on out to California for a successful fund-raiser. Lew Wasserman [head of MCA] helped overcome boycotts by some Jewish leaders who did not like our Middle East policy. I talked about human rights and our Mideast effort—a very tough and controversial issue.

OCTOBER 23   We flew to Minneapolis and picked up Senator Humphrey and [his wife] Muriel after visiting with his family. Although he has terminal cancer, as I saw him there with his family and how much the Minnesota people loved him, I didn't think about pity or sorrow. I thought how lucky a man he was. He's one of the finest people I ever met, and today he was particularly exuberant and excited about going back to Washington, particularly on Air Force One. He's a man that's easy to love, and I'm proud to have him as a friend.

MONDAY, OCTOBER 24 (VETERANS DAY)   I stayed in the mansion for the first time since I've been here during a weekday—long enough to eat breakfast with Rosalynn. Then we had an NSC meeting on South Africa and decided to take stern action short of an economic boycott. Met with Harold Brown on nuclear encoding matters. All in all, a leisurely day.

We decided to vote for the Egyptian resolution against Israeli settlement provided they remove objectionable language referring to Palestinian lands. NBC announced that Israel was making permanent six settlements in the occupied territories, but later they denied the story.

OCTOBER 25   At our congressional leaders breakfast we discussed almost exclusively the energy legislation. I particularly wanted Scoop Jackson and Russell Long there so we could have it out among Democrats concerning their differences, very deep and personal. I thought Russell acted moderately and like a gentleman, but Scoop acted like an ass. At the same time he's supporting my positions more closely than Russell.

Scoop Jackson was a brilliant and competent senator, a genuine expert on the Soviet Union and arms control. He was an early and persistent defender of the rights of Jews who were being persecuted in Russia. He and I had been good friends since 1971, when he first visited me in the Georgia governor's mansion as a candidate for president. I was honored when he asked me to nominate him at the Democratic National Convention in Miami.

An inevitable rift came when we competed as presidential candidates in 1976. His last major effort, supported by other candidates, was in the Pennsylvania primary, when I won a convincing victory. I seriously considered him as my vice presidential running mate after I was nominated, and I can only surmise that Scoop resented my choice of Walter Mondale. His later attitude made it obvious that he considered himself to be better qualified than I to be president.

In the Congress, Senator Jackson was the core around whom the most vitriolic anti-Soviet forces coagulated. Their premise was that the Soviets were enormous ogres who were poised to take over the world. This group looked on me as weak and naive because I argued that the Soviet Union was rotten to the core and that over time our promotion of peace, human rights, and accommodation on arms control would be detrimental to the Soviets and beneficial to our nation.

Then I met with Prince Saud, foreign minister of Saudi Arabia, to discuss the Mideast. He's a strong advocate of the Arab position, quite defensive of Assad and the PLO. I let him know we were on the verge of failure to get a peace conference convened, but I was not going to rewrite our working paper, which has been reluctantly accepted by the Israelis and criticized but not rejected by Sadat and Assad. The Syrians are insisting that the PLO be designated as such to participate in the conference. This is impossible. I agreed to make a statement that the Palestinian question would be pursued on an equal basis with withdrawal and definition of peace.

I talked to Cy and Andy about South Africa. Although some of our Western allies are a little shaky, there's a general consensus that we impose a strict arms embargo plus additional economic and trade restraints. Apparently South Africa is taking a politically suicidal attitude as far as the outside world is concerned.

OCTOBER 26 Frank Moore came to discuss the Senate struggle between Jackson and Long, which endangers our energy tax proposals. We're trying to stay aloof but get the conference committee to pass viable legislation.

Cy Vance spent the morning briefing Jewish congressmen and about seventy Jewish leaders from around the country. He has tremendous patience and is willing to take an awful lot of abuse.

OCTOBER 27 I talked to Zbig about my sending a message to Torrijos concerning democracy in Panama. He's going to work with Bob Pastor [national security advisor on Latin America] on this letter, which will be private.

It had become a primary goal of mine to see Panama follow in the footsteps of many other nations that were already scheduling democratic elections. Torrijos promised to do so but died in a plane crash before taking action. I led a delegation to monitor the election in 1989, but a military oppressor named Manuel Noriega attempted to steal the election. When he was overthrown and imprisoned, the elected leaders took office. Since then, democracy has flourished.

I met with about 150 House and Senate members concerning the steel industry, and we had a very tough discussion. I let them know there were no easy solutions, we couldn't erect trade barriers or abandon our commitment to pure air and water, tax reform measures, or antidumping laws. I would work with them and the industry to try to help it as much as possible.

We had a news conference today, and there seems a general sense among the press that they've been excessively critical. I think they're beginning to see that we've laid all our controversial and very difficult questions out for public debate and it's going to take a long time to resolve some of these historic questions—and we've not injected any of them into the Congress or the public that didn't need to be confronted.

[Illinois Democratic congressman] Dan Rostenkowski came by—a great guy who's really been a staunch supporter of ours. Dan feels that we ought to get our cabinet members on Capitol Hill more often to visit with congressmen who are most intimately involved with their agencies. And I'll do that.

A group of Bavarian musicians came by who had been rained out of their performance for the South Lawn Oktoberfest. Rosalynn brought them to the Oval Office, and they played music that sounded like a polka to me. Rosalynn and I danced with them in the Oval Office. Probably a first. I really enjoyed it.

In the evening I read Howell Raines's novel *Whiskey Man*—better than I expected, nothing extra.

OCTOBER 28   Spent two and a half hours with Jim McIntyre, Charlie Schultze, Fritz, Stu, couple more people to go over the budget for 1979 and the projection through 1983. It's going to be very difficult to balance the budget, but I'm not going to give up on it. If I don't hold firm, no one will. It was a very instructive, somewhat discouraging, session.

We went to Camp David in the afternoon and invited our top staff members from Georgia: Frank Moore, Hamilton, Jody, Stu, and Bob Lipshutz. (Jack Watson couldn't come.)

OCTOBER 29–30   We abstained on the UN vote on Israel without any scars. The vote was unanimous except for Israel.

Had one of the most pleasant weekends we've ever had at Camp David. Amy enjoyed having the Eizenstat, Moore, and Powell children to play with. It helped to have our senior staff there together for the first time.

I read four books over the weekend and had plenty of time to watch movies, play tennis, ride bikes, swim, and have long bull sessions with the top staff people. The last book I read was *Herzog* by Saul Bellow. One of the better novels I've read in several years.

MONDAY, OCTOBER 31   Cy Vance called, and we decided to vote for the general condemnation of South Africa and for the arms embargo, but against other resolutions sponsored by African nations. I think all our Western allies will go with us.

Had a private letter from Sadat, handwritten by him and sealed. Said he's going to take bold action to strip away the argument about semantics and get down to the real issues of Geneva. He didn't indicate what he would do.

I decided to speak to the World Jewish Congress and spell out the obstacles to peace in the Middle East. I'm going on television Thursday night to talk about energy to the American people.

I asked the cabinet to continue their effective speeches on energy around the country, to set aside time each week to visit the Congress, to continue work on the paperwork and reporting reductions, and not expect to exceed the budget limits I gave them. I cautioned the staff and the cabinet to be prepared to see a constant animosity in the press, but not to be paranoid about it—to go directly to the people and bypass the news reporters and columnists. As usual, we discussed twenty-five or thirty different items.

Senator Harrison Schmitt called. He's an ex-astronaut and one of the biggest jerks in the Senate, and talked to me about the interrelationship between the telecommunications satellite system and the Panama Canal treaties.

Griffin Bell reported that our plan on handling the [case of] Richard Helms [former director of Central Intelligence] had worked out perfectly. He's pleading nolo contendere to two misdemeanors to avoid a trial that would have been devastating in revealing our intelligence network procedures.

In one respect, this case parallels those of the accused terrorists that have been incarcerated in Guantánamo and other prisons. If our government brings them to trial, top-secret evidence against them will potentially be exposed to public knowledge.

The governor of Oregon, Bob Straub, described problems with excessive shipment of whole logs to Japan, which was robbing the American sawmills of work and letting the Japanese buy finished lumber at a very cheap price.

Being a timber producer myself, I was familiar with this issue. It was much better for our country if we processed the whole logs ourselves, using many American workers, and then sold the finished lumber to foreign buyers.

I directed Hamilton to look at all the projects we've got planned for next year and put them in an orderly schedule so we might emphasize them one or two at a time.

The Senate passed the energy bill 52–35. I called Senators Byrd, Long, Jackson, and Baker to thank them.

NOVEMBER 1   Kirbo reported that some of the oil executives were ready to help with our energy package, but they didn't have adequate access to the administration. Schlesinger will consult with them, and we'll decide whether I should meet with them directly.

I signed the minimum-wage bill, a process that began thirty-nine years ago with Roosevelt. Six other presidents have signed minimum-wage legislation [each increasing the level].

Met with [White House assistant] Midge Costanza, who's been quite concerned about adverse publicity lately. She's been buffeted badly, and I reconfirmed my confidence in her and asked her to stay closer to me. I've been concerned about her involvement in the abortion and gay rights business, but she takes a tremendous burden off me from nut groups that would insist on seeing me if they couldn't see her.

We had our congressional leadership meeting at supper instead of breakfast so Senator Humphrey could attend. I congratulated each of them on doing a good job this year, and then Senator Humphrey rounded out the evening by making one of his typical very fine fifteen-minute presentations on the Democratic Party. (The fifteen minutes wasn't typical.)

The amount of legislation passed by the Congress was extraordinary, and I was deeply grateful. We had support for our proposals from a wide range of Democrats and Republicans, all of whom had visited me in the White House. Committee leaders and their key staff members had worked closely with Stu Eizenstat and his team in drafting all the major proposals, which therefore had good momentum when they reached the Congress.

NOVEMBER 2   Senator Byrd called. He's concerned about the Middle East question being a partisan issue and not having enough support for my position. He said there was a lot of quiet majority support, and I told him my problem was that it was too quiet. He asked for a copy of my speech [to the World Jewish Conference] before I deliver it, and he'd try to add some supportive words and get some other senators to do the same.

NOVEMBER 3   Jody's facing a barrage of questions, of course, about the Helms decision, which I think was the best way to handle a very difficult question.

Fritz had a luncheon for the Chinese ambassador, Huang Chen. I went over and shook hands with him. This was unprecedented and perhaps a little excessive in view of the negative attitude the Chinese government has taken since Cy's trip over there.

There was a surprising incompatibility between Secretary Vance and the Chinese leaders, which I never really understood. This personal estrangement seemed to carry over during the much more harmonious months that followed.

We received a message from Sadat proposing that a summit meeting be called in East Jerusalem, and urging my immediate response to the idea. We all decided to respond negatively.

NOVEMBER 4   The biggest congressional action today is the Senate consideration of Social Security. The Congress is almost spineless when considering extra benefits for special interest groups, in this case retired people. They are on the verge of putting the Social Security fund back into bankruptcy by eliminating restrictions on earnings levels for SS recipients, which would cost $3 or $4 billion a year. We spent all day working to get these amendments eliminated, and finally succeeded.

Clark Clifford came to discuss the Cyprus question—almost impossible because the Greeks and Turks are maneuvering the puppet leaders on Cyprus and trying to pretend they're not. It's vital to NATO strength to bring Turkey and Greece back into it in a strong and supportive way.

I asked Sam Nunn to be my Senate floor leader on matters that related to defense and foreign affairs, and he agreed.

Senator Nunn was my neighbor and friend in Georgia, having served in the state legislature when I was governor. He defeated my Senate appointee, David Gambrell, in 1972, and rapidly became one of the Senate's most respected leaders on defense issues.

NOVEMBER 5   I handwrote a letter to the senators about supporting the Panama Canal treaties and describing their terms to the people in their states. I quoted a *New York Times* poll that showed by more than two to one the American people would support the treaties if they thought we had the right to defend the canal, which is of course the case. The public just doesn't know it.

Jim Schlesinger thinks John Connally is the most likely Republican nominee for 1980 because of his charisma and its effect in the Republican primaries, even though he's not the favorite of the Republican Party functionaries. Of course, he knows that he's just guessing.

This handsome, eloquent, and well-financed Texas governor launched his campaign in January 1979, and for some reason he repeatedly said that "no one should vote for Jimmy Carter because he takes a cold shower each morning"—which wasn't (and isn't) true. Despite his apparent advantages, Connally ultimately set a world's record for the most money spent to acquire a single delegate's vote—$11 million.

I invited Senator Byrd to discuss what I might do to help heal the very serious problem between Jackson and Long. He said we need the Republican votes, and that Long would know what was necessary to acquire them. Out of twenty-five issues, there were two or three that Long wanted resolved his way, and he would be willing to trade off the rest of them. Byrd didn't yet know what issues Long felt were important.

He expressed an inclination to support us on Panama. He and seven or eight other senators are going down there next week. He said the major thing was for me to go to the people and sell it. He commented that if he and Baker were both for it, it would pass; if they were both against it, it would fail; and if he was for it and Baker against it, it would be a tough fight.

He was somewhat critical of Israel, particularly that Israel's military strength was becoming excessive compared to their neighbors.

NOVEMBER 6   I taught Sunday school—fourth chapter of John—and enjoyed it. We have 200, maybe 250 people in class when I teach, although we don't publicize it. Fred Gregg invites one other class to join us.

We discovered when we got to church that the dam had broken above the Toccoa Falls Bible Institute [in Georgia] and thirty or forty people had been killed. We called to arrange transportation, and Rosalynn went down to spend the afternoon with them.

Scoop Jackson came by Sunday afternoon for a couple of hours, pointing out that we need to work together in confrontation with Russell Long in the Senate. He said we could trust China, but the Soviets are quite different. Chinese were confident; the Soviets were insecure. The Soviets have shown good progress in increasing the number of Jews who leave to about two thousand a month.

Scoop said he might help us on Panama. On nuclear issues he takes the position that he and his staff are intelligent and well-informed; [that] I, the State Department, NSC, and my staff are ignorant and have no idea what's going on, and he's going to save us from our problems. Byrd had said that in general Scoop may not agree with me on things, but on specifics he was with me. As we ticked off each item, Scoop claims in general to be for me, but on specifics against me.

Rosalynn called from Georgia to tell me we were to eat supper with Bob Strauss at 6:00. Amy and I went over, and Rosalynn came by after she got back. Strauss is a very knowledgeable political animal, and so is his wife, Helen. I like him, although as I told him when I first met him as a governor, I was ill at ease with him and a little afraid of him and all the big wheeler-dealer Democrats.

We had the interview shows covered Sunday with Fritz, Mike Blumenthal, and Harold Brown on the major networks. We need to do more of this because the distortions through the Washington press corps are absolutely gross.

MONDAY, NOVEMBER 7   Andy Young attended the senior staff meeting this morning. His stature in the press has gone up substantially, and I was thinking of my Georgia staff and cabinet members who've been put through an ordeal by the press: Griffin Bell, Andy Young, Jody, Jack Watson, Hamilton,

Frank Moore (perhaps worst except for Bert Lance), even Bob Lipshutz concerning the identity of some of his old legal clients. The members of my cabinet who are not from Georgia have come through surprisingly unscathed, and I'm thankful for that. With the exception of Bert, we've all survived fairly well.

At our cabinet meeting we discussed about forty or fifty items, including the Soviet Union. (Zbig made an interesting comment that under Lenin the Soviet Union was like a religious revival; under Stalin like a prison; under Khrushchev like a circus; under Brezhnev like the U.S. Post Office Department.)

I met with the Council on Drug Abuse, and we're making some progress under Dr. Bourne's leadership. The heroin purity on the streets is the lowest in seven years, the price is up 25 percent, and this year the National Crime Index is down 7 percent. We're moving on legal drugs like barbiturates, Valium, and others, and trying to make some progress on the treatment of drug and alcohol abusers.

Fritz and I agreed to list our 1978 agenda by priority and schedule it carefully. It's unbelievable how many items will be on the program for next year.

I spent hours working on the energy speech—the final draft. What I generally do is to get recommendations from staff and speechwriters, take all those recommendations and write my first very rough and brief draft, then submit it back to them for additional comments. I put all those comments together in a final rough draft, let them make last-minute comments, and then it goes to final form. This is the best procedure I've been able to evolve on speechwriting. It's time-consuming, but at least the speech winds up being mine.

I have always preferred to do my own writing—whether working on speeches, editorials, or books—although I still solicit ideas and comments from others as described above. This is my twenty-sixth book, and all the words are mine.

NOVEMBER 8   Met this morning with [former Israeli prime minister] Golda Meir. Earlier Cy had called to say she was obnoxious last night at a supper for her. The vice president said the same thing. He finally had to get up and offer a toast just to restore some balance to the meeting. When she met with me she was very friendly and deferential, and I enjoyed the meeting. She doesn't think there is any Palestinian question, and she takes a much more hard line on almost everything than Begin. Perhaps it's because she's representing a party that's out of power, or maybe she's always been that way. She has a deep feeling of hatred, and after meeting with her I could understand the political pressure on Begin from the right wing of Israeli society.

In the afternoon I signed a resolution passed by the Congress approving the Alaska-Canadian natural gas pipeline. This is possibly the largest construction project I've undertaken. Still, it will provide only about 1 percent of our energy needs.

NOVEMBER 9   The congressional comments and the news coverage on the energy speech were good. My own feeling is that I ought to make a fireside chat about every two months, on subjects of most interest at that time.

The air cargo deregulation legislation is the first success we've had in this field. I hope to deregulate air passenger service, and also trucking and other transportation.

Some of my staff are concerned about the return of the crown to Hungary. This is not a particularly popular thing with some Hungarian Americans, but former prime minister [Imre] Nagy and the Church hierarchy think it's a good thing. I do too, and I intend to go ahead with it.

The Crown of Saint Stephen, a religious and political symbol since the twelfth century, is considered to represent the sovereign nation of Hungary. More than fifty kings of Hungary were invested with legitimacy by wearing the crown. With the threat of Soviet occupation at the end of World War II, patriots delivered the crown and other royal regalia to American troops for safekeeping, and these treasures were stored in Fort Knox, the repository of U.S. gold. The intense debate was whether they should be returned only after Hungary was free of occupation or returned by me as a symbol of Hungary's sovereignty and an inspiration to those who cherished freedom.

We spent a couple of hours working on national health insurance policy. This can be a very ineffective, expensive program, or it can be a major step forward. It's going to have to be slow in implementation and thoroughly discussed. We've got a calendar for the first of next year. Califano's going to Germany and England—he's already been to Canada—to learn as much as he can about their national health programs.

Comprehensive health coverage was one of our major goals. My commitment was to work intimately with leaders of the six committees in the House and Senate who would be involved in the decisions when our final proposal was formulated. Because of tight budget constraints, a phased implementation would be necessary, and our goal was to announce detailed plans in June 1979.

Talked to Secretary Brown about activities of Paul Nitze in trying to block a SALT agreement and the fact that he had access in a consultative role to all our secrets and used this to pursue his own anti-SALT positions. I don't know what can be done about it.

NOVEMBER 10   At my bimonthly news conference they were surprisingly interested in domestic affairs. Nothing on SALT, China, a few questions on the Mideast and the attacks by Israel on Lebanon, which I thought were gross and completely uncalled-for. I had to restrain myself from blasting Israel because of this brutality. They used thirty planes and bombed and shelled ten villages — killed about 120 people because some PLO had fired a few mortar rounds into a little village on the coast.

I met with Soviet foreign trade minister [Nikolai] Patolichev, who said Brezhnev wanted to meet with me soon, and that trade was easy compared to SALT, the Middle East, comprehensive test ban. I told him that in our country it was just the opposite because Congress had a substantial role in trade and I had the initiative in foreign affairs and defense, but that they all were interconnected in our minds. I thought progress would be general if we continued the trends of the past few weeks.

NOVEMBER 11   At our foreign affairs breakfast we talked about how the Soviets have been moving on Jewish emigration and about the Hungarian crown. Fritz is quite worried about it. I'm the strongest to go ahead and move, and Cy and Zbig nervously agree with me. The best thing is get it returned early and without timidity. I don't want it to be a rallying point for all the dissident groups in this country.

Mother called me from Ireland. She's really having a good time and would like to stay longer. She said if she could stay an extra month she could resolve the problem between the Catholics and Protestants.

I met with thirty-five or forty editors. Although they were from some of my most severely critical newspapers, almost all the questions were positive and constructive. There's something about the aura of the White House that holds down at least overt animosity toward the president. This is another project that I didn't want at first, but it's turned out to be very good — meeting with four or five hundred editors this year for about half an hour with each group.

NOVEMBER 12   I sent a personal letter to Sadat thanking him for being so helpful in the Mideast negotiations.

We went to the Navy–Georgia Tech game. Navy won by four points. I pardoned the midshipmen who had demerits. Apparently the Naval Academy's making some progress on improving their curriculum, even approaching the point where they can satisfy Rickover.

Read [John] le Carré book Saturday night and watched Jupiter. We saw three of its moons on Jeffrey's little telescope we gave him in high school. Jeffrey's really doing well in college, and I believe likes his work.

Our youngest son studied geography and the then relatively new subject of computer science and later combined them in a project with his professor that provided plans for expansion of major cities in Asia, including Manila and Seoul.

NOVEMBER 13   Somalia cut ties with Cuba and ordered Soviet advisors to leave the country. We are trying to mount a propaganda effort concerning the Cuban intrusion into Angola, Ethiopia, and Mozambique. We ought to have a propaganda capability in case we ever need it, but we certainly don't have it now. This Cuban effort will be a test case.

MONDAY, NOVEMBER 14   I'm in the midst of detailed budget sessions, and I'll spend about twenty-five hours on this with the OMB officials. Then OMB goes back to the departments, and I've set aside ten or twelve hours for appeal meetings. We're trying to hold on overall funding level — about $500 billion, with a projected deficit of about $25 billion.

By way of comparison, the proposed federal budget for 2011 is $3.8 trillion, almost eight times as great, with a projected deficit of $1.3 trillion, fifty times greater.

My insistence on tight budget restraints was a continuing irritant to Speaker Tip O'Neill and the more liberal Democrats, as were my increases in defense budgets during this post-Vietnam era.

I asked Dr. Press to get us a small telescope to use at the White House. Both Jeffrey and I are interested in astronomy.

Harold Brown reported on a meeting in which the Chinese were particularly critical of our changing from a two-and-a-half-war capability to a one-and-a-half-war capability, but when Harold pointed out that the other war plan was designed against China, their criticisms were attenuated.

Fritz and I talked about the Federal Reserve chairmanship. All of my advisors want me to get rid of Burns. I'm probably more conservative than any of them on fiscal affairs, and I need some powerful person along with me to be primarily concerned about inflation.

Bob Byrd gave me a very excited report on his trip to Panama. He was favorably impressed with Torrijos, and I believe all senators who went down there will ultimately vote for the treaty.

NOVEMBER 15   We've agreed to relay a message from Begin to Sadat inviting him to speak to the Knesset.

I came over early to prepare for the shah [of Iran] and his visit. There are a large number of demonstrators around the White House, and about half pro- and half antishah.

During the arrival ceremony the demonstrators had a serious clash. Ten or fifteen people were injured, including police officers. The police fired tear gas canisters, and just at the conclusion of my welcoming address the tear gas came across the South Lawn. It was *really* rough. I think I took it perhaps better than anyone else, because I didn't want to admit that it was hurting me so bad. Most of the press, the shah, the two wives, and all the visitors had to break out handkerchiefs to control the tears.

They presented us with a tapestry that's remarkable. About 160 tiny little knots per square centimeter—a portrait of George Washington with the presidential seal above it. Took them two years to do it. It's really a great gift to commemorate our bicentennial.

The shah expressed admiration for Sadat's courage and thought Israel was not adequately cooperative in the Mideast settlements. Israel had made some proposals to him, but he could not cooperate unless they showed more inclination toward peace. He said that the Baaths, the militants, still want to evolve an Arab empire and threaten him and Israel. This was centered in Iraq and Syria, and they were not cooperating [with each other], but if they did in the future, it might create a serious problem. These were the people that provided havens for terrorists, and the Soviet Union was providing them with arms.

At supper the shah and Empress Farah seemed to be at ease. He's concerned about the public image of Iran, very proud of what has been accomplished, and, in my opinion, has done an excellent job. Now, though, he's strong enough to do some overt things on the human rights issue.

This is what I wrote at the time. Later entries will reveal the shah's serious mistakes and fallibilities.

We had Dizzy Gillespie and Sarah Vaughan give an excellent jazz concert. Earl "Fatha" Hines went up to play two pieces and almost stole the show. Brought back old times when I was an avid jazz fan.

This big event was held on the South Lawn. I went on the stage with Dizzy Gillespie and joined him in a rendition of "Salt Peanuts." It was a high point in my life when The New York Times *complimented my singing!*

NOVEMBER 16   The general reaction to Sadat's going to Israel is excitement and anticipation. Sadat is a tough and courageous man, and I think the rest of the Arab leaders are afraid to tackle him, particularly if we stand with him. This might be the opening we've been waiting for just to break the ice, and it's the first Arab recognition that Israel is a nation or has any authenticity in its existence. Officially Israel and Egypt are still at war. We've encouraged this meeting and are trying not to let it drive Syria away from an overall conference to settle the Middle Eastern question.

I had my follow-up meeting with the shah. We discussed the sale of nuclear reactors to Iran. He's already bought two and ordered four more from the Germans and two from France, and is going through Paris tomorrow to consider additional purchases from them.

This was the beginning of Iran's nuclear power program, which has now become of worldwide interest and concern. As a signatory of the Nonproliferation Treaty, Iran has a right to have atomic power and also to reprocess uranium to be used as fuel. The problem is that now Iran appears to be planning to use its highly enriched uranium to build nuclear weapons.

I took him in my private office and talked to him about the human rights issue. He was quite embarrassed but shared my concern. The crux of the matter is that they have a law in Iran, which he's not willing to repeal, that makes it illegal to be a Communist, and if someone is accused of being a Communist they are tried in a military court, sentenced, and put in prison. He thought it quite a liberal move just to admit civilian attorneys for defendants.

In this and subsequent discussions, the shah expressed concern that the United States and other Western nations were too lenient toward demonstrators, all of whom he branded as "Communists." Unfortunately, his secret police, SAVAK, had recently fired into a crowd of demonstrators, killing a large number. It seems, in retrospect, that this was the beginning of his downfall.

Jeffrey and I got a seven-inch telescope from one of the astronomers, and we're going to have a briefing on black holes, stars, and planets before long.

NOVEMBER 17   The big international question is Sadat's visit to Israel. We're putting as much pressure as we can on our European allies, Arab leaders, and also on Begin to make Sadat's visit successful, and trying to prevent their condemnation of him before he gets there. So far, with the exception of nuts like Libya and Iraq, they have been fairly moderate in their criticism.

Harold Brown and I discussed the latest SALT positions with Cy Vance and Paul Warnke. We're making good progress with the Soviets. They've yielded on some major points, and we have been quite inflexible up till now. I think they see that our positions are to their advantage; it's not a matter of our browbeating them into compliance.

During this meeting Begin called, extremely excited about Sadat's visit; complimentary of me. I pointed out the necessity for him to help Sadat, particularly with the other Arab leaders, by not letting it be an Israeli-Egyptian negotiation involving the Sinai.

We had a delightful reception for the American Film Institute at the White House for the producers, directors, actors, and composers who made the film industry great. I really enjoyed meeting Lillian Gish, Olivia de Havilland, Henry Mancini, Henry Fonda, and many others. Afterward we went to the Kennedy Center, where they recognized the fifty outstanding films of the last seventy-five years, and the best of all was *Gone With the Wind*.

Afterward we went up on the balcony with Jeffrey and looked at some of the galaxies, Jupiter with its full moons, and we saw a number of flights of ducks and geese going over the White House, illuminated by the Washington lights. This was one of our most pleasant evenings.

I later wrote a poem about this experience, included in Always a Reckoning, *a collection of my poetry.*

NOVEMBER 18   There's increasing pressure on Sadat from the Arab countries not to go to Israel, but there's no doubt that he's going. I called to give him my encouragement, my admiration. He was overly effusive in his thanks to me. Although there are some very serious dangers in a disruption of the Mideast peace negotiations and even danger to Sadat's life, certainly his administration, he's sure of himself, very much at ease, and I have confidence in him.

Admiral Rickover came over to talk to me about participating December second in the Shippingport [Light Water] Breeder Reactor going on-line to produce electricity—the anniversary of the first atomic reactor at Stagg Stadium in Chicago. He only stays about fifteen minutes, really husbands my time, and gives me a lot to think about.

This power plant would operate for twenty-five years before being decommissioned, always producing more nuclear fuel than it consumed.

Ambassador Dobrynin came by, and I told him we need an early reply from the Soviets concerning the Middle East conference; Sadat's visit to Israel was on his own initiative, we support the visit, and hope that the Soviets will join us in minimizing criticism of Sadat. I want to cooperate with the Soviets, but if they take a negative attitude we will have to pursue a Middle East settlement unilaterally.

The letter from Brezhnev was positive, and he encouraged me to make our exchanges more frequent. He wants to ban nuclear weapons tests of all kinds, to pursue a simultaneous halt in the production of all nuclear weapons by all states, and to reduce the stockpile of weapons. In the past there have always been some hookers in the Soviets' proposal; they sound good on the surface, but you never get to the specifics. Lately, though, they've shown some more forthcoming attitudes.

Then I went over to meet with about twelve hundred of our friends, both Democrats and Republicans, who have formed a national Panama Canal citizens group. They've come in from all over the country at their expense to help us sell the Panama Canal treaties.

NOVEMBER 19 Jim Schlesinger came to talk about a wide range of subjects. I enjoy doing this every few weeks. We discussed bird-watching, SALT, energy, and the need to expand the Outer Continental Shelf exploration without hurting the environment.

Schlesinger, who had served as secretary of defense under Presidents Nixon and Ford, had wanted to be my secretary of state or defense. He graciously accepted my decision not to appoint him, but we also agreed, with all good humor, that he and I would meet at his request on occasional Saturday mornings to discuss an unlimited range of subjects. I enjoyed these private sessions, and later, as secretary of energy, he became one of my favorite cabinet officers.

Henry Kissinger was disturbed about some of the things Dr. Brzezinski said to the Trilateral Commission in Bonn, and Zbig and Henry will have lunch and try to understand each other better.

I watched Sadat's arrival in Israel—a very moving ceremony, particularly when he met Golda Meir. Her joy was obvious to me.

Rosalynn returned from the women's conference very pleased with it, pleasantly surprised at the enthusiasm and fairly good harmony among the women.

NOVEMBER 20 Reverend [Charles] Trentham arranged a special prayer service for 8:15 in the morning, for Middle East peace, so that we could come home and watch the speeches by Sadat and Begin. Sadat's speech was very good. It was complete; spelled out very firmly the fact that they accepted Israel as a part of the Middle East community in peace, permanently. But also laying out the necessity for Israel to withdraw from occupied territory and resolve the Palestinian issue. I was disappointed with Begin's speech, which was primarily a rehash of what he had always said. [Labor Party leader Shimon] Peres went as far as he could in meeting

Sadat without separating himself too much from Begin. My concern and prediction is that both Begin and Sadat have an inclination to negotiate privately and to the exclusion of Syria, and we've been trying to get them, publicly at least, to disavow this inclination.

In the afternoon we went over to St. Patrick's [Episcopal] Church to hear Amy's violin class give a recital. I had dreaded it all week, but it was really a delightful afternoon. These children use the Suzuki method of violin instruction, where they start very young and work with their mothers as though they were learning a language, and the quality of the performance was startling and very pleasant.

MONDAY, NOVEMBER 21   The general reaction on the Mideast visit was that nothing much was accomplished. I'm afraid that our fears concerning their inclinations to deal bilaterally might be confirmed. It's going to be hard to hold Syria, and some Syrian leaders have even called for Sadat's assassination.

Mrs. Annie Duitscher from Baltimore came by. In 1882, when she was eleven years old, she saw President [William] McKinley going up the street and moved forward to shake hands with him. Her father said, "We're just common folks. You can't shake hands with the president." And now she's 106 years old and came by to shake hands with me. She's very lively and witty, and I enjoyed meeting with her.

Fritz and I discussed the problem we have with Israeli ambassador [Simcha] Dinitz wanting to deal directly with him, Eizenstat, Lipshutz, and Hamilton and bypass Zbig and Cy. Fritz will meet with Zbig and Cy to work out ground rules for the future.

Some of our supporters for canceling unnecessary water projects came to meet with me, Eizenstat, and OMB people. They just wanted to plan mutual strategy on a water policy acceptable to them and to me. These are [advocates for] forestry, fishing, wild rivers, environmentalists, Friends of the Earth, Audubon Society, Izaak Walton League, Rachel Carson Club, Sierra Club, and so forth. Good people and natural friends.

Prime Minister Begin called, still excited about the trip. He reported good results that he couldn't tell me about on the open phone, but said he was sure there would be no more war between Israel and Egypt. He was overly effusive in his thanks to me for making the Sadat visit possible. He said Sadat had little interest in procedural matters relating to Geneva.

NOVEMBER 22   French ambassador [André] de Laboulaye stated that the prime minister of France was going to Syria this week and would try to induce Assad to cooperate in the Mideast settlement. The French have been very cautious and have not helped us when it took any courage and have made sure they didn't do anything to aggravate the Arabs.

NOVEMBER 23–27   There's general confusion in the Middle East about specifically what we should do next; the same confusion exists in the White House.

I sent a handwritten letter in Spanish to General Torrijos, following up the senators' visit there to assess the Panama Canal treaties and also to express my hope that in free elections the Panamanian people might have a chance to vote for him for president in the future.

Rosalynn and I went to Stevens School to have Thanksgiving lunch. Amy and the other students prepared it. It was my first visit to Stevens. Apparently doing a good job, and Amy fits right in with the other students without any embarrassment or special status.

Although Sadat's visit has been good, I don't think he can go very far toward resolving the basic problems. I hope he can, of course. They have a new independence from us which I think is good.

Senator Byrd sent me word that we ought to move now on Panama.

MONDAY, NOVEMBER 28   In the afternoon, Harold Brown, General [George] Brown, Fritz, Zbig, and I went through the SIOP [Single Integrated Operational Plan] procedures, walking through several drills. This is the first time any president has done this, which is unbelievable. We've tried to simplify the process greatly since I've been in office.

I was culpable also, in that it had taken me eleven months to schedule this detailed drill procedure—which rehearsed our response to the use of nuclear weapons—and be sure that all participants attended. I consoled myself with the knowledge that I had insisted that, for the first time, the vice president be briefed along with me even before Inauguration Day about action to be taken in case of a nuclear attack.

NOVEMBER 29   Senator Long and the House conference leaders would be meeting at 9:00, so I called and informed Russell that we all looked on him as a key person in the energy negotiations, but that he had not exerted any leadership. They had not made much progress, primarily because of his unwillingness to participate actively. I pointed out that there were some things he wanted that I could not accept. He, of course, denied that he had any influence, but said he would try to bring the bill in by the fifteenth of December.

I had a long talk with Jody about our poor relations with the press — particularly concerned about the NBC program last night when they treated us with disdain and betrayal, since we had done them a favor and they came in to do an obvious gut job on me and the staff. He suggested that Fritz and Frank and others look at the program and then we would try to see what if anything we could do.

This strained relationship with the news media developed into one of our most serious and persistent problems. Thanks primarily to Jerry Rafshoon, our entire White House team attempted to improve relations, with frequent press conferences, an unprecedented degree of openness and access, and a continuing series of private suppers and long discussions with key reporters, columnists, and executives. These efforts helped, but minimally.

I got a report that Torrijos was getting quite nervous in Panama — that he'd do anything we wanted, but the whole nation was suffering because of delay in our ratification of the treaty.

NOVEMBER 30 Messages from both Assad and Sadat through our ambassadors indicated they consider it crucial to continue to work with and through the United States in resolving the Mideast question. This is the first substantive message we've had from Assad since the Sadat visit to Jerusalem.

I told Mike Blumenthal that oil companies should pay taxes on their overseas profits. In other words, payments made to foreign governments should be treated as royalties and not tax payments. This involves multibillion-dollar figures.

In April 1979 I asked Congress to "close foreign tax credit loopholes that now give unnecessary benefits to the major oil companies." This did not pass the Congress, even when the windfall profits tax was adopted in 1980. At

that time, I imposed an oil import tax by executive order, but, as with Presi-
dent Ford, this was overridden by Congress.

Had lunch with Secretary Brown, the Joint Chiefs of Staff, and Brzezinski. I wanted to know if they feel adequately involved in the decisions
being made about defense and to a secondary degree about politics. They
wanted Brzezinski to come and give them and the CINCS (the command-
ers in chief) a strategic briefing on the worldwide situation and then [re-
peat this] monthly. It's important for me to have them on my side on
difficult political matters and also helpful to have a military input into
some of the questions that we have to decide concerning Okinawa, Panama, Cyprus, sales of military weapons, NATO, plus of course the obvious
matters of SALT and comprehensive test ban. It was a very good and constructive meeting.

DECEMBER 1   At Senator [John] McClellan's funeral Frank talked to
Baker about him and [John] Sparkman getting the Panama Canal treaties
out of the Foreign Relations Committee without delay. The calls coming
into the White House have shifted almost unbelievably toward a favorable
ratio on the canal treaties.

DECEMBER 2   Cy, Fritz, and Zbig, and I discussed the arms sale list for
1978 fiscal year—a substantial reduction below '77, but it would include
perhaps a comprehensive package with F-5s to Egypt, F-15s to the Saudis,
and F-16s to the Israelis.
   We heard that David Owen, who goes up and down like a yo-yo, is
back with us on Rhodesia and is committed, again, to holding firm.
   I decided to return the crown to Hungary about the seventh of January,
provided they meet requirements concerning public display, involvement
of the Church in its return, et cetera.
   I met with Admiral Rickover and Jim Schlesinger to bring the Shippingport Light Water Breeder Reactor up to 100 percent power in a little
ceremony. This is the thirty-fifth anniversary of the Stagg Field sustained
nuclear reaction and the twentieth anniversary of the first stationary power
plant, also at Shippingport.
   We went to a tremendous fund-raising banquet for Senator Humphrey
to establish an institute of government in Minnesota. I spoke about ten

minutes, primarily using the experiences we had had with him since his impact on Georgia with his civil rights speech in '48; his coming to campaign in 1964, and Rosalynn, Mother, and [my sister] Gloria being with Muriel when she wouldn't go to a nonintegrated reception; his coming back as vice president to give a report on Europe; Amy getting brownie crumbs on his face when I was governor; how so many people wanted him to be elected in '68, but his closest friends didn't support him adequately; and what he had meant to me in office. It was a fine affair and raised several million dollars. Helen Reddy, Frank Sinatra, and Alan King entertained the group.

DECEMBER 3 Jim Schlesinger reported progress on the energy package. They've been in a virtual stalemate since September on Social Security, natural gas, crude oil, conservation measures, and rate reform.

Rosalynn and I went out and played tennis. I've not seen daylight all week.

DECEMBER 4 After Sunday school, I spent most of the day and night working on paperwork, which piles in every Friday. Rosalynn and I did bowl four or five games.

MONDAY, DECEMBER 5 I had a three-hour budget review on foreign aid, State Department, intelligence. We didn't get through, and I told Tim [Kraft] and Hamilton there was no way I could stay up with all the paperwork they pile on me.

My biggest problem with foreign aid was inducing a reluctant Congress to approve my requests. I had several sessions with a large number of key members, attempting to convince them that the aid I proposed was a sound investment for the United States. In particular, I was convinced that we should do as much as possible to help increase agricultural production in poor countries. Unfortunately, during the next twenty-five years, Western aid dedicated to this purpose was reduced by 50 percent. My commitment to this issue remains: beginning in 1986, The Carter Center helped sponsor a program in fourteen African nations to teach more than 8 million small family farmers to double or triple their production of basic food grains.

Paul Austin called, asked that I not eliminate deferral of foreign income tax payments, and said Kirbo would be contacting me about it. I don't appreciate that kind of call.

As the CEO of Coca-Cola and a fellow Georgian, Austin had direct access to me. This request displeased me because it was a less-than-subtle effort to derive financial benefit for his company from this personal relationship.

DECEMBER 6   With Califano I went over elementary- and secondary education proposals for 1978. Our educational system is discouraging. We ought to go into a rigid testing program, emphasize reading capability at the fourth-grade level and mathematics at a higher level, broaden representation of the poor in the educational process, equalize state funding, include parents in the teaching process, restore school buildings to the center of community activity, et cetera.

Among the goals I named in this conversation with Joe Califano were several that we had addressed successfully in Georgia. I felt that a key to our reform efforts would be the establishment of an independent Department of Education with a cabinet-level secretary, which we accomplished in 1979.

We went over the HEW budget requests. This is really a discouraging experience to see so much waste and so many programs passed by the Congress with practically no controls on them—a tremendous amount of overlap, duplication. Califano does very well. He's got a worse job than I have, and I sympathize with him. Each congressional subcommittee has its own pet projects, and they prevail because of legislative courtesy.

I talked to Cy about his trip to the Middle East. We're both concerned that Sadat, who was really on top of the world for a while in public esteem and appreciation, has now lost a lot of that by his irrational, unpredictable actions and statements. In Cairo, we want as much responsibility as possible to be on Begin and Sadat.

DECEMBER 7 (PEARL HARBOR DAY)   We've been lucky so far this year in not having any serious military threats, although there are enough trouble spots around the world.

Sadat sent me a message wanting me to urge Begin to make a public statement on withdrawal from occupied territories and working toward a solution to the Palestine problem. We'll pursue this, either directly to Begin or through Vance's personal visit later this week.

DECEMBER 8   I spent about eight hours getting ready for the Defense [Department] budget review meeting, which lasted about three and a half hours. This was probably the best I've been prepared, and when Harold appeals any of my decisions I'll be familiar enough to discuss it with him intelligently.

DECEMBER 9   Spent a couple of hours on a budget for the Energy Department—on a broad range of subjects, including the development of nuclear weapons. The department's just been formed and still in a state of flux, and we don't yet know what the Congress will do with my national energy proposal.

Mark Chona came over representing Zambian president Kaunda to warn me to be very cautious over the Christmas holidays.

This was one of a series of visions that came from Zambia about my future well-being.

DECEMBER 10–11   Dr. [Dabney] Jarman, Senator Humphrey's personal physician, went to Camp David with us, and we had an opportunity to talk at length, just the three of us. Hubert seemed to be in good spirits. Although he's getting weaker by the day, he looks better than he did a year ago when he came to Plains. We discussed his relationship with Johnson at some length, particularly while he was vice president. In general, he speaks well of President Johnson, and blames the disharmonies and his exclusion primarily on the pressures of the war in Vietnam. He felt he was treated at least as well as Johnson was by Kennedy and had as strong a role to play in government as other vice presidents.

He knows it was nothing like the responsibility I've given to Fritz and the closeness with which Fritz and I have worked. He really tries to speak well of everyone, except [former senator] Gene McCarthy, and he tries there but fails. He looks on McCarthy as a cynic, completely without integrity or moral commitment, and extremely superficial and disloyal. Humphrey suffered a great deal during the Vietnam War because of the animosity of the people toward him and Johnson. He can't comprehend why the blacks didn't support him in 1972 against [George] McGovern, who had had no role to play in the civil rights movement. He feels, as I do, that he should have been elected president in 1968 or 1972, but shows very little bitterness about it now.

He's begun to appreciate the small things: how birds feed and the colors of leaves, the sound of music, his newfound relationship with his daughter whom he hadn't seen very much the last twenty or so years. He gave me a great deal of advice on different members of the Senate. He admonished me about being overly concerned with daily aberrant criticisms; just to commit ourselves to a policy, make sure that it is well-advised, and then stick with it and try to ignore the harpings of the press.

He was quite relaxed and seemed not to have any pain except in his right leg where one of the glands was being pressed by his cancer. We went to church Sunday, and all in all it was one of the most enjoyable and interesting weekends I've ever spent.

Late Saturday night, Zbig called with a proposal that Begin has made concerning the Palestinian question. He wants to present his ideas to the cabinet, come here to see me, and then review where we have come and what we ought to do to correct political mistakes and lay a firmer base for the '78–'80 elections.

My first year as president had proved to be a valuable learning process, and by this point our domestic and international agenda for my term in office had evolved considerably. Moreover, I now knew the key Democrats and Republicans in the Congress personally, and we were working intimately with committee chairmen and their staffs on our major legislative proposals. My opinion poll ratings were holding up well, despite the confusion created by too many agenda items and too few final successes. We had involved the public in issues including energy, human rights, Middle East peace, Panama, and nuclear arms control; we were working with Congress on health care; and we were secretly moving toward normalizing diplomatic relations with China. Our greatest disappointment was Congress's failure to finish legislation for a comprehensive energy policy; we were also quite concerned about inaccurate and unfair coverage by the news media.

MONDAY, DECEMBER 12   We had a private meeting with just cabinet members and went over the 1978 agenda, which was received well. They were almost unanimous in their praise of the White House staff, having seen that I meant business in prohibiting my staff from giving orders to cabinet members. I told them we would work out how they could use Camp David, sometimes when I'm there, most of the time when I'm not there.

Senator Kaneaster Hodges and his family came in, and I had a delightful visit with them. He's going to make a good [Arkansas] senator but can only serve twelve and a half months. [Arkansas limits an appointed senator to the unexpired term.]

I called George Meany to congratulate him on reelection as president [of the AFL-CIO]. Sometimes he has to posture for the benefit of the public and his members, but although he's very conservative in his attitudes on some questions and too liberal on others, his advice has always been sound to me, and I respect him.

DECEMBER 13 I spent most of the day working on the executive order to establish the new intelligence administration. My primary inclination is to give the director more authority than the proposals submitted to me would give to Stan Turner.

We decided to announce the return of the Hungarian crown later this week.

DECEMBER 14 Had a breakfast with the Joint Chiefs of Staff and secretary of defense on the military budget, one of the most productive meetings I've had. The Joint Chiefs were at their best, talking about strategic and tactical needs without posturing or exaggeration.

Cy's report from Syria showed that Assad was quite negative, and [Foreign Minister] Khaddam was worse, but they both are willing to leave the door open.

I talked to Ham in some depth about the politics of 1978, domestic and foreign issues. He feels very strongly that he or someone like him should be involved in discussion of foreign questions when they impact on domestic attitudes. We also considered who might be the Democratic national chairman.

Had another typical meeting with a group of black leaders: NAACP, SCLC, [National] Urban League, et cetera. They were fairly friendly, acknowledged that we had done something, and demanded a great deal more. That's their profession, and I still feel at ease with them.

I met with about seventy-five women who serve in my administration, who gave me an outline of the International Women's Year Conference. They were friendly, and I enjoyed the meeting.

I went to meet the members of the Business Council, fifty-five of the most influential business leaders of the nation. I spoke to them for about twenty minutes and answered questions for another ten minutes or so. It was unstructured and kind of rambling, but Bob Strauss and Juanita Kreps, who called me later, were euphoric about the reaction among the business leaders. Maybe it was better than I thought—or maybe they just didn't expect much.

DECEMBER 15   I had breakfast with Scoop Jackson and Sam Nunn to talk about several things, primarily SALT. Scoop is adamant on this as on almost everything else. He thinks he has known from the beginning what would occur in the future. He has definite ideas on what must be done to satisfy the Congress, without any regard to what the Soviets will accept. Sam is more flexible but tends to follow the leadership of Senator Jackson, at least so far. They finally agreed to send me a memorandum outlining their specific concerns. Sam was not familiar with the history of SALT negotiation; didn't realize adequately that we had inherited an inequity and were trying to correct it. Later I told Brzezinski to give Sam a briefing from 1972 to date.

The news conference's major topic was the Mideast. I predicted that Social Security legislation would pass today, which it did, and expressed expectation that energy legislation would pass early next year.

I met with the Arab American leaders, who have given all my advisors a hard time. They talked about the PLO recognition question, definition of homeland, what we could do about Lebanon, deprivation of Arab refugees, and human rights. I was fair and staunch with them, gave the same responses as to the Middle East heads of state.

I had budget appeals this afternoon from HEW, a very difficult session. It's always hard to know where to draw the line at different levels of aid to poor people, when the additional costs are enormous but the need is evident.

We had several calls during the budget session concerning the prospective defeat of Social Security in the House, but everybody went to work, the tide turned, and we won. Immediately afterward the Speaker, John

Rhodes, Byrd, and Baker called and asked for permission to adjourn sine die. I congratulated them on the year's good work and approved.

Cy returned from the Middle East and reported that Sadat would have serious problems unless Israel was forthcoming with a viable peace proposal, that there was surprising support throughout the Middle East for Sadat's initiative, that he was quite vulnerable if he failed, and even Assad was much less critical than had been indicated through his public statements and made no personal criticism of Sadat. The Saudis are supportive, short of a public endorsement. We discussed how to handle Begin tomorrow morning if his proposal is superficial.

DECEMBER 16   Begin came over and presented a proposal for the Sinai region, giving up Sharm al-Sheikh and the route from there to Eilat, withdrawal of Israeli troops, and demilitarization east of the passes by Sadat, which I think is acceptable to us and the Egyptians.

His proposal on the West Bank is not acceptable, although it's a step in the right direction. He's willing to recognize the sovereignty of Israel only within the territories occupied before the 1967 war, leave sovereignty of the West Bank area in doubt, give the residents of this region an administrative council to be freely elected in a democratic process, turn over authority for all domestic affairs, including immigration, from the military government to the administrative council, and reserve the right of Israel for security in this region. He's not willing to commit to withdraw from occupied territories.

We are going to analyze his proposition, trying to resolve some legal differences. One is that we would like for the UN or both Israel and Jordan to turn over authority to the administrative council (not just Israel or its military government) to make sure the yielding of authority is permanent, not tentative, and to make sure this is considered to be an interim proposal.

Begin stated that he wanted peace with all his neighbors, and there would be no separate peace with Egypt.

I expressed my concern that his proposal was inadequate, which might cause the downfall of Sadat. I urged him not to make any public statement about it until after Sadat had a chance to assess it. He promised to do this. I then called Sadat and gave him a brief outline of what had occurred.

I had a two-hour budget appeals meeting concerning Defense, where the overall figure is politically important and individual items are of lesser significance. I decided that $126 billion would be adequate.

DECEMBER 17   I met with Begin, who has come a long way. What apparently made the most impression was my private comment to Begin that his idol Jabotinsky had been a pattern for Sadat's action — bold, reaching to the final conclusion without the incremental negotiations. That seemed to prey on his mind, because I'm sure he would like to be identified in world opinion as following Jabotinsky's philosophies. [Ze'ev Jabotinsky was a founder of the underground Zionist organization, Irgun, of which Begin became leader.]

Begin called for home rule in the West Bank territories. I suggested he use the phrase "military government would be ended," and he even agreed to the word "abolished." He had very little to offer in Jerusalem. I think the minimum is a Vatican-like autonomous area to encompass the holy places, extending as far as possible into eastern Jerusalem. Another question that has to be resolved is the criteria for entry to the West Bank/Gaza Strip area by Arab refugees.

We agreed that the expropriation of land should be a right guaranteed to the elected administrative council. He said that whatever rights the Israelis had to settle in this territory, the Palestinian Arabs would have the same rights to settle in Israel. He also disavowed any special status for the Israeli settlements. All in all, he's much more flexible than we had feared. After our regular meeting, he wanted to talk to me privately for a few minutes. He has a plan that Israel, Saudi Arabia, Ethiopia, Egypt, and Morocco could form a base for common strength in the Middle East.

This flexibility and political courage by Begin was very impressive to me and was a major reason why I came to believe that I could have a fruitful meeting involving just Begin, Sadat, and me.

DECEMBER 18   After supper with Fritz and Joan, Dr. Carl Sagan gave us a presentation on outer space with emphasis on whether or not there would be life on a distant planet.

The reaction to Begin's proposal has been fairly good in the press. This puts Sadat somewhat on the defensive, which I'm sure was Begin's plan. We'll have to be cautious about any endorsement, although the Israelis have characterized our reserved reaction as approval.

MONDAY, DECEMBER 19   I talked to Jody about recent attacks on Hamilton. He and Stu had been the only ones left from my Georgia delegation who haven't been seriously roughed up by the news media. Looks like Hamilton's time has come.

DECEMBER 20   I asked Zbig for briefing books for the trip so I can study during Christmas holidays. The Soviet Union has come back fairly strongly on our role in the Middle East. We approved a final version of a letter to Brezhnev.

I signed the Social Security Act, which I hope and expect will put the system on a sound basis for the next forty years. It's a substantial tax increase for those who are above twenty-thousand-dollar income levels.

The soundness of the Social Security system is as crucial now as it was when I was president, and any necessary action, no matter how unpopular, must be taken to preserve it. This includes tax increases like this one, raising the age limit for benefits, or reducing payments to wealthier retirees.

Jerry Ford came by and thought we ought to move much more strongly on Panama, that the national tone was shifting toward it. Expressed some concern about SALT, having got a briefing yesterday from Paul Nitze. He'll be meeting tomorrow with Paul Warnke, Zbig, and David [Aaron]. My sense is that the Republican hierarchy has decided to go along with us on Panama and fight us on SALT. We'll take them one at a time. Privately with me he [Ford] said he thought our tax level was okay, but later publicly called for much higher reductions in taxes.

We had a reception for about twelve hundred members of the White House press with their wives, and Rosalynn and I shook hands with all of them. We had a dance with Billy Eckstine and the Marine Band, and I danced with about one hundred of the wives, a brief time each. They just lined up to break in on me, and I really enjoyed it.

DECEMBER 21   There won't be any energy conference agreement this year. I made final decisions on the budget and we left, on the way home.

DECEMBER 22–25   We unpacked in the middle of the floor, since there was no closet space available. I put on my dungarees, walked in the fields for a couple of hours, then down the street in Plains, casually visiting friends.

I went quail hunting twice with Frank Chappell [a farmer who had been keeping my bird dogs]. We found five or six coveys—we didn't shoot well and got seven quail. I really enjoyed being in the open fields, looking at my woods, watching bird dogs, getting into fresh air, and also being with Frank. The Secret Service rode on the back of the Jeep, along with Dr. Lukash, but they don't intrude into our privacy.

I met early Saturday morning with farm strike leaders from Georgia, Florida, and Alabama. They were quite nervous about meeting with the president and read a brief statement. I was sympathetic and then told the press that prices for fertilizer and fuel had gone up 200, 300, 400 percent, and the price of farm products hadn't gone up much, if any. I thought inevitably in the future the farmers would have a better income. I sympathized with them, but I didn't make any promises. The farmers seemed to be satisfied.

Afterward, Rosalynn and I went over to R. D. [Laster's] farm to walk in the fields and found nine beautiful arrowheads. She found six of them.

Christmas morning we went to Mother's house at 6:30, from there to Miss Allie's [Allie Smith was Rosalynn's mother], then to church and Sunday school, and back to Miss Allie's for lunch. I called Sadat and Begin, the Speaker, the majority leader, Martin Luther King, George Meany, Hubert Humphrey, and others.

During the afternoon I worked on the trip notebooks and the executive order reorganizing the intelligence community.

We had a good Christmas but didn't get any rest, with everyone in the same house. I never saw the floor from the time we got there till we left because of the piled-up clothes and presents.

MONDAY, DECEMBER 26   Monday morning Prime Minister Begin called, and although I think the meeting in Ismailia was something of a disappointment, he was quite pleased. He said he and Sadat were closer together than indicated.

When we got back to Washington it was a great relief to walk into a spacious mansion practically alone.

DECEMBER 27   My choices for Federal Reserve Board chairman boiled down to William Miller with Textron and Bruce MacLaury, head of Brookings. I met with both of them and called several people—Bert Lance, Irving Shapiro, Reginald Jones, Clark Clifford—to get their advice. There was unanimous and overwhelming support for William Miller. Bill had not been eager to get the job, had tried to give me all the reasons why he shouldn't be chairman, but said he would honor my request. I also called Dr. Burns and asked if he could talk to me tomorrow afternoon so I might tell him about my decision.

I met with John White and asked him if he would be chairman of the Democratic National Committee. He said he would.

DECEMBER 28   Zbig said Sadat was hopeful that I could stop briefly in Aswan on the way from Saudi Arabia to France. He feels isolated, there's some threat that the Saudis might cut off his economic aid, and he needs some public support from me. We will consider it.

I went over the inventory of nuclear warheads, which is a sobering experience.

I met with Jim McIntyre to consider final details of the 1979 budget. He and his staff are unanimous in believing we should not insist that we can balance the budget by 1981, but that we can begin to cut down on the deficit substantially after this year. We now project, if our goals are reached, about a $15 billion surplus in 1981 — but this is tenuous at best. The trade-off is between giving tax reductions and keeping the money to balance the budget. This past year we gave a $6 billion tax reduction, in 1978 we'll give about $25 billion, and in 1979–80 probably another one.

Chairman Burns flew up from Florida. I really dreaded this encounter, but it was enjoyable and constructive. I told him in my first sentence that I had decided not to reappoint him for chairman; expressed my admiration for him; I would be glad if he stayed on as a member of the board; and if he had some alternative I'd like to have a chance to meet his desires. He responded well. I told him that my choice was a man whom he may not even know, named William Miller. He immediately responded, "Mr. President, that is a wise and worthy choice. I know him well. I have worked with him as a member of my board in Boston. I know his interest in international trade, his executive leadership is unsurpassed, and I am very pleased at your choice." I was quite relieved. I think Chairman Burns left here feeling good.

Dr. Burns was gracious enough to introduce Bill Miller at the Federal Reserve building to his top staff and also to come over here for the press announcement, where he made some very favorable comments. It was a gracious thing for him to do, and should provide maximum approval and continuity as the announcement is assimilated in the stock market and overseas.

On the morning of December 29, we departed for Poland, the first stop on a multinational journey. This was a long, difficult, and somewhat frantic trip, with changes in the itinerary being made en route. The accompanying news reporters sometimes did not have time to file their stories or to be adequately briefed about what occurred at each stop. Some of the following entries were dictated after each visit.

DECEMBER 29–30   We've just left Poland. We got along well with First Secretary [Edward] Gierek and the Polish officials. We discussed the importance of arms sale restraints and mutual and balanced force reductions. The Poles had suffered four successive crop failures and have a severe shortage of feed and food grains and also meat. We're trying to help them.

Rosalynn and Zbig went to visit Cardinal [Stefan] Wyszinski. He referred to Gierek as a true Pole and a righteous man. When I described this conversation to Gierek, he was quite pleased and informed me that he had recently visited Wyszinski. I suggested to him, somewhat seriously, that he should visit him more often and become a Christian believer like the cardinal and myself. Although Gierek was taken aback, I think he was impressed. He replied that as a Communist he also learned how to serve his fellow human beings. I told him that it was never too late to become a believer.

When I made one remark that the Poles were highly nationalistic, he very quickly corrected me and said that was not a proper word to use, that "patriotic" would be a better word. He says that Brezhnev is a gentleman and a compassionate man, and genuinely wants a SALT agreement. I told him he didn't want it any more than I. I think he was convinced, and told me as I left that he would immediately call Brezhnev and encourage him to make a renewed effort to cooperate with us in reaching this agreement on strategic bombs.

In my arrival ceremony statement, we discovered later that we had an interpreter who used outmoded Polish words and phrases, and something of a Russian syntax. We changed the interpreter after that.

The entire visit was delightful, and I came away with a renewed understanding of the horrible suffering of both the Soviets and the Poles in the war. They have a remarkable degree of religious freedom, and about 90 percent of the Poles profess to be Catholics.

DECEMBER 31 We left Poland in a heavy snow and enjoyed the flight to Tehran, flying over some very interesting terrain. Although it was a clear day, we never were sure whether or not we saw Mount Ararat to the north.

We had a cordial welcome in Tehran from the shah and Empress Farah, a delightful banquet, and adequate time to discuss the Middle East and nuclear power affairs with the shah. I met with King Hussein for a while and then just at the stroke of midnight went back in and joined the party of the Iranians and the Americans—a few of the top newspeople. So we offered toasts, drank champagne, exchanged kisses, and danced for a while. Went home about 1:00.

During the routine exchange of official banquet toasts, I made this comment: "Iran, because of the great leadership of the shah, is an island of stability in one of the more troubled areas of the world." Understandably, this was derided when the shah was overthrown thirteen months later.

1978

JANUARY 1   Early the next morning I met with King Hussein of Jordan and then drove to the airport with the shah. All three of us agreed that we ought to give Sadat our support, and on the basis for a Middle East peace. Both the shah and King Hussein said that they want to go after I do to Saudi Arabia and Egypt to try to get support for Sadat.

On the trip from Tehran to India, which was about four hours, I spent most of my time preparing the five or six speeches I'll have to make in India.

At the enormous square in New Delhi (Ramlila Grounds) they had hundreds of thousands of Indians assembled, and I made a speech about democracy and its relationship with human rights.

We had quite an argument with the staff concerning whether Rosalynn should join Cy in delivering the crown back to Hungary. I would like to be there myself because it will be such a historic event, but the ultimate decision was that she couldn't go to Hungary because the queen of Belgium has already arranged to have social affairs for her at the same time. [Indian] prime minister Morarji Desai has put my unscheduled visit to a village on a personal basis, saying that it's part of the heritage of Gandhi and Nehru, and he's practically insisting that we do go.

We [Desai and I] discussed unsuccessfully our legal requirement that nuclear fuel be provided to a country only if it accepted full-scope safeguards. He thought this was an encroachment on their sovereignty. I pointed out that Canada, Germany, Switzerland, Brazil, and Japan all accept the same safeguards and we were putting our civilian plants under similar inspection procedures. He was quite adamant and said that only after all nations quit producing weapons, including ourselves and the Soviets, could India accept such restrictions or inspections.

This has continued to be a preeminent issue thirty years later. I and the three presidents who followed me all maintained the same position, but President George W. Bush reversed this policy. An agreement was announced in 2008, but Indian prime minister Manmohan Singh has not yet gained the necessary parliamentary approval, and the U.S. Congress is still considering some unresolved details. In effect, we have agreed to provide India with nuclear fuel and technology as long as it guarantees to maintain safeguards and give access to the International Atomic Energy Agency.

JANUARY 3   The last day in India we went to a village named Daulatpur, about fifteen miles from Delhi. Large numbers of farm families were alongside the road to wave at me and the prime minister, and they apparently owned tiny portions of land—probably less than an acre per family. They seemed to be happy, genuinely friendly. We were able to go into the homes unannounced. In fact, the homes seemed to be open, with people and cows walking through them almost like passageways. They appear to be very proud of the way they live, apparently not knowing much about a comparative way of life.

We visited a farmer who had one hectare of land. He was very proud of a methane-producing vat where he takes cow dung from a fifteen-cattle herd, mixes it fifty-fifty with water, puts it in a tank in the ground, and in the winter adds some warm water. It ferments, methane gas comes off the top, and he uses the methane gas to cook. The remaining wet cow dung is drained into a pit, where it eventually dries. He claims it's even better manure after the methane gas is removed and the dung is fermented. They honored me with a gift of a carved cart and oxen, and they changed the name of the village to "Carterpuri," which means Carter Village.

After an elaborate departure ceremony, we flew to Riyadh. I was pleasantly surprised at the vigor and involvement of King Khalid. Each day he has open court, so any citizen of his country can come and visit with him. When he eats both dinner and supper, his table is open for common people to dine; each evening when he goes back to his home palace he permits women to come in to meet with him. In the desert and among the Bedouins he carries a large hospital mounted on five or six Mercedes trucks, and they treat a hundred or more patients each day. This is the custom of the Al Saud family, and he said no king could ever renounce it without danger of being overthrown.

Crown Prince Fahd, who takes care of most of the details, and I spent several hours talking about the Horn of Africa, the Middle East settlements, the value of the dollar, and the oil trade. They're the only leaders I've met who want to see an independent Palestinian nation formed. Others pay lip service to this, because of their reluctance to antagonize the Saudis. We were very frank about this point. We told them we saw a real danger in an independent Palestinian state.

Although sometimes they make public statements of concern, their private commitment is absolute to what Sadat is attempting to do. They're deeply worried about a possible conflict in the Middle East that might spill over into Saudi Arabia, strongly anti-Communist, and eager to accommodate us on almost anything I request.

JANUARY 4   We left Riyadh two hours early to go by Aswan. This was perhaps the most exciting visit because of my strong friendship toward Sadat and worldwide interest in our resolving the Mideast disputes. Sadat and I have no differences between us. Now the main problem is the Palestinian question. We agreed with the Arab position: that Israel ought to withdraw completely from the occupied territories with minor adjustments in the western part, that there should be self-determination of the Palestinians short of an independent nation, and genuine peaceful relations between Israel and each of her neighbors.

Immediately after leaving Aswan we called Begin, who seems to be under great pressure from his right-wing allies and the settlers concerning expansion of settlements in the Sinai and West Bank. We'll have to prevent this disrupting the entire peace process.

For me the French visit was the high point of the whole trip. Even back in May I had liked Giscard d'Estaing more than many of the other European leaders. I gave him a thorough report on the Middle East. He's very strongly in favor of the Arab position and against Israel. Begin had wanted to come to France, but when Giscard outlined the public statements he would make, Begin refused to come.

JANUARY 5   The most moving part of the trip was to the Normandy beaches—five of them; Omaha [was] where we lost so many men during the initial invasion of Europe. Then the trip to Bayeux was like a massive political rally on the eve of an election victory. With the playing of taps at the American cemetery I commented that the Americans in World War I, when they landed, said, "Lafayette, we are here." It was a very emotional time for me.

Giscard was gracious at Normandy in pointing out that we had liberated France, and even made his speech in both French and English. Obviously [Charles] de Gaulle would never have considered this.

The response at the Palace of Versailles was also remarkable. He invited a fairly good list of people, thinking that maybe fifteen hundred would come, and more than four thousand showed up. One extra-nice thing he did was ask [Marc] Chagall to paint an original design for the cover of the banquet menu.

JANUARY 6   On a seven-hour visit to Belgium, we had a delightful meeting with the king and queen, Baudouin and Fabiola. We had a good reception when we got back to the White House. It was nice to have a sure feeling while I was gone that Fritz and others could take care of my duties.

JANUARY 10   Read a misleading message from Begin concerning Israeli settlements and sent a strong reply pointing out that what he was doing was an obstacle to peace and also violated what he and Dayan had told me earlier.

In the afternoon I discussed with Ham the abominable quality of news reporting during this past year and the need for us to take every opportunity to go directly to the people through news conferences or radio call-in shows, fireside chats, and travels around the country.

JANUARY 11   The unemployment rate, which is down greatly, was announced this morning. It's good news for a change and corroborates the feeling we've had that the unemployment rate was bound to come down because the number employed has gone up more than ever in history—4.1 million this past year.

The unemployment rate was 7.5 percent when I took office, 6.4 percent in January 1978, 5.9 percent in January 1979, 6.3 percent in January 1980, and 7.5 percent in January 1981.

Senator Byrd suggested that instead of having a fireside chat on Panama that I deliver the speech in the Senate chamber. George Washington did this a couple of times, and Byrd said he'd be willing to have television cameras there to cover it as a news event. First he wants to check with [Alan] Cranston, Baker, and others, but it's an intriguing and interesting proposition.

Inducing two-thirds of the senators to ratify the treaties seemed almost hopeless at the time.

I met with Judge William Webster from Missouri, whom we're considering for FBI director. He said he'd be willing to serve if I asked him.

I met with state commissioners of education and told them if I could go out of office with every fourth-grade child knowing how to read, I would consider my administration to be successful.

JANUARY 12   The shah's visit with Sadat was constructive. He was amazed at Sadat's flexibility, and determined to help force the Israelis to be adequately flexible. He has a great deal of influence on Israel because he supplies oil to them.

JANUARY 13   Met with a group of business leaders and pointed out that unemployment had gone down about 1.5 percent, employment up about 4 million, GNP increased between 5 and 6 percent, business investment in real terms up about 8 percent, corporate profits up 11.3 percent, inflation dropped to 4 percent. We're tackling energy, Social Security, minimum wage, and welfare controversies and had solved a couple of them, and had good prospects for energy. In all, 1977 was a good year. We were trying to reduce the percentage of GNP collected and spent by the federal government from 23 percent when I came in office down to 21 percent.

General Torrijos urged me to call Goldwater because he thinks Goldwater will support the treaties. This would be a big step forward—almost as good as the John Wayne endorsement.

We were trying to get to Camp David to rest from the trip, but Fritz called and said that Senator Humphrey was on the verge of death, and later in the evening he did pass away. This is a sad day for me.

Humphrey was a mentor of Fritz Mondale and a hero of mine. He was the originator of the Peace Corps and the Nuclear Test Ban Treaty. Although despised by many southern political leaders for his successful sponsorship of the Democratic Party's unprecedented civil rights plank in 1948, he was later reconciled with conservative senators because of his honesty, perseverance, and oratorical skills. Georgia senator Herman Talmadge once said to me, "Hubert is the only person I know who has more answers than there are questions."

MONDAY, JANUARY 16   I came to work on the State of the Union and met with Senator Baker. He's decided to support the Panama Canal treaties, wants to work closer with me because his father-in-law, Senator [Everett] Dirksen, did this with presidents. I'll make every effort to accommodate this offer and see if it's in good faith.

JANUARY 17   Prime Minister Begin made a ridiculous and abusive speech at a banquet concerning the Egyptians. Cy and Foreign Minister [Muhammad] Kamal were there, were embarrassed by it, and I was aggravated when I saw it on the evening news.

JANUARY 18   President Sadat withdrew his whole delegation from Jerusalem. I called Sadat and asked him to leave his negotiators there. He refused but will keep an open mind re the military negotiators to come to Egypt.

After we got home, about 10:15, Sonny Carter [my cousin Hugh] called me and said that Uncle Buddy had died. They were going to have the funeral on Friday. I told him if they would move it until Saturday morning, that Rosalynn and I would attend and that we would like to.

This was Alton Carter, my father's only brother, who lived in Plains and had been like a father to me during my years after leaving the U.S. Navy. He was a shrewd country philosopher, with a wonderful sense of humor. He had been the patriarch of the Carter family, and all of us called him "Uncle Buddy."

JANUARY 19   I met with Senator Russell Long, which is always a complete waste of time. I have to admit it's entertaining and enjoyable, which, as contrasted with Al Ullman, is a complete waste of time and not entertaining or enjoyable. Russell put an embarrassing quantity of special interest provisions in the energy bill, which I think is abhorrent, and has a deep personal financial interest in the outcome of it. He's brilliant, knowledgeable, and shrewd and in general has not been supportive of me or my programs, but someone you have to respect politically.

I feel more at home with the conservative Democratic and Republican members of Congress than I do the others, although the liberals vote with me more often.

I took a nap and went over the speech one time on teleprompter, and that evening delivered the State of the Union message. I felt at home going back to the House chamber. There was genuine relief at the good reception by the Congress.

JANUARY 20   We went down to Atlanta. Rosalynn and I tried to shake hands with all 2,100 people who paid five hundred dollars to come to the fund-raiser. Bert Lance was in charge of one of the most successful fund-raisers in the history of our party. Then we flew to Musgrove Plantation — about as tired as I've ever been.

JANUARY 21   This morning we flew to Plains on the helicopter to go to Uncle Buddy's funeral. Then back to Musgrove again.

JANUARY 24   We got word that the Soviet nuclear-powered satellite would fall in Canada, and I called Pierre Trudeau and woke him to let him know it would impact just east of Great Slave Lake.

I met with the congressional leadership. There's a general growing support for the Arab position and against the Israelis because of their insistence on the illegal settlements. We want to keep this momentum going if possible.

I finally signed the executive order for the intelligence community and expressed my confidence in Stan Turner. It was a major step in the right direction. Now we have to constrain the congressional committees from passing an overly restrictive intelligence charter.

JANUARY 25   Mayor Dennis Kucinich came by from Cleveland. He's young, a supporter of mine, and a highly visible, very innovative young man.

Had lunch with just Kissinger, me, and Rosalynn. He's proceeding with his book [*The White House Years*], having finished four hundred pages. I asked if he had gotten through the swearing-in ceremony yet. He said his biggest difficulty was trying to correlate his memory with what the documents showed at the time. He said he only kept a diary for the first six months, thought it was impolite to record what he and Nixon had said to each other, and only found out later that Nixon was tape recording all their conversations.

I moved my memoir notes over to the residence and started my secure place. Later I don't want any misunderstanding about whether they belong to me or to the government.

This is an interesting entry, in part because I don't remember whether my conversation with Kissinger precipitated this decision.

JANUARY 26   We watched a film of a Soviet agent receiving information from the State Department, for which he was expelled from our country. We have an escalating expulsion process going on with the Soviets, and we're trying to put a stop to it. This guy was the one that the Soviets disputed, and we recorded his involvement in espionage and showed it to the Soviets.

JANUARY 27   We'll have a meeting in Malta soon with [Zimbabwe revolutionary leaders Joshua] Nkomo and [Robert] Mugabe, the British, and some of the frontline nations' representatives to try to work out the Rhodesian question. In the meantime the pressure is on Smith and the internal African leaders to reach an agreement.

I've been meeting with a lot of congressional leaders one at a time, and Frank Moore says these are very productive. During 1978 I won't have to do the hundreds of hours of detailed study of issues that I had to last year, since I'm now fairly familiar with most of them. I'll have more time to work with Congress directly, which I think is productive—and I enjoy it in a way.

I had lunch with Herman Talmadge. He's a very strong and able man. I asked him if he could help us with the Panama Canal treaties, and he said he might hold his nose and vote for it.

Talmadge did so, and this unpopular vote contributed to his defeat in the next election.

JANUARY 28   I've spent a great deal of time with the military this year—more than any other president—and have tried to involve top Pentagon officials in my strategic decisions concerning foreign policy and national security. This has helped me have their perspective and also tended to reduce greatly the friction that formerly existed among the Pentagon, National Security Council, and State Department.

MONDAY, JANUARY 30   We believe the pressure we're putting on with the Anglo-American Plan is forcing Ian Smith to negotiate for the consummation of majority rule in Rhodesia, with free elections.

Begin is under tremendous political pressure, but he obviously is breaking his word of honor to me that no new settlements would be permitted in the West Bank. The government did not authorize a new settlement at Shiloh, except for an archaeological site, but they've already moved twenty-five families in there—with Begin's knowledge—and he's too timid to remove them.

JANUARY 31   I'm still quite concerned by the Israeli settlements. My word of honor is at stake with the Arabs because I repeated the Israeli promise to them.

Senator Joe Biden came and covered three points: Ted Kennedy is running for president in 1980 and is already lining up support; the Jewish community has a deep distrust of me because I'm a Baptist; and Hamilton needs to spend more time with the members of Congress. I responded to each one of these in a mild way. Joe also asked that I help him with a fundraiser in Delaware, sometime this spring, which I will try to do.

As a young senator, Joe Biden had been my most effective supporter during the 1976 campaign. Joe's report proved to be quite accurate. This was the first indication I had about Kennedy's presidential plans, but they were soon to become more evident as he marshaled opposition to many of my proposals.

Ruth ate lunch with us. I asked her to contact James Dickey, who has a very serious drinking problem.

My youngest sister, Ruth Carter Stapleton, gained worldwide fame as an author and evangelist before I decided to run for president. She spoke to audi-

*ences of many thousands, delivering a calm, loving, and personal Christian
message that appealed to suffering people and also to world leaders in many
nations. The poet and author James Dickey was a family friend who spent a
lot of time in Plains with my mother. He wrote my inaugural poem, "The
Strength of Fields."*

FEBRUARY 1   We reviewed the transcripts of my meeting with Dayan, and it
was very clear that Dayan said that at the end of a year there would be no
more than six settlements, all of which would be within military boundaries.

FEBRUARY 2   I met with Ed Koch and Mike Blumenthal concerning
New York City. I promised to prevent bankruptcy, but I and the Congress
would insist that local/state officials, local banks, labor unions, and retirement funds would have to do their share.

FEBRUARY 3   We had quite an argument, with me on one side and Fritz,
Cy, Zbig, and Ham on the other. I think we ought to move much more
aggressively on the Middle East question than any of them, by evolving a
clear plan, discussing the various elements with Sadat, encouraging him
to cooperate with us, preventing any major surprises in the future, and
inducing him to understand Begin's position. The plan has got to be one
that can be acceptable by Begin in a showdown if we have the full support
of the American public. I don't know how much support I have, but we'll
go through with this effort.

*We had two choices: abandon our peace efforts or become much more active
and forceful in dealing with both sides. My search for a bolder approach
and a growing realization that we might have to move independently of the
Soviet Union led to a decision to invite Begin and Sadat to meet privately
with me at Camp David.*

Paul Austin came by. We're sending him on an important mission to
Cuba in a very confidential way.

*I wanted Paul, as a private citizen, to explore with Castro the prospect of our
moving more boldly toward U.S.-Cuba reconciliation. I had lifted travel
restraints, but Cuba was still involved militarily in several African coun-*

tries. The economic embargo was hurting the Cuban people, not Castro,
and there was a potential strategic advantage in breaking Cuba away from
the Soviet Union.

President Sadat and his wife, Jehan, came to Camp David. He was
quite tired after a trip from Egypt to Morocco to Washington, so after supper they went to bed early.

FEBRUARY 4   Sadat recalled a personal letter that I handwrote to him and
sealed and sent to him, urging him to take dramatic action to start some
progress toward peace, since we were bogged down in details. Sadat described the sequence of events since our last April meeting. He said he
asked [President Nicolae] Ceauşescu of Romania if Begin was for a genuine peace and if he was strong enough to implement one. Ceauşescu
thought the answer to both questions was yes.

Sadat listed the things Israel really wanted—direct negotiations with
Arab leaders, recognition as a permanent entity in the Middle East, and to
live in peace—and the true definition of peace—which all the Arabs had
until now rejected. He said the Israelis never dreamed that Egypt would
approve these points, but he decided in one fell swoop to accomplish all
these Israeli desires and get the U.S. Jew lobby (as he refers to it) off my
shoulders. He thinks his initiative to go to Jerusalem took the Israelis by
surprise. They were not ready for peace and possibly still are not.

He said he's changed the Arabs with his visit and even the rest of the
world, but at Ismailia he was completely disillusioned with Begin's ridiculous position. When Begin raised the question of settlements in the Sinai,
Sadat said he thought it was just a joke, and when Begin spelled out his
self-rule proposal, which was different from the one he spelled out to me,
it was obvious that Egypt could not accept it.

Sadat said he's going to announce to the National Press Club Monday
that they are discontinuing participation in the military or political talks;
they've given Israel everything they possibly could have dreamed of a year
ago. He said Israel only had one friend that propped them up, and that's
the United States. He was convinced that Israel never intends to change.

I pointed out, helped later by Vance, Brzezinski, and Mondale, that
this would be a very serious blow, would make Begin look good and Sadat
look like an obstacle to peace. We finally convinced him not to make this

statement but to put it in positive terms that he was ready to recommence discussions when Israel agreed to abide by [UN Resolution] 242 and not insist on the illegal settlements.

He spelled out a six-point security plan for Israel but said settlers could not stay in the Sinai even if the UN provided them security. He said he would accept ten thousand Israelis (former Egyptians) who wanted to move back into his country. I recapitulated what Sadat had told me to make sure there was no language problem, and we decided he would make a positive speech to the Press Club on Monday.

This was another threatening episode in the continuing drama. There is little doubt that Sadat's originally planned speech would have been a serious, perhaps fatal, blow to any peace agreement.

FEBRUARY 5   Sadat and I had another serious discussion, and we went over the principles concerning the West Bank and Gaza, and the Palestinian question. He basically agreed and said he did not want Jerusalem to be divided but there had to be joint sovereignty over one square mile where the religious places were located.

FEBRUARY 7   Leonard Woodcock met with me privately to discuss our China policy. He thinks that after the elections in the fall we ought to move, and that Deng's interview with the news media was more hard-line than he is likely to take if we get down to serious negotiation.

Kissinger, Ribicoff, [Jacob] Javits, and Strauss will get together Thursday morning to go over the Mideast situation and encourage Israel to move. Sadat apparently is making good progress with the American public, the news media, and Congress concerning the Israeli settlements, the need for a rapid movement to conclude a Mideast peace agreement, and Egypt's need for offensive airplanes.

FEBRUARY 8   I announced a new college tuition program that brings the total to about $5.2 billion next year, enough for 5 million students. This is done in part to prevent a much more expensive and less equitable income tax credit for the wealthier families.

My barber, Rod Morales, and his wife gave me a nice leather jacket which I couldn't accept. I sent it back to him with a heartfelt thank-you note. He was very excited that I was chosen best-coiffed world leader for last year!

For supper I had nine Jewish leaders: Phil Klutznick, Ed Sanders, Max Greenberg, Alex Schindler, Richard Maas, Frank Lautenberg, Ted Mann, Arnold Picker, David Blumberg. I spelled out the relative flexibility of Sadat's position and the intransigence of Israel. With the exception of Schindler, who always acts like an ass, the rest of them were constructive. We discussed primarily the illegal settlements, the short time frame in which to negotiate, and the need for Israel to recognize that UN 242 applies to the West Bank/Gaza Strip.

FEBRUARY 9   I met with Doug Fraser, who heads up the UAW, one of the best organizations that I've worked with since I've been president. They're unselfish and also politically competent. He wanted to discuss labor law reform, how he could help us with the Panama Canal treaties and work closely with us on the evolution of the national health insurance program later this year.

FEBRUARY 10   I met with Howard Baker, which is always a pleasant experience and constructive. He's a shrewd politician and sly, I know, but he's genuinely helpful on the Panama Canal treaties, and when I asked him also for help on energy discussion, he said he thought it was about time to move, and he was sure we would get a bill.

Howard Baker personified the bipartisan cooperation that existed in those days. A respected leader among Republicans, he did his best to support my proposals, including some that were anathema to his right-wing peers. When he later sought the Republican presidential nomination, his support for the Panama Canal treaties, my energy package, and normalization of relations with China were used by Ronald Reagan and others against him. He later served as Reagan's chief of staff and as U.S. ambassador to Japan.

FEBRUARY 11–12   We had a good weekend at Camp David and got some rest for the first time since early December. I watched Dayan's television program, when he insinuated that we were anti-Israel and no longer could be honest brokers. He insinuated also that Cy Vance in his opposition to the settlements was different in that position from my own. All of that is inaccurate, deliberately—so I think.

MONDAY, FEBRUARY 13   We had a regular cabinet meeting and discussed the coal strike, which could create some very serious problems if it's not handled soon. The production of coal has dropped by 60 percent, and by early April we could have at least 5 million people unemployed. We also had a discussion about whether the percentage of incompetent lawyers was 20 percent or 50 percent. I personally sided with Chief Justice Burger, who chose the higher number.

I listened to Bob Byrd's speech concerning the Panama Canal treaties, emphasizing the need for leadership and not just to assess the public opinion back home. He said if you went by public opinion polls and telephone calls or the volume of mail, you could replace senators with an adding machine or a set of scales.

FEBRUARY 14   I approved authorization to the attorney general for electronic surveillance but tightened up on the notification of me and insisted that in every possible case warrants be obtained.

I discussed with Stan the certainty of our verification procedures on different SALT facets, and he gave me a secret message showing that Helmut Schmidt had been extremely critical of me personally and also of our country. Schmidt seems to go up and down in his psychological attitude. I guess women are not the only ones that have periods.

Nelson Rockefeller called to say that the Mideast arms sales package was "a brilliant move"; that he'd been working on it for thirty-seven years and he admired what we were doing. He's talked to some of the Jewish leaders, including [Louis] Lefkowitz, and says there's growing support in the Jewish community for our position in the Middle East, particularly relating to the settlements.

FEBRUARY 16   Fritz called from Aspen. He said he's working hard to improve our relationship with the western states by talking to individual people on the ski slopes.

FEBRUARY 19   I needed a rest and got one. After going to Sunday school and church, I read a couple of books. One was *Watership Down*, about a group of rabbits, kind of an allegory similar to Tolkien's books and *Alice in Wonderland*. Then I read John McPhee's latest book about Alaska.

McPhee is a personal friend and one of my favorite writers. I have almost all the books he has written.

FEBRUARY 22   The CIA reports that Israel is continuing with plans under the urging of [Minister of Agriculture Ariel] Sharon to develop new and larger settlements in Gaza, Sinai, and the West Bank. This is going to be a source of real confrontation if Begin doesn't honor his agreement with me. He has also apparently reversed the policy of the Israeli government and now claims UN Resolution 242 does not apply to the West Bank. This is a drastic change and a serious problem.

I described to Sid Yates [senior congressman from Illinois] these latest developments, and he was sympathetic. He's the leading member of the House on the Mideast, and I think everyone trusts him and he can be a very valuable ally.

FEBRUARY 23   John J. McCloy [former U.S. high commissioner for Germany] expressed concern about the relations between Germany and us, and Zbig suggested that he go to Germany to try to get Schmidt to keep his mouth shut for a change.

FEBRUARY 24   At our foreign policy breakfast we discussed Schmidt's irrationality and that his own cabinet had begun to criticize him because of his remarks about me and the U.S. government.

I signed the Endangered American Wilderness Act, adding about 1.3 million more acres of wilderness lands, and encouraged the Congress to act expeditiously on the Alaska proposal.

Chief executives of the National Council of Churches brought me a list of things they didn't like about government. I responded in a polite but firm way that when you compared social programs, human rights, civil rights, between the government and churches, that by far the best record was with the government. I, being a member of both, was in a position to make an objective analysis.

FEBRUARY 25   Got some recordings of selections that [Vladimir] Horowitz will play tomorrow. Saturday afternoon we went down and listened to him practice. He thought the room was too "live," so he and I spread out some carpets around the piano platform. He's a very nice, friendly man whom I liked instantly.

One of my most remarkable presidential responsibilities was personally to drag large carpets out of the halls of the White House and then join the pianist Vladimir Horowitz on the floor of the East Room. With our butts in the air, we grabbed the edges of the carpets and adjusted their locations to soften the sound. He would play a few loud notes, and then we would move or add more carpets.

FEBRUARY 26   After Sunday school and church, I bowled three games with Dr. Lukash, averaging a little better than 180 in my first and best score of its kind. Then I introduced Horowitz and attended a superb concert. I told Rosalynn this is one of the best afternoons of my life. It was exciting to be with him, Toscanini's daughter, Rostropovich, Robert Shaw, Segovia, Isaac Stern, and about two hundred other people who were either performers or who had done good work for music in the country.

Rosalynn arranged an unprecedented series of performances by great artists in the White House and on the South Lawn. They included dozens of superb performers, ranging from Willie Nelson, John Lennon, and Dolly Parton to Mikhail Baryshnikov, Vladimir Horowitz, Leonard Bernstein, and Beverly Sills. She was able to induce PBS to broadcast many of the performances live throughout the nation, and they were recorded for later enjoyment.

MONDAY FEBRUARY 27   We're trying to stop Sadat from sending Begin a message that he's going to terminate the Sinai agreement, which expires this October. Also, we decided to convince Begin that he can't trade away his establishment of illegal settlements for any substantive concession to Egypt or us.

FEBRUARY 28   I announced the final phases of our 1978 education program: the first, a new Department of Education, and the second, a massive student aid effort—with elementary and secondary standards. I think it's one of the best in history.

I asked Cy about the advisability of sending Zbig to China in April. He is strongly opposed.

MARCH 1   CIA gave me an analysis of the Soviet negotiating techniques, primarily to be adamant and unchangeable, look on the negotiating process as an end in itself, and keep the finger on the pulse of the negotiating opponent. They have departed from this procedure to some degree, in SALT, because of the importance attached to it.

MARCH 2   Mike Blumenthal and Joe Califano asked that I drop plans for national health insurance for this year. I told them that my commitment was too deep to reverse myself, but we could work out with Kennedy, labor, and others a presentation of principles in April, specifications in July or August, and a final legislative proposal before the Congress adjourns. If it's handled right, individual members of Congress could benefit politically, and it won't interfere with work on tax reform and other bills.

MONDAY, MARCH 6   As has been the case recently, the cabinet meeting was devoted to serious problems without any apparent solutions.

MARCH 7   In Israel there's been a fairly uniform condemnation of Begin and his rejection of 242 as it applies to the West Bank/Gaza Strip, which may have some effect on his position when he comes here next week.

President [Josip] Tito (of Yugoslavia) arrived, and I gave him a warm welcome. He has been helpful to me and a close friend through continuing correspondence. He's an amazing man—eighty-six years old, appears to be about sixty, vigorous, very confident of himself, good hearing, strong voice, and helpful with advice concerning the Soviets, Ethiopia, Somalia, Korea, Egypt, and eastern European countries. We had the largest press contingent since I've been president to witness his arrival. Tito described his island zoo, how he made wine, his early days as a freedom fighter, and that he saw George McGovern's B-24 crash in a barnyard adjacent to his headquarters on the island of Vis.

Tito and his partisans helped McGovern return to combat duty during World War II.

MARCH 8   Frank Moore and others reported that we now have fifty-nine sure votes on the Panama treaties and varying degrees of success projected for [Senators] [John] Heinz, [Henry] Bellmon, [Wendell] Ford, Nunn, Talmadge, Long, [Jennings] Randolph, [Edward] Brooke, [Dennis] DeConcini, [Mark] Hatfield, and [Edward] Zorinsky. Byrd met with a few of them today, and they want some amendments that would be either embarrassing to me or to the Panamanians. I urged him to hang tough, and said I would rather yield on something important to the U.S. like the sea-level canal than go back on my commitment to Panama.

MARCH 10   I had a report from a Cuban American dignitary who visited Castro that he's eager to meet with me or Brzezinski and is willing to be flexible on releasing the 2,500 political prisoners (to use his figure) and on the subject of Cuban involvement in Africa. We will approach this cautiously.

Defense Minister [Ezer] Weizman came, and we had a thorough discussion. He is charming and the most levelheaded and able Israeli official I've met. He's in a somewhat sensitive position, having to be loyal to Begin—which I would expect from my own cabinet members—and at the same time having a better understanding of Egypt and the outside world than the prime minister.

Frank came in to tell me that Herman Talmadge's staff had asked us to call off the dogs; he was willing to go with us on the Panama Canal treaties without amendments.

We had a pleasant evening with Peter Bourne and Mary. This is the first time since we've been in Washington that Rosalynn and I have been out together for supper with friends.

MARCH 11   We [Cy, Zbig, and I] discussed the visit of Begin and decided to emphasize the positive consequences of peace to the entire Middle East, importance of our permanent friendship with the modern Arabs, necessity of implementing 242 on all fronts, and danger of continuing with settlement activity. We want to give Begin credit for his positive proposals, although he's backed off on some. If we have a breakdown, which is most likely, then we'll go ahead with a major public statement on the Mideast and the recruitment of public opinion to our position. We also decided that in the future it might be necessary to offer a United States–Israel security treaty.

MARCH 12   I called senators who are considered fairly hopeless on Panama: [William] Roth, [Quentin] Burdick, [John] Melcher, [Ted] Stevens, [Howard] Cannon, [J. Bennett] Johnston, [Dewey] Bartlett, [Robert] Dole,

[Robert] Griffin, [Milton] Young, [Pete] Domenici, [Barry] Goldwater, [Clifford] Hansen, [Richard] Lugar, [Dennis] DeConcini. I made some progress, but I didn't get any sure commitments.

Lately Rosalynn and I have been bowling a good bit. My average is up now to about 150 to 160. She's doing about 120 to 130. Gives us a chance to be together and also to get some exercise on bad days.

MONDAY, MARCH 13   Cy said that Ribicoff was with us re Israel. [Hyman] Bookbinder, [Phil] Klutznick, and some others expressed their support for our position if we keep the high road and don't put them in a defenseless position.

Ray Marshall [secretary of labor] reported an agreement on a coal contract. It's hard for me to concentrate on anything expect Panama.

MARCH 14   We're still short on sure votes for the treaties. I asked Cy to spend full-time on the Hill, and also Henry Kissinger, Harold Brown, the Joint Chiefs, Fritz, Stu Eizenstat, Cecil Andrus, Jim Schlesinger to devote as much time as possible to this effort. President Ford promised to use his influence. Rosalynn called Mrs. Hatfield in Montana, Mrs. Zorinsky, and she even got Landrum Bolling [CEO of the national Council on Foundations] to call Senator Dick Lugar, which is kind of a hopeless case. I have a feeling that I made an impression on Senator [John] Stennis, and in a showdown he won't let me down. This has been one of the worst days of my political life, knowing that we were lost, regaining a little hope. I still haven't given up, but it's going to be an extremely close vote.

Jim McIntyre called to say that he had met with his friend Henry Bellmon, who had been planning a trip to Oklahoma to see about a desalinization plant. He asked if [I would veto the plant] just because it was a water project. I told him [I would not]. McIntyre said that under those conditions, Bellmon would support the treaties.

MARCH 15   I went to bed about 10:00 and got up late, about 6:00 this morning, to get some rest.

DeConcini came in to tell me that he would support the treaties.

I had to call General Torrijos, who was planning to blast the Senate and reject the Panama treaties because of some amendment language of DeConcini. I don't like the language either, but it doesn't change the meaning of the treaties. I agreed to send [Deputy Secretary of State] Warren Christopher and Hamilton Jordan to Panama tomorrow after the votes to explain the complete action of the Senate to Torrijos rather than having him overly concerned about one sentence in the Resolution of Ratification.

I talked to Cy, Zbig, and Fritz about the Israeli invasion of South Lebanon. We're going to give them twenty-four hours and then call for their withdrawal. They are using American equipment for invasion of foreign territory, which is illegal.

A PLO faction had traveled on March 11 from the Lebanese port of Tyre and attacked the coast of Israel. An American photographer and thirty-five Israelis were killed and seventy-one wounded. I expressed my outrage over this "cowardly and senseless attack on a group of civilians." Israel's retaliation began on March 14; the villages of the attackers were destroyed, but most of them escaped. Bombardments left thousands of peaceful Lebanese citizens homeless. Moshe Dayan, in his memoirs, criticized the way the response was conducted and said that pictures of families fleeing "scarred our good name."

MARCH 16   President Ford called. He had contacted Brooke, Heinz, and Bellmon, really after they had made their decisions, but I appreciate his help. He's done everything he promised.

I informed Cy and Fritz that Zbig would go to China, perhaps as early as next month.

I notified the Israelis that we would introduce a resolution in the United Nations calling for their withdrawal, and for UN forces to keep the peace in Lebanon. They're using our equipment illegally to invade a foreign country, and they overreacted seriously by killing hundreds and hundreds of civilians in Lebanon in their massive attack.

During the day Bellmon and Hatfield announced for the treaties; Senators Ford and Zorinsky announced against. As of 1:00 we've got sixty-seven votes, plus Randolph if we need him. After lunch I called Senator Cannon, and he finally decided he would support the treaties. This gives us sixty-eight votes, if no one changes.

I listened to the treaty vote in my little private office and was really pleased and relieved when the vote came through—but the vote on the second treaty is going to be even more difficult.

The first treaty returned the Canal Zone to the Panamanians and expired at the end of the century. The second was effective in January 2000 and pro-

vides for U.S. ships to have priority in using the canal during times of emergency and lets the United States defend the canal against outside threats.

MARCH 17   We spent the day on the 95,000-ton USS *Eisenhower*, with a complement of about 6,300. It and the *Nimitz* are the largest warships in the world. It was an exciting display of professional competence by a very young crew. The F-15s and five other kinds of plane put on a good demonstration, and we were accompanied by a Spruance-class destroyer, a fleet frigate, and the nuclear cruiser *Virginia*, which also demonstrated their firepower. In spite of the impressiveness of the display, I don't believe we need to build another nuclear carrier, which costs about $2.5 billion and enormous quantities of money to operate.

Aircraft carriers were very popular with the Congress, and I had to veto the entire defense authorization bill to prevent their construction and so ensure that limited funds would be spent more efficiently. We prevailed against an all-out effort to override my veto.

MONDAY, MARCH 20   When I returned to Washington Monday evening, we had a meeting on the enhanced radiation weapons. A lot of momentum had been generated to produce and deploy these neutron bombs. My cautionary words since last summer have pretty well been ignored, and I was aggravated. The general sense is that it protects buildings and kills people. That's a gross oversimplification, but I decided to work out a way to cancel the idea without giving an image of weakness to our European allies, who don't want it anyhow.

I talked to Arthur Goldberg about his interpretation of UN 242, which is the same as ours, and completely contrary to the Israelis, who have been trying to get him to certify falsely that it doesn't necessarily apply to the West Bank.

MARCH 21   The response was excellent regarding our resolution calling for Israeli withdrawal from Lebanon. As Goldberg pointed out last night, this is the first Security Council resolution the U.S. has successfully sponsored in more than ten years. The Israelis did their best to prevent our sponsorship of the resolution. They grossly overreacted in Lebanon to the terrorist attack on some Israeli citizens, destroying hundreds of villages, killing many people, and making two hundred thousand Lebanese homeless.

I met with Begin [and Dayan and had an intense discussion of all the issues.]

MARCH 22   I got a scratch pad and wrote down the specific points for discussion with Begin. I then read to Begin and his group my understanding of their position: they're not willing to withdraw politically or militarily from any part of the West Bank; not willing to stop the construction of new settlements or the expansion of existing settlements; not willing to withdraw Israeli settlers from the Sinai, nor if they stay to permit UN or Egyptian protection for them; not willing to acknowledge that UN Resolution 242 applies to the West Bank/Gaza Strip area; and not willing to grant Palestinians a voice in the determination of their own future.

Begin said this was a negative way to express their position, but didn't deny the accuracy of any of it. For the first time, over their strenuous objections, the true position of the Israeli government was revealed. Dayan tried to put the best face on the Israeli position. That they did not want to have any political control over the Arab population. He went as far as he could to leave some hope open without being disloyal to Begin.

MARCH 23   I met with the Senate Foreign Relations Committee in a very sober, even moving, interchange concerning the Mideast. They seem to be unanimous in their support of me, even people like [Richard] Stone, [Jacob] Javits, and [Clifford] Case. We got word that Weizman in Israel would propose a peace coalition government, probably naming Begin as prime minister.

After lunch I told Jim Callaghan my concerns about the neutron bomb. He said it would not be deployed in Great Britain and that it would be the greatest relief in the world if we announce that we weren't going to go ahead with it.

After lunch I met with Harold Brown concerning the five-year navy construction program. We decided to do what we could to prevent Congress authorizing another nuclear carrier. This is going to be very difficult. We'll average around fifteen new ships per year for the next five years, with at least one new Trident submarine per year.

Senator Dick Stone called to say he was disappointed with a meeting he had with Begin and he would support our Mideast policy.

Sections of the following entry, about a trip to South America and Africa, were dictated after each stop. I realize that my description of these visits may come across as self-congratulatory, but they do portray a dramatic change in our nation's image in the Third World. Much of this was due to our approval of the Panama Canal treaties, a goal that had long been a top priority of many less-developed countries. Another factor was the good impression made by Andrew Young's service as our ambassador to the United Nations. Further, our strong human rights policy was popular in many countries around the world.

MARCH 28–APRIL 3   I realized before we left on our trip that the last U.S. officials to visit Venezuela were attacked. Nixon had his life endangered, almost had his car turned over, and Nelson Rockefeller met the same fate. When Eisenhower went to Brazil eighteen years ago, there were massive demonstrations of students and working people against him. When Kissinger tried to get permission to come into Nigeria two or three years ago, he was refused. I hope the time of the "Ugly American" is over, and from the reception we received, apparently this is true. I never saw a critical poster or banner or gesture among the hundreds of thousands of people along the highways and in the crowds during this entire trip.

In Caracas, I made the welcoming address and also a talk at Simón Bolívar's tomb in Spanish. Later the news media said it's the first time a president has ever made a speech in a foreign country in a foreign language. It was very easy for me after the speech was drafted and put into simple Spanish words. I met with former president [Rómulo] Betancourt, who thinks our human rights emphasis is the best thing that's happened in this hemisphere in his lifetime.

We also had a good visit to Brazil. Foreign Minister Silveira was amazed at the number of people who came out to the highway to greet us, at the friendliness of their reaction. I personally liked President [Ernesto] Geisel very much. He's an older gentleman, military, frank, honest, blunt, cool at first in his welcoming remarks, particularly. I rejected Zbig's suggestion that we be cool also, and made a very warm statement.

The two major issues are our insistence on human rights, which are abridged in Brazil but on which progress is being made, and the concern we have about Brazil putting in a nuclear reprocessing plant which we don't think they need. In both instances Brazil has considered this position of the United States an unwarranted intrusion into their affairs.

We went to Rio for a day and night of recreation, and thoroughly enjoyed the city. Had a meeting with Cardinal [Paulo] Arns and the bishop from Rio, and a major industrialist newspaperman and the head of the Brazilian bar, to discuss human rights.

At first I was confused about who Cardinal Arns was, since he acts so modest. Afterward I invited him to ride to the airport with us. He was going to return to São Paulo, and I thoroughly enjoyed his private conversation. He's an extremely good man, and I would certainly like for him to be pope someday. He's extremely courageous. Because of him the newspapers in São Paulo are under tight constraints, which is rare now in Brazil. Some of his students have been arrested. He said the political prisoners in Brazil have dropped about 90 percent, to around two or three hundred, but there are still ten thousand political exiles who have been forced out of Brazil.

He published a book the day before I arrived in Brasília on human rights, and got thirty-two other church denominations to publish a similar book and distribute it and five hundred thousand pamphlets on human rights the day after I left in honor of my visit. My guess is that our paying attention to him will not help with Geisel, but I think it's important in Brazil and worldwide for me not to back down on this subject that arouses intense interest in other countries.

Amy enjoyed the whole trip and was a delight to have along. She's a good ambassador.

Again, we had a great welcome on our arrival in Lagos, Nigeria, particularly in view of the fact that until recently we had been the villain in the news media and in statements made by all public officials. Now there's a genuine sense of sharing, responsibility for peace in Africa. President Obasanjo and I went to church together. He's a Baptist, he read the scripture, and I gave a prayer and read the responsive reading. The religious affiliations on this trip were quite significant. If the Christians can get together, particularly with an enlightened pope, the enhancement of human rights throughout the world would be very profound.

We made a brief trip to Liberia, because they have been a historic friend. President [William] Tolbert declared a national holiday, and the crowds to welcome us were unbelievable. He's an active Baptist preacher, for five years head of the World Baptist Alliance—the first black who had this very important position. His vice president, whom he said God asked him to choose, is a Baptist bishop.

This was the first visit by an American president to sub-Saharan Africa.

APRIL 4   It was good to get back home. I called to give our best wishes to John Wayne, who's had open-heart surgery. He had a pig heart valve installed, and it seems to be doing well.

APRIL 6   I had a heated meeting, surprisingly, with Ted Kennedy, Doug Fraser, George Meany, and others concerning national health insurance. Apparently Kennedy and Califano had a real run-in about it. I told them to let us work it out between now and May, and I would present principles that I would be responsible for and no one else in the administration. I believe Kennedy was posturing in front of the labor leaders.

MONDAY, APRIL 10   We've got a horrible problem throughout the country on retirement. The total unfunded retirement debt exceeds the national debt, and there are at least five major corporations whose unfunded retirement obligations exceed their total common stock values. This is an area we haven't entered yet.

Griffin pointed out that the omnibus judges bill is likely to pass, giving me 150 new judges to appoint, which I certainly don't want. In this four-year term I will have appointed more than half the total federal judges in the United States.

In the evening I had Tip [O'Neill] and [his wife] Millie over for supper. Tip is very downhearted about the *New York Times* article alleging his unethical conduct, which seems to have no substance to it. Instead of talking congressional business, we had a couple of good, strong drinks and kind of a social affair. I enjoyed it, and so did he. He's so supportive of me in his speeches that sometimes it's almost embarrassing.

Tip O'Neill filled the congressional seat formerly held by John Kennedy, and was famous for saying, "All politics is local." Although my personal friend, Tip was a liberal Democrat, and he was often bothered by my commitment to conservative budgeting and a strong defense, and by my failure to support his proposals for massive federal programs. Very loyal to me during the first three years, he was more supportive of Ted Kennedy during the 1980 primary season.

APRIL 11   I called Mike Blumenthal to tell him I want Bob Strauss to be the anti-inflation coordinator, and he blew his top. Said it was encroaching on his prerogatives as secretary of treasury. I was surprised. He and I

always have had a difference about the authority of the secretary of treasury. He thinks he ought to be my chief economic spokesman, chief negotiator with business, labor, and the Congress on any matter, and also my
chief advisor. I look on him as a cabinet officer who is my chief financial
spokesman, but I think Juanita relates to business, Ray relates to labor,
Charlie Schultze is my chief advisor, and Bob Strauss does the negotiating. It's a sincere difference of opinion.

*Blumenthal and his family were refugees from Hitler's Germany, and they
lived in Shanghai before immigrating to the United States. Mike was a brilliant and accomplished administrator, with prior experience in government
and as a top corporate executive. He returned to the business and academic
world after leaving office.*

APRIL 12   The Israelis, in their attack on South Lebanon, where more
than a thousand civilians were killed and two hundred thousand made
homeless, used cluster bombs [CBUs] in direct violation of an agreement
that we've had.

*Almost thirty years later, Israel took the same action when it invaded Leba-
non in 2006. When I traveled to Lebanon in April 2009 to monitor its election, thousands of tiny unexploded cluster bombs were still scattered
throughout the country. A proposed demand by the UN that Israel reveal
the location of the dropped bombs is still being debated.*

APRIL 13   Ceauşescu relayed [North Korean dictator] Kim Il Sung's desire to improve relationships with the United States. Wanted direct communications with us, a reunion of Korea confederation between North
and South Korea, letting them maintain their own political systems.

*Ceauşescu was popular in the West in those days because he maintained
independence from the Soviets, but he was a worse tyrant in his own country
than Brezhnev was in the Soviet Union.*

APRIL 15–16   The weekend was devoted to the second Panama Canal
Treaty vote, which is still very doubtful. We have a couple of flighty senators, [S. I.] Hayakawa and [James] Abourezk, who are attempting political
blackmail against me on completely nonrelated items.

MONDAY, APRIL 17   We had an excellent country music concert/reception, sponsored by the Country Music Association on their twentieth anniversary. Tom T. Hall, Loretta Lynn, Conway Twitty were the main performers, and then Larry Gatlin, James Talley, Gary and Terry Morris, Charlie Daniels all performed in an impromptu way. It was a very good evening, except that I was constantly on call about the Panama Canal treaties.

On Sunday and Monday we had a retreat with our top staff and cabinet officers, designed to share frank opinions with each other. After opening the Monday session with my own comments, I kept notes and later dictated the following entries. Vance and Brown were in Europe.

CARTER: We've had good progress in international affairs, with success in human rights, nonproliferation. Every time a world leader comes and talks with me, he wants to let me know what they've done with human rights. Unbelievable progress on Panama, which has been the most difficult, aggravating, and time-consuming issue—much more difficult and unpleasant than a presidential campaign.

We've undertaken some very challenging questions. I don't think Roosevelt, for example, ever put forward a series of comprehensive efforts like we have: the Mideast, Panama, Africa, energy, urban policy, tax reform, water policy, Alaska lands, federal lands, irrigation supplies, national health insurance. The country has shifted to a more conservative attitude; everything we do is contrary to people's inclinations. Sometimes we are too slow making decisions. We have a lack of Washington experience. Some staff are too loyal to me, while others have inadequate communication.

My complaints regarding the cabinet. There are times you don't support White House policy, when I make final decisions contrary to what you recommend. Important that Congress feel this is administration policy and what we're supporting. Staff and I need to know before you come out with a highly controversial decision. You haven't handled expeditiously the White House correspondence referred to you. We call re one out of twenty letters re a response. Commerce is best with average delay of seventeen days, which does not include a five-day transmittal! The worst is Interior—forty-two days. This is inexcusable.

Political involvement. This is an election year, and I think every one of you should bend over backwards to help Democrats—go the second mile. If we lose thirty-five votes in the Congress, we'll be castrated.

Leaks. There was a top-secret document leaked from the Defense Department. One hundred and four copies of the document were xeroxed at Defense, forty-eight at State, eleven at NSC, and fifteen at ACTA [Arms Control Disarmament Agency]—and we have a lot of leaks out of the White House.

Summary. I like the way things have progressed. Today I've concentrated on complaints.

VICE PRESIDENT MONDALE: We've gone beyond the leak stage to a tidal wave where everything is in the press. There was a classified cable received the other day which carried the highest restrictions, and [William] Safire quoted from it the next day in paper. The president will always be the loser. We all lose. The system gets chilled. We must find the leaks and move them out. Must get much tougher on leaks but not develop a siege mentality.

JIM SCHLESINGER: You spend more time on detail than any president in our history. Suggest spend less time on detail, use time wisely.

CARTER: I don't have too many burdens on me. I do read memos and look at details.

BOB STRAUSS: There is no one for the Carter administration now. Business, labor, Hispanics, Jews. Some are not against, but not for us. Maybe the educators—NEA. We deserve better. We've sent a list of accomplishments to Congress, and they were astounded. We're positioning you in too many places where you'll come out a loser. I've never seen an administration with so many people willing to speak negatively about it.

DR. BRZEZINSKI: The basic problem is that the historical profile of this administration is not clear. In past, circumstances dictated a clear profile—the Depression, World War II, even Eisenhower. Society is more conservative, [whereas] your administration is innovative and creative.

CARTER: I recommend [Robert] Donovan's latest book on Truman. He suffered constant problems with staff, cabinet, leaks, press, Congress. In retrospect you can see what he was trying to do, but you couldn't then. We need to let the public know what we're trying to do in broad theme.

CHARLIE SCHULTZE: You're not tough enough on us.

PATRICIA HARRIS: We have an attitudinal problem. I don't find leaks accidental, but explicable and predictable. We've achieved many of your campaign promises. I agree there is a lack of a theme. Everything we've done is impersonal. Don't agree that people have become more "conservative"; they're less naive and more intelligent. Until the "Pogo" theme ["We have met the enemy and he is us"] is met, we may not get to real problem.

MICHAEL BLUMENTHAL: We have not clear enough focus on our priorities. Once you have stated our responsibilities, let us work on the details. You'll come out looking good.

CARTER: Direct communications are important, and you can always reach me within two hours. Most of time would rather you submit things that have impact on other departments to Stu or Jack. This saves my time.

BOB BERGLAND: Two motivating factors are faith and fear. Nixon used fear. I think we've gone the other way, extreme. We should be permitted to crack political heads. You should be more distant. People on the Hill respect you personally but have nominal respect for office of the president.

JUANITA KREPS: We can't solve all problems. Primary domestic goals are jobs and anti-inflation, and into those we must put everything.

RAY MARSHALL: Thought we had a good theme: government being responsive to the people and to simplify government.

JOE CALIFANO: Always will be plagued with leaks but can cut down on them. Important to have candid communication with you. Most of what we do now is highly sanitized. We need friends whom we can call in rough times and say "Hang on." Examples are Israel and Middle East; black community. They need to understand and trust you better.

CECIL ANDRUS: We've zeroed in on negative aspects today. There are successes. We live in Washington, where society plays in an international flavor, but most people in the country care about where you're going to put the highway or hospital. There should be more publicity in regional areas.

STRAUSS: Secretaries of state, treasury, and defense—the three most prestigious members of your cabinet—they're wrong to think they're free from politics—can help more than they're doing.

HAMILTON JORDAN: We've got an active Democratic president when the mood of the country is passive and nonpartisan. We don't have an obvious and pressing national agenda. The reason Jimmy Carter was elected is because people wanted better government and not more government. People want the programs managed better. Public consensus is that this president is not tough and we're not managing well. People on the Hill are politicians; lack of respect politically; no reward for friends; no fear of retribution. Problems are real and deep. If not confronted in three to four months, we cannot govern effectively for the rest of the term—and if we don't have successes in elections this fall, we'll have it twice as hard for the last two years.

CARTER: I feel like a referee between cabinet and staff. Ninety percent can be resolved by staff knowing cabinet better. Once I sign off on a policy, I expect you to carry it out.

STU EIZENSTAT: We have tried too much, too fast, too comprehensively, in foreign affairs and domestically. Moving too fast is contrary to Congress and to people around nation.

JODY POWELL: If you have a run-in with one another, don't tell whoever is around your office. Go home and talk to your wife. President Carter is the best example of letting things roll off his back.

JIM MCINTYRE: Congress has same desire for success that we do, and wants some successes for campaigning. We have mutual interest.

JACK WATSON: The administration is not perceived as tough. If this image of incompetence persists, we will be having the most competent president in history and having it said that his administration is incompetent.

MIDGE COSTANZA: Special interest groups aren't used to someone who acts on the merits of an issue. Right wing affects a lot of what we do. We should help those people who helped us.

CARTER: I wanted you here because I could see a deterioration of our esteem in the public eye, and I don't disagree with the public. What has bothered me is lack of cohesion and team spirit, which is almost inevitable. We have a damn good administration, a fine cabinet, a good staff. I wish you knew each other as well as I know you.

Although we had regular cabinet meetings, they were devoted almost exclusively to reports of activities with no opportunities for self-criticism. This was an extraordinary session, especially for its frankness and the preponderance of negative assessments. I concurred with the comments, except as indicated by my responses, and have no reason to change my opinion thirty years later. There is no doubt that this frank exchange resulted in better understandings among my White House staff and cabinet officers.

APRIL 18   I came over early to work on the Panama Canal treaties. We're two votes short, and we decided to go all out today to get Hayakawa, Abourezk, or Cannon. Talked to Fritz about the possibility of my having to go to the Hill in case we don't have the votes. We began to get good reports on

Hayakawa and Cannon. Abourezk is trying to blackmail me on energy legislation, but there's no possibility of that succeeding.

I talked to Howard Cannon, who's moving our way. He's concerned about the church attitude in Nevada and about the newspaper. I called Salt Lake City to get a report. [Mormon leader] Ezra Taft Benson is the only one who's spoken out against them, but as he [Cannon] pointed out, both Mormons and Baptists have people for and against the treaties.

Abourezk is demanding that I not let cabinet officers attend any congressional meetings behind closed doors. I can't police the House and Senate; I told him no. He said he hated to do what he had to do, and hung up. Later I got word from Prince Sultan in Saudi Arabia that Abourezk would vote for the treaties.

We were planning for massive violence in Panama if the treaties were defeated, but were fairly sure we would have all three doubtful senators with us, and that's the way the vote came out—exactly the same as on the first treaty.

It was a cliff-hanger for twenty-four hours. The Senate really performed well. I called the key members and congratulated them, made a statement in English and then one for Latin Americans in Spanish. Then called General Torrijos.

It was an interesting experience, getting the Saudi Arabians to help us with Abourezk, calling the local news editors and leaders in the Mormon Church to encourage Cannon to support us, and reading Hayakawa's book on semantics so I could discuss it with him to get his support.

Senator Hayakawa, former president of San Francisco State College, became famous and politically popular when he stamped out student demonstrations on the campus in the late 1960s. He was a noted semanticist, the author of Language in Thought and Action. *I read the book carefully and asked him to come to the White House to discuss it with me. Somewhat suspicious, he asked me a few questions about the text and was surprised and convinced when I answered them correctly. I think it was this encounter that got his vote.*

I never wanted to know exactly how the Saudis convinced Abourezk to change his mind.

APRIL 19   In retrospect the statements by Torrijos and CIA reports show that we were on the verge of a major military confrontation with Panama had the treaties been defeated. It would have debilitated our efforts in the

Middle East and Africa, SALT, and our relationships with the developing world. It's the most significant vote perhaps in my entire administration, and I think deserved the effort that we put on it. At the [congressional] leadership breakfast this morning the feeling was that with the remaining problems we have concerning SALT, energy, tax reform, welfare reform, civil service, airline deregulation, anti-inflation, Mideast arms sales, Turkey arms embargo, congressional relationships—every one of these difficult issues will be made easier by the result of the Panama Canal Treaty vote.

I directed Jody to issue a statement about Cambodia, condemning the genocide that's been taking place there. He'll work it out with the congressional leaders, and we'll do it this week.

The situation in Cambodia was both disturbing and confusing to us. Pol Pot and his Communist regime stigmatized urban dwellers and began moving them en masse into rural areas, where they were treated almost as slaves. Many died from starvation, and many were executed. Those of Vietnamese heritage were especially abused, and in January 1979 Vietnam military forces invaded Cambodia and took the capital, Phnom Penh. As we continued to study the issue, it became increasingly obvious that China was supporting Cambodia. Only years later did the full horror of Pol Pot's crimes become known to the outside world. When I visited Hanoi and Phnom Penh in November 2009, Pol Pot's leaders were on trial for their human rights abuses.

I had a meeting with about twenty top business leaders to encourage them to do something on anti-inflation. They were primarily eager to point out what other people could do, with most suggestions of benefit to their companies financially. I hope I convinced them that they needed to make a strong positive statement in complying with our deceleration proposal; hold down executive salaries; [mount] advertising campaigns on inflation; [have a] quarterly meeting with me; meet directly with labor leaders to seek out common approaches to inflation; and so forth. Almost everybody around the table was making more than $500,000 a year, and one or two almost $2 million a year, but they were not willing to put a freeze on executive salaries. I was disappointed.

My primary economic concern during the last two years of my administration was the threat of inflation—quite a different economic challenge than those we face in 2010, which include high unemployment, skyrocketing defi-

cits, and low inflation. Excessive executive compensation, however, is another problem that has persisted, but it is now perhaps one hundred times worse, given some of the extraordinarily high salaries and bonuses paid by banks and other large institutions. Boards of directors and managers have formed coalitions that perpetrate this practice, in effect bypassing any opportunity for shareholders to learn about or control excessive compensation. Many bonuses reward short-term gains rather than strategic improvements that benefit both the shareholders and customers.

APRIL 21 I wrote the owner, Joe Allbritton, a personal note about *The [Washington] Star* and its completely false and abusive article about Amy. He called back later to tell me he understood my problem and would do what he could to correct it.

The article said that a Secret Service agent had stolen a trophy and given it to Amy, who had finished last in a relay race. The story was totally false.

The Hornes [Billy and Irene Horne, personal Georgia friends] came by to try to talk to me about Taiwan. I told them it was a serious mistake for Taiwan to give my friends expensive things such as trips and it was inappropriate to act as an ambassador for me or for the Taiwanese.

As the prospects for normalizing our relationship with China improved (eight months later, we formally established diplomatic relations), the leaders of Taiwan began to pour favors—such as free trips, lodging, and expensive gifts—on our close friends and relatives in the hope that they would secure my continued support. Rosalynn and I finally forbade any immediate member of our family to be seduced, but there is still a small Taiwanese garden on Main Street in Plains, donated during that year.

Had lunch with Sam Nunn, who is really growing in stature. We discussed the Panama Canal treaties, a successful SALT agreement, the political aspects of Africa. He said he would make a moderate statement on Korea calling for a reduced rate of troop withdrawals below what I had advocated. This is what we have in mind.

MONDAY, APRIL 24 Met with Griffin Bell and his deputy, Ben Civiletti, concerning criminal justice reorganization proposals that we'll introduce.

There are 110 different agencies in the federal government now involved in crime control, with tens of thousands of employees and a confused jumble of responsibility. We'll consult with congressional committee chairmen, who are much more interested in protecting their turf than are the cabinet members involved.

APRIL 25 Jody's begging me to speak to the White House Correspondents' banquet. My preference is not to do so. They are completely irresponsible and unnecessarily abusive. I see no reason for us to accommodate them every time they want me to provide entertainment for a half hour.

APRIL 26 The seven major items that we'll be pursuing [in Congress] are energy, tax reform, civil service reform, Mideast arms sales, air deregulation, hospital cost containment, and Turkey arms embargo removal.

I called several members of the International Relations Committee. Every one of them thought our arms sales package was advisable, and they resented deeply the Jewish demands being put on them. Half of them said they would give me their support; the other half said they didn't know if they could stand up against the pressure.

APRIL 27 I talked to Cy about the *Washington Post* story that accused him of trying to block Brzezinski's trip to China, and about his apparent "four hours' waste of time yesterday" talking to Dayan.

I received the final report of the Commission on Mental Health. Rosalynn and her twenty members really worked hard and did a good job. They got an enormous amount of publicity on radio and television, also the news, and I'll do my best with their recommendations.

APRIL 28 Planted a cedar from Lebanon on the White House grounds and talked about how much that country suffered.

APRIL 29 There was some newspaper flap because they claimed I was the first president who had not attended the White House Correspondents' banquet. I was determined not to go. They almost exert blackmail on me to attend, but I am not going to do it in the future. I don't see how the White House press could be any more negative under any circumstances, and I'd rather show a sign of strength. And besides, I wanted the weekend off. Jody took my place and let them know basically how we felt about them, and other staff members who were there say I didn't miss anything. We didn't see any aftereffects from my absence.

MONDAY, MAY 1   I met with Begin for about thirty minutes privately. He's a small man with limited vision, and my guess is he will not take the necessary steps to bring peace to Israel—an opportunity that may never come again. I'm determined to put maximum pressure on him but will have to judge the political situation closely to maximize the possibility for success.

Then we had a White House reception, which I had opposed [for Begin]. I finally agreed to meet with two hundred rabbis to celebrate the thirtieth anniversary of Israel. Twelve hundred showed up, and Begin and I made somewhat emotional speeches to them, although brief, and then shook hands with everyone. The result of the whole affair was very positive.

It was on this occasion that I announced the formation of a commission to establish an American memorial for the victims of the Holocaust. Eventually we recruited thirty-four members, with Holocaust survivor Elie Wiesel as chairman. The commission's work led to the creation of the excellent Holocaust Memorial Museum in Washington.

MAY 2   Zbig and I talked about his trip to China: he would go as far as he could toward normalization without a final agreement.

I called Jim Fallows in and told him that I was not satisfied with the speechwriting quality. The Law Day speech for Los Angeles I've had to write almost myself, with assistance from Stu Eizenstat. The draft I got from Fallows was completely inadequate.

MAY 4   I made a major speech to the L.A. Bar Association—a hard-hitting speech, highly critical of the legal profession. It was patterned to some degree after the Law Day speech when I was governor.

MAY 6–7   Rosalynn went to Chicago to campaign with Danny Rostenkowski at a Polish-American Day parade. Danny said it was fantastic how well she did. Then she left to go to Costa Rica, to stop back by Guatemala.

MONDAY, MAY 8   Jody has caught hell from the press about his talk at the correspondents' banquet. *Time* had another bad article this week. I think the press deserved it.

Jeffrey graduated from college cum laude, which was difficult for him under the circumstances.

Jeffrey, our youngest son, was not the only family member whose life was disrupted during my time as president. The private lives of all three of our sons and their wives were strongly affected, both positively and negatively, by my political campaigns and official duties. They were integral members of my campaign team in 1976 and 1980, and I called on them, Rosalynn, and my mother to represent our family on many official occasions, both in our country and overseas. In addition, they received many invitations to public events and accepted the ones they considered either interesting to them or helpful to me.

MAY 9　Last night at a meeting of American Jews, Senator Lowell Weicker [Connecticut Republican] made a ridiculous statement accusing Brzezinski of anti-Semitism, paralleling him with Hitler, and accusing our administration of not being supportive of Israel. Senator Pat Moynihan and Bob Lipshutz responded. Shows how sick the situation can get.

MAY 11　The vote's to come Monday on Mideast arms sales, and the Israeli lobby is going to be working overtime all weekend.

MAY 12　We had a regular foreign affairs breakfast and discussed normalization with China this year. Our selling arms to Taiwan and our uncontradicted statement concerning a peaceful resolution of the P.R.C.-Taiwan issue would be mandatory.

MONDAY, MAY 15　Friday evening we only had forty-three votes. The lobbying pressure is the most intense that anyone had ever seen on the Hill. It's unbearable for some people, like [Frank] Church, Gary Hart, [William] Hathaway, Tom McIntyre, Birch Bayh, Wendell Ford, Floyd Haskell, and others—all of whom agree that the proposal should be approved, but can't stand up against the pressure.

The controversy was primarily over sales of F-15 aircraft for the defense of Saudi Arabia. (Aircraft were also to go to Egypt and Israel.) They were not in any way a threat to Israel, but the Israeli lobby, AIPAC (the American Israel

Public Affairs Committee), made an all-out effort to prevent congressional approval. A number of reelection campaigns counted on large sums of money and other support from AIPAC, and any member of Congress who contradicted the lobby was likely to be targeted for defeat in the next election. This was to be the first occasion in my administration when members of both the House and Senate had to withstand this political pressure, and I was determined not to lose. So far as I know, AIPAC's policies are always congruent with those of the incumbent Israeli government. It was and still is extremely effective, but the lobby has recently been challenged by a new organization known as "J Street," which seems to be dedicated to bringing peace to Israel and its neighbors as a means of supporting the best interests of Israel.

The Republicans really came through. I guess I changed ten or twelve votes. Had we lost this vote, my ability to make progress in Mideast peace would have been almost terminated because it would have proven that Begin's intransigence was what the Senate preferred, and moderate Arabs rebuffed. Senator Baker said after the vote that he was tired of being right. One of the most difficult votes was cast by Muriel Humphrey, who had replaced her husband in the Senate. Ribicoff made the greatest speech and also showed courage. I was proud of the Senate.

MAY 16   The aftermath of the vote was not as bad as I anticipated. We've been concerned this would be interpreted as a major defeat for Israel and a wedge between us and them, but it is a defeat for the Israeli lobby, who hurt themselves badly with their pressure techniques.

I decided that we would move on normalization this year if the Chinese are forthcoming, after the November election.

I met Jerry Rafshoon and asked him to be in general charge of all access to the media, help with speechwriting, and work closely with Jody.

Rafshoon had been my media advisor when I served as governor, as well as during my gubernatorial and presidential campaigns. This decision involved bringing him into the White House on a full-time basis. Like Jody Powell, he knew me intimately, and a special benefit was his knowledge of television, film, and the arts community.

MAY 17   I watched a demonstration of laser capability and was impressed.

MAY 18   Zbig left for China. I met with Long, Talmadge, and Ribicoff concerning national health insurance programs. They are concerned about the cost and bureaucratic problems of a more comprehensive health plan.

MONDAY, MAY 22   At Oak Ridge [Tennessee], I visited one of the gaseous diffusion plants and saw fluidized bed coal combustion demonstration—a lot of work on environmental quality.

MAY 23   It's going to be very difficult to hold to a $540 billion spending level with roughly a $37.5 billion deficit for 1980. I'm determined to hold as long as I can.

At a dinner with the National Alliance of Businessmen, one of them asked me my two biggest disappointments in the White House. I told him the inertia of Congress and the irresponsibility of the press. The evening news is a complete distortion of what happened, with each White House correspondent trying to be the cutest, and, with the exception of *The New York Times*, none of the newspapers make any effort to be accurate.

MAY 24   We had a reception for the USO with Bob Hope as guest of honor. Hope made a lot of jokes about being a Republican comedian. I teased him about how much time he'd spent in the White House, that Amy had invited him to spend the night with us and hoped that he could climb up the tree to get to his bedroom, and so forth. It was pleasant.

MAY 26   Zbig came back from China, overwhelmed with the Chinese. I told him he had been seduced.

MAY 27   We had a three-hour meeting with Gromyko, interrupted by a brief visit with Mrs. Rose Kennedy. He told me several outright lies, which concerned me very much, and had a sharp exchange with Cy afterward. I guess I should not have been surprised that he didn't tell the truth since he was the one who told Kennedy there were no missiles on Cuba when we had photographs of them lying there. He said that my figures were ten times too great; my figures are very accurate. He claimed there were no Soviet generals in Ethiopia. We monitored communications about General [V. I.] Petrov in Ethiopia once he got ill and they had to delay a military operation. The East Germans have helped train the Katangans, but he claimed he never heard of East Germans being in Africa, and so forth. I believe he left here knowing the seriousness of our concern.

As we sat across the table from each other, Gromyko continuously made false statements. I knew he was lying, and he knew that I knew he was lying. For him, the "truth" seemed to be whatever the Kremlin policy was at that time.

This was my worst week since I've been in the White House, although most things turned out all right. I've never been so tired as I was Saturday at noon. I just haven't had any time to rest or think.

MONDAY, MAY 29   I spent almost all day Monday working on the briefing books for the NATO conference and my bilateral meetings with the different leaders. The volume of study material for a conference like this is overwhelming.

On *Meet the Press*, Zbig was very abusive against the Soviets— excessively so—and I chastised him about it. He was quite upset. I don't want to create sympathy for the Soviets among the European allies, or to drive them away from continued negotiations with us on SALT and the comprehensive test ban. The saving grace about it is that Zbig's always had a reputation of being anti-Soviet. I told him our relationships with the Soviet Union were much more important than those with China as far as the safety of our country is concerned—the prevention of war—at least for the rest of this century.

MAY 30   After Fritz asked me to give him four days off, he took eight days, and I didn't realize he was going to be gone all the way through the NATO meeting when I'm completely absorbed with it and have no one to take care of Congress. We have a vote on hospital cost containment coming up Thursday with three or four votes short, and I just don't have time to take care of it.

The unity and harmony in NATO after twenty-nine years is very impressive.

MAY 31   The NATO meeting seems to be going well; all the press reports are highly distorted, particularly around Washington. I made the final analysis on what the meeting had accomplished. It was a very fruitful session — candid, common purpose, demonstrating unity, dedication, strength. We've considered the long-term East-West relationships, how to cooperate in development and production of common weapons, and committed ourselves to a fifteen-year long-term defense program.

JUNE 1   I spent a good bit of time studying the background on national health programs, which is going to be a very difficult political decision — contrasting the need to bring order out of chaos and avoid future waste of money by proposing any increase in health expenditures. There's an intense interest in this matter by a good many of the cabinet officers, most of whom don't want to see us make any moves on national health.

My challenge was when and how to phase in a comprehensive program compatible with budget restraints. Stu Eizenstat and his staff continued to work with congressional leaders who would be responsible for legislation when we decided to introduce it.

The IRS, after auditing our 1975 and 1976 income tax returns at an expense of thousands of dollars to us for auditor fees, finally discovered that in '75 Rosalynn and I owed $180 and in '76 we owed nothing but got an eight-thousand-dollar refund.

Cy Vance came by to express his deep concern, in a very friendly way, about the relationship between him and Zbig and the fact that we had too many voices speaking on foreign policy — myself, Jody, Zbig, Andy, and him — and it was creating confusion. I agreed with him and will take it up at the Friday morning breakfast and put a clamp on so many diverse voices.

Our weekly breakfast meetings gave me a perfect opportunity to ensure that all my key people participated in reaching a common decision involving international affairs. I wanted Cy to be fully involved in shaping any public statements, except those I personally approved (with his knowledge) for others to make. These would be rare exceptions.

JUNE 4   Sunday evening I met with Vance, Brown, Brzezinski, Jordan, Mondale, Young, and Turner on the Soviet speech. They went over the individual paragraphs — about sixty — that I had written, and the results were surprisingly harmonious. There were no material changes, and we decided to put the paragraphs in the most effective order. I think it will be a good speech, tough but well-balanced.

JUNE 7   Reaction to the Soviet speech [at the Naval Academy] was good. It will provide a benchmark for our decisions in the future, and we've sent a copy of the speech to the State Department and all our embassies with the points to be emphasized. Most reporters played it as tough, which is good. If it's tough at home and the Soviets consider it mild, that's perfect.

JUNE 8   New York City loans: we had an overwhelming vote in favor of it in the House, still have problems in the Senate.

JUNE 9   Castro called in our Latin American desk secretary and spoke positively about the Annapolis speech, but criticized the Zairian peace-keeping force.

JUNE 11   I'm discouraged at the differences I have with the Democratic Congress about their pressures to spend more money on defense, water projects, public works, transportation, education, health, labor—almost across the board. Public opinion will be on our side. It's going to be bad for us to have a confrontation, which seems to be inevitable.

Also, whenever I tighten up a little on the Soviet Union or Cuba, the liberal press erupts with a spate of criticism. This is happening after the Annapolis speech.

MONDAY, JUNE 12   I met with congressional leaders who supported us on water projects, and told them I made a mistake last year in not vetoing the final appropriations bill. We'll have three amendments: strike out eight of the dams I disapproved last year; limit new starts; require front-end funding in the budget of the total cost of the dam, not just a tiny increment to get it started.

JUNE 13   Castro has blamed all the problem concerning Cuba and the Shaba Province raid on Brzezinski. He's joined the Soviets and Israelis and everyone else—when they have a problem with me, to blame it on Zbig.

The Shaba Province of Zaire had recently been raided by separatists from Angola. The United States and Cuba blamed each other for the problem but eventually I helped orchestrate negotiations that resulted in a nonaggression pact in October 1979.

The Washington Post for ten days has kept the Castro question on the front page with headlines. AP, UPI, and *The New York Times* have ignored the subject. This is typical of *The Washington Post*—childish and irresponsible.

I met with Prime Minister Desai of India and emphasized Pakistan's concern about India's military strength and about Afghanistan. We discussed an Afghan-Iranian-India-Pakistani agreement to preserve peace in that area. Desai showed some interest in it. I asked him about an agreement also for that region against nuclear weapons. This may be a possibility. He and I discussed nuclear fuel for their Tarapur reactor, which will be prevented by American law unless India adopts safeguards. His position is that they have a long-standing contract that the U.S. can't violate and that India will only adopt safeguards if the major nuclear powers agree on a comprehensive test ban and drastically reduce our commitment to nuclear weapons.

These four countries are still closely and even more dangerously interrelated. The Taliban and Al Qaeda freely cross the Pakistan-Afghanistan border, Iran has become much more influential in the region since the U.S. invasion of Iraq and because of its threat to develop atomic weapons, and a long-term military standoff between the two nuclear powers, India and Pakistan, continues. After eight years of nonproductive military effort in Afghanistan, U.S. forces are now being greatly increased in the southwest region.

Paul Warnke and I decided to do everything to expedite the comprehensive test ban. We can go with a three-year total test ban and a limited number of monitoring stations—better than a five-kiloton threshold for five years. On SALT, the two remaining issues are the Backfire bomber, which is kind of superficial, and the real issue of new missiles. Warnke is doing an excellent job, but his somewhat pompous attitude aggravates the members of Congress, particularly people like Scoop Jackson who are pompous themselves.

Warnke was an experienced international lawyer who had served in the Defense Department under both Kennedy and Nixon, gaining special experi-

ence in arms control. He supported a strong U.S. defense capability but had been an outspoken opponent of the Vietnam War and of further increases in nuclear armaments or doubtful weapons like the B-1 bomber. On almost every issue, he was on the opposite side from Paul Nitze, and the two were lifelong adversaries.

JUNE 15 Still a serious problem with the American Jewish community. We're having to reach out for new contributors, which may be healthy if we can get the American Jews back and keep the new ones we obtain.

The Senate committee voted overwhelmingly for the New York City financial aid package.

JUNE 16 We went down to Panama City [to exchange the treaties] with a few senators plus David McCullough, who wrote *The Path Between the Seas.* I had five speeches to make while in Panama, a couple of which were in Spanish. Although we had typically exaggerated reports from the news media about violence and animosity in Panama, it was an extraordinary reception for both me and Torrijos. The news media even acknowledged between two and three hundred thousand people in the Cinco de Mayo Plaza.

JUNE 17 At breakfast I had thirty minutes privately with just Torrijos and an interpreter. I pushed him as much as possible on the democratization of the government of Panama, and he thought the new constituent assembly, being elected in August, would be a proper body to draft a new constitution and move toward Democratic elections. But he did not give me any firm commitment.

We took a helicopter trip over the canal. I spoke to about five thousand Americans about responsibilities of the Zonians and how we appreciated what they had done and the difficulties they envision from the treaties. I told them I was in the navy for eleven years, and they booed. I told them that we depended on the army to keep the canal open, and they cheered. Later the news reports said there were boos and cheers during my speech.

Back home Saturday evening, really tired but convinced that the Panama Canal treaties were worth all the effort. When Pérez returned to Venezuela, he said this was the most significant advance in political affairs in the Western Hemisphere in this century—maybe a slight exaggeration.

JUNE 18   Sunday afternoon we had the best party we've ever had—the Newport Jazz Festival twenty-fifth anniversary. About eight hundred people came, and we had a collection of jazz musicians that was really remarkable. Amy performed on the violin, which was a real hit.

MONDAY, JUNE 19   The cabinet discussed regulatory reform. We estimate that government regulation cost $100 billion this year—about 5 percent of our GNP. We're trying to cut down on regulation, having had remarkable success in the airline industry—maybe a good example.

JUNE 20   I listened to Rosalynn's speech and Q&A at the National Press Club. She did very well and got excellent publicity because she answered [Aleksandr] Solzhenitsyn's attack on the quality of Americans.

JUNE 21   I spoke at the opening session of the eighth General Assembly of the Organization of American States.

I tried to do everything possible to strengthen U.S. ties to Latin America, and the fact that I delivered personal addresses at the OAS annual assemblies was quite significant. Some presidents who succeeded me either ignored these sessions altogether or sent a cabinet officer for a brief appearance.

Had supper with Strauss, Bob Byrd, and our wives at Paul Young's restaurant, without any press notice. Rare to be out in a public place to eat.

JUNE 22   This morning was about as full and frustrating as any I've spent. I met with energy leaders in the House and Senate, then those from sugar-producing states, then Frank Church re the Turkey arms embargo, then Russell Long re labor law reform, then Speaker [Sayed] Marei of Egypt's congress, then Gerard Smith, who's on the way to South Africa to pursue our nonproliferation policy. After that I met with a large number of Greek American leaders. I presented my case, and they publicly disagreed. Many of them, after it was over, gave me a standing ovation, pressed my hand, and said that they were for me and understood my position. In the Arab arms sales, Jewish Americans worked to arouse the Congress. In this case it's the other way around: a few members of Congress trying to arouse the

Greek American community to oppose me when they have no real feelings on it. Obviously, a few of them do.

JUNE 23   I directed Cy over his opposition to change Soviet documents
on SALT from a treaty to an agreement. The Republicans would use the
two-thirds vote in the Senate as a way to obstruct the SALT agreement. I
might eventually go with a treaty, but I want to keep the option open.

MONDAY, JUNE 26   I sent word to the vice president to let me go over his
Israeli speech to be sure it's tough enough. Later met with Joe Califano.
What has existed in HEW is nauseating—lack of enforcement of the law
and no administration of very costly programs. One example is the student
loan program, where, before we came in office, HEW did not even send the
students a bill to repay their loans. In some colleges they have an 80 percent
default rate.

After my regular news conference I met with Ted Kennedy. Told him
that we were interested ultimately in a comprehensive health program,
but because of the constraints of inflation and the budget it would be years
before we could impose it. I'll make a speech on prevention of illness, and
perhaps Kennedy could have some hearings on this, along with cost containment later this year.

*At this time, I was working closely with Kennedy and the other chairmen
of the key committees in the House and Senate who would be involved in
health care legislation.*

JUNE 28   The Supreme Court ruled on the *Bakke* case, which is highly
exaggerated by the press in its importance. It pretty well confirmed present policies against strict racial quotas for affirmative action programs.

Had a private meeting with Clark Clifford, Sol Linowitz, Bill Heckler,
Irving Shapiro in the Map Room, where they gave me counsel on what I
should do as president. Clifford thought we ought to stay as aloof as possible from direct involvement in the Mideast negotiation—that it was a
losing proposition.

JUNE 29   Rosalynn, Amy, and I went fishing with Cecil Andrus off the
coast from Virginia Beach and caught three sizable tuna (25–30 pounds).

Amy reeled in one by herself. We needed the rest and spent an entire week at Camp David.

JULY 6   Went to Gettysburg, Charlottesburg, and Harpers Ferry to review my Civil War history. [Historian] Shelby Foote spent the night and made the trip with us. One impression I got from Gettysburg is that I should handle the federal government more like Longstreet advocated [circuitous] instead of the way Lee acted [frontally].

Like many southerners who had military training, I was familiar with more than a century of arguments about General James Longstreet's performance at Gettysburg. He demurred when General Robert E. Lee decided on a frontal assault by General George Pickett's men, quoting himself as saying, "General Lee, I have been a soldier all my life . . . and should know, as well as any one, what soldiers can do. It is my opinion that no fifteen thousand men ever arranged for battle can take that position." Longstreet advocated, in effect, a more circuitous attack. He carried out Lee's decision, however, with terrible losses to the Confederate army. This may have been the turning point of the war.

MONDAY, JULY 10   Cy, Fritz, and I had an extended discussion about the Mideast. Our conviction is that Israel does not want any peace agreement if it involves giving up part of the occupied territories; Egypt does want an agreement. [We discussed] the circumstances under which we would put forward a proposal and how we would deal with failure.

JULY 11   Had a meeting with Senator Dick Clark re farmers' attitudes. Their income, exports, and prices have improved dramatically since the passage of the 1977 farm legislation, but the more their prosperity goes up, the lower his and my popularity goes in Iowa.

JULY 12   Mother arrived to spend two or three days [with Amy] while we're gone [to Europe]. She's traveling a lot, making speeches throughout the country. She'll go to Italy to receive the so-called Ceres Award and to the Sahel area of Africa to assess the devastation of drought and starvation.

Mother made more than five hundred speeches after returning from the Peace Corps, never had a text, and sometimes shocked her audiences with the frankness of her extemporaneous remarks. We tried, unsuccessfully, to prepare some simple texts for her while I was president, because often she was considered by foreigners to be representing me. When she landed in Rome on this trip, she brushed aside a suggested arrival statement with the comment, "I've already thought of something to say."

Surrounded by news media, Mama declared, "I am delighted to be in Italy for three reasons: first, I understand you have just elected a fine young president whom I'm eager to meet, since my husband passed away [President Sandro Pertini was two years older than Mama]; second, as a Methodist and now a Baptist, my highest religious ambition will be realized when I meet the pope; and third, I have never met an ugly Italian!"

JULY 13   We departed for West Germany, with fairly low expectations concerning the economic summit. Schmidt broke protocol and met us at the airport in the late evening. He was in a good mood, stating that being chancellor would be very enjoyable without the Bundestag and without the press.

JULY 14   I then laid a wreath at the war memorial and went to the Rathaus (City Hall) and made a speech to a very large crowd. The mayor said it was half again as large as the crowd for the queen [of England], which surprised him; it was a friendly group appreciative of what the U.S. means to the independence and security of the Federal Republic. The older people were particularly emotional when I went down to shake hands with them.

JULY 15   We flew to the Rhein-Main Air Base in Frankfurt. Helmut and his top executives met me there, and he and I spoke to several thousand German and American troops. There's a growing interest in standardization of weapons. The German Leopard tank and their personnel carrier are both superior to our own; in other areas our weapons are better. We've wasted a lot of money in duplicating weapon systems, and ammunition is not interchangeable.

I flew to Berlin and went to the Kongresshalle, where I had the town hall meeting, answering questions for an hour. This was covered live by all German television stations. It went off without a hitch, and I did not make a mistake.

I was told in advance that, for the first time, this give-and-take session would be designed for the interests of Germans living on both sides of the Berlin

Wall. East Germans were quite interested in my foreign policy, especially as it related to promoting human rights and dealing with their Soviet occupiers.

We then drove back to the central part of Berlin. This is probably the largest number of people that ever came out, and they were friendly and even emotional. I sat on top of the car, and Rosalynn and Schmidt also waved to the crowd.

JULY 16   In Bonn, I went to the Palais Schaumburg for the economic summit, much better than the one in London last year—better preparation, more constructive, more specific, more thorough. It was primarily hard, tedious work. As in London, I had an advantage with the German public because I had two days of an official state visit and was better known. This may be the case in Japan next year.

It's always surprising how different the relationship among heads of state is compared to what the press reports. We feel like members of a fraternity; we share problems and political analyses, try to understand different national perspectives, and cooperate. We don't lecture each other or chastise each other, and there's a great mutual admiration and respect, at least among this group.

Jim Callaghan is a dove, even proposing that there might be some Yalta-type agreement with the Soviets to divide up our influence in Africa. I objected strongly to this and said I was not willing to accept any Soviet presence in Africa that was superior to our own in any country. At the luncheon on Sunday we worked up a commitment to cease all flights to and from a country that did not return hijacked planes or the hijackers to the country in which the crime was committed.

This was a somewhat cryptic entry that referred to a secret agreement among us to deal as a group with any threat of terrorism. Five nations, all enemies of Israel, had announced that hijackers of commercial airplanes would be received in their airports. Libya was the worst offender, so all of us sent independent letters to Mu'ammar Gadhafi telling him privately that if this should occur again, all air traffic to and from his country would be terminated. He canceled the practice immediately.

MONDAY JULY 17   The four Western Berlin powers discussed the possibility of meeting in some Caribbean hideaway with just our wives, no press coverage, and spend a long weekend together. When Giscard and I agree, we can prevail. There is a substantial difference in the attitude of the others toward us two presidents, compared to prime ministers. Germany and Japan are much more independent of the United States than they formerly were. This is good. When Giscard objected to trade negotiators bragging on themselves, Strauss quoted Dizzy Dean: "If you done it, it ain't bragging." The translators had a problem with this.

Rosalynn and I and Amy slept all the way home. They both did very well on the trip.

JULY 21   Cy sent me a report on the meeting in Leeds, where the Israelis again insisted that they would keep the West Bank. Kamal [Egypt's foreign minister] got emotional about the Israeli intransigence.

MONDAY, JULY 24   Congress is getting down to some important issues: airline deregulation; all four of our energy bills; Alaska lands; civil service reform; the Helms amendment on Rhodesia; Turkey arms embargo; and tax reform/tax cut—which is in the worst shape of all.

Talked to Cecil Andrus about our vacation. We'd like to go down the Salmon River and also visit some of the national parks which we've never seen.

I told Hamilton and Jody to tell the staff that anybody found using drugs of any kind would be gone. Jody called Jack Anderson to tell him about this action. Anderson said he's dropping the investigation, but if anything happens after my memo, *he's* going to reveal the names. Jody told him they would be names of people who used to work here.

Ham, Jody, Jerry, Strauss, and I had a thorough discussion about politics, and we all agreed that from now on one of the major considerations would be the 1980 elections. Most of our politically damaging decisions are over, barring some unforeseen developments. We'll concentrate on improving our relationships with the Congress, the press, the public, and with special constituency groups.

JULY 25   I'm pleased at the vote in the Senate to remove the Turkey arms embargo. Still have a fight in the House.

Russell and Carolyn Long came over. Russell's a master at circumlocution, but it's easier for me to understand him now than before. He hasn't quite made up his mind on natural gas, but he subtly puts in the sugar problem. He has a reverence for his father, and I think he has supported us on key foreign affairs issues because he thinks I'm a populist and foreign affairs don't concern him. It's hard to get down to specific agreements with him—in fact impossible—but after our discussions in the past, he's always come through and helped us. The evening was a success.

JULY 26   Got a message from U.S. ambassador [Richard] Gardner in Italy describing the superlative job that Mother did. She couldn't have had a better diplomatic success.

Had our second supper for news media leaders, this time [Jack] Germond and [Jules] Witcover plus the top commentators and executives in NBC: Fred Silverman, Les Crystal, John Chancellor, David Brinkley. We had a much better discussion than with the *Time* magazine people, who seemed to be more interested in polls and frivolous things.

JULY 27   Kennedy is upset because of the time schedule and some other factors involving the national health system.

I met with Democratic members of the Ninety-fourth Congress, who have been supportive but are restless. We had a frank discussion. Congressman Robin Beard was almost abusive when he said my low standing in the polls was caused by taking on controversial issues like the Mideast, Rhodesia, Panama, Turkey arms embargo, and that I was causing him and others some political problems. I told him I was sympathetic, but his re-election was not the most important thing in my life.

Ted Stevens came to give us his proposal on Alaskan lands. It's not adequate, but we might make some progress this year. We're in the driver's seat because we can control the amount of land tightly constrained by decisions in the Interior Department.

Had a thorough discussion with Schultze, McIntyre, Eizenstat, and Califano concerning health care. Primarily we agreed to accept Kennedy's principles but explain to him our interpretation of what they mean. Stu talked to Kennedy, who didn't like my decision. We'll just have to hang tough. I talked to Kennedy at length in the afternoon, and he insists we send up legislation before the election. I insist it will not be sent up because the Congress members couldn't stand up under pressure from the AMA, Hospital Association, Chamber of Commerce, NAM [National Association of Manufacturers], and others and it would take months to marshal support for a plan. I'll see how much of it we can send for Kennedy's consideration late this fall.

I met with Cecil Andrus, and we decided to spend three or four days going down the Salmon River on a raft beginning the twenty-second of August and then come back through Plains to the Georgia coast. This would be our vacation this year.

JULY 28 The most unpleasant experience of my presidency was a breakfast with Tip O'Neill, who was so emotional about Bob Griffin that he could hardly speak. When he did speak, he was extremely abusive toward me, Frank, Hamilton, and Jay Solomon [director of the General Services Administration], and did it in the most personal way.

I told the Speaker this man had caused me more trouble than any other personnel matter, that he was a good, decent, honest, competent civil servant but was incompatible with the two administrators who had been at GSA—one of whom had already resigned because of Griffin, and the other one who was threatening to resign. I did not assuage his feelings at all. He said that Frank Moore was barred from his office permanently, and that he would instruct his staff not to speak to Frank anymore. I think that this will be tempered in the future, but he was very emotional.

Griffin was Solomon's deputy, and he'd been retained by the GSA at Tip's insistence. Tip's threat was of great concern, because Frank Moore was in charge of everyone on my staff who worked with the Congress. Obviously, the Speaker was the key person in deciding whether my legislative proposals would be seriously considered in the House of Representatives. But Tip and I had a natural affinity, and despite the contentious conversation described in this entry, we were soon cooperating as before.

Mark Chona came by, representing Zambian president Kenneth Kaunda, to give me another cryptic message about a threat against me between the twenty-eighth of September and the second of October, concerning my number two and number four people. This is the third message that he's sent to me.

Kennedy had a press conference to blast us on the health care system. I thought he betrayed my trust because he specifically asked us to delay our press conference from Friday until later so he could study my proposal. Then without letting us know, he scheduled his own. In the long run, though, it helped because we've been dreading the liberal image of putting forward an expensive health care system, and Kennedy made us look responsible and conservative with our plan.

MONDAY, JULY 31   I had the weekly foreign affairs breakfast at Camp David Monday morning and decided to send Cy to the Mideast in spite of Sadat's rejection of any further negotiations, and suggest that the two men come to Camp David for a meeting directly with me. We understand the political pitfalls involved, but the situation is getting into an extreme state and I'm concerned that Sadat might precipitate a conflict in October, as he has hinted several times.

This decision would prove to be a turning point in our effort to remove the only serious military threat to Israel's existence, and to provide a blueprint for peace in the Middle East. At the time, prospects for progress were dismal. A Geneva conference in partnership with the Soviet Union was no longer feasible, Israel was embedded in obdurate positions regarding the West Bank and the Sinai, and Sadat was talking to other Arab leaders about military action. I was fairly confident that Sadat would cooperate with me, but I had no idea how Begin would react to my invitation. Also, we had not evolved a clear concept of the role we would play or what specific proposals to espouse even if a meeting should take place.

The Speaker said he was not going to vote on the Turkey arms embargo but hoped we won, and that the altercation with Griffin would not affect his relationship with the administration.

AUGUST 1   I had a briefing from Stan Turner re all the religious and ethnic groups than comprise Lebanon—their organizational structure, strength, strategy, and tactics.

Lebanon's culture and politics were so complex that I needed regular instruction, especially when some factions were either aligned with or deeply antagonistic toward Israel. Later, when Iran's government began coming apart and the Iraq-Iran war erupted, I also received intensive personal briefings regarding the teachings of the Koran and differences among the various Islamic sects.

Missouri senator Tom Eagleton [Democrat], who's been very helpful, advised me to end this year all proposals that had a liberal tint, and in the next two years spend time with a limited legislative program and an emphasis on the moderate to conservative image. This, of course, suits me fine, and it's compatible with what we've been planning.

We won the Turkey arms embargo vote in the House by a squeaker. It was hung up at 205–205 about five long seconds. It seemed like hours, and then Bill Lehman and Butler Derrick changed votes, and we won.

I finished the handwritten letter to Begin, which Vance will take to the Middle East this weekend, and I will do a similar letter to Sadat.

AUGUST 2   There are security leaks in the government relating to Nationalist China—we know they are there relating to Israel—and probably to some of the opponents of SALT, who are American citizens.

Some people within our administration had dual interests, and they considered it proper to leak secrets if it would help further their own special goals. Much later, in January 2009, when Presidents Clinton, George H. W. Bush, George W. Bush, and I met with President-elect Barack Obama, we all laughingly agreed that there was no way to prevent any secrets being shared with Israel if they were known by more than two people in the White House, State or Defense departments. I had the same problem with leaks by some in my administration who were intensely loyal to Taiwan, and others who were deeply antagonistic toward the Soviet Union.

At supper for *Washington Post* and *Newsweek* executives, I asked them an innocent question: if I had a major event to discuss with them off the record and in depth, with whom could I discuss it? It precipitated a one-hour argument among them, with Kay Graham and Phil Geyelin being eager to have a background explanation, and with Howard Simons and Ben Bradlee expressing some concern about it, along with Ken Auchincloss [managing editor of *Newsweek*]. I didn't push it. I just let them argue. They finally decided that Ben Bradlee would write me a letter with their answer. We have this relationship with *The New York Times* through Scotty Reston. He trusts us and we trust him to handle the information properly. The editorial policy of *The Washington Post* has been very good; the news policy has been abominable—and *Newsweek* is the most inaccurate periodical that I read. Maybe they'll improve.

AUGUST 5 Went to Norfolk Navy Base, my old home, to commission the USS *Mississippi*, a nuclear cruiser.

As newlyweds, Rosalynn and I had lived in Norfolk while I served on the old battleships Wyoming *and* Mississippi. *The crews on these ships were involved in the most advanced research in gunnery and fire control immediately after World War II, and I was electronics officer. The worn-out and leaky hulls were decommissioned soon after I served on them, and now one of the names was inherited by our navy's newest ship.*

AUGUST 6 In the evening we got word from Vance that Begin had responded enthusiastically, almost emotionally, in favor of the summit meeting at Camp David. Cy will now go to Egypt to meet with Sadat.

MONDAY, AUGUST 7 We've got a serious problem concerning energy legislation with the conferees unwilling to sign their own report! It shows the ridiculous childishness of Congress and their subservience to lobbying pressures.

Jody, Hamilton, Zbig, and I discussed the handling of the Mideast summit if Sadat agrees. It's almost impossible for me to restrain them blurting out the news, but I will try to honor the confidentiality Sadat and Begin and I agreed to maintain.

I had a third supper for news executives. We had the Goldensons (ABC), the Arledges (ABC), the Smiths (ABC), Barbara Walters (ABC), and the Wickers, Frankels, Smiths, and Restons from *The New York Times*. This was the best session we had, but they've all been good. During supper Brzezinski called to tell me that Sadat accepted the invitation to the summit meeting, and September fifth was the date he suggested. After the other guests left, I confidentially told Scotty Reston about our plans.

AUGUST 8 We began briefings with congressional leaders [regarding our Camp David plans]. I told them about my own initiative and the favorable replies from Begin and Sadat. The response of congressional leaders was positive, with the possible exception of Howard Baker and with the exception of Scoop Jackson. Howard was leaving his options open for criticism in the future. Scoop was reticent because he was in a one-person minority. President Ford when I called him was very supportive, as has always been the case.

We had a superb visit in New York. The bill signing [providing bailout loans] was a major political achievement, and we enjoyed my first Broadway play—*Ain't Misbehavin'*—in fifteen or twenty years.

AUGUST 9   Griffin Bell refused to go along with our negotiated agreement with the Maine Indians. I called Kirbo and asked him to consult with Interior lawyers.

After playing tennis with Dr. Lukash, we had a dinner with CBS officials, including Walter Cronkite and Carl Rowan. Cronkite is really a fine gentleman, one of my favorite people, my favorite news person.

AUGUST 10   Rosalynn left for Rome to attend the funeral of the pope [Paul VI, whose successor, John Paul I, served only thirty-three days].

Cy came back with a very happy, almost euphoric, report on his trip to Israel. When Cy met with Begin there was an instant acceptance of the proposal for the summit. Cy gave him permission to talk it over with Dayan—the only two who knew it—in the closed cabinet meeting.

[At Camp David] we'll ask religious leaders to set aside a week of special prayer, build a special prayer tent for Sadat at Camp David, use every influence we have to make it successful, not put a time limit on how long we stay there, have no press contact except minimal through one spokesman (Jody), and hold down expectations.

AUGUST 12   The State Department and the CIA are doing a psychological analysis of the key negotiators who will be at Camp David.

Compiled by historians, political scientists, and psychiatrists, these two briefing books covered the entire lifetimes of Begin and Sadat, including their formative years, role of parents, early political involvement, public statements, current political environments, and influence of families, friends, and allies. The briefing proved to be both interesting and valuable as I dealt with the two men under the tensions and stresses of difficult negotiations. One memorable difference was how they acted under pressure. Begin would resort to minutiae, arguing for hours about the meaning of individual words. Sadat tended to respond by generalizing about a proposal of mine and discussing its likely impact in broader realms, such as the entire Arab community or worldwide. Sadat cared little about semantics, while Begin seemed to have no regard for anything except his own people. At times, this let me correlate the different opinions of the two men, like intertwining the fingers of two hands.

Rosalynn made a fine statement in Rome, looked beautiful, and did a good job.

MONDAY, AUGUST 14   We got word that Israel was planning five new settlements in the West Bank, which is typical, and fired off a quick letter to Begin.

AUGUST 15   Begin sent a fairly contentious reply, saying they had called off the settlements until after Camp David, settlements had not been a problem between him and Sadat, they had a right to establish such military settlements, but Israel would do nothing to prevent success at Camp David.

I had a one-hour *Newsweek* interview, which was a waste of time. Ninety percent of their questions involved public opinion polls.

We had a meeting on the defense authorization bill, which should be vetoed because of its wastefulness. The Congress changed $5 billion of what we and the Defense Department had recommended, including $2 billion for an unnecessary nuclear aircraft carrier.

We had another dinner for media representatives including [Arthur] Sulzberger and [Abe] Rosenthal from *The New York Times*; [Robert] Mac-Neil and [Jim] Lehrer; Don Carter and [his wife] Carolyn; and [Marvin] Stone and [John] Mashek from *U.S. News & World Report*. These people represent responsible media where the emphasis is more on what an interviewee actually says than twisted interpretation. *The New York Times, U.S. News & World Report*, and the television interviewers all have this characteristic. This policy makes them fairly lonesome among news media.

AUGUST 16   I went to the CIA for briefings and made a speech to the employees. Most of them preferred to stay inside instead of coming out in the open where photographs could be taken.

AUGUST 17   I had a news conference, which everyone characterized as the best we've had. I felt relaxed and confident, a little aggressive.

AUGUST 18   Rosalynn's birthday. I gave her luggage, and Billy had arranged a party for our family when we got home to Plains.

AUGUST 19   I got up early, picked up Mother, and we went over to my farm to fish. We caught twenty-five or thirty very nice bream, and I thoroughly enjoyed spending two or three hours with my mama in the boat. She's in better spirits than I have seen her in the last fifteen to twenty years. Rosalynn and I went through the Plains business district shaking hands with friends, neighbors, and dozens of tourists. In the afternoon we had a softball game between my team (Secret Service agents) and Billy's (news media representatives). We won a very narrow victory—6–5—and arranged for a rematch on Sunday afternoon.

MONDAY, AUGUST 21–AUGUST 24   We went to Idaho and spent three days on the Middle Fork of the Salmon River [with our sons Chip and Jack]. It was among the best three days of my life. We were almost completely isolated from the press—Secret Service nonintrusive, caught a lot of fish, beautiful scenery, good companionship, good food. I had daily reports on international affairs. We saw mountain sheep, golden eagles, chukar, red grouse, and otters. The last day our boat caught fifty-nine trout. I used a fly rod and was really pleased to get back into that habit. Rosalynn will try it when we get to Wyoming.

We flew to Jackson Hole, Wyoming.

AUGUST 25–30   In Wyoming, we fished, sailed, rode horses, visited Yellowstone, and went to a rodeo. [I studied the psychological profiles of Begin and Sadat.]

AUGUST 31   [Back in Washington] I caught up with paperwork and prepared letters to senators re natural gas. I had lunch with [Hermann] Eilts and [Samuel] Lewis, our ambassadors to Egypt and Israel, to brief me personally on what to expect from the leaders of those countries. Both ambassadors report that Begin and Sadat are surprisingly optimistic.

I think we ought to move on Vietnam normalization. Ham feels that it might be a serious political problem, but I believe the country is ready to accept it now that they've dropped their demands for reparations or payments.

All the briefing books from the State Department, NSC, and CIA had set our expectations too low. I want to insist to the Middle East leaders that we resolve as many problems as possible at Camp David, not just come out with a declaration of principles leading to further negotiations. If we can't solve anything at this summit level, it's highly unlikely that foreign ministers and others can do so later on.

SEPTEMBER 2   I decided to go on to Camp David Monday and spend the isolated hours getting ready for the negotiations.

MONDAY, SEPTEMBER 4   This was a hurried morning, with everybody wanting to give me last-minute advice or information about the summit. I went over responsibilities of the coming week while I would be away: defense veto override, passing civil service and natural gas legislation. The rest of the day [at Camp David] I spent studying the voluminous notes, maps, past history of negotiations, psychological assessments of Begin and Sadat.

Throughout the many days of talks with the Israelis and Egyptians, cabinet members came to Camp David to discuss current issues. Fritz Mondale went back and forth to Washington and represented me in the White House. I was pleased to hear that we were making surprisingly good progress on a number of issues with the Congress.

I kept detailed written notes during all the discussions at Camp David (September 5 to 17), and from them I dictated entries in my diary a couple of times a day. Many of the scratched notes are available to scholars in the Carter Presidential Library.

Camp David, which is managed by the U.S. Navy, is a completely isolated mountaintop area of about 125 acres. In addition to swimming pools, bowling alleys, and tennis courts, there are eleven residence cabins and a large assembly hall, all named for species of trees. These sites are connected by wandering paths through the forest.

My early conversations with Begin and Sadat outlined the basic issues and differences with which we would be occupied during the remaining time together. After my entries covering the first two days I abbreviated those covering the remaining days as much as possible.

DAY 1, TUESDAY, SEPTEMBER 5   Sadat, on arrival at Aspen, emphasized that he was eager to reach agreements, total if possible, not just to establish procedures for future negotiations. He stated that Begin did not want an agreement and would try to delay as much as possible. Sadat said he would back me in all things and has a comprehensive proposal "here in my pocket" that would include establishment of diplomatic relations and end the boycott against Israel. He needed a rest, preferred my seeing Begin tonight, and wanted to meet me tomorrow morning.

I told him I would delay any U.S. proposals until after he and Begin explored all the differences. He said he would try to protect me by putting forward good proposals and make it unnecessary for U.S. proposals. I told him he needed to understand Begin's problems and attitudes. He seemed to be somewhat impatient of Begin, distrustful of him, determined to succeed, perhaps overly bold and inclined to acquire my partnership against Begin.

The next conversation was with Begin after his arrival—quite a different attitude. Begin was immediately interested in the techniques of Camp David discussion: times, places, how many aides at the meetings, and so forth. He pointed out that this meeting was historically unprecedented, that there had not been an agreement between a Jewish nation and Egypt for more than two thousand years. He said he wanted tonight to discuss Lebanon.

I told him we three principals could not expect others to settle major issues if we couldn't, that all the issues should be addressed at Camp David, and that Sadat had a concern about Begin's preoccupation with details instead of the major issues. Begin said, "I can handle both." Begin was amenable to my meeting with him tonight, with Sadat tomorrow morning, and then tomorrow afternoon with us three principals. He seemed eager to have aides participate as soon as possible.

My next meeting was with Begin at Aspen, 8:30 p.m., just he and I. I described my understanding of Israel's problems and positions, and the importance of the meeting. We had plenty of time, were isolated at Camp David, should not depend upon references of problems to subordinates to solve, we would have no bilateral secrets, and I would not give to Sadat or to Begin and Sadat together any U.S. proposals without discussing them first with Begin. We should seek complete agreement on issues or else define the differences; we could make unilateral statements in the final document on unresolved issues; the maximum interrelationship should exist between Sadat and Begin; I reserved the right and had the duty to put forward the U.S. position as a compromise, but without surprises. I emphasized our awareness that Israel's security was paramount, that he could not be satisfied with hazy guarantees.

I outlined the agreements between Sadat and Begin: "no more war" and my hope that Sadat would repeat this commitment; Israel must have security, including a military presence on the West Bank; there should be no independent Palestinian state; UN 242 applies to the West Bank, and although there were differences in definition, this includes withdrawal. There should be a phased implementation of some aspects of the agreement after two, four, or perhaps five years; Jordan and the Palestinians on the West Bank should have a negotiating role; an early warning system would be important, possibly including Israeli airplane overflights; and disputed areas should be demilitarized. There were differences between Egypt and Israel about the definition of Sinai and West Bank areas. They had agreed that the military government should be terminated and there should be a united Jerusalem.

Begin described again without modification his previous position on the Sinai, emphasizing that the settlements were important as a buffer between Gaza and Egypt. He wanted a complete agreement with Egypt at Camp David but first needed an agreement with the United States. We all need patience—not years, but perhaps a few months—to work out remaining differences. The Egyptians suspect Israel of deliberate delay, but this was not true.

Begin pointed out that Israel had never proposed a separate peace treaty with Egypt, but they did think an agreement on Sinai might come first and then later more complete agreement on the West Bank. The Sinai needed to be demilitarized, with three airfields kept for three to five years, then one or two under civilian control with Israeli right to use them.

I pointed out that this is not something we desired, but if both Israel and Egypt desired it, we would consider it favorably.

He proposed that the question of sovereignty on the West Bank/Gaza Strip be left open, and that Israeli defense forces would have to be kept there. He was willing to give the Palestinians full autonomy.

I pointed out that if he, Sadat, and I agreed on anything, we were strong enough to prevail even if others disagreed with aspects of a settlement. I had no objection to an Egyptian-Israeli treaty signed in the absence of other Arab nations, but it would have to include crucial elements in the West Bank/Gaza Strip. I said that Sadat would not yield on the Sinai settlements; I had tried unsuccessfully to get him to do so.

I emphasized that there should be no new settlements, and he disputed our long-standing position on this. He said that in pursuing Israeli settlements there would be no confiscation of land, and [that Israel] could be restricted to a military presence only in furtherance of the security force to be retained in the West Bank.

In general the conversation was discouraging. He simply repeated the old Israeli negotiating points, and I could find no inclination toward flexibility. At least I made the points clear that we wanted conclusions at Camp David and that we were going to put forward our own positions forcefully.

DAY 2, WEDNESDAY, SEPTEMBER 6 *Meeting with Sadat, 10:00 a.m.* I informed Sadat that I had met with Begin, the meeting was basically nonproductive, with former positions reaffirmed. It was important that we not bypass Begin or put him on the defensive. Unless our proposals were eminently fair to Israel, his ministers and the Israeli people would certainly support him if the peace talks broke down.

He responded that Begin was a very formal man, difficult to approach, and that he was bitter and inclined to look back in ancient history rather than deal with the present and the future. He said he would go to extremes in the Egyptian proposals in order to expose Begin, and that Camp David was inevitably going to be a trap for Begin.

I pointed out that Begin was a man of integrity and honor, with deep and long-standing opinions that were difficult for him to change. I did not want to cause anybody to be embarrassed or defeated, but wanted a positive result at Camp David that would benefit all parties involved.

Sadat said there were two points on which he could not be flexible: land and sovereignty.

I interrupted to ask how he assessed the difference between sovereignty on the Golan Heights and Sinai versus West Bank/Gaza Strip, and he said there was a difference. I asked him where he ascribed sovereignty in the West Bank/Gaza areas. He said among the people who live there—not either Israel or Jordan. He was not interested in a declaration of principles but wanted a firm framework for permanent peace and to deal with specific issues while we were at Camp David—then let the aides draft a peace treaty over a period not to exceed three months.

He brought up the question again of his disagreement with Begin on Egyptian strike forces not exceeding the passes as an example of Begin's distortions. He mentioned that an Austrian Jew named [Karl] Kahane and other major financiers of Israel were all concerned about Begin's intransigence. When Kahane visited Begin in his office and asked, "What do you want?" Begin placed his hand on the West Bank portion of a map and said, "I want this."

Sadat said he could not accept any partial agreement or a separate agreement with Israel. He could not isolate himself from the rest of the Arab world. He was a spokesman for all Arabs, and if he betrayed their trust in him, then Egypt would be isolated and the Soviets would win in the Middle East. He said he had a carefully prepared proposal to put forward, and read the proposal verbatim and said he would keep it as an Egyptian paper because he did not want me to be responsible for its wording. He would give it to Begin at our three-person meeting.

As he read the proposal, it was obviously very harsh and unacceptable to Israel. He said he was careful not to refer to the '67 borders. He realized that the Jews are great scientists, and that Israel already had nuclear weapons. The peace treaty should be signed three months from now. When he completed reading the Egyptian proposal, I told him this was too demanding to be accepted by Begin, his advisors, or the Israeli people. There had to be more flexibility than that. He said, "I understand that perfectly, and I have some extra items for the United States to propose."

He cautioned me not to reveal these to anyone, but said that he could accept some modifications [and then outlined them].

When I told him there had to be additional flexibility, he said, "Any interim agreement will be satisfactory with me. I can sell this to the Arabs. I have no fear of their displeasure, but the permanent agreement will have to include more completely the Arab provisions that I have described."

We then agreed to meet with Begin at 3:00 this afternoon. When I proposed that we meet with advisors and aides this evening after supper, he said his position should be assessed by Begin before aides were brought in. I told him I was sure the meeting this afternoon was going to be unpleasant and nonproductive, and we were better to include Dayan and Weizman. He finally agreed, with some reluctance, to meet with advisors tomorrow morning. He said he would present his written plan to Begin and me this afternoon.

My assessment is that Sadat feels Begin is hopeless. He looks for a propaganda victory at Camp David based on genuine proposals and principles, hoping that others in Israel or Begin's successor might be forced to accept the Arab position, which would be ostensibly endorsed by us.

Begin and Sadat, 3:00 p.m.   I met earlier with Begin to tell him two things: I had sent Assad a personal message calling for peace in Lebanon;

and for Begin to expect a very tough proposal from Sadat and not to over-react to it.

Sadat arrived, and I described the wide differences between them and called for both to be flexible. I asked Sadat to begin, and he asked Begin to do so. Begin said that the Israeli peace plan of last December was not final, but a basis for negotiations, and that differences are so broad that a few months of negotiation by technicians are needed, working five days a week. We agreed that, at Camp David, Saturday would be the only day we'd take off; except for religious services on Sunday and Friday we would work. Begin said we need to forget past differences. Sadat agreed.

I then asked Sadat to respond. He said we must seize this opportunity at Camp David and reach a firm framework for peace, not avoiding any controversial issues. This would outline the broad terms of a peace treaty, then aides could work out the details using directives from the top, in a month's time.

Begin made a comment that when the Catholics chose a pope, they said, *Habemus Papam*. He would like for us to say *Habemus Pacem*. Sadat said he hoped the spirit of King David, the great leader of Israel, would prevail at Camp David.

I outlined again in the strongest terms what I hoped to see accomplished. I reserved the right to put forward suggestions for resolution of differences. I hoped they would use me not only as a mediator but as a basis for proposals that neither of them could put forward on their own, and which neither of them could accept from the other nation but might be able to accept from us.

Begin said that the concept of a framework was okay, that Israel made a proposal in December and was looking forward to hearing Sadat's counterproposal. I asked Sadat specifically, "Are you willing to act in the administration of the West Bank and to conclude an Arab-Israeli treaty if Jordan is not willing to participate?" He said, "Yes, we are." I asked him if he was willing to negotiate a Sinai agreement at the same time that a West Bank/Palestinian treaty was negotiated. He said yes, but he would not sign a Sinai agreement before a West Bank/Palestine agreement was reached.

Sadat then began to read his proposal, requesting that Begin should not respond today but discuss it with his people first. Sadat read the very tough set of proposals, word by word. Begin listened without expression. There was some tension when he got through. I suggested to Begin that if he was ready to sign the document as presented, it would save us a lot of discussion and debate, and expedite a successful conclusion of Camp David. He said, after a few minutes of laughter, "Would you suggest that I do so?" And I said, "No, I think we both need a chance to discuss with our own advisors the terms of this proposal." There was a remarkable relaxation of tension. Both men appeared happy, friendly. We adjourned in good spirits, with Sadat and Begin patting each other on the back.

Later in the evening I met for an hour or so with my own advisors and staff to go over the meaning of Sadat's proposal and to discuss what has transpired so far. The general consensus was that Sadat's tough proposals had broken the ice and the meeting tomorrow between Sadat and Begin in my study would be the first real opportunity for an extended direct negotiation between Israeli and Egyptian leaders.

DAY 3, THURSDAY, SEPTEMBER 7   *U.S. and Israel, 8:30 a.m.*   [In attendance were] President Carter, Secretary Vance, Dr. Brzezinski, Prime Minister Begin, Minister Dayan, Minister Weizman.

I made the following points: Sadat's proposal is more rigid than I anticipated; the U.S. has not been active in the preparation of either [the] Israeli or Egyptian proposal.

BEGIN: The document smacks of a victorious state dictating peace to the defeated. Sadat was ill-advised to submit this document—not the basis for negotiations.

PRESIDENT CARTER: Sadat was reiterating established Arab position.

Begin then insisted on going through Sadat's paper in detail, refuting dozens of points. I tried to convince the Israelis that the Egyptian proposal included its maximum demands and to trust me and let me know what they actually needed for security and to comply with international agreements they had already accepted. Sadat had proposed minor adjustments in the pre-1967 borders. What did Israel propose? Expansion of settlements was the crucial issue.

CARTER: I believe I can get what you really need, but I don't feel I have your confidence.

WEIZMAN: We wouldn't be here if we didn't have confidence in you.

CARTER: You are as evasive with me as with the Arabs. The time has come to throw away reticence.

BEGIN: I will ask Sadat to withdraw the paper.

CARTER: Everyone should be free to submit anything they want. You can be equally effective by saying it is unacceptable.

BEGIN: Okay. We will not ask for withdrawal. We'll simply say it is unacceptable.

Begin and Sadat, 10:45 a.m.   At the very beginning I decided to stay present but withdraw from the discussion, and I looked at other papers or made notes so they would talk directly with one another.

Begin assessed the Egyptian document in great detail. He was brutally frank, discussing [every detailed issue]. Sadat could restrain himself no longer, and there developed a heated discussion. It took me fifteen minutes to assure them that neither side was insinuating that the other was a defeated nation. Sadat was particularly aggravated about Israel taking Egyptian oil.

Begin said that there were 24,000 square miles of territory, and that they were returning over 90 percent of it [the Sinai]. They were postponing the sovereignty question over the other 2,340 square miles [the Gaza Strip and West Bank].

Sadat said that we needed to discuss basic principles, not details. He said the phrase "inadmissibility of acquisition of territory by war" was one of those principles—words from the 242, 338 UN resolutions. He said the essence of the whole question was "You want land," and he used the example, very fervently, about the Israeli settlements in the Sinai.

Begin repeated that no Israeli leader could advocate the dismantling of those settlements, and there were four other conditions for the return of the Sinai.

Sadat pounded the table and said that the land was not negotiable, in the Sinai and the Golan especially. There were thirty years of desire by the Israelis for full recognition, no Arab boycott, security, and so forth. He was giving them all of that. He said, "Security, yes! Land, no!" In the Suez there was no restriction on navigation; in Tiran Straits the same. There would be an end to belligerency, but he could not continue the discussions if Begin continued to prove that he wanted land.

Begin said he had demonstrated his goodwill by changing a long-standing policy of Israel concerning the Sinai land between Eilat and Sharm al-Sheikh. Begin had agreed to yield all the territory in the Sinai to Sadat, and their continuation of the settlers' homes there was not an infringement on sovereignty.

Sadat then said that self-determination by the residents of the West Bank/ Gaza was the only measure of sovereignty. Sovereignty rested in them, and this sovereignty would ultimately lead to a Palestinian entity, or state. It should not be independent or have military forces. His recommendation was that it be linked to Jordan, and he was willing to put in the treaty on his word of honor that the Palestinians must choose a link with Jordan. Begin said that self-determination applies to nations and not parts of nations.

They then got sidetracked on a long discussion of Lebanon: Sadat saying that only Israel was causing the disturbance; Syria was in Lebanon because of Israeli influence on behalf of the Christians; King Khalid could force Syrian withdrawal in twenty-four hours, with only a message from Khalid to Assad.

After a temporary interlude Sadat said that many of the feelings he'd had at Jerusalem had been destroyed because "minimum confidence does not exist anymore since Prime Minister Begin has acted in bad faith." I pointed out that this mutual feeling of bad faith was something that I would like to correct; they were both honorable, decent, courageous men, and I knew them both well. Mutual respect was warranted.

The discussions were very, very bitter—open and unrestrained. I refereed and explained what was meant when it was obvious that a misinterpretation had occurred. Strangely enough, every now and then laughter broke out. Once, for instance, when they referred to kissing Barbara Walters in Jerusalem and what their wives might think, and when they argued about who was permitting hashish to go through the Sinai to Egypt or to Israel.

Before we adjourned I insisted on listing the remaining problems: demilitarization of the West Bank and Sinai and what "demilitarization" means; settlements in the West Bank and Sinai; the independent Palestinian state; Israeli defense forces in the West Bank and Gaza; termination of military rule; devolution of power; nature of the succeeding government; West Bank borders; whether they should be monitored and by whom; self-government for the West Bank/Gaza; Jerusalem—whether it should be divided or united, and how administered.

Sadat said he had no thoughts of a divided Jerusalem, but Begin said Sadat was advocating two sovereignties in different parts of Jerusalem.

Next, definition of "peace": end to the embargo, enhancement of trade, open borders and waterways, diplomatic recognition, ambassadors . . .

Sadat interrupted to say he had formerly been committed to open borders and full diplomatic exchange, but because of Begin's bad attitude he was reconsidering that position.

I mentioned next the refugees, how many would return to the occupied territories, what refugees would be permitted, and who would monitor this return; recommitment to "no more war"; Sinai airfields; definition of "Palestinian people"; participation by Jordan and other Arabs; delineation of early warning systems; borders, demilitarized zones; and mutual defense treaties that might involve the U.S.

They agreed this was a definitive list, we have a long way to go, but are making progress at least in defining issues.

They adjourned in a little strain. Begin said he had complete confidence in Sadat; Sadat did not respond.

Afternoon with me, Begin, and Sadat.   The meeting began very stilted, left over from tension of the earlier meeting. Begin said, regarding Sinai settlements and airfields: we should turn it over to the military leaders who will meet for a week or two, resolve the differences, and refer their answers back to heads of state for approval.

Sadat quickly said there was no need for this, a complete waste of time. There was no way that [General Muhammad] Al-Gamasy could negotiate for him. He was not going to yield on the settlements or have military presence on Sinai territory. Begin said Egypt would get the Sinai back in its entirety, but after two to four years. Sadat said no military control would be permitted; he would be glad to see Israel plow up the airstrips.

Begin asked about navigation in the Tiran Straits. Sadat said of course, he would keep his commitment. Sadat said he had tried to provide a model of friendship and coexistence for the rest of the Arab leaders, but instead he had become the object of extreme insult from Israel, and scorn and condemnation by other Arab leaders. This had worked against the others being willing to attempt peace with Israel. His initiative came not out of weakness but out of strength and self-confidence. He still had hopes that on Mount Sinai there could be a meeting of the three political leaders representing three religious beliefs. Begin agreed to the Mount Sinai proposal. He pointed out that in the thirteen settlements in the Sinai there were a total of only 2,000 to 2,500 people.

The discussion then deteriorated, and Sadat said a stalemate had been reached, and he saw no further reason for discussions to continue.

I then made an analysis of all areas of agreement and pointed out that the United States had a strong security interest in Mideast peace that could, if violated, cause a worldwide conflict. I would learn all I could from them through tonight, meet with the Egyptians and then with Begin, and prepare a summary of the status of the talks. I would make a strong proposal to both sides about what should be done. If they were willing to reject the entire peace agreement because of some minor difference, I didn't believe their people would accept it.

I pointed out to Begin that if [the reason for] his rejection of the treaty effort was the Sinai settlements (two thousand Israelis on Egyptian soil), this would be a serious matter. If he approved it, he could certainly sell it to the Israeli people. He denied this, saying there was no way he could sell a closing of the Sinai settlements to the Israeli people. It would cause the downfall of his government, which he was willing to accept if he believed in it, but he didn't believe in it.

I encouraged them not to break off their talks, to give me a chance to use my influence, to have confidence in me. Sadat reluctantly agreed; Begin agreed easily. We adjourned.

Meeting with the Egyptians, 10:35 p.m.

CARTER: You are probably discouraged. The main issue today was the settlements, and Egyptian and Israeli positions are incompatible.

SADAT: We have had three long sessions. I cannot compromise on land and sovereignty. Begin is not saying anything today that he might not have said prior to my Jerusalem initiative. The man is obsessed, a hopeless case—but we are not defeated. Begin is not ready for peace.

CARTER: Begin is a tough and honest man. He sees his proposal as a starting point, his control over the Sinai derived from wars which Israel did not start. His approach is more forthcoming than his Labor predecessors. On the settlements, Begin wants them to continue; our position is that they are illegal. On airfields, Begin wants some transitional control. This might be worked out.

SADAT: I had two discussions with Dayan and Weizman. Dayan said he was ready to abandon the Sinai for peace. Weizman said the Sinai settlements are only important as precedent for the West Bank. As to the airports, Weizman agreed that they are not needed. Begin wants the West Bank; originally he was prepared to turn over Sinai to me in return for the West Bank. I must have also resolution of Gaza/West Bank. I cannot do the Sinai alone.

CARTER: Sovereignty issues differ from Sinai, Golan, and West Bank. We should be able to work something out, but I don't agree about Begin.

He is an honorable man, tenacious. The Israelis want us to play a more active role. If Begin refuses to terminate Sinai settlements, then I am prepared to make that a test of Begin's leadership.

SADAT: I am willing to give two years to phase out the settlements.

CARTER: It is necessary to be flexible—two or three years.

SADAT: Okay.

CARTER: The U.S. will not negotiate for Syria or Jordan, so language on the West Bank has to be somewhat general. On the Sinai, it must be more specific because you and the Israelis can negotiate with each other.

SADAT: I agree to withdrawal to agreed security points.

CARTER: We must find a formula that both Egypt and Israel can accept. I intend not to fail.

Later I met Zbig on the path, and he pointed out that both Israelis and Egyptians were frustrated about whether any progress could possibly be made. The Egyptians are contemplating leaving because of the intransigence of the Israelis, primarily on the settlements issue. I asked them both if I could come to their cabin. Begin, because of protocol, said he must come to call on me. Sadat said OK.

DAY 4, FRIDAY, SEPTEMBER 8   *Meeting with Begin 2:30 p.m.*   We went into my little office, and I thought we had made real progress on several issues; when I had outlined them to both leaders, they had not disagreed.

Begin says there was one issue that caused him particular problems: the settlements in the Sinai. Not only Sadat but Vance, Brzezinski, and Mondale were insisting that the Israeli settlements be removed. He pointed out that the Sadat paper wanted to impose the harshest possible requirements on Israel.

I went through a detailed analysis of the difference between the two men: Begin's position was the same privately or publicly; Sadat approached it a different way. His proposal was not his final position; he knew that neither Israel nor the United States could accept it, but he had to get on the record a comprehensive Arab position. He had told me privately that some items would be handled in a more moderate way. Begin said he didn't understand how an honorable man could put forward one thing publicly and another thing privately.

I said there were some things that could be accepted reluctantly by Sadat if I proposed them. Begin discounted this statement, saying that

Sadat was demanding things that were unreasonable. He pointed out that even Brzezinski had called the Israelis "colonialists" in establishing settlements on the Sinai. Then he said, "I will never personally recommend that the settlements in the Sinai be dismantled."

He then turned to me and said, "Please, Mr. President, do not make this a United States demand." I said, "Mr. Prime Minister, we cannot avoid addressing the most contentious issues, and this is the one on which the entire Camp David talks have foundered so far. I can't let Sadat tell me not to discuss Israeli security on the West Bank. I cannot let you tell me not to discuss Israeli presence on Egyptian territory."

I told him I could not reach any agreement with him not to include the settlements, and asked him bluntly if he objected to our producing a U.S. proposal. He said he did object, that we would become the focal point of all dissension and disagreement. There was no likelihood that our proposal would be accepted by the Jews or Arabs, and those who disagreed would take out their displeasure against the United States. It might turn the entire Arab world against us.

I told him I was prepared to face that eventuality; the alternative might lead to war that would involve the security of my own country. Political considerations, even the loss of some friendships, were not my paramount concern.

I repeated that I saw no possibility of progress if the U.S. left the negotiations up to direct contact between the Egyptians and Israelis. I said we were going to present a comprehensive proposal. I would not surprise either Begin or Sadat, would go over the proposal when it is drafted tomorrow with Begin first, let him comment, then give it to Sadat.

That seemed to end the conversation. He asked if Rosalynn and I would join him and the other Israelis for the Friday evening meal, and I accepted.

Begin had requested that kosher meals be prepared for the Israelis, and our Filipino stewards learned to do this in our cabin, known as Aspen. Begin and his wife usually ate in their own cabin. When it was known that the prime minister would eat in the general dining hall, called Laurel, the stewards would prepare large quantities of kosher food for the Israelis who ate "proper" food when he was with them.

Meeting with Sadat, 4:05 p.m.   I outlined the problems we faced, and he assured me of his patience. I said we could not afford to have the American initiative rejected by both sides, and I had just come from Begin and was convinced of Israel doing so. I outlined to Sadat the exact procedure I would use and which I had also outlined to Begin. I told him the time for the three of us to meet was passed. I would like to spend the Jewish Sabbath working on a text, submit it to Begin and then to Sadat, receive their views, relay their views to one another, meet with Begin and then Sadat again, and continue that until I was satisfied that we had the best compromise proposal. And then we would all meet with our advisors.

He said, "This is a final meeting?" I said, "Well, it might be in more than one session, but it would be the final type of meeting."

He said if I did not include violation of land and sovereignty issues regarding Sinai and the Golan Heights, he would support any reasonable proposal put forward. He said we must not have a U.S.-Egyptian failure to agree. I told him I would honor his confidence, would be sure not to violate the rights of the Palestinians or the Arabs or put him in an embarrassing position, but he had to be flexible. He assured me he would be flexible, and he would stay with the negotiations as long as there was hope for success.

He said he had no objection to U.S. troops being in the Sinai. That was a private matter to be discussed between me and him. Whenever I wanted this to be done, if ever, to let him know privately, and he would make a public request that this be done.

He said he had no animosity toward Begin or the Israelis, did not want to put him in an embarrassing position, wanted success, and not a victory over the Israelis. And we parted company.

DAY 6, SUNDAY, SEPTEMBER 10

By this point, the tensions were so great I had decided to continue the discussions without any direct talks between Begin and Sadat. We planned a trip to nearby Gettysburg by all the participants who wished to visit the Civil War battlefield. I laid down some ground rules, including no discussion of the Middle East peace issues. I sat between the two leaders on the drive and attempted to orchestrate a harmonious conversation. At the battle site it soon became obvious that almost all the major participants were quite familiar with this crucial conflict, since most of us had been through advanced military schools where a detailed analysis of the tactics was required.

Rosalynn and I noticed that Begin did not participate in the excited discussion among the Egyptian and Israeli cabinet members, most of them former generals. When we arrived at the site of Lincoln's Gettysburg Address, however, Begin began to speak in a quiet voice. Soon everyone became deathly quiet, and we were transfixed as he quoted the words verbatim.

After this excursion, Begin and Sadat did not see each other again until after the consummation of the peace talks. I continued to go back and forth between the two sides, working with a single document, checking off items as agreed, and persisting until I reached acceptable compromises on all of them.

Meeting with Israelis after returning from Gettysburg, 4:03 p.m.

CARTER: I stressed how important the meeting is — the culmination of our efforts on behalf of peace. Consequences of failure are clear. We have put in writing a reasonable document for bringing peace to the Middle East. There are phrases in it which both you and Sadat will find difficult to accept, because of positions previously taken. My task will be hopeless if you now reject the language of UN 242. Sadat doesn't believe Israel wants to sign an agreement; that you really want land. I told him he was wrong. Finally, an agreement between Egypt and Israel would preclude a successful attack against Israel by other Arab countries, a major source of security, a first step to agreement with the Arab states. This document, which I am about to hand you, will be given tonight to Sadat. I would hope you will be flexible and minimize your proposed changes.

(Everybody reads the document.)

BEGIN: This may decide the future of the people of Israel. We ask that you defer giving this to Sadat. I will leave this room deeply worried because of some numbers in it.

CARTER: The document was not proposed with the idea that either side would alter it substantially. I have kept in mind what Israel wants and needs. I don't expect exact words to be settled tonight. Anything you and Egypt can agree on, we will welcome. I think I can get Sadat to accept this basic document.

We adjourned for supper and resumed at 9:35 p.m. and talked until 3:00 a.m. about the applicability of UN 242, the Straits of Tiran, the definition of "Palestinian," political and military control over West Bank, self-government, the right of return, and Jerusalem. I agreed to make nonsubstantive changes in the text before presenting it to Sadat.

DAY 7, MONDAY, SEPTEMBER 11   At 3:00 in the morning, I asked Dayan to walk with me. I described the problem: that Begin was unreasonable and the obstacle to peace; that I had doubts about his commitment to an agreement. I asked Dayan to help me with these phrases when the Israelis meet again. Dayan told me that the question of Sinai settlements was the most serious. I told him I would bring this up with Sadat, but I didn't think there was any chance for success. Dayan is a levelheaded, competent person, and if he or Weizman were prime minister, we could long ago have reached a resolution. It's becoming clearer that the rationality of Begin is in doubt.

We were extremely tired. Dayan only had one eye, and as he turned away to leave me he walked directly into a tree. He was shaken, his nose was bleeding, and I helped him to the main path. After a brief nap, I revised my master text while the issues were fresh in my mind.

Meeting with President Sadat, 10:30 a.m.   We were not quite ready with typed copies, so I probed for some flexibility re Israel's settlements in the Sinai. One proposal was to let Israelis live in one settlement, Yamit, acknowledging that it was in Egypt, just as Jews lived in Cairo or Alexandria. [Sadat] was adamant, saying that the homes could be left or destroyed when the Israelis withdraw. This single settlement was to be the most difficult but crucial issue.

When our document came, Sadat read it aloud and suggested several changes. The most troublesome was that if Israel had armed forces in the West Bank/Gaza Strip, Egyptian and Jordanian forces should be permitted. This is a major setback that has not previously been discussed. He insisted that otherwise we would be perpetuating Israeli military occupation. He was hesitant to put into the document a few other items like diplomatic, economic, and cultural relations with Israel, saying that if anyone else was prime minister he would do it, but with Begin he was not willing. We had quite a discussion about Jerusalem. He then said he would let his legal advisors go over the document and we would get together tonight.

With the exception of the armed forces question, very serious, the changes he suggested were modest. Cy is convinced that his [Begin's] legal advisors will have many technical proposals because they are known as the worst nitpickers he knows.

Meeting with Weizman and General [Nadav] Tamir, late afternoon. I asked Weizman to outline to me the status of negotiations between him and Gamasy on military arrangements concerning the Sinai. He did so and said the primary problems are airfields along the Israeli-Sinai border. The primary one the Israelis want to keep is Etzion, because it's near Eilat. Sadat is only willing to let them have this for three years; they want it longer. Israeli general Tamir, who's looked upon as an almost unreasonable hawk, said that joint Israeli-Jordanian patrols might be beneficial along the Jordan River and even south of the Dead Sea, going down to Eilat. Weizman said that he was having a hard time finding a place to park all of the U.S. military equipment that they had got and were getting, including tanks and airplanes. Weizman didn't think we were going to get any document signed at Camp David.

Cy called during the meeting to say that the Egyptians requested a twelve-hour delay so Sadat could spend more time with his advisors. This is a bad sign.

My next meeting, about 8:00 p.m., was with Dayan and [Attorney General Aharon] Barak. I was quite sleepy, since I had not been to bed much in the last thirty-six hours. I found Dayan to be a little more optimistic but willing to accept failure rather than yield completely on the Sinai settlements because of political considerations in Israel. This also would set a precedent for full withdrawal on the Golan Heights. This is what we've long suspected, but the Israelis have never admitted any of these things. I guess it is a sign that they now are more trustful of us.

I outlined to them the consequences of failure. They informed me that Begin was not going to reject the paper out of hand but would have several levels of action: acquiescence in an issue; approve it, but get cabinet and Knesset confirmation; disapprove it, but let the Knesset make the ultimate decision. Dayan suggested I proceed with a proposal Sadat might accept. At least it would clarify the issue.

DAY 8, TUESDAY, SEPTEMBER 12   *President Sadat, 10:30 a.m.* Sadat was in a heated discussion with his advisors on the porch and got here about five minutes late. He was sober and concerned.

I told him I was increasingly troubled about the entire Middle East with the threat of the Soviet Union, South Yemen, Afghanistan, Ethiopia, Libya, Iraq, Syria, and possibly Sudan. It was imperative that he and I begin resolving those more serious issues. Therefore the successful resolution at Camp David was imperative. I pointed out that he had five divisions lined up along the Suez, and a relaxation of tension with Israel would let everyone know that those forces were available to fight Egypt's battles.

He was also concerned about the overall Mideast position. He said it was apparent that the Israelis were not going to negotiate in good faith but were trying to prove to the Arab world that they could twist and control us. It was imperative that the Arabs give us their confidence and support. The American document as drafted would cause grave doubts among the Arabs of our intentions and would weaken this key link to our own security and prosperity in the future.

I reminded him that the words used to describe Palestinian rights and borders were his own words evolved with us at Aswan, and with Peres in Vienna concerning borders. He acknowledged this but seemed inclined to back off from that wording. I pointed out that our word of honor was at stake; after reaching an agreement with him on these two issues, I had let the Israelis know we would stand by these words. For me to reverse myself was unacceptable.

He said the document must be something that he and I could both accept, and which the Arabs in other countries could accept even with reluctance. I pointed out that he had already crossed the bridge of Arab displeasure when he went to Jerusalem.

We were both quite concerned with the attitude of each other at this point. I told him we would try to incorporate as many of their ideas as possible. Where they would be unacceptable to the Israelis and/or to us, we would have to reject them. We could turn toward more general language if there was a deadlock, but it was imperative that there be a commitment to continue the discussions.

I then described to him our language, which has not yet been revealed, on the West Bank settlements: they should not be expanded or the number increased.

I pointed out the difference in leadership. He was a strong and courageous leader in the forefront of a movement toward peace, but restrained by his advisors' concern about the rest of the Arab world. In the Israeli delegation it was just the opposite: Begin's personal courage and integrity was unquestioned, but he was wedded to past positions of himself and his party. He was the obstacle to progress, and his advisors were more forthcoming.

I told him we had to delay some questions: permanent borders in the West Bank; permanent status of the Palestinian Arabs; permanent status of Jerusalem. Palestinian Arabs might after five years — if there was a genuine self-government and genuine autonomy — prefer, with Israeli and Jordanian withdrawal, to keep the interim government intact. He said he would keep an open mind about it and accept that possibility in the language to be drafted.

Sadat and I were both relieved at the end of the conversation, compared to the first half hour, when it was obvious that he might refuse to sign anything other than his hard-line Arab paper. I'm a little too influential on Sadat when we are together, and I hope that his attitude when he left will be maintained. His advisors always try to harden his position to accommodate the feelings of the Arab leaders in other countries.

After this conversation with Sadat, I went back to my cabin and looked again at the detailed maps of the Middle East I had been studying for the last few months. All of a sudden, I felt fairly confident that I could get both leaders to agree to a general proposal that could resolve all the long-term differences concerning the Sinai, and also provide the basis for a future treaty between the two nations. The only exception was the Israeli settlements, which remained a crucial problem. Within about a half hour, I had jotted down my thoughts on a yellow pad.

President Sadat, about 4:30 p.m. I went over and met with Sadat. I only had a rough scratch copy of my concept. He read it over carefully and made only two suggestions for changes, involving the width of the demilitarized zone and the delay in implementation of the agreement after it was concluded. I agreed to have that typed up, make one copy, and let him look it over before it was submitted to the Israelis. The meeting lasted about fifteen minutes.

Meeting with Prime Minister Begin, 8:00 p.m. As we prepared to eat supper at Laurel, Begin said he wanted to see me as soon as possible for the most serious talk we had ever had. I tried to induce him to wait until tomorrow after the drafting session, but he insisted.

He opened by saying that this is the most serious talk in his life except one with his idol, Jabotinsky. He went into an impassioned speech about the use of the words "inadmissibility of acquisition of territory by war" and

tried to rationalize why, although it's in the text of UN 242 that his government adopted and repeatedly confirmed as applicable, he was unwilling
to accept [it]. He said Israel could not agree to any document that included that phrase, and he would not sign it. Then he spent the rest of the
evening talking about settlements in the Sinai. At the end he said if they
can't reach an agreement, we might issue the following statement: "We
had met at Camp David, and Israel and Egypt appreciated the invitation
they had received from the United States." Or we could just list all the
items on which we did agree and disagree.

He repeatedly claimed that he would like agreement, but the people
of Israel and their will must be represented. I pointed out that I had seen
public opinion polls every two or three weeks where a substantial majority
of the Israeli people would be willing to accept a peace treaty with an end
to the settlements, the removal of settlements in the Sinai, and the yielding of substantial portions of the West Bank now under the Israeli military
government.

It was a heated discussion, unpleasant and repetitive.

I pointed out that he was willing to give up a demilitarized zone of
forty kilometers along the Sinai border; no attack forces through the
passes; free use of the Suez Canal and the Straits of Tiran; peace with
their only threatening enemy; full diplomatic recognition and an end to
the boycott; economic cooperation; a chance to negotiate with Jordan and
others for a comprehensive peace settlement; ability to keep adequate security forces in the West Bank/Gaza Strip; and an undivided Jerusalem—
he was willing to give all these to keep a few settlers in the Sinai.

As he left, he said Israel didn't want any territory in the Sinai or in the
West Bank—"for the first five years!"

*After these intense confrontations with both leaders, I decided to hold on to
my draft agreement regarding all outstanding issues on the West Bank and
Gaza and to concentrate on negotiating details of an agreement regarding the
Sinai. I would work directly with the Egyptian Osama El-Baz and the Israeli
Aharon Barak, who seemed to have the most confidence of their leaders.*

DAY 9, WEDNESDAY, SEPTEMBER 13   After a very satisfactory meeting with
Barak and a very unsatisfactory meeting with Osama, I asked Osama if Sadat was reversing himself. Osama finally admitted that he had not discussed
the issues with Sadat. I told him to go and let Sadat know I wanted to see

him tonight, to see if he wanted to deliberately cause a deadlock. It was quite early, but they sent word back that Sadat had already gone to bed.

In the meantime I went to thank Begin for their very constructive attitude today—the first time I ever felt the Israelis were really trying to resolve difficult problems. He said he would like to withdraw any mention of settlements from the major document. I told him that would not be reasonable.

DAY 10, THURSDAY, SEPTEMBER 14   I walked for an hour with Sadat. I complained about the adamant attitude the Egyptians had taken yesterday, and asked Sadat to be more flexible on the West Bank and Gaza. We discussed the questions of Jerusalem and self-determination. I reminded him that we had worked this out together at Aswan, and he said it could be in the implementing section of the agreement. He was interested in having an international highway connect the Sinai and Jordan near Eilat and was willing to have the Etzion air base used for the supply of Eilat so long as it was operated by the Egyptians and not the Israelis.

Later, Dayan and Weizman came by. We discussed the entire Sinai question. It ultimately resolved into the same subject—the settlements near Gaza. I told them I would draft language letting this be a matter open for negotiation, to be resolved during the three-month period.

I drafted a new Sinai settlement proposal and took it to Sadat. He immediately responded that there were preconditions: the airfields not being used for military purposes, and the settlements. He would negotiate when— not if—the settlements should be withdrawn. I discussed with him the procedure to be followed if the Israelis won't agree on the settlements issue in the Sinai, and he said he would like to sign the document anyway, because it described his proposal. I discussed the same question with Dayan, who said he would like to see us prepare a paper describing the items on which agreement was reached and not reached, so that the ten days of negotiation would not be in vain and the world would know what differences remain.

DAY 11, FRIDAY, SEPTEMBER 15   I met in my cabin with the American delegation and decided we should spend Friday getting the last proposals from the Egyptians and Israelis, spend Saturday drafting, and Sunday adjourn, issue a joint communiqué, and put an embargo on further public statements until noon Monday. I handwrote this message, and Fritz delivered it to Begin and Sadat and they both accepted it.

Then I began a meeting with Secretary of Defense Harold Brown. After fifteen or twenty minutes, Vance walked in with his face white, saying that Sadat had decided to withdraw completely from the negotiations and leave Camp David.

Sadat had abruptly decided that our discussions would never yield an acceptable agreement and asked for a helicopter to take him to the airport in Washington. This was one of the worst moments of my life. I went to my bedroom, knelt down, and prayed, and—for some reason—decided to change from my sport shirt and jeans to a suit and tie.

I went immediately to see Sadat, who was on his porch with a group of people, including five or six of his ministers. He and I walked into his cabin. I explained to him the serious consequences of his breaking off the negotiations: it would damage severely the relationship between the United States and Egypt and between him and me; he would violate his word of honor to me—the basis on which Sadat and Begin had been invited to Camp David. He was adamant.

I pointed out that the Sinai language was completely compatible with what he desired, that we were making good progress on the West Bank and Gaza, that difficult issues in the general framework were nothing new to the Arab world, that Sadat had crossed those bridges (and displeased the rejectionists) when he visited Jerusalem and made his Aswan and Vienna statements, that an acknowledgment of defeat would now be the worst of all worlds for him—with his own people, with the Arab world, with the general international opinion, and certainly with me and the American people. I told him that he had to stick with me.

He was shaken by what I said, because I have never been any more serious in my life. He said that the reason for his decision to quit the negotiations was that Dayan had said the Israelis would not sign any agreements. This had made Sadat furious. It would leave the Egyptians vulnerable if he signed with me and the Israelis withdrew. Subsequent negotiations would provide the Israelis with an opportunity to say, "The Egyptians have already agreed to all these points; now we'll use this as a basis for future negotiations."

I thought very rapidly and told him that he and I would have a complete understanding, specifically in writing, that if the Israelis rejected either document then none of the proposals of the Egyptians or us would stay in effect. Sadat said that if I would give him the statement I had described, he would stick with me as he had promised. We shook hands. I left.

Friday evening Fritz and I went over to join Sadat for a social visit, and [Sadat agreed, in effect, to] confirm again all the promises he's made to me.

I told him that if we signed agreements here, although he's never asked me for anything, I'd like to do something for the Egyptian people. After a brief discussion we decided what they needed most was food, namely wheat and corn. I told him that on my own initiative I would meet this need.

We then watched the [Spinks-Ali] heavyweight fight and enjoyed it. We put in a call for Muhammad Ali and finally talked to him about 1:30 a.m. He said he was going to keep the championship for six months and then retire. I talked to his ten-year-old daughter and invited her to visit Amy. Ali was excited to know that Sadat and I had watched the fight.

DAY 12, SATURDAY, SEPTEMBER 16   I got up early and listed all the things that the Israelis could possibly use as arguments on the Sinai document, and then went for a walk with Sadat. I told him I needed him to give me some flexibility on the Sinai settlements. He said he would be willing to accept UN forces in the settlements area, agree not to dismantle the settlements, be flexible on the time of withdrawal of Israeli settlers—but he could not be flexible on the principle of their withdrawal.

I decided to discuss the settlements issue with Dayan, and other matters concerning the general framework. The negotiations are primarily about whether UN 242 applies to all aspects of the discussions in the West Bank. On the West Bank settlements, he thought we could handle it with no new settlements, but that's something I would have to work out with Begin. He said that Begin felt somewhat excluded, and this evening I should meet with just Begin and Barak, since Weizman had met with Sadat this morning.

Weizman walked down to Aspen with me and [gave me] his overoptimistic reports to Sadat of what Begin will do—and vice versa. When I have to tell them the harsh facts, I'm the villain. So we have three opinions in the Israeli delegation re settlements: Begin wants no withdrawal; Dayan is willing to withdraw after an extended period of time; and Weizman, Sadat, and I all agree that the settlers should be withdrawn.

At lunchtime, Sadat delivered to me papers saying that Weizman's report was completely erroneous. They would not negotiate, and all agree-

ments were null and void unless Israel agreed ahead of time the settlements would be withdrawn.

Meeting with Sadat and El-Baz. Got the final papers typed up just
before that. The meeting was constructive. I went over my draft on Sinai
with him, and also the general framework. I outlined all the advantages he
would derive from a success at Camp David; everything that he would
lose if we failed.

To summarize: Begin agrees for the first time to accept 242 in all its
parts applicable to all its neighbors including the West Bank and Gaza; to
end the Israeli military occupation; to accept the principles of withdrawal
on the West Bank/Sinai; to recognize the international border; to withdraw
all armed forces and ensure that Egypt would exercise its full sovereignty
over the entire Sinai; to consummate a full peace with demilitarization,
limited elements, and economic benefits. In the West Bank the Palestinians would have "full autonomy" up to the 1967 lines for five years; before
the five years expired there would be a permanent resolution of issues involving the West Bank/Gaza. It would have the first Palestinian self-
government ever, with a very strong local police adequate for them to care
for their own affairs. The Israeli military government would be replaced by
self-government. The Palestinians would be a separate party to the negotiations on government, refugees, and displaced persons. I would try to get
them a chance to ratify the agreement concerning all these things, giving them in effect a veto, and let them be part of the negotiation of a
Jordanian-Israeli treaty. Palestinians [are] to have their legitimate rights recognized by Israel, and to solve the Palestinian problem in all its aspects.

The Israeli security presence would be immediately and demonstrably
reduced, as agreed. We would have a framework that would apply to all
the confrontational states, fulfilling Sadat's promise for a comprehensive
settlement. Peace would release Sadat's armed forces for other, more useful
purposes than confrontation with Israel. This entire Camp David agreement would demonstrate finally that Sadat's historic Jerusalem initiative
was successful. There would be no new settlements in the West Bank/
Gaza Strip. It would reestablish firmly Sadat's leadership politically and
militarily in the Arab world. It would demonstrate U.S.-Egyptian harmony. There would be a commitment not to use a threat or use force in
relationships. It guarantees future U.S. involvement in the talks. Israel, for

the first time, has recognized and accepted the UN Charter—something they had always refused to do in the past.

On the Sinai we are substantially in agreement. Sadat was willing to say "international waterway" relating to the Strait of Tiran. He insisted that full diplomatic relations and open borders would apply only when the interim withdrawal was complete. He accepted the question of settlers by expressing the Egyptian and Israeli positions and then to let the Israelis decide—to go ahead or to fail. Sadat was in a sober and constructive mood.

Meeting with Begin.   Also Dayan and Barak, the two best ones he could have brought. After I described all the benefits to Israel if the Camp David meetings were successful, Begin responded, expressing deep concern about all the compromises they had had to make. We then discussed many issues, including the site of negotiations, Sharm al-Sheikh, and earlier diplomatic relations. Then we had to focus on settlements, and Begin was shouting words like "ultimatum," "excessive demands," and "political suicide." I proposed having the Knesset make the final decision on settlements, and he seemed to agree. I said if the Sinai agreement was approved with the exception of the settlers, it would be a great step forward, and they agreed.

On the framework for peace in the West Bank/Gaza, there was a surprisingly amicable discussion. We went over every word. I insisted the Palestinians should participate in the determination of their future, and Dayan proposed, "We'll let the Palestinians join the Jordanians during the negotiation of the peace treaty with Israel." We agreed on all principles and provisions of UN 242 being applicable. On West Bank settlements, we finally worked out that no new Israeli settlements would be established after the signing of this framework. The issue of additional settlements would be resolved by the parties during negotiations. On refugees, they finally agreed to take into account the United Nations resolutions.

We then agreed to abbreviate the Sinai language and not modify it [until] later, depending upon the Sinai agreement.

After the Israelis left, we discussed the progress, and both Vance and I believe that it was far more than we ever anticipated. The only remaining major issue, barring some unforeseen development, is on the withdrawal of the settlements, and this will be submitted to the Knesset for a decision before the peace treaty negotiations commence in the Sinai. And there's at least an equivocal attitude toward this on the part of Begin and Dayan. Weizman will strongly support approval. We'll use our political influence in the American Jewish community and Congress and in Israel to get them to approve this language; so if the Knesset acts favorably, Camp David will have been a complete success.

DAY 13, SUNDAY, SEPTEMBER 17   Sunday morning I went to discuss the final draft of the Sinai agreement with Sadat. He does not want to meet in El Arish as long as it is under Israeli control. He was pleased with the submission of the settlement question to the Knesset prior to negotiations. He said that he would make these concessions, as he calls them, only if the Palestinians can participate in negotiations on the Israeli-Jordanian treaty, and he would like to delete the entire paragraph on Jerusalem!

We had promised Sadat a letter stating that the U.S. supports the UN position on Jerusalem. The Israelis went into an absolute furor, stating they would not sign any document if we wrote any letter to Egypt on Jerusalem.

After redrafting the entire Sinai document for perhaps the eighth time, I discussed the remaining issues with the Israelis, especially the settlements. Dayan was absolutely certain that the Knesset would *never* vote for withdrawal of the settlers prior to negotiations on the Egyptian-Israeli treaty. I emphasized that equivocating about details of the Sinai agreement was inappropriate because the major issues, except the settlements, had already been resolved.

It was obvious to me that Weizman was eager to submit this issue to the Knesset and was going to fight hard for it as a campaign effort. He apparently looked on this prospect with relish as a way to become prime minister.

I went over the entire draft of both documents again, trying to discern some means to resolve the remaining issues. Now the Jerusalem issue seemed fatal. I read texts of what our UN ambassadors ([Charles] Yost, [Arthur] Goldberg, and [William] Scranton) had said concerning Israeli occupation of East Jerusalem—all very critical of Israel. I asked Barak to go over the text of our letter, and he was as adamant as the other Israelis on this point, saying that it was hopeless.

Earlier, [my secretary] Susan had brought me some photographs of myself, Sadat, and Begin. Sadat had already signed them, and Begin wanted me to sign them to give to his grandchildren. Susan decided to get the actual names of his grandchildren. I personalized all the photographs and walked over to Begin's cabin with them. He was sitting on the front porch, very distraught and nervous, because the talks had broken down at the last minute. I handed him the photographs. He took them and thanked me, then looked down and saw that his grandchild's name was on the top one. He called her name and then looked at every photograph individually, repeating the name of each grandchild that I had written on it. His lips trembled, and tears welled up in his eyes. He told me which was his favorite grandchild. We exchanged a few words in an emotional way about grandchildren and war.

This proved to be a turning point in Begin's attitude toward reaching a peace agreement, from obdurate objections to an obvious desire to be successful.

Then he asked me to step inside his cabin for a few minutes and closed his door. He told me he was sorry, but there was no way he could accept the Jerusalem letter from us to Egypt. I told him we had submitted a new version of it, told him to read it over, and call me and let me know what he decided. I could not go back on my commitment to Sadat to write the letter, and the entire peace negotiations depended upon my keeping a commitment once I made it. I was willing to let the talks fail, rather than to violate my promise to Sadat. Begin said he would call me in about fifteen minutes, and I went back to Aspen, very dejected.

Sadat was there, and we went over the entire text of the Sinai and the West Bank/Gaza framework. Sadat made a few minor suggestions, which I knew would suit the Israelis. Begin called to let me know they would accept the Jerusalem letter, which removed the last major obstacle with Israel! [Or so I thought.]

In the meantime, we were making tentative plans to go back to Washington. A thunderstorm was taking place. As we were making final plans for helicopters, or automobiles if the rain didn't stop, Barak came over with Begin's draft of the West Bank and Sinai settlements language, which was completely unsatisfactory and in violation of what they had agreed the night before. I told Barak that both letters were unsatisfactory and to take them back to Begin. Barak agreed with me that the language that I reread to him from my documents was accurate.

In a few minutes Begin called to tell me that he could not accept my language on the Knesset because it put the Knesset under a threat. I was adamant, and he finally agreed to say that the peace negotiations would not commence until after the Knesset voted on the issue. I wrote it out on a piece of tablet paper and gave it to Fritz to go and let Sadat and Begin check the language.

A few minutes later I went into the front room, and Fritz was still there, saying that Begin was at Sadat's cabin and he hated to interrupt him with a message. I decided to go myself, because I thought it was crucial for me to intercede if they were arguing. It was the first time they had been together for ten days, except the trip to Gettysburg.

I ran out the front door, and Begin was just leaving Sadat's cabin in a golf cart with Barak. Begin was quite happy, saying they had had a lovefest, and that Sadat had agreed to Begin's language on the Knesset vote. I knew this was wrong, and every time I asked Barak to tell me exactly what Begin and Sadat had said, Begin would interrupt him and not let him reply. Finally, I asked Prime Minister Begin to please let Barak answer. What Begin had asked Sadat was: "Do you think the Knesset should be under pressure when they vote?" Sadat said, "No, I don't think the Knesset should be under pressure." This was the total conversation. Begin therefore assumed that he could write any language he wanted concerning negotiations versus the Knesset vote.

I asked Barak to come with me. Begin excused him, and we went to my cabin. I checked their language very carefully and finally thought of a way to say it that was in the final letters and satisfactory to both Begin and Sadat. Susan typed it up. I wrote a note to all our people: "This is the exact language to be used. Do not use any other language on or off the record." We firmed the issue up, literally at the very last minute. Only then did I realize that we had finally succeeded.

Just changing the language from a positive option ("the negotiations will commence when . . .") to a negative one ("the negotiations will not commence until . . .") was enough to convince Begin. There were several other semantic differences concerning territory or describing people, and I agreed to exchange letters with the two sides. Although there were some differences in nuance, both leaders agreed to accept this exchange as adequate. In addition to the official "framework," these ancillary letters expressed either Begin's or Sadat's personal interpretation of language. I induced both men not to let any minor differences deter them from signing the overall agreement.

Sadat and Begin met me at the front of my cabin, we embraced enthusiastically, went to the helicopter, and flew to Washington together.

I had placed a call to President Ford before we left Camp David, and all three of us talked to him on the phone before we landed at the White House and had our press conference.

It was the first time I've ever been glad to leave Camp David and come back to Washington.

Other notes. I called Senator Byrd and Tip O'Neill about addressing a joint session of the Congress Monday evening, and then called Howard Baker to let him know that we had better news than anyone had expected. I did not go into any detail about the agreement.

The exact wording of the Camp David Accords and the large number of separate letters were much too complicated to explain in a press conference or in a conversation with congressional leaders. For instance, Begin insisted on referring to the occupied territories as "Judea and Samaria," and to the Palestinians as "Palestinian Arabs." We three leaders and our close advisors, of course, had the texts in all three languages, which permitted some semantic flexibility. Fortunately, we all agreed that the English version would prevail.

I told Rosalynn earlier not to return to Camp David from the White House, where she had attended the Rostropovich concert with Mrs. Begin and the two ambassadors' wives.

Mother called from Little Rock—almost as excited as I've ever heard her. Quite emotional about what had been accomplished [at Camp David].

We had a superb team effort. I never saw any evidence of jealousy or disharmony among us. Our discussions were freewheeling. I worked closely with Cy and got my best advice from him, Fritz, and Zbig. We stayed cooped up in the small room in Aspen, sometimes for hours and hours. Often late in the afternoon we would break away for a couple of sets of tennis—Cy, Fritz, Ham, Zbig, Dr. Lukash. When Rosalynn was not there with me, I ate at Laurel with the American group. Sadat always ate in his own cabin. Begin ate frequently at Laurel with the Israeli group. I went swimming two or three times; long walks with Sadat, bicycle rides with Rosalynn, and walking from one cabin to another was the exercise that I got. Some of the most unpleasant experiences of my life occurred during these thirteen days. Also, of course, at the end, one of the most pleasant achievements of my life.

We had not planned such a long and isolated stay. In addition to helping me with the peace talks and entertaining about 130 people at Camp David, Rosalynn had to go back and forth to Washington to fulfill our scheduled social obligations at the White House. When appropriate, Mrs. Begin accompanied her.

The easy, gentle atmosphere was very helpful. It kept tensions down. We tried to impose a dress standard that was informal: I wore blue jeans most of the time, sometimes slacks and a sweater; Sadat wore very attractive lounge suits for walking and for negotiating; Begin almost always wore a suit, white shirt, and a tie.

On one of my walks with Sadat, we discussed that my being from the South gave me a sensitivity to the problems of the Middle East. My region had suffered, lived under an occupying power, for generations had been torn apart by racial prejudice, and was resurgent. The South had overcome its problems, and we might be able to do the same thing for the Middle East. It was an interesting conversation.

Sadat's book, *In Search of Identity*, is a remarkable expression of a highly idealistic philosophy, particularly during the time he was in prison. I came to respect him more and more as time went on.

Begin had his strong points, too: intense feelings, courage, sure knowledge of history, a clear concept of what he wanted, and in the end a surprising flexibility that made it possible for us to achieve success. He had a realization that a majority of Israelis, other than his old revolutionary friends, would support what he was doing. I read that Israeli teachers who were out on strike, having heard about the Camp David agreement, voted unanimously to go back to work.

MONDAY, SEPTEMBER 18   We planned our strategy on contacting the other Arab leaders. I discovered that [King] Hussein had canceled his visit with Sadat scheduled for Morocco. I was quite concerned and told Cy I wanted him to go to the Mideast to talk to Hussein and Fahd. [At the request of Fahd] Assad agreed to see Vance.

Late in the afternoon it became obvious that Begin was making an ass of himself with his public statements. Sadat, of course, was very responsible and moderate. I talked to both of them in the presence of several people and repeated my request that they not aggravate the situation by making crazy statements. It had very little effect on Begin, who continued to do so until he finally left the United States. They should have left a nursemaid with him — either Dayan or Barak or Weizman. This makes it very difficult for Cy's mission to be successful, and for Sadat.

In the evening I addressed the joint session of Congress, and there was bipartisan support and gratitude. Older members of Congress said they had not seen such a response since Churchill spoke to the Congress during the Second World War. This was appreciation to all three of us leaders, not, of course, just to me.

I had Fritz talk to Sadat about any items to put in the speech that would help him with the Palestinians or the Arabs. He [Sadat] said the only thing he wanted was not to aggravate the Jews, who are quite excitable and unpredictable people. He was completely self-assured and confident. The most emotional part was when I quoted Jesus, "Blessed are the peacemakers, for they shall be called the children of God." In Israel the headline was "Blessed are the Peacemakers."

SEPTEMBER 19   I met with the Senate and the House leadership for breakfast. Re energy, Byrd said that we'd get between fifty-five and sixty-five votes on recommittal. Turned out later that we got fifty-nine. Tip said he would like to make the House vote on all [energy] bills at once, which would help us greatly if we can get it through the Rules Committee. Discussed taxes. I expressed my thanks for the civil service reform vote. Airline deregulation coming up on Wednesday; the prospects look good. I outlined the campaign efforts that I, my family, and my cabinet were making. I repeated to them that inflation was the worst problem, and that the House and Senate had to cooperate with me, business, and labor in holding it down.

I had an interesting meeting with Ambassador Ch'ai Tse-min, from China. There are obvious compatibilities between the two [nations] if we want to normalize relations. The key issue from our side is that we will continue to sell defensive weapons to Taiwan, and we would make a public statement that the issue should be settled by peaceful means. We would expect China not to contradict this in an aggravating way.

Later Begin came by, and I gave him a little plaque that said SHALOM Y'ALL. In the privacy of the Oval Office, with Rosalynn present, I told him how extremely damaging his statements were, and asked him to restrain himself. He made a noncommittal reply. A flap developed between us on the West Bank settlements. He's trying to welsh on the deal.

Although I was very tired, we had a meeting with media representatives from the *Los Angeles Times* plus Bill Moyers, and I gave them a personal account of what occurred at Camp David.

SEPTEMBER 20   Henry Kissinger called and said he found it very disturbing to make the statement that he had in mind for me. Then said that not only did I do as well as he could have done, but that he had to admit that I did even better. We laughed about it, and he said he thought the entire Camp David document was superb.

SEPTEMBER 21   Zbig suggested that the vice president go to New York to talk to Begin to calm him down, but I decided not to send him. He [Begin] has already done enough damage to the peace treaties—denying the agreement we worked out Saturday night, on which I have a complete record and a perfect memory.

The understanding Sadat, I, and our American team had was that Israel would build no additional settlements during our negotiations about Palestinian autonomy, which we needed to complete successfully before we could consummate the Camp David Accords. Begin later claimed that he meant that no settlements would be built just for a three-month period. There was an honest difference of opinion, but it dealt a very serious blow to the Middle East peace process.

I met with Geraldine Ferraro, Democratic candidate in the Ninth District in New York. Very attractive; facing a difficult battle in an Archie Bunker–type community.

The House passed airline deregulation overwhelmingly.

SEPTEMBER 22   I had a message from Sadat saying not to worry about reaction from the other Arab leaders; he was not worried about it.

Met with a group of editors attending a seminar on Latin America and got the same basic question I had from several others: for handling major problems re labor or Latin America, would I take a group to Camp David and stay there until we solved it? I told them no; in the future, my preference was to enjoy Camp David with my wife, not with [a labor leader, like] George Meany or [Frank] Fitzsimmons, or with [Nicaraguan president Anastasio] Somoza.

SEPTEMBER 24   During the afternoon and night I worked on the Sinai settlement: wrote out all of the points of dispute for the peace negotiations using large maps of the Sinai. I decided we ought to move rapidly. The Knesset is likely to vote within the next seven days.

We watched Vladimir Horowitz on a live broadcast from New York and called to congratulate him.

MONDAY, SEPTEMBER 25   The judgeship bill has passed; we need to set up an unprecedented screening procedure, because we have more than 150 federal judges to choose.

At the cabinet meeting we discussed the '78 elections. I, my family, and the cabinet will participate in over one thousand key elections between Labor Day and Election Day.

SEPTEMBER 27   The news came that the Knesset voted to approve the Camp David agreement and remove Israeli settlers from the Sinai. This was a remarkable demonstration of political courage by Prime Minister Begin, who had to go against his own previous commitments and against his closest friends and allies. I really think a lot of him after that vote but anticipate being aggravated again as we start on the West Bank.

SEPTEMBER 30   I had an interesting meeting with Gromyko. I described my desire for better relations, et cetera. He responded at length: our relationships had gone down lately, but public statements were better; the Soviet Union was blameless; all problems were American; no Soviet intent to interfere in our relations with others (meaning China) provided there was no threat to the Soviet Union; we didn't recognize the importance of the Soviet Union; the Camp David Accords contributed to danger in the Mideast; they were against separate deals; the Israelis won everything, Sadat lost everything; the Soviets want stable peace, legitimate rights of the Palestinians, and Israeli rights, but Israelis were working against their own rights.

Strangely, all this sounded reasonable compared to a year ago— apparently a pro forma Soviet political line.

I outlined our SALT position, as far as I'm going to go. The primary questions are: how many air-launched cruise missiles per bomber; range limits; time for Soviets to dismantle excessive missiles. My feeling was that Gromyko responded favorably.

Afterward he and Cy had lunch with me, one of the best meetings I've had with a foreign leader. Gromyko seemed to want my advice on where we should go from here. No posturing or polemics on his part. I recognize their problems re potential nuclear adversaries—ourselves, Britain, France, and China—whereas we face only Soviets and perhaps to a tiny degree China.

At the time, Andrei Gromyko was, perhaps, the most experienced diplomat in the world. He had served as the Soviet ambassador to the United States and the first permanent representative to the United Nations. He was then foreign minister for twenty-eight years and also an intimate confidant of a long series of Soviet leaders. There was never any doubt that he could speak with absolute authority for the Soviet government. He rarely smiled and was widely known as "Mr. No" because of his generally negative response to proposals from any foreign source. Like other Soviet leaders, he always spoke in Russian when discussing official matters, but in private conversations with Rosalynn and me, he spoke perfect English and could be charming and humorous.

OCTOBER 1   We flew to the Kennedy Space Center in Florida, on my birthday, [for an award ceremony.] To meet the first [American] man in space [Alan Shepard], the first to go around the earth [John Glenn], the first to land on the moon [Neil Armstrong], and see future plans was a very thrilling experience for me, Rosalynn, and Amy. They gave me a space photograph of the Sinai, with a battle quote on it. One of the emotional experiences was when we gave the Medal of Honor to the widow of Virgil Grissom [the second American in space, killed in 1967 in a prelaunch training mission].

OCTOBER 3   I had a meeting with the Democratic leaders, and my public works veto cast a pall over everybody. Later I met with Republican leaders.

I was determined to control excessive spending to prevent further inflation, but the public works bill had been filled by members of Congress with their pet local projects. This particular legislative process was almost sacrosanct, and my veto was a shock and serious aggravation to them. The top leaders were determined to override my veto, which required a two-thirds vote in both House and Senate.

Kirbo spent the night with me, and we discussed handling 150 judicial appointments that will result from new legislation.

OCTOBER 5   I made sixty telephone calls and got word we had won the public works veto with a margin of fifty-three votes, almost unbelievable. Tip O'Neill came by, was quite chagrined, saying I was guilty of overkill, that we had it won all the time. We later got their vote counts, and they thought they had it won until the day before. In the last part of the meeting we relaxed, and as we approached the elevator we embraced, pledged our lifetime friendship and cooperation.

OCTOBER 8   We attended the Leontyne Price concert in the White House. She's by far the most accomplished singer we've ever had.

OCTOBER 10   At my news conference I was asked about the Soviet defector whose girlfriend claimed he was paying her five thousand dollars a month for sexual favors. I told them I disapproved because this kind of payment was highly inflationary! The CIA's paying him a standard fee for consultant services.

I spend all my time calling members of the House and Senate on key legislation.

OCTOBER 11   I've been dreading meeting with Senator Byrd since he got furious about my successful fight against a veto override. He had been tearing up my letters and giving my emissaries a hard time. After I said I had confined my efforts to the House because he had me beat in the Senate, we both relaxed.

These days I'm signing a lot of legislation, now that I've shown I can sustain difficult ones such as public works and defense. Members of Congress now work avidly to eliminate objectionable features, when in the past they've often ignored my position.

I met with editorial cartoonists, who gave me a book of my face by more than a hundred of them—interesting, humorous.

Lunch with Senator Adlai Stevenson, very disturbing. He was almost completely negative about himself, me, my staff, the House, Senate, and politics in general.

OCTOBER 12   We enjoyed having John Travolta with us last night. He's a delightful young man, twenty-four years old, possibly the most popular young movie actor in the country, and all of us just enjoyed talking to him about his own life. He was quite at home with us.

I met with Long and Ullman to go over the tax bill. I told them they would have to comply with my total tax cuts, drop accelerated depreciation and capital gains indexing, clean up deferral of capital gains at death, take the best of both bills on minimum tax, have equitable distribution of capital gains cutbacks, delete tuition tax credit, and so forth. They were sober, argued somewhat, but they know I'll veto the bill if it's not acceptable.

I signed a bill that will give us twelve inspectors general in as many agencies, appointed by me, confirmed by the Senate, protected by the Hatch Act, responsible to detect and root out waste, mismanagement, corruption, fraud.

We had the opening ceremony for the Egyptian-Israeli peace talks, adjourned, and negotiators went with Cy Vance to Blair House to conclude a treaty.

Lunch with Rosalynn. CBS is doing a special on her. Her duties in some respects equal or exceed my own: meeting with groups; campaigning for Democrats around the country; pursuing mental health; relationships with the elderly; volunteer groups; urban renewal — plus all the White House receptions and parties.

Spent time with Scotty Reston on a mood piece re what we've accomplished the first two years and how I feel about the future. I was upbeat, but he said I looked tired. I told him since the Camp David meetings began I had no time off and the frantic final days of Congress were burdensome, but I enjoyed it and felt good.

OCTOBER 13   Had a delightful signing ceremony for the civil service reform bill. Everybody was proud of the achievement, which I think is momentous.

This day has been a nightmare, with repeated crises evolving in the Congress, Mideast discussions, Vance leaving for South Africa, arguments about SALT, members of Congress desperately afraid I'll veto their pet bills. The crucial vote on energy passed 207–205, with last-minute support by Republican congressman Tom Evans, who cracked up afterward when I called him on the phone. The abuse he received from the Republican leadership was excessive, to say the least.

OCTOBER 14   The last day of the congressional session, I pray. Bob Byrd came by and said he'd been in the Congress twenty-seven years and had never seen such tremendous legislative achievement, nor such harmony between the Congress and a president.

I've really been tired the last few weeks and look forward to some rest at Camp David.

Chip was attacked yesterday on a Texas college campus by Iranian students. He was protected by campus police, a small Secret Service group, and some college football players and black students. The Iranian students are getting out of hand in some cases. They are helping the shah more than they hurt him.

Both in Iran and the United States, opposition to the shah was growing rapidly among young militants. Since all the Iranian students in our universities had been selected and approved by the shah's regime, most of them were loyal to him, but a small minority were very vocal and took advantage of our legal freedoms to demonstrate, sometimes violently.

OCTOBER 15   About 7:00 in the morning the House started voting and passed the omnibus energy bill without any problem. We went to Camp David, really exhausted. Other than swimming, biking, I just read a couple of books and slept.

MONDAY, OCTOBER 16   Came back to Washington. Had a report about Mideast negotiations and unresolved questions.

All of us were excited about the selection of a new pope. Brzezinski knows him, and I was flooded with requests from Polish Americans to go to the investiture ceremonies. I decided to let Brzezinski and Ed Muskie [Democratic senator from Maine] go, and we'll decide on the others tomorrow.

OCTOBER 17   Stan Turner's intelligence briefing was a videotape of the South African nuclear test site episode that showed data collection through satellites, photography, and electronic signal analysis, [and it was] superb. Personnel or human intelligence is very poor compared to what it should be.

The Israelis had the nerve to ask me to finance the cost of moving the illegal settlements from the Sinai. I told them this was ridiculous.

OCTOBER 18   I received a report on the bogged-down Israeli-Egyptian peace treaty negotiations. None of the problems seem to be insurmountable, but I may have to intercede more directly and personally. It is obvious that the Israelis want to trade their peace treaty approval for U.S. financial contributions and are claiming their military expenditures will be greater after a peace treaty is signed than before!

OCTOBER 19   Ted Stevens came to discuss with me the Alaskan lands bill. They [the Alaska congressional delegation] prevented the bill being passed, but we can be even more restrictive than our bill would have permitted. He blames the breakdown on [junior Alaskan senator Mike] Gravel, when I think that he and Gravel are equally culpable. I told Cecil Andrus to be very strict on Alaska, and we got a commitment from Stevens to help us pass our basic proposal early in 1979.

Ever since Alaska had become a state in 1959, dividing up its land was such a controversial issue that final decisions were repeatedly postponed. How much would be owned by the state, private citizens, Inuits, native Indians, and the federal government and what access and control would be exerted over each parcel was extremely complicated and sharply debated. The two senators were aligned with oil and other commercial interests, and I was determined to set aside large areas for forestry, parks, and wilderness areas.

OCTOBER 20   Because of the negative attitude of Israelis, the peace talks are about to come apart, and I've been trying to figure out what to do. The only thing I can think of is some negotiations with me present. If the Israelis will be at all forthcoming, we can get problems solved.

I signed the ERA extension. The women are very happy and enthusiastic, and maybe we can put this across in the future. Fifteen states have not ratified it; still three to go before we have the requisite thirty-eight.

The Equal Rights Amendment was approved by Congress in 1972 but had to be ratified by thirty-eight states. This legislation extended the deadline for ratification from 1979 until June 1982. The ultimate rejection of the amendment to our Constitution was a great disappointment for Rosalynn and me, since we had supported it actively while I was governor and president. Despite widespread public support for granting American women equal rights with men, some church leaders — Catholic, Protestant, and Muslim — opposed the amendment. By exerting their influence, they probably made the difference. The discrimination by male religious authorities, who erroneously claim it is the will of God, is one of the root causes of the worldwide abuse of women and girls.

OCTOBER 21   After working with both sides, I think we've put together the Israeli-Egyptian peace treaty text.

I'm getting ten to fifteen bills a day that passed during the last hours. Some major bills were written after Congress went home; they just voted on outlines, and the congressional staffs did the writing.

I went to Kansas and then to Minnesota to campaign. Don Fraser supporters have the same attitude that Gene McCarthy supporters took in 1968 when they blocked Humphrey's election and put Richard Nixon in office. This is one group of Democrats with whom I feel uncomfortable. They have a commitment to political suicide in order to prove some far-left philosophical point. It is really disgusting.

OCTOBER 22   I worked almost exclusively on the anti-inflation text and put it on tape.

OCTOBER 24   I signed the airline deregulation bill, which is a major step in the right direction. I'm proud of having turned this hopeless case into success.

Cy's report from Moscow is what I expected. There are still the same remaining issues. Brezhnev was in a good mood and much more vigorous and healthy. He wanted SALT II to be concluded early, for us to have a summit meeting, to proceed on SALT III, comprehensive test ban, and mutual and balanced force reductions. Most of these can be resolved, with some flexibility on both sides.

OCTOBER 25   Iran has decided to break a lot of its relationships with Israel. They've been a major purchaser of Israeli weapons, and so far as I know they will still sell oil to Israel. The Israelis' major effort, in my opinion, is still to acquire as much American money as possible for signing a peace treaty. The cabinet decided to approve the treaty with several revisions.

The PLO want to discuss the West Bank/Gaza arrangements with us, but first they'll have to approve UN 242.

In 1975, Secretary of State Kissinger had made a binding commitment to the Israelis not to meet with or negotiate with the PLO until after they recognized Israel by confirming UN Security Council Resolution 242. It was an unpleasant and increasingly unnecessary restraint, now that we had, in effect, negotiated on their behalf and made it possible for Palestinians to have full autonomy and join in negotiations to "determine their own future."

We have growing hints at least of Saudi-Jordanian support for cooperation in the West Bank/Gaza settlements in the future.

The CIA gave me an analysis of the economic and political problems of Iran. The shah has asked for advice on how to handle the trend toward democracy and liberalized society. He has alienated powerful groups: the right-wing religious leaders, who don't want any changes; the radical left, some of whom are communists; and the new middle class in Iran, who are now wealthy but have no voice in the government.

Rosalynn and I flew up to Camp Hoover [in Virginia's Shenandoah National Park], the first time a president's been there in forty-five years. I liked it very much and will go there next spring when the weather warms up. During the winter, the trout stream at the head of the Rapidan River has little water in it.

OCTOBER 26   Iran is running into serious trouble because of strikes preventing shipment of oil to foreign markets. The shah will have to take action soon.

Israel, again, has tried to throw a monkey wrench into the peace negotiations by announcing they were going to expand their settlements no matter what anyone else said, and Begin might move his office into East Jerusalem. We sent Begin a very firm letter on this subject. We have to support the Camp David agreements, even when Israel tries to violate them.

I realized, of course, that Begin was under great pressure from his political supporters.

I signed the Ethics in Government Act, a real step in the right direction requiring full financial disclosure for all GS-16s and above [senior civil service], all executive branch officers, federal judges, and members of Congress. The next step should be public financing of congressional races in the general election at least.

OCTOBER 27   I signed the Humphrey-Hawkins bill.

I sent Begin and Sadat a congratulatory message after they received the Nobel Peace Prize jointly. Sadat deserved it; Begin did not.

OCTOBER 28   The Israelis are backing down from some of their ridiculous demands on the peace treaty text. Cy is a tough and good negotiator.

I made a campaign trip to New York, Connecticut, and Maine for Democratic candidates. Back to the White House to discuss a serious run on the dollar and then late at night to Camp David.

OCTOBER 29   I got more rest at Camp David than I have in two or three months.

MONDAY, OCTOBER 30   I jogged, swam, played tennis, read [William Warner's] *Beautiful Swimmers* and a lot of magazines.

I returned to the White House for paperwork, signing bills, and a Halloween party for the WH staff.

OCTOBER 31   Had a letter from Begin, sealed, no one to read it but me. He said his actions on West Bank settlements were to assuage the feelings of his former revolutionaries and political allies who have now turned against him. I got a report quoting Dayan saying they did not intend to carry out the West Bank portions of the agreements. I called a meeting tomorrow morning to decide how to handle this.

NOVEMBER 1   We sent a stern message to Somoza in Nicaragua, saying that we agreed with the outline of the settlement for his stepping down. I asked him not to reject it out of hand.

The family of Anastasio Somoza Debayle had ruled Nicaragua since 1936, and he had been the nation's dictatorial leader since 1967. Our government had been deeply involved in the country for many years—we had several times sent troops when it seemed that revolutionary forces might prevail—and I felt responsible for helping to orchestrate a peaceful resolution of the armed conflict between Somoza's military and the Sandinistas. I attempted to induce both sides to accept a national referendum, to be monitored by the Organization of American States. This effort ended when Somoza fled to Paraguay; he established a residence there and was assassinated in 1980.

We've gone about as far as we can in pushing the Egyptians on language. The Israelis keep coming back over and over for additional concessions, and lately Dayan has said he couldn't negotiate for Israel anymore; we'd have to check with Begin on every sensitive question. I instructed Cy and Zbig not to make any commitments on financial arrangements without my personal approval.

Zbig and Cy have evolved an erroneous impression lately that Sadat doesn't care about the West Bank/Gaza settlements. Obviously, Sadat wants his own territory back very badly, but even more than that, he considers himself the political and military leader of the Arab world. His word of honor is at stake. He's promised his people he would not betray them, and I have never doubted his sincerity.

Our drastic steps to stabilize the dollar had an immediately beneficial reaction.

I sent Sadat and Begin a photograph of a new planetoid discovered while we were at Camp David. It was named Ra-Shalom.

Griffin Bell and Bob Lipshutz are squabbling about how to choose the 152 federal judges authorized by Congress. I established guidelines re method of selection, quality of candidates, and a fair sex and race allocation.

NOVEMBER 2   The shah expressed deep concern about whether to set up an interim government, a military government, or perhaps even to abdicate. We encouraged him to hang firm and count on our backing.

I took off for a two-day trip to New York, Michigan, Illinois, Oregon, California, and Minnesota. This makes thirty-one states I will have visited this year for campaigns.

MONDAY, NOVEMBER 6   Over the weekend, I sent the shah a message that whatever action he took, including setting up a military government,

I would support him. We did not want him to abdicate, which he had threatened to do. He is not a strong leader but very doubtful and unsure of himself.

NOVEMBER 7   Election Day. The House encouraging, governors as expected, lost a few senators, the worst loss being Dick Clark.

This was a hard-fought midterm election, and my family and I had spent a great deal of time campaigning for Democratic candidates throughout the nation. Our party's prospects had looked very bleak earlier in the year, but the Camp David Accords and the success of our legislative agenda significantly improved our position. In the end, Democrats lost three seats in the Senate and fifteen in the House, but still retained a 58–41 advantage in the Senate and 277–158 in the House. This result encouraged me as I considered what we hoped to accomplish in the coming year.

NOVEMBER 8   I decided to let the leadership in Israel and Egypt know we were through devoting full-time to this nonproductive effort. It's obvious the Israelis want a separate treaty with Egypt, to keep the West Bank and Gaza, to get as much money as possible from us, and use the settlements and East Jerusalem to prevent involvement of Jordan and the Palestinians.

NOVEMBER 9   I signed the energy legislation—five major bills. This is encompassing about 60–65 percent of the energy savings we had projected originally. The main omission is the refusal of Congress to authorize a tax on oil that could be refunded to the American people immediately. This is something that we will pursue through administrative or congressional action next year.

When the Congress later adopted our proposed windfall profits tax legislation, we achieved our goal of passing a comprehensive energy package. We prevailed over the powerful lobbies of energy corporations and automobile manufacturers, but that didn't prevent them from maintaining their influence in Washington. An unaroused American public is no match for the legions of tenacious and well-funded Washington lobbyists.

  Soon after I left office, the sweep and impact of our energy package was substantially diminished by President Reagan, and some of its beneficial effects were attenuated over the years by executive orders of other presidents,

*their selection of cabinet officers who were unwilling to enforce the laws,
and of course legislative action by both houses of Congress.*

NOVEMBER 10   Somoza has offered to have a plebiscite, and I'm inclined
to agree along—provided it is supervised by some objective body like
the OAS.

NOVEMBER 12   I spent almost all day on the Mideast peace negotiations,
which are apparently coming apart. I talked to Cy several times and to
President Sadat. Later in the day I got Begin on the phone, who was very
abusive, who denied that Israel had changed their position, who said that
Weizman had no authority to speak for Israel. I reminded him that the
previous agreements concerning the interim withdrawal schedule and
other things were committed not only by Weizman but by Dayan, Barak,
the attorney general, and others. He still insisted that they had not changed
their position and that the cabinet was the final arbiter, saying several
times that he was only one member of the cabinet.

During the afternoon we went to Cedar Point Farm to meet with [Sena-
tor] Harold Hughes and his wife, [Senator] Pete Domenici, Senator and
Mrs. Lawton Chiles, Senator Dewey Bartlett, General David Jones, [Chris-
tian leader] Doug Coe, and a few others—a Christian fellowship meeting.

*This group of Christians later became known as "The Family." A book by
that name argued that the fellowship represents a secret movement at the
"heart of American power," and that the members use the name of Jesus, not
the Christ, as the one under whose auspices their work is to be done. The leaders were said to believe that God chooses to advance his kingdom through
specially anointed powerful men, regardless of their personal morals or chosen religion. Their inner circle includes political, military, and financial
leaders, both in the United States and in foreign nations. I was surprised by
some of these statements. I attended the annual National Prayer Breakfasts,
sponsored by the group, but I never heard anything about secrets and just
saw an effort to focus on shared positive values.*

MONDAY, NOVEMBER 13   Arthur Goldberg called, quite concerned about
Israel's attitude, and thought I might have to get Begin and Sadat together
again, which is a horrible prospect. Sadat sent word that if there was no link-
age between Sinai and West Bank/Gaza, he would not sign a peace treaty.

NOVEMBER 14　Schlesinger reported that Chinese leaders are strongly opposed to normalization of relations between ourselves and Vietnam. I told him we had no intention to do this before similar action with China, provided they didn't deliberately delay.

I took Morocco's King Hassan on a tour of the second floor. We stopped by Mother's room. She had recently been to Morocco and said she smelled all the twenty-one types of perfume in the dressing room where she stayed. He [King Hassan] offered to give her some more perfume, and she said no. Mother laughed and said, "You damn foreigners are all alike." He laughed also, put his arms around Mother, and gave her a kiss. I doubt the king's been called a "damn foreigner" before, and I don't know anyone else who could get away with it. Mohammed, his oldest son, went with him everywhere and was almost an assistant king.

I outlined to him the importance of progress on the Mideast peace settlements. He said that my apparent discouragement was unjustified, that he thought what we had done was irreversible, and that there should be no abandonment of the peace effort.

NOVEMBER 15　I was disturbed at the Joint Chiefs' leak concerning MiG-23s in Cuba. I called Harold Brown and discovered that a top-secret document that we treat with great care in the White House, making no copies, was given to the Joint Chiefs and they made fifteen copies, one copy of which I guess routinely is routed to the news media. My displeasure has been registered in the Pentagon; we'll see if it has any effect.

I was told later that Paul Nitze, Scoop Jackson, and a few others had orchestrated the leak and subsequently aroused fears of a Cuba-Soviet threat to the United States—all of which was designed to prevent acceptance of any SALT agreement.

NOVEMBER 16　[Hosni] Mubarak [vice president of Egypt] made a good impression. He said Camp David resolved 90 percent of the problems, 75 percent of the remainder were resolved, but the remaining few were very important.

NOVEMBER 17　I met with the Judicial Selection Committee of the American Bar Association. We've chosen 62 judges and have 152 more approved by new legislation, so we'll be working very closely with the bar in the screening of potential candidates. I told them they need to modify their procedures to accommodate the need for more minority and women appointees. They seemed to agree.

NOVEMBER 18   We had a crisis in Guyana with Congressman Leo Ryan and five other Americans being murdered by a religious sect headed by Reverend Jones, from California. Several hundred of his followers committed suicide at his urging. We helped evacuate the dead and wounded.

More than nine hundred members of this American cult group led by Jim Jones died from cyanide poison in Jonestown, a community in northern Guyana. Leo Ryan was the only U.S. congressman ever murdered in the line of duty.

I talked to Begin to encourage him. He's under intense pressure from right-wing elements in Israel. His car was splattered with eggs and tomatoes, and his car windshield smashed at his own party conference.

I have been jogging regularly, twenty-five or thirty minutes at a time, which is about three and a half miles.

MONDAY, NOVEMBER 20   We are concerned about the shah's courage and forcefulness, and he seems to be excessively isolated.

NOVEMBER 21   His ambassador told me there was no concept the shah had given the Iranian people of what he could accomplish. He had no PR program, no advisors to prepare such an effort, and no political structure to succeed if and when elections are held.

We were in an increasing quandary with respect to the shah. He had been a dependable ally of the six presidents who preceded me, and the revolutionary forces opposing him were completely unpredictable. Instead of reaching out to his people and strengthening his control of the government agencies, he was becoming more isolated, oppressive, and ineffective. After much thought and discussion, I decided to give him as much support as possible without directly interfering in the internal affairs of Iran.

Begin reported the cabinet had approved the peace treaty as presently drafted. He claimed this was a momentous decision. The reluctance of Israel to get pinned down on the West Bank/Gaza is still a key problem.

NOVEMBER 22   Phil Klutznick gave me a report on his work as president of the World Jewish Congress. He said the Israeli people were overwhelmingly in favor of peace and he hoped I could understand the criticisms from the American Jewish community. I told him I was relatively impervious to their criticism, had grown accustomed to it, and my commitment to a Mideast peace treaty was permanent.

NOVEMBER 26   In Nicaragua most of the moderate activist [groups], twelve out of fifteen, want to have a fair plebiscite. Three of them, the most vocal, do not want to have any plebiscite unless Somoza steps down first, which he will not do.

MONDAY, NOVEMBER 27   We were surprised that [Japanese] Prime Minister [Yasuo] Fukuda was defeated by Mr. [Masayoshi] Ohira—whom I had met earlier and was my favorite.

NOVEMBER 28   Our foreign affairs group discussed the MiG-23s in Cuba and agreed that a mountain was being made out of a molehill.

NOVEMBER 29   Went over the first list of about twenty federal judges jointly recommended by Griffin Bell, my own staff, and involved senators. We did not act on some states where women and blacks have been ignored.

Sadat was very, very negative in his attitude. He said he would never accept a treaty with the present articles 4 and 6 included. I think personally that Sadat has yielded to pressure from the Baghdad conference, and Assad and Hussein are prevailing.

NOVEMBER 30   I met with Joe Califano, one of the best and strongest members of the cabinet.

We had the newly elected House Democrats in for briefings. It was surprising how many gave me their personal thanks for my mother's help [during their campaigns].

I ran another five miles, much easier than running two miles three weeks ago.

My brief entries covering the following two days—which happened to occur over a weekend—indicate vividly some of the key international areas with which I had to deal: Cuba, Nicaragua, nuclear arms control, relations with

China, Middle East peace, and Iran. Thirty years later they are still in the
news—and on the president's agenda.

DECEMBER 1   I authorized NSC and State to send Bob Pastor and [Peter]
Tarnoff to Havana to negotiate the release of the four American prisoners.

Both sides have accepted the plebiscite in Nicaragua, but their terms
are in direct conflict. It's better to negotiate how a plebiscite should be
held than to see bloodshed.

On SALT, we have gotten to the point where the Soviets will have to
either fish or cut bait. They're taking our latest position back to Moscow,
and we expect a response early next week.

The P.R.C. are making good noises about normalization. In effect,
we've given them a prospective date of January first.

I had a harsh message from Sadat, and I sent him the same proposal I
had given Mubarak. None of my staff or cabinet thinks this will work, but
I have a gut feeling Sadat will accept. My guess is that Israel will not accept because they don't have any intention of carrying out the Camp David Accords on West Bank/Gaza.

We had final fitting for cross-country skis, and I continued running—a
little over seven minutes per mile.

DECEMBER 2   I'm increasingly concerned about Iran, with holy days beginning Sunday and [Ayatollah Ruholla] Khomeini [Iranian religious leader
in exile in France] calling for massive bloodshed.

MONDAY, DECEMBER 4   Spent the morning going over the Defense budget. I was disappointed by Secretary Brown. He's not followed my guidelines
re zero-based budgeting. Other departments have done well, and Brown
himself has used this technique with his individual services.

Griffin Bell notified me that the FBI officers will be punished. We hope
the public and FBI will accept this final conclusion of a divisive question
about how to punish agents and their superiors when they violate the law.
We will punish superiors and admonish lower agents carrying out orders.

The problem was what to do about sixty-eight FBI agents and supervisors
who had violated federal laws while searching for members of the Weather-
men in the early 1970s. Agents had burglarized homes, tapped phones without
warrants, and monitored mail. Griffin Bell, FBI director Bill Webster, and I

believed that when a serious crime such as this one occurred, those who ordered or approved the action should be punished, and not their lowest subordinates.

This is the worst time of the year for me, with the Mideast, SALT, China, South Africa, Nicaragua coming to a head and preparing the 1980 budget—all onerous and dispiriting—nothing pleasant.

DECEMBER 5   We kicked off the Humphrey scholarship program, designed to bring graduate students from developing countries over here for a year.

This has been a remarkably successful program; young professionals from other nations come here for additional education and training and in the process become familiar with the United States. During the academic year 2009–10, for instance, 187 fellows from ninety-four countries received training in seventeen U.S. universities. As a professor at Emory University, I lecture and answer questions from several dozen Humphrey Fellows each year.

Rosalynn and I went to New York to help Abe Beame with a fund-raiser, and to attend the opera *Aida.* It was remarkably good, compared to previous performances we had seen, and the first time any president has attended an opera at the Metropolitan.

DECEMBER 6   Abe Ribicoff, as a UN delegate, made a strong statement concerning Palestinian rights, based almost exclusively on the text of the Camp David Accords, and it was well received by Arafat and others.

DECEMBER 8   I spoke in Memphis, shook hands with two thousand people, and put a wreath at the site of MLK, Jr.'s assassination.

Congressman Don Young from Alaska said my protecting the territories was a violation of their human rights.

DECEMBER 9   I called Mother to ask her to represent our nation at the Golda Meir funeral.

MONDAY, DECEMBER 11   Our NATO allies had a tough debate about our human rights policy and almost unanimously decided it was good for the Western world as a counterbalance to Communist propaganda.

Brock Adams and I discussed deregulation of trains, trucks, and possibly buses.

We are flooded with refugees: 150,000 from Vietnam, 3,500 Cubans, and 1,000 from Lebanon.

DECEMBER 12   Senator Byrd gave me a great report on his mission to Egypt, Israel, Jordan, Saudi Arabia, Syria, and Turkey—a definitive book. I've gained an ally because his views on how to treat the Mideast questions are compatible with mine.

President Ford came by. We discussed the Mideast, the dollar, inflation, SALT, China. I will need him on SALT. I explained the contentious items; how we had resolved them. He seemed to be in complete agreement.

My leg has healed up from a sprain, although I still wear an elastic bandage when I run. Monday I ran seven miles without any strain, and this afternoon five miles in thirty-eight minutes.

DECEMBER 13   Teng [later Deng Xiaoping] surprisingly accepted our draft communiqué, and we are trying to expedite the process. I told Bob Byrd, and he said that anytime I brief senators it wouldn't be a secret more than five minutes. We worked until quite late on the words for the joint communiqué and our unilateral statement.

Cy Vance reports that he and Sadat have reached agreement on the treaty text. Later he reported from Israel a very cold and negative reaction.

DECEMBER 15   The big day for the China announcement. We were favorably impressed with Teng and the rapidity with which he moved and agreed to accept our one-year treaty with Taiwan, our statement that the Taiwan issue should be settled peacefully would not be contradicted by China, and that we would sell defensive weapons to Taiwan after the treaty expires.

Two days later, Deng Xiaoping announced that China would adopt profound changes in its basic political and economic structure, which made possible its unprecedented free enterprise system, the opening of trade with many other nations, and the loosening of tight restraints on the movement of citizens, their right to worship, and granting of other freedoms.

These decisions within China, as well as those affecting the relationship between our two nations, have resulted in perhaps the most important changes in the worldwide economic and political landscape during the past thirty years.

Ed Sanders, speaking for American Jews, came by. He's had a flood of bitter recriminations against me, which is typical every time we have a disagreement with Israel. I outlined the recent negotiating history and told him to get everyone to calm down.

Vance came back, extremely bitter against the Israelis, for the first time I've ever seen him this way. He had drafted a rough press release for me, but even Zbig thought it would be a mistake to issue it, it was so critical.

We notified many leaders about China, and with the exception of the Israelis, the worldwide response was either neutral or enthusiastic. There were celebrations in China. Some small demonstrations against us in Taiwan, but in general everybody realizes this is a historic development which will contribute to world peace and the opening of China even more to the outside world.

Normalizing relations with China required that we travel a long, difficult path to a politically unpopular but correct decision. The extremely powerful Taiwan lobby had continued to prevail even after Nixon announced in Shanghai that there was only one China—without taking action. Ford, Reagan, and other Republican leaders had insisted on continued diplomatic relations with Taiwan, which was governed by the Chinese Nationalist political descendants of Chiang Kai-shek. Also, ties between Taiwanese and American news media, business, financial, and commercial institutions had proved to be unshakable.

We successfully avoided potentially disastrous early news leaks from the State Department by routing all negotiating messages to Leonard Woodcock through the White House. Fortunately, the U.S. Constitution gives the president exclusive authority regarding diplomatic recognition, but I had to honor the one-year phasing out of the treaty with Taiwan, which had been in effect for almost thirty years.

DECEMBER 17   Cy was on *Meet the Press* and did a good job holding firm on the Mideast in spite of building press criticism of me for being "even-handed."

When I called Zbig to tell him about my conversation with Nixon about China, I asked him if they had heard that the Chinese had canceled our agreement. He almost fainted before I could tell him I was joking.

President Nixon was both surprised and delighted by the news that we had normalized relations with China. Although he had been deliberately avoid-

ing the limelight, he accepted my invitation to come to the White House for the prospective ceremonies. This would be the first time he returned since his resignation.

MONDAY, DECEMBER 18   The shah wants to remain as commander in chief, let a civilian government share defense responsibilities, and let one of the leaders form a coalition government without his interference.

I made up my mind on SALT. We've got a darn good agreement. The issues on which we yielded are insignificant, and we have a good prospect of prevailing on the issues important to us.

Paperwork this week is unbelievable. I work from 5:00 a.m. and can't clean out my in-box before I'm exhausted, and have something scheduled almost every night. Everybody's under a lot of tension, and tempers are high.

DECEMBER 19   Cy came to describe some problems between NSC and State. I think he was just speaking up for subordinates who have made a mistake or are overly sensitive about press reports. I had a meeting, and I think the air was cleared. There will be a weekly luncheon including Cy, Zbig, and their deputies.

The great event of the day was the birth of Sarah Rosemary Carter, our first granddaughter!

DECEMBER 20   I had a horrible attack of hemorrhoids, but I couldn't stop working because I had to prepare all the directives for Cy for the SALT and the Mideast negotiations, wrap up the budget problems and the China problems. We had a Christmas party for all of our staff members, and when I finally got down to the reception for the White House press corps, I could hardly bear the pain.

DECEMBER 21   I didn't get any sleep Wednesday night in spite of very strong antipain medication, so I just canceled my Thursday schedule and asked Fritz and others to take it over. Dr. Lukash gave me some Demerol injections, which finally put me to sleep.

DECEMBER 22   The pain has gone down some, and I worked all day. Cy reported he was making excellent progress with Gromyko. We flew to Atlanta to see the baby, a beautiful redhead, and then home.

DECEMBER 23   There were many demonstrators in Plains. I walked in the woods carefully, because of my rear end. I stayed in touch with the Soviets, Israelis, Egyptians, and we're walking a tightrope in Iran, giving the shah every assurance but encouraging him to be decisive. He's been just the opposite, which has aggravated an already bad situation.

MONDAY, DECEMBER 25–SUNDAY, DECEMBER 31   On Christmas Day the Egyptians prayed that my hemorrhoids would be cured because I was a good man, and the following day they were cured. I was tempted to make a public announcement thanking the Egyptians but decided that we'd had enough publicity with my ailment.

Back at Camp David, I read two books on China. Its leaders have really acted like gentlemen these last few weeks.

When Warren Christopher arrived in Taiwan, he was greeted with an abusive public demonstration obviously encouraged by President Chiang Ching-kuo. I let him stay there for two days of unsatisfactory meetings.

The situation in Iran varies from bad to terrible. We instructed [Ambassador William] Sullivan to tell the shah that if he couldn't form a civilian or military government that would restore peace and reduce bloodshed, to consider a regency council—which means he would have to abdicate. He responded fairly well to this suggestion. I asked if he could find asylum in the United States. Sullivan replied affirmatively.

We finally straightened out questions in the budget, and we won't have any problem meeting our $30 billion maximum deficit figure.

We recognize that there are significant religious issues and emotions sweeping the Mideast, in particular within the Muslim world, primarily between the Shiites, the Sunnis, and others, and I directed Cy and Zbig to give me an analysis of these religious movements.

I also authorized Clark Clifford to explore with potential new Iranian leaders some means of communication. They had made the proposal indirectly. We also need some way to communicate better with the Palestinians.

While at Camp David I began running again. The first day a mile and a half, then five to eight miles.

As midnight approached on New Year's Eve, Rosalynn, Amy, and I had a party with sandwiches and champagne. This is the first time we've stayed up till midnight in a long time.

1979

MONDAY, JANUARY 1   I came back to Washington for a long discussion about Iran and the need to move Americans out if the violence escalates. We all thought the shah would have to leave, and he needs to be decisive in doing so.

By now we were reasonably certain that the shah's regime would be replaced by a revolutionary government, whose character and policies we could not anticipate. At this point, however, the reports from our ambassador in Tehran were fairly sanguine about what the consequences of this change would mean for the United States and the Middle East.

JANUARY 2   [Iranian prime minister Shapour] Bakhtiar will try today to establish a cabinet leading to a regency council. He has a good background with both labor and students, basically French educated. He's not endorsed by Khomeini, who indicated he might return to Iran and would be receptive to friendship with the U.S.

JANUARY 3   Andy Young said that the most important political influence in the United Nations, according to Senator Ribicoff, was the Palestinians—a group whom we have basically ignored.

Ambassador Sullivan recommended that we advise the shah to abdicate. I decided to send a squadron of F-15s into Saudi Arabia after the Bakhtiar government is established, and to let the shah know that he has a haven here on the Palm Beach estate of Mr. [Walter] Annenberg if and when the Bakhtiar government is established.

I've noticed the inclination by a few people to present me with unacceptable proposals in a time of crisis just to create a record for themselves, warning of impending doom. One who's never done this is Secretary Vance.

The two most memorable examples of this ploy occurred when I was contemplating going to Camp David to meet with Begin and Sadat, and later when I was trying to decide whether to go to Egypt and Israel to conclude the final terms of the peace treaty between the two countries. In both these cases, several members of my administration predicted that pursuing these initiatives would have dire consequences—and in both cases they were wrong. On the other hand, some of my political advisors said that addressing so many controversial subjects in my first term would alienate voters, and those predictions proved accurate.

JANUARY 4   We [Rosalynn, Amy, and I] left Washington in something like a holiday mood on the way to Guadeloupe to meet with the three European leaders, and I assessed their potential attitudes. My easiest and friendliest relationship is with Callaghan, and Giscard is the best liked. When we arrived, Helmut was in a very bad mood, saying that Germany was suspect because of Hitler.

In the evening, Fritz, Cy, and I spent a good bit of time talking [among ourselves] about the Iranian problem. Some [Iranian] military leaders had told Sullivan, "We will not permit the shah to leave Iran; we plan a coup to take over the government." Cy wanted to stop any such move, but I insisted that we retain our relationships with the shah and the military—our only two ties to future sound relationships with Iran.

My own belief, difficult to prove, has been that the shah, Shapour Bakhtiar, and the military are acting in concert. We are sticking with the shah until we see some clear alternative, since we can't force the shah to leave and the military must be kept cohesive.

This coalition did exist at the time but dissolved of necessity when the shah decided to abdicate. Some of Iran's military leaders also went into exile, while

others shifted their loyalty to the revolutionary forces who assumed power.
Bakhtiar, after serving as prime minister for five weeks, was branded a traitor
by Ayatollah Khomeini; ultimately he moved to Paris and was assassinated
by militant Iranians in 1991.

JANUARY 5   The shah tells Sullivan he has complete control over the military, and that he's leaving to help Bakhtiar in accordance with the Iranian constitution. [U.S. Air Force] general [Robert "Dutch"] Huyser met with the military and said they support Bakhtiar. Sullivan's assessment is that if the shah leaves, Bakhtiar has a chance; if the shah stays in Iran, Bakhtiar has no chance.

I met with Helmut, Jim, and Valéry, and their first order of business was for me to assess the world political situation. I emphasized the U.S. relationship with China; that we believe a stronger relationship with the Soviets and the P.R.C. might eventually avoid excessive disharmony between the two nations. I described our new interest in Africa; how much Andy Young had helped—which drew a frown from Valéry. We were treating the South American countries as individuals; trying to mediate the Nicaraguan dispute; keeping down violence between Argentina and Chile. We were trying to improve relationships with Brazil; to overcome our Vietnam image. I thought there had been setbacks in the Horn of Africa, Afghanistan, and Pakistan. We needed to improve Pakistan's orientation to the West and prevent Afghanistan from becoming anti-West.

It is important to remember that during the Cold War our relationships with
almost every nation were colored by intense competition with the Soviet Union.
In many ways, we considered the issues involving Afghanistan and Pakistan
to be interrelated, since they traded with each other and shared tribal connec-
tions and a lot of history. Later, when the Soviets invaded Afghanistan and
threatened, if successful, to move farther into the oil-rich Gulf region, I felt
that this was a direct threat to the security of our country.

We needed help from them [our European allies] in Turkey, Greece, and Cyprus—and in keeping the nonaligned movement from slipping under the control of Cuba.

Schmidt was very critical of Ceaușescu, saying he was conducting a dangerous and idiotic policy in arousing the Soviets against him. He considered Tehran and Bucharest to be similar, and he had long known that the megalomaniac shah would be brought down. He saw Norway shifting stronger toward domination by the Soviet Union. His whole attitude was very negative.

Valéry said the Soviet army was increasing its influence at the expense of the Politburo, that Brezhnev in his meetings was almost incoherent and approaching senility, and he thought the strain between the Soviet Union and China was beneficial to the West. When I asked him specifically, "Would you rather have a war between Russia and China or reconciliation?" he immediately said, "War would be better than reconciliation." Gromyko had said to Valéry that the Soviet Union was against reunification of Germany, did not trust the Germans under any circumstances, and the Soviets wanted to have a "special relationship" with France. He said the strain between the U.S. and Germany was uncomfortable. He also reported that China wanted to buy five hundred Mirage 2000 airplanes, a request considered grossly excessive.

I asked Helmut if he considered Valéry's statement concerning U.S.-F.R.G. strains to be true. Helmut said most of the problems have been alleviated, but the uranium supply question was the bone of contention. I explained our nonproliferation policy, similar to Canada and Australia. Helmut said it was a uranium cartel, and that Canadian and Australian policies were dominated by the U.S. Callaghan said this was not true, that world opinion was shifting toward nonproliferation.

Helmut said a strong F.R.G. military and economy was a problem with the West, that Germany was still not trusted by other European nations.

I was impressed and concerned by the attitude of Helmut toward appeasing the Soviets—much more than the other three of us.

In general, I thought this discussion was helpful in understanding our mutual attitudes and concerns.

This was a truly remarkable occasion; rarely do the leaders of the top four Western democracies spend time together in a completely informal setting. We were able to relax with each other and, I believe, to eliminate all restraints that inherently exist when we deal with issues through bureaucratic intermediaries and are concerned that the news media will report every encounter. The recent trend has been in the opposite direction, with the G7 adding Russia to make G8, and now moving to the G20, with China, India, Saudi Arabia, Brazil, South Africa, Indonesia, and other influential countries included. The reason, of course, is that international political or economic events can no longer be shaped by only a few nations.

At our second session I gave a complete rundown of SALT II. We had a long and tough conversation when I raised the issue of their defending themselves. [We discussed all the nuclear and conventional weapons systems.] Helmut was quite contentious, Jim was cooperative, and Valéry minimized French involvement. The meeting was inconclusive, but everybody seemed to think the Germans would have to cooperate and we would evolve a way to do it without arousing the concern of other North Atlantic members.

JANUARY 6   I was still concerned about the nuclear threat to Europe and said I would be glad to send David Aaron there to consult and also give a report on Deng's visit.

I then discussed Iran and found little support among the other three for the shah. They all thought the civilian government would have to be established and the military kept strong and intact. They were unanimous in saying the shah ought to leave as soon as possible. Valéry reported he had decided earlier to expel Khomeini, but the shah thought it best to keep him in France instead of letting him go to Iraq or Libya, where he might stir up even more trouble. Therefore Valéry kept Khomeini there.

My three associates at Guadeloupe never had any sympathy for the shah and continued to be more compatible with the revolutionary forces than I. Later, it was difficult for me to induce them to support our embargo when American hostages were being held captive in Iran. They valued their trade relationships, especially access to oil supplies.

Valéry said that two years ago Israel would have accepted UN 242. I replied that this was not the case because Israel had always been deeply committed to avoiding giving up the West Bank/Gaza, and I thought the Camp David Accords were the best avenue to realize the Palestinian hopes and to reduce the Israeli influence in the occupied territories.

At our last luncheon together, with topless women bathers walking on the beach below us, Jim complained strenuously that his back was turned to the beach.

JANUARY 7–9   We enjoyed scuba diving, and I was glad Rosalynn joined me. I went down about fifty feet, stayed down until my air tank gave out. I had to shift over to the reserve supply. Amy went down with a large air tank floating around on her back with some of the Secret Service agents staying very close to her. I stayed at the helm of the trimaran almost all day Tuesday—one of the most enjoyable times I've ever had.

JANUARY 10   Back in Washington, I had a meeting with Vance, Brown, Mondale, and Brzezinski on Iran. Giscard would inform Khomeini in Paris that France and the U.S. desired for Khomeini not to disrupt the establishment of the Bakhtiar government. We would encourage the shah to leave Iran without delay, support the Bakhtiar government, and encourage the military to stay cohesive.

We had a report that Arafat sent a delegate to Fahd requesting that Hussein be spokesman for the Palestinians in carrying out the Camp David Accords.

This was good news. Since we were restrained from dealing directly with the PLO, I was pleased that the Palestinian leaders had examined the Camp David Accords and wanted to see the provisions implemented. Having the Saudis involved was also an asset.

Jim McIntyre reported that, not counting Real Wage Insurance, we would have a $26 billion deficit, a notable achievement.

Had an unbelievable cable from Ambassador Sullivan, who apparently lost complete control of himself because we approached Khomeini through the French instead of directly as he had pushed. My inclination was to recall him, but Cy said he was just hot-tempered and we decided to leave him there for now.

JANUARY 11   Had a half-hour or so interview with James Reston. I was impressed with the extremely high opinion of Reston held by the European leaders in Guadeloupe. He's the best columnist in our country as far as judgment, experience, soundness, and integrity are concerned.

Griffin Bell brought a list of recommendations for federal judge appointees, but senators have refused to include women nominees, especially liberals from Connecticut, Wisconsin, Illinois, Michigan, Ohio, and Iowa. I didn't approve any nominations and told Hamilton and Griffin to meet with

Sarah Weddington and other women to work out some way to start pressuring senators to let me appoint women to these judgeships.

JANUARY 12   General Huyser is making daily reports from Iran, which relieves me because I've lost confidence in Sullivan.

General Robert Huyser, a combat hero who was trusted by the secretary of defense, combined excellent diplomatic skills and a natural rapport with top Iranian military officers. It appeared that his reports on the changing situation in Iran were quite accurate, while those of Ambassador William Sullivan were biased and erroneous. What mattered most to me was that Huyser followed orders whereas Ambassador Sullivan was insubordinate.

We discussed the need for some relationship with the Palestinians. Fritz looks on this with abhorrence, but there's no other way we can implement the Camp David Accords.

I met with the Women's Advisory Committee, a fruitless meeting. Bella Abzug had already issued a 100 percent negative press statement. I decided to ask her to resign from the committee and the chairmanship. This women's group could be helpful but has been a pain in the neck. After I pointed out all the problems with them, they applauded.

In the middle of the night, Prince Sihanouk of Cambodia came to our mission office in New York and asked for asylum. He's done an extremely effective job in presenting the anti-Vietnam/Soviet/Cuba position in the UN, deploring Vietnam's invasion of Cambodia, and also the abuses of the Pol Pot regime. He's blamed all the problems in Cambodia on Nixon and Kissinger. He seems to be a very discerning man.

JANUARY 13   A full working day, with piles of paperwork and problems re firing Bella Abzug. Cy asked me to call Giscard to encourage Khomeini to stay in France and not go to Iran after the Bakhtiar government is formed, and I agreed.

JANUARY 14   I called Giscard d'Estaing, and he was willing to cooperate but had no way to prevent Khomeini leaving France. His government's only policy was to support the Bakhtiar government. He believes a visit by the shah to the United States would be a mistake; much better to a more neutral country. Later he called back and reported that Khomeini has no current plans to leave Paris. He is afraid he might lose his life, but his final aim is to overthrow the Bakhtiar government. Huyser is making good reports to us and seems to have the confidence of the Iranian military.

I went to Atlanta for the Martin Luther King birthday celebration at Ebenezer. Some are against [his wife] Coretta's sapping away from the SCLC [Southern Christian Leadership Conference] publicity, money, and nationwide support. Andy rode with me and said the King crusade was always subject to sharp abuse from other black leaders, even when Dr. King was alive, so this was nothing new. I called for the designation of January fifteenth as King's birthday and a national holiday.

MONDAY, JANUARY 15   I didn't get any rest this weekend, and I'm a little tired. This is not a good time, with the Congress coming back and increasing problems concerning inflation.

JANUARY 16   Breakfast with congressional leaders, and I told them the shah left this morning at 5:45 from Iran on the way to Aswan, and from there he would come to California.

Although Giscard d'Estaing had recommended that the shah not come to the United States, at this time I saw no problem with it because Walter Annenberg had offered his home as a safe place for the shah and his family to reside until the fluid situation in Iran could be clarified.

Lunch with Rosalynn and Drummond Ayres, who is writing an article for *The New York Times* about her. He has done several months of work and was primarily interested in her impact on me and her involvement in my activities as president.

During this weekend we were thinking again about how Rosalynn has changed in the last couple of years. She's gotten younger, healthier, prettier, more enjoyable to be around. And she's doing a lot of things that she would never have considered before: skiing, swimming, tennis, jogging. She just seems to be more relaxed and more sure of herself, even than when she was first lady of Georgia.

JANUARY 17   We are pushing hard to keep Khomeini out of Iran, and we have direct contacts with persons on his staff in France. So far the Iranian military have weathered the shah's departure fairly well.

JANUARY 18   At the annual Prayer Breakfast, Bishop Fulton Sheen made a very good talk, and then I talked about the interweaving of religious beliefs, sometimes misguided, into the modern world. The three top stories of last year were Jonestown, election of a pope, and Camp David. The top news this year might very well be religious—fervor in the Persian Gulf.

Some political scientists predict that cultural and religious differences will lead inevitably to global struggle. I fervently hope this will not occur, but it has become increasingly obvious since my time as president that the inter-relationship between religion and major political events has become more intimate—and deadly. The Iran-Iraq war was partially caused by differences in Islamic belief. The two U.S. invasions of Iraq, the terrorist attacks of September 11, 2001, and the war in Afghanistan all pitted Western forces, largely Christian, against Muslim opponents. The same general orientation is obvious in Sudan and less clearly divided local conflicts, as in Somalia. A long-lasting conflict with great negative influence on world peace is caused by the continued Israeli presence in Palestine, Syria, and Lebanon, and the sometimes violent reaction of the occupied Arabs.

I've been worried about Billy and called him. He's had a lot of cancellations since the Libyan-Jewish altercation. He was very apologetic about any embarrassment to me, but I'm more concerned about him.

In my absence from Plains, Billy had become my surrogate among farmers, local news reporters, and thousands of tourists. He was naturally outspoken on almost any subject; now his excessive drinking sometimes led him to make inappropriate comments, and often enough they were distorted or taken out of context—which is what happened when he defended his attempt to sell oil from Libya.

JANUARY 19   Israel has reinvaded Lebanon, even going beyond the Litani River, which makes the UN force look foolish and encourages them to withdraw.

We agreed to reassess the South Korean troop withdrawal issue, but Harold and I both said they should continue to be withdrawn. Although North Korea has built up additional forces, a countervailing factor is the extremely good economic circumstances in South Korea, which lets them defend themselves, plus the restraint that China might place on North Korea.

I had been a submarine officer in the Pacific arena during the Korean War, and the area was of special interest to me. I very much wanted to reduce U.S. military forces gradually and let the South Koreans build up their own strength accordingly; unfortunately, we were never able to accomplish this. South Korean leaders were opposed to our plan, in part because they feared their neighbors, but also because they wanted us to pay the major costs. There were very close ties between military leaders in our two countries, so a lot of pressure also came from the Pentagon and the CIA. I was somewhat skeptical of intelligence reports that North Korea had doubled the size of its military within a few years, but had no way to disprove them.

Although not able to make progress in the Korean peninsula while in office, I accepted Kim Il Sung's invitation to Pyongyang in 1994 and negotiated with him an agreement that resolved (at least for six years) his threat to purify nuclear fuel adequately for weapons. He also agreed to a summit meeting with the South Korean president. (Details of these negotiations and their aftermath can be found in my 2007 book, Beyond the White House.*)*

I'm reading Barbara Tuchman's book A *Distant Mirror,* about the fourteenth century, which is good.

JANUARY 21 The shah decided not to come to the U.S., which suits me fine.

MONDAY, JANUARY 22 I met with fifteen of the top executives of the American Trucking Association. Of course, they're against deregulation, and they made clear their economic difficulties as they sat around the room with large diamond rings, gold cuff links, four-hundred-dollar suits, and silk shirts with monograms. There needs to be an end to the antitrust exemption for them to set their own rates, and to have more liberal entry policies so new competitors could serve the routes.

The highlight of the day was Rosalynn's being chosen among the ten women in the world who have the most sensuous and elegant legs!

JANUARY 23 I was pleased with a message from Bakhtiar that he's going to stand firm, and the military would support him in preventing Khomeini from coming into Iran this Friday as scheduled. He'll close the airports and permit Khomeini to enter only if he promises to do so as a religious leader, not as a political heir.

I made a briefer, clearer, more balanced State of the Union address this evening. I thought the delivery was relatively poor, but it got good reviews. At least that chore is out of the way for another year.

Earlier in our nation's history the president merely reported on the state of the union to the Congress, as required by the U.S. Constitution. Washington and Adams reported in person, but Jefferson and his successors sent a written report until 1913, when Woodrow Wilson delivered a verbal report to a joint session. This has now expanded into a speech with live worldwide television coverage. The number of interruptions for sustained applause is considered by news media analysts to be a measure of the president's current popularity, so exciting verbiage and oratorical skills are quite important. I made a written report in 1981.

JANUARY 24   CIA gave us an assessment of Deng Xiaoping, his psychological profile, background, prediction of what he is going to discuss with me when he comes next week.

This visit, and its cause, was truly historic: until this point, our nation had never had diplomatic relations with the People's Republic of China (P.R.C.). Since the P.R.C.'s founding on October 1, 1949, the United States had maintained diplomatic ties exclusively with the political remnant of Nationalist China's forces that had been driven from the mainland to the island of Taiwan. This relationship had become deeply embedded in the commercial, media, political, and military establishments of our country. During this time, the P.R.C. was almost invariably referred to in political debates as "Red China" and "Communist," which had a negative connotation similar to the one "terrorist" has today. To me, Deng Xiaoping's welcome in Washington was an early indication of approval for the decision I had made to shift official diplomatic relations to mainland China.

In my meeting with Senator Ribicoff and a large group of senators, I was taken aback by the animosity toward the Soviet Union of senators who had been there. Ribicoff said that the Soviets don't understand the Senate, Bellmon said they were two-faced, Javits said they're not willing to give up anything for SALT, and others around the room had a very negative attitude. I responded that we've negotiated this treaty for six years. It was a benefit to ourselves and the Soviets. We had preempted their influence in Egypt, India, Indonesia, China, Yugoslavia, Romania, Scandinavia, Somalia, Angola, Hungary, North Korea, and the Mideast, where the Soviets have been rooted out altogether. We had to be fair and also recognize the terrible consequences of a Senate rejection of the treaty once it was negotiated. Détente would be destroyed, our allies and the rest of the world would look upon us as warmongers, we would have no chance to control nuclear proliferation, and our own people would lose faith in the nuclear weapons control process.

As will become evident, an unwarranted furor over the revelation that some Soviet troops remained in Cuba and the justified condemnation of the Soviet invasion of Afghanistan would preclude Senate ratification of SALT II. In time, however, the Soviet threat dissipated: internal human rights pressures, a continuing weakening of worldwide Soviet influence, and later the leadership of Mikhail Gorbachev would bring about changes that would result in the fragmentation of the Soviet Union into Russia and about a dozen separate nations.

Afterward Ribicoff called me on reaching home and said he had been overwhelmed by my argument and that if I would meet with small groups of senators in that tone it was a most important way to get SALT ratified.

Immediately thereafter I met with Scoop Jackson, as usual a very discouraging and aggravating meeting. Scoop knows everything—in fact knew everything that was going to happen five or six years before it did happen. He is unappreciated by my cabinet and staff, who in general are worthless and incompetent, is against helping us with most-favored-nation [status] for the Soviet Union and the P.R.C., and is against SALT—but other than this he's happy with me and my administration and wants to help!!

This most-favored-nation status would mean that their terms of trade with the United States would be as unrestricted as possible.

JANUARY 25   I had a good meeting with Muskie and Robert Giaimo [Connecticut Democrat] on the 1980 budget. We urged them to hold the spending level at $532 billion and not use tricks to permit expenditure of additional funds.

Later I finished seven miles and felt good enough to finish ten—in eighty-eight minutes, including two slow miles with Rosalynn.

JANUARY 26   I had my regular meeting with editors from around the country and another news conference. When we come out of one without making big news, that's a major success.

Kennedy's laying the groundwork for a campaign, although he has stated publicly and repeatedly that he's not going to run and will support me. Every day he takes some tiny thing out of the budget and issues a press release condemning me, which is getting tiresome.

We had no doubt at that time or subsequently that Ted Kennedy would be a candidate for president in 1980. What made this challenge so troubling was that, as a Kennedy, he had instantaneous access to the news media, so that a critical comment that would be ignored from any other source would be given headline coverage. At the time, he was an overwhelming favorite in public opinion polls; increasingly, a number of my supporters began to align themselves with him as the prospective next president.

MONDAY, JANUARY 29   I was favorably impressed with Deng. He's small, tough, intelligent, frank, courageous, personable, self-assured, friendly, and it's a pleasure to negotiate with him.

I outlined five basic factors that shaped U.S. opinion and the lives of our people: (a) enhancement of U.S. strength and influence for the benefit of our people and those in the rest of the world; (b) awareness of an increasing desire throughout the world for a better quality of life, more political participation, independence or liberation for peoples, and a desire for freedom from the domination of outside influences; (c) power shifting from a few nations like ourselves and the Soviets to be shared among many nations, with regional leaders emerging like Mexico, Venezuela, Brazil, Nigeria, India, Indonesia, and China; (d) our future American security was tied to good relations with these developing nations; and (e) the rapid increase in Soviet military strength. We have maintained U.S. military parity, and the Soviets were weak politically, economically, ideologically, and their inferiority complex caused a potentially unstable attitude toward the rest of the world. We wanted to join with China to use the positive elements in the world to deal with the negative ones.

Deng stated that the world was "untranquil," and the U.S. and the P.R.C. had many common interests. Mao [Tse-tung] and Chou [En-lai] long ago had described along with him three worlds. The First World was the Soviets and the United States, and the Soviet Union was the main danger. He thought the U.S. should join the Second and Third Worlds to oppose the Soviet Union.

The P.R.C. recognized Israel's existence, but when I asked him if there was a possibility of establishing communications with Israel, he said, "No, at the present time this is not a possibility." He said the Mideast problems were likely to spread to Iran, Saudi Arabia, and other countries unless they were headed off.

His prediction was accurate. It is likely that a factor in the animosity of these nations toward Israel was the unresolved plight of the Palestinians.

During the day we discussed about twenty nations, including India, Turkey, Afghanistan, Iran, and Vietnam. He supported SALT II but said it would not control a Soviet buildup. China needed a long period of peace to realize its full modernizations.

I said we wanted to have the Soviets be a responsible nation and not isolated from the rest.

Deng requested that we meet privately in the Oval Office on the Vietnam question. He outlined all the reasons and then said they were contemplating a punitive action across the border into Vietnam. I pointed out the adverse impact of this; it was best to continue the isolation of Vietnam.

We then went to the state banquet, which was a delightful experience. During the banquet I discussed religion and human rights with him. The overriding issue among the American press was Nixon's attendance at the banquet.

During a quiet moment, Deng expressed his appreciation for my direct involvement in the reconciliation process and asked if I had any personal desire regarding China. I told him I was a Christian, and that as a child I had given five cents a week to help build hospitals and schools for Chinese children. Baptist missionaries to China were our ultimate heroes. I realized that religious freedom was not guaranteed in China, Bibles could not be distributed, and foreign missionaries were prevented from entering the country. I asked that he consider changing these policies. He seemed surprised, laughed, and said he would reply the next day.

He later said he would grant two of my wishes, concerning religious freedom and the distribution of Bibles. On missionaries, however, he was ada-

mant, saying they had exalted themselves and tried to change the culture of Chinese converts, and China would never again permit this to happen.

He kept his promise. Bibles were being freely distributed when I visited China in 1981, and some Christians told me the government had helped obtain special paper for their printing. During the 1982 National People's Conference, religious freedom was guaranteed. Although congregations are required to register with the government, even this restricted system has brought about astounding results. The National Catholic Reporter *magazine recently claimed there are ten thousand new Chinese Christians every day. To put this number in perspective, it equals ten conversions for each million people, or one per one hundred thousand. Chinese Christians may soon constitute a greater number than in any other nation.*

At the Kennedy Center we had another delightful experience. He and I, [his wife] Madame Zhuo Lin, Rosalynn, and Amy went on the stage with the performers, and there was a genuine sense of emotion when he put his arms around little children who had sung a Chinese song. He kissed many of them. The newspapers later said that many in the audience wept. Senator [Paul] Laxalt, who's been a strong opponent of normalization, said later that we had them beat; there was no way to vote against little children singing Chinese songs.

JANUARY 30   The next morning I wrote a letter concerning our objection to a punitive strike against Vietnam, and the letter was read very carefully to Deng. I offered him an intelligence briefing on troop placements around China, and he responded eagerly.

In our final meeting I discussed the claims-and-assets question, with claims against China much greater. He said, "Do you want to resolve it today?" I said, "Yes." He outlined the problem carefully and accurately, said [Ambassador] Huang Hua would work with Blumenthal and have it worked out before tomorrow.

I outlined the problem with most-favored-nation legislation. He said there was no relationship between China and the Soviet Union. He said, "If you want me to release 10 million Chinese to come to the United States, I'd be glad to do so." Everyone laughed. I told him he offered me 10 million Chinese, I offered him ten thousand journalists; he disagreed quickly with that proposal.

We had had a problem with his approval of certain students. I told him we wanted to have maximum student exchange. He said there was a limit to their accommodations but China was strong enough to withstand a few students, and they would not screen them because of ideology. We wanted to exchange journalists. He said there would be some limited travel but not any censorship.

JANUARY 31   Had an excellent breakfast with the Democratic leadership and discussed the advantage of having most-favored-nation treatment given to both China and Russia. Allan Cranston said we could win this issue in Congress even if Jackson opposed. I told them Khomeini had decided to go back, Bakhtiar permitting him.

I had my final meeting with Deng Xiaoping. We signed agreements concerning consular offices, trade, science and technology, cultural exchange, and so forth. After discussing the political problems I had in normalization, Zbig asked him, "Did you have political opposition in China?" Everybody listened very carefully when Deng said, "Yes, I had serious opposition in one province in China—Taiwan."

He was helpful on Taiwan, saying they were patient, wanted to resolve it peacefully, and outlined the offer that Taiwan could retain its cultural life, political independence as an autonomous state, and also its own military forces. But he was insistent that they negotiate with China.

U.S.-China relations have continued to be peaceful and relatively friendly for thirty years. The relatively open and free economic system that evolved has brought China enormous wealth, while our country has steadily grown more deeply in debt to the Chinese because of our negative trade balance and because we have financed a substantial portion of our huge budget deficits by selling U.S. bonds to China. We now owe the Chinese almost $1 trillion. During this same period, China has expanded its influence in international political affairs, and its rapid industrial growth has driven it to become a major purchaser of raw materials from many developing nations and the greatest exporter of goods.

In its political system, China has maintained the authoritarian structure of communism, depriving citizens of the right to choose their leaders. Human rights activists criticize these policies and also the adverse effect of government policy on the culture of ethnic groups, especially the Tibetans and Uighurs.

FEBRUARY 1   Khomeini returned to Iran with a minimum of violence. The military are keeping their powder dry. Huyser was instructed to stay there, and we have a C-130 standing by to bring him out.

During the evening we had a superb session with about twenty key senators—all experienced in foreign affairs. The discussion was led by me, Cy, Harold, and Zbig. Muskie, Kennedy, and [John] Culver all said it was the best evening they ever spent at the White House. We'll continue with more of these evening sessions.

FEBRUARY 2   I went to New York for the memorial service for Nelson Rockefeller. It was very moving, and Happy was very friendly and attractive. The only person who was emotional and weeping openly was President Ford. I presume he felt bad having kicked Rockefeller out of the White House as he prepared for reelection. Rockefeller's contributions were indeed impressive in politics, business, art, and public service.

I knew Nelson Rockefeller when we were both governors, and liked him very much. His wife, Happy, was especially delightful. I will always be grateful to Rockefeller for granting me a great personal favor: in 1973, he made it possible for me to move the remains of William Few, a Georgian who signed the U.S. Constitution, from New York to Augusta, Georgia.

There is little doubt that Ford's decision to replace Rockefeller with Bob Dole on the 1976 Republican ticket—a decision made largely due to pressure from right-wing southern Republicans—was a fatal political mistake. Dole was a flop on the campaign trail, and he alienated the African American community, which would have supported the Republican ticket if it included Rockefeller, who was their hero for his generosity to them. The shift to Dole also cost the Republicans New York, and a win there could have given a Ford-Rockefeller ticket the victory in 1976.

FEBRUARY 3–4   I directed Huyser to return from Iran to give me a personal report.

We enjoyed skiing in and outside Camp David.

MONDAY, FEBRUARY 5   World oil supplies have deteriorated since our predictions in April of 1977. At that time we were looked on as doomsayers. I told Transportation to hold firm on the fifty-five-mile-per-hour speed limit and cut off federal funds if states violate it.

Fritz and I discussed the need to address the Democratic attacks on me. Kennedy is the worst violator, and Frank Church is taking cheap shots, trying to raise money from American Jews.

General Dutch Huyser came in to give me a private report. He said there was a remarkable difference in interpretation of American policy between himself and Ambassador Sullivan. I told him this had been evident. He pointed out that both he and Sullivan read the same dispatches, but Sullivan thought we ought to permit Khomeini to take over, that it would lead to democracy; Huyser thinks it would lead to communism. Sullivan thinks the military is very weak; Huyser thinks it's strong. Sullivan thinks the military ought to stand aloof and not participate in political processes; Huyser thinks the military should support the constitutional government of Bakhtiar while democratic processes permit the writing of a new constitution and free elections.

Sullivan has almost been disloyal, in my opinion, and we sent a deputy assistant secretary over to try to get him straightened out or remove him.

Huyser thinks the military have made adequate plans to protect the installations. Originally, when the shah left, the military was determined to have a coup, but he dissuaded them. [U.S.] general [Philip] Gast is qualified to take over from Huyser. The military refer to the shah now as a has-been, and there is growing belief in Iran that Khomeini is part of the problem.

Unfortunately, no one at that time had a clear understanding of what was going on in Iran, nor did we receive accurate predictions of what would happen in the future.

FEBRUARY 6 Thailand prime minister [Chomanan] Kriangsak and I discussed refugees. We've accepted about 170,000, plus 58,000 more that are coming [from Vietnam and Cambodia]. The Thais, with their much smaller country, have accepted 140,000. Most of theirs are by land, primarily out of Laos.

When I met with Cy's people, I laid the law down to them as strong as ever in my life. The situation in the State Department has become intolerable. I described my procedure for making decisions, how difficult they were. Once I made a decision, it had to be carried out loyally, even if they disagreed. The only alternative for them would be to resign. If I had another outbreak of misinformation, distortions, and self-serving newspaper leaks as had occurred in the Iran situation, I was going to direct Cy to discharge the leaders who were responsible, even though some innocent people may be punished. I told them I realized the press was sometimes guilty, but I knew from years of experience in politics that almost always there was a source even for an inaccurate press story. I told them again either to be loyal or resign. Then I got up and left.

FEBRUARY 7   Ted Kennedy called to say that Rosalynn was the most eloquent witness they ever had and was magnificent. [Rosalynn was testifying about the recommendations of a task force that I had established on mental health.] Although some of the reporters said she was nervous at first, there was no doubt that she knew all about mental health and made an impression on the Senate Health Committee members.

I met with Zbig's key leaders and criticized them for an attitude of contention and competition with State. Zbig is too competitive and incisive, Cy is too easy on his subordinates, and the news media aggravate the inevitable differences. I hardly know the desk officers in State but work very closely with NSC people.

It was a rare occasion when I received an innovative and helpful suggestion from the State Department while I was president. The driving forces that shaped our foreign policy originated mostly in the White House and occasionally from the Defense Department. On the other hand, desk officers at State provided cautionary restraints which, I have to admit, were sometimes well-advised.

I met with Henry Kissinger privately, and we had a good discussion. On the Mideast he thought a top-level meeting was probably necessary, but believed we will get a peace treaty. On Iran he said the shah feels betrayed. He had serious thoughts about Ambassador Sullivan. He said we only have two options: either a military coup or another Libya or Algeria. He said in a time of revolution, force was absolutely necessary; compromise was permissible only before or after the crisis.

The reason I invited him was to discuss SALT. Kissinger will meet with Republican senators tomorrow and then go to Mexico for a month to finish his book. He said he couldn't criticize the details of SALT since he had negotiated 60 or 75 percent of the agreement. He would like a briefing when he returns from Mexico. He doubted the willingness or the capability of U.S. armed forces to act in a troubled region. He said, for instance, "Thirty percent of the soldiers are black. Will they fight in Africa?" And the third concern he had was Soviet adventurism since 1975. He said he would not be unhelpful, and reminded me that his concerns were not insuperable. He said Germany was moving toward the Soviet Union no matter what we did. My hope is that my meeting with him will give him some caution about criticizing the SALT treaty itself.

I decided to appoint former senator Dick Clark to coordinate our refugee program. I would like refugees to be in a special category as briefly as possible after they come to our country.

FEBRUARY 8   We [Rosalynn and I] had lunch with Frank and Bethine Church. He's been a pain in the neck for me as chairman of Foreign Relations. I outlined what I could and could not accept, and he said he had been inclined to go too far and too fast and would back off and consult more closely with State.

Frank Church had a notable record in the Senate, and although he was not always a reliable ally, he was very helpful to me with some issues. He had been a leader in opposition to the Vietnam War, and his committee had revealed serious crimes committed by the FBI and CIA. This led to the passage of the 1978 Foreign Intelligence Surveillance Act (FISA), which I supported. It severely restricted surveillance of both foreigners and American citizens, and required that covert surveillance receive prior approval by a panel of judges. After the terrorist attacks of September 11, 2001, President George W. Bush circumvented some of these restraints.

FEBRUARY 10–11   We did a lot of skiing [around Camp David] in some very rough terrain. All of us came back with bruises, but we enjoyed having Hamilton and Jody, Cy and Gay Vance with us.

I spent a lot of time working on my speech to the Mexican Congress and monitoring changing events in Iran, where the military withdrew their support for Bakhtiar. He resigned, and [Mehdi] Bazargan apparently will be in power. Our primary interest has been to increase our interrelationship with Bazargan in order to protect Americans. So far we've been successful—one of the few successes we've enjoyed in Iran lately.

MONDAY, FEBRUARY 12   The Bazargan people have been very helpful, protecting our embassy, protecting General Gast, and sending messages that they want to have continuing good relations.

FEBRUARY 13   Today's report is much better. Khomeini is likely to go to Qom, leaving Bazargan to run the government. Most of his ministers have been educated in or have direct ties with Western nations.

Elie Wiesel came by. He'll be chairman of the Commission on the Holocaust. He brought me four books he had written, and seemed to be pleased that we were going to recognize this tragedy.

I talked to Griffin briefly about the appointment of judges. We're still trying to build up appointment of blacks and women, over the opposition of senators and even some Judge Selection Committee members that I appointed. The American Bar Association has shown that the minority and women appointees we have chosen measure up very well in quality compared to the white men.

FEBRUARY 14   I had a report about 3:00 a.m. from Cy concerning a difficult situation with our Iranian embassy, but Khomeini sent some forces for its protection. Two marines were slightly wounded.

Also called Mrs. Adolph Dubs, the wife of our ambassador to Afghanistan, to express my condolences to her because her husband was killed in a shoot-out with three terrorists who had kidnapped Ambassador Dubs. We thought the Afghanistan officials, advised by Soviets, were too peremptory in their showdown with weapons and probably caused the death of our ambassador. He was a fine man, strongly supportive of my policies. I authorized his burial at Arlington Cemetery.

Arrived in Mexico City to a welcome—deliberately cool, arranged by [President José] López Portillo. We went to the National Palace for a discussion on foreign policy. My assessment of Portillo is that he is an academic, philosopher, strong, honest, emotional, likes to pontificate, postures for news media, extremely egotistical, born with a silver spoon in his mouth. His nation is shifting from a developing country to one with substantial oil wealth; the sharp division between his kind of life and the average Mexican's is undoubtedly a root of future trouble. He's covering this up by blaming Mexico's trouble on the U.S. It was difficult not to respond sharply when he postured in this tone for his domestic benefit.

He wanted to speak from the viewpoint of a developing nation. He expressed concern about an absence of clear U.S. policy and said that Central America should have been a federation, as Mexico became. They didn't have any oil. Cuba may become a model for them in the future. Economic systems were disrupted and social problems ignored. Mexico's position was one of aloofness, nonintervention. The problems in Nicaragua were not Mexico's but the fault of the U.S. The free world had neglected its area of influence, whereas the Socialist countries have taken care of theirs.

I replied that the United States had a clear but complex policy. Stability was important to us; instability was important to the Communist nations. We did not divide the world up between the Soviet Union and ours as far as hegemony was concerned. The U.S. was the strongest nation, and we enhanced our strength by close ties with allies, which were being made even more secure. Our goal was peace for our own people and others. We wanted to get along with both China and the Soviet Union, and improve our relationships with the Third World. We were successful in these efforts, and trying to control nuclear and conventional weapons and the possible nuclear proliferation. In Latin America we were treating nations for the first time as individuals and as equals, working for peace, human rights, democracy. One example of this was the Panama Canal treaties having been concluded.

We were afraid the Nicaraguan problems would spill over and adversely affect their neighbors. We were trying to strengthen the OAS and other regional groups. Mexico should take a growing responsibility in Central America, and since they had such a good relationship with Cuba, they should talk to Castro about his interventions in Africa; their [Cuba's] rapid buildup of armaments; and their refusal to control nuclear weapons by signing the Treaty of Tlatelolco.

At lunch, he had handed out his remarks in advance and made some very abusive statements, cautioning us to play clean and honor the independence of Mexico. The toast was completely inappropriate, but I responded positively. Most of the news coverage was about Portillo's abusive comments, and this image hung over my entire visit.

I had my own troubles with the media on this trip: in my impromptu response to López Portillo's toast, I made a joke about having diarrhea on my first Mexican visit, in 1963, which didn't help the situation.

FEBRUARY 15   Portillo took me on a tour of the mansion and grounds. It was unbelievable what he has spent: separate houses for each of their children; a personal gymnasium that must have cost hundreds of thousands; electric cars, outdoor and indoor swimming pools, portraits of himself throughout the mansion. I left Los Pinos [the president's residence] and went to Ixtlilco El Grande, a small village about sixty-five miles southeast of Mexico City, and felt much more at home.

That night Leonard Bernstein conducted one of the Mexico City symphony orchestras, a good performance, but a little ragged on some passages I knew well in Beethoven's Fifth.

FEBRUARY 16   I went to Los Pinos for a final breakfast meeting with López Portillo and told him I didn't think we should have a general discussion. The situation was so bad between us because of his first day's toast that we ought to repair the public relations damage. His face was pale, and he suggested that we go to his study together. I told him, with only an interpreter present, that our country was not accustomed to being chastised publicly, especially when we were guests in another nation. We respected the independence of Mexico, and headlines in Mexico City to the contrary were of great concern to me.

I told him I had studied Mexico and its problems extensively before coming and had admiration for him and his family. There was a good attitude in the U.S. toward Mexico, but he had caused damage. We both had problems, but his were not caused by us. It was important that we reopen negotiations on gas, fisheries, and other things they had terminated, and I would like to meet him in the summer, somewhere in Texas, where we would show American hospitality. I wanted the press and the public to know after I left that we cleared the air and were ready to move forward to resolve problems.

For the first time he did not posture but responded soberly that he would hold a press conference immediately after my plane departed. I told him we would leave the American press to hear his remarks, and I would do my part to put a good face on our meeting. He said he would meet with me anywhere I wanted in the summer.

I then went to the Chamber of Deputies, was well received, made a speech in Spanish, announced to the group that López Portillo and I were going to meet in the summer, and then I went to the airport. Portillo's press conference was very good. I was told that Jody Powell could not have done better.

Relations between the United States and Mexico remain quite sensitive, especially on issues involving immigration. When I left office, there were 2.2 million Mexican immigrants in the United States; this number has now grown to 11.5 million. The inherent difference in personal income creates powerful incentives for Mexicans to cross the border, legally or not, to obtain employment and transmit earnings back to their families. They provide much-needed workers in less-attractive jobs but in recent years have been the target of condemnation and abuse from news commentators and members of Congress. Laws have not yet been passed that would make it possible for the United States to accept needed workers, restrict excessive immigration, guarantee humane treatment, and accommodate those who have lived and worked here for many years.

Back in Washington I got a brief report from Harold Brown on his trip to the Mideast. It was successful in assuring them of our staunchness. The Arabs were on the defensive because we want a closer relationship than any of them want. They obviously don't want Israel to be assigned any major defensive role and don't want an American military base on their land. They do want excessive American military sales and/or financial aid.

Later, beginning in the 1990s, large U.S. military bases were established in the region. The building of bases in Saudi Arabia was condemned strongly by some as a sacrilegious intrusion and was later cited as justification for violence against the United States and its allies.

FEBRUARY 18   The temperature [at Camp David] was below zero, but we skied a lot. Late in the afternoon it began to snow heavily. We were going down a very steep slope on the new highway, it was almost dark, the trail was quite narrow, and the snow was in our eyes. My right ski went under the ice sheet and I fell on my face, which was cut badly—forehead, upper and lower lips, and chin—and bled profusely. We looked around for Dr. Lukash, but he was not there. We called on the radio and asked him to come down the mountain on a snowmobile, but he was doctoring the National Park superintendent who had had an identical spill and cut his face even more severely. I rode back to Camp David on a snowmobile, and Dr. Lukash treated my face.

MONDAY, FEBRUARY 19   We skied again Monday.

Before leaving for a trip to Atlanta, I spent at least an hour having extensive makeup applied to my face. It was so thick and heavy that I couldn't smile without having it crack.

FEBRUARY 20   I made a foreign affairs speech at Georgia Tech and got the first honorary degree they've ever given. They had to pass a special rule by the Board of Regents that an honorary degree could be given by a college in the university system only to an alumnus of the college who had become president of the United States.

FEBRUARY 22   As usual, at lunch with Rosalynn we discuss issues parallel to the ones I discuss with my major foreign and domestic advisors, plus a few personal matters, quite often financial in nature; our family interrelationships; White House entertainment; guest lists for state dinners and other events; and she brings me correspondence of interest to both of us.

FEBRUARY 23   Cy reported from Camp David that [Egyptian prime minister Mustafa] Khalil and Dayan were having difficulty reaching agreement on some items [concerning the peace treaty]. Khalil is authorized to act, but Dayan will have to go back and report to Begin and the cabinet. We told them to conclude their discussions Sunday evening, and we'll let them know I'd like to meet with Begin and Sadat next week.

I told Joe Califano to announce that we will propose a comprehensive health plan to the public and the Congress, but we'd only move this year on the first part. He will continue consultations with liberal members of the Congress, convincing them that Kennedy's proposals would be excessively expensive and impossible to pass.

We went by to see Baryshnikov rehearsing [in the East Room]. He's really a remarkable dancer and will perform Sunday afternoon.

We were going to the Moscow Philharmonic performance Saturday but discovered they refused to bring Rostropovich's sister over [to the United States], which is a human rights problem. After Rosalynn discussed it with Rostropovich, we decided not to go.

MONDAY, FEBRUARY 26   We've brought all U.S. citizens out of Iran who are willing to leave. The Congress seemed to be in better shape this year than ever before. The Senate approved Leonard Woodcock as ambassador to China.

FEBRUARY 27   The Israeli cabinet refused to let Begin come over to negotiate with the Egyptians. For months now the Israelis have refused to negotiate on any reasonable basis. It's hard for us to understand their motivation. We decided that I would call Begin and Sadat and brief congressional leaders on what has occurred [in the peace talks].

I approved twelve more judges, with three blacks, three Hispanics. We're having some success in affirmative action but still a terrible time getting senators to agree to appoint women.

During my tenure, I appointed 56 judges to the courts of appeals and 203 to the district courts. I was able to increase the number of women appellate judges from one to eleven, and district judges from five women to twenty-nine. This was five times more than all my predecessors. In addition, thirty-nine of my appointees were African American. Accomplishing this was very difficult and my efforts were strongly opposed, but ultimately we convinced everyone involved that I was adamant in my commitment to ensure fair representation among the judicial appointees.

Khomeini sent his representative to pledge increased friendship and cooperation, and to make sure that we were supporting a stable government in Iran. We gave him that assurance.

My decision at the time was to recognize the revolutionary government as legitimate and to exchange diplomatic emissaries. There were more than eight thousand American citizens living and working in Iran, and, as would soon become known throughout the world, we had a complement of diplomats and staff in our Tehran embassy. I have always believed that the ayatollah intended to honor these mutual commitments and was taken by surprise when, nine months later, young militants acted independently by seizing the American embassy and holding hostages.

I had an interesting meeting with Dobrynin, to emphasize the fundamental importance of our relationship with the Soviet Union. I told him we were demanding that China withdraw from Vietnam. Also, I thought

Vietnam should withdraw from Cambodia. We wanted to draw SALT to a conclusion. He thought the SALT discussions could be concluded in two weeks, with a summit to be scheduled immediately thereafter.

The reactions of Begin and Sadat were predictable. Begin said he did not want to go to Camp David, was not bringing any cabinet member with him, and would not discuss substantive issues. Sadat was willing to negotiate at any time but insisting on the comprehensive nature of the Camp David agreement being preserved.

Still have some problems with the Yemenis. The Saudis have called all their military people back from leave and have announced it's an international crisis. I approved the early delivery of some of our previously contracted weapons to North Yemen.

There's increasing turbulence in Afghanistan from tribal leaders and religious groups who don't favor the Russian-supported Communist government.

MARCH 1   I spent the afternoon preparing for Begin's arrival. When he got off the plane he made some very combative statements: the talks were in deep crisis, he refused to let us force him to sign any worthless document that would be an obstacle to peace, and so forth. Apparently he was extremely nervous, and I did everything I could to put him at ease. He wanted to speak first. He had suffered personally from the Camp David concessions he had made. He was willing to go through with the agreement, but Egypt's demands were irresponsible, and contrary to the Camp David Accords. He said at Camp David Dayan now had full authority to negotiate, but Khalil had no authority. He then said the Russians were not human. There was a woman in Russia who slept with a knife under her pillow because the Russians were rapists, and this was typical of their attitude.

I replied that the U.S. and Israel had many mutual interests, and a strong Israel was of value to the Middle East and to us. Camp David had been a historic first step toward recognizing the interests of Israel and the United States in the entire region, but our national interests extended beyond Israel. The unilateral buildup of Israel as a powerful military force would be considered a threat to the Arab world. There was no way that a threat could be successfully mounted against Israel. The threat was from Palestinian militants who had been encouraged by the events in Iran, and Saudi Arabia and Egypt had been a major restraining force on the PLO and others. The major long-range threat was from the Soviet Union toward the Middle East, and I hoped Israel could join with the moderate Arab nations in meeting that threat.

I pointed out the isolated nature of Israel; in five years I would like for Israel to have as good a friendship with France as with us. It was not good for them to have to rely almost exclusively on the U.S. for their security, although our support of Israel was permanent and staunch.

I proposed that Israel and Egypt move expeditiously toward elections in the West Bank/Gaza and exchange of ambassadors. He accepted the West Bank/Gaza part, and that the ambassador exchange be as agreed.

My judgment is that he's completely inflexible on the treaty terms. Maybe we ought to put together a comprehensive package, including a peace treaty, a defense agreement with Israel, and increased aid; let them accept it or reject it, and then [I'll] go to the American public and explain that we've done the best we could.

MARCH 2   We met with Begin and his people in the Cabinet Room, and he was very strong, negative, apparently confident, making unreasonable demands and adamant statements. He said Sadat still wants to destroy Israel.

I emphasized that Begin had made no proposals to resolve the differences, therefore there had been no progress. Prospects were dismal, and Sadat had heavy pressures to withdraw from the negotiations. Egypt had given Israelis everything they originally wanted, and Israel had continually raised demands. We did not need a Mideast policeman; the Arab nations had more fear of Israel than they did Soviet influence. The security of Israel was paramount for us. If we had a peace treaty, increased security capability for Israel would be warranted. We have gone as far as we can in compromise language with no constructive response from Israel. Begin seems to have very limited concepts of any future events or strategic problems.

That night I thought about how to break the obvious impasse, caused by Begin himself. I've not been able to penetrate past him to other members of the cabinet, the Knesset, or the Israeli people. He deliberately distorts our position and spreads lies through the news media. We have a problem with the U.S. public in not bringing this thing to a conclusion. It's sapping away our strength.

So I decided to pursue the possibility of going first to Egypt, getting together with Sadat, and then going to Israel. If we're not successful, just describe what we proposed and what they've given up, and let the whole thing shift to the UN.

MARCH 3 Cy, Harold, Zbig, Jody, Hamilton, and Fritz worked on my proposal. Except for Zbig and Hamilton, they're all concerned about it. Begin came to the White House and was moody and sullen, and after two hours he left with a total absence of progress, but with a clear picture of our concern and willingness to break off the negotiations.

MARCH 4 I taught Sunday school from Romans 8. I told the class, and later the reporters, that Begin and I had made no progress.

I drafted an identical letter to Begin and Sadat explaining how I proposed to resolve remaining differences based on the nuances of our treaty text, and including guarantees of U.S. action in case the agreements were violated in the future.

MONDAY, MARCH 5 Begin called to say that the Israeli cabinet had accepted our treaty proposals. I called Sadat and told him about the Israeli acceptance but did not go into detail on language. I told him I was prepared to come to Egypt, and he was overjoyed. I then sent for Begin and informed him that I was going to Egypt and would also like to come to Jerusalem. He guaranteed me a good reception.

Begin told me he couldn't sleep after my meeting with him Saturday night, and I presume he saw a serious deterioration in U.S.-Israeli relationships because of his adamant position. I decided to send Brzezinski to Egypt with the advance team and informed Sadat. He replied, "Great! Your trip will be a wonderful event and a complete success."

Throughout the morning we watched real-time photographs come in from Jupiter, remarkable achievements in our Voyager program.

MARCH 7 We've gotten very negative reports from the Saudis and others concerning my Mideast trip, with threats to cut off aid to Egypt and even reduce their sale of oil. I sent messages to a few of the more reasonable ones asking them to support our peace efforts.

I instructed Vance to hold firm on Taiwan legislation. If it violates my commitments to China, I will have to veto it, leaving it illegal to deal with Taiwan.

I was in control of this situation because I had presidential authority to form new ties to China and sever the treaty relationships with Taiwan. The Congress, meanwhile, had more limited authority: they could pass legislation that authorized our country to continue trade and commerce with Taiwan, but only as a province of China.

Kissinger congratulated me on my going to the Mideast. He predicted success, and we both agreed that the problem was with the Israelis.

MARCH 8   We went to Egypt. I had assurances from Sadat that he would be helpful, but doubted if Begin wanted the peace treaty. Our only hope was to convince the Israeli people, the Knesset, and the cabinet. As I've said many times, I have never been pleasantly surprised by the Israelis.

In my private visits with Sadat, he emphasized that his main concern was about me. He wanted my trip to be a "smashing success" but directed me to negotiate fairly, in the best interests of Egypt and Israel. I reminded Sadat that Begin is both courageous and basically honest, but in his mind he went too far at Camp David. Sadat said, "I don't know how you performed this miracle at Camp David." I told him it was his giving me flexibility to negotiate and Begin's desire to represent the Israeli people's inclination toward peace. I reminded Sadat that it's been very difficult for Begin because he's had to go back home to the condemnation of his old friends. Sadat understands that Begin may wish to back out if he gets a chance, or wait until after 1980 when there's a president in the White House who may not be so balanced between the Israeli and Arab interests. Sadat and I worked out all the agreements necessary between us and Egypt; in effect, I had complete authority from Sadat to negotiate as I saw fit.

MARCH 9   In Alexandria the crowds were the largest I've ever seen. I told Sadat this was one time a politician didn't have to exaggerate the numbers.

MARCH 10   I left Egypt with confidence because I had authority from Sadat to conclude an agreement.

I drove from Tel Aviv to Jerusalem with Begin and President [Yitzhak] Navon, whom I really liked. We arrived in the outskirts of Jerusalem after dark, and Mayor [Teddy] Kollek and the chief rabbi served me bread and wine. There were angry demonstrators, and the Secret Service warned me that we would be pelted with eggs, but we were not.

There were many signs, mostly negative, but I remember one large one that said, WELCOME, BILLY'S BROTHER!

We went to Begin's residence, and he told me he could not sign *any* agreement. I would have to conclude talks with him; let him submit proposals to the cabinet; let the Knesset have an eight- to ten-day debate on all the issues; and only then would he sign the documents. I couldn't believe it. I stood up and asked him if he thought it was necessary for me to stay any longer. We spent about forty-five minutes on our feet in his study. I asked him if he actually wanted a peace treaty, because my impression was that he did with apparent relish everything he could do to obstruct it. He came right up and looked in my eyes about a foot away and said that he wanted peace as much as anything else in the world. It was almost midnight when I left. We had an extremely unsatisfactory meeting, equivalent to what we'd had the previous Saturday night at the White House.

I have rarely been so disgusted in all my life. I was convinced he would do everything possible to stop a treaty, rather than face the full autonomy he had promised in the West Bank/Gaza.

MARCH 11   I told President Navon what had occurred the previous night. He had never heard of any such commitment by the prime minister to the Knesset.

Ham and the others advised me not to take my frustration with Begin out on the cabinet, that I must stick with my original reason for coming to Israel: to go over Begin's head to the cabinet, the Knesset, and the Israeli people. We spent hours with the cabinet, with Begin negative on every subject. He asked me first to preside and then rudely interrupted, wouldn't let his own cabinet officers or anyone else speak without interrupting them. It was a fruitless session. [Shmuel] Tamir, minister of justice, was impressive, and so was [Ariel] Sharon, minister of agriculture. He's tough, a former general, an avocado farmer—a nut on Jewish settlements but seemed to have substance. [Archaeologist and Deputy Prime Minister Yigael] Yadin was also very good, but they all were dominated by Begin.

In the banquet hall I shook hands with the opposition leaders, [Shimon] Peres, [Yitzhak] Rabin, Abba Eban, and others. Navon gave a nice toast, after which Begin gave one that was inconsiderate and very negative.

MONDAY, MARCH 12   I worked on the Knesset speech and then met with the cabinet, but they were not flexible or constructive. All were present— sixteen plus Begin. They seemed to have a genuine concern about oil supplies.

We had a few minutes at the hotel, and then I departed for the Knesset and gave my speech. There was quite a buzz when I said the people were ready for peace but the leaders had not yet shown the courage to take a chance. Begin apparently resented this comment, but it was accurate and needed to be said. When Begin got up to try to speak, he was interrupted by shouts and rudeness. He seemed to take delight in it, beaming with pleasure every time it occurred.

Peres had made an excellent speech, about a third devoted to the rights of the Palestinians. Begin thought this was not a good thing to say, and claimed the Labor Party had turned against Peres, which was not true. During Begin's and Peres's speeches, I wrote down the two basic issues that needed to be resolved: oil and Gaza access. I told Cy to meet with the cabinet and get these key issues settled.

I then met with the Foreign Relations Committee and then went back to the hotel, as tired as I've been in a long time.

Zbig and Cy came to tell me that they made no progress with the cabinet, and we were astonished to hear that Begin claimed substantial progress, with only a few issues to be resolved.

I decided to invite Begin for breakfast tomorrow morning, and to call Sadat and report my lack of progress.

Shortly afterward, Dayan called Cy to say that he and several other cabinet members—Yadin, Sharon, Tamir, Weizman—had gotten together to see how to salvage the talks, which apparently were doomed to fail. They were all concerned about Begin's intransigence.

MARCH 13   We had an early session [before breakfast] to go over the prospects. The cabinet, even the more conservative members, seemed to want a settlement before I left at noon, with Begin holding out adamantly.

With Begin I outlined our position on oil: nondiscriminatory sales directly to Israel with us guaranteeing oil supplies. He was evasive, said he

"I [decided to] walk from the Capitol to the White House on Inauguration Day . . . I thought it would be a good demonstration of confidence by the new president in the people of our country as far as security was concerned, and also would be a tangible indication of some reduction in the imperial status of the president and his family." (January 20, 1977)

Vice President Walter Mondale was kept thoroughly informed about the most sensitive and difficult subjects, and I trusted his judgment, honesty, and frankness. He never deviated from my policies in his actions or statements, he was careful not to usurp my authority as president, and I never failed to honor his suggestions on how his partnership with me could be enhanced.

Among all my cabinet officers, Secretary of State Cyrus Vance was philosophically closest to me, but his first loyalty was to the State Department. On numerous occasions, he threatened to resign when he felt someone else might be given too significant a part to play in foreign affairs. Cy and I remained good friends, though, and after I left office, I would visit with him and his family on my trips to New York.

As a college student, Hamilton Jordan had volunteered to help me in my campaign for governor in 1966; four years later he became my top political leader. In the White House, he effectively served as my chief of staff, although he did not want any title. Everyone in my administration—and in Congress—recognized Hamilton as the most influential of my advisors in Washington.

On all issues, foreign or domestic, Press Secretary Jody Powell always spoke with my full confidence and complete understanding of my position. Jody had been my constant traveling companion and, except for Rosalynn, the closest person to me for many years. He was never excluded even from the most sensitive discussions, and his judgment about how much could be revealed was impeccable.

Mother became quite well-known when I was governor and then president, and took full advantage of her fame to become friends with notable people, enjoy worldwide travel, and appear as a frequent guest of Johnny Carson on *The Tonight Show*. She delivered numerous speeches, never had a text, and sometimes shocked her audiences with the frankness of her extemporaneous remarks.

My mother always said that Billy was her most intelligent child, and none of us disputed her. He devoured information of all kinds and made a lot of money on wagers about esoteric facts, historical events, or sports statistics. Billy had a great sense of humor—sometimes seemingly crude when repeated by others—and formed intense friendships. I am confident that he had ten times as many close friends as I.

"Rosalynn has changed in the last couple of years. She's gotten younger, healthier, prettier, more enjoyable to be around." (January 16, 1979) "Rosalynn returned from Peru, quite excited about her trip. She's an outstanding diplomat in that she can broach without embarrassment subjects that are very difficult to raise through an ambassador or the State Department." (July 29, 1980)

Amy, who was born fifteen years after her youngest brother, Jeff, was nine when we moved into the White House. She had attended a racially integrated school in Plains, and we enrolled her in a similar public school in Washington. Thoroughly engaged in politics, she joined in our often heated family discussions during mealtimes. Amy was naturally shy and always wanted to avoid the limelight.

Known as "the Father of the Atomic Navy," Admiral Hyman Rickover is widely considered to be the greatest engineer of all time. Other than my father, he shaped my life more than any other man. He always demanded perfection, never admitted satisfaction with any level of my performance, and worked harder and more hours than anyone I ever knew.

Senator Hubert Humphrey was a hero of mine. Although despised by many Southern political leaders for his successful sponsorship of our party's civil rights plank in 1948, he was later reconciled with conservative senators because of his honesty, perseverance, and oratorical skills. Georgia senator Herman Talmadge once said to me, "Hubert is the only person I know who has more answers than there are questions."

On April 18, 1977, I delivered one of the most important speeches of my presidency. I began by saying that the energy crisis was "unprecedented in our history," and that with the exception of preventing war, it was "the greatest challenge that our country will face during our lifetime." I then said: "This difficult effort will be the 'moral equivalent of war,' except that we will be uniting our efforts to build and not to destroy."

Before becoming president, I studied the original agreement regarding the Panama Canal, which had been in effect since 1903. It was obviously unfair, and my commitment to furthering justice and human rights made me determined to negotiate a new treaty; it was also important to ensure the long-term safety of the canal. Securing the Senate ratification of this agreement was to become the most difficult task of my political life.

Zbigniew Brzezinski had been my primary foreign affairs advisor during my presidential campaign and continued in this role as national security advisor. He and I were in close contact throughout each day and had an excellent personal relationship.

Bert Lance had been one of my most intimate friends for many years, and as director of the Office of Management and Budget he was my primary contact with the business community. He became engulfed in a controversy involving his actions while president of a small bank in Georgia, which ultimately led to his resignation in September 1977. Later, all the allegations were either withdrawn or disproved.

In the fall of 1977, Dizzy Gillespie and Sarah Vaughan gave a jazz concert on the South Lawn. I went onstage with Dizzy and joined him in a rendition of "Salt Peanuts." It was a high point in my life when *The New York Times* complimented my singing!

As a young senator, Joe Biden had been my most effective supporter during the 1976 campaign. In January 1978, Joe came in to see me and told me that Ted Kennedy had decided to run for president in 1980 and was already lining up support. This was the first indication I had about Kennedy's presidential plans, which were soon to become more evident.

"Welcomed President and Mrs. Anwar Sadat this morning and had my first meeting with him. At first he was a little shy, or ill at ease, . . . but it soon became obvious to me that he was a charming and frank and also very strong and courageous leader who has never shrunk from making difficult public decisions . . . I believe he'll be a great aid if we get down to the final discussions on the Middle East." (April 4, 1977)

"Begin had his strong points [during the negotiations at Camp David]: intense feelings, courage, sure knowledge of history, a clear concept of what he wanted, and in the end a surprising flexibility that made it possible for us to achieve success. He had a realization that a majority of Israelis, other than his old revolutionary friends, would support what he was doing." (September 17, 1978)

"I described the wide differences between them [Sadat and Begin] and called for both to be flexible . . . Begin said we need to forget past differences . . . Sadat said he hoped the spirit of King David, the great leader of Israel, would prevail at Camp David." (September 6, 1978)

"The signing ceremony [marking the Egypt-Israel peace treaty] was well attended, exciting, and pleasant. Sadat was effusive in his praise of me; did not mention Begin at all. Begin made a longer speech. All of them were adequate, with a sense of the historic importance of the treaty. I just pray that we can keep this same sense of cooperation in the future." (March 26, 1979)

Despite transient ill feelings toward Henry Kissinger when he made disparaging remarks about my policies or actions, I respected his knowledge of international affairs, his experience, and his sound judgment. He gave me very helpful support during some of the most crucial times, and I continue to value his wisdom and advice.

My relationship with Gerald Ford transcended political or partisan differences—in fact, Ford and I once challenged historians to find a closer friendship between presidents. One of his last phone calls to me was a request that I deliver the eulogy at his funeral. Startled, I responded that I would do so if he would make me the same promise. Delivering the eulogy at Ford's state funeral in January 2007 was a sad duty but a great honor.

It was a remarkable occasion when Helmut Schmidt (chancellor of West Germany), Jim Callaghan (prime minister of the United Kingdom), Valéry Giscard D'Estaing (president of France), and I met in January 1979 for two days of discussions in Guadeloupe. Rarely do the leaders of the top four Western democracies spend time together in an informal setting.

Deng Xiaoping's visit to the United States in January 1979 was truly historic: until this point, our nation had never had diplomatic relations with the People's Republic of China (P.R.C.). To me, Deng's welcome in Washington was an early indication of approval for the decision I had made to normalize relations with the P.R.C.

Senator Robert Byrd was remarkably effective and was, overall, a great asset to me as Democratic majority leader. As president pro tempore of the Senate and third in line for the presidency, he was very protective of his status. In 1971, he narrowly defeated Ted Kennedy in a contest for majority whip, and he let me know that he still remembered every senator who voted for or against him

Speaker of the House Tip O'Neill filled the congressional seat formerly held by John F. Kennedy, and was famous for saying, "All politics is local." Although a personal friend, Tip was a liberal Democrat, and he was often bothered by my commitment to conservative budgeting and a strong defense, and by my failure to support his proposals for massive federal programs.

A scholarly assessment after I left office showed that I had the most unfavorable press coverage of the century, with a net of negative news stories every month except for my first one. Despite frequent news conferences and a concerted effort to meet privately in the White House with all the key reporters and media executives, I was never able to turn them around.

Senator Ted Kennedy played a complex and important role while I was president. When he decided to run against me for the Democratic nomination in 1980, he was the overwhelming favorite. Despite his popularity, I remained confident that we could beat him, and although we knew it would be a tough political fight, we took pains to treat him with personal respect.

The cooling system malfunction and subsequent partial meltdown of the reactor core at Three Mile Island in March 1979 was a serious nuclear accident and presented significant technological challenges. Because of my training under Admiral Rickover, I was familiar with the design of the reactor and understood the steps necessary to correct the problem.

"I talked to Rosalynn after she met with the pope at the Vatican. She was somewhat disappointed and surprised that he didn't discuss any religious issues but was primarily interested in politics . . . I asked if she got an endorsement out of him for 1980, but she said she forgot to ask for it. She's meeting today with almost all the top political figures of Italy and this evening with the president." (May 10, 1979)

"I met [Soviet President Leonid] Brezhnev at the president's palace, and we agreed that it had been too long that we had delayed getting together . . . He and I both agreed that success [in our negotiations to limit nuclear weapons] was necessary for ourselves and for the rest of the world; and he said a very strange thing: 'If we do not succeed, God will not forgive us.'" (June 15, 1979)

When I was president, Andrei Gromyko was the most experienced diplomat in the world. There was never any doubt that he could speak with absolute authority for the Soviet government. But for him, truth was a casualty of Kremlin policy. I particularly recall a meeting in May 1978 when Gromyko sat across from me and continuously made false statements. I knew he was lying, and he knew that I knew he was lying.

The address I made to the nation on July 15, 1979, was one of the most dramatic and memorable events of my administration. Although initially praised, it was later characterized as a speech about America's "malaise" because I pointed out some of our nation's problems and discussed the challenges that could be overcome by bold action. Since then, however, the speech has often been called prescient.

Andrew Young, the congressman and civil rights hero who became my ambassador to the United Nations, played a key role in maintaining and improving relations with African nations and other countries that were susceptible to Soviet enticement. He was a close friend, and accepting his resignation in August 1979 was one of the most heart-wrenching decisions I had to make as president.

In the summer of 1979, facing reelection, I made a momentous decision when I put Paul Volcker—an independent and outspoken banker—in charge of the Federal Reserve Bank, and so essentially removed White House influence from this crucial element of the American economy. But more than political benefit, I wanted the strongest possible effort to control inflation, which was dangerously high.

When Ed Muskie became Secretary of State in May 1980, he was at first inclined toward the equivocal debating style of the U.S. Senate and was reluctant to engage in the sharp exchanges needed to deal with a master diplomat like Soviet foreign minister Andrei Gromyko. He learned rapidly, and earned the Presidential Medal of Freedom.

On November 4, 1979, Iranian students seized the U.S. Embassy in Tehran and took more than sixty Americans as hostages. Initially, I expected the hostages to be released quickly; it was inconceivable to me that the Iranian militants would hold our embassy personnel for any length of time. I had no way of knowing, of course, that this would prove to be the most important event of my last year as president. (AP Images)

In December 1979, the Soviet Union invaded Afghanistan. The Iranian hostage issue was to cause me more personal anguish and concern, but the Soviets' occupation of Afghanistan was a threat to the security of America. If they had consolidated their hold and moved into adjacent countries, I would have been forced into military action against them. (AP Images)

After accepting the Democratic nomination, I was relieved to have the primary season behind me. Now Rosalynn and I would have a chance to rest and begin concentrating on the general election campaign against Ronald Reagan. "It's become more and more obvious that Reagan and I have perhaps the sharpest divisions between us of any two presidential candidates in my lifetime. Also, his policies are a radical departure from those of Ford and Nixon." (July 31, 1980)

"Pat [Caddell] was getting some very disturbing poll results, showing a massive slippage as people realized the hostages were not coming home. The anniversary date of them having been captured absolutely filled the news media. By Monday, only a tiny portion—19 percent—thought the hostages were going to be coming home anytime soon. Almost all the undecideds moved to Reagan." (November 3, 1980) (AP Images)

On November 20, 1980, I met alone with President-elect Ronald Reagan in the Oval Office and we had a friendly and unrestrained discussion. Only two successive presidents could have covered the range of sensitive subjects we discussed that day. Surprisingly, however, the entire Republican transition team subsequently refused to participate in or even be briefed by us on the most politically controversial topics.

"On the inaugural platform, [I was concerned] that at the last minute the hostages might not be released. I watched the ceremonies as a somewhat detached spectator . . . As we passed the [Secret Service] agent I was informed that all the hostage planes were on the way to the Turkish border. This was one of the happiest moments of my life, and colored the entire day—indeed the week—making it enjoyable." (January 20, 1981) (Courtesy Ronald Reagan Library)

While working on this abbreviated version of my White House diary, I have been surprised by the number of subjects that were of common interest to me and other presidents. At times, we presidents have reacted to similar events in much the same way; at other times, we've responded quite differently.

There is no way to describe the relationship that Rosalynn and I have with the small town of Plains, Georgia. Both our families have lived in the community for five generations, and when I was four years old and she was a baby we were next-door neighbors. This is where our families have worked, worshiped, been educated, intermarried, and are buried. Whenever we are away, there is always a quiet yearning to come back home.

These later years have been busy and enjoyable for Rosalynn and me. We have been deeply involved in the work of The Carter Center, the Rosalynn Carter Institute for Caregiving, Habitat for Humanity, and the affairs of our hometown of Plains and our expanding family. Almost every aspect of our lives has been affected beneficially by having served as America's First Family.

couldn't give me any commitment on that. I then covered Gaza, including moving Israeli military out of Gaza populated areas, but he said this is a military issue; he couldn't resolve it. He said there were seven problems when I arrived in Israel, and four had been resolved. He seemed to think this was adequate. I repeated our position on the three items and asked for his opinion. He said he would not express an opinion because this would imply a cabinet commitment.

As we stood to depart, I reminded Begin that all his cabinet members had approved my proposals, and that this was the last chance to consider them before we departed for Egypt. With obvious frustration, I made one final effort.

I asked Begin the three questions re Gaza, oil, and ambassadors, and he said yes. I went over the statement to be issued in Egypt, and he approved. He said he would come to Washington to have the signing with me and Sadat.

I was, of course, delighted with Begin's final acceptance of the treaty terms, especially since he was the lone holdout among government leaders. This was his standard negotiating technique—refusing to budge until failure seemed inevitable—but I had not been at all sure that we would reach an agreement this morning.

As the Begins, Rosalynn, and I descended from my suite with two security agents, the elevator stopped six feet above the lobby floor. After trying unsuccessfully for about twenty minutes to get it started, security forces and hotel employees finally tore the door off with a large pry bar, and we climbed down on a ladder. We were surrounded by hundreds of diplomats and news reporters, all eager to know the result of our breakfast meeting, but we did not make any comment.

At the airport, Begin and I gave a much more upbeat departure statement than most people were expecting. I would still have to get Sadat's approval for the concessions I had made.

When I got out of the plane and stepped on the ground, I blurted out, "I feel like I'm coming home." I was fairly confident with Sadat. I told him, "You will be pleased." I told him Begin had been his usual self. Sadat said, "I sympathize with you." He also said, "My people in Egypt are furious at how the Israelis have treated our friend Jimmy Carter." I told him it wasn't bad.

I read him a message from Fahd, which expressed concern when he thought our negotiations had broken down. We both agreed that Fahd tells the people what they want to hear.

Ham suggested that I call Begin, so I gave him a call and told him Sadat had agreed to all the provisions.

We then went to the plane and flew back to the United States. On the plane I called Fritz, who was quite discouraged, then very happy. I called Bob Byrd, who had been praising my trip that morning in Washington, thinking it would be a failure. By the time I got Tip O'Neill he had already heard about the agreement, and said, "Mr. President, you're not just a deacon anymore but a pope."

The transient accolades were nice, but I knew better than any of them that we still had a long road ahead of us. It would prove to be very challenging to put into precise diplomatic language all the verbal agreements we had reached.

MARCH 14   We consider the trip to be very successful. I resolved to do everything possible to get out of the negotiating business.

CBS, quite often a spokesman for Israel, accused Jody of deliberately misleading the press Monday evening, when all of us thought the talks were over. They also reported that the peace treaty was bought at a cost of $10–$20 billion, which is completely erroneous. I told Jim McIntyre, Cy, and Harold to get some good estimates of what we would pay to Israel and Egypt over the next three years.

I was drowsy all day but prepared for a meeting with congressional leaders for a briefing at 5:00. We decided on a rough estimate of $4 billion in additional military and economic aid for both nations combined over a period of three years.

These funds were to be used to cover the exceptional costs of removing Israeli installations from Egyptian territory, and to reimburse Egypt for the expenses it would incur in implementing the peace agreement. Since 1971, annual U.S. aid to Israel had been about $1.4 billion. Later, in 1985, annual assistance was increased to about $3 billion; it has been maintained at that level since then. This does not include special loans and forgiven interest payments.

MARCH 15   I authorized Vance to notify the shah that he could not come to our country because of threats to Americans still in Iran. We offered the

shah earlier a haven here, and he decided on going to Egypt and Morocco. Now King Hassan wants him out of Morocco. We'll try to help find
a place within Latin America, Israel, or Canada.

Kissinger called to congratulate me on the trip. He said I was working
him out of his career of criticizing the government because I was not leaving him much to criticize.

MONDAY, MARCH 19   We spent all day discussing economics and energy.
Inflation was higher than we had anticipated, but the economy was stronger and budget response has been outstanding. Monetary system is much
more stable on an international basis, but we still have too much protec-
tionism with special interest groups prevailing whenever a proposal is
made to control inflation. Inflation is also up among the nations who are
our major trade partners.

We're now in our fifth year of expansion, and we're straining industrial
capacity. Consumers are in a buying mood. The economy's cooling off
enough without any outside additional effort.

We decided to offer the oil companies complete deregulation if the
Congress will pass a severance tax or an excess profits tax.

MARCH 20   Some disturbances in Afghanistan with conservative Muslims threatening the Soviet-backed Communist government.

The Israelis insist on violating the agreement on early withdrawal from
the Sinai and are endangering the commitment of Egypt to exchange
ambassadors!

I got a letter from Brezhnev, primarily a plaintive message, because
the Soviets have been left out of the Mideast discussions. He accuses us of
violating agreements made in 1977 that we would work together. That
effort came to a dead end when the Arabs and PLO refused to cooperate.

MARCH 21   I met with Doug Fraser, a fine man, and went over our plans
to announce tomorrow a comprehensive health policy, but to move on
the first phase only. Doug was positive and constructive.

I told Cy to find the shah a place to go. Kissinger and Howard Baker
are beginning to complain because the shah doesn't come here.

Had a pleasant visit with Kennedy. Told him about my 1980 plans. He
wished me good luck and said his statements still prevailed about his
support. We discussed health proposals; it's almost impossible for me to

understand what he talks about, but there's a basic difference in his approach and mine. He wants a mandatory collection of wages from everyone to finance the health program, which is different from what we have in mind.

Israel's Knesset approved the peace treaty by a vote of 95 in favor, 18 against. Maybe we'll get to use the big tent after all.

MARCH 23   I directed Cy to strengthen our embassies' security for the next few days following the peace treaty signing, as we expect acts of terrorism against us and Egypt, perhaps Israel.

I spent most of the afternoon in an energy meeting. There are not any easy answers. It's a difficult political decision on the degree of deregulation versus the inflationary impact that might result. We're getting hurt politically because of a reputation of inaction.

Kennedy was disappointed that Califano announced our health policy without Kennedy knowing the details. He's emotional about this issue and also knowledgeable. But he's come a long way and has been more flexible than some labor leaders and aged groups, with whom he works.

MARCH 24   The Soviets are getting in more difficulty in Afghanistan. To keep their puppet government in power they have to condemn the activities or influence of Pakistan, Iran, and most of the Arab world. We got a lot of publicity about cautioning the Soviets not to become directly involved in trying to control Afghanistan's political affairs.

I had an exciting and delightful trip to Elk City, Oklahoma. The people there were euphoric about my visit, and it was something of a love-fest. The Dallas newspaper later reported that it was a welcome like a new Baptist preacher coming to a small town.

Of the many local town hall meetings during my presidency, this was best. These overnight stays with local families and public town hall sessions were a great help to me in explaining our policies and learning the attitude of the public through their unrestricted questions on current issues.

MARCH 25   I got up early to run three or four miles around the periphery of the local airport. The Secret Service stayed at the hangar, so this was the farthest I have been away from other people since I got protection in October 1975. I enjoyed the solitude and the exercise.

The Secret Service agents are highly trained, not only to provide security but to maximize the privacy of those being protected. When I was president, they knew when Rosalynn and I preferred to be alone and undisturbed. Like other former presidents, I still receive Secret Service protection, and even now the agents learn quickly how to watch out for us. For instance, when we are fishing in a trout stream, they are careful not to get so near that they disturb the fish. Some of the agents become close companions, especially those who have run relatively long distances with me or skied cross country or down mountain slopes. The younger agents usually serve with us only for about three years, and it is often a sorrowful occasion when their career advancement requires that they be transferred to other posts.

MONDAY, MARCH 26   President Sadat came, and said Begin was like a grocer, quibbling about every detail. He reported that when Mubarak went to Saudi Arabia, Fahd said the only problem was that the peace treaty had been delayed, and therefore threatened to disturb the tranquillity of the Mideast. Sadat was relaxed and pleased.

I then met with Begin, and we discussed the same items as with Sadat. He said the statement at the signing ceremony this afternoon would be the third written text he had ever used in his life. The first one was when he came out of imprisonment, and the second when Sadat came to the Knesset. He said he would avoid any inflammatory actions or statements in the future.

I emphasized to both of them the need for harmony and expressions of friendship and generosity, but they still are not in that mood yet.

The signing ceremony was well attended, exciting, and pleasant. Sadat was effusive in his praise of me; did not mention Begin at all. Begin made a longer speech. All of them were adequate, with a sense of the historic importance of the treaty. I just pray that we can keep this same sense of cooperation in the future.

The Camp David Accords, concluded the previous year, provided a framework for regional peace, concentrating on the rights of the Palestinians. This treaty was just between Israel and Egypt; it concerned Israel's withdrawal from the Sinai and placed specific restraints on both countries as a way to preserve the peace.

After the ceremony I met with key members of Congress to go over with them the aid package. It actually amounts to expenditures of only

$1.47 billion [for both countries]. The Israelis are already mounting a campaign to liberalize these terms, but I asked the congressional leaders not to do so.

The evening banquet was delightful, with superb entertainment. [Itzhak] Perlman and [Pinchas] Zuckerman and Leontyne Price were particularly good. I said a prayer for the first time at a state banquet, but I think the religious overtones of the event made this acceptable. The whole day was exciting, historic, and inspirational, I believe to all of us.

Thirty years later, not a word of the treaty has been violated. There have been no warlike actions or threats against Israel by any of the surrounding governments.

MARCH 27　I went over the energy situation in its entirety and finally listed our goals: a regular market price on fuel; maximum domestic production; equity in distribution of wealth from oil supplies; minimal imports; maximum production of new sources of energy. We'd have to phase deregulation and wage a fight to get a tax on the oil industry's excessive profits, about 75 percent allocated to more efficient transportation and development of alternate energy sources.

I told Joe Califano to support the Department of Education legislation, since quietly he's been opposing it.

Califano was a very experienced and effective cabinet officer who sometimes had an agenda of his own. I had a sound relationship with him, but he tended to ignore suggestions or directives that were relayed to him by my White House staff. Correctly or not, some of my staff believed that he would take his arguments with my policies directly to The Washington Post *and was the source of some damaging leaks.*

The Soviets have continued a high rate of Jewish outmigration— something like five thousand last month. Begin asked me to ask Brezhnev for direct plane flights from the Soviet Union to Israel so émigrés couldn't stop in Vienna and change destinations from Israel to the U.S.

MARCH 28　We're deeply concerned about Argentina's continued violation of human rights. They have arrested and killed about fifty people per month. Now they claim they have reformed, but have made this claim in the past.

I had breakfast with the Joint Chiefs, a very productive meeting. David Jones and others pointed out some problems with existing agreements, and I reassured them. They want further reductions, at least 10 percent, in missile levels at the summit, even before SALT II is signed. I explained to them that we had worked harmoniously on military and political strategy concerning Turkey, Taiwan, China, NATO, Panama, Mideast arms sales, Iran, the Israeli-Egyptian peace treaty, and Philippine bases. They had acted like statesmen. I had always accepted and accommodated their advice and their concerns. When I meet with Brezhnev, I want Jones to be present. I outlined the serious, even tragic, results of any detected cheating on the SALT agreements, that this was highly unlikely unless the Soviets had the intention of going to war.

I sent another message to General [Muhammad] Zia [in Pakistan], asking him on humanitarian grounds to spare the life of [former president Zulfikar Ali] Bhutto.

Bhutto was hanged on April 4.

MARCH 29   We spent the afternoon putting final touches on the energy speech for next week. I feel at ease with the decisions, although there's not going to be any political benefit from the announcement.

MARCH 30   The shah is scheduled to go to the Bahamas, and there's a good chance he can stay permanently in Mexico.

Throughout the day I stayed in touch with the nuclear reactor problem on Three Mile Island near Harrisburg, Pennsylvania. Apparently the core was damaged more than we thought. There is more careful monitoring and coordination now, and we've finally gotten control of the situation. There's a large gas bubble brought about by the hydrolysis of water in the containment vessel that prevents cooling water from completely covering the nuclear rods. The primary cause of concern is how to vent that gas.

The cooling system malfunction and subsequent partial meltdown of the reactor core was a serious nuclear accident and presented significant technological challenges. Because of my training under Admiral Rickover, I was familiar with the design of the reactor and understood the steps necessary to correct the problem. My diary notes about the incident are quite detailed, and I was soon able to ascertain that the situation was stable, temperatures were under control, and threats to people were nonexistent. In the meantime, however, the news media, led by The Washington Post, *engaged in irresponsible scare tactics designed to terrify the public and, not incidentally, sell newspapers. One headline described an impending explosion inside the reactor core, and another advocated mass evacuation of hundreds of thousands of people. I consulted with Dr. Harold Denton, who was at the site, and with Rickover, and decided that I needed to act personally to let the truth be known.*

MARCH 31   I decided to go to the power plant tomorrow and to take Rosalynn with me, to show our confidence in what is going on and for me to learn firsthand from the scientists about prospects of resolving the incident.

I approved a refugee level of about ten thousand refugees per month—seven thousand from Southeast Asia and three thousand from other places around the world, particularly Jews from the Soviet Union.

APRIL 1   I talked to Denton. The situation is improving, but slowly, and there's still a sharp difference of opinion about what to do with the gas bubble in the top of the reactor. This particular problem has never been assessed by anyone in the nuclear industry—with a small breakdown of fuel rods, release of heat, and hydrolysis of water, the collection of vapor in the top of the reactor container, pressing down to prevent cooling water from being effective, and no way to vent the radioactive gases.

After Sunday school and church we flew to the reactor site, and we went into the control room, primarily to demonstrate the safety of it. We were getting about one-third as much radioactivity in the control room, one hundred feet away from the reactor, for instance, as a passenger in an airplane at an altitude of thirty-five thousand feet.

I felt much better when I left the site, and made a statement to reassure the public. We've had 480 cumulative years of operation of atomic power plants in the U.S. with no loss of life or serious injury, and this is the first overheating of any reactor core. This is a remarkable safety record, but I'm very concerned that the extremely high publicity and emotional nature of the nuclear power question will cause severe damage to nuclear power plant construction.

I felt then, and now, that nuclear power would inevitably become an increasing source of propulsion and power production. With standardized and simplified designs of reactors and strict standards of safety and personnel training, such power plants are perfectly safe. They are being installed on a massive scale in other industrialized nations.

MONDAY, APRIL 2   Hospital cost containment is making progress along with a comprehensive health program. Russell Long has now gotten interested in passing a fairly substantial package this year. For this first step, he, Kennedy, and I might reach a close agreement.

I talked to Bob Strauss about a possible role in the Middle East, and his response was, "I've never even read the Bible, and I'm a Jew." I told him it wasn't too late to start reading, and Kissinger was also a Jew.

I talked to Denton. The bubble size has gone down to about fifty cubic feet, and the explosion threat is now moot. Radioactivity within the dome is still high, but the source is probably iodine, which has a half-life of only nine days.

APRIL 3   I received a long telephone call from Sadat reporting a productive meeting with Begin.

APRIL 4   I asked Fritz to join with Mubarak in promoting fund-raising efforts for a religious shrine on Mount Sinai, which is of such great interest to Sadat.

Sadat pursued this project while we were at Camp David, and we discussed it further when Sadat and then Begin came to visit Rosalynn and me at our home in Plains after I left office. Unfortunately, the plans for this shrine failed to be realized after Sadat was assassinated in October 1981 and Begin and I were no longer in office.

The CIA briefing was primarily on Afghanistan, with detailed maps showing the spread of dissident strength and the interrelationship between the Soviet Union, Afghanistan, Pakistan, Iran, and the ethnic groups in the Soviet Union.

After leaving office, Rosalynn and I visited Pakistan on a health mission for The Carter Center, and President Mohammad Zia-ul-Haq arranged for us to go to the Khyber Pass. Several thousand Afghan freedom fighters assembled under a large tent to welcome me and express thanks for American assistance in their struggle against the occupying Soviets.

The PLO are sending feelers to us from various sources wanting a means by which to consult. We will do as much as possible within the bounds of our promise to Israel.

APRIL 5   My annual physical examination showed my weight down nine pounds since last year because of running, with pulse rate down to forty. Some remaining hemorrhoid problem but no worse than it's been most of my adult life.

APRIL 7   Vance reported that Dobrynin had in effect accepted my proposals on SALT, and a likely time for a summit is the middle of May.

APRIL 8   We jogged from Camp David to Cunningham Falls, and Rosalynn completed the run—3.7 miles with the last .8 of a mile severely uphill. I was proud of her.

MONDAY, APRIL 9   David Rockefeller came in, apparently to induce me to let the shah come to the United States. Rockefeller, Kissinger, and Brzezinski seem to be adopting this as a joint project.

This effort was to develop into a nationwide appeal, and its leaders recruited everyone whom they thought had any influence with me. I still felt, as a matter of caution, that it would be best for the shah to stay in some other country.

APRIL 11   Russell Long called to tell me he wanted to conclude a health care package early enough to start payments of benefits the first of January. I relayed this information to Stu and told him to follow up. I told CEOs of health insurance companies that I wanted them to increase [positive] advertisements, hold down health costs, work with us on hospital cost containment, and support key elements of the upcoming health care package. They and we have common goals re holding down costs.

President Ford called and also wanted me to provide a haven for the shah. I told him why this was a problem, with potential kidnapping of American diplomats and Iranians, and also because we wanted to get [control] of our satellite observation sites in northern Iran. He seemed to agree once I explained the situation to him.

The CIA briefing was on the unhappiness of King Hussein of Jordan [about the agreements between Israel and Egypt], Idi Amin's government about to fall, and that a plane had crashed in Zambia. An American parapsychologist had been able to pinpoint the site of the crash. We've had several reports of this parapsychology working; one discovered the map coordinates of a site and accurately described a camouflaged missile test site. Both we and the Soviets use these parapsychologists on occasion to help us with sensitive intelligence matters, and the results are unbelievable.

The proven results of these exchanges between our intelligence services and parapsychologists raise some of the most intriguing and unanswerable questions of my presidency. They defy logic, but the facts were undeniable.

The Israelis are lobbying to see if they can get a more liberal aid package. We agreed to fight this.

APRIL 12–19   We left Washington with a great sense of relief, never so ready for a vacation, and went to Sapelo Island. We sailed, fished, jogged a lot, had picnics on the beach, and slept. We had a delightful visit with the Hog Hammock Baptist congregation. They have two Baptist churches for about 170 people who live on the island. We joined them when I was governor for worship, and have many friends among them.

APRIL 20–22   Then we went to Plains, which was packed with news media, and enjoyed visiting Mama, other kinfolks, and friends. Then to Calhoun and back to Washington. It took me a couple of hours each day to deal with government business.

MONDAY, APRIL 23   The multilateral trade negotiations have now been initialed. Strauss predicts that this legislation will pass and that every section of the country will enjoy job gains because of it.

I was committed to reducing trade barriers and attempting to understand and accommodate the special needs and concerns of other countries. Despite the complexity of these trade issues and the intense competition among nations for advantage, Bob Strauss was able to reach a consensus and then to achieve near unanimity within the Congress on their ratification. By lining up overwhelming support before the proposals came to a vote, Bob removed the drama—and also the opportunity for publicity—from his achievements. Bob's ability to negotiate successfully and to win congressional support was unequaled.

At the cabinet meeting, everyone agrees that the inflation control effort is really being helpful but is almost universally panned by the press.

I met with Cy, who said he was ready to go ahead with the appointment of Strauss as the Mideast negotiator. I then met with Strauss, who said he was ready to go but wanted to report directly to me and not be part of the subcabinet bureaucracy.

Most of the afternoon and night was devoted to drafting speeches for the week and the squabble between Strauss and Vance about the interrelationship between the two. Strauss has been enjoying the status of cabinet officer, and it would not be proper to demote him. Vance wants to be sure that the State Department is not bypassed in Middle East negotiations. I instructed Fritz to bring Strauss, Vance, and Hamilton out to his house in the evening to work out an agreement. Vance threatens to resign if he's bypassed.

APRIL 24 We learned that the Indian cabinet directed Foreign Minister [Atal] Vajpayee not to yield on safeguard inspections for their nuclear plants; they are prepared to receive fuel from another source after 1980—maybe the Soviets—and go ahead with their reprocessing of plutonium. I met with Vajpayee and let him know that what we did with our own fuel was constrained by U.S. law. There was little prospect for sales of fuel unless India complies with international standards. I thought Pakistan and India were destined for a nuclear arms race unless they themselves restrained their inclination to go ahead with reprocessing and enrichment. He was sobered, but in view of the instructions from the cabinet and his own previous inclinations, I don't think changed.

I went to the Capitol Rotunda to make a statement commemorating the Jewish Holocaust. It was a moving experience for all of us who were present. Elie Wiesel really castigated our country because of our silence during this time—something that has rarely been done, but which I think was justified.

During the morning we finally worked out the relationship between Strauss and Vance without my having to get involved in it. I called Begin, Sadat, and a few congressmen on the reasons for selection of Strauss. If anyone can keep these negotiations on track and protect me from the Jewish community politically, it's Bob Strauss.

I talked to Sadat about Bob Strauss, and he said, "The man [Begin] told me about this when he was in Egypt," which was something of a surprise to me. And then he said, "That man has changed for the better."

APRIL 25   I met with the commission on the Three Mile Island accident and gave them a charge to preserve their integrity and reputation for openness and honesty, explore the accident thoroughly, and give me a report within six months. This commission really takes a burden off me because there's an intense interest in nuclear safety now.

APRIL 26   We completed negotiations with the Soviets on prisoner exchange. Alexander Ginzberg, Georgi Vins, and three others will be released, and Anatoly Filatov will not be executed; we'll commute sentences of two minor spies.

The Senate did a superb job yesterday in protecting our budget. I thanked Ed Muskie, who has become perhaps the foremost statesman in the Senate.

I thoroughly enjoyed having Dr. Joe Pursch and Billy with me. Billy was relaxed, proud of himself, has superb confidence in Dr. Pursch, and seems to be very determined to succeed with his battle against alcoholism. Joe said that often in a hotel lobby or restaurant strangers would come to him and say, "Take care of that boy, we really think a lot of him." It became obvious to Joe that Billy is indeed a folk hero.

Dr. Pursch was an expert in the rehabilitation of people addicted to drugs or alcohol. Until the end of his life, Billy never took another drink, and he and his wife, Sybil, became extremely effective in working with thousands of alcoholics in combating their affliction. Among other things, they contracted with large corporations to help troubled employees.

My mother always said that Billy was her most intelligent child, and none of us disputed her. He devoured information of all kinds and made a lot of money on wagers with acquaintances about esoteric facts, historical

events, or sports statistics. He was a "walking encyclopedia" of baseball in-
formation. Billy had a great sense of humor—sometimes seemingly crude
when repeated by others—and formed intense personal friendships. I am
confident that he had ten times as many close friends as I.

APRIL 27   We're proud of the exchange of prisoners. Baptists, Jews, and I
think the entire country will be pleased. We let some Ukrainian leaders
come in to see [Valentyn] Moroz and some Jewish leaders come in to see
the three Jewish dissidents. Vins was quite remorseful that he had left the
Soviet Union, even though his family's going to follow him. He felt that
other Baptists and Christians there should not have been abandoned by
him. The prisoner exchange was a highly emotional experience, and I think
one of the most significant things in a human way that we've done since
I've been in office.

   We learned that the five prisoners were awakened at 4:00 in the morning in their individual prison cells, informed that their Soviet citizenship
was revoked, they would leave the Soviet Union, and their families would
not be punished and might be joining them. They were transferred to an
Aeroflot plane and kept in a small compartment with two security guards
alongside each prisoner. All their heads were shaved except Vins, who's
been living in so-called exile. They demanded two ramps going into the
plane at the New York airport. They wanted the American prisoners walking up one ramp while the five Russians walked down the other ramp.
This kind of quibbling caused some delay.

APRIL 28   Jody, Pat, and Rosalynn came over, and we discussed basic deep-
seated and growing concerns among the American people about the future, and what I as president might do about it.

Pat Caddell's penetrating opinion polling revealed that our country was
still affected by the assassinations of Martin Luther King, Jr., John Ken-
nedy, and Bobby Kennedy; embarrassed by our military defeat in Vietnam,
Watergate, and Nixon's impeachment; and felt vulnerable due to the effec-
tive Arab oil embargo. I was particularly interested in what the polling re-
vealed about our efforts to promote energy conservation; until this time, the
Congress had not been able to overcome the powerful interest groups and
pass my comprehensive energy policy. Caddell's polling helped us under-

*stand that additional speeches about energy would not be effective, but we
still did not know how best to advance our agenda.*

APRIL 29   Up early to prepare my Sunday school lesson, from 1 Kings
21—about Ahab, Jezebel, and Naboth. Since Georgi Vins was with me,
the parallel between this lesson and his persecution in the Soviet Union
was remarkable.

*Vins sat next to Rosalynn and later pulled off his shoe, lifted the inner sole,
and showed her a photograph of me that he had kept while in prison. He
said many prisoners knew of our human rights policy.*

This man is really a courageous martyr—calm, strong, sure of himself.
I told the Baptist leaders who were present to let him rest, think, pray,
consult with his wife, and then make a decision about what he wants to
do. I think the Soviets underestimated the impact of their [prisoner] release
on American and world opinion.

MONDAY, APRIL 30   Brock Adams discussed with me the need for a massive industry-government effort to develop a more efficient and economi-
cal automobile. I agreed to meet with automobile executives in May to
explore some possibilities.

MAY 1   The Speaker was critical because of my lack of consultation with
him, although investigation showed we had consulted constantly with his
staff. The Speaker has a selective memory; basically he doesn't favor any
effort to balance the budget or have fiscal restraint. His measure of success
is passage of new or expanded social programs. He's running counter, I
believe, to the attitude of the Congress and the American people—
certainly counter to me. He's still a valuable ally.
    Vance called to say the Soviets agreed on four of five items on SALT,
and the other issue is of no importance to me.

MAY 2   Prime Minister Ohira [of Japan] and I had what all of us agreed
was one of the most productive diplomatic sessions of our administration.
Subcabinet negotiations will continue, and we will establish a group of
distinguished "wise men" to advise government leaders.

This group evolved into a remarkably successful mechanism for resolving the multitude of trade disagreements that were inevitable as labor-intensive manufacturing—of such things as textiles and shoes—left our country and moved to the East. The group also addressed recurring disputes about television, radio, automobile tires, and lumber. During my presidency, these three "wise men" from each side would meet regularly in Washington, Tokyo, or Hawaii and spend days developing balanced proposals to make to top government officials. This ended what often had been an unpleasant relationship with Japan.

I decided on new ambassadors for ten or twelve countries. We've been maintaining between 70 and 75 percent professionals and the others "political" appointees—all of high quality.

MAY 3   I discussed with Zbig the possibility of getting North and South Korean leaders together when I visit with [South Korean president] Park [Chung Hee] in June.

MAY 5   In L.A., I went to see John Wayne, who's lost a terrible amount of weight, and another cancer is debilitating his strength. He was in good spirits, appreciated my coming, and said the left-hand part of my hair had improved the shape of my head—that he was a professional and recognized things like that instantly. He wished he could share his lunch with me but only had one straw!

While vacationing on a Georgia island, I had decided to change the part in my hair from right to left. When the news media noticed it several weeks later, my failure to announce it was a big story.

MAY 8   The Begin government is being criticized by other Israeli leaders for trying to establish excessive control over the West Bank.

Vance reported a final agreement on [key issues in] SALT, and on the summit [to be held] in Vienna, fifteenth of June.

MAY 10   I talked to Rosalynn after she met with the pope at the Vatican. She was somewhat disappointed and surprised that he didn't discuss any religious issues but was primarily interested in politics. She liked him. I asked if she got an endorsement out of him for 1980, but she said she forgot to ask for it. She's meeting today with almost all the top political figures of Italy and this evening with the president. Later she called to say she had made a mistake by telling the president of Italy that I would meet with Brezhnev on June fifteenth. I had told her this was confidential, but she misunderstood. I teased her by saying that I had just gotten word from Brezhnev that he was canceling the SALT agreement because we leaked the date too early.

The top staff meeting was devoted to SALT. There's a general feeling that the press will be more supportive than on any other issue since I've been in office—which, by the way, does not say much.

A scholarly assessment after I left office showed that I had the most unfavorable press coverage of the century, with a net of negative news stories every month except for my first one, after my family and I walked down Pennsylvania Avenue to the White House. Despite frequent news conferences and a concerted effort to meet privately in the White House with all the key reporters and media executives, I was never able to turn them around. We finally decided to accept the situation and plow ahead with our programs.

Even in retrospect, I do not understand the reason for our failure in public relations. Contributing to it, perhaps, was the fact that I had proposed a diverse agenda to the Congress, and many of the issues on it were quite controversial and potentially unpopular. Our overall successes were often obscured by defeats on details of the legislation. Energy was preeminent among domestic issues, and we received negative press about many of our initiatives, even though the crisis we were facing was (and still is) real. Meanwhile, each facet of our encounters with the Soviet Union, Panama, China, and the Middle East aroused intense criticism from some vocal sources. We were ultimately successful on all these fronts, but the negative aspects of the extensive debates always seemed to prevail.

MAY 11–13   Rosalynn and Amy arrived, very pleased with their trip, and we flew to Camp Hoover—very beautiful, rustic, and quiet. We caught a number of eight-to-nine-inch brook trout and saw two black bears.

MONDAY, MAY 14   We left [Camp Hoover] after three days, went to the top of the mountain, and flew to Virginia Beach. With Cecil and [his wife] Carol Andrus we caught fifty bluefish and then stopped—running eight to twelve pounds. They're really great fighting fish. It rained most of the day, and we were really cold when we arrived back at the dock.

In the evening I sent a message to Giscard D'Estaing, Mrs. Thatcher, and to our ambassadors in Arab countries like Saudi Arabia, [asking for support in] urging Khomeini not to assassinate any more Jews. They have convicted and killed one prominent Jewish industrialist simply because he was friendly toward Israel.

MAY 15   Rosalynn and I and Califano announced the Mental Health Systems Act, which was being sent to Congress to revise those programs and to increase allocation of funds for research, development, prevention, and so forth.

Charlie Pride and Willie Nelson gave me the Country Music Association Award for my interest in and support of country music.

MAY 16   Ed Muskie gave me a report on his trip to Europe: nothing significant except a remarkable lack of loyalty in [European allied commander Alexander] Haig. He takes every opportunity to castigate me and my administration.

I had the first 1981 budget meeting. Our goal is a total expenditure of $580 billion, which puts us in striking distance of a balanced budget if the economy stays reasonably strong.

MAY 18   [Former deputy secretary of state] Phil Habib will be coming back to help Cy. I want him to go to South Korea and explore possibilities of a significant meeting between me [and] the North and South Koreans while I'm over there.

I met with leaders of General Motors, Ford, Chrysler, and American Motors to work out a basic research program between their industry and government. They were highly defensive of whether they had been innovative. It's obvious to me they have not. They were remarkably chastened by the knowledge that the energy shortage was permanent and that large cars were going out of style. They were even eager for me to discuss the basic research program with foreign leaders and to bring in foreign automobile manufacturers.

While I was in office, my administration made considerable progress in our efforts to persuade the automobile industry and the country as a whole that the energy crisis posed a serious threat to our future. But Ronald Reagan's premise during the 1980 campaign—and for the eight years he was in office—was that there was no energy shortage, our great nation did not need to make any sacrifices, and the restraints I was imposing on the automobile and oil industries were unnecessary.

MAY 20   I went to Amy's violin recital, where she played Bach's Minuet no. 1 as a solo. She did quite well.

MONDAY, MAY 21   Had a cabinet meeting, with *The New York Times* covering the first few minutes. We discussed the 1979 and '80 Congress budget proposals, which came out almost exactly as we had advocated—within less than one-half of 1 percent. Out of twenty issues, energy comprised five of them. My guess is that gasoline shortages might evolve into the most explosive political issue of 1980, and so far the Congress has done nothing to cooperate.

MAY 22   I met with Rafshoon to go over general themes in the 1980 campaign. He thinks I should run as an experienced outsider and try to tie these two apparently contradictory terms together. We'll select certain themes to pursue, campaign among small groups as a president struggling to stay close to the people, avoid details and specifics of legislation, dwell on potential strengths, be prepared to meet any challenger, be willing to attack the establishment, which might include the Congress and the press, and start our publicity effort in key states perhaps as early as October.

Although I restricted my efforts early in the 1980 campaign year because of the hostage crisis, I followed most of this advice later, during the general election.

MAY 23   I called Don Daughenbaugh [a guide whom we had met while vacationing in Wyoming last summer] and told him to set up the trout fishing trip to Pennsylvania for just south of State College, a half-hour flight from Camp David.

MAY 24   I had a depressing breakfast with economic advisors, who don't know what to do about inflation or energy. I told them we would hammer out a policy that the other major consuming nations might adopt [at the G7 meeting].

MAY 25   I was really peeved when I got the memorandum from Zbig on the Vienna summit with Brezhnev, with the same timidity as before the

Camp David/Mideast talks. Every presumption was that we would fail, with analyses of how we would cover up failure. I told him to set maximum goals and work toward them; at least we would have done our best. I wasn't just interested in going to Vienna to the opera.

MAY 26   We flew up to Spruce Creek, in Pennsylvania, on Wayne Harpster's farm. This is some of the best fishing in the United States. The creek was high and a little bit murky, but we caught maybe twenty nice trout as good as western trout. They averaged fourteen inches, browns and rainbows.

This opened a new era of pleasure and friendship for my family. We formed close family ties with the Harpsters and have often returned to Spruce Creek during the subsequent thirty-three years. Wayne has accompanied us to China, Japan, Venezuela, Argentina, Russia, and many sites in the United States as a fishing companion, and to Georgia for hunting and other outings. They were our special guests in Oslo for the Nobel ceremony when I won the Peace Prize in 2002.

MAY 29   I enjoyed my fiftieth news conference today, although there's a blackbird-type movement among the press to say how despondent the White House is these days.

Mayor Koch called just to say everything was going well in New York, that I had a friend forever in Ed Koch, that he was with me in 1980 and available for any help he could give.

These would prove to be short-lived promises. When the mayor later went to Miami, ostensibly to help with my reelection campaign, I learned that his almost exclusive message was a condemnation of my policy in the Middle East. His loyalty to me was at best intermittent; shortly before the 1980 general election vote, for instance, Koch ostentatiously invited Republican candidate Ronald Reagan to his home, Gracie Mansion, which was widely interpreted as an endorsement of Reagan.

In the evening I gave a speech to the National Conference of Christians and Jews. They gave me a citation, and I talked about discrimination that still remains against blacks in southern Africa, Palestinians in the Mideast, the poor and minorities in our own country, and the constant threat of anti-Semitism.

MAY 30   We had a strange private dinner to assess the depth of despair, hopelessness, discouragement, and fear among the American people, to see if it was inevitable and what I as president should both know and do. It was remarkably nonproductive, with [Professors] David Bell and Christopher Lasch being too erudite for their comments to be practical, [Reverend] Jesse Jackson the most levelheaded and constructive, [former White House press secretary] Bill Moyers a little too preachy but somewhat helpful, John Gardner [founding chairman of Common Cause] levelheaded and concerned, [journalist] Haynes Johnson not quite so knowledgeable, and [*Washington Monthly* editor] Charlie Peters negative. The whole session ended in confusion, but there was a general belief that I should be not so involved in details, be more inspirational, be frank about analyses of problems, assume the role of the American people as much as possible, emphasize the strength of our country and our ability to resolve problems if we work together.

My administration was still searching for a better understanding of how to address the disturbing public opinion poll results that Pat was finding. That evening's discussion did not provide much illumination.

JUNE 3   In the afternoon I went to a memorial service for A. Philip Randolph [the leader of the nation's railroad porters and a pioneer defender of civil rights] in the Metropolitan AME Church. The high point was when Leontyne Price sang the Lord's Prayer. I wept, as did many other people, in the middle of the final phrases, and the audience erupted into spontaneous applause. Bayard Rustin said Randolph had never said a critical word about another human, and his net estate was five hundred dollars and a broken TV set.

MONDAY, JUNE 4   I was disappointed with the weekly memoranda on MX missiles—nauseating to confront the gross waste of money going into nuclear weapons of all kinds.

I told Cy to condemn very strongly the Israeli settlements in the West Bank, which are cutting the legs out from under fruitful negotiations with Egypt.

[Foreign Affairs Minister Jean] François-Poncet from France stopped by. The French have a violent dislike for Israel, don't think our separate treaty approach is going to be successful, but did promise to help prevent other nations from punishing Egypt.

President Ford called and reported that if I would pay some attention to the Republicans they would help me on several key issues. They have done this in the past. I told Frank to set up a breakfast between me and the Republican leadership.

Throughout my term, I had surprisingly strong support from Republicans. As I lost support from liberal Democrats who supported Kennedy against me for the Democratic nomination, I worked more closely with Republican leaders Bob Michel in the House and Howard Baker in the Senate.

JUNE 6   Averell Harriman [former diplomat and New York governor] came by to tell me that the Soviets have more respect for the U.S. president than for any other world leader; Brezhnev considered the Vienna summit as one of the great events of his life; they've done everything to avoid failure; and Brezhnev's firm commitment was to keep war away from the Soviet Union. It's important that I not embarrass Brezhnev and treat him as a friend, because quite often he's not well-informed on individual matters. He's human and emotional. They believe, along with us, that the nonproliferation policy must be implemented globally. Brezhnev has been disappointed in our Middle East policy of going it alone. The Soviet Union will not back down on their support for liberation movements. They believe in this as intently as we do our human rights commitments and giving aid to our allies. The CIA pointed out that the Soviets value the negotiating *process* very highly; we look on negotiations as an aggravating procedure toward a solution.

I met with Russell Long. We've reached general agreement on the basic principles of health legislation. He wants weaker hospital cost containment; a strong and early commencement of payments for catastrophic illness.

JUNE 8   At the budget appeals meeting—the last one, I hope—I decided on a balanced budget for 1981, which is going to be strict and not leave expenditures low enough to permit a tax reduction.

MONDAY, JUNE 11   In the evening we had another briefing for about ninety members of the House on Panama implementation legislation, similar to the previous meeting, but better. The House members are sober; their main concern was not about right or wrong, but about the political consequences of voting in any way favorable toward Panama. Most of those who spoke out against it were shamed by the responsibility of the others. We're making some progress; still don't have the votes to stop crippling amendments.

JUNE 12   I announced a new health insurance program with Jim Corman, Charlie Rangel, Harley Staggers, Russell Long, Abe Ribicoff, Gaylord Nelson, all of whom vowed to support the proposal. Kennedy, continuing his irresponsible and abusive attitude, immediately condemned our health plan. He couldn't get five votes for his, and I told Stu and Joe Califano to fight it out with him through the public news media. It's really time to do something about health care, catastrophic illness, the problem with the very poor not having health care at all, also prevention for children, prenatal to the one-year age level. This kind of coverage is lacking in our country, and it's needed. We want to implement this by 1983. Russell Long wants to move the catastrophic [coverage] up to next year, but I want to have a balanced budget in 1981.

Our national health plan was the result of two years of work by my cabinet officers, economic advisors, White House staff, and congressional leaders. We had full support from key members of the House and Senate, all of whom had been involved in its preparation. Our plan protected all Americans from catastrophic illness costs; extended comprehensive health coverage to all low-income citizens; gave total coverage to all mothers and babies for prenatal, delivery, postnatal, and infant care; promoted competition and cost containment; and provided a clear framework for phasing in a universal, comprehensive national health plan. Its total start-up costs were included in my annual budget proposal, and it was to be fully implemented over a period of four years, with funding assured. (Details of the plan can be found in Public Papers of the Presidents: Jimmy Carter, 1979, *pp. 1028–31.)*

Ted Kennedy, chairman of one of the six key committees, also cooperated with us until the very end, when he decided to oppose the proposal—as had become his custom after deciding to run against me in 1980. Kennedy's opposition to our health plan proved fatal: his was a powerful voice, and he and his supporters were able to block its passage. We lost a good chance to provide comprehensive national health care, and another thirty years would pass before such an opportunity came again.

I met with Rosalynn and other top advisors to talk about the political situation. I told them they should screen their entire staffs and tell everybody we were faced with difficulty now. It was very likely to get worse in the future. If they couldn't take the pressure, to get out. I felt personally confident that we were doing a good job for the country, and that we would prevail again in this Congress as we had in previous years. I would win in 1980 no matter who ran against me, I was going to fight to a last vote, and I had no timidity about Kennedy running or anyone else.

I agreed to let Ham be chief of staff (everybody wants him to) and let Stu, Jack, and others have more direct control over the cabinet.

JUNE 13   I met with the Joint Chiefs, who in general approved the SALT II agreement. Bernie Rogers said they thought for a military interest it was a wash, but for the national interest it was advantageous. Lou Wilson said for military he thought it was a negative, but overall for national interest it was very positive. The other three said it was militarily and nationally an advantage to have SALT II. This is my last meeting with them before the summit meeting, but they wanted to review their thoughts to me personally.

I told Harold Brown to handle the military registration and draft question that Sam Nunn is pushing, and to leave me out of it.

JUNE 14   I worked all the way to Vienna, and we divided responsibilities among us. In SALT III we will discuss deep cuts, limit on throw-weight, verifiability, survivability, air defense buildup, and perhaps a prohibition against building any more atomic weapons, a declaration against the first use of force—even conventional, mutual visits by top military persons, prior notification of all test firings, and cooperation to monitor test flights, including the use of aircraft and listening stations in third countries. We'll push on comprehensive test ban, leaving the British out if necessary to make progress, and have a clear understanding on antisatellite negotiations.

JUNE 15   I met Brezhnev at the president's palace, and we agreed that it had been too long that we had delayed getting together. I asked him if he has enough newspeople in Moscow, pointing out that we had more than two thousand with us in Vienna. He said he had too many to suit him. He and I both agreed that success was necessary for ourselves and for the rest of the world, and he said a very strange thing: "If we do not succeed, God will not forgive us."

JUNE 16 I will outline briefly his statement: "There's a special responsibility on the Soviet Union and the United States because we are such powerful and influential nations. Relationships between the two countries now can be classified as good, since at least we have not had a world war. In the last few decades we have experienced both good and bad relations. We moved from World War II allies into a state of sustained cold war. It has not been easy to reverse the cold war trend and arrive at the present state of cooperation." Then Brezhnev laughed, pointed his finger at Vance, and said, "This man disagrees." And everyone laughed at Cy, who was quite discomfited.

Brezhnev continued, "We must have a sense of equality between the two nations, a mutual sense of security, noninterference in the affairs of others, and peaceful coexistence. But first we must control nuclear weapons. The statements by President Carter and others that competition and cooperation must exist together provide a formula which rests on quicksand, and we are disturbed to have leaders in the U.S. refer to us as an adversary. The Soviet Union does not desire dispute but looks forward to the future. The major question is: Shall we have good and stable relationships as equals? The Soviet adage is: Don't have a stone under a shirtfront."

I then reported that Brezhnev and I had agreed yesterday there was an excessive delay in our meeting, and we would not wait this long again before the next. I pointed out that Brezhnev had said, "God will not forgive us if we fail." Brezhnev looked embarrassed, and Gromyko stated, "Yes, God above is looking down at us all."

I continued: "Many of our differences result from a lack of understanding and consultation. Foreign ministers meet frequently. It is true that Mr. Gromyko and Secretary Vance have not always contributed to progress." People laughed. I pointed out that [the American and Soviet] heads of state have only met ten times since World War II. Some of these summit conferences were not productive. The heads of [our militaries] have never met with each other since 1946, and military meetings would be helpful.

"We will discuss SALT II and III at the next session. Some competition between us remains, and this is inevitable, but there are some elements of competition which are of deep concern and potentially destabilizing. Neither nation can dominate the other. Each is too powerful to permit this to happen. There's a race in both nations preventing regional hegemony by the other. The Soviet Union is a great and powerful nation—not afraid but confident. The United States is a great and powerful nation—not afraid but confident. The world looks to both of us as leaders. There cannot be any proof of superiority or victory in a nuclear war.

"Arms control is a centerpiece, and verification of agreements is crucial. This includes SALT II, comprehensive test ban, antisatellite agreement, the conventional arms agreement, the mutual and balanced force reductions [MBFR], and SALT III. I'm very eager to understand your concerns and to cooperate with you."

All of us were impressed with the vigor of Brezhnev as compared with the reports we had heard, his ability to make extemporaneous remarks, and his obvious although heavy-handed attempt at humor. He moves with difficulty. At first his speech is slurred and his upper and lower jaws seem to be close together, but as he talks and becomes more animated, this speech defect seems to go away.

The afternoon meeting reconvened at the American embassy. Brezhnev again spoke first: "Progress has not been easy, often delayed, not because of obstacles created by the Soviet Union. Amendments would not be acceptable; only the treaty as signed would be effective."

I pointed out that there would be no deployment of weapons that would be excluded from national verification. I emphasized the mistake the Soviets were making in not having the treaty effective when signed, a departure from international custom, and from our experience with the limited test ban, still not ratified, the Vladivostok agreements, never presented in formal language, and the extension of SALT I beyond its expiration date. Brezhnev seemed to be confused by this, but Gromyko continued to prevent Brezhnev from agreeing for an immediately effective date on SALT II.

We then went back to the residence, and Brezhnev, Gromyko, [Konstantin] Chernenko, and [Dmetri] Ustinov joined us. They immediately wanted a drink, and then Brezhnev impatiently asked for supper to be served—not rudely, half joking, but somewhat strange behavior. Brezhnev raised frequent toasts during the meal and bottomed up his glass of vodka each time. The meeting started out quite formal and restrained, became easier as the evening progressed, but there was never a time for discussion of issues.

JUNE 17   At the Soviet embassy, I made the first statement, pointing out that SALT II set ceilings and some reductions, but it permitted continued buildup of nuclear weaponry. The U.S. is ready to consider a 5 percent reduction per year.

Brezhnev responded very similarly to my comments. We must halt and reverse this tendency, but the U.S. and the Soviet Union cannot go on and on while others build up nuclear forces. There should be a treaty describing a complete ban on all new weapons tests.

I told them their statement on Backfire was unacceptable. They had agreed ahead of time that production would not exceed thirty per year. After quite an altercation, Brezhnev interrupted to say, "The Soviet Union will not produce more than thirty Backfires per year." I told him this was completely acceptable.

The Backfire was a supersonic strategic bomber that could deliver nuclear weapons, although its limited range would preclude an attack on any U.S. region except Alaska.

I recapitulated our key points, and on the ride down the elevator I agreed to give Brezhnev a written copy of my proposals concerning SALT III. He said this was the most important thing, and we could further discuss this Monday.

In the afternoon we discussed trouble spots around the world: the Persian Gulf and the Arabian Peninsula; military activities of Cuba; the Mideast; Palestinian rights; China. They all perked up, although they had listened with intense interest during the whole presentation. I said that after thirty years, normalized relations with China was overdue. This would lead to peace and stability—not only for our two countries but for that entire region, and perhaps the world—but these improvements would never be at the expense of relations between the Soviet Union and the United States.

Brezhnev then responded: He's surprised at the lackadaisical way that the U.S. refers to the remote region of the Persian Gulf and Arabia as being of vital interest to our country. World War II was an unbelievably terrible experience for the Soviet people, still the paramount consideration for a Soviet citizen. We need a non-first-use-of-arms treaty between the Warsaw Pact and NATO. In the Mideast, the Soviet-U.S. statement has been violated, the Egyptian-Israeli treaty has failed and has led to Israeli war against Lebanon. The Soviet Union will counter the illegal Israeli-Egyptian accord. Cuba—the Soviets are strictly observing a 1962 agreement not to build up any forces that would be a threat to the U.S. U.S. bases are at the doorstep of the Soviet Union in South Korea, Japan, and the Philippines.

We decided not to respond to individual points, since it was late.

We moved to the banquet room, and it was greatly superior to the supper we had the night before. Brezhnev was very proud of this. Two interpreters kept the conversation lively, Zbig and Harold seemed to speak good Russian, and several of the Russians spoke English.

Brezhnev offered frequent toasts. The first time I didn't turn my glass bottom up, and he made a big issue of it. From then on I got a smaller glass [specially made in advance] and drained the glass with each toast.

There was a good bit of jovial banter. Ustinov said the U.S. should be able to afford a uniform for Harold Brown as secretary of defense. I told him I had promised Harold the uniform if he was able to solve the MBFR question with Ustinov this afternoon, but since Ustinov was so stubborn, he was the one who deprived Harold of a uniform.

I asked Gromyko if he was sincere about the other three permanent UN members being involved in future SALT III talks. He gave an equivocal answer, and I suggested that I would be responsible for France and Great Britain if he would be responsible for China. He threw up his hands in semi–mock horror at the thought. It was really a pleasant evening.

MONDAY, JUNE 18   I got up quite early to work on my notes for the day, to finish the signing statement and the speech for Congress this evening.

I went to the American embassy, where Brezhnev joined me for our private discussion. He suggested that he read his entire statement before I responded, seemingly eager to get to the part of his speech that comprised 90 percent of it—about China and the consequences of our normalizing relations. He had no objection to normalization but warned about any anti-Soviet attitudes; this would be a serious mistake and lead to woes for the mistaken nation. Then he quickly referred to human rights, saying that the Soviet Union is not against this subject as a discussion on ideological grounds, but there is a problem if it is discussed as official state-to-state policy. There can be no progress if trade is related to human rights; they have not related trade to the unemployment rate in the United States, nor racial discrimination, nor the violation of the rights of women. This is a sensitive subject for the Soviets and not a legitimate ground for discussion between him and me.

I replied that the U.S.-China relationship was good for the United States, for the Soviet Union, and for the world. He shouted, pleasantly enough, "Certainly not good for the Soviet Union!"

I then said, "Yes, it would be good for the Soviet Union because our influence will be used to preserve peaceful relationships between China and Russia." This was our pledge. We would never use U.S.-China relations to the detriment of the Soviet Union, we would keep him informed, and I would like him to keep us informed about their relations with China.

I told him there was one more difficult subject I wanted to raise. And he brightened up and said, "Only one?" And I said, "Yes."

I then said that the question of human rights was important to the people of our country. I was a Baptist, one of 14 million who were deeply gratified and felt greater friendship toward the Soviet Union because Mr. Vins and his family had been released. One of the best things the Soviets could do would be to continue this process by releasing such dissidents as Sharansky. He thought his previous statement on human rights was adequate, and Brezhnev added that Sharansky had been tried and convicted for espionage, and that as leader of the nation he was bound to support the laws of his country. I reminded him again of the importance of this issue to us, and that we were determined to have progress made without overt confrontation.

The signing ceremony [of the SALT II treaty] was very impressive and well conducted. When we finished signing the documents and handed them to one another, I shook hands with Brezhnev warmly, and, to my surprise, he leaned forward and put his cheek against mine for a more intimate embrace. We were both somewhat emotional. Then we left for the airport.

Brezhnev was obviously not well, but he was mentally alert and careful to carry out the decisions made in advance among Gromyko, Chernenko, and other Politburo members. He was eager to expand nuclear armament controls and very sensitive about China and human rights. The Soviets had made major concessions regarding Jewish emigration but were drawing the line—for the time being—on Sharansky and some other famous dissidents. It was obvious to all of us, but unmentioned, that Soviet influence in many regions of the world was dissipating.

On the way, [U.S. ambassador] Milt Wolf told me that [Austrian chancellor Bruno] Kreisky had decided not to permit any Jews to emigrate from Russia through Vienna who might wind up in an illegal Israeli settlement on the West Bank. This is quite a significant decision.

JUNE 19   We're assessing what we can do on Nicaragua, which is becoming increasingly difficult for us. We'll try to prevent the deterioration into a Cuban-sponsored Communist government on the one hand, and direct American military intervention on the other. Our thrust will be through the OAS.

JUNE 20   At the congressional leadership breakfast, the Speaker reported on pending legislation. The Department of Education bill does not seem to have the Speaker's support, primarily because of opposition from Catholic bishops. Hospital cost containment [bill] is stalemated because of the health lobby.

At this breakfast for Democratic congressmen, one of the more liberal members asked me what I would do about reelection if Ted Kennedy decided to run for president. I responded, "I'll whip his ass." Predictably, my comment was leaked to the media and then widely publicized.

I had lunch with Fritz, who thought my comment concerning whipping Kennedy's ass was ill-advised, but his is a lonely voice. Some of my staff members say it was the best thing for morale since the Willie Nelson concert.

After lunch I inaugurated the West Wing solar system and announced the solar policy message that has gone to the Congress.

With fanfare, Reagan removed the solar panels from the White House. Using his executive powers, he also reversed many of the conservation measures taken by my administration, including automobile efficiency requirements.

Fortunately, most of our important conservation measures were embedded in laws passed during my administration and impervious to executive orders. As a result, our oil imports were reduced from 8.6 million barrels per day to half that amount within five years. By 2007 we were importing over 12 million bpd.

We're becoming concerned about recession combined with high inflation, brought on primarily by the OPEC price increases, irresponsible and abusive to consuming nations. I hope we can do something about this in Tokyo.

I monitored House votes on the Panama amendments, which were very favorable. This has been one of my most difficult issues, potentially very serious and always in doubt.

JUNE 21   The final vote on implementing the Panama Canal Treaty was 224 to 202, but we blocked a crippling amendment by only three votes.

There's a growing concerted effort in Congress, Europe, among American Jews, and certainly in our administration to put pressure on Begin concerning illegal settlements in the West Bank. I discussed this with Bob Strauss before his visit to the Mideast and told him how important it was.

Then and now, it was clear that building these settlements in Palestine was the major obstacle to a comprehensive peace for Israel and its neighbors. George H. W. Bush understood the importance of this issue and exerted great pressure on the Israelis, but unfortunately Presidents Reagan, Clinton, and George W. Bush basically ignored the problem. Construction was especially rapid during Clinton's term.

Early in 2009, President Obama seemed to recognize the paramount importance of the issue and insisted on a settlement freeze as a precursor to substantive peace talks. But he soon backed away from this commitment.

I presented a proposal to the OAS that Somoza step down, let a provisional government be established; peace be restored; elections be held; and an OAS peacekeeping force be established.

JUNE 22   We spent a lot of time on the refugee question. We now take about 70 percent of all the Southeast Asia refugees—about seven thousand per month.

Cy gave me a report on Latin American governments' attitude toward Nicaragua. Mexicans, Jamaicans, Panamanians, and Grenadans want to let the [revolutionary] war continue, hoping the Sandinistas will prevail. Guatemala and Paraguay, however, want the war to go on for the opposite reasons, hoping Somoza will prevail. Costa Ricans are doubtful. The Andean group is searching for a compromise. Almost everybody wants Somoza to step down, but the question is whether all Nicaraguans can express their views freely or whether Sandinistas should be given privileged status since they have been the ones to fight for the overthrow of Somoza.

I wanted to let the people of Nicaragua make this decision, and my admin-istration attempted to orchestrate a national referendum, with the Organi-zation of American States monitoring the process to ensure its fairness.

JUNE 23–24   We decided to go to [the G7 meeting in] Japan through Alaska, arriving with some trepidation because of the uproar in Alaska concerning the lands issue and my establishing seventeen national monu-ments with over 50 million acres to protect natural areas in the absence of congressional legislation. Governor Jay Hammond and [Senator] Ted Ste-vens were on hand to meet me. Mike Gravel was not there; I presume he only goes back to Alaska on election year. Jay Hammond gave me a mule driver's whip, since he said I might need it to whip somebody's ass.

MONDAY, JUNE 25   We went to the Akasaka Palace, and I was surprisingly excited about meeting the emperor. He was such a tiny little figure, bow-ing and saying the same thing over and over to everyone he met, that I was somewhat disappointed, but later my respect for him built. He's a delight-ful conversationalist, a fine amateur marine biologist, and has ruled the country from a nonpolitical position for more than fifty years with great sensitivity. I talked to him about air and water pollution, and his marine biology research.

The Japanese emperor stays out of politics but is not without influence. For instance, the Diet passed sweeping legislation to control air pollution because one day he remarked, "There are no more butterflies around the palace."

At the prime minister's residence, Ohira and I agreed that Japan will assume 50 percent of all the costs of the U.S. effort on refugees [from Vietnam and Cambodia], and we would double our induction rate from seven thousand per month to fourteen thousand. Our cochairmen for the wise men's group will be [former U.S. ambassador to Japan] Robert Ingersoll and [former Japanese ambassador to the United States] Nobuhiko Ushiba. At the Meiji Shrine, the priests wanted me to throw in some coins, bow twice, and say a prayer. I refused, and afterward my interpreter said he was a Christian and was proud that I did not worship heathen gods.

At the emperor's banquet I sat between the emperor and Crown Prin-cess Michiko, and thoroughly enjoyed my discussion with her. She's the first commoner who ever married a crown prince, and I can see why he married her. [Both she and the emperor knew my sister Ruth quite well.] I stated that had there been such a U.S.-Japan wise men's group fifty years ago, the tragic turn of history might have been averted. The emperor agreed wholeheartedly. Later, I gave Rachel Carson's books—*Silent Spring* and *The Sea Around Us*—to the emperor.

JUNE 26   We went to the same tiny restaurant where [the *New York Times* journalist] Richard Halloran and I had eaten four years ago. The place specializes in "yakitori" chicken. It only seats about twenty to twenty-five people, and this turned out to be the most important symbolic thing we did for the whole trip—letting me be identified as a man of the people. We enjoyed the meal, drank a lot of sake, and there was laughing, clapping of hands, and toasts between me and all the Japanese citizens.

I told the proprietor that I would return if he wouldn't change the place, and he kept his promise. The restaurant became famous and made the proprietor a rich man, and eventually he opened several large restaurants around To-kyo. Each time we visit his restaurant he places a small brass plaque on the table where we eat. There are now thirteen of them.

JUNE 27   In a Shimoda town hall meeting, televised throughout Japan, the questions were primarily related to family, my background, Amy's education, the proper duties of a mother, and whether I would marry a black woman. This showed, I think, the interests of the Japanese people—family life of Americans and how a little boy from a Georgia farm could become president.

Later, we invited Mrs. Thatcher and Prime Minister [Joe] Clark to come over [to the U.S. embassy]. He came first, and I liked him immediately.

JUNE 28   This first day of the economic summit was one of the worst days of my diplomatic life. We had specific goals [regarding the energy crisis] that I thought had to be reached in order for the conference to be significant. The Europeans had locked together in [a prior] meeting and were adamantly against any individual national commitment [on energy issues]. I spoke early, outlined our specific goals, and said we must commit ourselves on an individual national basis. Our luncheon was bitter and unpleasant. Schmidt got personally abusive toward me, alleging that American interference in the Mideast on a peace treaty had caused problems with oil all over the world. Eventually Ohira proposed a compromise that I thought the Europeans accepted: the Europeans later this year would assign individual nations their quota and monitor it. It seemed quite clear to me, but later Schmidt, Thatcher, [European Union president Roy] Jenkins, and [Italy's Giulio] Andreotti tried to wiggle out of it. Valéry helped hold it together, pointing out that we had reached a superb agreement based on complete misunderstanding.

In the afternoon we did not accomplish anything and wasted at least twelve hours of work. We adjourned in bad spirits, directing our representatives to work out a joint communiqué with differences in brackets. The relationships among us were strained during the receiving line and the banquet.

I sat next to the crown prince and found him to be intelligent and interesting, careful to avoid any comment on international or domestic politics. He would be the 126th member of his family to serve as emperor of Japan. The entertainment was a long, strange snake dance, but the music was relatively good, with the musicians being descendants of Koreans or Chinese.

JUNE 29   All the news from home was bad, with the truckers' strike, long gas lines, and the apparent stalemate in our summit. The OPEC decision amounted to a 60 percent increase in prices since last December, which will cut our growth rate maybe 2.5 percent through the end of 1980, increase the inflation rate 2.5 percent, and cost us eight hundred thousand jobs. I was determined, along with the others, to have a strong blast against OPEC for the first time in history, if we could do it in concert.

Although we strongly condemned OPEC, it had no effect on their decision greatly to increase the price of oil. It was clear that there would be a serious adverse effect on the Western economies. The impact later was exacerbated by the Iraqi-Iran war, which reduced supplies of oil coming from these two countries, creating an additional world shortage.

We had our "Berlin Breakfast" [just the seven leaders], and this helped alleviate the tension between me and Schmidt and Thatcher. We had an interesting and profound analysis of the ultimate prospective showdown between Western nations and OPEC countries.

When the conferees reconvened, we had resolved most of our differences. Our position prevailed in every instance, but the tension was still there. The Europeans were still squirming: Andreotti said he could not accept individual quotas for 1985; Thatcher came out with a carefully prepared amendment; and Roy Jenkins gave a little speech, obviously prearranged, putting all the European countries back in the same basket. I was adamantly opposed to it, Valéry supported my position, Helmut stayed quiet, Joe Clark and Ohira supported me, and we came out with a substantive final communiqué. Condemnation of OPEC was unanimous, and perhaps significant for the future. Margaret also tried to weaken the refugee communiqué.

Valéry is a strong, competent man—still my favorite; Helmut is strong, somewhat unstable, postures, drones on and on, giving economic lessons, strongly protects German interests, popular in his own country; Andreotti is a smooth politician, compromiser, subtly tries to get special advantages for Italy, plays on sympathy about Italy's weakness; Thatcher is a tough lady, highly opinionated, strong-willed, cannot admit that she doesn't know anything; Joe Clark had done his homework and protected Canadian interests but was willing to accommodate the ultimate conclusions when necessary; Ohira is one of my favorites, but his language gap prevented his being a good presiding officer.

In the final press conference I emphasized the significance of our condemnation of OPEC; the devastating blow of OPEC's decision on developing nations; the importance of restrictive and specific national consumption goals from 1979 through 1985; our independent and collective commitment to alternate sources of energy; improvement of marketing procedures to prevent wild fluctuations in the oil market; our willingness to double the number of refugees admitted to the U.S.; and that we had long, tedious arguments but ultimately arrived at the boldest and most constructive position. The conference was a success.

We then went directly to Korea, where I helicoptered with General [John] Vessey around Seoul and then to Camp Casey, quite late. When I looked at tomorrow's schedule I didn't see how I could possibly survive, but we had already made arrangements for me to run with the troops at 5:15 the following morning.

JUNE 30   Up, feeling surprisingly good, I joined a group of Signal Corps troops. Brigadier General Bruckner and I were in front to run one and a half miles to another camp and then back. After the first mile, they reported it was eight minutes and five seconds. I thought it was faster, and decided to pick up the pace. Toward the end the troops couldn't keep up, and television crews reported their falling behind. It was an exciting run,

I guess in about twenty-two minutes, which was very easy for me. I shook hands with all the troops, and as they went by they were supposed to shout, "Fit to fight!" but about half of them couldn't speak. Then [I] changed clothes and went to the parade ground for commander-in-chief honors. I made an inspirational short talk and promised that the next time I would run in combat boots and let them wear running shoes—but would not race anyone less than fifty-five years old.

We then drove to Seoul for the most impressive welcoming ceremony I've ever seen. I was surprised at how small [President] Park was, and how beautiful his daughter was. We rode into Seoul, and I believe the biggest crowd I've ever seen was there to welcome us, apparently in a genuinely friendly spirit. One newspaper said 1 million, the other said 2 million people—my guess is 1 million.

At our first meeting, I was prepared to be very forthcoming on troop commitments, but Park read an abusive harangue for more than an hour. I was so angry that I decided I would respond in generalities and request that he and I meet in private.

I did make a fairly strong statement that we stood by our commitments, had worldwide obligations that we always met, our military, political, economic strength was unsurpassed, and I could not understand how a tiny nation like North Korea could surpass so greatly a large and strong South Korea, even with forty thousand American troops and superb air cover, and I was deeply disturbed about this trend.

We then went in for a private meeting, which was unsatisfactory. Park was unwilling to commit himself to a specific increase in the percentage of GNP to be spent on defense, and he continued to be evasive on human rights. I did not indicate what I would do in the future.

I told President Park that I had come with the sincere intent to work closely and had been taken aback by his adamant demand that U.S. force levels not be changed when the numbers involved were only one-half of 1 percent of the total defense forces available to South Korea.

PARK: We do not plan to increase the number of ground forces. We have a 1954 agreement with the U.S. that freezes the level at six hundred thousand.

CARTER: Do you want the limit removed?

PARK: We would prefer to concentrate on equipment. The North Koreans, for example, have over 2,000 tanks. We have about 850.

CARTER: Our impression was that you had 1,050.

PARK: The number may have changed slightly.

CARTER: General Vessey told me this morning that you have more than 1,000.

PARK: That may be true.

[We then had an equally frank discussion about Park's human rights abuses.]

JULY 1   We welcomed key Korean religious leaders for prayer and a discussion. [Baptist pastor] Billy Kim asked me to talk to Park about becoming a Christian, and I promised to do so.

Everywhere we went we pushed human rights, including with Prime Minister Choi [Kyu Hah] and then with President Park and his daughter—the most important unresolved issue. Only 17 percent of Americans support military action to defend Korea, because of unfavorable publicity about human rights. Park thought for a long time and said, "I understand your concern, and I will try to act to alleviate your concern."

In the car going to the airport, I asked him about his religious belief. He said he had none, his two daughters were devout Catholics, and his son had indicated some interest in Buddhism. I said I'd like for one of the Baptists to explain our faith, and would send Billy Kim to see him. He said, "I will invite him myself." And I said, "I'll let Billy Kim know." I asked him how he would react to the U.S. establishing relations with North Korea when South Korea established relations with China. He said this was the desire of the government of South Korea. It was a good and frank discussion—helpful to me.

We departed for Hawaii, and home, exhausted. Good trip.

Rosalynn and I had planned to spend a few days in Hawaii—my duty station as a submariner—but pressing issues at home, including a truckers' strike and rising concern about the energy crisis, were too serious for me to delay our return.

MONDAY, JULY 2   Strauss called from Jerusalem, eager for me to address the Kreisky-Begin dispute about processing Jews emigrating from Russia. They had crafted a letter making Vance admit he was mistaken in the past. I revised the letter just saying we were against illegal settlements, in favor of maximum Jewish emigration from the Soviet Union, and urging Kreisky not to take action until after he discusses it with Begin.

JULY 3　North Korea reacted negatively to my visit to South Korea, and so far to the tripartite talks.

My wishes while president to bring about peace between North and South Korea were frustrated. It was not until June 1994 that I finally went to Seoul and Pyongyang and arranged a summit meeting between the two. Although South Korean president Kim Dae Jung received the Nobel Peace Prize for his subsequent reconciliation efforts, the continued ostracizing of North Korea and its development of nuclear weapons have prevented success. An official state of war persists.

I had an interesting meeting with Omar Torrijos re Nicaragua. Our proposal was that all military assistance be stopped, Somoza step down, and a ten-person provisional government be set up, then elections under OAS auspices. Torrijos responded favorably.

We will reveal GNP for 1979 will decrease by .5 percent, which indicates a recession; prospects for next year will be 2 percent growth; the consumer price index this year will increase 10.6 percent and for 1980 8.3 percent, and unemployment likely up to almost 7 percent.

JULY 4　At Camp David, I got up early and read Pat Caddell's memorandum—one of the most brilliant analyses of sociological and political interrelationships I have ever seen. The more I read it along with Rosalynn, the more I became excited. I think we two are the only ones that are reasonably sold on his premises. It will take a lot of courage. Pat thinks it would be a serious mistake to make the speech Friday night just on energy; the problems of the nation are much broader and deeper. Our trust among the American people is low, and the number of people who listen to my voice is minimal.

I got a copy of the energy speech and told Rosalynn I couldn't deliver it. Pat suggested that I speak just on the mood, attitude, or problems of the country, but it was our idea to have people come to Camp David and consult with them. I felt a remarkable sense of relief and renewed confidence after I canceled the energy speech and began to shape the thoughts I would put into the next week's work.

Our country and others were facing an economic onslaught from OPEC, which had brought about long gas lines, economic stagnation, and world-wide inflation and unemployment. One result was a strike by truckers, who were heavily afflicted by the fuel crisis. The Congress, deeply divided between states that produced or consumed oil and gas, was refusing to give serious attention to my repeated calls for comprehensive energy reform.

I needed frank advice from the best thinkers in our society and also average citizens. Rosalynn and I decided to stay at Camp David and spend as much time as necessary consulting with a series of visitors before I delivered a carefully drafted speech to the nation that would encompass what we had learned. I wanted my words to be incisive, accurate, and hopefully inspirational.

JULY 5   I had Jody, Jerry, Fritz, Hamilton, Pat, and Stu come [to Camp David] to talk to me. Stu and Fritz were adamantly against what we proposed, and everyone else reluctantly agreed. I finally told them we were going to do it; I needed their support.

I took a walk around the Camp David fence with Fritz, to get him cooled down. He was quite distraught. I told him that my mind was set, that I had to have his support—but we didn't really get it after that. Stu came around quicker, but Fritz was extremely fearful about the consequences of what we were planning to do.

We then decided to list people to come up—governors and political wise men and women. We had a frank discussion in the evening about the cabinet officers. There was a unanimous recommendation among Fritz and the top staff people that Califano, Blumenthal, and Schlesinger should be replaced. I did not agree with them and defended the three cabinet secretaries.

JULY 6   I called Bob Strauss in Egypt at 4:30 a.m. and got a report on the Mideast. He was surprised at Sadat's high opinion of Begin. I told Bob to tell King Hussein to get off his ass and help us, that I was not going to invite him to come over here and give him a White House forum to blast me about the Mideast peace effort.

The governors arrived to spend the night. I felt a new kinship with them I had never felt before, and found them surprisingly supportive of what I was trying to do.

JULY 7   They agreed to make supportive statements; to outline that I was well, happy, strong, confident, determined, searching for answers to some basic issues affecting America, and they were willing to help me. This is our thirty-third anniversary. I called Rosalynn on her way to Louisville to tell her that I loved her. She's been a tower of strength and fountain of wisdom throughout this Camp David stay.

In the evening we brought in the so-called wise men and one woman. We talked before and during supper, while I sat on the floor and took notes. We assessed the cabinet and my staff. Their criticisms of me were much more severe, including the basic question: Can I govern the country?

JULY 8   One interesting feature was that there never was a positive state-ment made about the American press; they were universally negative. By the way, by today the news media are beginning to cover actually what is going on. The statements made by the governors have done a lot to as-suage outside concern.

At the end of the meeting I told Jim Schlesinger it was time for him to step down, since he had submitted his resignation on two previous occa-sions. I offered him a major diplomatic post, but he said he couldn't take seven children overseas. We parted company in a very friendly spirit.

MONDAY, JULY 9   This was a long day, with two congressional committee groups and a morning session on energy. I've never seen so much coop-eration among this group who have been fighting for two years. They pledged their readiness to move on a comprehensive energy program, and the environmentalists and oil state leaders were remarkably compatible. I spent 90 percent of my time listening. The only dissident was the Speaker, who cannot accept the idea that the Great Society days are over, and that all the problems of the nation can't be solved with massive spending pro-grams, public works, et cetera.

I worked hard all week, some of the most strenuous mental work of my life. Also, it's not easy for me to accept criticism, and to reassess my ways of doing things, to admit my mistakes. This was a week of intense reassess-ment. I ran every day from three to seven miles and swam afterward.

June figures for prices and unemployment were reasonably good: un-employment went down to 5.6 percent, and OMB estimates a $28.1 billion 1980 deficit.

JULY 10   The worst session of the week was the economic meeting. When you get bankers, labor leaders, economists, financiers around the table, they are so eager to posture and repeat the analyses they've already evolved that it's not helpful. But we had to go through the rote process. In general, they thought we ought to hold firm on economic policy; some thought we should decontrol gasoline; some didn't; some thought we ought to prepare for a tax reduction, not move on it now.

The best meeting may have been with the religious leaders. They made very moving and deep analyses of the problems of our nation and helped shape my Sunday night speech more than anyone else. [Terence] Cardinal Cooke impressed me most, Rabbi [Marc] Tanenbaum next, and the others were very helpful.

JULY 11   I talked to Tip [by telephone] about the Department of Education, and it passed narrowly.

Then I met with state and local leaders. It was too large a group but was very constructive. They were honored to come. One of them said it may not help my credibility to be at Camp David, but it certainly helped hers.

JULY 12   Rosalynn and I spent almost all day working on Sunday night's speech. I have gone through my conversations with everyone and used exact quotes that I think are pertinent. In the evening we flew over to a Pittsburgh suburb called Carnegie to Bill and Betty Fisher's house. It was hard to keep them answering questions, they were so eager to ask me questions. It was constructive and helpful, and gave us an image of not being secluded at Camp David, but also dealing directly with people in their own homes.

JULY 13   We flew over to Martinsburg, West Virginia, to visit the home of Mr. and Mrs. Marvin Porterfield, and about fifteen or twenty of their friends. We came back [to Camp David] and met with a group of top news reporters: John Chancellor, James Kilpatrick, Marvin Stone, Joseph Kraft, Hugh Sidey, David Broder, Carl Rowan, Tom Wicker, Frank Reynolds, Jack Germond, Max Frankel, Meg Greenfield, Brandt Ayers, Anthony Day, Jim Lehrer, Ed Yoder, Walter Cronkite. They were pleased to come and impressed, I believe, with what I had to say, and interested in the procedure I had followed. We put my exact quotes off the record, but let them express the tone of what I was saying. They did it very accurately. I think it turned the media assessment of Camp David around in a positive fashion.

JULY 14   I authorized Schlesinger to send a million barrels of kerosene to the Iranians.

I went over the speech several times and practiced it once. Of course, I had to work on the speech for Kansas City on Monday to the county commissioners group and on Monday to the CWA [Communication Workers of America] convention.

JULY 15   I made the speech in the evening, and the response was very good. Instantaneous poll results on the West Coast were the best they've ever had for a half-hour program, and I think the people were getting the message. About 100 million people watched this speech.

This entire episode was one of the most dramatic and memorable events of my administration. Although initially praised, my speech was later characterized by Ted Kennedy, Ronald Reagan, and adversarial news reporters as a speech about America's "malaise," because I pointed out some of our nation's problems and discussed the challenges that could and would be overcome by bold and direct action on my energy proposals. Down through the years, however, the speech has often been called prescient and praised for its honest analysis of the troubled mood of our nation.

MONDAY, JULY 16   I got my energy speech revised by the time the helicopter took off for Kansas City, and delivered it strongly and well. Got an overwhelming response from the county officials, about 4,500 of them. Went to Detroit and had a good session with the CWA.

During the process of the last few days, we've decided that some changes must be made in the White House staff and the cabinet. We need to let the public know, perhaps with another semishock, that I'm trying to get control of the bureaucracy, particularly within my own administration.

JULY 17   I met with the staff and then the cabinet. They reached a consensus that all would resign orally, since they served at my pleasure anyway, and all seemed pleased with this arrangement. Brock [Adams] made his peculiar statement again [that he would resign or stay on], Mike [Blumenthal] and Joe [Callahan] said they did not have the support or confidence of the White House staff. The rest of them all made supportive statements.

Soon after delivering my speech about the challenges facing our country, I made a mistake when I mishandled the decision, already made, to change a few members of my cabinet. As a pro forma step, I accepted a recommendation from the attorney general that all cabinet members submit resignations so that I might accept those that should leave. This announcement to the press created an impression of crisis and sent the wrong message about my confidence in the remaining cabinet members.

JULY 18   The news reports, predictably, made a crisis of the cabinet offering their resignation, ignoring that the cabinet resigned in support of me to give me a clear hand in handling replacements.

Somoza had agreed to my complete package in Nicaragua, involving a temporary replacement for him in Francisco Urcuyo. There was to be no further bloodshed; cessation of warfare; blending of the revolutionary army with the National Guard; et cetera. In addition, Somoza was to be given safe haven in Florida. Under the urgings of Somoza, Urcuyo, once in office, restarted the war. I got very angry and notified Somoza that his staying in this country was contingent on his carrying out the complete agreement. He raised hell but complied.

I asked Pat Harris if she would take HEW, and she agreed. Califano came by, and we had a harmonious meeting. I told him that he had done a good job but I wanted him to resign. I offered to let him go to Camp David this weekend, and I would be glad to meet him there so we could talk over his future.

Reg Jones [CEO of General Electric] talked to me about secretary of treasury. He thought that either David Rockefeller or Bill Miller would be good.

JULY 19   Joe came by and said he would give me his letter of resignation today. He seemed to be in a good mood. I told him Pat would be taking his place. He preferred to visit his parents rather than go to Camp David, and I told him that later I'd be glad to have him and his children go to Camp David to visit with us. I talked to Schlesinger, who said he was ready to go in an orderly fashion.

David Rockefeller came down. Told him I wanted to interview him for secretary of treasury. He asked me a number of questions, as though he was interviewing me for a job. I said he would be the economic spokesman for my administration, and suggested since he had qualms to talk it over with Reg Jones. Then I called Bill Miller, who said he would be glad to serve anywhere I needed him. I told Hamilton to tell Rockefeller to cancel his meeting with Reg Jones, that it would be better for him not to serve in the Treasury Department. Mike Blumenthal and I immediately and jointly decided that he should leave. I called Brock Adams, who had said he didn't know if he wanted to stay or not, that his staying would depend upon my support for his programs and whether or not my staff would be responsive to the American people. I called Brock and told him that he should step down. This will, I hope, complete all the resignations. Only three really are under any sort of restraint: Adams, Califano, and Blumenthal.

JULY 20   The Nicaraguan question has been substantially resolved. We don't know what the junta and other leaders will do, but we are concerned about the spread to neighboring countries of the revolutionary impact. El Salvador is weakest, but Honduras, Guatemala, and even Costa Rica could be vulnerable.

I met with Jaime Roldós, president-elect of Ecuador, who was very grateful that we had made it possible for him to win [an honest election]. He's pleased that Rosalynn will attend the inauguration. The democratization of Ecuador, and perhaps Bolivia, are two more strong steps that may have resulted from our effort on human rights.

When I became president, most of the regimes in South and Central America were military dictatorships. Historically, the U.S. government under both Democratic and Republican presidents had supported the dictators and strongly opposed—often with U.S. Marines or army troops—any popular uprisings of indigenous or minority citizens that threatened the status quo. The reasons for this were obvious. Many of the leaders had been trained at West Point or Annapolis, were fluent in English, conversant with our free enterprise system, and eager to form lucrative partnerships with American corporations that had an interest in natural resources of the country involved. These included bananas, pineapples, bauxite, tin, iron ore, and exotic lumber. It was politically convenient to brand any indigenous people or other groups as Communists or simply revolutionaries. Catholic priests who supported the poor and subjugated citizens were condemned by the Vatican as practicing "liberation theology." We became strongly involved in promot-

ing human rights in all these countries, condemning injustices, interceding with abusive leaders, using economic pressure, and giving public support to human rights activists.

I met with Mike Collins, Buzz Aldrin, and Neil Armstrong in ceremonies observing the tenth anniversary of the moon landing. I pointed out that this had been a major goal; we had a similar one now on energy security and had the same national strength and technological ability that would permit success.

JULY 21   In the evening we went to Wolf Trap to hear Rostropovich and André Watts. Their Rachmaninoff Second and Beethoven Seventh were superb, and the newspapers reported that we got a "tumultuous welcome." When people shook hands and spoke to me, they said, "Stick with it, Mr. President; don't back down." It was reassuring after facing the Washington press the last two days.

MONDAY, JULY 23   I met with Hedley Donovan [retired editor in chief of *Time* magazine]. Described what I wanted—a senior advisor with maximum flexibility—a nonpaying position. He would work directly for me, not as a member of the staff. He said he'd let me know in a couple of days. [Donovan later accepted the position.]

JULY 24   During the day the multinational trade bill passed 90–4 in the Senate. This is a notable achievement, almost without notice.

Paul Volcker came in with Bill Miller. He was enormous in size, stubborn, opinionated, committed to controlling inflation and preserving the value of the dollar, intelligent, highly trained, very experienced. I was surprised to find that he was a Democrat. Bill Miller and I decided that Paul could work harmoniously with us.

Facing reelection, I was about to make a political decision of momentous importance, and my advisors were very concerned. Putting someone as strong, independent, and outspoken as Volcker in charge of the Federal Reserve Bank and thus monetary policy would basically remove our White House influence from this crucial element of the American economy. Paul and I agreed that I would not try to interfere with his decisions but would expect to be kept informed as appropriate.

What I wanted more than political benefit was the strongest possible effort to control inflation, which was dangerously high and about to go higher. (In the months ahead, the inflation rate would go up to 13.6 percent in the United States—18 percent in Great Britain—primarily because of the rapid increase in oil prices.) Our trepidation about Volcker's appointment was later justified, when the Federal Reserve, under his leadership, curtailed the supply of money and therefore raised interest rates to very high levels—which ultimately achieved his goal of reducing inflation but also brought about a severe recession. These economic restraints and their consequences were a negative factor in my 1980 reelection campaign; Reagan gained considerable political advantage, for instance, when he condemned my projected deficit of $33 billion. (During Reagan's tenure, the deficit continued to grow; by 1986, it had risen to $220 billion, while the total accumulated debt grew from $749 billion to $1,746 billion.)

JULY 25   I discussed Moon Landrieu [former judge and mayor of New Orleans, for HUD] and Neil Goldschmidt [former mayor of Portland, Oregon, for Transportation].

I asked Paul Volcker to be chairman of the Federal Reserve, and he accepted. The results were as anticipated, even better, with almost unanimous, enthusiastic support.

JULY 26   I spent a long time going over judgeship appointments. Out of 153 authorized, we have 20 left.

Sam Nunn made a statement that he could find nothing in particular wrong with SALT II, he wanted it tied in with adequate defense budgets, and insinuated that the Carter administration had not been for adequate budgets. In fact, in my first two years the Congress has cut my proposals by $5 billion. We don't want to get in an argument with Nunn, but I'm not going to lie down and roll over for him.

JULY 27   We [Dr. Lukash and I] ran the 10K below Camp David on the terrible up-and-down hills, very slowly in fifty-three minutes [and next day in fifty minutes].

JULY 29   I called Kissinger about his SALT testimony, and he assured me it would be constructive. He called back later to say he perhaps misled me; it is not going to be so pleasing. He said he would try to modify it to be helpful.

AUGUST 1   We're still exploring ways to get the PLO to accept UN 242 and Israel's right to exist. This is developing as a UN flap.

AUGUST 2   Lunch with Rosalynn. We discussed her trip to Latin America, primarily [later canceled]. It's surprising how excited the leaders are when Rosalynn will visit their country. It's also gratifying to see how many of those Andean nations are moving toward democratic governments.

AUGUST 3   Had a long discussion about the Palestinian UN resolution, and how we could move toward peace without committing political suicide. My preference is that Strauss deal with the Israelis, American Jews, and Arabs, but Cy said he'd just as soon resign if he's going to be a figurehead. Later he cooled off a little. There's no advantage for me or Vance to be in the forefront of this difficult issue. We can set the policy; Strauss can carry it out with more political impunity.

I met with Bill Miller, Jim McIntyre, and Stu Eizenstat on the Chrysler bankruptcy situation. We will help in a very cautious way with a guaranteed loan, only if we have the preeminent position and if Chrysler can show they are doing their best to resolve their fiscal problems through the free enterprise system.

Our government was heavily dependent on Chrysler as a major defense contractor, and bankruptcy would have cost an estimated two hundred thousand jobs at a time when unemployment was already 6 percent. This was another difficult legislative battle. Chrysler was suffering from enormous financial losses, a fleet of inefficient cars, and high fuel prices. After tough negotiations, Chrysler's management, labor organizations, local governments, and creditors agreed on $2 billion in concessions, and I approved a loan guarantee of $1.5 billion. The results turned out to be remarkably successful. We monitored compliance with the agreement, and the loans were repaid, with interest.

I also agreed on financial bailouts to prevent bankruptcy of New York City. In both cases, we closely supervised expenditure of funds and took a preeminent position to guarantee the integrity of our loan. Both grantees recovered, complying with strict fiscal discipline imposed and monitored by

Secretary Bill Miller. The interest rates we charged were high, and with Chrysler's recovery its CEO, Lee Iacocca, insisted on an early repayment. I recommended against this, and the federal government collected its full financial profit.

President Obama has been forced to deal with the bailout of major banks, insurance companies, and automobile manufacturers—obviously on a much larger scale than I confronted. Faced with an economic crisis, he did not have the same negotiating leverage I enjoyed in getting a good deal for the federal government.

AUGUST 5 Since Sapelo Island will not be available for vacation, Rosalynn and I discussed a trip down the Mississippi on the *Delta Queen*, starting in the Minnesota area, plus a few days in Plains, and then to Camp David.

MONDAY, AUGUST 6 Met with Cy, Strauss, Zbig, and Ham. We agreed that Israel does not want to include any Palestinians in the West Bank talks, nor do they want the PLO to endorse UN 242 or the right of Israel to exist. I don't feel inclined to back down.

AUGUST 7 We've had 192 judges [including 39 vacancies] to appoint within the last nine months, and we are down now to maybe 15 that are fairly noncontroversial. We've done the best we could with women and minority groups. It's been difficult because they have such a small portion of the lawyers in the country and most of them are fairly young, not having had much experience. The ABA has been remarkably cooperative in certifying some doubtful blacks or women.

As the surprise victor in 1976 with practically no support from the "power structure," I had made no promises regarding judges, cabinet officers, or ambassadors before assuming office. Attorney General Griffin Bell, on the other hand, was deeply involved with many of the leading members of the American Bar Association, with ties of friendship to deans of law schools and senior members of major law firms. He knew many of the would-be judges, as did members of the U.S. Senate. Despite strong original opposition from him and some senators, I was able to choose a large number of women and minorities. These appointees, carefully assessed, brought a fresh spirit to the federal judiciary and performed superbly.

AUGUST 8   In a one-and-a-half-hour luncheon with Ambassador [Ephraim] Evron of Israel we had a very frank discussion about recent attacks on me and our country, which were unwarranted, false, and unacceptable. I told Eppie I would not be swayed by political considerations in the U.S., do not have to be reelected, and would do what was best for our nation and Israel. They were in danger of becoming international pariahs if they continue bombing civilian communities in Lebanon and refuse to help resolve the Palestinian question. We are their main friend, and when they can't get along with us it leaves them almost isolated. Eppie is a good man, and I trust him—a remarkable improvement over his predecessor, who was a liar and could not be trusted.

AUGUST 10   Cubans are offering to release about five hundred more prisoners. We've only been processing three or four per day, so I instructed the attorney general to expedite the process.

MONDAY, AUGUST 13   I met with food processors and distributors, who seem to be cheating the public. Although pork prices peaked last February, it was more than four months before retail prices started going down. The spread between the farm price and retail price on meat has increased 109 percent, fresh fruits, 90 percent. Top officials in the food chains mouthed a lot of inaccurate data, but I think they realize my analysis was correct.

AUGUST 14   I learned that Andy [Young] has gotten himself into serious trouble by meeting with the UN PLO representative. This is understandable because Andy is president of the Security Council, but when interrogated about it by the State Department he told them a lie. Later he told the Israeli ambassador the truth and the Israelis very unwisely made this fact public, although Andy's meeting with the PLO was certainly designed to help the Israeli cause. This is an almost impossible problem to resolve without Andy leaving.

While I was out jogging with Rosalynn, Vance came with Warren Christopher, Hamilton, and Jody, to say that in his opinion Andy would have to leave. Cy's implication was that the choice was between him and Andy [a threat to resign that Vance repeated many times during his tenure].

CEO Tom Murphy of General Motors told me they would no longer fight against air pollution or efficiency standards but would turn out automobiles that would exceed our requirements. This would cost them

$6 billion, and they would transfer part of their technology to other manufacturers.

AUGUST 15 During the afternoon, Andy decided he would resign today. We responded reluctantly, with praise for him. Jody wept when he read the letter to the press accepting Andy's resignation. Andy was not penitent at all, saying he had done what he thought was right. It is absolutely ridiculous that we pledged under Kissinger and Nixon that we would not negotiate with the PLO; but our country's honor is at stake, and we will do the best we can. I instructed Cy and Zbig not to make any more reassurances that we were not meeting with the PLO; if the Israelis couldn't trust us, they could find another "trustworthy" partner.

Accepting the resignation of Andrew Young was one of the most heart-wrenching decisions I had to make as president. He was a close and intimate friend, and the prohibition against meeting the PLO was preposterous, as this group was a key to any comprehensive peace agreement. He would have retained his position if he had been truthful to the secretary of state.

AUGUST 16 Went to the Justice Department to participate in the ceremony to swear in Ben Civiletti and tell Griffin goodbye. They are both outstanding men and have really added integrity to the Department of Justice.

AUGUST 17–24 Over Senator Harry Byrd's strong objections, I told him the fourth judge in Virginia would be black.

We [Rosalynn, Amy, and I] left for Saint Paul with a remarkable degree of excitement, and went aboard the *Delta Queen*.

We had small but adequate quarters on the stern, just above the paddle wheel and below the calliope. We had anticipated only four stops, not realizing we had twenty-six additional stops at locks where our stay was an hour or more—plus several towns along the way where we took on water and discharged trash and garbage—which all became full-scale rallies. Nor did we anticipate the number of small towns where large crowds would gather, the *Delta Queen* would turn upstream, slow down, get in close to shore, and I would make a speech from the deck with the spotlight on me at night. By the end of the trip I had made forty-eight appearances with speeches to the crowds, day and night, who lined the banks to watch the *Delta Queen* go by.

At all the locks, regardless of the time of day or state of the weather, we had several hundred or several thousand people come to see us, sometimes waiting as long as six hours and walking as far as two miles. The people were in good spirits. Friendly. Excited. I went down for every crowd. Rosalynn generally slept after midnight. In spite of all this activity we got enough rest, fished a little, read a lot, had meals with the different passengers. Rosalynn's birthday was 8/18, so we received a lot of small gifts, including three large paintings of the *Delta Queen*. We jogged every day. The first morning I got up early and jogged around the deck, but disturbed people with the running. So after that we found places on the different locks, generally early in the morning, to run between four and five miles.

At lock 24 [August 23] the attorney general called re an allegation against Jody, Hamilton, and Tim taking cocaine in Studio 54 in New York.

Past lock 26 there were more than thirty tow boats waiting. The authorized construction project had been held up fifteen years, by the railroads primarily, who have recently been joined by environmentalists.

All of us enjoyed the trip—remarkably beautiful, in northern places looking like European rivers, with high bluffs, mountains in the background. I spent a lot of time in the pilothouse learning about the Mississippi River, while reading *Life on the Mississippi* by Samuel Clemens.

Back at the White House [August 24], Jody and Hamilton denied the allegations, apparently from some owners of Studio 54 nightclub under indictment and attempting to plea-bargain. I'll stay aloof and let the lawyers handle it.

The charges against all of them were eventually proven to be unfounded.

AUGUST 29   I had Don McHenry in for a long talk and was favorably impressed. I asked him to accept the ambassador's job at the UN.

AUGUST 30   At Georgia Tech we had a very good seminar on new developments in energy. Energy use versus GNP growth has dropped 40 percent in the last three or four years. I then went to Emory to speak about American morality and ethics, dedicate a religious center named for Bishop William Cannon, and receive an honorary degree. I then flew to Tampa for a reception in a pouring-down rain and a town hall meeting, The advantages of campaigning as incumbent are obvious. The disadvantages of being an incumbent are also obvious. I had been wet three times and was exhausted when we got to Plains at midnight.

AUGUST 31–SEPTEMBER 2   There are not as many tourists in town as before, and I think the character of the town can be preserved. Rosalynn and I caught a lot of fish on fly rods [in our pond], jogged all the way home, seven miles. Sunday afternoon, I played softball—three hits out of four times at bat!

MONDAY, SEPTEMBER 3   When we got to Washington we had a picnic for about one thousand people representing labor organizations.

SEPTEMBER 4   Fritz gave me a glowing report of his visit to China and is very pleased re his responsibilities. I told him they were unlimited; if he came up with anything additional, I would approve it.

    Bob Byrd expressed concern about Soviet troops in Cuba and thought this might be a fatal blow to the SALT treaty. I told him there was no way to mandate that the Soviets withdraw [their] troops, that in the 1960s they had twenty thousand there—ten times what they have had for the last fifteen or twenty years.

SEPTEMBER 5   The major concern during the day was the Soviet troop presence in Cuba—which is obviously not a threat to our country or a violation of any Soviet commitment, but politically devastating to SALT.

    I spent four hours answering ridiculous questions from Paul Curran [special investigator appointed by Griffin Bell] about the warehouse, and after I got through answering all of them in good spirit, I told Curran that I thought it was a travesty of justice. The main problem is not with him but with a weak attorney general and our system of justice.

SEPTEMBER 6   The evening news was a wild exaggeration of the Soviet troop situation—both within the media and also Congress. The Soviets have responded reasonably.

SEPTEMBER 7   Charlie Schultze went over the extreme impact of energy price increases on our nation's inflation rate. There's no good news in the economic forecast except that inflation will probably moderate toward the end of the year.

I announced our assessment of the Soviet troops—good, accurate, and treated favorably in the news media.

SEPTEMBER 8   We [Dr. Lukash and I] ran twelve miles, which convinced me that I do not want to be a marathoner.

MONDAY, SEPTEMBER 10   The Israeli cabinet was split sharply on the settlements issue between Sharon and Yadin.

The Soviets claim there's been no substantial change in the numbers [of their troops] since 1962. Their mission has always been the training of Cuban officers, and they are respecting all the 1962 agreements, not trying to test my will, and willing to work with us to alleviate this problem.

SEPTEMBER 11   The general feeling in the White House, our campaign headquarters, and the DNC is stimulation and excitement since the increasing speculation about Kennedy's candidacy. We're ready to meet him.

SEPTEMBER 14   I went down to Mobile, Pascagoula, Pensacola, to assess the damage by Hurricane Frederic—much worse than I dreamed, with damage exceeding that of Hurricane Camille ten years ago. For miles along the Gulf shore, all homes were destroyed. Almost five hundred thousand people were evacuated along the coast, so deaths were held to a minimum. John Macy, head of FEMA, our new [Federal] Emergency Management Agency, has done an outstanding job. There was a minimum of confusion and a maximum of careful and thorough preparation.

In creating FEMA, we brought together about thirty previously uncoordinated agencies into one, with three vital characteristics: a highly competent administrator, direct responsibility to the president, and unlimited emergency funds. Later, President George W. Bush abandoned all these with an incompetent administrator, doubtful bureaucratic status, and insufficient funding, which led to a human and political disaster when Hurricane Katrina struck the Gulf Coast in 2005.

SEPTEMBER 15   I made a serious tactical mistake in the ten-thousand-meter race on Catoctin Mountain by deciding to cut four minutes below my best previous time. I overexerted and had to drop out of the race. I came through it okay, attended the awards ceremony, handed out the prizes, and, although I felt a little weak, didn't have any aftereffects. We should have played it safe to make sure we finished.

Predictably, this incident became a major news media event. Many commentators seemed eager to suggest that my excessive striving and failure to finish the race had deep metaphorical meaning.

MONDAY, SEPTEMBER 17   Lunch with Fritz. We discussed the Kennedy challenge, which seems to be more sure. I told him that Rosalynn and I felt remarkably at ease about it, and so did he. The main issue Kennedy is raising is leadership. We assessed our record on NATO, the Mideast, jobs, steel, agriculture, Panama, and compared Kennedy's record. As a student he was kicked out of college; he's my age but unsuccessful; as majority whip in the Senate, he was defeated after his first term; his preoccupation with national health insurance while never able to get the bill out of his own subcommittee in twelve years, et cetera. When the issues are debated we will be okay, but the weekend newspapers were unbelievable, practically anointing Kennedy as the president and claiming the 1980 election is already over.

These comments about Kennedy seem harsh, but it must be remembered that they were written in the midst of a political campaign that pitted me as the incumbent president against a Democratic challenger who had killed comprehensive health care and was opposing almost all my other legislative proposals and foreign policy decisions.

SEPTEMBER 18   We had a regular meeting with Democratic leaders. The energy package is in good shape, but there is slow progress on the mobilization board and the windfall profits tax.

At the staff meeting we discussed how to handle the Soviet troop problem—one of the most complicated nonsubstantive issues we've ever addressed.

SEPTEMBER 19   I discussed with Brzezinski the situation in Afghanistan and told him to move on deploring the Soviets' potential increased presence there.

Rosalynn and I worked on fourteen speeches she will make during the next two days in Florida. I always keep her up-to-date on all current events so she can answer questions. People are more and more looking at her as part of our administration, and media heavyweights go with her.

SEPTEMBER 20   The House has been ridiculously irresponsible this week, voting down the budget resolution, Panama Canal legislation, their own salary increase, raising the debt limit, et cetera—just a bunch of disorganized juvenile delinquents, with Tip having little influence or control.

SEPTEMBER 21   I authorized the Nicaraguan junta members to come to Washington, and I will meet with them for a brief courtesy call.

The basic inflation rate has increased up to about 8.5 percent. The major uncontrollable impact has been OPEC price increases, which amount to about 100 percent annual rate.

SEPTEMBER 22   There was indication of a nuclear explosion in the region of South Africa—either South Africa, Israel using a ship at sea, or nothing.

SEPTEMBER 23   We had a delightful party for members of Congress and their spouses. Several of the members said they are going to help me out.

MONDAY, SEPTEMBER 24   I told all my people to pursue the concept of a split party and possible Democratic defeat if Kennedy is an active candidate.

Lou Brock came by to visit with me. We joked about his breaking Ty Cobb's stolen base record, but he said no one would ever break Ty Cobb's four-thousand-hits record.

I asked Pat Caddell to talk to me about Soviet troops in Cuba. I would rather be defeated than pull down or endanger SALT in any way, so my guiding premise will be what's best for ratification of SALT.

SALT II was designed to have a life span of five years, and it was meant to be succeeded by SALT III, which would encompass much more drastic reductions in nuclear arsenals. Because of the Soviet invasion of Afghanistan, SALT II was never ratified, but its terms were honored by us and the Soviets for seven years, until Reagan negotiated what was called START (Strategic Arms Reduction Treaty).

SEPTEMBER 26 We're making an all-out press for the Department of Education. The opposition is formidable with abortion, busing, private schools, and other issues being foisted on the bill. Frank [Moore] and his staff said we could not change any votes, but I got aggravated and we started trying again. I spent a lot of time calling members to support our legislation.

Panama implementing legislation passed 233–188. This has been a bitch ever since more than two years ago.

SEPTEMBER 27 The education bill passed, by fourteen votes.

SEPTEMBER 28 We had a visit by López Portillo, and we were both on our best behavior. He gave me a remarkable portrait that looks like me from a distance but is made up of buildings and flags of all the states in the Union, the house that I grew up in, ships, and so forth. There's no human feature at all about it.

In my presidential library and museum, this painting by Octavio Ocampo became the most popular item among all the gifts I ever received. Many visitors purchase copies of the original.

SEPTEMBER 29–30 [Preparing for address to the nation] Because the issues were so profoundly complicated—ourselves, Cuba, the Soviets, SALT, Congress, politics—this has been the most laborious speech preparation of my life.

MONDAY, OCTOBER 1 The speech went over well, and the general result was exactly what we wanted: to defuse the Soviet troop issue and let the nation realize the importance of SALT. It was a quiet but good birthday.

The speech described the complex and inseparable interrelationship among the six issues I named, with the target audience being more thoughtful viewers who would take time to consider what I was saying.

OCTOBER 2 Had lunch with country music stars Dolly Parton, Johnny Cash, Tom T. Hall, Ronnie Milsap, et cetera—enjoyable! During the evening we went to Ford's Theatre for the country music gala.

OCTOBER 3   I think we're in better [political] shape than anybody realizes—not only in Florida but in New Hampshire and perhaps Iowa. The schedule of 1980 primaries and caucuses is arranged to our satisfaction.

OCTOBER 4   Overseas reaction to the Cuba speech was good, except in Israel. We're making progress in the Senate, where there's almost a unanimous commitment to move on with SALT.

I called Rupert Murdoch, publisher of the *New York Post*, to tell him I want to have lunch with him when he gets back from Australia. His paper is potentially a great ally or a great knife in the back. We prefer the former.

Strauss returned from Florida with a positive report from Dade County Jews. It would help if they ever made a positive statement in support of what I've tried to do, but I guess this is expecting too much. Eppie Evron, however, is doing a good job for us when he travels around the country, and Dayan made a great statement before he went back to Israel.

OCTOBER 5   Carl Yastrzemski came by, and I congratulated him on his 3,400 hits and 450 home runs. He's a nice guy.

OCTOBER 6   [My notes on the following conversation are unusually complete.] Pope John Paul II arrived and was warm and friendly, put his arms around Amy, kissed her, and remembered the visit [of Rosalynn and Amy] to the Vatican at the time of his investiture. He was grasped at and his hand was shaken more this day than ever before according to his people.

On the north side [of the White House] we spoke to members of the cabinet, Congress, Supreme Court, and their close friends—about three thousand, plus the ones in the park. Then he said he preferred to be alone with me, without anyone to take notes.

He had some difficulty understanding English, so I spoke very slowly and distinctly, and we got along well. He said he was somewhat tired but had a country retreat that he could visit about two months a year. I told him I would say a prayer that he could spend four months next year.

I asked him if he wanted to talk as officials or just have a personal conversation. He said personal. I asked him if he had difficulty with the pomp, ceremony, and adulation that he experienced. He said it was his greatest problem, and he spent hours praying for the humility that Christ exhibited.

We discussed Deng Xiaoping, and Deng's report that there were several thousand Catholics including bishops and priests in China. The pope mentioned a possible letter I might send to Hua Guofeng so the relationship between Rome and the China Catholic Church might be reestablished. I agreed to help with this. He said that of all continents, the two Americas were the most deeply committed Christians, and that western Europe was moving toward secularism; eastern Europe had a deeper faith in comparison.

It was important for the U.S. to reach out to eastern Europe and bypass government obstacles in every way. We agreed that our common Christian belief was a significant tie. I told him about my efforts in Poland to convert [First Secretary] Gierek just after he visited Rome. He said, "I doubt sometimes Gierek's nonbelief, but his faith in communism and atheism may be stronger." We discussed the success of Protestant evangelism in South Korea, and he said Catholics were not as strong there.

I told him I would like him to make a trip to Jerusalem. He replied that this is a sensitive subject for him. I said at times I felt lonely trying to resolve the Mideast problem, as the only outsider involved in working toward a comprehensive peace. My belief is that a visit by the pope to Jerusalem would reassure Christians and be well received by Arabs, indicating that Jerusalem was not exclusively a Jewish place to worship. He said there was the opportunity there for embarrassment. I told him it would not be a catastrophe for the pope to be embarrassed if acting in a good cause.

I told him the Jerusalem issue was indeed sensitive, even at Camp David; that Begin and Sadat had reached accord on a paragraph concerning Jerusalem, and I promised to send him this paragraph and a copy of the Camp David Accords. I told him the Jews in our country thought he was biased because he had never mentioned Israel in his speeches. He replied, "I have mentioned Jerusalem." I replied, "This is not adequate for the Jews." He said, "Okay, I will mention Israel sometime in the future." And then he smiled and said, "Once."

I suggested to him on behalf of Zbig that there should be one common prayer that was said all over the world in Latin, maybe the Lord's Prayer. He didn't seem to respond too well to this suggestion. I asked him if the Church was getting stronger or weaker in the last five years or so. He said it had a dip following Vatican II because of the dramatic changes made in Church procedures and the sense that the Church was too liberal, but it was regaining in some parts of the world.

We discussed the common doubt among poor people toward wealthier people, and that the U.S. was the epitome of wealth in the minds of most poor or hungry people. He was interested in autonomy of Baptist churches and how rapidly we were growing and our evangelistic spirit. He said that in Poland the Church was stronger than the government in a showdown, and the government knew this.

He had been surprised at his reception in the United States. I told him I had been amazed at the universality of his acceptance here even among those who had not wanted to be associated with the Catholic Church. We discussed his statements to the bishops the previous day, and I agreed that on celibacy of priests and the right to live, his statements had been in accordance with what Christ must have said had he been on earth in this modern day. I told him it was difficult for me as a politician sworn to uphold our laws to live with the concept of permissive abortion.

Then we went out on the South Lawn to make more personal and warm speeches to the six thousand or so people who had assembled. I called him primarily a pastor, and we joked about that. After we had finished our talks, somebody shouted, "Let the pope bless the audience!" and I told him it would be okay. His cape was blowing up over his head, and I held it back for him. When he went through the crowd it was amazing to see sophisticated leaders almost collapse, often in tears, when he approached them.

Leontyne Price sang the Lord's Prayer and "America the Beautiful." He was really impressed by her and her voice, which I still think is the best. Then he had to go to another ceremony. I told him to get some rest and come back to see us.

MONDAY, OCTOBER 8–WEDNESDAY, OCTOBER 10   I worked with Congress and left on a trip to a number of western states.

OCTOBER 11   Ray Marshall was remarkably popular when I introduced him to labor leaders in San Diego. He said all over the country he has stated flatly to labor conventions that I had the best record of any president with the possible exception of Franklin Roosevelt. He's asked them to challenge that statement, but no one has done so.

OCTOBER 12   We are concerned about the Mideast talks becoming stagnant, which may be the best state for them until Sadat gets his land back and we solidify our political support among American Jews.

We decided there was nothing we could do except continue to oppose strongly Pakistan's nuclear explosion effort. Most of us doubt that Pakistan has the ability to do it anyhow, but they're posturing and getting a lot of prestige by doing so.

Still shaky on SALT, with a group of weak-kneed senators holding their fingers up to the political wind. Our hope is to convince them it's politically expedient to vote for it.

I told Cy to go ahead on establishing diplomatic relations with Equatorial Guinea. We all agreed it was a mistake not to try to woo former Soviet allies away from them, like this country, Uganda, Somalia, Angola.

OCTOBER 13   During a radio call-in show, twenty-nine people asked a total of forty questions—half on energy, a fourth on inflation, with none on politics or Kennedy—a remarkable difference from the frivolous questions at White House press conferences.

During the day we got reports from Florida [a straw poll]. We did well against the Kennedy and labor challenge. We should wind up with about 65 percent, Kennedy 30 percent.

OCTOBER 14   The Washington press typically distorted the Florida results, squeezing as much equivocation as possible out of a sure victory for us.

MONDAY, OCTOBER 15   Flew out to Kansas City, then to Chicago. [Mayor] Jane Byrne made a good speech of support for me. I gave a relatively poor speech in delivery but said the right things. All in all, it was a very successful day.

OCTOBER 16   I talked to Bill Miller and told him to start selling gold on a flexible schedule, instead of regularly scheduled times.

[Special Investigator] Paul Curran's report said that our warehouse operation was okay.

Joe Biden called to say he had polled fourteen senators up for reelection in 1980, and none of them wanted Kennedy to run except [John] Durkin.

OCTOBER 17   We had a big and good ceremony putting the new Department of Education bill into law. We flew to Baltimore for the seventh game of the World Series, which the Pirates won. Willie Stargell set a world record of seven extra base hits in one Series.

OCTOBER 18   A district court ruled I did not have power to terminate the Taiwan defense treaty, and we're appealing immediately.

Hedley [Donovan] brought up State versus NSC. I pointed out the lethargy and inertia of State—the almost total lack of initiative or innovation, and that I couldn't deprive myself of stimulation of Zbig and his people. He'd like to talk to both Zbig and Cy privately.

I worked on the Kennedy library speech and in the evening saw a movie about James Agee, part of which was recorded with me in 1976.

I've always said that James Agee's Let Us Now Praise Famous Men *is my favorite book, and have participated in several documentaries about Agee's life.*

OCTOBER 19   Amy's birthday, and I gave her a child's thesaurus. She was happy with it and will also get some nice leather boots, which is what she wants.

Phil [Wise, my scheduler] came to say that we carried Florida delegates in the final count by 61 percent compared to 30 percent for Kennedy. I guess two-to-one is adequate.

In the afternoon Schultze came by to tell me the prospects for inflation and unemployment were dismal for the next sixteen months, with near double-digit inflation and unemployment going up maybe 2 percent.

We [my advisors and I] met on the Caribbean and Central America, and I was disgusted with the proposals, recommending military action, gunboats, intelligence activities, how we can manipulate elections, et cetera. My judgment is all of this is counterproductive, and we ought to let the people know that we want to be their friend and their best interests are a major factor in our decisions. We need to replace the neocolonialist attitude and also reach outside of government to universities, business, labor, governors, churches, farmers, medical people—and take the onus off us as an intervening power.

I was fed up with the White House, so we [Dr. Lukash and I] went out on the towpath and ran five and a half miles.

OCTOBER 20   We flew up to Boston, met by the entire Kennedy family, who were friendly and hospitable. Had the [John Kennedy] library dedication ceremony. I made my speech, which went over very well, even getting rave reviews later on from [columnists] Mary McGrory and David Broder!

I told Brzezinski to permit the shah to go to New York for medical treatment and just inform our embassy in Tehran that this would occur. The State Department had suggested that I try to get permission from the Bazargan government to do this.

We notified Iran's prime minister and foreign minister of the shah's need for treatment. They said they would protect the embassy but worried about hostile demonstrations. This was to be one of my most significant decisions, made with great reluctance and only after the shah was diagnosed as fatally ill with cancer.

MONDAY, OCTOBER 22   We assessed the prospects for U.S. senators up for election next year, and they are dismal. Many are quite weak or very liberal. Bob Byrd and I will see what we can do to help them.

Jim McIntyre told me that the 1979 deficit would be about $26 billion—much better than we had thought—but the '80 deficit, because of high interest rates and lower receipts, would be about $8 billion more than expected.

OCTOBER 23   I met with the Women's Advisory Committee on ERA re six or seven states where it might be ratified next year. They lack basic competence in assessing a situation, deciding what to do, dividing responsibility, and checking progress. I'm eager to help, but they don't know what they want. If we don't succeed in 1980, the chances of ever getting it will be doubtful.

OCTOBER 24   We had a cabinet meeting—first time in quite a while. Energy legislation [proposals] on Energy Mobilization Board, rationing, windfall profits tax, solar bank, and Security Corporation are in good shape on the Hill. Schultze gave a reasonably sanguine report on the economy: stronger than anticipated, unemployment staying down, growth rate staying up, inflation still the biggest threat.

I told Hamilton and Jack to move on Shirley Hufstedler for Education and Luther Hodges for Commerce.

Zbig told me that Cy became almost emotional about his [Zbig's] stopping by to see King Hassan [in Morocco], and this really aggravated me. Cy's so extremely jealous, it's ridiculous—but I didn't interfere.

OCTOBER 25   Rosalynn came back in, kind of late, after I had run for a while. She looked especially beautiful and exciting, flushed with the success of her trip to New Hampshire and Boston.

OCTOBER 26   At the foreign affairs breakfast we went over the South African nuclear explosion. We still don't know who did it.

I met with Austrian chancellor Kreisky, who assessed East European politics and then said the Austrian people had little interest in the Mideast, but he did, and thought Camp David was very important. Sadat had made a mistake in thinking that other Arabs might join him. Palestinians are the most important factor in Arab countries, much more so than Sadat—and also less expensive; Syrians are blocking any relationship between the PLO and the West; and it was impossible to talk with Begin.

Got word that President Park in South Korea had been assassinated. I told Harold to alert armed forces throughout the western Pacific, and to notify the Soviets, Chinese, and North Koreans that we would not permit any disturbance in South Korea.

OCTOBER 27   Jane Byrne announced that she would support Kennedy, violating a direct unequivocal commitment to Jack Watson, to Rosalynn, and to me personally. This is a rare event in politics, when somebody deliberately lies.

Jane Byrne was mayor of Chicago, a position that under her predecessors had resulted in almost complete control over the outcome of voting, especially in Democratic primaries. Her violation of a well-known promise was very damaging to her influence, both in the contest between me and Kennedy (which I won) and also in her later reelection campaign (which she lost).

Since August, Kennedy had made it clear that he would be a candidate, and by the time he made his formal announcement on November 7 in Boston's Faneuil Hall, he was a two-to-one favorite. I understood why he chose to run. He had always felt that, somehow, he was entitled to be president because of the tragic legacy of his brothers, and to be presented with an almost certain victory in the Democratic race was a temptation too attractive to resist. Further, a number of the more liberal Democrats were increasingly disaffected with my insistence on a balanced budget and a strong defense— and they never gave me their support in the 1980 campaign.

Kennedy's understandable opposition, for political advantage, to our legislative proposals and my decisions on foreign policy and health care would add additional complexity to my efforts to deal with these issues. Despite his popularity, I remained confident that we could beat him, and although we knew it would be a tough political fight, we took pains to treat him with personal respect.

OCTOBER 28 We're going to go all out to win in Iowa and New Hampshire, and convince the American public that a vote for Kennedy in the primaries is equivalent to a vote for him for president. According to polling, Kennedy has the qualifications of an exciting candidate but very negative image as an actual president. The more we change toward a general election attitude, the better off we'll be.

MONDAY, OCTOBER 29 I met with Judge Shirley Hufstedler and asked her to serve as secretary of education.

OCTOBER 30 I discussed the possibility of Strauss leaving the Mideast and going to the campaign, and that Sol Linowitz would take Strauss's place as the negotiator.

We got the report from the Kemeny commission on Three Mile Island. It will take several days for me to assess the forty-four recommendations and report to the public and Congress on what needs to be done.

Tom Eagleton complained because we [my campaign staff and I] had gone to a black-owned restaurant in Kansas City, bypassing a friend of his who owned a string of restaurants. I suggested that he and his family meet us at the White House with the restaurant owner and his sons and let them bring a barbeque meal and we'd all eat together. This partially assuaged his displeasure.

OCTOBER 31 Sol Linowitz agreed to take the Mideast negotiation post. We decided to move on the Chrysler proposal, with half the financing required as a government guaranteed loan, our part not to exceed $1.5 billion.

I had a budget review of 1981 that was very discouraging, with the prospect for everything getting worse: economic growth, inflation, balance of trade, budget deficit, employment, and no viable proposals that might give the American people some hope for the future.

NOVEMBER 1   Billy Graham and his wife, Ruth, had supper with us, and we liked them very much. Billy doesn't believe any evangelistic group could possibly support Kennedy because of the moral issue.

NOVEMBER 2   [California congressman Henry] Waxman, who's supporting Kennedy, seems to be trying to obstruct a vote on hospital cost containment, but we are pushing it to a vote as well.

I warned my staff not to be too liberal with Chrysler but to hold the line. Frank says we'll have to push hard to get anything for Chrysler through Congress.

On drugs, we've done fairly well stopping brown heroin from the South, but white heroin flooding Europe from Pakistan, Iran, and Afghanistan is likely to come here later on. The attorney general is getting prepared.

NOVEMBER 4   I spent hours on the phone talking to political leaders around the nation, but early in the morning was quite disturbed to learn that [Iranian] students with the [subsequent] encouragement of Khomeini had taken over our embassy and captured fifty or sixty of our people. Without the protection provided by the host government, it's almost impossible to do anything if one's people are taken.

It was an unprecedented act for a host government to support invasion of the sovereign diplomatic territory of another nation and hold diplomatic staff members hostage. Initially, I expected the Iranian students to release the hostages quickly; it was inconceivable to us that the militants would hold our embassy personnel for any length of time. We had no way of knowing, of course, that this disturbing incident would evolve into the most important event of my last year as president.

We had received assurances from Prime Minister Bazargan and Foreign Minister Ebrahim Yazdi of Iran that our embassy would be protected. Their only condition was that the shah refrain from making any political statements while in our country, and the shah accepted this restriction.

We watched a CBS special Sunday night about Kennedy, which I thought was devastating to him. It showed him not able to answer a simple question about what he would do if elected or why he should be president.

During the day we discussed the possibility of Rosalynn's going to

Thailand to learn at first hand what might be done for the starving people there [in the enormous refugee camps].

MONDAY, NOVEMBER 5 The students are still holding our people with the public approval of the idiot Khomeini.

I signed the Gas Rationing Act, which sets up authority for states to develop emergency procedures in case of fuel shortages, and the Senate will vote on the Security Corporation and synthetic fuels program this week.

I directed Civiletti to investigate increasing Ku Klux Klan activity.

NOVEMBER 6 This was Election Day. Democrats did very well all over the country, electing governors in Kentucky, Mississippi. The press interpreted the southeastern state votes as a victory for me against some strong Republican challenges.

Although we had assurances from Prime Minister Bazargan and Foreign Minister Yazdi that our hostages would be taken care of and released, they resigned because Khomeini would not permit the action and continued to encourage the students to keep the hostages. I spent most of the day, every spare moment, trying to decide what to do about Iran. I decided to send William Miller and [former U.S. attorney general] Ramsey Clark over to some staging point [eventually Ankara, Turkey] to try to get permission from the Revolutionary Council to come and negotiate with Khomeini. We began to assess punitive action against Iran. We still have 570 Americans there, and I directed the companies who employ these people to get them out.

We also asked the Algerians, Syrians, Turks, Paks, Libyans, PLO, and others to intercede on behalf of the release of our hostages. It's almost impossible to deal with a crazy man, except that he does have religious beliefs and the world of Islam will be damaged if a fanatic like him should commit murder in the name of religion against sixty innocent people. I believe that's our ultimate hope for a successful resolution of this problem. We will not release the shah, of course, as they demand.

NOVEMBER 7 We got word that Khomeini would refuse to see Clark and Miller, but the PLO announced from the UN that they would send a delegation to Iran to get our hostages released. The pope agreed to help us with Khomeini but didn't want publicity.

I made calls and developed support for the Energy Security Corporation over opposition from oil and coal companies, the NAM, Chamber of Commerce, and others seeking a future monopoly in energy production.

NOVEMBER 9   Rosalynn called [from Thailand], having been to one camp with about 28,000 refugees, many of them dying. They were expecting between 100,000 and 200,000 more in the same camp over the next few weeks. Ambassador [Morton] Abramowitz had given her a list of twenty-two things that needed to be done. I told her to be very aggressive with the UN officials responsible for services to Cambodia.

SALT was voted out of the Foreign Affairs Committee, 9–6.

I met with family members of the American hostages in Iran, who issued a beautiful statement supporting what I'm doing and calling for the American people to be calm.

NOVEMBER 10   Rosalynn returned from Thailand, tired but pleased with her trip. She was given top treatment by General Prem [Tinsulanonda], Prime Minister Kriangsak [Chomanon], the king, queen, and others. She'll make three basic reports: to me about what can be done through the U.S. government; to the American people, primarily seeking assistance for starving people; and privately through the UN, and I'll help her get this done. Her number one recommendation is a single coordinator responsible for all the relief activities in Thailand and Kampuchea [Cambodia], now fragmented among many groups.

Khomeini will see the pope's representative, and the Syrians, Swiss, and others were permitted to see the hostages, who seemed to be in good condition.

MONDAY, NOVEMBER 12   Rosalynn and I discussed the Kampuchean question with [UN secretary general] Kurt Waldheim, and he promised to do what Rosalynn recommended.

We also agreed that our government would provide a large contribution, and that [Notre Dame University president] Father Theodore Hesburgh and Rosalynn would mount a public drive for donations.

Rosalynn and I decided that if we don't have the hostages back, our vacation to Sapelo would be canceled and I would not make public appearances for political purposes even during the announcement week.

At this point I was working almost full-time on the Iranian hostage crisis, exploring every possible way to establish communications with Khomeini and secure the hostages' release.

I worked on hospital cost containment [bill] in the afternoon, calling the members of Congress, many of whom have been bribed by the hospital industry. This is the worst example of a powerful special interest that I've seen since I've been in office.

"Legally bribed" might have been more technically accurate. But a major reason why reforming health care in our country has always been so difficult is that collectively, the health industry—pharmaceutical and insurance companies, hospitals, nursing homes, doctors—has almost unlimited funds to give to members of Congress, ostensibly in the form of campaign contributions.

NOVEMBER 14   At 5:45 a.m. Bill Miller called to say that Iran had ordered withdrawal of their funds. I told him to impound all Iranian assets until we could ascertain what Iran owes us in every possible form. I told Cy to assess the status of the shah but not encourage him to leave the U.S.

I enjoyed the meeting with Republican congressional leaders as we discussed Iran, health care, energy, Kampuchea, and Panama. There will be opposition re the Chrysler loan. I met with NASA re the space shuttle, an extremely complicated project. The first orbital mission may slip till next December. From Chicago, Senator Richard Newhouse and state comptroller Roland Burris are committed to support me. The vice president and I had a discussion about Iran and politics—his substituting for political speeches and trips I had planned.

NOVEMBER 15   I, Fritz, the cabinet, and everyone worked on hospital cost containment [bill] during the day. In the afternoon the House voted it down. This was a blow against the American people and a victory for special interests of the most selfish possible kind. I'm going to do everything I can administratively to put controls on hospital costs.

This single health bill, directed at hospital charges, would have saved the American people more than $50 billion in the first five years, while leaving

hospitals free to raise prices 50 percent above the prevailing inflation rate.
The American Medical Association alone paid an average of more than
$8,000 to each of the 202 members who voted against the bill, and 48 of them
accepted over $16,000. Since then, the cost per vote has gone up considerably.
Several key Senate leaders considering President Obama's health reform pro-
posals have received more than $2 million from the health industry.

NOVEMBER 16   I told Zbig to look at Esfahan, the oil refinery that's being
built in Iran, and discussed with Harold the mining options, and how we
might handle the Iranian students who are still in Texas training as aviators.

NOVEMBER 17   The Iranians announced that sixteen of our people [then
thirteen females and blacks] would be released, hopefully by Thanksgiving.

NOVEMBER 18   Khomeini made a confusing statement that the others
would (or might) be put on trial. Castro agreed to help in Iran through the
nonaligned movement — in a clandestine way.

NOVEMBER 20   I decided that another carrier be brought to the Arabian
Gulf, a replacement moved to the Philippines, refueling capability be
increased on Diego Garcia, and large helicopters be transferred to the
carriers. The mosque at Mecca was attacked, and the imam killed. Saudi
Arabia is isolated and keeping the attack as secret as possible. Sadat said
any attack on Iran should be two-pronged, one to come from Egypt.

NOVEMBER 21   Our embassy in Islamabad, Pakistan, was invaded, with a
mob in the compound. Their shouts indicated a false report that we were
involved in the Mecca mosque situation. The mob was eventually under
control, but the embassy burned — after our cryptographic machinery was
destroyed. Zia extended his apologies to me and the American people, and
offered to pay for the damage. Khomeini had apparently caused the problem by saying, "It is not inconceivable that the United States and Zionists
are to blame for the occupation of the mosque in Mecca." [Saudi crown
prince] Fahd ordered that maybe 1,500 people occupying the mosque be
shot and killed, and has privately told our people that this is a good way to
get rid of these militants.

NOVEMBER 22   [At Camp David] This was the quietest day I've had in a long time, and did some reading, swimming, jogging, and fishing. Then spent a while with Jody and Ham going over the Iranian situation in all its complexity—the first time they had been briefed on all aspects because we had compartmentalized the discussions severely.

NOVEMBER 23   Up early to work out my own thoughts on Iran before the advisors—Fritz, Cy, Harold, David Jones, Stan Turner, Jody, Zbig, and Ham—arrived. We discussed mining of the ports and restricting shipments to Iran of goods by our allies if the hostages are put on trial. There was some opposition from Cy. I finally told him to notify Khomeini through sure channels that any trials of our hostages would result in severe restrictions on Iranian commerce, that no negotiations through the UN would be conducted, and that any harm to our hostages would result in direct retaliatory action. So far our allies have not done anything that might endanger their relationships with Iran. Perhaps the threat of interrupting their commerce will get them to give us specific and real help. I directed Cy to notify the four leaders in Japan, France, Germany, and Great Britain that this message was delivered to Khomeini.

I made sure that Khomeini got word from me that the trial of any hostage would result in a blocking of Iranian commerce with the outside world, and the death or injury of a hostage would mean direct retaliation against Iran. He never again threatened such action.

Kissinger, who has made a personal crusade of getting the shah to the U.S., is trying to force us to ask the shah to leave. We all agreed that Kissinger is irresponsible and must be dealt with in some way.

NOVEMBER 24   Cy expressed his displeasure with Henry Kissinger's lies and other activities, and I told Cy to call him in and let him know about our feelings concerning his role. I told Cy not to trust him or say anything that Kissinger could twist around, and to have a witness present.

Despite our transient ill feelings toward Henry Kissinger when he made disparaging remarks about our policies or actions, all of us respected his knowledge of international affairs, his experience, and his sound judgment. As is apparent from other entries—both before and after this one—Henry gave me very helpful support during some of the most crucial times, and I continue to value his wisdom and advice.

The Joint Chiefs came, and in general all were pleased with what I had done since I've been in office. They thought the '81 budget now being discussed was adequate, and that there had been fifteen years of neglect prior to my administration.

NOVEMBER 25   I worked all Sunday on paperwork and telephone calls. We prepared our case for the Security Council meeting. Political phone calls were very good in Illinois, Iowa, New Hampshire, not so good in the far West [of the U.S.], okay in Maryland, New Jersey, New York. Holding our own with mayors and governors. National opinion polls showed Kennedy two-to-one ahead of me.

NOVEMBER 27   Released hostages [reported that they] had been threatened with loaded guns, kept bound, not let speak a single word, not let go outside, bathe, or change clothes. I told Jody to let the public know how the hostages are being treated.

Cy read the ticker tape, came in, and threatened to resign [once again], claiming I said we would put our nation's honor above the hostages' release. This was in effect true, but what I said was there were some things we could not do in order to get the hostages released.

The hostage crisis occurred before CNN or other cable news services provided current news, so the Associated Press and other wire services were the primary sources of such information over teletype machines. They often sent out little more than headlines or brief summaries, which sometimes caused inaccurate readings of the news. As I told Cy Vance that day, what I had actually said was that we would never apologize to Iran, never deliver the shah to them to be put on trial, and never pay reparations.

Billy had the Libyan chargé meet with Zbig, the first time the Libyans have been in the White House since I've been here. They promised to do everything possible with Khomeini.

NOVEMBER 28   The foreign minister of Iran was dismissed, and a guy named [Sadegh] Ghotbzadeh—Iran's Jody Powell—was made foreign minister. Every time one of the Iranian government officials shows any sign of rationality, he's incompatible with Khomeini and is replaced.

In the press conference my purposes were to show firmness and re-solve, encourage Americans to have patience, let the Islamic world know we have respect and reverence for their religious beliefs, and isolate Khomeini as one who believed in kidnapping, extortion, blackmail, and the abuse of innocent people.

The P.R.C. wants to have an official accord on helping with monitor-ing [military activities in the Soviet Union]. We want to keep this on a verbal but confirmed basis so we won't have to reveal details to the Con-gress and therefore to the public.

This was a highly secret electronic monitoring site in western China that gave us valuable observation of the eastern portion of the Soviet Union. I was reluctant to inform any members of the Congress because of the likelihood of revelation and a serious response from Moscow. I soon decided to inform just the chairmen of the intelligence committees in the House and Senate.

NOVEMBER 29   Civiletti reported there would be a special prosecutor in the Hamilton Jordan case. He gave a ridiculous reason: there had not been enough evidence to warrant any sort of prosecution, and the special pros-ecutor was needed to decide whether the accusers were guilty of perjury!

After a long and painful investigation that cost Hamilton more than $250,000, the special prosecutor found him completely innocent, whereas the Studio 54 officials were guilty of perjury.

I went out to run along the canal and told the Secret Service to meet us at Fletcher's boat landing about two and a half miles from town. I ran past Fletcher's in freezing cold weather one and a half more miles and came back. The cars were caught in traffic and not there. I stood there about ten minutes while I fumed, then ran back into town. I was really furious, and my hands almost froze because we were dressed lightly and didn't have gloves. Part of the problem was caused by [my orders to] the Secret Service to keep my running a secret.

NOVEMBER 30   At the foreign affairs breakfast, we discussed what to do about the six Americans who are being given asylum in the Canadian embassy in Tehran. We'll be very cautious so they don't get caught trying to leave the country.

I had a personal report from Lloyd Cutler [counsel to the president] on a visit with the shah, who was very bitter about López Portillo's reversing a decision to welcome him to Mexico. He said he would rather go to Egypt temporarily, and as a last resort to Argentina or South Africa.

We won our Taiwan treaty appellate court decision, certifying that I had the right to terminate the treaty.

DECEMBER 1–2   Zbig and Cy have not done anything to prepare an alternative place for the shah to go. Zbig has been too much a part of the David Rockefeller community and has always wanted the shah to stay in this country. Kreisky started equivocating about letting the shah come in [to Austria]. I called [Egyptian] ambassador [Ashraf] Ghorbal, and he said Sadat's advisors are very concerned about the consequences of the shah going to Egypt. The situation is that I want him to go to Egypt but don't want to hurt Sadat. Sadat wants him to stay in the United States but doesn't want to hurt me. It's a decision for me to make. I called Fritz re two basic options: Egypt or one of our military bases. Fritz preferred Egypt. Harold Brown reported either Fort Sam Houston or Lackland Air Force Base—both near San Antonio—would be best if we have to keep him here. I told Cy not to talk to me any more about it, but to move the shah to Lackland, and it was done.

MONDAY, DECEMBER 3   Kennedy made a ridiculous statement condemning the shah and our country for accepting him as a refugee.

The major [energy] legislation left is windfall profits tax. We think we'll get a compromise agreement at the level of about $185 billion. The Chrysler bailout is in trouble, but Byrd will probably bring it up after the windfall profits tax.

John Lewis came to resign from ACTION so he could run for Congress in Atlanta. He told me he would not support Kennedy under any circumstances. The evening news played up Kennedy's attack on the shah and the responses very heavily, and also the new Harris poll results with me a couple of points ahead.

DECEMBER 4   I announced as a candidate for reelection in a heartwarming small ceremony.

We had an important NSC meeting. I told them that domestically we are in good shape on Iran, but our position around the world is slipping, with our allies getting more and more timid. We need to institute stronger economic measures, let the world of Islam know we are not at odds with them, and find a good home for the shah. Cy objected strongly to AWACS going to Egypt, but I want them there before we launch any mining or other action against Iran.

These extremely valuable "airborne warning and control systems" were installed in large airplanes that could circle at a high altitude over a region and monitor weather and all air traffic throughout a very large area.

DECEMBER 5 I met with Prince Bandar, who brought a message from Crown Prince Fahd. They were eager to pursue the Mideast peace settlement by establishing a Marshall Plan–type fund of about $20 billion, recognizing and lifting the embargo against Israel, reestablishing ties with Egypt, provided Israel would carry out the spirit of the Camp David Accords and pledge to take care of the Palestinians and withdraw from occupied territories. They made it plain they were not talking about all occupied territory.

The Saudis were inclined to tell me what I wanted to hear, but this was a profoundly important offer, almost exactly the same as the one made later, in 2002, by Saudi king Abdullah and adopted by all twenty-one Arab nations and then by all fifty-six Islamic countries, including Iran. This offer is compatible with the Camp David Accords, international law, and the Road Map of the International Quartet, which spells out a step-by-step achievement of peace in the region. In 2007, President George W. Bush and his secretary of state, Condoleezza Rice, announced that it would be the basis for comprehensive peace talks. These talks still have not been held.

I met with about one hundred members of Congress, primarily about Iran. They were heavily inclined for me to do more than we had, and I explained what was going on behind the scenes.

DECEMBER 6 Dobrynin suggested that somehow we continue negotiations on nuclear arms, and my preference is on future SALT III cuts.

At the staff meeting we discussed the unexpected success of our fund-raising banquets around the country. The National Farmers Organization has been very critical but now is extremely supportive of our farm programs.

DECEMBER 7   Dayan [who had left the government in October because of disagreements over the territories issue] commented to Linowitz that the present autonomy talks were not going to be successful, and the best way to handle it was to let the Palestinians have their own elections without interference from Israel. This might evolve in the future.

The first Palestinian election finally took place in January 1996, authorized by the Oslo Accords of 1993. The Carter Center monitored this election, in which Yasir Arafat and eighty-eight legislators were elected; the center has monitored all other Palestinian elections as well.

Cy proposed that the national Christmas tree only have the star of hope on its peak and other lights out until the hostages are released.

I announced my decisions on the [Three Mile Island] Kemeny report, encouraging strong conservation, increased energy production, and pointing out that there was a real and continuing place for safe nuclear power.

I told Harold to keep our AWACS planes moving around in Europe and North Africa, ready to be sent to Egypt if we need them in a military action.

DECEMBER 8   An AP and Gallup poll are both surprisingly good for me. Gallup jumped from 30 percent approval to 61 percent in one month.

DECEMBER 9   The Iranian UN ambassador stated that the shah's return to Iran was a moot question, and that personal trials for the hostages were not a real option. I hope this is an accurate report from Khomeini.

MONDAY, DECEMBER 10   The evening news reported that the ayatollah had come out against me for president, which will give another boost to our campaign.

Congress is still dragging on [key legislation]. Our inclination is to move strongly and publicly against the Congress if they don't act. It would be unacceptable to me and the nation if they go on a thirty-day vacation with all this work undone.

DECEMBER 11   South Africa and the Bahamas said they would not take the shah, which leaves Panama.

The crazy women's organization NOW [the National Organization for Women] announced they would support anybody for president except me. Their attitude is indicative of the reason that ERA has not passed.

Ham called from Panama saying that Torrijos was firmly committed to receiving the shah, and I told Ham to wrap it up.

DECEMBER 12   The shah and shabanou are willing to go to Panama.

The new Gallup poll showed that we were ahead of Kennedy 48–40, and far ahead of Reagan and Ford. Kennedy is almost even with Reagan and behind Ford. This should remove the last remaining argument that Kennedy had when he announced as a candidate.

I talked to Clark Clifford about the advisability of Kennedy's withdrawing from the race. He said the excellent poll results were probably transient, and the best thing that had happened to us was for Kennedy to become an opponent. It would be a great achievement for me to defeat Kennedy, with momentum going into the general election. An opponent like Kennedy kept us on our toes.

He mentioned the fishermen who caught a delicious fish called turbot, but found that in the tanks in their vessels they got fat and lost their flavor. Putting one small barracuda in the tank kept the thousands of fish lean and tasty, and the barracuda only ate three or four fish.

Clifford had been a personal lawyer for the Kennedy family but decided to support me in the 1980 campaign. He had been instrumental in Truman's decision to give immediate recognition to the new nation of Israel in 1948.

Paul Volcker thinks interest rates will continue to come down. The money supply for the last two months has not increased very much, and the dollar has shown surprising strength in the adverse circumstances of Iran and OPEC oil prices.

Rosalynn's in New York speaking to the foreign affairs conference on Cambodia, going to Koch's birthday party, and appearing on the *Today* show. Amy is in trouble because she and some friends let the American flag fall on the ground, and they have to write one thousand words on how to treat it with respect.

DECEMBER 13   Kissinger and I discussed SALT and other things. He had some provisos—not difficult to fulfill. He said he wanted to see SALT passed and would help when the time came. We discussed his criticisms of our administration and vice versa. He said his [critical] interview was given before the hostages were seized. He said Schmidt was shifting toward neutralism between us and the Soviet Union.

Fritz raised hell about Zbig's comments that the Vietnam complex was over. He thought this was a psychiatric analysis of people like him who had been against the Vietnam War. Speaking of psychiatric problems, the president of NOW would be chaining herself to the fence this afternoon. However, the weather report calls for rain, so she apparently doesn't feel that strongly about the issue. I met with representatives of fifteen or twenty women's organizations (not NOW), and it was harmonious and constructive.

Had another pleasant discussion with President Ford concerning SALT. He was looking for ways to support it. He thought Bush was doing better than Baker, and was extremely anti-Reagan.

The Supreme Court ruled with me on the abrogation of the Taiwan treaty.

The National Christmas Tree Lighting was an emotional experience when Amy threw the switch and the lights did not come on the big tree, except the star of hope on the top. It was on national television, and I got more comments about this than almost anything I've ever done.

Muhammad Ali called from Las Vegas. He was with Mother and said he'd do anything we needed, including radio tapes for our campaign.

DECEMBER 14   I decided to send someone to meet with Soviet leaders, without delay. I feel that our relationship is deteriorating unnecessarily. We'll continue to publicize the fact that the Soviet Union is increasing its troop placement in Afghanistan.

I instructed that an analysis of the Saudi proposal be prepared and to work with Sol Linowitz. Sol gave me a surprisingly sanguine analysis of his Mideast meeting with Begin and Sadat. He was pleased at their attitude and had made some progress on specific items—emphasizing the things on which they agree, not on how they disagree.

Bob Byrd reported they had worked out a $178 billion compromise on windfall profits tax, which would break the filibuster and lead to rapid passage. I didn't approve, but acknowledged the information.

DECEMBER 15 I woke up early and decided to call the shah. I gave him my best wishes and told him he would like Panama. He said he was doing well, was pleased with the arrangements, and had really been ripped off in Mexico and the Bahamas.

MONDAY, DECEMBER 17 I met with the Hassidic rabbis of New York. They have about one hundred thousand voters in the city plus another one hundred thousand throughout the country. We've a good chance to get their support. In the evening I participated in a ceremony to light the menorah for Hanukkah, then had an enjoyable evening with Margaret Thatcher. We liked the giving of toasts before the banquet.

Historically, toasts at White House state banquets had been given after the meal, although heads of state, sometimes including me, were nervously anticipating their speeches during the entire ceremony. In our meetings with the Soviets there was the additional problem of excessive alcohol consumption. The solution was to make sure that all the speeches were given at the beginning of the meal. Rosalynn decided to change the format, and it has worked well ever since.

The evening news from Iran was negative, with Khomeini siding with the students and against Ghotbzadeh about the possible release of our hostages before Christmas.

DECEMBER 18 I urged Democratic congressional leaders to move on windfall profits, the mobilization board, synthetic fuels, and Chrysler. Tip said in the heart of Boston a poll showed Kennedy with 38 percent, I had 32 percent, and 30 percent [were] undecided.

DECEMBER 19 We had the vote today on the Chrysler aid bill and were successful.

DECEMBER 21 The Soviets continue their buildup in Afghanistan. I signed a finding to maintain contact with those who might want a more responsible and democratic government in Iran. I instructed Zbig to keep Congress out of the decision-making process on findings I issue for covert operations around the world. This is none of their business; they are to be informed, not consulted.

In the case of some decisions involving intelligence or military issues where public revelation would be embarrassing or damaging, it is necessary for any president to be very careful about maintaining secrecy. In a few instances, a relatively unpopular decision must be made unilaterally, without involving members of Congress or even cabinet members. The decision to maintain contact with anti-Khomeini Iranians was one such case; another involved setting up the secret post in western China that allowed us to observe events in the Soviet Union.

We discussed how to handle the twenty-six senators who are still doubtful about SALT.

Rosie Grier [former football player who had served as Robert Kennedy's bodyguard] came by to pledge his support to me. We thought he would undoubtedly go with the Kennedys. We then went to Camp David, carrying piles of paperwork and a couple of hundred telephone calls to be made, primarily about Iowa.

DECEMBER 22   I had Jim McIntyre and his staff, plus Stu Eizenstat, come to Camp David. We made final decisions about the 1981 budget—fairly restrictive, with a deficit of about $15 billion, a strong commitment to defense, an innovative program on youth employment, political balance among constituency groups, fiscally conservative, no tax cuts, and a token increase for the Mideast peace package.

Bob Hope called to tell me that he would make an attempt to go to Iran for Christmas Day entertainment of the hostages. He just wanted to let me know, not ask me to do anything to help.

MONDAY, DECEMBER 24   We're preparing our case for the UN on Iran, calling for sanctions if they don't release the hostages.

I decided, over [my staff's] opposition, not to participate in the debate against Jerry Brown and Ted Kennedy in Iowa. It's inconceivable to me that they would pursue this matter, because it's obviously counterproductive politically. When we decided to do the debate, it was just me and Kennedy, Kennedy was two-to-one ahead of me in the polls, and we didn't have the Iranian crisis on my shoulders. Now all those factors have changed. Rosalynn thinks I'm right.

By this time I had decided to minimize my public campaign activity as much as possible until the hostages were released. I asked Rosalynn, our son Chip, and Fritz Mondale to fill my obligations as a candidate.

It's relatively lonely at Camp David—just Rosalynn, Amy, and I. This is the first time in twenty-six years that we haven't been with our folks for Christmas—since the year my daddy died. I told all the senior staff at the White House and the Filipino stewards to bring their families up for Christmas Day.

DECEMBER 25 Amy wanted to get up at 5:30, which we did. We exchanged gifts, called our folks at home, and had photographs with families of the staff and stewards. We didn't make many [political] telephone calls because we've run out of calls to make.

DECEMBER 27 I decided during the evening that we would return to Washington because the Soviets have begun to move their forces in to overthrow the existing Afghan government. They have had 215 flights, moving 8,000 or 10,000 people in—an extremely serious development.

DECEMBER 28 This is a radical departure from the reticence the Soviets have shown since they overthrew the government in Czechoslovakia. We're determined to make this action as politically costly as possible. I sent messages to our allies, key nonaligned leaders, plus all the Muslim countries—urging them to speak out strongly against the Soviet action and to share their thoughts about what should be done. I also sent on the Hot Line the sharpest message I have ever sent to Brezhnev, telling him that the invasion of Afghanistan would seriously and adversely affect the relationship between our two countries. We'll continue to let the SALT treaty be considered, trying to make the point that regardless of our relationships with the Soviets, SALT is advantageous to us.

Down through history, Afghanistan has been a quagmire for foreign forces. The British invaded the country in the 1840s, the 1880s, and 1921. Their first intrusion ended in January 1842, when 16,500 British soldiers engaged in a major battle and only one survived. More recently, Russian and American forces (with UN allies) have found it relatively easy to invade Afghanistan, but it has proven difficult or impossible to prevail and then withdraw with any semblance of victory or lasting impact.

I called Jim Gannon in Des Moines—the editor of the newspapers—to tell him I would not participate in the debate. I would guess that the newspapers will condemn my action, but I have no doubt it's right.

DECEMBER 29   Bob Strauss said he had been wrong about the Iowa debates. Even the owner of the newspapers thought it would have been a serious error for me to debate at this time.

We have a problem with the Iran sanctions vote in the UN, and I agreed to call some of the countries involved [with good results in Nigeria, Zambia, and Jamaica]. The Iranians have agreed to see Waldheim.

MONDAY, DECEMBER 31   We were pleased when the UN vote was cast to get eleven affirmative, no negative, and four abstentions.

I had a one-hour interview with Frank Reynolds of ABC. He's going to chop up the interview into four or five sections and broadcast them on prime time the rest of this week. Jody thought the interview was great, and I think it was a very good one.

I gave Senator Byrd a briefing. He thought it was highly likely that we'd have to pull down the SALT treaty. No one can do it except the Senate, but I can request that the action be taken.

In the ABC interview, one answer was highly publicized. Frank Reynolds asked if I was surprised by the Soviet invasion of Afghanistan. Although we had been monitoring developments meticulously and could see preparations for the invasion evolving, I responded, "Yes," meaning it was fruitless, counterproductive, and highly damaging to the Soviets. Also, the Soviets had been working closely with us on SALT, Cuba, and other strategically important issues, and their invasion would abort all this progress.

There is little doubt that we had the votes lined up in the Senate to ratify SALT II, but the Soviet invasion sent a clear indication that they were not to be trusted.

Rosalynn and I welcomed in the New Year by ourselves, which is the best way for us to do it.

1980

JANUARY 1   A new public opinion poll showed we were leading Kennedy 58–38.

I called Begin, and he said the January 7 meeting in Aswan was very important. He thanked us for the $200 million increase in loan assistance to Israel, but said they need much more. When I called Sadat, he was prepared for Aswan and said, typically, he was absolutely committed to help on any issue, militarily or politically.

JANUARY 2   On SALT, we decided to keep it on the Senate calendar, but there's no way to vote on it now. European allies, Canada, and ourselves all agreed that the invasion [of Aghanistan] is a major new dimension in Soviet policy. [We approved a litany of more than twenty punitive steps.] The two most difficult are grain sales and participation in the Moscow Olympics. I'm inclined to restrict grain sales, but the Olympics issue would cause me most trouble and be the most severe blow to the Soviets. Only if many nations act in concert would it be a good idea.

JANUARY 3   This is the most serious international development that's occurred since I've been president, and unless the Soviets recognize it has been counterproductive for them, we will face additional invasions or subversion in the future.

The Iranian hostage issue was to cause me more personal anguish and concern, but the Soviets' occupation of Afghanistan was a threat to the security of the United States. If they consolidated their hold and moved into adjacent countries, I would have been forced into military action against them.

CBS and the *Chicago Sun-Times* reported a poll in Illinois: I was 69, Kennedy 18; in Cook County it was 73–15; in Chicago, 75–14. It's difficult for us to maintain the posture of an underdog!

After much debate, my inclination is to stop all grain sales to the Soviets above the 8 million tons guaranteed by an international agreement—all for animal feed. Fritz very strongly opposed.

I went to a reception for American poets in the White House, quite an elaborate affair; about twenty poets read their own works to a large group. The first time this has been done.

JANUARY 4 We discussed aid that might go to Pakistan and therefore to the Afghan rebels. My preference is to send them weapons they could use in the mountains, primarily against tanks and armored personnel carriers. We need to get as many other nations as possible to join us so the Paks won't be seen as dependent on or subservient to us.

I addressed the nation on January 4 to describe what the Soviets had done in Afghanistan and the retaliatory action I would be taking. Obviously, I did not mention these secret weapon sales.

This military assistance was steadily increased during my term in office. For many reasons, it was a highly secret operation, and I decided to furnish the Afghan rebels with weapons manufactured in the Soviet Union so it wouldn't be apparent that they were coming from us. Soviet weapons were available in many nations, but we procured them primarily in Pakistan, Egypt, and Saudi Arabia. This contribution to ejecting Soviet troops was continued and expanded under Ronald Reagan, and ultimately became known to the public.

After Gorbachev withdrew troops from Afghanistan in 1989, the United States and other Western nations almost totally abandoned the Afghan peo-

ple and failed to assist in the rebuilding of the ravaged country. To fill the resulting political and economic vacuum, some of the militant elements who had resisted the Soviets evolved into the Taliban, welcomed financial aid from other sources (including Osama bin Laden and Al Qaeda), and precipitated the subsequent international crisis.

The Waldheim mission to Iran was a complete failure. He didn't make any progress and was treated rudely, even put in danger of his life.

On Afghanistan, State has been stronger than NSC. Brzezinski was remarkably sober about our future relationships with the Soviets. Chuck Percy reported that in a TV response system in Seattle, [the Afghanistan address] was the highest-watched presentation I'd ever made, with almost 100 percent approval. However, we expect serious adverse reaction from Midwest farmers, particularly in Iowa.

JANUARY 5 We watched the Iowa Republican debate. [Howard] Baker came out worst, [Philip] Crane and [John] Anderson best, [John] Connally bombed out, [Bob] Dole looked and acted like a hatchet man, and [George H. W.] Bush looked [weak]. The winner was Ronald Reagan, who didn't show up.

JANUARY 6 Kurt Waldheim spent the first hour [of a meeting with me] in a very emotional and excited recitation of his horrible experiences in Iran. Kurt felt that his life was in danger on three different occasions while he was in Tehran. He's convinced there is no government there, the terrorists are making the decisions, Khomeini is unapproachable, the Revolutionary Council is ineffective and timid, and Ayatollah Beheshti [supreme court chief justice] is the strongest man on the council.

MONDAY, JANUARY 7 We discussed the advisability of moving the Olympics to Montreal, Munich, or perhaps permanently to Greece, but this could only be done in the future.

An economic analysis showed housing and auto sales down, consumer spending and business investment steady. OPEC price increases have cut our GNP growth by 3 percent and added 5.5 percent to the inflation rate.

I had lunch with Fritz and tried to assuage his concern about the action we took against the Soviets. Met with Muhammad Ali and his father,

Cassius Clay, Sr. He told the press he was instructing his 75 million followers in the U.S. to pull the lever for me and Fritz.

I signed the Chrysler loan guarantee legislation!

Mrs. Gandhi is winning in India. I'll try to be friends with her, but I think she's inclined toward the Soviets.

JANUARY 8   Billy is really helping with country-and-western stars. Tom T. Hall and about seventy-five others had a fund-raiser in Nashville and will support me.

A few members of Congress tried to use the grain embargo to get special privileges for farmers—100 percent parity, et cetera. I told them if I didn't get any farm votes and no allies supported me, my action was proper and necessary and I would carry it through.

Obviously, there were many times when it was necessary and desirable to compromise. For instance, almost all our major legislation was drafted in the White House or by cabinet officers and then submitted to the Congress for assessment, debate, amendment, and final passage. Our constant duty throughout this process was to decide when changes to our proposal were acceptable, when we should intercede to modify them, and whether I should sign or veto final legislation. In my decisions involving foreign policy, the requirement for consultation with Congress was much less of a factor—a blessing for me and other presidents.

Brezhnev has told me that the troops are there [in Afghanistan] temporarily, but our presumption is that even our economic and political steps will not force them to withdraw.

JANUARY 9   I met with about forty-five of the top-ranked political advisors in our country: [Averell] Harriman, [George] Ball, [James] Schlesinger, [John] McCloy, [Arthur] Goldberg, [Bill] Scranton, and so forth. They were highly supportive of our action in Iran and Afghanistan and thought we should, if anything, be even more forceful.

Ham reported a good situation in Iowa, although Kennedy's focusing his nationwide effort there, whereas we have strong programs going in Maine, New Hampshire, Florida, Alabama, Illinois, et cetera.

Cy reported that Dobrynin had asked us not to do anything else to the Soviet Union before he returns [to Washington].

JANUARY 10   Castro sent word that he would like to have a high-level discussion in Havana because of the Soviet invasion of Afghanistan. I sent Bob Pastor and [Peter] Tarnoff, and instructed them to warn Castro against subversion in Latin America; to reemphasize the requirements we would have for improved relationships with Cuba; and primarily listen to what he has to say.

Begin called to give me a report on his meeting with Sadat. They will go ahead with normalization this month, including ambassadors, air transportation, telephone and postal service, et cetera.

JANUARY 11   We decided to send Pakistan defensive weapons to repel an attack, and which might also be effective inside Afghanistan against the Soviet invaders. We will pursue the possibility of moving the Olympics and interrupt high-tech sales to the Soviet Union.

Grain markets were *very* good, which is quite a relief to me. I don't know why the news from grain markets on Wednesday was so depressing, but it was one of the low points of my administration.

Corn was up twenty-three cents, wheat thirteen cents, soybeans eight cents. Unbelievable!

This entry is somewhat surprising to me. I presume I was affected so deeply because my work before (and after) the presidency was as a farmer, and I knew from personal experience how these dramatic market variations would have a direct impact on American citizens whose livelihoods depended on agriculture.

Iran made an unacceptable UN proposal: General Assembly to meet; a delegation to go to Iran; and the UN confirm with a two-thirds vote that Iran's claims against the shah and us are justified—then the hostages will be released.

MONDAY, JANUARY 14   I decided to emphasize U.S.-Soviet relations and threats to peace in my State of the Union speech and draw a line: "This you can do peacefully; beyond that line there will not be peace. We will protect our interests."

Interesting meeting with [Prime Minister Adolfo] Suárez [González] of Spain. We have underestimated Spain's importance, both in Latin America and in the Middle East. He described some of the Islamic nations as "Allah above, oil below, nothing in between." To a remarkable degree, [the] Afghanistan, Iran, and Palestinian problems are interrelated.

JANUARY 15   Lunch with Fritz, who is more cautious and concerned about Iowa than the rest of us. He's doing an excellent job in getting labor unions, local officials, et cetera, to support us. He enjoys that kind of work, and I don't.

Iranians are expelling all American news representatives, which is a good move toward resolution of the hostage question. Zbig had a disappointing meeting with Giscard; [France's] relationship with the Soviets will continue as usual, different from what he told me last week.

Harold Brown had a successful visit to China but reported they are tough negotiators: "Our one-night stand is over; now we must explore a more permanent relationship."

[Senior hostage] Bruce Laingen reported that sanctions against Iran really hurt and are the best approach to their release.

JANUARY 16   I got a letter from one of the hostages which remarkably was mailed in Iran and not censored. After being captive for fifty-three days, he reported they were denied basic human rights; confined in a semidarkened room without sunshine or fresh air; given no news; hands tied day and night; bright lights burning all night; constant noise so they are unable to sleep properly; not permitted to speak to another American. He had slept on a hard floor for thirty-three nights, had only three brief periods of exercise outdoors, and had his personal mail withheld. He's not been visited by any representative of the U.S. government or any other country. When the clergymen came in on Christmas Eve, none of the prisoners were permitted to worship privately—obviously a propaganda charade by the Iranian kidnappers.

Bruce Laingen was held separately from the large group of hostages and had opportunities to communicate on rare occasions. Messages from the others were quite rare; presumably they were taken from the compound by some friendly cook or other servant and sent through the regular mail system.

JANUARY 17   I told our people to quit talking about the Olympics. It's beginning to be an obsessive story, and I want Lloyd [Cutler] and me to handle it in a legal and proper way.

New polls show the American people support our positions very strongly: delaying SALT, 71 percent; no technology to the Soviets, 78 percent; grain embargo, 77 percent; UN action, 86 percent; Olympics not going to Moscow, 55 percent; Iranian action, 61 percent; U.S. military bases in the region, 61 percent; sanctions against Iran, 82 percent. They don't want a U.S. blockade or an ultimatum delivered to Iran. We've had good support from Europeans, except the French, with Giscard all over the lot. Thatcher has expressed strong concern about the Olympics being held in Moscow.

I met with Ted Gleason, president of the longshoremen, who were refusing to load feed grain for the Soviets. I put maximum pressure on him, as a matter of patriotism and national security. I don't have any idea that he'll help.

JANUARY 18   I had my physical exam—all okay with pulse rate forty-two.

My decision on the Olympics: send a message to the International [Olympic] Committee and major allies that unless the Soviets withdraw their troops from Afghanistan within a month, there can be no participation in Moscow. We will seek alternative sites and support that effort financially and otherwise, and express our preference for a permanent location of the Olympics in Greece beginning in 1984. I'll reveal this position on *Meet the Press* Sunday.

Our emissaries to Cuba reported startling frankness in an eleven-hour discussion with Castro. He described his problems with the Soviet Union, his loss of leadership position in NAM [nonaligned movement] because of his subservience to the Soviets, his desire to pull out of Ethiopia now and Angola later; his involvement in the revolutionary movements in Central America but his aversion to sending weapons or military capability to the area; and so forth. He's deeply hurt by our embargo and wants better relations with us, but can't abandon the Soviets, who have supported his revolution unequivocally.

Throughout my term in office (and now), I thought it advisable to have normal diplomatic relations with Cuba, stop the embargo, and terminate all travel and trade restrictions. We made some progress with free travel, the release by Castro of hundreds of political prisoners, and the opening of "interest section" offices (not embassies) in Havana and Washington. Castro's injection of Cuban troops into African trouble spots, promotion of revolution in this hemisphere, and dumping of criminals and other undesirables into Florida made it difficult to make additional progress.

We agreed that SALT II observance [ratified or not] was in the best interest of our country, the Soviet Union, and the world, and would be the position of our government.

JANUARY 19   I decided to move on registration for the draft—registration, not draft.

MONDAY, JANUARY 21   A half hour after the caucuses commenced in Iowa, networks announced that we would win by two to one, much better than we ever anticipated, and undoubtedly a severe blow to the Kennedy campaign. We carried all ninety-nine counties except Page, and farmers three to one.

JANUARY 22   We're having practically a rebellion from Stu and Fritz against registration for the draft, same timidity as on the "malaise speech," changing of cabinet, withdrawing from the Iowa debate, the grain embargo, et cetera. This is worse.

I had a breakfast with evangelical leaders. They're really right-wing: against ERA, for requiring prayer in school, against abortion (so am I), want publicly committed evangelicals in my cabinet, against the White House Conference on Families. In spite of all these negative opinions, they are basically supportive of what I'm trying to do.

Sol Linowitz is going on a ten-day visit to the Mideast. We'll push hard to get some movement on Jerusalem and the West Bank prior to the May deadline.

JANUARY 23   I practiced the State of the Union speech. Up until the last minute I had to fight off the draft dodgers in my group who didn't want registration, but Harold, Cy, Zbig, Jody, Hamilton, Rosalynn, Lloyd, Jerry, all agree with me. The declaration that any foreign attempt to take over control of the Persian Gulf area would be a direct threat to the vital interests of the United States and would be met by armed military force was the most significant single thing in the speech. The speech was better received than any I've ever made. The biggest applause was when I repeated that we would not go to the Olympics.

We could not afford to have the Soviets move into adjacent nations and, in effect, control much of the oil supply in the Gulf region. The statement re-

garding the potential use of military force in the Persian Gulf region became known as "the Carter Doctrine" because it implied the use of all our strength.

One of my most difficult decisions was supporting the boycott of the summer Olympics. With the Soviets still occupying Afghanistan, the U.S. Congress voted almost unanimously to do so, as did sixty other nations. The U.S. Olympic Committee overwhelmingly adopted our proposal to move the Olympics away from Moscow, with an emphasis on a one-year delay or postponement. However, despite a sixty-one-nation boycott, restricted Olympic games were held.

JANUARY 24   The big media coverage was on draft registration and "the Carter Doctrine."

JANUARY 25–27   I signed a [secret presidential] finding regarding our six people and Canada. we will attempt to get Americans out of Iran who have been kept in the Canadian embassy.

Rumors are that Kennedy will get out of the campaign, having closed down offices and canceled visits to Maine and New Hampshire. He's broke. He'll make a major speech Monday. He asked for briefings on foreign affairs and intelligence, and I approved.

JANUARY 25   I told Cy and Harold that Kennedy could do anything from withdrawing to mounting a vicious attack on our foreign and defense policy, and to be cautious in their meeting.

Congress is back in session. We discussed energy, defense, intelligence, youth employment, et cetera.

I went to Camp David and to bed. Ham reported a good meeting with the Frenchmen, who reported a completely different version of Waldheim's visit to Iran than he had reported to me.

During the hostage crisis, Hamilton Jordan held a series of clandestine meetings with people inside and close to the Iranian revolution. His reports became my most accurate source of information about what was actually occurring in Iran, and he also provided my best communication with Ayatollah Khomeini and other leaders. Sometimes Ham wore a wig, mustache, and other disguises when he met with his contacts in Paris or other European cities.

MONDAY, JANUARY 28   I got a report that the six Americans were out safely from Iran.

This was a most dramatic episode. Six of our American diplomats evaded capture by militants in the compound and made their way to the Canadian embassy. Out of concern for their safety, we concealed their existence. After receiving approval from the Canadian parliament (in its first secret session since World War II), Ambassador Ken Taylor decided to smuggle the Americans out of Iran, disguised by the CIA and using Canadian passports. As meticulous plans were made, we maintained the fiction that all American diplomats were being held hostage. On January 27, after we received indications that their concealment was known, the six diplomats left the embassy, boarded a Swissair flight, and flew to safety. The Canadian embassy was then closed, with Ken Taylor and his staff returned to Canada. We did not admit any U.S. involvement in the rescue until some months later.

Ambassador Taylor was subsequently awarded the Congressional Gold Medal, and Americans responded to the liberation of these hostages with a tremendous expression of appreciation for the Canadians.

Kennedy's speech was a hodgepodge of proposals: wage and price controls, no registration for the draft, an "inflation freeze" for six months, I was too hard on the Soviets, immediate gasoline rationing, et cetera. We decided to let Bob Strauss answer, since it was nonsubstantive and obviously political.

JANUARY 29   Averell Harriman told me we should make public the consistent and repeated warnings we gave the Soviets before they went into Afghanistan and publicize that they were using chemical warfare. He's afraid they may be tempted to repeat this action unless world condemnation and adverse consequences are very clear. He said their primary motivation is that they have never let a Communist government loyal to the Soviet Union fall, and this was an important factor.

Sophia Loren came to say privately that the Europeans were looking to me for leadership and she wanted to help in every way possible with the Italian American vote for me. She was even more beautiful than I had expected.

I met with Simone Veil, president of the European parliament. She said the leadership I had shown was a strengthening factor among the entire European community. She's an impressive, quiet, strong woman.

JANUARY 30–31   LeRoy Neiman gave me a copy of an oil painting of the [Egypt-Israel] peace treaty signing. He's made three hundred copies to be sold for three thousand dollars each, with the funds going to the DNC.

I approved judges, and Mrs. Ginsburg wanted to be on the Second Circuit Court or the D.C. Court. She's been a matter of some controversy.

Ruth Joan Bader Ginsburg was chief litigator for the ACLU and considered excessively liberal. She served well and became an associate justice of the U.S. Supreme Court in 1993.

Amy had a dirty word written in her hand, and we deprived her of television entertainment and visitors for three days. She's a remarkably well-behaved child, doing really well on the violin, but doesn't like the lessons.

With Republican congressional leaders, Jake Garn said he would filibuster any attempt to register women for the draft. We argued about defense spending the last ten years, which went down all through the 1970s until 1977 [when I took office]. Since then it's been increasing in real terms and will until 1985.

FEBRUARY 1   Muhammad Ali will be visiting African nations on our behalf. We're making an all-out effort to bring Greece back into NATO. I authorized Cy to send a message to Gromyko, giving them an avenue back into international respectability if they withdraw from Afghanistan, and not humiliating them any more than necessary.

We welcomed the six people from Iran. They were overwhelmed with the love that Americans had exhibited toward them, and all of us were almost emotional in our joy that they had returned safely.

FEBRUARY 3   One [CIA] agent whom we had sent into Iran with a false German passport was questioned by customs because instead of using a full middle name, we used the initial "H." Apparently the Germans never use a middle initial. When questioned about it, the agent very quickly said, "I'm ashamed of my middle name, which is Hitler." The Iranian said, "Well, under those circumstances, I can understand why your passport is different from all the others in Germany."

MONDAY, FEBRUARY 4   We had an Iranian response. Apparently [President Abolhassan] Bani Sadr is sending word that he wants to proceed with a resolution of the hostage question, but to be known as a revolutionary, protecting the interest of Iran against both superpowers' threats.

FEBRUARY 5   Had a hard-hitting meeting with Democratic congressional leaders, who are not doing anything except dragging around and blaming one another for lack of progress. They will be vulnerable unless they act incisively and without delay. I let my views be known, and most of them agreed.

Ham got a call from his people in Iran. They've been meeting regularly with Ghotbzadeh and Bani Sadr, and say everything seems to be on track. There are some minor differences, which may become major when they are revealed to us. The Revolutionary Council announced that Bani Sadr has become its new chairman.

FEBRUARY 6   Bani Sadr is isolating the militants from the public and condemning their action as a detriment to Iran—hopefully part of preparation for releasing our hostages.

The Saudis want us to play the lead role in protection of the Persian Gulf region. They want to give us quiet backing but not be associated with us publicly—which might hurt them with their Muslim brothers. This is characteristic of weak countries—to have as many other nations love them as possible and let strong countries like us defend their interests, both privately and publicly.

FEBRUARY 7   I gave a speech to the National Prayer Breakfast, primarily about spiritual and personal growth, pointing out the need to pray for our enemies, thank God for our trials and disappointments, and have in our hearts love for others; only through prayer could we grow in God's sight.

Speaker Tom McGee of Massachusetts came by to pledge his support and offered to endorse me whenever I asked him. He said that no leadership person in the Massachusetts legislature was for Kennedy.

These last few days have been among the worst I've spent in the White House because of the multitude of responsibilities and issues and lack of time to prepare for each succeeding meeting, to keep up with paperwork, negotiations with allies, work with the Iranians, management of the campaign, and dealing with Congress, budget items, and legislation.

For some reason, I have always been able to "hunker down" under multiple challenges, to assess each problem on its own merits, and to think more clearly. Also, I resort to prayer that my judgment will be sound and conducive to peace and justice. When questioned about my presidential experiences, I've often said that I prayed much more during this final year than at any other time.

FEBRUARY 8 Sol tends to exaggerate agreements that Egypt and Israel have reached on a few relatively insignificant points on West Bank autonomy, and I think he underestimates the firm opposition of the Saudi Arabians to the negotiating trends now. The bottom line with them is East Jerusalem and the Palestinian issue, and we have not yet reached the point of resolving either of those.

Cecil Andrus reported that the Senate was postponing a vote on the Alaska lands bill until after July fourth. I instructed him to protect the remaining areas of land with executive orders to be issued Monday.

Mama called from Plains, a little nervous about going to Maine. I told her she would find a good reception and to enjoy it, not to knock Kennedy but just let people know how much we appreciated their support and how busy I was in Washington. She'll be leaving there and going to Nashville, where Tom T. Hall, Johnny Cash, and others are having a fund-raiser for us.

At Camp David I was really tired. Talked to Hamilton about his trip to Europe. He'll use the name Phillip Warren, since we do not want people to know he's in Europe.

FEBRUARY 9 I worked all day on the serious problems the French have caused with their changing policy on the Soviet invasion—at least five different public positions. I was aggravated when Giscard told [Australian prime minister] Malcolm Fraser that it would be an affront to France to meet with a country like Canada or Italy [led by a mere prime minister] on an equal basis.

Got a good report from Hamilton in Bern, Switzerland.

FEBRUARY 10 Made ski runs all the way down the hill, a couple of miles. Cy and Gay were with us.

Reports from Maine showed five or six times more voters than in 1976. The press predictably presented it as a marginal victory for me and better than Kennedy expected—although two weeks ago Kennedy said he had to win in both Maine and New Hampshire following his Iowa loss.

MONDAY, FEBRUARY 11 I met with Muhammad Ali, who had just re-turned from difficult trips to China and India. I had also asked him to go to five nations in Africa because he had decided quite early that American athletes should not go to the Soviet Union while invading troops were in the Muslim country of Afghanistan. He went to present our case, which he had done very well. Ali said it was a lot tougher to be a politician and a statesman than a boxer, but he was pleased at the outcome of his trip.

Ali had become a special friend of my mother, and she suggested that he offer his services to me. As an extremely famous black Muslim he had access to almost any world leader; he proved to be very eloquent and persuasive. His only failure as a volunteer diplomat was that he was not permitted by Ayatollah Khomeini to come to Iran to discuss the release of our hostages.

Cy, Ham, and [Assistant Secretary of State] Hal Saunders had a good meeting with Kurt Waldheim, settled on members of the Iran commission, and got positive reports from Iran. Kurt will issue his statement tonight, and the Iranians will respond that they accept the commission, which will go there within a week. There will be no interrogation of hostages. The hostages will be removed to a hospital, and a report will be made by the commission to the UN and published. Then the hostages will be released, and Bani Sadr will make statements as agreed ahead of time.

FEBRUARY 12 I met with senior advisors on the apparently new policy from Israel concerning Jews settling all over the West Bank. Again we'll rap Israel for this settlements policy, which is designed by Begin to aggravate us and to keep the Palestinians from becoming moderate and cooperative.

I announced our nuclear waste management policy, signed an execu-tive order, and appointed a coordinating committee headed by Governor Dick Riley. This is thirty years overdue.

With a naval background in this subject, I recognized the need for a na-tional policy on the disposal of spent nuclear fuel. The policy would involve providing guidelines for burial of spent fuel on individual sites and choosing a central and secure underground storage facility. Preliminary research suggested that Yucca Mountain in Nevada would be best, but not until 1987 was this choice approved by law. Because of strong political opposition, President Obama decided in 2009 not to proceed, leaving the disposal question unanswered.

Southern Baptists gave me an Outstanding Christian Service award.

While I was out running, Jody said *The Washington Post* had a story concerning our feeding military equipment to Afghan rebels through Pakistan. If this story is published, it would be very damaging to our relationship with Pakistan. We finally decided that Cy would talk to [publisher] Don Graham at the *Post* to hold off the story. They only agreed to do it for twenty-four hours.

We had a postmortem concerning Maine. The essence is that Kennedy put all his forces in Iowa and lost, all [remaining] forces in Maine and lost, and he'll have to decide how to channel his limited effort. We're keeping a full-court press in every state. Pat pointed out that many people are supporting Kennedy to keep him from dropping out, not because they want him to be president.

FEBRUARY 13   The Iranians in their proposed draft included interrogation of the hostages. Cy let Waldheim know that we could not go along with this.

I talked to Bess Truman on her ninety-fifth birthday. She's getting along all right, a little hard of hearing, and she was at the beauty parlor.

FEBRUARY 14   Ben Bradlee [editor of *The Washington Post*] came in, a little chastened. He was cooperative and promised that the story would be handled in an appropriate way.

I had an interview with the *Boston Herald*, which has at least treated us fairly in comparison with *The Boston Globe*. The *Globe* headline after Maine, for instance, was "Carter Fails to Get Majority." The *Globe*'s been wanting an exclusive interview, and Jody sent them a message: "Since you're the favorite newspaper in Boston, we had a poll on our staff. The *Globe* got 47 percent, the *Herald* got 39 percent, the *Phoenix* got 11 percent. Since you failed to get a majority, we consider that the *Herald* was the winner."

FEBRUARY 15　We decided not to initiate a rescue mission for the hostages at this sensitive time, and to terminate our Iran covert operation, since we are satisfied with Bani Sadr until now.

FEBRUARY 16　Hamilton reported he was doing very well in France with Ghotbzadeh, [Argentinian Hector] Villalon, and [French attorney Christian] Bourguet [all with access to Iranian leaders].

The Afghan army continues to deteriorate, with its members defecting to the rebels. The Soviets are fighting against their units around the major cities.

We finally got the Iran commission approved by the Iranians and by countries represented by the members. The Iranians have to accept the membership, their coming to Iran, and the commission's seeing the hostages without interrogating them or accusing them of anything.

Cy will make sure that when the commission gets to Iran, they will not leave until the hostages are removed from control of the militants and transferred to a third country or, more likely, to the Iranian government itself.

FEBRUARY 17　Ham made a written report on his visit with Ghotbzadeh in Paris. Ghotbzadeh criticized Bani Sadr severely, was equivocal about a time schedule for releasing the hostages, asked Ham if we would assassinate the shah, claims to be the preeminent confidant of Khomeini, and said he has been catching hell all over Europe because they are holding the hostages. The fanaticism of Khomeini seems to dampen any prospects of responsibility being exhibited by Bani Sadr, Ghotbzadeh, or others whenever they go to him for approval of an action or a policy.

FEBRUARY 19　Both Tito and King Khalid are on the point of death.

I spoke to the American Legion, and of eight hundred people there I doubt if two of them would vote for Kennedy or Brown.

I came back and had lunch with Rupert Murdoch, the Australian news publisher, and really liked him. He was interesting, friendly, and promised me full support of the New York Post in the primary campaign.

Chip called from New Hampshire to tell me about Jack's representing me at the National Rifle Association meeting. Jack not only told them I was a hunter all my life and a good shot, but also said in a loud voice, "My daddy will approve anything you want to do in the woods." When they later asked Chip if he agreed with Jack's statement, Chip said, "Anything but incest!"

The key words were "in the woods." The NRA, basing its argument on the Second Amendment to the U.S. Constitution regarding the right to bear arms, has acquired tremendous influence within the U.S. Congress and among state and local governments. I have publicly opposed the NRA's successful promotion of the alleged right to carry concealed weapons, to possess them in national parks and even churches, and to sell and own automatic assault rifles and armor-piercing bullets, since their only designed purpose is to kill people. Overwhelmingly, police and other law enforcement people oppose putting this firepower in the hands of criminals.

FEBRUARY 20   I was called at 3:30 a.m. and informed that the Iranians had made a crazy statement that the commission was to investigate the "crime and corruption of the shah and the United States." I told Waldheim to say the commission would proceed under the terms of the agreement, and to quote it verbatim. The Iranians later asked for a three-day delay in the commission's visit, for technical reasons.

Paul Volcker came on a routine visit. He joined me in deep concern about the increasing inflation rate.

Civiletti came to let me know that there is a suspect in NSC who is providing information. They are checking on some of the intercepts to see if this suspicion is justified.

The deadline ran out for Soviet withdrawal of troops, so we announced we would not be attending the Moscow Olympics. We still do not have U.S. Olympic Committee confirmation, but in my judgment they will do so at their meeting in April.

FEBRUARY 21   Lloyd Bentsen gave me a report on his trip to the Philippines, Taiwan, and South Korea, where the Japanese are beating us on business investment and trade. He's concerned about our antibribery actions being overly severe.

The Congress had accepted my proposal that the granting or acceptance of a bribe to conclude a commercial agreement would be a crime. This initiative was strongly opposed by many of our top business leaders, who claimed they could not compete with companies in other nations who bribed bureau-

crats or influential politicians to buy U.S. airplanes or weapons, or to sell tin, bauxite, timber, or other raw materials. For at least twenty years we were the only country that had such legislation, but the European Community and others have finally begun to impose similar restraints on these illicit business practices.

FEBRUARY 22   We've been pleased that there has not been an adverse reaction in the Senate to our observing SALT II pending ratification.

All Americans celebrated when the U.S. ice hockey team defeated the Soviet Union [at the Winter Olympics]. It was an emotional moment. I immediately called the coach, Herb Brooks, congratulated him, invited him and the team to the White House Monday. He responded that he strongly supported our not attending the Moscow Olympics in the summer.

FEBRUARY 23   Khomeini made a disturbing statement that parliament would decide on the hostages, which means a delay until April in their release.

FEBRUARY 24   We discussed lowering the oil import target, possible imposition of an oil import fee, purchase control by the government to restrain buying overseas oil, sharp cuts in the 1980 budget, restrictions on retail credit, et cetera. Volcker was supportive.

MONDAY, FEBRUARY 25   I spoke to the United Jewish Appeal and got a rousing response.

Andrés Segovia came, and invited me to come to Madrid to visit him. Then we went to his concert at the Kennedy Center.

FEBRUARY 26   I sent word to Bob Byrd about the adverse consequences of a continued Kennedy campaign; if he was out of the race, we could bring the Democratic Party together and start raising money to support senatorial candidates in the fall. So far Byrd's public statements have been critical of me and supportive of Kennedy. I don't know why.

Our son Jeff is doing well with his computer analysis company. He's going to Seoul and Manila on behalf of the World Bank to impose guidelines for major construction projects, averaging about a quarter of a billion dollars each in World Bank loans.

With a relatively rare dual major in geography and computer science, Jeff formed a partnership with one of his professors and they helped plan major expansions in these huge cities to accommodate future population growth.

New Hampshire returns were much better than we had anticipated, with 49 percent [for me], 38 percent for Kennedy, 11 percent for Brown. Reagan surprisingly whipped Bush more than two to one. In Minnesota Kennedy wound up with only 8 percent.

President Sadat called, pleased that they had exchanged ambassadors [with Israel] today with no adverse consequences, and wanted me to get involved again in the negotiating process. Eppie told me that if it became obvious in May or June that Begin did not genuinely want a peace settlement, Dayan and others would bring down the Begin cabinet, hopefully preserving the Knesset, but shifting to a more progressive effort toward autonomy for the West Bank.

FEBRUARY 27   We have a growing belief among our scientists that the Israelis did indeed conduct a nuclear test explosion in the ocean near the southern end of Africa.

FEBRUARY 28   Rosalynn's going to get some rest at Camp David, and I told the campaign staff to leave her alone, because she's really worn-out. She's been filling in for me and for other people, and making last-minute appearances, radio call-in shows, telephone calls. She's the most enthusiastic member of our campaign effort. She and Chip are extremely effective.

Chip was a natural politician and had been more effective than anyone except Rosalynn during the 1976 campaign. As president, I used him for many sensitive foreign missions.

Iraq has sent word that they'd like to improve relationships with us, but I think it would be predicated on a possible fragmentation of Iran. I'd like to go along, but not on this basis. We want Iran to be united and stable.

Ham reports there's a showdown concerning whether the UN commission can see our hostages, and the struggle is between Beheshti and Bani Sadr. We understand Khomeini has ordered the militants to let the commission visit all the hostages.

I told Fritz, Zbig, Cy, and [Soviet scholar] Marshall Shulman that I wanted to send a personal message directly to Brezhnev, not backing down on our position but letting him know that if they get out of Afghanistan, we'd go along with a one-year postponement of the Olympics. Zbig and Fritz objected to our taking this initiative, but I feel a responsibility even though we are rebuffed. We have evidence that the Politburo is split on the advisability of the Afghan invasion. This would be a secret message delivered personally by Marshall Shulman to Brezhnev, with his staying there to bring a reply back to me. If the reply is negative, we haven't lost anything; if the reply is positive, we can follow up by letting Cy meet with Gromyko.

FEBRUARY 29　I discussed with Gus Speth [chairman of my Council on Environmental Quality] some global issues on environment: loss of land to deserts and erosion; loss of rain forests and one hundred thousand species of animals and plants; a 50 percent increase in world population; acid rain threats; carbon dioxide buildup. These will take place during the rest of this century.

MARCH 1　[At Camp David] Chip and I took Chip's son James out, put him in the fiberglass sled, and gave him a little push on some thin snow, and he hit the grass, and instead of slowing down, the sled speeded up and went flying down the hill on the golf course. I ran and tried to catch it, dove at the sled to keep it from going down in the woods, and missed it. I fell down the hill on top of the sled, which was on top of James. Luckily he didn't get hurt, but he was quite frightened—not nearly as badly as Chip and I.

MONDAY, MARCH 3　[Fritz and Ham] told me that the Israelis and American Jews were extremely upset about the UN vote on the settlements in Jerusalem. I told them that the Jerusalem references had been deleted. They showed me a copy of the resolution as it was passed, with "Jerusalem" being mentioned six times. I couldn't believe it. I called Cy in Chicago. He said he thought "Jerusalem" had been deleted. We issued a statement saying the vote at the UN was cast through error.

My understanding with Begin was that we would let the issue of Jerusalem and the issue of dismantling existing settlements be resolved in the peace negotiations. That's why the error was serious, but I'm convinced that even though it's embarrassing to admit a mistake, we resolved it okay.

I met with leaders of the World Jewish Congress and explained to them my clear opposition to any settlements in the West Bank, the fact that the establishment of new settlements was an obstacle to peace and a direct violation of the law. We thought the Jerusalem issue and the dismantling of settlements in the West Bank/Gaza should be settled through negotiation, that Israel's security was paramount and her right to live in peace was a high priority of my administration.

MARCH 4   The election results from Rhodesia came in. Mugabe won a clear majority, and apparently the British and South Africans will approve of his taking over as prime minister.

Mugabe was then a hero as one of the revolutionaries who overthrew the apartheid regime of Ian Smith and triumphed over others who joined in the struggle for freedom. Subsequently, he served well for about twelve years and then became an oppressive leader of a corrupt regime. He was responsible for the effective end of democracy and the financial ruin of his country.

MARCH 5   I reassured Helmut Schmidt [on a state visit] about our firm commitment to force the Soviets out of Afghanistan. He said we need "both a carrot and a stick," and I told him it was not beneficial for the Europeans to expect us to provide the stick and for them to compete with one another about providing the biggest carrot. He disavowed my assessment, but it's fairly good and accurate.

MARCH 6   The militants announced that they would turn the hostages over to the Revolutionary Council. The prospect developed that the commission would see them this weekend, the hostages would then be examined by physicians, and perhaps moved to a hospital.

We will recognize Zimbabwe when the new government is established.

MARCH 7   We'll make a special effort to get Greece reincorporated back into NATO, but it's not going to be easy. In fact, I'm coming more and more to the realization that nothing is easy.

There is no doubt that this last year of my term was the most difficult and unpleasant. Hamilton Jordan commented that during this time there were "two White Houses"—one dealing with the Iranian hostage crisis and the other with all normal duties of the presidency.

We have [made good progress] on trucking deregulation, Energy Security Corporation, windfall profits tax, fair housing, and how to finance registration under Selective Service.

I told Schultze to brief the press on the unfortunate news about the Producer Price Index and to emphasize that other nations are in the same boat—that energy prices went up 7.5 percent in February alone.

Hamilton called to say that the hostages would be transferred to the Revolutionary Council tomorrow morning.

MARCH 8   Ham called early in the morning to say that Khomeini made a public announcement that he had not supported the transfer of hostages. The militants were now going to delay their action.

I met with Ed Koch and his budget director. One issue was the guarantee that I would stick with him on keeping the New York City budget balanced. And he talked about the distrust of American Jews toward me, the sense that [UN ambassador] Don McHenry was a Third World pro-Palestinian advocate and the State Department pro-Arabist. To carry the election, I [needed to state] that I made the policies and that we were committed to the security of Israel. He pointed out that the Jewish community would be very reluctant to see any second-term president elected because it would remove their leverage in anticipation of a reelection campaign.

Reports from Iran were that there's a struggle between the militants and the Revolutionary Council. Our increasing concern is that there's some reason Khomeini and the fanatics don't want the UN commission to see the condition of the hostages, and Khomeini will make the ultimate judgment.

MARCH 9   My guess is that during the next few weeks we'll see whether Begin wants a peace settlement or not. Politically, this is not a good time to have the issue come to a head, but I see no way to avoid it.

MONDAY, MARCH 10   Khomeini instructed the Revolutionary Council not to let the UN commission visit the American hostages unless the commission first condemned the United States and the shah for illegal acts. He will permit them to visit a few of the "American spies" ahead of time.

This is obviously unacceptable. The UN commission must return, and it shows there is no government in Iran other than the fanatics. We'll impose economic sanctions when the commission is clear of Iran, and investigate confiscating Iranian assets in addition to just impounding them.

MARCH 11   In the Illinois primary we won in every category, every geographic area, and with more than 90 percent of the delegates. It was sweet to defeat Kennedy and [Mayor Jane] Byrne simultaneously.

I briefed the New York constituency meeting, my twenty-third, about Iran, Afghanistan, energy, inflation.

During the late afternoon we discovered that Israel had confiscated eleven hundred acres of land in East Jerusalem. Even the mayor of Jerusalem condemned the Begin cabinet for taking this secret action.

Ed Koch made a disgraceful statement in New York, referring to Vance, Brzezinski, McHenry, and Saunders as a Gang of Four out to destroy Israel. Cy called him and had some heated words. Koch is almost acting like a fanatic this last couple of days.

MARCH 12   We carried Hawaii by almost four to one. Hawaii being a very liberal state, this was a pleasant surprise. We carried Washington two to one and Oklahoma three to one, but not Alaska, where people decided to go uncommitted.

MARCH 13   I think Bani Sadr is weak, and the only control is in Khomeini, who has hidden because of age and timidity and illness, hoping that the issue would not come to him. The militants forced it on him, contrary to earlier orders to let the hostages be visited. He ruled with the militants so they, Khomeini, and the Communist Party were the only ones that stood together. He brought discredit on the Islamic republic he was trying to establish by cutting the legs from under the elected president and others in the government.

The windfall profits tax passed overwhelmingly!

I met with Jerry Ford, who made a profound apology for his speech attacking me last night, saying it was not personal but partisan rhetoric. He hoped I understood. I told him accurately that it didn't bother me.

Gerald Ford and I had evolved a lifelong friendship that transcended any possible political or partisan differences. I recall that at the ceremony to cel-

ebrate the two-hundredth birthday of the White House, Ford and I spoke of our close personal relationship and challenged any historian to find a closer friendship between presidents. One of his last phone calls to me was a request that I deliver the eulogy at his funeral. Startled, I responded that I would do so if he would make me the same promise. Delivering the eulogy at Ford's state funeral in January 2007 was a sad duty but a great honor for me.

[Bavarian president] Franz Josef Strauss said that when he met with the French to talk about the Soviet invasion of Afghanistan, they told him that the Soviet invasion was an expression of weakness, not strength. Strauss's reply was, "How many expressions of weakness will be necessary before Soviet troops are in Paris?" I liked him, but I can understand why in the election campaign he prefers to let [Helmut] Kohl, the president of their party, be the public spokesman, while he takes a more moderate posture as a candidate. He could frighten people.

I met with key Senate and House Democrats re the anti-inflation package. They were so proud of themselves that it was really an emotional experience. They worked six to ten hours a day for the last week, and the outcome will be a good anti-inflation proposal.

MARCH 14 Rosalynn's hotel in Kansas had to be abandoned because of fire, and she left in her bathrobe. She was not injured, but her room filled with smoke.

MARCH 15 At Camp David, we had six to eight inches of snow, frozen real hard on top. When the sun softened up the crust we had the most enjoyable cross-country skiing of the year. The temperature was a little above freezing. We went about five hard miles up and down hills, including a complete trip outside the fence at Camp David.

MONDAY, MARCH 17 Lunch with Fritz. Neither of us could understand what Kennedy is trying to accomplish, since he is going down in all the elections throughout the country.

MARCH 18 I called Sadat early in the morning to see if he could come over here the first part of April. He responded enthusiastically. I then invited Begin, and he agreed to come. We decided to announce it tomorrow at noon.

In Illinois we beat Kennedy almost ten to one in delegates.

MARCH 20   Rosalynn is going to Connecticut today and New York tomorrow and Saturday. She stays remarkably well briefed by specialists as necessary. There's no one else in the government, with the possible exception of Jody and Fritz, who can speak with more accuracy for me.

I gave Sol Linowitz instructions before he goes to Israel and Egypt tomorrow: the same tactical approach we had at Camp David, to devise a package of proposals that would be acceptable to me, Sadat, and the Israeli people, threatening to bypass Begin—and hopefully forcing him to either join in with us reluctantly or let other leaders take over.

MARCH 21–23   I spent a lot of time worrying about the shah's spleen operation.

To Camp David, and Cy and Gay went with me. I know he's had a difficult week with the [attacks on] him.

After I talked to President Sadat, the shah flew to Egypt on Sunday, and Dr. [Michael] DeBakey will treat him there. I was extremely reluctant to let him go to Egypt, but Sadat insisted that it would be no problem, and would be pleased if he came.

On Saturday we had a five-hour NSC session and went over the rescue operation in detail. I authorized surveillance in Tehran and an airplane flight to check on details, but did not let any momentum build up for the rescue itself, because it would undoubtedly result in substantial loss of life on both sides. I authorized the expelling of Iranian diplomats, imposing sanctions, inventory of all Iranian assets in preparation for confiscation, and notification of our allies that we need them to break diplomatic relations with Iran if they don't release our hostages within two weeks after the Majlis [parliament] is formed. Otherwise, we'll reserve the right to take more drastic action, involving mining and so forth.

By this time we were seriously considering an alternative to securing the release of the hostages through diplomacy or UN intervention, and now we began making definitive plans for a rescue operation. The first step would be to locate a remote place in the Iranian desert (known as Desert One) where we could safely land C-130 transport planes and large helicopters without their being detected. Six helicopters would be required to evacuate the rescue team and fifty-two hostages; to provide a margin of safety, we decided to send eight helicopters from the carrier Nimitz, *located in the nearby Indian Ocean. The helicopters would be refueled and flown closer to Tehran, to be met there by Rangers, who would then overpower the militants, extract the hostages, and bring them to a nearby air base for evacuation.*

We had learned from a discharged Greek cook the location of every hostage and the habits of their captors, which had become somewhat lackadaisical. We were confident that our Rangers—who would be thoroughly informed and operating with night-vision equipment—could succeed with a surprising and rapid assault on the embassy compound.

MONDAY, MARCH 24   Everything we've done lately has hurt me in New York: cuts to bring about a balanced budget, the UN vote, and Cy's fumbling explanation to congressional committees. It's a unique state, with a habit of sucking at the federal budget tit more than anyone else in the country.

As expected, Kennedy won in New York by 59–41 percent and in Connecticut by 47–41. Political analysts said the enormous popularity of his brothers, my loss of Jewish support because of the UN vote, and an inclination to keep Kennedy in the race were the major factors. We gained more in Virginia than we lost in the two northeastern states, however, so by this point in the campaign Kennedy would have had to win 63 percent of the remaining delegates to secure the Democratic nomination—a practical impossibility.

MARCH 25   I was distressed to hear that Archbishop [Oscar] Romero in El Salvador had been assassinated. He's one of the finest human rights activists in the world, very effective in using his influence as a churchman to bring about reforms in his troubled country.

I met with Christian Bourguet and Hamilton for a discussion of the situation in Iran. I wrote Bani Sadr a brief memorandum that said this is what we want: release of American hostages unharmed and quickly; normal relations with Iran when the Iranian government desires this; recognizing the fact of the revolution; and an opportunity for Iran to air its grievances, either in the UN, the International Court of Justice, or through the world press.

After I sent this tough message to Bani Sadr, he and Ghotbzadeh tried to deliver on the release of the hostages. As a consequence, I held up on sanc-

tions, but when Khomeini vetoed our basic proposals, I terminated our support for the procedure on April 7.

MARCH 26   Moshe Dayan came to see me and said we will never make progress as long as Begin is heading the government. His belief is that private discussions or negotiations with the Palestinian Arabs will be successful in unpublicized withdrawal of the military government from increasing elements of Palestinian life. He also proposed some ultimate plans for Israeli settlements: if Israelis want to put in twenty or thirty settlements with a total of 4,000 or 5,000 Israelis, the Palestinians will be assured that 50,000 to 100,000 of their people could come back and settle in the West Bank. He has proposed this in the Knesset, and it has real possibilities for the future.

MARCH 27   The PLO seems to be determined to take a resolution to the UN Security Council or General Assembly concerning the establishment of a Palestinian state.

This proposal remains alive. In July 2009, European Union foreign policy chief Javier Solana proposed that the UN recognize the state of Palestine after a fixed deadline, even before any clear negotiated boundaries have been established. This would permit many nations to establish diplomatic relations with this sovereign nation and put great pressure on the United States and Israel to complete the peace agreements. As part of Solana's proposal, Arab states would recognize Israel.

Windfall profits tax passed—a major victory—and congressional leaders asked that I sign the bill as soon as possible.

MARCH 28   I authorized Commerce not to permit any shipment of goods to Moscow for the Olympics, and prohibited NBC from making further payments concerning Olympics TV coverage.

MARCH 29   The vote of Arabs who live in East Jerusalem is an important issue. Sol made the point in Israel to Begin that they have the right to vote in Jordanian elections, and it was illogical to forbid their voting in elections concerning the West Bank. At first Begin didn't believe this was a fact, but after investigation among his own advisors found it was true.

MONDAY, MARCH 31   I signed the financial reform legislation, a landmark law, which completely revises the handling of deposits, the paying of interest, and the management of commercial banks, savings and loans, credit institutions of all kinds.

This legislation was designed to increase the existing savings rate among Americans—it was just 3 percent in 1979—and to stabilize credit for housing construction, provide competition among lending agencies, and strengthen the Federal Reserve System. Unfortunately, all these cautionary measures and those remaining from the 1930s were removed in a series of bills passed during the Clinton administration. A key provision in one of these bills was to permit almost unrestricted interrelations between banks and the insurance companies that were supposed to guarantee bank loans. The economic meltdown of late 2008, caused by trillions of dollars of unsecured debt, was aggravated by a zero savings rate among Americans.

APRIL 1   Rosalynn has been through her worst week. She was really nervous and discouraged about the election, and Hamilton was predicting that we would lose in Wisconsin. Pat called to say the exit polls showed 56 percent for me, 30 percent for Kennedy, 12 percent for Brown—exactly what the final return was—and we carried Kansas by the same margin. We took every county in Wisconsin except one, and I believe we carried every county in Kansas. Jerry Brown withdrew from the campaign following his defeat.

APRIL 2   The Otter mission was successful in looking over a landing place in Iran.

The Otter was a small plane that flew into the staging area. This news meant that we had completed the first step in carrying out the hostage rescue mission: we had ensured that the ground at the remote Desert One site was firm enough to bear the weight of C-130 airplanes carrying the rescue team, fuel, and equipment.

Schultze predicted a drastic reduction in the CPI after July, so [inflation] figures before the election in November should be good. We had a signing ceremony for the windfall profits tax. Everybody was exhilarated with this victory, recognizing how much trouble we've had with it for the last twelve months.

APRIL 3   Two members of the Revolutionary Council, after meeting with the militants, announced that the hostages would be turned over to the government on Saturday. Bani Sadr said the hostages would be transferred, but that the council would take no action without Khomeini's approval. He told ABC, "Don't worry, the transfer will be carried out." There's no way for us to know what will actually happen, but experience would indicate caution and doubt.

Ronald Reagan had been wavering on the Olympics, but he issued a statement that the boycott should be upheld and we should use every persuasion short of legal action to keep the athletes from going individually. The leadership in the House and the Senate sent letters to the U.S. Olympic Committee urging them strongly not to participate.

I called Harold and told him to check on putting the decommissioned *Nautilus* [the first nuclear submarine] in Groton [Connecticut] instead of in the Washington Navy Yard. [Governor] Ella Grasso wants it. This is the kind of issue on which I spend an awful lot of time.

APRIL 5   In Louisiana we got 56 percent, to 22 percent for Kennedy.

APRIL 6   On Easter Sunday we began with a sunrise service at Camp David, the daddies [including some White House staff] hid eggs, we played tennis, and I went fishing. Caught four nice trout and kept two of them to eat.

MONDAY, APRIL 7   We came back from Camp David for the NSC meeting, and I decided to break diplomatic relations; expel all Iranian diplomats; declare an embargo against shipment of any goods to Iran except food and medicine; make a census of claims against Iranian assets which we hold; and expedite through legislation a conclusion of those claims. We then discussed various military operations among the statutory members of the NSC.

The "various military operations" meant the planned hostage rescue mission, with which I had decided to proceed. All the punitive steps were predicated on my conviction that we could no longer hope to negotiate successfully with the conflicted Iranian leaders.

We had a political meeting, and most of our people opposed any resumption of campaigning on my part—saying it would damage my credibility. Rosalynn and Fritz backed down.

APRIL 8   Yesterday, when the Iranian ambassador was meeting with [State Department director of Iranian affairs] Henry Precht, he claimed that the hostages were well taken care of and under complete control of the Iranian government. Precht responded, "Bullshit." The Iranian ambassador stalked out and complained to the American press about the abuse and the language. I wrote Henry a note, saying that one of the elements of good diplomatic language was to be concise and accurate and clear, and his reply to the Iranians proved that he was a master of this technique.

President Sadat arrived and said he was going to posture with the Israelis to encourage action, but the May 26 date [for Israeli withdrawal] had no significance to him. The only significant date this year was the November election in the U.S., and he would do everything he could to get me elected. As far as I was concerned, I had carte blanche in how to handle the negotiations. Egypt was doing well economically, thanks to the aid package and $2 billion in oil revenues they were deriving from the wells returned to them under the peace treaty. He offered again to provide water to Israel's Negev, saying that the tunnel under the Suez would be completed this week.

Iran and Iraq are squabbling along the border, with limited military action. They are waging a diplomatic propaganda effort against each other.

APRIL 9   The Israeli cabinet has ostentatiously instructed Begin not to negotiate on key issues like settlements and voting rights for people who live in East Jerusalem. All of this sounds like a broken record.

APRIL 10   The Iranian terrorists are making all kinds of crazy threats to kill the American hostages if they are invaded by Iraq—whom they identify as an American puppet government.

I never approved any diplomatic relations with Saddam Hussein—who came to power in mid-1979—and strongly condemned all Iraqi attacks against Iran. A major reason I did so was that such an attack would further complicate my efforts to secure the release of our hostages.

APRIL 11   I told Warren to notify Begin that if Israel did not withdraw from Lebanon, we would vote for the UN Security Council resolution condemning them for their invasion.

APRIL 12   In Colorado Springs, by more than a two-to-one vote, the USOC [U.S. Olympic Committee] decided not to send a team to the Olympics.

MONDAY, APRIL 14   Sergeant [Samuel] Doe in Liberia seems to be planning at least a partial bloodbath. He's parading cabinet officers down the street nude, has already beheaded Tolbert's son and killed President Tolbert. We don't want to turn Liberia toward the Soviet Union and Cuba, but we want to demand from them some kind of civilized performance in their government. I told Warren to check to see what military forces we had that we could move into the ocean off the coast of Liberia in case the five or six thousand Americans in our facilities there are endangered.

Beginning in 1990, The Carter Center played an active role in promoting peace and democracy in the war-torn nation of Liberia. In 2005, Ellen Johnson Sirleaf won the presidential election monitored by our center, and became the first woman president in Africa.

At the staff meeting we all agreed that the press was particularly savage lately in their attacks on us.

I told [DNC chairman] John White to get Tip to help us with the apparent plans of Kennedy to disrupt the convention, change the rules, and try to get himself nominated in spite of the vote in the primaries and caucus states. He wouldn't be successful but could disrupt the convention and split the party.

We were uncertain about Kennedy's ultimate goal. Was it to be elected himself, or did he just want to prevent my reelection? It had been obvious for several weeks that he could not become the Democratic nominee, and our opinion polls showed that support for him as a potential president was weak. Reagan, meanwhile, had won ten of fourteen primaries and was now the favorite, but we were not yet paying much attention to the Republican contests.

APRIL 15   We spent the morning with Begin and his group. My own prediction was that Begin had no intention of carrying out the provisions of the Camp David Accords and would do everything he could to block progress on this visit. However, I was somewhat encouraged at the progress we made. The remarkable thing is that the Camp David Accords have actually become almost a sacred document, in that the exact language, the punctuation, the nuances, are studied meticulously to see who will prevail in an argument. I've never yet seen an instance when the actual text of Camp David did not prevail.

As soon as I left office, Begin and the Israelis began to assume that the Camp David provisions concerning the Palestinians would no longer be enforced by the United States. President Reagan made little effort to achieve peace in the region, except when Israel's invasion of Lebanon forced the United States to become involved in what would prove to be a political and military debacle, resulting in the death of 241 American servicemen in 1983 when their barracks were bombed.

I was pleasantly impressed with Dr. [Josef] Burg [Israeli chair of autonomy negotiations], who seems to have a good sense of humor and I believe is sincere in trying to work out an agreement. Begin refused to move on anything that concerned Jerusalem, [not] even giving the Palestinian Arabs who live in East Jerusalem a right to an absentee ballot. He points out to me accurately that Israel is now paying Egypt $650 million for oil that they used to control themselves, Israel spends 31 percent of its GNP on defense where we only spend 5 percent, and so forth. Our inflation rate is too high, but theirs is more than 100 percent.

APRIL 16   I talked to Begin privately to let him know about my deep concern over the settlements, and asked him to declare a moratorium. He fervently asked me to withdraw my request, and I finally agreed not to specifically ask him, since he wouldn't have done it anyway, but at least he knows how disturbed we are.

We're having some trouble with Oman in getting planes to fly through on some of our missions farther east. We had a two-and-a-half-hour briefing session in the Situation Room about the Iranian problem and explored opportunities that we have to resolve the issue. I was particularly impressed with Vaught, Gast, and Beckwith, and their dedication to resolving the question. Beckwith is from Ellaville, Georgia, and used to play football at the University of Georgia.

This was a definitive briefing on details of the hostage rescue mission. General Jim Vaught was the top military commander responsible for the rescue attempt, Lieutenant General Philip Gast was the top field commander, and Colonel Charles Beckwith was the founder and commander of an elite Ranger group known as Delta Force. Secretary Vance participated in all these planning sessions. It was convenient for us to fly over Oman to reach our rendezvous point at Desert One, even without permission.

APRIL 17   Vance has been extremely despondent lately. Warren Christopher advised me to meet with him late in the afternoon to add some personal concern to his problem. I called Cy in for an extended discussion. For the third or fourth time, he indicated that he might resign. This happens every time we get into a real crunch and have to make a difficult decision, but after he goes through a phase of uncertainty and disapproval, then he joins in with adequate support for me. He said he would stay on but afterward would reserve the right to say that he disagreed with some of the policies on Iran.

Bob Byrd is concerned that we were consulting inadequately with the Congress because of the rash of newspaper stories about possible military action against Iran. He's always been an advocate of restraint and patience. Although the War Powers Act has never been accepted by any chief executive, I would consult with the Congress before imposing a blockade or a mining operation against Iran.

APRIL 18   At our foreign affairs breakfast we had quite a discussion about how to deal with the congressional leadership and the European Community on the Iran decisions. Fritz was insistent that we not make any prior revelation of a possible action to the Congress, being sure it would leak. Cy took the other position, and I basically agreed with Fritz.

APRIL 19   We got a message from Laingen [our senior hostage] advocating very strong action against the Iranians.

MONDAY, APRIL 21   Our Iranian plans are going on as scheduled. I had Cy, Zbig, Harold come by to see me, to talk about the question of consulting with Congress and how to handle the postoperative time.

The Methodists at General Conference passed an embarrassing resolution mentioning Western imperialism and so forth. Bishop [William] Cannon, D. W. Brooks, and three others want to come in and see me sometime this week, to encourage us not to take military action. I told Cy I wanted him to meet with them, and he said he could not do it. I stood up, and the three men [Cy, Zbig, and Harold] left.

I met with Cy at 6:00, and he urged me to consult with Congress, and also submitted his resignation because of his attitude concerning the Methodist bishops' meeting, since he could no longer support my policy toward Iran. I took his letter, said I would keep it, and would talk to him later about whether we should implement his decision. I would not try to talk him out of it.

APRIL 22   During the day I got reports from Pat Caddell and others who said the Pennsylvania primary was too close to call. And that's the way it turned out, with only a ten-thousand-vote difference out of a million and a half who voted. We split the delegates equally in Pennsylvania, got sixty in Missouri with ten for Kennedy, and lost by two delegates in Vermont. So overall we had a good day.

APRIL 23   I met with the delegation from the United Methodist Conference, who made a very distasteful recommendation to me, ignoring the fact that the Iranians are holding American hostages and violating the laws and norms of society. I restrained myself with difficulty, did not respond, and said we would give them our response in writing tomorrow morning.

Stan Turner opined that the hostages would not be released in the next five or six months, and he and Harold Brown reported progress being made [on the rescue] without a hitch.

APRIL 24   I met alone with Shimon Peres, chairman of the Israeli Labor Party. He said he had asked Begin for approval of a meeting with King Hussein and Begin refused. Peres had Jim Callaghan ask Hussein, "Would you be willing to negotiate with the Israelis on the basis either of a partition or shared responsibility for the West Bank for a period of time?" Hussein's response was yes. He proposed an informal meeting of the U.S. with the Saudis, Jordan, and Egypt re a resolution of the Mideast crisis, and then a report of the results to Israel. He repeated his belief that a Gaza-first arrangement would be preferable.

The following account of the rescue attempt is drawn from a number of entries in my diary.

The sole objective of the operation was to position the rescue team for the subsequent effort to withdraw the American hostages, which required my approval before [the team] executed the rescue itself. No such approval was requested or given because, as described below, the mission was aborted.

Beginning approximately 10:30 a.m. EST on April 24, six U.S. C-130 transport aircraft and eight RH-53 helicopters entered Iran airspace. The C-130 aircraft carried a force of approximately ninety members of the rescue team equipped for combat, plus various support personnel. There was room for all the hostages.

From approximately 2:00 to 4:00 p.m. EST the transports and six of the eight helicopters landed at a remote desert site in Iran approximately two hundred miles from Tehran, where they disembarked the rescue team, commenced refueling, and began to prepare for the subsequent phases.

During the flight to the remote desert site, two of the eight helicopters developed operating difficulties. Of the six helicopters that landed, one developed a serious hydraulic problem and was unable to continue with the mission. The operational plans called for a minimum of six helicopters in operational condition able to proceed from the desert site. When the number of helicopters available to continue dropped to five, it was determined that all our people could not be extracted from Tehran and the operation could not proceed as planned. Therefore, on the recommendation of Delta Force commander Beckwith and my military advisors, I canceled the mission.

During the process of withdrawal, one of the helicopters accidentally collided with a C-130 aircraft, which was preparing to take off, resulting in the death of eight personnel and the injury of several others. Altogether, U.S. forces remained on the ground approximately three hours. The five remaining C-130s took off about 5:45 p.m. EST and departed from Iran airspace without further incident.

At no time during the presence of U.S. forces in Iran did they encounter Iranian military forces of any type, and Iranian leaders were unaware of the presence of U.S. armed forces until after their departure from Iran. In carrying out this operation, the United States was acting wholly within its right, in accordance with Article 51 of the UN Charter, to protect and rescue its citizens where the government of the territory in which they are located is unable or unwilling to protect them.

The cancellation of our mission was caused by a strange series of mishaps, almost completely unpredictable. The operation was carefully planned and the men well trained. We had every possibility of success, because no Iranian alarm was raised until two or three hours after our people had all left Iran.

I was exhausted when I finally got to bed, after calling Rosalynn in Texas to tell her to cancel her campaigning for tomorrow and come home. She was most disturbed because she had no way to know what was going on, but knew from my guarded comments on the phone that we had had serious problems. Of course she expected the worst, like a war with Saudi Arabia, or something like that.

APRIL 25 I got up early in the morning and made a TV statement at 7:00. Henry Kissinger called and made a superb statement to me of full support and admiration, and offered to help in every way possible. I told him to call the networks, which he did. Cy told Lloyd [Cutler] and Fritz about his decision to resign.

I met with the Senate and House leadership and gave them a briefing. They were quite supportive, although a couple had been acting like asses beforehand: Frank Church the worst, and Scoop Jackson second. The early morning phone calls were better than 70 percent favorable, and jumped to 80 or 85 percent after I made my TV statement. The following day [they rose] to 90 percent favorable, but I think this is temporary support that will probably fade away.

Harold and I decided not to tell anyone anything about the rescue plans that were to be carried out.

APRIL 26 I met with Stan, Harold, David, Zbig, and Jim Vaught. We made an assessment of what occurred in Iran and made plans for another rescue operation.

APRIL 27 We visited the Delta crew and some of the representative groups from the Ranger squadron, the C-130s, and the helicopters, taking off from the vice president's home and returning to Anacostia. There was no knowledge of our trip by the press or the public. Before we took off, Vance told me he wanted his resignation effective tomorrow, and I said that would be all right with me.

I had an inspirational and thrilling meeting with the rescue team, who were dedicated and eager to plan for another rescue mission. Beckwith said that after they lost the third helicopter he was absolutely committed to the termination of the mission.

On the trip, I told Harold and Zbig about Cy's resignation. They did not know about it ahead of time in any specific terms, although they both had suspected it was coming.

After we returned, I asked Harold to ride into the White House with me and discussed with him possible replacements for Cy. His first choice was Ed Muskie—the same as mine. His second choice was Warren Christopher—the same as mine. When we returned, I met with Kirbo, Rosalynn, Jody, Hamilton, and Fritz, and all agreed.

I then called Ed Muskie to see if he would be interested in being considered as secretary of state. He said he was interested, but he would like to check with his wife and key staff members the following day without making any commitment to me.

This choice was difficult for me. Warren Christopher, my deputy secretary of state, was—as I said the following year when I gave him the Presidential Medal of Freedom—the best public servant I had ever known. At this time, however, I needed a secretary of state who had great stature in the U.S. Senate, and Muskie, as a former vice presidential and presidential candidate, was both highly regarded by his colleagues in the Senate and well-known to the public. Christopher later served well and honorably as Clinton's secretary of state.

MONDAY, APRIL 28 I met with Muskie, who seemed to be eager to have the job, and wanted to go to Maine to meet with Governor [Joseph] Brennan. Later I called Warren Christopher and told him about my choice of Ed Muskie. He was pleased at the choice and said he would cooperate fully. Cy left in good spirits but suffering from an attack of gout.

APRIL 29 An Iranian C-130 approached the *Nimitz*, and we sent up two F-14s to escort it back to its home base, where it belonged. No shots were fired, although the Iranians claimed there were.

The senators and House members whom I called on the phone about Muskie were extremely surprised—astonished—and also very pleased. The only two cool reactions that I got were from Frank Church, who ought not be in the Senate, and from Scoop Jackson.

MAY 1   We got a completely negative report from Linowitz concerning Begin. This is the most difficult he has ever been, and that's really saying something.

     I told Jack Watson to be thinking about how we might get Cuba to cooperate on the flood of refugees coming out of Mariel seaport. The Cubans are having a lot of trouble also, as would inevitably be the case when 10 percent of a nation's population wants to escape.

This proved to be a very challenging problem. We had long had a govern-ment policy of accepting any Cuban refugee who reached the Florida coast. But some of the thousands of new refugees were known criminals or other-wise troublesome, so we arrested them and held them in detention until their legal status could be determined. At the same time, I was attempting to convince Castro to stop the exodus of his citizens.

     The press have had a remarkable number of irresponsible and deliber-ately false articles concerning the Iran rescue mission—claiming that the Defense Department program was slashed back by me and therefore made inoperable, that Colonel Beckwith and his men wanted to go for-ward with the mission and I terminated it, and so forth. So Charlie Beck-with had a meeting with the press shortly after lunch. He's a good man and did well with the press. He and I have a great personal relationship. He told his men that the president wasn't about to back out on a mission— that I was "as tough as woodpecker lips."

MAY 2   I took Muskie, Christopher, and their wives to Camp David. They spent all afternoon together going over questions concerning the State Department organization—while I went fishing and caught seven trout. I'm learning how to use the fly rod, the flies, and also getting acquainted with the stream.

MAY 3   For several hours, Zbig, Harold, David Aaron, Henry Owen, Tony Lake, Peter Tarnoff, Ben Read, and David Newsom joined the three of us. We discussed the relationship between State and NSC, Defense, the White House, and Congress. I emphasized that I wanted to work with the deputy and assistant secretaries in State so I could have some benefit from their proposals, other than just to have a conglomerate watered-down, lowest-common-denominator recommendation—which has always been the case. It became more obvious as we discussed the situation that Cy had been bogged down in details and captured by the State Department bureaucracy. Everyone felt good after the meeting, and it resolved a lot of problems that could have been handled a long time ago had Cy been willing to let anyone penetrate the State Department shell.

Among all my cabinet officers, Cy Vance was philosophically closest to me, but his first loyalty was to the State Department bureaucracy. He always finessed my suggestions that I come over there and have a direct session with his subordinates, and he threatened to resign on numerous occasions when he felt that Harold Brown, Bob Strauss, Sol Linowitz, Zbig Brzezinski, Warren Christopher, or anyone else might be given too significant a part to play in foreign affairs. It was almost impossible for me to get an innovative idea from State, and its primary role seemed to be to put brakes on any proposal that originated elsewhere.

Cy and I remained good friends, and I had him join me when we welcomed our hostages back to Wiesbaden, Germany, immediately after I left office. Later, I would visit with him and his family on my trips to New York.

The Texas voting returns were very good for us. We got about 56 percent, Kennedy 22 percent, Brown 3 percent, and the rest uncommitted— better than anticipated. I thought we'd lose Colorado, but we beat Kennedy 41 percent to 26 percent.

MAY 4   Tito died, and we have already made plans to send Mother and Fritz to head the funeral delegation.

At a meeting with editors of the *Baltimore News-American* someone asked if I would step aside for Fritz. I told them I would do so if I was dead or incapacitated, and under those circumstances Fritz would obviously be my first choice.

MAY 6   I met with the Florida congressional delegation on the Cuban-Haitian refugee problem. They've been telling Cuban Americans they want everybody to come in, telling other citizens they don't want anybody to come in, and then blaming the whole problem on me.

Turner briefed us on U.S.-Soviet relative military strength. We're much better in quality of aircraft, air- and sealift, technological innovation, and so forth. They are stronger in medium-range ballistic missiles, the number of tanks, et cetera. Both sides have the capability to destroy each other after a preemptive nuclear strike is completed. The Soviets are spending much more heavily than we are.

Secretary General Joe Luns of NATO is very supportive. When the Danes complained about our mounting a rescue mission without consulting them, he asked if they wanted me to announce to the world, "After close consultation with Copenhagen we've decided to mount a rescue operation in Iran." They quickly dropped the proposal to delay economic sanctions against Iran.

Linowitz called from Israel. He's having a very difficult time with the negotiations. We'll have to start preparing for a total failure, and how to extricate ourselves from the negotiations—shifting it to the UN or some other forum if necessary.

We had excellent news from Tennessee, North Carolina, and Indiana—even D.C., and will gain about 165 delegates, which will put us over the 1,500 mark. Pat says the rescue mission seemed to have helped, rather than hurt.

MAY 7 We had a celebration marking the inauguration of the Department of Education. Shirley [Hufstedler] and I spoke briefly, and Amy unveiled the department's flag.

To see the establishment of an independent Department of Education had been a goal of mine ever since I served as chairman of our county's board of education in the 1950s. For years, the vital subject of education was overshadowed by health and welfare; when HEW did focus on education, most of its attention was dedicated to judicial contests regarding such issues as busing students, equal opportunity for female athletes, and the role of the federal government in state and local education systems. My hope and expectation were that the new department would devote almost all its resources to making an effective contribution to education and supplementing the primary roles of state and local governments.

MAY 8 We had a session in the Situation Room concerning a parapsychology project where people can envision what exists at a particular latitude and longitude, et cetera.

MAY 9   I instructed Muskie that when he meets with Gromyko to discuss the overall U.S.-Soviet relationship, Afghanistan, Iran, Cuba, TNF [theater nuclear force], MBFR [mutual and balanced force reduction], SALT, and possibly Yugoslavia. I will tell him in writing what to discuss and give him advice on how to deal with Gromyko.

I told the [NSC] group to set up a meeting on the Mideast Monday morning, and to call back our ambassadors from Israel and Egypt, with Sol, so we can decide where to go from here.

We had a moving, emotional ceremony at Arlington National Cemetery for the eight servicemen who died in the Iranian desert. The families were more solicitous about my feelings than about their own sorrow.

MAY 10   Bill Miller called to say that they were on the verge of approving the Chrysler loan that would at least keep them afloat for a while.

MAY 11   Bob Byrd makes a habit during his Saturday morning press conferences to stick a knife in my back. Every statement he makes is a pro-Kennedy statement. This weekend he said that Kennedy was helping the party by running against me, and called for me to participate in a debate with Kennedy.

Senator Byrd was remarkably effective and was, overall, a great asset to me as Democratic majority leader. As president pro tempore of the Senate and third in line for the presidency, he was very protective of his status, determined to channel as much financial assistance as possible into his home state of West Virginia, and proud of his ability as a bluegrass fiddler. In 1971, he narrowly defeated Ted Kennedy in a contest for majority whip, and he let me know that he still remembered every senator who voted for or against him.

We respected him and attempted in every way to remain in his good graces.

MONDAY, MAY 12   We are getting more problems with refugees, with about three hundred to four hundred criminals coming in and a general dissatisfaction around the country with our being too liberal in our acceptance of the Cubans.

On the ERA calls, some of the legislators are very bitter. One said he has already cast thirteen votes for it and does not intend to vote for it anymore.

I understand that the Cook County delegation might very well change toward ERA, so we have a fighting chance to get it passed in Illinois.

MAY 14   We hammered out a decision concerning how to defuse the [Cuban] refugee issue. We'll set up a registration office in Miami to let Cuban Americans list their close family relatives who may be qualified to enter, plus those who have been political prisoners and have sought refuge in our own interest section [office] there and in the Peruvian embassy. We'll work closely with the UN, OAS, and others to encourage or force Castro into cooperating on an orderly exodus of those who want to escape Cuba. We'll lease ships and aircraft to bring Cubans who have been screened to the U.S. and will order the flotilla of boats going back and forth between Key West and Cuba to cease bringing passengers in, with severe fines and seizing the boats if they do not obey this order. We'll begin expulsion of criminals and other undesirables that Castro has foisted off on us.

I spent two hours with representatives of the automobile industry—labor and management—and the key members of my own administration about high unemployment in the industry, restraint being needed on Japanese automobile imports without raising excessive protectionist barriers, how to deal with credit, government regulation, tax incentives, administration of customs, SBA [Small Business Administration] and bank loans, and so forth. The CEOs and presidents of GM, Ford, Chrysler, American Motors, and Volkswagen in the U.S. were here, along with Doug Fraser and a group of people from the UAW. It was an excellent meeting, and we'll schedule a follow-up at the end of roughly six weeks.

MAY 15   I went to the Pentagon to meet with the C-130, helicopter, communications, and planning groups in the Iran rescue operation, and also some clandestine workers who penetrated Iran to prepare for the mission. Again, it was an emotional meeting.

I then briefed the national cabinet of the United Jewish Appeal. They seem to be supportive when I'm with them, but the Jews voted four to one against me in Maryland.

MAY 18   We returned to Washington in time for Amy's violin recital. She played a solo and did very well. She's getting more interested in the lessons now and is making much more rapid progress than before.

MONDAY, MAY 19   Muskie gave me a report on his European trip. He's been received like a hero in Maine.

I discussed with Don McHenry the UN Mideast attitude and can't find any fault with it. McHenry represents what our nation ought to do, perhaps more accurately than I do. I asked him for a memorandum re the almost weekly UN Security Council resolution condemning Israel for military adventure into Lebanon or some violation of Palestinian rights.

New senator George Mitchell from Maine came by to see me with his wife and daughter.

I had earlier appointed Mitchell as U.S. attorney in Maine and then as U.S. district judge. In Ed Muskie's conversation with Maine's governor after being named secretary of state, Muskie had requested the appointment of Mitchell to replace him as senator. Because of his superb ability, Mitchell became majority leader in 1988 despite his relatively junior status.

MAY 20   At the staff meeting we discussed the oil import fee and the good progress on truck and rail deregulation.

I was appalled when I read Muskie's talk with Gromyko. He was weak and apologetic, and Gromyko ran all over him. Rosalynn couldn't believe the transcript. This sends an uncertain signal to the Soviets on our strong defense; persistent condemnation of their actions in Afghanistan; resolve to meet Soviet challenges in Europe on theater nuclear weapons; and our displeasure at their interference in the Iran hostage question. Muskie conveyed the sense that my strong positions were a reaction to public opinion during an election year.

I had known Ed Muskie since 1972, when he visited the Georgia governor's mansion to request my support as a presidential candidate. He had been Hubert Humphrey's running mate in 1968 and was an early Democratic favorite in 1972, but his campaign faded during the primary contests. I seriously considered him as my vice president before finally choosing Fritz Mondale. As a new secretary of state, Muskie was still inclined toward the equivocal debating style of the U.S. Senate and was reluctant to engage in the sharp exchanges needed to deal with a master diplomat like Foreign Minister Gromyko. He learned rapidly and earned the Presidential Medal of Freedom.

Interestingly, Ed Muskie held the highest political position of any Polish American. (His immigrant father's name was Marciszewski.) My life was also strongly affected by two other men of Polish heritage: Admiral Hyman Rickover and Zbigniew Brzezinski.

MAY 21   I decided to visit Washington and Oregon to see the damage done by the Mount Saint Helens volcanic eruption. It's much more extensive and serious than I had thought, with the Portland harbor [reportedly] filled in with silt, several inches of silt in Spokane several hundred miles away, and serious damage to timberland, crops, and possibly to the health of the people who live there. Just six hours later, we took off. I had the secretaries of interior, agriculture, the army, the director of FEMA, the National Institutes of Health, plus science advisor Frank Press to assess the problems with the explosion and eruption.

MAY 22   In the morning we took helicopters down the Columbia River to the Kelso area, where the Toutle and the Cowlitz rivers dump into the Columbia. The surge of ash carried by the rivers had clogged up the Columbia ship channel from a depth of forty feet down to only twelve feet. We are moving dredges in to open the channel because a number of ships are trapped.

We then went up Toutle Valley—first seeing large quantities of the white ash and then where the blast had directly burned the trees. Fifteen miles from the volcano the trees had been burned instantaneously with power at least equivalent to a ten-megaton nuclear explosion, leveling every tree in an area of 150 square miles. One cubic mile off the side of the mountain had been pulverized, and ash had flowed down the mountain, carrying large chunks of ice, large rocks, and molten lava. The top 1,200 feet of the mountain was missing. Spirit Lake was filled with 400 feet of this ash and lava; its level rose 150 to 200 feet.

This is like nothing I had ever seen—much worse than any photographs of the face of the moon. It looked like a boiling cauldron; icebergs the size of houses were buried underneath hot ash and lava; the icebergs were melting, the surface of the ash was caving in, and steam from the melting ice was rising. There were a few fires about, but there was nothing much left to burn. Eighty-five or ninety people were dead or missing, including, unfortunately, some geologists who were handling the seismograph stations and inclinometers to assess the mountain's volcanic activity before it erupted. We couldn't get all the way to the mountain because of heavy steam and cloud formations. When "Whitey," the helicopter pilot, decided to turn around, he didn't get any argument from me. Frank Press says this is by far the biggest natural explosion ever recorded in North America in the last four thousand years.

My inclination is not to clean up anything we don't have to that's not directly affecting human life, but to let nature take its course in the valley region and around the mountain, which now has a completely different geologic configuration.

Recovery of the region around Mount Saint Helens continues. Twenty-six years after the eruption, Rosalynn and I were building Habitat for Humanity homes in Michigan when a timber company delivered a large truckload of lumber to us from trees that had sprouted at the base of Mount Saint Helens after the eruption.

The House committee passed the trucking deregulation bill in very good form.

MAY 23   At the foreign affairs breakfast, we talked about the Mideast—the fact that we are not making any progress, that Begin is carrying out his effort to subvert the Camp David agreement by keeping the West Bank, and he's captured the Jerusalem issue and is clinging to it.

I directed an analysis of how to keep SALT II basically in place and, without necessarily ratifying it, jump over it and go into SALT III and TNF. This may be the only option to keep alive the nuclear weapons control effort.

MONDAY, MAY 26   We flew from Camp David over to Norfolk and landed on the *Nimitz*, returning from the Indian Ocean after 144 days at sea— escorted by the *Texas* and *California*. I made a speech to several thousand of the *Nimitz* crewmen and met a representative group from the other two ships. It was a gratifying and exciting way to commemorate Memorial Day.

MAY 27   Charlie Schultze reported the recession will be steeper than expected but shorter lived, with interest rates dropping, fairly good recovery later this year, embarrassing data on unemployment, and the inflation rate may go down to 6 percent or lower.

Fritz is just back from a fishing trip in northern Minnesota. He thinks that Kennedy has as a major goal the defeat of the Democratic ticket in

November, and I think he's probably right. It's hard to explain Kennedy's actions any other way.

Hedley Donovan came by. I had asked him what we should do about recruiting back the northern liberals. He said first of all their problem was they were naturally prejudiced against me because I'm a southerner, a devout Christian. The liberals are more liberal than I am—a natural difference that can't be healed. He notices that when I do something that is liberal in nature, I generally cloak it in conservative language. He says it's probably a hopeless case trying to move very many of them to me that are not already friendly.

MAY 28   We won all the elections: Kentucky, 67–23; Arkansas, 60–18; Nevada, 38–28; Idaho, 64–22; with the other votes for uncommitted or minor candidates. According to AP, we have 1,644 delegates and need 1,666 to put us over the top.

I sent some extra troops into Fort Chaffee in Arkansas to make sure we didn't have additional problems with the Cubans there. [These were illegal immigrants believed to be criminals released from prison by Castro.]

MAY 29   I had breakfast with the congressional leadership. Bob Byrd was obviously very peeved concerning my opposition to the budget resolution. Although openly polite, he was filled with venom. I don't understand him, and neither do any of my congressional relations people.

I took off for Columbus, Ohio, and had perhaps my best day of campaigning that I remember. This was the first and only time that I had campaigned as a president, and the aura of the office plus the enthusiasm of a well-organized campaign effort make a good combination. I had five events during the day, plus two extended interview sessions.

I spent a lot of time discussing what to do about visiting African American attorney Vernon Jordan, who was shot down in Fort Wayne, Indiana, by a rifleman across the road from his hotel. I talked to the doctor and to Vernon's wife, Shirley, and decided to visit him over the weekend.

MAY 30   At our foreign affairs breakfast, Muskie was trying to avoid making the Mideast peace speech, and I finally decided he would make it next week. We need to spell out the American position to encourage Begin and Sadat to get back together and hold off the European allies who are trying to modify UN Resolution 242.

Ed sent a letter to Gromyko after I approved the text spelling out our position on Afghanistan: that with the withdrawal of Soviet troops and assurance that Afghanistan would be nonaligned and could choose a government of the people's liking, we would help guarantee the neutrality of Afghanistan and encourage a peacekeeping force to be established under the aegis of the United Nations.

After another long, hot squabble between the French and Italians concerning a quadrilateral meeting in Venice, I decided not to have such a meeting but to let the seven leaders discuss matters of political and strategic importance. If the French don't want to attend, we'll let the other six have the discussions.

I met with the National Spelling Bee finalists. The staff in the briefing paper misspelled the name of the winner [Jacques Bailly] as Pailly.

The happiest thing that happened this week was that Hamilton was found to have no reason for charges to be leveled against him. I don't have any doubt that the people who accused him perjured themselves, and I hope the attorney general will prosecute them.

MAY 31   During the morning I had an interview with a new cable news network being put into operation by Ted Turner. This is for the inaugural day, Sunday night. Daniel Schorr was one of the interviewers. I spent about an hour with them.

No one at the time realized what a profound change the inauguration of CNN would bring to domestic and worldwide news coverage. Soon, whenever I visited foreign leaders, whatever the continent, they would almost inevitably be tuned to this channel—even though the telecasts were in English.

JUNE 1   Jack Watson reported more trouble at Fort Chaffee with the Cubans leaving the camp. Several people were wounded when the military had to use force to get them back in.

This incident in Arkansas would prove to be a special aggravation to Governor Bill Clinton, who would later maintain that my permitting Cubans to be incarcerated there was a major factor in his failure to be reelected in 1980. Ultimately, though, it may be that this setback and his remarkable political recovery worked out well for his career.

MONDAY, JUNE 2   I spent almost all day working on volumes of paperwork and trying to get my oil import fee veto upheld. Bob Byrd has turned against us and released all those that had pledged to support me. I don't think we can uphold the veto in the Senate and probably not in the House.

Of my thirty-one vetoes, two were overridden: this one and another in August 1980 providing salary increases of 38 percent for Veterans Administration doctors and dentists.

When Rosalynn returned from a good day in New Jersey and Rhode Island, we celebrated her last campaign trip of the primary season.

JUNE 3   Jack Watson reported to me that a Panamanian ship was coming to the United States overloaded. I told him to confiscate the ship, put the captain in jail, charge all the Cubans on board with violating immigration laws, and seek some cooperation from the Costa Ricans and others to accept any future ships coming our way and not to permit them to come into U.S. waters. Also, to give me an immediate report on what I can do to deport the Cuban criminals and other unacceptable characters who are coming into our country.

Zbig reported that a false signal into some of our computers had triggered early stages of response to a Soviet missile attack. None of our sensing devices picked up any launches so no damage was done, but we need to find out how to prevent this occurring in the future.

[Actor] Burt Reynolds came by to offer his support for me politically, and to help us with our energy conservation effort. He's quite interested in Lake Tahoe and was pleased at the steps we've taken to protect the quality of life there.

In the last eight states, we picked up enough delegates to get a seven-hundred-delegate margin over Kennedy—a tremendous achievement, compared with what we expected seven or eight months ago. I asked Fritz Mondale if he would run with me again. He responded immediately yes. I went across the street to a tavern called "The Buck Stops Here" and thanked all my supporters who have made a custom of meeting there on election nights. I told them that when I asked Fritz if he would be a candidate for vice president again, he said he would if I would debate him.

I placed a call to Senator Kennedy, just to wish him well, before the returns started coming. His staff reported that he was resting and could not be disturbed. I can imagine how he must feel after thinking he had the election won back in the fall, and then failing so miserably. We wound up winning more than two-thirds of the states and a clear majority of all the votes, compared to about 37 percent for Kennedy. It's been a long, tough, tedious, divisive primary season.

JUNE 4   We had a congressional leaders meeting, and I was very abusive toward the irresponsible and disloyal Democrats and outlined all the legislation still pending. Most of them acknowledged that we have a serious problem, and the outcome of the meeting was very good in that we all pledged ourselves to help one another.

JUNE 5   I met with Kennedy, who came in apparently completely obsessed. It took him about an hour to fumble around and say we still had issues dividing us and needed to have a personal debate in front of the TV cameras in order to resolve those differences. However, he would not agree to support me and Fritz even if we had such a debate, saying that there were still some economic matters to be worked out. It was a fairly friendly meeting. I told him we would treat his people fairly at the convention, that I intended to get a majority of the delegates, and the best way to resolve any differences between us on issues was through the platform process, including an open floor debate before the delegates vote. This is the first time the Kennedys have been rebuffed by the electorate or by anyone else.

It was obvious to me and our political team that we still faced the formidable task of holding the Democratic Party together. Despite our best efforts, this was to prove an impossible task.

JUNE 6   At the foreign affairs breakfast we discussed the Mideast peace talks. Begin is shaky and we don't want to do anything to prop him up because he's a major obstacle to success, but we've got to show our leadership, keep the Camp David process alive, and stop the abandonment of the process by Egypt.

Senator Howard Cannon came by to present a documentary film and photographic scrapbook of the 1977 inauguration. The promptness of the delivery and the quality of the product are both indicative of the character of the Congress.

All my advisors are seeking the lowest common denominators as an excuse not to do anything under the guise of protecting me from political controversy. It's increasingly difficult to get any action. Even Zbig and Ed have formed such a close friendship, exchanging mutual congratulatory letters, that the incisiveness and innovation of the NSC has been abated. This in balance is a good thing because of the harmony involved, but we are sitting in the doldrums in our entire administration.

It was impossible to separate completely the pressures of an ongoing political campaign from those of managing the domestic and international affairs of our nation. In fact, they were inextricably mixed.

JUNE 7   We went up to Spruce Creek on the farm of Wayne Harpster. I caught a couple of trout, and just as we were getting ready to see the fly hatches come off after sundown, we had storm warnings and had to get back into Camp David.

JUNE 8   I worked on Muskie's Mideast speech, talking points for his appearance on *Meet the Press*, and volumes of paperwork.

MONDAY, JUNE 9   Ed finally made his Mideast speech to the Washington Press Club after I dragged him kicking and screaming over the starting line. He thought he came out very well, and the subsequent reaction from the press and the Middle East was surprisingly good.

We flew to Seattle for the U.S. Conference of Mayors convention. At the last minute Kennedy tried to move his appearance time. [My assistant] Anne Wexler objected, and so Kennedy canceled his acceptance. Again, a news flap.

JUNE 10   I got a report on the Mount Saint Helens situation. The cleanup cost will exceed $900 million. The geologists tell me that the mountain is still swelling, and another eruption is almost inevitable. We're still trying to keep people out of the region.

After my speech to their convention the Democratic mayors passed two resolutions: one urging party unity and for Kennedy to get out of the race; and the other endorsing me.

Back in Washington, I went to a convention of the [National] Mental Health Association, where they gave Rosalynn the award as Outstanding Volunteer of the Decade. The ceremony was beautiful, and so was she.

JUNE 11   The Democratic House leaders promised that the other energy bills would be to me by the Fourth of July. I'll have to see it to believe it.

We had one of our finest parties on the South Lawn—the annual congressional picnic, with food from different regions of the country and different bands and choirs singing. It was a festive, enjoyable, relaxed occasion. The Congress was in a good mood because they had cleared up the budget resolution, supported fair housing legislation, and the Senate invoked cloture concerning registration for the draft.

JUNE 12   The press response to the move of Hamilton, Jack [Watson], and Gene Eidenberg has been almost perfect. Jack's gotten good reviews in *The New York Times* and other media.

When Hamilton moved over to run my reelection campaign, Jack Watson became chief of staff. Watson had served as secretary of the cabinet and was in charge of dealing with all matters concerning federal programs and their relationship with governors and local officials. His many successes had been widely publicized, and his new appointment was popular with the news media and public. Eidenberg became secretary of the cabinet.

JUNE 13   Begin's response to Ed's speech included the phrase that the Jerusalem issue was negotiable (although Israel's position was firm) and that ten more settlements would be the last of them. This is unacceptable to the Egyptians but better than expected from Begin.

I told the leaders at the foreign affairs breakfast to help with the Democratic platform and future plans. Ed is a tremendous improvement over Cy in dealing with this kind of question.

Chip, Jack, and I went by Camp David, picked up our fishing gear, and took off for Spruce Creek. We fished until 10:00 at night, just knocking off briefly for supper—one of the best and most enjoyable twenty-four-hour periods of my life. We put into practice all the things we've been reading about and studying in the books and magazines. This was particularly exciting after dark when the trout were feeding.

JUNE 14   We were on the creek at 5:15 in the morning and fished until about 4:00 in the afternoon. I caught twenty trout and released all but six, which Wayne insisted that we keep.

JUNE 15   I came back to the White House after lunch because I had voluminous briefing books to read for the European trip, plus seventeen speech texts to approve for the entire period.

MONDAY, JUNE 16   We prepared a veto hit list and let Congress know I'll disapprove bills that would break the budget.

JUNE 17   A good meeting with King Hussein—perhaps the most difficult critic of Camp David—surprisingly harmonious. He seemed to be eager to accommodate our views, and we met him halfway. He deplored the Iranian capture of our hostages and its contradiction of Islamic tenets of fourteen hundred years. He seemed sure the PLO would desire a confederation with Jordan and not an independent nation, and that Jerusalem [must] be undivided, under Arab sovereignty, with free access to the holy places guaranteed. He agreed with everyone else that little if any progress can be made with Begin as prime minister.

I told him that Jordan's criticism of the Camp David effort was particularly surprising and painful for us. He replied that he was particularly hurt that we included Jordan in our agreements with Egypt without consulting him.

Civiletti told me that Billy ought to acknowledge if he was an agent of Libya. There would be no punishment for him, but Billy was unwilling to do so because he claimed he was not an agent.

The United States had diplomatic and business relations with Libya, but its dictatorial ruler, Mu'ammar Gadhafi, was considered to be aligned with the Soviet Union, a strong supporter of the PLO, and a protector of airplane hijackers. Unfortunately, a Georgia state senator approached Billy and induced him to attempt to sell some of Libya's oil to the state of Georgia. They exchanged visits, and Billy's family members now state that Libya paid for some of his travel expenses but he did not receive a fee. Billy never asked for my advice or help in any of these matters, and I learned about what he was doing from the newspapers.

The Justice Department asked him to register as an agent of Libya, but his lawyers advised him that this was not necessary. In the spring of 1980, it was learned that Billy had accepted more than $200,000 from the Libyan government, which Billy claimed was a loan to be repaid from commissions on future oil deals. The Justice Department, the IRS, Congress, and the

media all descended on him, making wild accusations that he had improp-
erly used his influence with my administration. This was untrue and we had
nothing to hide, but I was inundated with questions about my knowledge of
Billy's relationship with Libya and any involvement by members of my ad-
ministration. I finally decided to devote an entire evening news conference
to this subject, just before the Democratic convention.

Ben [Civiletti] admitted that the people who accused Hamilton had committed perjury, but three of them are in jail — and the other one, named [Barry] Landau, was unworthy as a human being even to fool with.

JUNE 18   At the staff meeting we discussed the problem of generals lob-bying on the Hill, independently of either me or the Pentagon, for defense contractors. I agreed with Senator Stennis, who said, "Anyone caught do-ing that should not be promoted." All promotions have to come across my desk and through his committee.

The Kennedy group has been completely uncooperative in drafting the Democratic Party platform. They apparently are determined to have a confrontation with us. We run over them because we have the votes.

JUNE 19   On the way to Rome I made telephone calls thanking key Con-gress leaders for their progress on [energy legislation]. They assured me it would be ready for signing when I return. I had massive briefing books for bilateral meetings with nine heads of government plus the pope and heads of the European Community.

JUNE 20–21   After meeting with top Italian leaders, opposition party lead-ers, and a delightful visit to the Vatican, we left for Venice. Shortly after arriving, I had an unbelievable meeting with Helmut Schmidt, who acted like a paranoid child — ranting and raving about a letter that I had written him, which was a well-advised message. He claimed that he was insulted, that he had never reneged on any of his pledges. I told him I knew that he had not reneged, and the letter was not insulting; I had merely pointed out erroneous press reports and stated that our nation would not agree to a moratorium or freeze on deployment of theater nuclear force weapons, because the Soviets were so far ahead. We dis-cussed the protocol on SALT II. He objected to it. I described why it was necessary.

He was quite emotional. When Zbig responded in a heated fashion, I tried to cool Zbig off. Ed Muskie then joined me in explaining to Schmidt why we all needed to support the TNF and not create confusion about it. Schmidt then said he would carry an accurate, firm message to the Soviet Union leaders in Moscow, and asked me if I would make a statement to the press that I did have confidence in him, and we agreed on theater nuclear force. We then went out, and I made a statement to the press as we had agreed. He said he confirmed everything I said, and then departed.

He's a strange man and a good leader of Germany. He's constantly critical of the United States, of our resolve, our fairness, our commitment, our honesty, and so forth. He knocks me and Brzezinski and Vance and Muskie and others. Later, when I saw [German foreign minister Hans-Dietrich] Genscher, he said he was thankful that I handled the difficult situation as I did.

My relations with Schmidt were erratic, at best. Our differences of opinion regarding human rights policy, dealing with the Soviet Union, and European armaments were often apparent to other leaders and the public. Helmut was frequently critical of my policies in his speeches and in press interviews, and this habit continued even after we both left office. In 2007, despite his general compatibility with Republican leaders in the United States, he issued a statement saying that the United States was a greater threat to world peace than Russia, and condemned the invasion of Iraq as "a war of choice, not a war of necessity." Though Schmidt's criticism of our country was often unwarranted, I agreed with this latter statement.

We took an evening boat trip through the Grand Canal. Venice is an exciting and completely different city that hasn't changed much in three hundred years, but from the water it seems quite dilapidated.

JUNE 22   After [I went] running alongside the water to the old spaghetti factory and back, we went to the Cini Foundation for the [G7] summit conference. At a private breakfast with just the heads of state, we discussed the predictable subjects: Afghanistan, Iran, détente, the Middle East. Schmidt was very friendly, as though nothing had happened.

My purpose at the summit is to induce the other leaders to make strong condemnatory statements about the Soviets' presence in Afghanistan; to support us on Iran; to recognize the need for harmony. Several other leaders expressed concern that Giscard, in order to keep the political support of the Communists in France, was inclined to be very amenable to Soviet suggestions. Schmidt also has an element in his own party in Germany that is pacifist in nature and extremely committed to "Ostpolitic" [Eastern policy, especially accommodating to the Soviet Union]. The Japanese, the British, and we stand very firm. The Canadians and Italians don't speak too much on this strategic struggle with the Soviets.

It seems amazing that we always reach unanimity in our public statements, having such a wide variance in general attitude. I think the reason is that politically it's valuable to each of us in our own country to be seen as being supported by the other leaders among the seven—and, of course, our strategic interests are parallel.

I pointed out that we have to make unpopular decisions at home in order to protect money, inflation, refugees, oil exploration, food, oil prices, and increase production. I wanted a strong commitment to conservation and development of new energy sources; inflation is our first priority; and we must include the Soviets and their bloc plus the OPEC nations in helping the LDCs [less-developed countries] survive economically.

Giscard wanted to condemn OPEC. He pointed out that five out of us seven had met the Tokyo goals, but Canada and Japan had not.

Schmidt lectured on economic matters and gave a history of Germany's great sacrifice to help other nations overcome their economic problems.

[Foreign Minister Saburo] Okita said Japan had carried out their commitments on previous summits, that coal and nuclear would be the major energy sources to replace oil.

Thatcher said oil prices were not necessarily the main cause of inflation; we need to exercise fiscal prudence, make massive investments, bring about increased productivity—that there was a major shift in world power toward OPEC.

Trudeau always takes the very liberal side of the question. He said that condemning OPEC may be counterproductive.

We agreed to go to Canada in 1981, to restrict the size of entourages, stay where we could all be together, and restrict participants to heads of state or government and foreign ministers.

After the economic session, I met with Giscard d'Estaing. He and I get along very well, as he looks on me as his only equal, since we are the two heads of state [the others were prime ministers, and Okita was a foreign minister].

MONDAY, JUNE 23   I had an early breakfast with the monks at Saint Mark's Basilica, a delightful experience. They formerly had 215; now only 12. They termed my visit there the greatest event since Pius VII was elected pope 180 years ago. They go there for life and apparently are satisfied.

We finished the text and had the press conference. The basic themes I've been describing all this year were adopted by the others: the Soviets' invasion of Afghanistan is a serious strategic thrust southward that we would not accept as was done in Czechoslovakia; it's not only a local but a global threat, and we demand total withdrawal; we've agreed on a program to reduce our dependence on OPEC by the end of this decade and to break the relationship between energy used and economic growth; we'll produce and export more coal; everyone will conserve; we'll help the developing countries produce more energy and withstand the shocks of OPEC price increases.

Later we went to a private dinner at a small Venice restaurant. There was a cloudburst, and water was running all over the floor. They had awnings to keep the rain from lashing in at us, and someone said you could tell it was a Venetian restaurant because of all the blinds.

JUNE 24   We [Dr. Lukash and I] got up early to run [as every morning], [and then] went swimming. [Later we] circled over Venice several times, and flew to Belgrade. The [Yugoslav] leaders are all eager to carry on Tito's heritage. [President Cvijetin] Mijatovic referred to it as "Tito's Yugoslavia."

JUNE 25   We flew to Madrid and were met by King Juan Carlos and Queen Sofia. They are very impressive, in particular the queen. I gave my state luncheon toast in Spanish, and the reviews were fairly good. I then had a talk with the king and Prime Minister [Adolfo] Suárez, who tended to dominate the Spanish side of the discussion. They wanted my reports on the summit, Afghanistan, Iran, the Mideast.

I then met with Felipe González, head of the Socialist Party and a very impressive young man. He has been to Iran, is trying to work out release of our hostages, and thinks he'll have a majority in the parliament after this year's elections. The prime minister and king are worried about it, and Juan Carlos didn't want me to meet with González, but I've made a practice of meeting with major opposition party leaders.

We visited the Prado—too briefly. We had probably fifty security agents between me and the paintings, but I still enjoyed seeing those by El Greco,

Velásquez, and Goya. It's quite an impressive collection. We'll attempt to put together an El Greco exhibition from Madrid, Toledo, and the U.S. museums and let it tour both Spain and the United States, maybe in 1982.

JUNE 26   We flew to Lisbon, where I met with Prime Minister [Francisco] Sá Carneiro and his foreign minister. There's intense competition between Sá Carneiro and President [António Remalho] Eanes. The prime minister is very impressive. He has learned English perfectly, alone with his wife, without traveling to an English-speaking country. I then met with Mario Soares, former prime minister. He and the PM want to eliminate the "Revolutionary Council" and change Portugal to a real democracy.

Eanes talked almost exclusively about Angola. He's a strange man, very boring, a compulsive talker, somewhat unsure of himself, an introvert, intense, a good friend of our country, and a war hero who has done a good job in bringing democracy to Portugal.

While I was gone, the Congress behaved well, passing the Energy Security Corporation and trucking deregulation legislation. We arrived home without fanfare, then flew to Camp David, exhausted.

JUNE 28   I talked to Billy about his refusal to sign the foreign agents permit [regarding his relations with Libya], but he and his lawyer don't believe he needs to file. This can become an embarrassing incident later on, particularly with American Jews.

We went to Owen's Mill Creek above Thurmont to fish, although they haven't been catching any trout. We just raked them in, using an "Irresistible" trout fly and the "Honey Bug" as a wet.

JUNE 29   I talked to Ed Muskie in Anchorage. We've got a serious question coming up concerning the UN Security Council vote on Jerusalem, and also the question of who will go to the Ohira funeral ceremonies.

MONDAY, JUNE 30   We decided to return to Washington, primarily for a meeting concerning the upcoming UN vote on Jerusalem.

The key passage in this UN Security Council Resolution was "All legislative and administrative measures and actions taken by Israel, the occupying Power, which purport to alter the character and status of the Holy City of

Jerusalem have no legal validity and constitute a flagrant violation of the Fourth Geneva Convention relative to the Protection of Civilian Persons in Time of War and also constitute a serious obstruction to achieving a comprehensive, just and lasting peace in the Middle East."

It's basically compatible with our nation's policy. Linowitz, who's supposed to be the objective negotiator, advocated that we veto the resolution. Fritz said there would be a worldwide explosion among Jews if we abstain, but Begin is not doing anything to further the peace process under any circumstances. I decided to abstain.

I decided to go to the Ohira funeral. Ohira was a special friend of mine in a strange way—a Christian leader of Japan who fought for stronger ties with our country against formidable political pressure. Also, it will be a good gesture for Asia, since we've spent a lot of time recently on the Mideast and European problems. Another factor—unrelated of course—is that Ed and I can stop over in Alaska for twenty-four hours to do some trout fishing.

We had a massive signing ceremony for the synthetic fuels bill, the best we've ever had.

JULY 1   I signed the trucking deregulation bill, which is a miracle achievement, since nobody thought it would ever pass—also a bill setting up a Vietnam veterans' memorial.

JULY 2   I signed the proclamation for initiating draft registration.

JULY 3   Left early in the morning for California to combine Democratic national fund-raising efforts with a presidential visit. I spoke to the NEA [National Education Association] convention in Los Angeles—a rousing event, like a political rally. They later endorsed me and Fritz with a vote of almost 80 percent. We visited the Oakland Port and saw how rapidly it is growing, then the much more decrepit San Francisco Port, where the Authority is composed of political appointees; the Oakland Authority being a professional organization. I told Mayor [Dianne] Feinstein this was probably one of the differences in the relative success of the two ports.

JULY 4   We had an exciting town hall meeting in Merced, which captured the spirit of the Fourth of July, then Modesto for a fund-raiser, then to Miami for a speech to the NAACP convention—and finally to Plains, the first time I'd been home in ten months. I was really glad to see our house.

JULY 5–7   I went fishing, skinny-dipping in the pond, divided our worship service between Maranatha and Plains Baptist, and played softball against Billy's team each afternoon. Big tourist crowds attend these games and all the press, but it's not as much excitement and competition as in the summer of 1976. Billy is feeling very good—not drinking, tanned, plays golf, harassed by the government on the Libya deal.

Since childhood, I had been a member of Plains Baptist Church, a member of the conservative Southern Baptist Convention. I was a deacon in the 1960s, when my family and I had been outvoted 50–6 (with 150 abstentions) on my proposal to welcome African Americans to worship. During the 1976 campaign, thousands of demonstrators filled the churchyard each Sunday, seeking publicity for their various causes. This disrupted the congregation and led to some more permanent divisions. Without our involvement, about two dozen of the church's more moderate members withdrew after I went to the White House and organized a new Baptist church, known as Maranatha (Come, Lord). When we returned home in 1981, we decided to join the new church, where both Rosalynn and I are deacons and I teach Bible lessons each week that I am in Plains.

MONDAY, JULY 7   I left home early enough to arrive in Detroit at 7:00 a.m. and met with automobile industry people, including labor, and made a statement to the press about the aid package we had put together. The Republicans raised hell because they said I was trying to steal headlines from them in Detroit.

Then we flew to Tokyo, a long trip, a lot of paperwork, and conversations with Muskie and Brzezinski on the future of the Middle East, our relationships with the Soviet Union, et cetera.

JULY 9   We arrived about noon, went to the embassy residence to be with [U.S. ambassador] Mike Mansfield, then to the funeral services for Ohira, which were very impressive, with 108 nations represented. I paid a courtesy call on the emperor and went to the Ohira residence to meet his family, which was a delightful visit in spite of the sad circumstances. I went to bed about 10:00 p.m. Japanese time—tired but not particularly affected by the time change. It seems to bother me less than anyone I know.

JULY 10   I met with Chinese premier Hua [Guofeng], who is likely to be removed from office in another month or so. Then we flew to Anchorage.

We got up at 3:00 a.m. and flew north by helicopter to Clarence Lake. The rainbow streams were overflowing because of heavy rains, so we decided to fish for grayling. We stayed at the lake for about six hours, and I had the best luck of all. My Irresistible dry fly worked wonders. I caught twenty-four grayling and was literally worn out from fighting the fish. We cooked just enough to have lunch, releasing the others. We left Anchorage about 1:00 p.m. and flew to Glynco, Georgia.

JULY 11   On Sapelo Island, I was glad to see Rosalynn and Amy. Lloyd Cutler called to say that Billy agreed to sign the Justice Department Consent Order on revealing his relationship with Libya, which is good news.

JULY 12   We jogged each day, swam in the ocean, and did some fishing in fresh and salt water.

JULY 13   We went to St. Luke's and enjoyed the singing and preaching. We left halfway through the service, after an hour and a half, to meet with our key political advisors.

Pat [Caddell] believes, as with Goldwater and McGovern, there's a chance that the people will reject Reagan as a competent president. This is a possibility which I doubt will materialize. If they once accept him, then it will be an even struggle between me and him. All of us agree that the press is highly prejudiced against us. At least at this moment, [Congressman John] Anderson [Illinois, Republican] is their darling. They're playing hands-off with Reagan, criticizing us in every possible way. Most issues are out of our control—like the hostages, inflation, unemployment, relationships with allies.

This proved to be a prescient analysis, very much in line with what was to occur about one hundred days later on Election Day—which, unfortunately for our campaign, was the exact anniversary of our hostages' capture.

We had an economic [policy] meeting. The team came down unanimous in asking me to approve a tax reduction and a moderate spending program to assuage Kennedy and stimulate the economy. I was adamantly against it and, after considerable discussion, prevailed. I think everyone left convinced we had made the right decision: to hold firm; oppose any tax reduction in 1980; permit it to be discussed, not voted on; and not to deviate from our strict commitment to a restrained budget.

JULY 15   After lunch we took off for Athens [Georgia] and on to Don Carter's fishing camp. We fished in Soapstone Creek, and I caught about twenty trout. I enjoyed being with Jack Crockford, who cooked the best venison I've ever eaten and gave me a beautiful handmade knife. I told him that when I got through being president I would join him in a retirement partnership where we would concentrate on training bird dogs, hunting, studying the mountains and beaches of Georgia, and tying trout flies.

After "retirement," Crockford and I have continued this outdoor partnership for thirty years.

JULY 16   Back on Sapelo we monitored a flap [at the Republican convention] about Reagan and Ford, where Reagan apparently promised Ford he could be almost an equal president if Ford would run as vice presidential candidate. They apparently reached agreement and then backed out. I was looking forward to running against Ford again.

JULY 17   I went to Jacksonville for a political rally, then to Fort Lauderdale, where I spoke to the International Congress of Transport Workers, then back to Washington.
    I called Reagan, congratulated him on his victory, and told him I would welcome a chance for several debates in different regions of the country. He responded favorably, and Fritz arranged to challenge [vice presidential candidate] George [H. W.] Bush to a debate also.

JULY 18   At the foreign policy breakfast we discussed the military coup in Bolivia. There's a flap in the Senate and the Jewish community about possible improvements to the F-15s we sold to the Saudis. I approved a letter stating that we would not permit these planes to be offensively capable against Israel. There is some indication in Afghanistan that the SA-7s [shoulder-fired antiaircraft missiles] are being used effectively against attack helicopters.

There's a lawsuit in Philadelphia to delay draft registration because women are not included. In the evening a three-judge panel ruled that registration for men only was unconstitutional. We will appeal to the Supreme Court.

For some reason I feel better about the political situation than a week ago. The Republican convention was not as successful as we had anticipated, although some of the press put the best possible light on the Ford debacle and a very poor acceptance speech by Reagan.

JULY 19 I presented the Medal of Honor to Lieutenant Colonel Matt Urban. We both had tears. He was an unbelievably courageous hero in 1944, but his records were lost for more than thirty-five years.

I then met with Richard Queen [hostage released because of illness]. He was excited, talkative, apparently physically weakened because of his imprisonment and his multiple sclerosis. He described in vivid terms the abuse they had suffered at the hands of the student militants—not beatings but incarceration for weeks in a basement without light or fresh air—which he called a tomb.

Chairman Paul Volcker came to let me know he'll be testifying next week, and his position is compatible with that of my advisors and some of the key Republican economists as well—and contrary, of course, to the position put forth by Reagan, [Jack] Kemp, and others.

I talked to Amy, who's making good progress at tennis camp, except her backhand.

JULY 20 We enjoyed having [actor] Kirk Douglas and his wife, Anne, spend the night with us. I taught Sunday school and worked on my acceptance speech. I called senators to promote the Alaska lands legislation on which they'll be voting this week.

Lloyd and Zbig called concerning Billy's relationship with Libya, and his contacts with the White House. I told them to research very carefully the telephone logs and other records and prepare a complete report on what had been done. So far as I could see, nothing improper has occurred.

MONDAY, JULY 21 I met with a large group of different interest group representatives supporting the Alaska lands legislation that we prefer. This is going to be a major battle in the Senate. Prospects, according to Dan Tate and others [congressional liaison staff], are quite poor.

Unresolved since Eisenhower's administration was the question of what to do with large portions of Alaska. I paid close attention to this extremely complex issue during my entire term. It provoked intense struggles among the state government, private landowners, Indians, Inuits, hunters, fishermen, timber interests, environmentalists, the oil industry, and their highly paid lobbyists in Washington. Working with Interior Secretary Cecil Andrus, we had been using the Antiquities Act of 1906 to set aside the most precious areas of the state by executive order, which gave us powerful leverage against opponents. Now we were approaching a legislative showdown.

I left the White House and flew to Evansville [Indiana] and then Henderson, Kentucky, for a fund-raiser. I stood in line after a brief speech and shook hands with five hundred people inside a tent, with the temperature outside over one hundred degrees. My necktie was dripping sweat off the end, and Governor John Y. Brown had to drop out several times to cool off, and eventually lay down in his own bedroom.

We then flew to Texas, visited a farm by helicopter, went to a Democratic Party rally in Dallas, then to [financial executive] Jess Hay's home for a fund-raiser that brought in more than $600,000. Got back home shortly before midnight—a successful day—good media, raised a lot of money.

JULY 22 Begin is again threatening to move his office to East Jerusalem within the next ten or twelve days, which might result in the termination of peace talks. It's hard to oppose the PM as he consolidates Israel's claim over Jerusalem.

The Olympics seem to be shaping up into a farce, with the Soviets winning all the gold medals except those in swimming that East Germany has picked up.

Byrd wants a congressional resolution for a tax cut in 1981, Jim Wright thought there should be no tax cut, and Russell Long, typically, said let the Senate pass a Christmas tree bill, the House a responsible bill, and if it was still irresponsible for me to veto it, I presume ten days before the election! Most of us took strong exception to this.

We'll have to defeat a [Scoop] Jackson effort to table the Alaska lands bill. I had lunch with Senator Gary Hart, one of the outstanding members.

JULY 23 I signed the "River of No Return" Wilderness Bill, protecting the area that we went down two years ago in rafts.

We had [president of the AFL-CIO] Lane Kirkland and his wife, Irena, over for supper. I told Lane we would accommodate Kennedy as much as possible and then beat him with delegate votes on everything else.

Begin is driving Israel into almost complete isolation among the nations of the world and even alienating a lot of American support that has been the salvation of Israel until now.

The Alaska lands bill support was so great that the opponents, particularly Ted Stevens, have now moved toward private negotiation to work out a compromise.

JULY 24 The prime news story is the Billy/Libya relationship. So far as I know, on behalf of me [and] my entire administration, there are no improprieties or illegalities involved. I spent hours with Lloyd and Jody, making sure that we had all the facts. I approved a statement that we would cooperate with the congressional investigation and would forgo any claim of executive privilege. My own belief is that we should let all of the information be known as completely and as soon as possible.

The mental health bill passed, gratifying to Rosalynn.

Harold Brown gave us a briefing on the SIOP revisions [Single Integrated Operational Plan, for use of our nuclear arsenal]; also on some of the new technological defense achievements that will be inevitably revealed in the future.

The major thrust of our Defense Department under Brown, former president of the California Institute of Technology, was the development of new and highly sophisticated weapon systems, including precision bombs and missiles and stealth aircraft that could not be detected by radar. This would revolutionize aerial warfare and was our topmost secret. As we were now approaching the test flight stage, however, thousands of scientists, contractors, and workers shared the information, which was bound to be disclosed.

JULY 25 We discussed the attitude of some who are trying to open the Democratic convention in order to help Scoop Jackson, Ted Kennedy, or some favorite governor. We'll have to face it and meet the challenge. Fortunately, the liberal "bed wetters," as Frank [Moore] calls them, called their meeting on Thursday and Friday when all of them are madly scrambling to go home. Gives us the weekend to work on it.

Kirbo called to say Scoop Jackson and Sam Nunn decided not to speak to the convention. Scoop is obviously trying to get himself promoted as the nominee.

JULY 26 At Camp David, I worked on the acceptance speech, inundated with suggestions from every conceivable source.

I talked to Rosalynn, who was quite upset about headlines in the paper concerning Libya, congressmen, and so forth. I told her to read the first verse in our Bible chapter last night—John 14 ["Let not your heart be troubled . . ."]—and she would feel better. She wanted me to calm her down before going to Peru to the inauguration of the new president.

Rosalynn hopes to strengthen our ties with the outgoing military group and also the new president, [Fernando] Belaúnde. She will prod the Chileans about human rights violations there.

In the afternoon I met [at Camp David] with a remarkable group of trout fishermen, fly tiers, rod makers, book writers, specialists on casting techniques, who assembled from all over the Northeast region of our country. It was one of the most pleasant two or three hours I've spent in a long time. They gave me some samples of what they had done, let me watch them tie the more difficult flies, and gave me some instruction on how best to cast.

JULY 27 Early in the morning I had a report the shah was dead.

MONDAY, JULY 28 We found that Bob Byrd had a luncheon meeting with a few senators and tried to induce them to come to the White House and discourage me from continuing my campaign for president. Some of our supporters in the committee objected strongly to his approach, and apparently he backed off from it.

JULY 29 I met with the Democratic congressional leaders and told them about the Libyan question: I was making available to the public and the Congress all the information I had, there was nothing about which we needed to be ashamed, and no secrets that would be embarrassing. I asked them to expedite the youth bill, rail deregulation, Alaska lands, fair housing, the Superfund to deal with waste dump areas, and not let the Republicans stop all confirmation, because some of them are crucial, like ambassadors.

We had a ceremony to mark the anniversary of the Helsinki Accords. I condemned the Soviets again for their invasion and for cutting down on Jewish outmigration, and for their persecution of [physicist and human rights activist Andrei] Sakharov and others.

Rosalynn returned from Peru quite excited about her trip. It was an extensive enough visit for thorough discussions with the leaders of Costa Rica, Spain, Peru, Colombia, Venezuela, and others. She's an outstanding diplomat in that she can broach without embarrassment subjects that are very difficult to raise through an ambassador or the State Department.

JULY 30   Cecil called to say that Alaska leaders Stevens and [Governor Jay] Hammond have gone about as far as they could publicly, but they might be willing to let the Senate rule over them on Alaska lands.

I told Ed, over some reluctance on his part, to go ahead and send a message to our European allies urging them to work on the hostage release now that the Majlis had chosen a Speaker, the prime minister had been nominated, and the shah's funeral was over. The State Department moves like cold molasses.

We also discussed the continued effort by Bob Byrd to get someone else, probably himself, to be the Democratic nominee.

Mark Hatfield called to let me know he was praying for me and referred me to Hebrews 11. I appreciated it. A lot of people think I'm a lot more burdened down and discouraged than I actually am.

JULY 31   The Israelis in the Knesset adopted the Geula Cohen bill, officially moving the government to East Jerusalem. This almost puts the final nail in the coffin of the Camp David negotiations between Israel and Egypt.

More than the West Bank, Gaza, or any other area, all Arabs and other Muslims cherish their unimpeded access to the holy places in East Jerusalem. Israeli encroachment is still a bone of contention.

I have a lot of problems on my shoulders, but strangely enough, I feel better as they pile up. My main concern is propping up the people around me who tend to panic (and who might possibly have a better and clearer picture of the situation than I do).

In preparing my own acceptance speech notes, it's become more and more obvious that Reagan and I have perhaps the sharpest divisions between us of any two presidential candidates in my lifetime. Also, his policies are a radical departure from those of Ford and Nixon.

Economic indicators were remarkably good, the highest in five or six years—increasing 2.5 percent in one year.

I signed an agreement between the U.S., Japan, and Germany to build a coal liquefaction plant in West Virginia and introduced Bob Byrd graciously in spite of his trying to stab me in the back politically.

Joe Biden and twelve other senators met at lunchtime to decide how best to support me. They called a press conference afterward that was very lightly covered—predictably. In general, it's been a very good day.

AUGUST 1   I'll interrogate the CIA on why they don't know more about the location of our hostages.

I met a large, excited, enthusiastic group of House members who came to repledge their support. Several of the defectors from our position were there, and impressed with the show of strength. We have weathered the worst of the shaky support, and things are firming up, unless something else happens.

At a staff meeting, we discussed the strange meeting between John Anderson and Kennedy yesterday, where Anderson announced afterward that he would withdraw from his campaign if Kennedy was the nominee.

AUGUST 2   I spent an afternoon and evening working on the report to the Congress [about Billy and Libya]. It was tedious and aggravating because there was no substance to the whole affair that affected me or anyone in my administration. The irresponsible press has made every effort to prolong the thing into another Watergate. When unwarranted allegations are made, coming from every direction, it's a lot more difficult to prove something never happened than it is to prove something *did* happen.

Sadat has demanded that for the peace talks to continue, Begin would have to agree that Jerusalem is negotiable, stop the settlements, and take care of the human rights of the Palestinians. I don't believe he [Begin] will do any of these things, and has dug himself a hole very damaging to Israel.

MONDAY, AUGUST 4   I spent almost the entire day getting ready for the news conference in the evening and put the final touches on all the statements and documents going to the House and Senate committees.

Everyone thought the press conference went well. My hope and expectation are that this entire process will help reestablish Billy in the public mind as a reasonably responsible person, but it really depends on how Billy handles the question of money from the Libyans and whether or not he tells the complete truth about it. All in all, it's been a very unpleasant experience.

AUGUST 5   Harold Brown reported that Greece and Turkey were approaching agreement on terms under which Greece would reenter NATO. He said Turkey had agreed to all but four words in a proposal, but the four words might be "Greece belongs to Turkey."

The response to the TV news conference last night was overwhelmingly good.

I met with a group of national religious leaders who are even more concerned than I about the right-wing radical TV religious performers who equate a belief in Christ with the embracing of right-wing South American dictators, opposition to ERA, and a move to abolish the Department of Education. They are a threat to the Christian faith and trying to promote themselves through political means into a nationwide force.

Klutznick and Goldschmidt are worried about the Jewish vote—as am I—but they don't have any easy solutions for it. I asked Fritz to take on Mayor Koch as a special project. He's been one of our biggest problems.

I presented a special gold medal to Simon Wiesenthal, an emotional experience. He's been the leader in hunting down Nazi war criminals and has done an outstanding job.

AUGUST 6   I went to New York to speak to the Urban League. Koch rode in the car with me, and I gave him hell for his daily stabbing me in the back. He pulled out a list of things that he said could be done only with a stroke of the pen. They involved changing the general revenue-sharing laws that had been in effect since Nixon's administration. I told him that with friends like him I didn't need any enemies, and with supporters like him I didn't need any Republican opponents.

It's interesting that the Ku Klux Klan has endorsed Reagan and made an announcement that the Republican platform could have been written by a Klansman.

I met with Lloyd Cutler and the people that worked with him and Al Moses [advisor on Jewish affairs] on the Libya matter. They were excited to meet me personally, and I told them that someday they might even be able to meet Billy!

AUGUST 7   Dr. and Mrs. Bailey Smith came by. He's president of the Southern Baptist Convention. He asked me about secular humanism and how I explained my attitude toward it. I told him I never had used the words and wasn't familiar with them. Apparently this is part of the attacks being made by the Jerry Falwell right-wing group. Falwell has lied in Alaska by claiming that he met with me in the Oval Office and I told him I had to have homosexuals on my staff because there were homosexuals in the United States that needed representation in my inner circle. I've never had a private meeting with him, he's never been in the Oval Office, and I've never had any such conversation.

Signs of change within the Southern Baptist Convention had become increasingly evident, and in 1979, more conservative leaders assumed control, turned hard right politically, and aligned themselves with the right wing of the Republican Party. The new leaders looked with favor on very few of my projects or commitments. I regretted this very much and attempted during the 1990s to heal the differences. About forty of us, including seven past or future SBC presidents, assembled at The Carter Center and made some progress, but it was short-lived. In January 2008, after working with former SBC president Jimmy Allen, Mercer University president Bill Underwood, National Baptist Convention president William Shaw, David Goatley, and other leaders of major African American Baptist organizations, we assembled the New Baptist Covenant, a large interracial group of North American Baptists.

AUGUST 8   I told Harold to send David Jones to see General Chun, the new dictator in Korea, concerning the Kim Dae Jung trial—to make sure they don't execute Kim. If they do, we should be ready to withdraw some of our troops from Korea.

Kim Dae Jung was a human rights hero, and I was determined to put as much pressure as possible on General Chun [Doo Hwan] to prevent his execution. Eventually we prevailed, and Kim was permitted to come to the United States "for medical purposes." He was later elected president of South Korea and won the Nobel Peace Prize for attempting reconciliation with North Korea.

I signed an executive order encouraging all federal agencies to help the black colleges. Benjamin Mays [president of Morehouse College] said I had done more for black people than any other president, including Lincoln—which surprised and embarrassed me at a big press conference.

I spent an uncomfortable lunch period trying to eat and answer questions at the same time from Jody, Zbig, Stu, Rosalynn, and Jerry—in preparation for the *60 Minutes* interview with Dan Rather. He sent word to me secretly by Jody that he was not going to ask negative questions but try to restore his image to be more as Walter Cronkite and not as a frivolous, slashing interviewer. He failed. Not only was it frivolous, but the way it was finally edited—all of his negative questioning and just brief snippets of my answers—was more like Sarah McClendon or Father [Les] Kinsolving than Walter Cronkite.

AUGUST 9   *The Washington Star* and *The New York Times* are running a story on Ruth's trip to Oman and other places in the Middle East and the Far East. *Time* magazine has a story about Jeffrey's little company signing a contract to do work for the city of Manila in the Philippines. The situation is really ridiculous. At one time or another everyone who is close to me in any way has been worked over by the press in an extremely exaggerated way.

I worked on the [convention] speech; its basic thrust will be the extremely sharp difference between me and Reagan and the threat of Reagan's positions to our energy program and to peace and the SALT process. Also, some brief enumeration of the major achievements of our administration, without seeming like we're bragging—concerning [10.5 million] job additions, energy policy, Mideast peace, normalization with China, Zimbabwe/Rhodesia, deregulation of major industries, et cetera.

AUGUST 10   The Kennedy forces threatened to filibuster Tuesday evening with a long demonstration for Kennedy. I told Hamilton to let them know we'll either take it out of his time or postpone his speech until after the business of the evening. The press is full of threats that we're going to be defeated on the rule vote and that Kennedy's going to take over the convention.

There's a flap concerning PD [presidential directive] 59, where I changed targeting of our nuclear weapons to permit more flexibility in case we are attacked—letting me destroy Soviet military and command control and communication centers instead of all their major urban centers.

MONDAY, AUGUST 11   Monday evening the convention began. There were heated debates on the rules question. When the vote came we did better than we had anticipated, getting 1,935 votes—about a 700+ vote margin over Kennedy. He called me shortly afterward to say he was going to withdraw his name from contention. I asked him if he was going to endorse and be on the platform with me Thursday night. He said that would depend on how we worked out details of the platform. I pointed out there were a lot of differences between us and we couldn't expect any substantial compatibility beyond what we already hammered out. He agreed and seemed to be in a good mood. Later, he announced his withdrawal from the campaign. This was a relief. It's been a long, drawn-out, bitter confrontation between me and him.

Tom Donilon, a young computer and delegate management expert, did a superb job. As he walked through the crowd of people in our command headquarters, I could hear them shouting, "Donilon for president!"

AUGUST 12   The story on Ruth didn't turn out badly. I watched her and Mother being interviewed by Walter Cronkite, and she did very well.

In the evening Kennedy made a stirring and emotional speech.

AUGUST 13   During the day at the hotel in New York, I worked on the speech draft and practiced once with the teleprompter. When I got to New York, I was informed that the MX [nuclear missile] vote was going to be lost by three hundred to four hundred votes. I told [our supporters] I did not want to lose that vote, and to go all out to win. I wrote a personal note to every one of the delegates, and we won the vote easily. In the evening we had the vote on nomination, and I won without any problem. I was pleased that Texas put me over the top.

AUGUST 14   We went to bed at 2:00, and I jogged in Central Park at 6:30. When I gave my acceptance speech I was amazed and disconcerted because I couldn't see the teleprompter at all—just a word here and there as it passed by a black spot in the audience with somebody with a dark coat on. I had to make the entire speech either from memory or from glancing down at my written text.

Afterward, Kennedy drove over from his hotel, appeared on the platform along with a lot of other people, seemed to have had a few drinks, which I would have probably done myself. He was fairly cool and reserved. I thought it was adequate, but the press made a big deal of it.

Ostentatiously, Kennedy refused to shake my extended hand, and this became one of the main news stories from the convention. Despite this, I was happy and relieved to have the time-consuming Democratic primary behind me and to emerge with a victory. What Rosalynn and I wanted and needed now was some rest and a chance to begin concentrating on the general election campaign against Ronald Reagan.

AUGUST 15   It was Mother's birthday, and [she joined us to visit] the Picasso exhibit. The breadth of his achievements is staggering, I think unequaled by any other artist.

I met with the Democratic fund-raisers and the National Committee group, then flew to Camp David and then to Spruce Creek in Pennsylvania. This is what I've been waiting for all week.

We have another of the UN Security Council resolutions on Israel — the tenth one in five months. That's all the jokers do over there. I can't say that Israel doesn't deserve to be condemned, but there are much more serious problems in the world.

AUGUST 16   Fishing all day.

AUGUST 17   Fished again until about 3:00. In reading the Sunday *Washington Post*, I couldn't believe the obvious hatred and vituperation leveled against me. It was as though I was a combination of Adolf Hitler and Goofy. I was incompetent and untrustworthy. They ignored the fact that we had beaten Kennedy, won the rules fight, had the nomination, prevailed well on the platform, and that Kennedy had endorsed. Really unbelievable.

MONDAY, AUGUST 18   Rosalynn's birthday. Our fondest expectations were realized in the polls. AP and NBC showed that we had come up within seven points of Reagan. This is a remarkable improvement, because of the favorable impact of the Democratic convention proving that the press analysis had been incorrect.

The Senate passed the Alaska lands bill, which is very gratifying. Now it's got to go back through the House, hopefully without an amendment. I don't believe we can get it through the Senate again.

I gave Rosalynn a beautiful little picture frame and put Ecclesiastes 9:9 in Spanish written in the frame as a message from me to her.

The King James version is "Live joyfully with the wife whom thou lovest all the days . . . which he hath given thee under the sun . . . ; for that is thy portion in this life and in thy labour which thou takest under the sun."

AUGUST 20 I worked on the American Legion speech and on the remarks Ed Muskie will make today on the UN Security Council Resolution concerning Jerusalem. Fritz gets very excited about these decisions that affect the American Jewish community.

In the evening I talked to Archbishop [John R.] Quinn about the Democratic convention platform plank on abortion. I told him that my position had not changed; that I disagreed with the platform and had expressed my disapproval specifically in my last Wednesday's remarks.

AUGUST 21 We decided to let Harold handle the stealth aircraft development, because the B-1 bomber decision was justified even absent any developments on stealth—because the cruise missiles are so superior. Reaction from the legionnaires was fairly good, not as enthusiastic as Reagan had gotten.

Billy testified before the Senate subcommittee on his Libyan relationships, and Frank Moore reported that the senators who are not on the subcommittee say that Billy deserves a Congressional Medal of Honor for the way he handled himself. I called and congratulated him.

AUGUST 22 At the foreign affairs breakfast we discussed Poland, Israel, oil, and Greece coming into NATO. Harold will explain the nonclassified part of the stealth plane today. Israel made an unwarranted attack on Lebanon, and more than sixty people were killed.

AUGUST 24 We discussed the poll results at our political meeting. With Anderson in the race we're about six points down. The convention and my speech had a tremendous impact on the American people and their opinion. Every issue I emphasized had a dramatic change in voter reaction.

All except Fritz thought my campaign appearances should be substantive in nature: in an automobile plant with new American cars; a steel plant that was being modernized; a synthetic fuel plant concerning solar power, coal mines, transportation, improved port facilities; the signing of bills like mental health in a major mental hospital; and so forth. Fritz thought the American people wanted to see me actually campaigning and asking for votes.

Most of Anderson's supporters steal the Democratic liberals who are disaffected with me. They don't yet recognize their incompatibility with Anderson's record and his basic philosophy because it's so chameleon-like. The campaign looks a lot better than it seemed to be prior to the convention. My main problem is still the opinion of the American people that I am not a strong leader and have inadequate vision for the future.

MONDAY, AUGUST 25   The Polish problem seems to have moved into phase two, which Zbig says is "from bread to freedom."

I met with Bob Byrd, House leaders, and Kennedy. We had remarkably good meetings, ironing out our political and personal differences.

AUGUST 26   With congressional leaders, I pushed on the youth bill, Energy Mobilization Board, rail deregulation, mental health, and Alaska lands. I described the situation in Poland, the difficulty the Soviets have either in intervening or acquiescing in the move toward free labor unions.

All of us, including [Democratic] members of Congress, feel much better now than we did four weeks ago. Reagan has kept his foot in his mouth every time he's been out in the last two weeks. We're trying to stay on the front of the debate issue, insisting on multiple debates, preferably most of them being with Reagan alone, but agreeing to debate the other candidates if necessary.

It became increasingly clear to us that Reagan wanted to avoid debates as much as possible, unless the third-party candidate, John Anderson, could participate as an equal. This was shrewd politics: he was well ahead in the polls, and any votes for Anderson, including those who had been Kennedy supporters, would come directly from those who supported me. Anderson had announced earlier that he would withdraw if Kennedy was the nominee, and he later ran in the general election as an independent, hoping to attract liberal Republicans and Kennedy Democrats.

AUGUST 27   Things are getting worse in Poland. I let the European leaders know about our concern, our basic support for the Polish workers, our intention to do what we can economically to stabilize the Polish economy.

The show of independence by Lech Walesa and his fellow workers was to be-
come a turning point in contesting the Soviet occupation and control of east-
ern European nations. Germany and some of our other NATO allies were
reluctant to join us in supporting those who were seeking independence.

We had a fairly emotional reception for Mugabe. The audience was
extremely supportive of the new independent republic and of Mugabe,
who was so courageous in fighting for that independence.

AUGUST 28   The strikers in Poland are making a lot of progress. Our information is that the Soviets are not inclined to intervene militarily.

I met again with a group of Jewish supporters from New York City, and
the session went well. Later they reported remarkable approval for what
I've said.

AUGUST 29   The situation in Poland seems to be coming to a climax.
We've been giving private support to the Polish strikers, through some of
our labor unions.

I told Sol Linowitz to be very firm in explaining to the Israelis how
their recent actions were damaging the peace prospects and to let Begin
know that he couldn't blackmail me just because it was an election year.

To Camp David. I caught the largest trout yet, plus others. Had a good
time, but I was surprised at how tired I was.

AUGUST 30   I spent most of the time working on five or six speeches. I
called Geraldine Ferraro and asked her to assume the deputy chairmanship of our election campaign. She said she'd be glad to do it, even if it
might cost her own election. I'm looking forward to this full week of campaigning.

MONDAY, SEPTEMBER 1   In Tuscumbia the day was great. We had the
platform filled with political leaders from Tennessee, Alabama, and Mississippi. Several of them said it was the biggest crowd they had ever seen at a
political rally. Estimates ranged from thirty thousand to fifty thousand.
When I saw the crowd I said, "That's big enough." I was pleasantly surprised
when I got the biggest round of applause with my attacks on the Klan. I
pointed out that Judah Benjamin, a Jew, was secretary of state of the Con-
federacy and that General [P. G. T.] Beauregard and many others were

Catholics. In Michigan, Reagan made the mistake of saying I had gone to the home place of the Ku Klux Klan to begin my campaign.

SEPTEMBER 2   There was really a furor about Reagan's Klan remark—the lead story in all three networks last night, and headlines in the paper this morning. Governors of seven southern states blasted him for insinuating that the Klan represented the South.

In Independence, Missouri, I visited with Bess Truman and went by the Truman Library, made a speech, and had a town meeting at Truman High School. The headlines were that I insinuated Reagan's nuclear arms stance might be contrary to peace. The overall press reaction was that Reagan and I were involved in a serious public verbal battle. I'll try to be more presidential, but he genuinely aggravated me with his Klan remark.

SEPTEMBER 3   Lane Kirkland is pushing for funds to help Polish workers. Ed Muskie and others are trying to dissuade him, because of the possible excuse for Soviet intervention in Poland. Apparently the Polish labor leader Lech Walesa made a public appeal for money, and Lane was not to be dissuaded.

Linowitz reported from Cairo that Begin and Sadat had agreed to start peace talks again.

SEPTEMBER 4   Reagan spoke to the B'nai B'rith last night and accused me of betraying Israel.

I got a report this morning on our Selective Service registration, and it's extremely encouraging. About 93 percent of all those eligible registered in a timely fashion.

We almost had a problem when Ed consulted with the Soviets and had not planned to meet with the Polish ambassador. Zbig found out, and Ed met with both.

Begin called to express his appreciation for Linowitz's constructive visit. He said he was looking forward to the recommencing of the peace talks.

Pat reported that Anderson is still running around 20 percent in the Northeast and 15 percent among all voters. I made the final speech to B'nai B'rith and thought the membership were cool until I told about giving photographs of Begin's grandchildren to him, which turned the tide at Camp David. The audience wound up in a warm standing ovation for me. Pat thinks we're ahead now with Jewish voters in the country, although there's still an inordinately high support for Anderson and a high undecided.

SEPTEMBER 5   We'll hold fast on our Kampuchea seat position which we've pledged to maintain to the ASEAN [Association of Southeast Asian Nations] nations, to Hua of China, and also to Fraser and others in the Pacific region. Some of our liberals want us to declare the seat vacant.

I had condemned the government of Kampuchea (Cambodia) under Pol Pot as "the worst violator of human rights in the world today." However, we could not accept Vietnam's invasion and occupation of Kampuchea. When the issue came before the UN, instead of voting to seat Vietnam's puppet government, the United States voted to allow the remnants of the Khmer Rouge to retain the seat. This was a choice between two evils, and we aligned ourselves with China, Australia, all the ASEAN nations, and Europe against the Soviet Union, Vietnam, Cuba, and a few of their allies. In doing so, I took the advice of Cy Vance and our regional ambassadors, although several of my best people in the State Department disagreed.

We went to Camp David and fished for smallmouth bass in the Potomac near Clear Springs, Maryland.

MONDAY, SEPTEMBER 8   Jesse Jackson came by and said he wants to endorse me. I look on this with some doubt, because he generally makes his living criticizing people, not supporting them.

SEPTEMBER 9   I [began to campaign more] regularly and characterized Anderson as a product of the American media who had not won a caucus or primary, had no party or convention, but who did take votes away from me and helped Reagan. In crucial states like Florida and Texas he only has 6 or 7 percent.

SEPTEMBER 10   With congressional leaders I listed remaining bills I want passed this year: youth, Superfund, Alaska lands, rail deregulation, child health, et cetera. I think we'll get a good portion of these.

[New York investment banker] Felix Rohatyn said he was going to get involved for the first time in a campaign. He looks on Anderson as a political nonentity and Reagan as a catastrophe and will support me for reasons that are personal, professional, and political—and because he's interested in the future of Israel.

I blasted Reagan for claiming our policies had cut U.S. energy production. Oil production is up for the first time in a decade, we produced more coal than ever in history, and we have more oil-drilling rigs going than ever before.

SEPTEMBER 11   I told Zbig to prepare a list of everything we have offered the Iranians to get the hostages home.

Proxmire is attempting to prevent any loans to New York, and I told Fritz to take charge and keep us on the side of the New York angels.

SEPTEMBER 12   We continue to get favorable messages out of Iran. With prior notification to us, Khomeini confirmed the earlier proposal made through the Germans, and the militants corroborated what Khomeini said, limiting the demands to the return of assets, return of the shah's assets, and agreement not to interfere in Iranian affairs. With high secrecy, we prepared for Christopher to go to Europe to follow up on the proposals.

These were demands we could consider. It was increasingly obvious to me and my political staff that my inability to end the captivity of our hostages was a crippling factor in my campaign. On multiple occasions, various leaders in the complex Iranian government seemed on the verge of making a positive decision, and we pursued each of these opportunities through the Germans, Swiss, Algerians, and as many other interlocutors as possible.

At the foreign affairs breakfast we discussed the need to develop specific action that might be taken toward South Korea if Kim Dae Jung is executed and to relay this threat that would be carried to President Chun in order to prevent this happening.

We had an NSC meeting on a threat about the Soviet Union toward Iran and decided that any Soviet invasion would precipitate a worldwide confrontation between the U.S. and the Soviets. Our military ability against thirty or forty invading Soviet divisions in Iran would not be good at all, but worldwide we could equal the Soviet force—and they are quite vulnerable on access to the seas, economics, and so forth.

Willie Nelson, [his wife] Connie, and their two daughters are staying with us. We jogged three or four miles and then went swimming. I like them very much. They are at ease with us, and vice versa. He's having a fund-raising concert tomorrow night.

SEPTEMBER 13   Tarnoff reported very favorable results of his discussions with Castro. He [Castro] will announce Tuesday that hijackers will be executed or returned to the United States immediately for trial. He will cut off the refugee flow on the twenty-fifth, send all the empty boats back home, and also hold down the rate of refugees coming to the U.S. to around one hundred per day between now and the twenty-fifth. He refused to accept anything in return. Told me not to take any action that would be harmful to me, and made it clear there was no quid pro quo involved in what he was doing.

SEPTEMBER 14   I worked from the time I got up until I went to bed, on reports, legislation, and a large number of speeches.

MONDAY, SEPTEMBER 15   I finished preparing my remarks for more than fifteen events to be concluded on a two-day swing through Texas, Georgia, South Carolina, and Ohio. We had good success with rallies and fund-raising.

SEPTEMBER 16   At Ebenezer Baptist Church, Daddy King, Coretta, and Andy [Young] participated in a rally of all the southeastern area black leaders, from Texas to Maryland. I commented that racism and hatred had been injected into the campaign because the Ku Klux Klan had become an issue. This is code-worded as "states rights." The press reported this as a statement that Reagan was a racist, which I denied.

In fact, Reagan had kicked off his campaign in the South in Neshoba County, Mississippi, where three young civil rights workers were assassinated in 1964. (Their bodies were buried in a dam near Philadelphia, the county seat.) As he and his campaign staff well knew, this place had strong symbolic meaning for southerners for whom the race issue was important, and the subject of his speech there was "states' rights."

SEPTEMBER 17   Christopher's conversations with [Sadegh] Tabatabai in Bonn were satisfactory. The biggest hang-up is going to be on the shah's assets. Our proposals are as forthcoming as possible and preserve the integrity of our nation and our courts.

This was the first time we were certain we were in direct contact with the ayatollah, and his position was both clear and rational. Tabatabai was fluent in German and was the brother-in-law of Khomeini's son. He gave us the four requisites for the hostages' release that were repeated verbatim by the ayatollah the following day: an apology for the U.S. historical role in Iran; unlocking Iranian financial assets; withdrawal of legal claims against Iran; and delivery of all the shah's assets. We would ignore the apology request, and we had no way of knowing the extent or location of the shah's assets.

Just in case we were successful, I directed Hamilton to draft the procedure for welcoming the hostages home that was eventually used—but much later than we anticipated.

At breakfast with congressional leaders we discussed [outstanding legislation]. When we have our worst confrontations, the aftermath has been that the Congress moves to resolve the issues.

A poll in *The New York Times*, CBS, showed that in the last month I've picked up in every area of the nation and every age group, every ethnic group, every special interest group, compared to Reagan. Anderson has either held his own or dropped a little bit.

SEPTEMBER 18   Somoza's assassination [yesterday] may have been by Argentine activists who fought in Nicaragua and are connected with the Sandinistas. We don't know yet.

SEPTEMBER 19   We're preparing our strategy in case the Arab League moves to expel Israel from the UN General Assembly.

We went to Spruce Creek, where Rosalynn joined me after a successful campaign trip.

SEPTEMBER 20   We fished the Trico hatch with George Harvey, from Penn State. The ways he can tie flies and use a fly rod are both works of art. Back at Camp David, I prepared for speeches and rallies in Illinois, California, Oregon, and Washington.

SEPTEMBER 21   We watched the Reagan-Anderson debate, which was really depressing, as they merely spouted statistics, et cetera. Anderson probably helped himself with liberals, and Reagan seemed ineffectual. But who knows? Pat will give me audience reaction tomorrow.

MONDAY, SEPTEMBER 22   Iraq bombed the Iranian airport where military planes were located. We'll decide how best to handle this, and how it might relate to the release of the hostages. The main thing to avoid is any Soviet intrusion into Iran.

I have always believed that the unwarranted attack and later invasion by Iraq was a major factor in preventing further progress on the release of our hostages. Some Iranians alleged that Saddam Hussein had U.S. support—which was not true at the time. Later, when Reagan became president, he gave diplomatic recognition to the Iraqi regime and supplied war matériel.

Beginning a two-day trip through Illinois, California, Oregon, and Washington. Kennedy's been in California for several days trying to raise money, with minimal success. We'll help him with a unity fund-raising event. In the meantime he'll be helping us around the country.

SEPTEMBER 23   Very serious problems on Iran-Iraq border—attacks are being made on the refineries in each nation by the other, also aerial attacks on Baghdad. Both countries have ceased shipment of oil through the Persian Gulf. This involves almost 3 million barrels of oil a day—most of it from Iraq—and cuts the overall world supply by that much.

In Los Angeles I raised the issue of war and peace with Reagan. Eight times in the last few years he's advocated gunboat diplomacy. The press jumped on it as a mean campaign tactic on my part, but most of them told Jody privately that they thought it was a legitimate issue and Reagan was both culpable and vulnerable on it.

SEPTEMBER 24   I conducted a National Security Council meeting. We agreed to do everything we could to terminate the Iran-Iraq conflict as soon as possible, to stay strictly neutral, to call other nations to stay out of the conflict and be neutral, and to keep open the Strait of Hormuz. My hope is that a cease-fire, with Iran still threatened, might be an inducement to them to release the hostages and repair their relationships with the outside world.

Mr. Stanley Walesa came by. He's the father of Lech Walesa, the Polish labor leader. Mr. Walesa expressed his support for me for president, but he's not yet a citizen and can't vote.

SEPTEMBER 25 Congress is making better progress on legislation now than I ever dreamed they would. We'll get half [those we want] before we adjourn next week and have a good chance to get the others after the election.

The League of Women Voters accepted our terms for a two-person debate with Reagan, followed with a three-man debate. Later, Reagan rejected this, saying he wouldn't debate without Anderson.

I called Paul Volcker, who is raising the discount rate. This will hurt us politically, but I think it's the right thing to do.

As mentioned earlier, my firm understanding with Volcker was that he would do his utmost to control inflation without regard to its effect on my campaign—and he did so, without equivocation.

SEPTEMBER 26 Castro has cut off the exit of refugees from Mariel Harbor, and 150 to 200 empty boats are on their way back now to Florida. He's done everything he promised.

France, Germany, and Great Britain foreign ministers have said they are concerned about the courage and will of President Zia of Pakistan. I told Muskie that his will was a hell of a lot better than their nations had indicated as a result of the Soviet invasion of Afghanistan.

I met with Jesse Jackson, who is volatile and demanding but has been of great help to us in the last couple of weeks.

We had a great time signing the Infant Formula Act with children all over the Cabinet Room. One of whom picked up my telephone at the desk, and I told him that Brezhnev wouldn't figure out what was happening, but to tell the Russians to get their troops out of Afghanistan.

Later we [Rosalynn and I] went to Camp David and watched a special that Bill Moyers had on the Moral Majority. Although he condemned it in the last four minutes, I thought he gave the religious nuts fifty minutes of uninterrupted bragging on themselves. It is a disquieting movement, its effect still difficult to determine.

Although I had received strong support from moderate Christian evangelicals in 1976, I was never supported by the more extreme right wing. These conservative evangelicals were now forming a political alliance with the right-wing elements of the Republican Party, one that would prevail for more than a quarter century. Opinion polls revealed that they supported Reagan by a two-to-one majority in 1980.

As one indication of the power wielded by this new alliance, that autumn a group headed by Jerry Falwell purchased $10 million in commercials on southern radio and TV to brand me as a traitor to the South and no longer a Christian. (We were limited to about $26 million for our entire national campaign.)

SEPTEMBER 27–28 We caught a lot of fish at Little Owen Creek [near Camp David], then I worked the rest of the weekend on phone calls, speeches, paperwork, and Congress re the New York loan guarantee. Also we [NSC and I] addressed how to handle the threat of expulsion of Israel from the UN General Assembly.

MONDAY, SEPTEMBER 29 Brown reported we could have four AWACS and fifteen F-15s in Saudi Arabia within forty-eight hours [if necessary].

The trip to New York was great, with a rousing speech and response with the ILGWU [garment workers]. I spoke against any expulsion of Israel from the General Assembly and pointed out that it would be difficult for us to stay in that body if Israel was expelled. I also pledged to guarantee New York a $300 million loan as soon as the congressional obstacles were removed. Rosalynn campaigned in Louisiana, Texas, and Mississippi.

SEPTEMBER 30 I had a good meeting with Ellie Smeal, president of NOW. I think we healed old wounds adequately.

OCTOBER 1 Fifty-six years old. If I'm reelected, I'll be sixty when I go out of office—a good retirement age.

Concerning the Persian Gulf War, we've handled it well. We forced Oman not to let Iraq launch an attack from their territory, forced the Saudis to assume a neutral position, sent the AWACS, and consulted on what else needs to be done to defend Saudi oil fields. We informed Iran that all these are peaceful moves to limit and end the war. They're even discussing the hostage release within the Majlis.

I took off on an all-day campaign trip—a constant series of happy birthday greetings and birthday cakes. Went to Detroit and inspected the five new automobiles, and the Ford plant at Wayne, which is making the small new efficient cars, then to Flint, Niagara Falls, and back home. We have an excellent chance to carry Michigan and New York.

OCTOBER 2   Mama fell and broke her right hip, and she's in the Sumter Regional Hospital. Apparently the insertion of a steel pin or plate is a fairly routine operation because of the high number of nursing homes in the area.

OCTOBER 3   I met with Zia and liked him. He's calm, I think very courageous, intelligent. He's willing to accommodate refugees coming into Pakistan from Afghanistan and needs to have his debts rescheduled. We'll sell them F-16s in the future.

I met with the National Association of Women Judges. They were very excited about what I've done to include women in the judiciary.

I then flew down to see Mother, who is in relatively good spirits. I enjoyed being with Billy, Gloria, and Ruth all at once.

OCTOBER 4   Rosalynn, Amy, [Amy's friend] Cricket, and I stopped briefly at Camp David on the way to Spruce Creek. The fishing was difficult, but all of us are much better with our knowledge of the stream and techniques. Wayne took us on a wild trip through his fields. We saw probably two hundred deer, several raccoons, a fox, and two skunks (Amy's favorites). The night before, Wayne and the [White House] stewards saw five black bears. It was cold enough for a big fire.

MONDAY, OCTOBER 6   There was an article in The [Washington] Star—a completely irresponsible rag—that Muskie was dissatisfied and wanting to resign. Ed said it was an absolute lie, that he was really enjoying being secretary of state and it was the best thing that ever happened to him. The irresponsibility of the news media is almost nauseating.

I campaigned in Wisconsin and Illinois, always accompanied by political leaders in Air Force One or my limousine. Christopher called with some potentially good news from Iran, which we'll pursue.

OCTOBER 7   We're pursuing the possible favorable response from Tabatabai and [Ali Akbar Hashemi] Rafsanjani [parliament chairman and later president], but there have been so many disappointments and frustrations that we have to prepare for every eventuality.

Rosalynn and I flew to Annandale, Virginia, to meet with Senator Kennedy and others to sign the Mental Health Systems Act of 1980. It was a pleasant, quick trip. We discussed the extremely negative twist that the press places on every comment I make concerning Reagan. We are disconcerted about it and want to focus the campaign on the issues. Reagan is coasting, staying almost in seclusion from the press or from any sort of interrogation, refuses to debate, and is somewhat ahead in the polls.

OCTOBER 8   I called Mama, who is heartbroken because the Dodgers were eliminated from pennant contention.

I told David [Aaron] and Zbig that SALT II ratification should be separated from the Soviet presence in Afghanistan. SALT II ought to stand on its own, and we need to start spelling out that concept now.

Pat reported that poll results in Illinois, Pennsylvania, and Texas were improving substantially.

OCTOBER 9   I had one of my best campaign days in Tennessee, North Carolina, and Florida. Christopher gave me an encouraging message from Tabatabai: "The American proposal has fallen on fertile ground."

OCTOBER 10   As usual, I got up early to run, then had a signing ceremony for the refugee assistance bill at the [Florida] State Capitol.

I went to Saint Petersburg to see John Pennington. It was an emotional experience. He weighs only about one hundred pounds, has cancer, and probably will not live more than a couple of months. We reminisced about Quitman County.

Pennington was a courageous reporter for The Atlanta Journal *who, in 1962, played a crucial role in my first political campaign, for the state senate. The ballot box had been stuffed against me in Quitman County, Georgia, by an unscrupulous political boss, with 126 people "voting" alphabetically, including many who were dead, in prison, or living elsewhere. The news coverage by Pennington made it possible for me to mount a successful challenge to the results, as described in my book* Turning Point.

Back at the White House I signed the Martin Luther King, Jr., [national] historic site bill and an act to resolve differences between the Maine Indians and the other landholders there.

OCTOBER 11   [My son] Jack and I fished in Little Owens Creek, then I worked all weekend.

I approved a message to the Iranians concerning an inventory of the matériel and spare parts they had ordered prior to the revolution which we could make available for shipment without delay.

MONDAY, OCTOBER 13   We learned that Hussein had induced Saudi Arabia to give support to Iraq. In fact, Iraq is an aggressor nation and is becoming identified as such in the eyes of the world.

Although guilty of corruption and terrible abuses of his own people, Saddam would receive the support of many Sunni Arabs in his war with the Iranians, who were Shiites.

I went on a three-state campaign tour. Scoop Jackson joined me for a rally in a [New York] Jewish center, and I was surprised at the lack of enthusiasm for Scoop in that audience. I marched in the Columbus Day parade, then flew to Marion, Illinois, going down about six hundred feet in a coal mine to meet with miners.

OCTOBER 14   Mubarak came and expressed Sadat's belief that the Iran-Iraq war was good for us and Egypt—a psychological defeat for Saddam Hussein and to convince the crazy regime in Iran that they cannot adequately protect the integrity of their own country without a strong and stable military and good ties with the outside world.

I signed the rail deregulation legislation, which is another major step forward in addition to financial institutions, oil and gas prices, airlines, and trucking. We'll move on communications, I believe successfully, in the months ahead.

This comprehensive deregulation effort brought about profound changes in the relationship between the federal government and the entire free enterprise system. Almost every major decision concerning transportation rates, charges, establishment of new companies or mergers with others, salaries of personnel, and routing of transportation systems had been controlled by government agencies. This had basically removed the element of competition and protected incompetent corporations from failure. An airline, for instance, could be profligate in granting salary increases and maintaining an excessive fleet of planes, knowing that an appeal to raise its rates would be guaranteed. To encourage competition in banking and financing, I authorized more flexibility but retained the strict controls necessary to prevent unlimited risk-taking or abuse of customers.

My remaining goal for deregulation included radio and television. We began the process of deregulating these industries during my administration, and Reagan made additional moves to withdraw oversight during his tenure as president.

OCTOBER 15   I decided that Muskie and I would declare publicly that Iraqi action against Iran was invasion or aggression, which is a fact.

I'm still campaigning every day. In Pittston, Pennsylvania, a little Jewish boy asked me in a town meeting if I thought God heard his prayers. This was an event that was emotional.

Bailey Smith, president of the Southern Baptist Convention, had recently made the ridiculous statement "God Almighty does not hear the prayer of a Jew, for how in the world can God hear the prayer of a man who says that Jesus Christ is not the true Messiah?" This was part of a new and much more exclusive theology that defined the fundamentalist trend. Under pressure, Smith later apologized.

Larry Klein, who headed my task force on economics in 1976, got a Nobel Prize, which did not surprise those of us who know him. I jokingly told Senator Kennedy on the plane [going to Connecticut] that Klein got the prize for giving me such good advice on how to control inflation and reduce interest rates.

OCTOBER 16   We had good news on the economy. Housing starts are up above the 13-million-per-year rate, and general building construction up 15 percent. GNP is going up now instead of dropping. I think the recession's over.

Despite these encouraging reports, the United States and all other countries were severely affected by the doubling of oil prices, exacerbated by the loss of supplies from both Iran and Iraq. This resulted in very high inflation, which high interest rates were designed to control. Unemployment, meanwhile, had risen from just under 6 percent the previous year to 7.5 percent.

Overall, the economy was not in good shape, which was yet another reason my campaign was an uphill battle.

OCTOBER 17   At our foreign affairs breakfast we discussed a script to follow if the hostages are released—dealing with Congress, the families, Cy Vance, foreign leaders, the press.

I talked to Eppie and told him that it would be a very serious thing if Israel annexed the Golan Heights. He agreed and assured me that it would not be done. He also said that the Jews in New York have turned around, and not to worry about them anymore. Our biggest headache up there is Mayor Koch.

OCTOBER 18   Harold reported that the Greeks and Turks have finally agreed to Greek reintegration into NATO. NATO will vote on it Monday.

OCTOBER 19   I spoke at a joint fund-raising unity dinner, a pleasant affair with the proceeds going to Kennedy's campaign debt.

MONDAY, OCTOBER 20   This will be a very difficult week, with a full campaign schedule, Greek integration into NATO, and the hostage negotiations approaching a climax. The NATO council voted on Greece, something we've worked on for three years.

OCTOBER 22   Good, enthusiastic crowds at all the stops, but this is probably the case with Reagan at this late stage of the campaign.

OCTOBER 23   Ham gave me an election analysis that looked fairly good. We have troubles in Florida, where we're five or six points behind, strangely enough. We also have trouble with American Jews. Reagan seems to have been picking up lately.

Harold has completed plans for sweeping mines if the Iranians should try to lay some in the Strait of Hormuz. An interesting satellite photo showed a gas station in Iran with automobiles waiting in a line several miles long.

I interviewed A. W. (Tom) Clausen for president of the World Bank. I offered him the job, and he accepted. Reagan and his people had agreed that Clausen would be acceptable to them.

A delegation of the New York Board of Rabbis came by to invite me to speak to their convention [on their] one-hundredth anniversary in May. I accepted. They are for me, which will help.

OCTOBER 24   The Iranians are still making favorable noises. I think they are playing with us to some degree, relishing the publicity as they've always done, confused internally, but no negative signals of any substance coming out.

At the foreign affairs breakfast we discussed the hostage situation, the possibilities of action if they [the Iranians] should come back with an acceptable proposal after their debate Sunday. Everybody agreed with me that Cy Vance would be a good one to head up our effort in making this a nonpartisan event, and we agreed that Vance might want to go over to Europe to meet with the hostages, since they will probably be there around five days for medical examinations, debriefings, et cetera, before coming home.

Ham reported some good poll results out of Florida for a change. This helps to counterbalance my bad feeling with a 1 percent increase in inflation last month. The only thing we can do is emphasize the highly inflationary nature of the Reagan-Kemp-Roth proposal and the noninflationary effect of our own tax proposals.

OCTOBER 25   I went to Grand Rapids, Michigan. I found out later I called it "Cedar Rapids." When Gerald Ford went out castigating me for it, he shouted to the TV cameras that apparently I didn't even know that Michigan was "one of the forty-eight states."

The political group prepared some talking points on each of the prospective eight or nine questions that will get into the debate. I spent several sessions with them.

OCTOBER 26   The Iranian Majlis is approaching the time of decision. None of the votes have gone against our position, but hard-liners are still trying to prevent the release of the hostages. Our object in all our statements is to play down the prospect of the hostages being released in order to lower expectations, but unfortunately they've built up anyway because the hostage issue dominates the news.

In our own assessments and in public opinion polls, it was obvious that the plight of our hostages was the dominant concern of American voters. Walter

Cronkite closed each of his CBS evening news programs by announcing the number of days they had been held, and ABC launched The Iran Crisis: America Held Hostage *in November 1979. (This show later developed into* Nightline, *with host Ted Koppel.) With the anniversary of the hostages' capture fast approaching, newspapers and all other media had a similar focus. It was increasingly clear to me and my advisors that if we could not secure the release of the hostages before the election—an unlikely prospect at best—our chances of beating Reagan were slim.*

I talked to Amy on the phone about the upcoming debate. I won't see her again for about a week. She said that the atomic bomb was the most important issue, and we had a discussion about what a kiloton was, what a megaton was. She discusses international issues, including the hostage crisis, almost like an adult.

MONDAY, OCTOBER 27 We moved out to Cleveland to get ready for the debate. Rosalynn is campaigning in the Northeast and will join me tomorrow.

I had benefited greatly from the three debates with Gerald Ford in 1976, and we had originally wanted multiple debates with Reagan in different parts of the country. He had shrewdly decided, as the clear front-runner, to limit our joint appearance to this one event, where detailed knowledge of issues would be of little benefit compared to an overall image of us two candidates. As a professional actor, he felt that this would be to his advantage.

OCTOBER 28 In the debate itself it was hard to judge the general demeanor that was projected to the viewers. Reagan was "Aw, shucks" . . . this and that . . . "I'm a grandfather, and I would never get this nation in a war" . . . and "I love peace . . ." He has his memorized tapes. He pushes a button, and they come out. He apparently made a better impression on the TV audience than I did, but I made all our points to the constituency groups—which we believe will become preeminent in the public's mind as they approach the point a week from now of actually going to the polls. Both sides felt good after the debate. We'll see whose basic strategy is best when the returns come in next Tuesday.

On balance, Reagan clearly gained from this single exchange, alleviating previous public concern that he would engage our country in war, introduce an extreme right-wing political philosophy, cut social programs, and create huge deficits. The debate provided me with my last opportunity to overcome the negative effect of the hostage crisis, and though I was generally pleased with my effort, it was not sufficient to improve my position in the race.

In June 1983, it was reported that a copy of my confidential briefing book had been stolen from the White House and delivered to Reagan's campaign team prior to the debate. The report (undisputed) was that Reagan's aides had used the notes to prepare my opponent to counteract my planned debate tactics.

OCTOBER 29   Still confusion in Iran. The Majlis votes in our favor, roughly 100–80, but it takes a two-thirds attendance for a quorum, and some of the members refuse to attend. Khomeini is apparently displeased because the Majlis has rendered itself ineffective by deliberately not having a quorum.

We had a town meeting in Pittsburgh, an exciting outdoor rally in Rochester, New York, then to Newark for a black church rally with the ministers of New Jersey, then to an Essex County fund-raiser, which they say was the best they've ever had. We then flew to Philadelphia to spend the night.

OCTOBER 30   Went to a Polish American meeting, a good Jewish meeting, then to New York for the annual Seventh Avenue Garment District Parade. We then flew to the upper peninsula of Michigan near Saginaw for a town meeting, then to Saint Louis, Missouri, for an outdoor rally where I emphasized the parallel between myself and Harry Truman, then to Columbia, South Carolina, where I spent the night with Governor Dick Riley, exhausted.

The postdebate figures on Pat's "internals" don't look good for us. Reagan apparently improved more than I did. Nobody knows.

OCTOBER 31   We then went to the Columbia Township Auditorium for a town meeting, then to Lakeland, Florida, for an outdoor rally, then to Memphis for a televised town hall meeting, where I emphasized agriculture and gave a response concerning the attacks on me by the Moral Majority. From Memphis to Jackson, Mississippi, where we had a rally in front of the Governor's Mansion, then on to Houston, Texas, where we had a very exciting rally.

My hands are getting scratched up on the back, because the crowd gets emotional and a lot of people weep. It's kind of a high-pitched shrill sound that comes out of crowds now. I'm sure that as the election approaches, something happens to other candidates, but there's a lot more intensity of interest than in weeks gone by.

NOVEMBER 1   After [I went] jogging as usual, we went to Brownsville, San Antonio, and to Abilene for one of the largest crowds they've had in West Texas, to the stockyards in Fort Worth. After that we flew up to Milwaukee, then to Chicago.

I was expecting a call from the State Department, because indications are that the Majlis will have a quorum when they convene.

NOVEMBER 2   Before I went to bed I was told that they have a quorum at the Majlis. They would debate three or four hours. At 3:45 [a.m.] Warren Christopher called to say that the Majlis had approved four points compatible with what Khomeini has announced and what Warren discussed with Tabatabai. They were transmitting the message to us. I met with Hamilton and Jody and decided to return to Washington.

The Majlis proposal is not acceptable. They've got words like "confiscate the shah's property" and demand that the U.S. government remove all private claims against Iranian assets. These are things we cannot do under our law, and they're not right anyway.

I went through the unofficial Majlis text, identified the problem areas, and prepared a response that goes as far as we can while honoring our nation's principles and law. I also drafted a statement saying that this was a good and constructive move; was a basis for resolving the differences; but emphasizing that we would not let the calendar affect me. We want to see the hostages released, but only if it maintains the honor and integrity of our nation. It's imperative that we tell the Americans the truth, but not build up expectations that might be dashed by the unpredictable Iranians.

Most public opinion polls show Reagan a little ahead of me and that he had a fairly great lead in states like Utah, the Dakotas, Montana, et cetera. I hope we can make up for this by coming slightly ahead in the states where the electoral votes are large.

Pat thinks the trend is in our direction, and CBS pollsters apparently agree. We are almost exactly even with Reagan—two points up on a two-man race—and had overcome all the loss we suffered immediately following the debate.

MONDAY, NOVEMBER 3   I got up at 5:00 and talked to Ed and Warren about developments in Iran. Khomeini met with the militant student leaders and told them he wanted the hostages turned over to the government. He needed the students to help defend Iran on the battlefront. They announced in some way that the Algerians would be "responsible" for the hostages.

A satellite photograph showed that outside the compound there were two large buses that had not been there before, which indicates that the hostages are likely to be moved to another location as the government assumes responsibility for them.

We started off on one final thirty-six-hour tour around the country, while Rosalynn and Fritz did the same thing. One of the themes that I pursued was to call for the Anderson voters to give me their support, pointing out the general compatibility between my views and theirs, and the sharp difference in philosophy between them and Reagan. In the Midwest, including Detroit, and on the West Coast and in Oregon and Washington the crowds were enthusiastic. Our people felt good.

But Pat was getting some very disturbing poll results, showing a massive slippage as people realized the hostages were not coming home. The anniversary date of them having been captured absolutely filled the news media. *Time* and *Newsweek, U.S. News,* all had front-cover stories on the hostages. By Monday, only a tiny portion—19 percent—thought the hostages were going to be coming home anytime soon.

Almost all the undecideds moved to Reagan. Strangely enough, my favorable [ratings] went up—both the way I handled the Iran situation and the percentage that thought it was used for political purposes. There was a general sense of rejection of incumbents.

It was hard to believe the dimensions of what Pat was telling us. But by that evening, as we campaigned in Oregon and Washington, we knew that our prospects for victory had faded away.

NOVEMBER 4   When I got home I talked to Rosalynn. We were remarkably at ease. I told my family what the situation was.

Most of the things we did that were difficult and controversial cost us votes in the long run: Camp David Accords, opening up Africa, dealing with Cuban refugees, Panama Canal Treaty, normalization with China, energy legislation, plus the hostages and the Soviet invasion of Afghanistan — particularly the hostages. Also, the Kennedy attacks for eight months hurt a lot. I spent a major portion of my time trying to recruit back the Democratic constituency that should have been naturally supportive: Jews, Hispanics, blacks, the poor, labor, and so forth.

After we voted, I made a speech on the depot platform, went over to see Mother, and flew back to Washington.

Warren Christopher reported no progress on hostages.

About 7:30 or 8:00, two of the networks called the election for Reagan. I called him about 8:30 and congratulated him, told him I would work with him harmoniously, and we would have a good transition period. About 9:30 I made a concession speech, went to bed, and slept till 7:30 in the morning.

Subsequently, there were news reports and books written about alleged efforts by Reagan supporters to induce the Iranians to hold the hostages until after the election. The most thorough analysis of this question was October Surprise, *written by Gary Sick in 1991. Gary is a retired navy captain who served on the National Security Council staffs under President Ford, me, and Reagan. I prefer to let the reader decide how much credence to give to his claims.*

NOVEMBER 5   We only carried six states. There was a massive shift away from us, and we also lost control of the Senate.

Reagan began the campaign with an 8 percent advantage over me, but I gained over the weeks and we were almost in a dead heat until the last few days of the campaign, when the public realized that the hostages would not be coming home. Reagan won the election with 50.7 percent of the vote, whereas I received 40.0 percent. John Anderson, who was supported by many Democrats who had been loyal to Kennedy, received 6.6 percent.

During the morning we prepared for the interim. I designated Jack Watson to be the head of the transition team.

I met with the press, just a going-away session to let them know we were in good shape and had no hard feelings or bitterness, I was going to have a good transition period, I would be supportive of Reagan if he seemed to make progress on matters important to me, like inflation, unemployment, SALT, and so forth, and reminded the nation that I was still the president until January twentieth.

Then we flew to Camp David to get some rest—both of us pretty well exhausted but in remarkably good spirits. We made a few phone calls, read awhile, walked, went swimming, and discussed the future.

Our first inclination was to have a place near Atlanta so Amy could go to school, but we soon decided we ought to go to Plains and let that be our home base, and set up a transition office and the library documents in the Atlanta area.

Chip and Jeffrey came up to Camp David, also Jody and Frank Moore and their families later on. We just relaxed with our children, extremely surprised at how well we all took the defeat.

The last year had been quite a strain and more unpleasant than the first three years of my tenure. I regretted very much losing the election, and Rosalynn and Amy were quite sorrowful. My efforts to reassure them were probably also a help to me.

The interval between an election and the inauguration of a new president lasts a relatively long time, and I was determined not to let anything interfere with my efforts to complete my legislative agenda and deal with pressing foreign issues. Of special interest in the Congress were a few remaining energy proposals, the Alaska lands legislation, and the Superfund bill that was designed to deal with toxic wastes. Bringing the hostages home, continuing our efforts to achieve peace in the Middle East, and the Soviet occupation of Afghanistan all remained urgent challenges. By the time of Reagan's inauguration, the domestic legislation on my agenda had become law, the hostages were safe, most of my staff had made plans for the future—and I was reconciled to life as a private citizen.

NOVEMBER 6   I spent all day at Camp David making four very complicated little fly line drying reels. I want to give one to fishing friends Wayne Harpster, Lloyd Riss, and George Harvey. I kept one for myself. They were more complicated than I had anticipated, but I thoroughly enjoyed working all day in the carpenter shop. Jody said his father left a completely outfitted carpenter shop in Vienna that he was sure his mother would like for me to keep for him—which would be very pleasant for me, too.

NOVEMBER 7   We flew up to Spruce Creek. Rosalynn and I spent the day on the stream, and all of our friends were there to see us. Not much talk or concern about the outcome of the election.

NOVEMBER 8   We fished and also shot some pheasants and quail. We're planning to have our trout fishing friends up to Camp David to spend one evening with us, to thank them for their hospitality and to enjoy being with them.

I approved and signed all the documents for Christopher to take to Algeria to try to get the hostages released. I made sure that the wording of them was not embarrassing to the United States.

NOVEMBER 9   Ham came up, and we discussed the future. We're going to stay in Plains, commuting to Atlanta. I'll keep a low profile for a few months. He'll work with Kennedy and Mondale to get an acceptable leader for the Democratic National Committee. Ham will teach at Emory, Jody and Frank will stay in Washington, and I asked Phil [Wise], Susan [Clough], and Rosalynn's assistant Madeline [MacBean] to be with us.

MONDAY, NOVEMBER 10   I made fifteen or twenty phone calls and will make another hundred or so in the future. We fished for a while and came back to Washington. Rosalynn was a little depressed during the evening, but I tried to cheer her up. The depression hasn't reached me at all.

Reagan (or his advisors) is backing off from all his politically attractive but controversial positions. His major points were lifting the grain embargo against the Soviet Union, abolishing the Department of Energy, repealing the windfall profits tax—I don't believe he'll do any of those. News reports say he's now backing off his commitment to eliminate the Department of Education; his Reagan-Kemp-Roth tax proposal to cut taxes 30 percent in three years—he's equivocating on that. It doesn't leave him much in the way of campaign commitments that he's going to carry out, but this assessment may be incorrect.

NOVEMBER 11   A holiday. Lloyd Cutler offered to help me with speaking and book-writing contracts, very encouraging. He said I have almost complete control over my presidential papers and will enjoy being an ex-president a lot more than being president.

Lloyd was correct. Later, I saw a New Yorker *cartoon that mirrored this sentiment. A little boy is looking up at his father and says, "Daddy, when I grow up I want to be a former president."*

I'll be finding jobs for all our people. There are business leaders, and we can help in universities around the country.

I worked on the next budgets, and then we spent a couple of hours watching the Voyager pass Saturn. This has been one of our best scientific efforts. The displays were going on a couple hours a day. I decided to approve the Venus radar probe to penetrate the shroud of atmosphere and see what the topography is like. This will be good news for NASA.

NOVEMBER 12   The Algerians sent a delegation to Iran last night, but no response back from them yet.

The newspapers are beginning to assess what's happened economically recently. Through 1978 for [the previous] fifty years there had been a steady increase in real federal spending, but for the last two years and continuing under my administration there's been a steady decrease in federal government expenditures per capita. The same thing applies with the effectiveness of the civil service system. In a senior staff meeting, Fred Kahn said we had shifted to a new role for the Democratic Party: one of economic realism combined with compassion. We agreed in international affairs we had accommodated the upsurge in Third World influence, dealt with the Soviet challenge, maintained the peace, opened up China, and strengthened our alliances.

The foreign minister of Algeria sent our response to Iran. If they reject [it], that's the end of it, because we can't go any further. The form or the procedures might be subject to some negotiation.

I told Ed to explore the possibility of selling medicines to Cuba and maybe establishing some sort of direct air flights.

The Alaska lands bill passed the Congress and was on the way to my desk for signature!

NOVEMBER 13   I gave Democratic congressional leaders an analysis of some of the factors in the election and how we need to address any changes that Reagan wants to make concerning Departments of Energy, Education, Kemp-Roth, grain embargo, personnel freeze, SALT, and so forth. Afterward, Muskie suggested the possibility of a Begin-Sadat summit with me before I go out of office. I'll see whether Reagan would be willing to commit to a possible summit after he is president. That would be the best way to keep the Camp David Accords going.

I met with Prime Minister Begin privately. He was ill at ease at first. I told him that I had accepted the result of the election with equanimity, and this had a surprising effect on him for some reason. I thanked him for his contribution to the Camp David Accords and peace treaty. I told him that it would be a serious mistake for Israel to annex the Golan Heights—an abandonment by Israel of a commitment to UN 242, and also a violation of the commitment made in the Camp David Accords. He didn't respond, but I think he was impressed. We then made a brief statement to the press, emphasizing the binding nature of the Camp David Accords and the peace treaty.

Sol Linowitz came to say that since I was such a young retired president I should open up a new and much broader scope for my future activities. I then met with Howard Baker—the best possible Republican leader we could have.

NOVEMBER 14   Fritz told me he may run for the Senate in Minnesota, or for president in 1984. He was quite critical of Kennedy—both the way Kennedy acted in the primary season and also the attitude of the Kennedy staff recently. It's gratifying and quite remarkable that Fritz and I have gotten along so well. I genuinely like him and respect him. He's a close friend, and we've had no serious disagreements. He's expressed himself, I believe, without restraint. We've not always agreed on every issue, but he's accepted my final judgment with complete loyalty. Our staffs have worked harmoniously, and he's performed well every task I've given him. Joan has been a great asset to our administration and to the nation. And I really wish him well.

I devoted the afternoon to telephone calls—thanking people.

NOVEMBER 15   Al Moses came to urge me not to build up the offensive capability of the F-15s, not to expedite their delivery, and not to sell AWACS to the Saudi Arabians. I told him I was really disgusted with the American Jewish community, making these kinds of demands. I had told them during the campaign that we would not build up the offensive capability of F-15s, and for him to come in here now and add additional requests was very aggravating to me. He said the Jewish community eventually would see the great contribution I made to Israel. I told him that may or may not be true, but it certainly was not indicated by the outcome of the elections, when the Hispanics and blacks with an overwhelming majority—better than 80 percent—supported me, and the Jews didn't even give me a majority. I told him I was not bitter about it, which I'm not, but that I would never understand it. He said it was Andy Young, Southern Baptists, and Billy-Libya issues. Al's an outstanding person and can't help the fact that most of the Jewish leaders eventually supported me but the rank and file didn't. I pointed out, though, that we spent an enormous amount of political time and capital trying to get the 45 percent or so vote that we finally did derive from the Jews. I would have been better off if I had ignored them, I think.

I still have deep regrets about the fact that I alienated many American Jews during my time as president, and over many years I have attempted to understand the reasons. The Israel-Egypt peace treaty has remained intact since it was signed in March 1979, but when I pressed Israel, during and after my presidency, to withdraw from other occupied Arab territory as a necessary prerequisite to peace, I was considered by some Jewish Americans to be anti-Israel.

NOVEMBER 16   I enjoyed teaching the Sunday school class. The visiting preacher, Dr. Broach, spoke very bluntly about the Moral Majority and its threat as ayatollahs of religion in our country.

MONDAY, NOVEMBER 17   Helmut [Schmidt] continues to make snide remarks about how glad he is to finally have a strong and consistent administration in Washington. I guess he can't resist the temptation.

NOVEMBER 18   At our weekly foreign affairs breakfast we discussed the hostages, Poland, Nicaragua, Mideast, Kim Dae Jung, and the Saudis' F-15s. The Saudis put tremendous pressure on David Jones, and no one could figure out how Al Moses knew about this before David got back home and reported it to Harold Brown. Zbig is eager to move forward on enhancement of the F-15 airplanes. This is a decision we can't make unilaterally, and I'm going to finesse it if possible and put the burden on Reagan, because it requires congressional approval and a twenty-day notification period.

I met with Danny Inouye, who was almost emotional in his friendship and support for me. He's been a staunch ally and a great man—probably my strongest supporter in the Senate or maybe the entire Congress. He thinks the Kennedy campaign not only cost me the election but also a number of Senate seats. He's very disappointed in Bob Byrd as the disloyal Democratic majority leader.

There was a nice reception for Cy and Gay Vance at the State Department, which we attended. I've been blessed with two fine secretaries of state.

NOVEMBER 19   In my address to the OAS (my sixth visit), I emphasized nonintervention in Latin American countries, ratification of the Tlatelolco treaty [this was done], economic development, long-range impact of the Panama Canal treaties, democratization, and human rights.

NOVEMBER 20   Because of all the critical statements Schmidt has made, both privately and publicly, Jody and Zbig refused to attend the [Washington] luncheon and participate in the conversation. Schmidt was negative about everything, but he and I both made a generous statement about each other to the press. I'm glad to deliver Schmidt and Begin to Reagan. Hans-Dietrich Genscher and other German leaders have been remarkably helpful to us, in spite of Schmidt's negative attitude. Also, the leaders of all other Western nations have been very constructive and basically friendly.

I met alone with Reagan in the Oval Office, and we had a friendly and unrestrained discussion. He listened primarily and made a few remarks, apparently excerpted from his basic campaign speech.

I told him he ought to set aside a day and a half or two days to be briefed on his responsibilities under the SIOP [Single Integrated Operational Plan, the procedure for deployment of nuclear weapons]; described special arrangement on intelligence with the People's Republic of China; agreements with Britain and France on the handling of nuclear materials and launching a nuclear attack; support for Afghan freedom fighters and Pakistan; achievement with stealth airplanes and the reasons why we did not need the B-1; importance of Strategic Arms Limitation discussions;

need for him to announce that SALT II would be effective until a more acceptable treaty was negotiated; and importance of the nonproliferation policy. I told him I would go ahead with the second round of draft registration before Inauguration Day to give him some time to decide the permanent status of draft registration.

I mentioned the Superfund disposal plan for toxic wastes and told him our personnel freeze had cut down sixty thousand or more permanent employees. I emphasized the need for the MX, which had taken ten years to develop. I brought him up-to-date on the hostage situation, told him we would keep his people informed. I asked him who would be his spokesman on foreign affairs and defense, and he said Richard Allen. I presumed that after he designates secretaries of defense and state that we can deal with them as well as Allen. I told him that Schmidt had refused to deploy neutron weapons unless a second Continental nation agreed, and predicted that Germany's orientation toward the East would be a continuing problem.

I urged him to continue the Camp David process, including having a summit meeting with Begin and Sadat after he was in office, and he said that would be a good idea. I described the question of the F-15 sales to the Saudi Arabians and told him he and I would have to agree before our nation adopted a policy. He said he understood and that we would have to be in harmony. I described the special problem with Kim Dae Jung possibly being executed, and thanked him for the message they [Reagan's staff] sent about the same issue.

The only original statement he made was that he was very envious of the South Koreans in the way they handled demonstrators, that when President Park was faced with students demonstrating on a campus he closed all the universities and drafted the demonstrators into the army. He described how envious he was of the authority that the president of Korea had.

We had some photographs made with Nancy, who had returned from touring the White House with Rosalynn, and then the Reagans departed.

Only two successive presidents could have covered the range of sensitive subjects Reagan and I discussed that day. Surprisingly, however, the entire Republican transition team subsequently refused to participate in or even be briefed by us on the most politically controversial subjects—including our hostages in Iran, the sale of F-15s to Saudi Arabia, the observation site in western China, and the succeeding year's budget.

I never knew whether the decision to forgo further briefings was made by President Reagan or whether his subordinates believed that this tactic would allow them to refuse to assume any responsibility for events or decisions that later might prove to be unpopular.

I talked to Howard Baker and Bob Byrd about getting Superfund legislation passed, and then we went to Camp David. All the trees and roads were covered with ice, so we couldn't run.

NOVEMBER 21   Christopher reported that the Iranians and Algerians would meet tomorrow, and the likelihood was that the Iranians would demand that we clarify our terms.

Muskie told me about plans to invite President Chun from South Korea to the inauguration. It's unbelievable to me, but I suspect that dictators around the world are rejoicing because of the outcome of the election. I received a message from Ed Meese that Reagan would not comment one way or the other on F-15 sales to Saudi Arabia. After lunch I ran and then our guests arrived—our trout-fishing friends. We had demonstrations on how to tie leaders, flies, how to make bamboo rods and dip nets, how to cast—with different types and weights of rods and lines. We saw some movies, and a lecture on how to handle the chalk streams in England. [Rod maker] Tom Maxwell brought me a bamboo rod that the people at Leonard Company had made—especially beautiful, and a delight to cast. Everybody got along well—even [fisherman and author] Vince Marinaro, who's an old curmudgeon. He brought along his six-foot, one-ounce split bamboo rod. It's a marvel.

MONDAY, NOVEMBER 24   I met with Fritz, Ed, Harold, and Zbig. We were taken aback that Reagan has refused to take a position one way or the other [on F-15 sales to Saudi Arabia]. It's necessary for us to work in harmony because a decision can't be concluded through the Congress until after inauguration. The Senate passed the Superfund bill, which is a major achievement.

NOVEMBER 25   Jerry Brown came to recommend Chuck Manatt as DNC chairman, and I added Moon Landrieu, Neil Goldschmidt, and others as okay with me. He had attended a party by Marty Peretz (editor of *The New*

Republic) and other prominent Democrats and said there was absolute disarray among them. I told him it was typical of Washington.

NOVEMBER 26   I'll be very strict with staff members on what documents they can retain, but will give them access to the files in Atlanta. Each staff member will have to sign an agreement to comply.

I told Muskie to express concern about the departure of South Korea from democracy. We've been too timid with Premier Chun.

I instructed Christopher to prepare a positive response to the Iranians that they could use for propaganda purposes—and have an addendum of the caveats through which we could deal with our legitimate claims against Iran.

NOVEMBER 29   We prepared our response for Iran. I don't want to get sidetracked on a claims settlement mechanism and decided that we should offer to the Iranians either the World Court or the International Chamber of Commerce as a claims settlement mechanism or offer a bilateral procedure. We still don't have any sure word as to who is in charge of the hostages. The militants claim they've turned them over to the government, but the government refuses to acknowledge that this has been done. They're all liars, so there's no way to tell what the facts might be.

MONDAY, DECEMBER 1   Christopher called this morning saying that he shared my message to Iran with [Algerian ambassador Redha] Malek. His suggestion is that we let the Iranians know this is our final proposal. They can either accept or reject it.

Stan Turner gave me a briefing on China's intelligence relationship. He recapitulated the advantages to our country of the SALT II agreement and the almost unbelievable explosion of missile production that would be available to the Soviets absent the SALT II restraints.

DECEMBER 2   At our final congressional leadership breakfast there was a degree of relief that Democrats will not be responsible for all the problems in the future. Tip came in very tense because in January we had to extend the debt limit, which would run out late in February. Bob Byrd informed Tip that Democrats in the Senate had decided to let the Republicans worry about it and let them scrape up the votes for a change. Tip was instantly astonished and relieved just to think about such a situation.

I signed the Alaska lands legislation, which is a very important achievement. Some people had been working on it even before Alaska became a state in 1958. A comparison of what we originally proposed early in my administration and what finally passed shows a remarkable compatibility. It was an exciting ceremony.

The Alaska National Interest Lands Conservation Act set aside for conservation an area larger than the state of California, including four national forests, ten national preserves, sixteen national wildlife refuges, and seven national parks. This doubled the size of our national parks, tripled our wilderness areas, and protected twenty-five free-flowing rivers in their natural state. It opened 95 percent of Alaska for unrestricted oil and gas exploration while providing special protection to an area known as the Arctic National Wildlife Refuge and prohibiting oil exploration within the refuge unless the president and both houses of Congress agreed to allow it. We never dreamed that Republican administrations would make opening the refuge to exploration a major goal, and I spent a lot of time and energy during the next thirty years helping to defeat all these efforts.

We're trying to get Superfund through the House as a last major objective.

Our package of energy proposals was passed almost in its entirety, with some details changed to accommodate special congressional interests. This legislation resulted in reducing imported oil from 8.7 million barrels per day (bpd) when I took office to 4.3 million bpd within five years. A strong commitment was made to increase the use of renewable energy, and there were mandatory improvements in efficiency of buildings, industrial equipment, and transportation. One concession was that motor vehicle efficiency requirements could be reduced or postponed by presidential action, and my successors permitted this to be done. Twenty-five years later, motor vehicle efficiency had not been appreciably increased. In addition, Reagan promulgated a public claim that the United States was too great a nation to be restricted in its uninhibited use of all kinds of energy, and refused to finance some of the authorized legislation. By 2007, the United States imported over 12 million bpd.

DECEMBER 3   I told Christopher in Algeria that the negotiating phase with Iran was over. They had to either take or reject our present proposal.

We had a last official meeting with the cabinet. It was pleasant, almost emotional. If we had had a tape recording of the brief reports the members made about what they've been able to accomplish in the last four years—and the American people could have heard it—we never would have lost the election. We reviewed the vast improvement in agencies formerly discredited, like GSA [General Services Administration], SBA [Small Business Administration], OSHA [Occupational Safety and Health Administration], HUD, EPA, and CIA. There had been no scandal, a restoration of federalism, quality of ambassadors, enhancement of international trade, involvement in government of minorities and women, relations with the Third World.

I reminded them not to be timid: we will run the government until January 20 and need not ask permission or consult with the Reagan forces unless they consider it advisable, but to keep the new team informed when appropriate.

I continued to meet with staff members to discuss the future.

Reagan hasn't even met with his senior advisors for the last ten days. This is inconceivable to me.

DECEMBER 4   Reagan's team asked for the use of the Situation Room so they can make a telephone call to Reagan, so maybe his official activities are going to pick up.

I sent a hotline message to Brezhnev and issued a statement. The Soviets are between a rock and a hard place. They can't afford to let their socialist system break down in Poland, but are outcasts partially because of Afghanistan and this would be the end of détente. I'd hate to be in their position, but we've got to do all we can to keep them from invading Poland.

DECEMBER 5   I decided to hold all aid to El Salvador because we have information the security forces were involved in the murder of several Catholic nuns, some of whom are Americans.

I directed Muskie to settle with the Israelis on compensation for their sinking the USS *Liberty* [in 1967].

Harold will visit South Korea and deliver a very strong message to Chun and military leaders about the adverse consequences of the execution of Kim Dae Jung.

DECEMBER 7   We went to Sunday school at our church, then to Georgetown to hear Billy Graham preach.

MONDAY, DECEMBER 8 [California congressman] Jim Corman came by to express his friendship and his conviction that my early concession [on election night] did not influence the western elections. I'll never be sure he's right, since he lost very narrowly.

Christopher called to say that the Iranians had asked us to define the shah's family, out to second cousins and grandnieces and so forth—which is ridiculous. Since this is the only question they've asked, it may be that they've accepted the other provisions of our proposal.

Ham and others want me to get involved in choosing a DNC chairman. Bill Clinton, Moon Landrieu, Chuck Manatt, and others are maneuvering for support. If Strauss, Tip O'Neill, and I agree on someone, we can probably prevail, but I'm inclined to stay aloof until the dust settles.

DECEMBER 9 The Algerians are actively pushing the Iranians to accept our latest proposal.

The leaders of FLAG [Family Liaison Action Group] brought me and Rosalynn some yellow roses and said we had performed exactly right in dealing with the hostage question.

DECEMBER 10 It seems obvious that the hostages have now been turned over to the government. They are sending letters to their families, fairly optimistic.

Rickover advised me to stay quiet for a good while—maybe a couple of years—and then run for president again. He thinks I would have no trouble in being reelected because Reagan is both dumb and incompetent, and like a congressman who votes for all the expenditures and votes against all the revenue bills and extension of the debt limit. He thought I won the debate with Reagan. He thinks the military-industrial complex is ten times more of a threat to this nation now than it was when Eisenhower went out of office.

Admiral Rickover never had much political judgment, but he understood the relationships among the Congress, defense contractors, and the Department of Defense as well as anyone. His long and distinguished career ended abruptly: in late 1981, Rickover's wife heard on the radio that President Reagan had retired the admiral, who was on a new submarine conducting sea trials, and she had to give him the news. Several weeks later, he was invited to the Oval Office and decided to don his full dress uniform. He told me that he refused to take a seat, listened to the president ask him to be his special nuclear advisor, replied "Mr. President, that is bullshit," and then walked out.

Bill Clinton came to see me. He's inclined to run for chairman of the DNC. I didn't encourage him or discourage him, but told him to make an all-out effort if he decided to get into it, and he'd have to forgo running for public office in 1982 and possibly '84.

I enjoyed having Walter Cronkite come by. He's getting ready to retire from his regular job, but he said he has enough requests even from CBS to stay busy almost on a full-time basis. He seemed primarily concerned about arms control and said he was genuinely disappointed when I was defeated. It was a deep feeling of his, aside from his professional inclination, to be objective, and he couldn't deny the fact that the press had been partially responsible for the outcome of the election.

DECEMBER 11 I signed the Superfund legislation—another landmark bill. I pointed out to the crowd how productive this so-called lame-duck congressional session had been.

Zbig expressed his concern, which I share, about the Finlandization of Germany, where they're an ally but everything is decided on whether it will or will not displease the Soviets. Intelligence is that the Soviets are preparing for an invasion of Poland. They are surveying invasion routes, have a complete communication system throughout Poland, and are doing reconnaissance flights out of Czechoslovakia and East Germany. The French have suggested that we have our foreign ministers meet immediately if the Soviets invade.

We continue to have long budget sessions. Now we'll have to put together my final decisions [absent Reagan's involvement].

My emissaries came back from El Salvador. They are going through a bloodbath there, having killed perhaps nine thousand people and buried them. They don't have anybody in the jails; they are all dead. It's their accepted way of enforcing the so-called law.

We went out to a party at [White House social secretary] Gretchen Poston's house, about twenty people there. Gretchen is one of my favorites, but once every two or three months is often enough for a party like this around Washington.

DECEMBER 12　Instead of our regular foreign affairs breakfast, with Harold and Ed in Europe, we drafted a response to Iran's two questions: claims against individual Iranians who damaged American property, and how to estimate the shah's assets in the United States. In effect, we finessed both of them but gave the Iranians some verbiage that they may offer to their own public as a claim of victory. I would estimate the shah's assets to be one thousandth as much as the Iranians claim.

I told Sol Linowitz on the phone to go ahead and get as much of a three-nation agreement as possible on what we've accomplished already, and what we still have to do. My belief is that the Israelis have boxed themselves in. Had Begin acted in good faith to carry out the Camp David provisions, they would have had permanent peace, good relationships with their allies, and guaranteed security. Maybe the Israelis will see this sometime in the future.

Jack [Watson] asked me if I wanted to have any special pardons for people, bypassing the regular processes. I told him no, but I'd like to see David Hall [Oklahoma governor incarcerated for mishandling retirement funds] pardoned if he can be approved through the regular process.

Nancy Reagan created something of a furor this morning when she said she thought it would be appropriate for me and Rosalynn to move out of the White House into Blair House early so she and Ronnie could decorate it before they move in. The female press is having a little field day over this, but Rosalynn is going to stay mute and not respond.

After a late departure for Camp David, Rosalynn and I jogged, got in the sauna, went swimming, had a drink, ate a good supper, and watched an excellent movie, *Competition*.

DECEMBER 14　We came back to the White House early to hear Amy play a solo in a violin recital. She was very good.

MONDAY, DECEMBER 15　The hostage families said they prefer no Christmas lights on the tree until the hostages come home.

Congress worked all night and finally passed the continuing budget resolution that is highly acceptable to us.

DECEMBER 16　I met with the Advisory Committee for Women. Lynda Robb has done a good job, and they are almost emotional in their approval for what we have tried and actually done. If they, the blacks, Hispanics, consumers, and environmentalists had been as friendly toward me a year ago as [they are] now that I'm going out of office, I would not have had any trouble getting reelected.

The White House is jam-packed full of visitors. I dread going over there for a meal, and I guess it's even worse on Rosalynn. It's like a hotel. Each one of the people is nice and welcome—but collectively there are just too many.

Strauss came by at my request to discuss the DNC chairmanship and said he had had fifteen hundred or more people urge him to run for president. I responded that being chairman would be a good route to a campaign of his own, and he said that if he ran he could be elected.

DECEMBER 17   The Polish Memorial Day for slain union members held in Gdansk went off very well. Walesa calmed down the labor movement and formed a fairly close relationship with the [puppet] Communist regime. This should defuse the threat of Soviet intervention at least for the foreseeable future. Bob Novak told Zbig that on his recent visit to Poland there was a general agreement that our administration was going out of office with the flags flying, having probably saved Poland from a Soviet takeover by the way we handled the threat.

Reagan announced that [Alexander] Haig would be his nominee for secretary of state. In my judgment this is a very serious mistake, for him and for the country.

Haig was to become most famous for his remark "I am in control here" after Reagan was shot and wounded in March 1981. Haig was also accused of giving a "green light" to Israeli leaders for their invasion of Lebanon in June 1982. He denied this but was replaced as secretary of state by George Shultz a month later.

At the NSC meeting I pointed out that we couldn't meet in this next ten years a direct Soviet intrusion into Iran with conventional ground forces, and that we had to make it clear to the Soviets and to the world that such an invasion would precipitate a worldwide confrontation between us and the Soviet Union and would not be necessarily restricted to conventional armaments.

I pointed out that the Defense demands for expenditures comprise a bottomless pit. One of the most serious problems that we have, as I've said many times to this group, is the inclination on the part of our military leaders, the Joint Chiefs of Staff, the civilian leaders as well, to savage themselves, denigrating American military capability. This hurts our own country, our allies' confidence in us, and encourages the Soviet Union.

A major continuing commitment to arms control is absolutely imperative — not only for us but for the Soviets — because the budget's going to be increasingly limited in the years ahead no matter who is serving as president.

I think if we can buy at least five or six years' time in getting along with the Soviets, at least on a shaky détente — the trends are moving against them, at least if my policies are continued by the next administration. Our emphasis on the Third World, human rights, peace, arms control — I think [these policies] would provide the prevailing influence, and the Soviets could not gain against us on that basis. We also need a strategy for economic warfare against the Soviet Union if it's necessary. We also need to build up our Caribbean military forces as a clear but quiet signal to everyone that we will protect our interests in that region. Based on these points, we'll develop a presidential directive to be issued secretly before I go out of office.

It was increasingly clear to us that the existing Soviet Union had serious weaknesses, as was later made apparent by its loss of influence within the international community and failure to conquer Afghanistan after nine years of occupation, even with two thousand tanks and one hundred thousand troops. During the same period, the Soviet economy was sagging and public dissatisfaction with the political system resulted in the choice of reformer Mikhail Gorbachev as leader in 1988. The Berlin Wall fell in November 1989, and in 1990 the other Soviet republics won the right to hold their own elections and soon demanded independence from Moscow, a process that was completed on the last day of 1991. Within the Soviet Union and its occupied nations, the demand of millions of people for increased freedom and human rights ultimately prevailed.

I had a feeling of alienation at the evening party for White House correspondents, about twelve hundred of them, but it was surprising how many individual members were genuinely supportive and friendly as they came through the receiving line.

Reagan and the press are playing up the so-called economic emergency. As a matter of fact, with the exception of interest rates, everything is going surprisingly well. Unemployment, inflation, retail sales, gross national product, value of the dollar, trade balance—all these things, even housing starts—are holding up very nicely.

DECEMBER 18   Lloyd and Al Moses came by to give me a briefing on the Billy-Libya case so that I can answer some questions for Justice tomorrow. This is one of the most aggravating things I have ever had to do.

There is nothing pleasant in the final budget review session. As a percentage of GNP and in real dollars the deficit is under very good control, but until the entitlement programs are addressed I see no way to have a balanced budget even with very stringent limits on spending.

The staff are planning to buy me a ten-thousand-dollar Jeep. I told Jack Watson privately that it was excessive and something that they ought not to do. He asked for alternatives, and I told him a television set—which we don't have—or some woodworking equipment for a shop at my house.

DECEMBER 19   I authorized [Don] McHenry to see the PLO representative if necessary, only in his role as Security Council president.

We received through the Algerians [an Iranian] demand for a large deposit, about $25 billion—obviously ridiculous and unacceptable.

Although we've done everything possible to protect Chrysler this year, Lee Iacocca was on TV saying he thought the nation would survive and prosper after January 20. I called Bill Miller to tell Iacocca that it was difficult for us to help him anymore. Iacocca admitted that he was a blabbermouth and said he was going to write me a letter of apology, but I'm not going to forget what he said.

Later, when I was on a nationwide tour promoting the sale of my memoir, Keeping Faith, I visited Iacocca in his office. He brought in his top executives, raised my hand, and said, "This is the man that saved Chrysler." I pointed out that I had just supported the efforts of Treasury Secretary Bill Miller.

DECEMBER 21   Gretchen had covered the White House front lawn with snow for the Peggy Fleming entertainment. We took the children for toboggan rides, and they had a snowman contest.

MONDAY, DECEMBER 22   There was a favorable ruling from the Ninth Circuit Court of Appeals on the legislative veto question. This is something we've been fighting for the last three years, and this may be one of the most profound decisions made in executive versus legislative rights and authority in a long time.

During my term and those of previous presidents, hundreds of laws were passed with the provision that executive decisions would not be final, but subject to later veto by one or both houses of the Congress. These laws confronted me with difficult choices: either to veto the legislation or to sign the bill and take legal action to strike down the veto provision. I had chosen the latter course, and the court ruled that hundreds of laws providing for congressional vetoes of executive-branch actions were unconstitutional.

I gave [White House chief usher] Rex Scouten a list of tree seedlings from the White House grounds that we might plant at home.

Kirbo talked about the warehouse and is also concerned about renting the farms next year, since we've had three crop failures in a row.

I had put all our business interests in the hands of Charles Kirbo, with instructions not to let me know about their status during my presidency. Before I became president, Carter's Warehouse had been a lucrative source of income for us, and our farms were devoted to the production of high-quality peanuts used exclusively for seed. We also had a cotton gin, storage warehouses, a large commercial peanut shelling plant, and we mixed and sold fertilizer. Now Kirbo informed me that we were about $1 million in debt and in danger of losing our business and much of our farmland, including about half of the land that had been in our family since 1833 and the rest since 1904. Luckily, we were able to avoid this outcome by selling the business soon after we came home to Plains. The purchaser was Archer Daniels Midland (ADM), a large corporation that decided, for the first time, to begin buying and processing peanuts.

Peggy Fleming's ice show provided entertainment for our final Christmas parties. She is the loveliest entertainer I've ever met.

DECEMBER 23   All the bridges and roads were frozen over and the helicopters couldn't fly, so we were delayed an hour and a half taking off for home. Mother was taking little steps with a walker, regaining strength faster than had been projected. Amy and I walked down through the woods and found a small but well-shaped Christmas tree, and also one arrowhead.

Rosalynn and I enjoyed looking around, trying to decide how to change our place when we get home. She wants a fence across the front yard, and I want a good woodworking shop, probably in the garage. We'll have to put a floor in the attic to hold more stuff. We've not really spent full-time here in fourteen years, since I began running for governor.

DECEMBER 24   The Algerians are seeing all the hostages, which is good news but no harbinger of a quick resolution of our differences.

DECEMBER 25   I gave Rosalynn a small television set, since we don't have one. She gave me a book on woodworking. The children gave me and Rosalynn good bicycles. We went out to Mama's house and had a good breakfast. Gloria was the hostess. She and Billy are getting along remarkably well. Mother's practical nurse Millie is a jewel and even gets along well with Mother. We then went to Miss Allie's [Rosalynn's mother], had another Christmas there, and [went] back home. We went back to Miss Allie's for lunch, then out to Billy's house and stayed about an hour or so. I enjoyed being with them.

DECEMBER 26   Mama is living in the isolated Pond House, so we decided to put our office in her downtown residence. We flew back to Camp David.

DECEMBER 27   With about two inches of snow on the ground we went out to ski and had a good run down to the old house. I was coming back up around the nature trail, and my right ski hit a rock. I fell and broke my left collarbone. Went in to Bethesda to get it strapped, and after about an hour I returned to Camp David. I spent the day signing the last bills the Congress passed this year, and vetoed a couple.

DECEMBER 28   I stayed fairly inactive to let the swelling in my shoulder and chest go down, took some codeine, and then shifted to Tylenol. No preaching because the roads were iced over.

The Algerians came to give me a report on their visit with our hostages, who were in good shape. The Iranians were quite accommodating and agreed to let mail go back and forth to American families. The Algerians are quite eager to help us negotiate the release of the hostages.

MONDAY, DECEMBER 29   I was mostly reading and sleeping—not my usual custom.

DECEMBER 30   A long walk, and feel much better. I began working on my farewell address. A draft sent up here by Rick [Hertzberg] and Jody is no good.

DECEMBER 31   Haig wanted to postpone a decision about the Saudi F-15s. He'd be better off being able to say that this was a joint decision we had made, and both Reagan and I stand behind it.

We returned to the White House and a mountain of paperwork—decisions to be made before the end of the year. We joined a few others at Jody's house to see the end of 1980, with no regrets. Everybody was in a good mood, looking to the future.

1981

——————

JANUARY 1   I put on a coat and tie for the first time, and we went down to Dobbins Air Base to pick up our Georgia friends, then on to New Orleans for the Sugar Bowl. I had to protect my left shoulder from being jostled [but Herschel Walker, Georgia's Heisman Trophy–winning running back, jerked it pretty hard. Georgia beat Notre Dame 17–10]. The first time Georgia's ever won a national championship. That night I was sore all over and went to bed immediately.

JANUARY 2   At the foreign affairs breakfast we discussed the French conviction that the Soviets are still going to move into Poland. I'm convinced that free labor unions and a totalitarian government cannot live together.

On Iran, I instructed my people to prepare for a breakdown in negotiations and possible hostage trials. I'll declare a state of belligerency or ask Congress to declare war against Iran. We'll freeze the Iranians assets permanently, go directly to the UN Security Council, and call for complete sanctions against Iran. I hope these actions won't be necessary but have had to consider them for the last fourteen months. Military action like a blockade or mining will probably come after these things are done.

Haig and Allen have refused to be briefed on the Iranian situation! We've had no contact with the Reagan people in Defense. [Designated secretary of defense] Cap Weinberger has not even been to the Pentagon and has not designated any deputy—neither has Haig. We've not been able to get any word back from Haig or Reagan on the F-15 sales to Saudi Arabia.

We've gotten favorable reports out of Korea concerning Kim Dae Jung, but the issue is still in doubt.

I discussed with Chip the possibility of his staying with me to help with personal affairs, but I want to leave him completely free to do whatever he chooses. It may be a good time for him to break away from us and be on his own, but we'll let him make that judgment.

JANUARY 4   I taught a lesson from the ninth chapter of Luke, about the service of others being the measure of greatness. It was amazing how some news media distorted what I said into personal references to myself.

I hadn't even chosen the lesson to be taught. In Baptist churches, the Bible text for each Sunday is preordained so that uniform study pamphlets can be prepared.

JANUARY 6   I've been jogging about a half mile and walking another mile, most of the time in heavy shoes, to get some exercise while my collarbone heals.

We assessed the Iranian response to our latest proposal, very close to an acceptance.

Chuck Manatt reported good progress on his campaign for DNC chairman. I promised to help him as chairman, but for several months I would not be involved publicly in affairs of this kind.

We met with Marvin Josephson, a literary agent, and his assistant Lynn Nesbit, who was very attractive to me and Rosalynn as someone with whom we could work. They explained the mechanics of contracting at least one book from me and one from Rosalynn.

JANUARY 7   [Mohammed] Benyahia, the foreign minister of Algeria, expressed concern about our reply to Iran, and I sent Christopher over there to meet with him.

I shook hands with about three hundred people on our staff. For some reason, standing in a receiving line and shaking hands hurts my left broken clavicle worse than anything else I do.

JANUARY 8–9 Economic news is relatively good, with unemployment and inflation going down and interest rates continuing to drop slightly.

We went to Plains to start preparing for the move home — mostly cleaning out to make room for our new stuff. We gave away a lot of clothes, et cetera, to our families and to the stewards who were helping us.

JANUARY 10 Christopher is continuing his effort in Algeria. All the signals coming out of Iran so far are good.

We can't find my two split bamboo rods — to me, two of the most valuable items I own. [They must have been stolen when our things from Camp David were repacked in the White House. The FBI helped look for them but had no success.]

JANUARY 11 I worked on the farewell speech, with the draft from the speechwriters really so disappointing that Rosalynn cried when she read it.

MONDAY, JANUARY 12 The Iranians have asked the Majlis to meet, authorize negotiations through Algeria to resolve the hostage issue.

Some of Begin's cabinet resigned, and he'll have to decide to step down and call elections or stay on as prime minister of a minority government. The results will be the same, one way or the other.

Sol Linowitz wants me to stay active in Democratic Party affairs and perhaps as a member of some boards of directors. He said publishers prefer one book but would be willing to discuss a separate one on the Mideast. If it can all be included together, that would be easier for me.

JANUARY 13 Although the Majlis didn't act yesterday, some of the top officials told the Swiss ambassador that he did not need to see Bruce Laingen and others because the hostages would be released by Friday. We take this report with a grain of salt.

Lloyd Cutler reports trouble with the twelve banks and the Iranian National Bank in clearing up questions concerning the transfer of the $4.8 billion. Also, there would be some delay in transferring the gold to

Algeria. The time's running out, and it would take three or four days after the Iranians agreed on all the issues before we could actually deliver the assets and get the hostages free.

After the hostages were taken, the United States confiscated large sums of Iranian money and about $2 billion worth of gold. Much of the cash had been deposited in U.S. banks, and now that I was ready to assume control of these resources in order to negotiate with Iran, a few greedy bankers were attempting to retain the deposits or extract more profit by making retrospective adjustments in interest. Another complication was that any final deal would have to be understood and approved by the Iranian National Bank.

Neil Goldschmidt delivered to me the report on the automobile industry. About half their problems derive from excessive labor costs, the other half from poor management and suppliers distant from the plants. Their recommendations are likely to cause some disturbance in the automobile industry.

I decided to give Fritz a special Ruger over-under shotgun as a going-away present.

Last night Slava Rostropovich gave an excellent little speech at our table, pointing out that the masses of people were often wrong, that what was significant was the personal relationship that developed between leaders or performers or artists and others, and that we had meant more than anyone in the United States to him and his family when they came here from the Soviet Union. He pointed out that the masses made a mistake on November 4 as they had when they rejected Beethoven's Ninth Symphony, rejected *La Traviata*, and in the first performance of *Tosca* the audience reacted against it so violently that they couldn't even raise the curtain for the third act. He said that history was going to treat my administration the same way they did Verdi, Puccini, and Beethoven.

At night, my shoulders hurt so badly that I had to let Rosalynn take off the strap.

JANUARY 14 I decided to try this day without my shoulder strap on, and Dr. Lukash said it would be okay if I was careful.

The Majlis approved legislation authorizing negotiations. I talked to Chris in Algiers and told him to stay there as long as necessary.

Bill Miller will move on the Chrysler loan, provided the suppliers, lenders, and labor unions will make concessions to keep Chrysler in as sound financial condition as possible. It would mean the reduction of about $1 billion in Chrysler's debt if he can put this together, which is doubtful; then the federal government would guarantee another $400 million loan.

As noted throughout my diary, I had serious problems trying to help the troubled U.S. automobile manufacturers. Except for the bailout loan we made to Chrysler, my experiences when dealing with American auto executives were generally frustrating. They used their influential lobbyists and nationwide panoply of dealers and parts suppliers to oppose every effort to improve efficiency of either production or operation of their vehicles. They seemed determined to produce the more profitable gas guzzlers, ignoring competitive imported cars, costs of very generous labor and retirement commitments, and extra transportation costs from distant parts suppliers.

Ultimately, the unwillingness of the car companies to adapt to the changing marketplace resulted in the bankruptcy of General Motors and Chrysler in 2009. Government mandates forced both companies to restructure and adopt significant reforms, and they are now struggling to recover.

I delivered the farewell address, and the response was good. I described the pressure of special interest groups, how they fragment the country. Primarily I emphasized, however, the threat of nuclear destruction, environmental issues, and consideration for human rights. These are the same themes I used in my acceptance speech in 1976, my inaugural address four years ago, and that I pursued when I was president.

On Iran, the challenge is to overcome the greed of the twelve American bankers and simultaneously keep the Iranian Majlis from throwing a monkey wrench into the whole process. I don't know which of the two entities is going to create the most trouble for me before it's over.

Zbig reported that Giscard said the influence of Germany was going to go down because they've been damaged by their equivocation concerning eastern Europe and Russia, and the pending financial problems that seem to be inevitable.

We sent out over fifty thousand thank-you items, and about one hundred letters to foreign leaders.

JANUARY 15 Eppie Evron came by, almost emotional, to congratulate me on my administration and to thank me for what I had done to help Israel. I told him I would stay active in the future, to restrain Sadat if necessary, and to pursue my concept of what Israel ought to be. I don't see how they can continue as an occupying power depriving the Palestinians of basic human rights, and I don't see how they can absorb 3 million more Arabs into Israel without letting the Jews become a minority in their own country. Begin showed courage in giving up the Sinai. He did it to keep the West Bank.

At this time I preferred to encourage ties between Jordan and the Palestinian territories, but later I supported an independent Palestine alongside Israel. Unfortunately, the situation in the Middle East has deteriorated during the past thirty years, in part because commitments pertaining to "full autonomy" and other rights for Palestinians have not been honored. Palestinians are divided into two major factions, Hamas and Fatah, and peace talks have not been fruitful. Acts of violence against Israel from Palestinians and militants in Lebanon have precipitated massive retaliatory strikes. Hamas controls Gaza, and Israeli military and political control of the occupied territories in East Jerusalem, the West Bank, and the Golan Heights is almost complete. Israeli settlements have far exceeded promises that there would be "no confiscation of land," and "Israel would be restricted to a military presence only in furtherance of the security force to be retained in the West Bank."

Happily, however, both sides have honored meticulously the terms of the peace agreement between Israel and Egypt, which has prevented another war between the two.

I told Lloyd to push the American banks hard, that I did not want them to hold up the hostage release because they were squabbling over who was going to get the money that Iran agreed to forgo.

We had a delightful supper that Lloyd and [his wife] Louise hosted for the cabinet and top staff persons. As I looked around the room, I recognized the tragedy of losing those people to government service for the group of jerks that are coming in to replace us.

JANUARY 16 We spent most of the foreign affairs breakfast talking about Iran. The Iranians made a good proposition to us yesterday based on transferring $8.1 billion to the Bank of England. They would then refund all except about $3 billion of it, release the hostages immediately, and solve the rest of the disputes over interest rates and claims through normal processes in the future.

Ten other banks are acting reasonably about paying a fair rate of interest to Iran on the money they kept for the fourteen months. The Bank of America and one small one are trying to cheat the Iranians, in my judgment, by claiming they couldn't invest all the money profitably and derive for themselves more than $130 million in unearned profits. They could have invested the money on a daily basis, the same as the other ten banks did.

We had a long discussion about this, and I decided to transfer the gold to the Bank of England; dispose of the treasury certificates and have the money in the Bank of England; and when we are sure the Iranians have accepted the proposition, issue an order for the American banks to transfer the funds to the British bank. Final transfers cannot be completed Monday, but at that point the Iranians could go ahead and release the hostages. They have requested that Algeria arrange for transportation and there be a team of Algerian doctors to examine the hostages before they get on the plane to certify that they are in good health. We [later] met executive officers of the twelve banks involved in the $4.8 billion in Europe and convinced them that the overall agreement was in their interest, but some banks held out as long as possible for the lowest possible payment to Iran. I considered bringing the hostages directly back to the U.S., but I figured in the end it would be better for them to go to Wiesbaden, Germany—where we've made arrangements for medical and psychological care.

At the staff meeting we deplored the lack of preparation Reagan's making for taking over next week. They probably won't have a secretary of state, haven't named the deputy, only four NSC staff members have been named, et cetera. This is completely different from the way we handled things when we were coming in.

We had a good Medal of Freedom ceremony. It was somewhat emotional because of the people involved. Warren Christopher, who is in Algiers, Earl Warren, Andy Young, Judge Elbert Tuttle, Mrs. Robert McNamara, Esther Peterson, Roger Baldwin, Walter Cronkite, Zbig, Ed Muskie, Kirk Douglas, Harold Brown, and Gerard Smith.

I talked to Lloyd, who said the banks are willing to pay the full amount of interest into the escrow account. We'll try for a Sunday transfer of the money and asked the Algerians to get the hostages ready to move—both transportation on the Algerian plane and the medical examination before they go to the airport. Lloyd said it was the most complicated financial transaction that he had ever heard of.

JANUARY 17   The Algerians' planes are standing by. I talked to Christopher, who confirmed he had had a tough day. He thought we'd have an agreement by Sunday noon, and the escrow agreement was okay.

JANUARY 18   In church, Bill and Lloyd called to let me know that we had moved on the problems well enough so that Mike Cardozo was bringing the executive orders for me to sign. Christopher reported that everything seemed to be nailed down. The Algerians will announce that they are willing to go forward. Christopher thought it would be better for me to go to Wiesbaden than to Algiers. I was talking to Thatcher and Schmidt when necessary, I called Reagan and gave him an update, and also four hostage family leaders and the widow of Captain Harold Lewis, who was killed in the rescue attempt.

MONDAY, JANUARY 19   Shortly after midnight; now Monday, we got word that two planes had left Ankara, Turkey, on their way to Tehran. About 2:00 a.m. we got word that the three declarations and the adherence had all been signed in Iran. Bill Miller said this is the first time in history that the Bank of England stayed open on the weekend.

About 5:30 a.m. I lay down awhile, and woke up with an uneasy feeling. I called [Deputy Treasury Secretary] Bob Carswell and learned that they still had not received from the Iranian Bank Markazi the technical instructions for transferring the deposits and payment of the recognized debts.

[Algerian minister of foreign affairs] Mohammed Benyahia sent a strong message to Iran, and we got negative reports that the Bank Markazi did not agree with the terms of the papers they had already signed, and were using this refusal to hold up the entire process.

In the meantime we got word that the medical exams have been completed, the hostages were at the airport, the airplanes were ready to take off—but still the Markazi officials will not issue the necessary papers.

Reagan called me at 9:20 to say that if the hostages didn't get out prior to inauguration, he would like for me to go over there in Air Force One and represent our country—which I appreciated very much.

I told Warren Christopher to remind the Algerians that my authority and my legal status would expire at noon on January 20. After that, the entire negotiating process might have to begin anew.

I had not been to bed since early Sunday morning, spending all my time in the Oval Office and sometimes lying down for a few minutes on the couch. I was constantly searching for new ideas, trying to understand clearly one of the most intricate financial and political problems ever faced by any nation. At stake were the lives of fifty-two precious people who had been imprisoned in Iran for 444 days—and almost $12 billion of Iranian assets. I could not afford to make a mistake, and time was an ever-present concern. All the financial and political messages were highly technical and had to be meticulously translated twice in each direction, since the Iranians spoke Persian and the Algerians French.

JANUARY 20   The final approval from Bank Markazi began coming to the twelve banks by telex at 2:00 a.m. and had to be absolutely clear and accurate.

The following entries are excerpted from my written notes about this extraordinary day.

2:23   Bill Miller reports, "It looks good!" [In fact, it was garbled, but Bill didn't have the heart to tell me.]

3:05   Miller: "The test number is correct, but we'll have to correct the errors."
I decide: "Tell the banks to use the garbled text."

3:16   Miller: "The money is moving to London." (Cheers.)

3:40   Carswell: "U.S. federal attorneys in Algiers refuse to sign the agreement."

I ask President [Anthony] Solomon of the Fed in New York to instruct the attorneys to sign. One of the attorneys in Algiers says that he is fainting and cannot discuss the situation further. Again I tell Solomon, "Have them sign the agreement." Solomon: "We can sign with some minor amendments."

4:35   Miller: "The money [from private banks] is in." A total of $7.977 billion has to be transferred from us to the Algerians—the last step before the hostages can be released.

4:38   Christopher: "Algeria will not accept any amendments unless they are first approved by Iran." I participate in a conference call and finally convince everyone that the total package is adequate.

5:00   Solomon to his attorneys: "Sign it!"

5:20   Miller: "It only took two seconds to transfer the money."

6:05   From Tehran control tower: "Line up Flight 133" [containing our hostages].

6:35   Christopher: "The Bank of England has certified that they hold $7.977 billion, the correct amount."

6:47   I place a call to Governor Reagan to give him the good news and am informed that he prefers not to be disturbed.

7:35   Rosalynn comes with a razor and a barber. She says, "Jimmy, you have forgotten to shave, and you need a haircut." The barber cuts my hair while I'm on the phone.

7:55   I get the word from Tehran airport, "Flight 133 ready for take-off!" We all knew that this flight was three airplanes: two 727s and the other to serve as a backup or possible decoy that would carry home the Algerian medical team.

8:28   From Operations Center: "The planes are now at the end of the runway. One Iranian F-4 is active. May be escort."

10:45   Rosalynn: "Jimmy, the Reagans will be here in fifteen minutes. You will have to put on your morning clothes and greet them."

I looked in the mirror as I put on the rented clothes, and wondered if I had aged so much as president or whether I was just exhausted.

I made arrangements for the Secret Service to keep me informed on the way to the inaugural ceremonies. Reagan seemed somewhat disconcerted that no one was in the reviewing stands and there were a large number of ERA banners. He told a series of anecdotes that were remarkably pointless. The one he considered funniest was about an old man who was asked whether he slept with his beard under or over the covers, and then he couldn't sleep. He suggested this might be a good punishment for Khomeini for seizing our hostages.

I consider him to be affable and a decent man, remarkably old in his attitudes. His life seems to be governed by a few anecdotes and vignettes that he has memorized. He doesn't seem to listen when anybody talks to him. He'll have my support and my sympathy when he's president. It's a tough job, and I think he'll have to rely heavily on his advisors and subordinates to make the ultimate policy decisions.

On the inaugural platform, my feelings were of regret that I had lost the election but a sense of relief to be free of the responsibilities for a while. Persistent, though, was my concern that at the last minute the hostages might not be released. I watched the ceremonies as a somewhat detached spectator, without any emotional feelings. I thought the speech was remarkably hackneyed, nothing new and just a collection of campaign material. I was glancing back at the Secret Service agent when the MC said, "Would the president and first lady please come forward." I had an involuntary inclination to stand up with Rosalynn, but I realized he was talking about the Reagans.

As we passed the agent I was informed that all the hostage planes were on the way to the Turkish border. This was one of the happiest moments of my life and colored the entire day—indeed the week—making it enjoyable.

Fritz and Joan joined us in the limousine to drive to Andrews Air Force Base. This is the first time the four of us have ever been in a car because only on very rare occasions did Fritz and I ride in the same vehicle, in order to avoid a catastrophe that might have affected me and him at the same time. The mood during the drive was one of excitement and levity. We made some disparaging remarks about the quality of Reagan's inaugural address, but in general it was a pleasant drive.

We arrived at Andrews, reviewed the troops, they fired a twenty-one-gun salute and played the National Anthem. I shook hands with a few in the crowd, although my shoulder was beginning to hurt pretty badly.

As I approached [what had been] Air Force One, the first person I met was Mrs. [Thomas] Schaefer, whose husband was the senior military officer being held hostage. I put my arms around her, kissed her on the cheek, and she looked up at me and said, "Mr. President, we thank you for what you've done. I hope someday you'll have a chance to meet my husband." I started to tell her that I would be with him tomorrow morning in Wiesbaden, Germany, and as I made the statement I broke down and began to cry, and so did she. It was a happy but emotional moment.

I then shook hands with the other members of our cabinet and senior staff. Everybody was close and friendly. When we arrived where Amy and [her friends] Courtney and Crickett and Emily were, they were all sobbing, so Rosalynn invited them and Nancy [Moore], Nan [Powell], and the children to come on board the plane, although all the seats had already been assigned. They crammed into our cabin for the takeoff. On the way down to Plains we had a chance to talk and make plans for a trip to Germany the following day. It was a genuinely happy flight.

Following the welcome and my remarks to a huge crowd in Plains, we slipped away and went down to the cotton gin, where Jack, Jody, Hamilton, and Frank presented me, on behalf of all the staff, [with] a beautiful collection of machinery and tools for my woodworking shop. I was overwhelmed. It was something I always wanted, and they had done an outstanding job in putting everything together.

At Billy's house I slipped into a back room and watched the hostages landing in Algiers. Benyahia made a statement on behalf of Algeria. Warren Christopher replied on behalf of the United States.

Following that, two good poets from Arkansas, who had been invited by Tom T. Hall [to come to Billy's house], read poems about me and my administration. I responded briefly, and we came back home.

James Whitehead and Miller Williams, the two poets who read that day, taught poetry at the University of Arkansas. Later, when I began writing poetry, they volunteered to accept me as a student. They worked with me for seven years, and in 1995 I published my book of poems, Always a Reckoning.

JANUARY 21   Because of the excitement, we didn't get much sleep. I left at 5:30 a.m., flew by helicopter to Robins Air Force Base [in Georgia], and joined the rest of our group on "Special Air Mission" 26000 [since Reagan now had Air Force One], which had flown in from Washington. Fritz

Mondale, Ed Muskie, Lloyd Cutler, Bill Miller, Rick Hertzberg, Mike Cardozo, Peter Constable, Henry Precht, Gary Sick—plus Phil, Hamilton, Jody, and Susan—made up the team.

About an hour out from Robins, I talked on the radio with Warren Christopher, who was about four hours out from Andrews Air Force Base. He gave me a report on the status of the hostages, and we exchanged congratulations. On the way over to Germany I wrote out on a tablet a fairly detailed report of my negotiations before the hostages were turned loose. Before we landed I went over photographs of each hostage and learned special characteristics of their wives or their history as hostages. I wanted to be as familiar with the individual members of the group as possible.

At the Rhein-Main Air Base in Frankfurt, I was met by Helmut Schmidt, other German officials, and Cy Vance. Cy cautioned me not to mention the rescue operation unless the hostages brought it up. This may have been colored by Cy's sensitivity because of his resignation. We got to the hospital about 9:00 in the morning, German time, and there were tremendous crowds of Americans both at Wiesbaden and at the Rhein-Main airport, very friendly, thanking me for the hostages' freedom.

Dr. [Jerome] Korcak said there were two basic things he wanted to tell me: the hostages had been treated much worse than anyone had anticipated or known; and I was going to be facing some hostility among the hostages toward me. I told him if they could think of any new criticisms that I hadn't faced already in the United States, I would be very surprised.

I went into the room with the hostages with some degree of trepidation, but mostly anticipation. Bruce Laingen met me right outside the door, and we walked into the small dining room. They were very stiff and formal, standing at attention, each one in front of his or her own chair. I had decided to meet each liberated American individually first, and as I reached the first one, we involuntarily embraced. As I went around the room, I spoke to each one, tried to say something about their background or their family, and then put my arms around them. Some of them kissed me on the cheek. I was relieved and pleased.

When I finished greeting all the hostages assembled there, Bruce said a few words, and then I made a short statement. We had prepared a text, but I spoke off-the-cuff, emphasizing to them how deeply they had been loved; how completely committed our nation was to their safety; how proud we were of them and considered them to be heroes; how inevitable it was that I, American officials, and they would make some mistakes in the long

ordeal of their incarceration; that it was better to forget about any statements or action that they took which they themselves might consider to
have been in error.

I told them that we had never considered apologizing or paying any
ransom, that we had seized between $11 [billion] and $12 billion in Iranian money, and that yesterday after their release we refunded less than
$3 billion of it to Iran. The hostages broke into enthusiastic applause.

I told them I had been worried that they might be angry because we
cheated Iran. They laughed. I told them that my attitude toward their lives
had been the same as the marine guards at the beginning—that we could
very well have killed a lot of Iranians, but it would have resulted in deaths
among the Americans.

I asked for any questions, and the first was about the rescue operation.
I explained it to them, told them about the heroism of the entire group,
who were all volunteers willing to give their lives for the freedom of the
American hostages. Eight of them had done so. I described the patriotic,
generous, and proud attitude of the families of the servicemen who had
died in the desert in Iran.

The second question was about the reason for letting the shah come in,
asked by Thomas Ahern. I explained the circumstances surrounding the
shah's admission: the fact that it was a decision that I made, that my advisors were unanimous in agreeing with the action, and pointing out that we
had the full commitment of the government of Iran that following the
shah's admission for medical treatment our embassy would be protected.

I considered the session to be a friendly one. We took a photograph
with me and each one of the hostages, later with the marine group, and
later with the entire group. One of the hostages had escorted my mother
when she visited Morocco, and he sent her his autograph on the back of
my speech notes.

As I went up the hall I entered the telephone room where direct lines
had been set up to America. I interrupted six or seven of the liberated
Americans who were speaking to their wives or mothers and spoke to the
family members back in the States. Two or three of the mothers said that
they were concerned that their sons had such long hair, and I assured them
that they had gotten haircuts—at least the ones in question. They looked
very neat.

I had encouraged the group to stay together, pointing out that the
strong ones were needed to help the weaker ones. But I reminded them

and the doctors that they were free Americans now, no longer prisoners, and if they insisted, they would be released earlier. The doctors seemed to think that Saturday or Sunday would be the best time for them to come back to the United States. Following the visit, I went out on the front steps of the hospital with Bruce Laingen for some photographs and then drove back to the airport at Frankfurt.

I made a ten-minute speech to the hundreds of news media representatives, which was carried live back in the States. Then I got on the plane while Jody and Lloyd and others gave the briefing to the press.

Later we assembled in the after cabin, and Lloyd opened some very good champagne (Cristal). The plane crew had brought some fine crystal goblets with the presidential seal on them to give me as a parting gift. We drank champagne from them, and I told everyone to keep the glasses as a souvenir of the trip.

JANUARY 22   We returned an hour or so later than anticipated because we spent more time with the hostages than we had thought, but we got back to Plains before sunrise on January twenty-second. Rosalynn said that almost the entire trip had been live on television, and they had been able to follow it very closely.

Chip moved my new tools to the garage while I slept. Later, Fritz called to say that he spent about five minutes giving Reagan a briefing on our visit with the hostages and delivered the letter I wrote him, which he didn't open before Fritz left.

Aftermath

I kept a diary after I came home to Plains, and I have included a few early excerpts to show how my life began to evolve after the White House years. Our first chore was to refurbish our twenty-year-old house and yard; to save money and to feel that I was doing something useful, I decided that we would do all the work ourselves.

I stayed in touch with the members of our staff who had remained in Washington, but decided that I would not comment publicly on political events, at least for the first year. I was a relatively young presidential "survivor," with a statistical quarter century of life remaining, and I needed to decide what I wanted to do. In a relatively naive moment immediately after my electoral defeat, I had told the media that I would not become involved in the commercial world, but that I planned do some lecturing, teaching, and writing. At the same time, I had an obligation to raise enough money to build and furnish a museum and library for the storage of tens of millions of documents, photographs, and other mementos of my public service.

I declined two opportunities to become president of a prestigious university in the South, but I was interested in teaching either in the Georgia university system or in a private institution. My first obligation was to pay off my personal debt, either by selling Carter's Warehouse or with a book contract.

As a former president, I had an allowance for a secretary and some office space; I also had a transition staff that would move and process material destined for permanent storage.

JANUARY 23   Chip and I started flooring the attic. There's hardly a board that goes down without having to cut a notch in it because of pipes, wires, and framing, but we need the floor space in order to store boxes and clothes.

FEBRUARY 11   I've been getting calls from Brzezinski, Bob Strauss, Warren Christopher, and more frequently from Jody. Strauss thinks the Reagan administration is making some very serious mistakes, and Zbig says that the NSC has been almost dismantled and that Reagan plays no role in the evolution of foreign policy.

FEBRUARY 12   We've received about sixty thousand letters since Inauguration Day—still getting ten to twelve thousand letters a week, much more than anticipated—almost all very strong, favorable, encouraging. We've got volunteers and an excellent staff being run by Dan Lee.

FEBRUARY 16   The Lanier people came to demonstrate the word-processing equipment. It's expensive, maybe worth the money.

*I had studied both typing and shorthand in high school and am a proficient typist. I had written my previous book (*Why Not the Best?*) and all my speeches by hand or on a typewriter, but decided it was time for me to change to a more convenient technique. The machine I purchased, which cost about ten thousand dollars, was a relatively rudimentary word processor; at the time, however, it represented the cutting edge of technology. I remember that I had to return the carriage at the end of each line, and there was no carryover from one page to the next. Later,* The New York Times *published an article about my experiences as a neophyte computer user.*

FEBRUARY 17   Kirbo informed me that we have a substantial primary and general election debt. This is the first time I knew about it. It is likely that the DNC [Democratic National Committee] will ultimately take care of the general election debt, but we'll need to raise some money to pay $123,000 to the Federal Elections Commission.

FEBRUARY 20   I went to Atlanta to meet with my literary agents Marvin Josephson and Lynn Nesbit, and the publishers at Morrow and Bantam. The Morrow people didn't act very interested, but the Bantam people did. I learned from both of them. They want a highly personal book, expressing my impression of the White House, the presidency, people with whom I met, the ordeal of making difficult decisions. Books written previously by Ford, Johnson, Nixon, even Truman, have been highly impersonal in nature, primarily a recapitulation of the daily schedule or written by a committee. I told them I was going to spend about a year writing the book and five or six months making sure the book was a commercial success, it would be personal, and I would write it myself. I think this is the main message they needed to hear.

FEBRUARY 26   I met with Jimmy Buffett, who's going to join in with Charlie Daniels and some others who are having concerts to help pay off our primary debt.

MARCH 6   We closed the deal on the warehouse with the ADM people and paid off all our debts—a great relief to me. For the first time in many years we'll be collecting interest instead of paying interest.

We still have two farms that have been in our family for several generations, and we have devolved ownership to our children and grandchildren. Rosalynn and I retain management control and work with two partners in the production of peanuts, cotton, corn, soybeans, wheat, and other crops. Our most reliable source of income is about eighteen hundred acres of carefully tended woodland that is a mix of both native trees and planted pines.

Josephson called regarding Bantam's latest offer: a $900,000 advance (half to be paid on delivery of the book), a paperback edition, a special-edition high-quality volume, and a Book-of-the-Month-Club offer—apparently great enthusiasm to let this be their first major hardcover volume. Holt, Rinehart has an equivalent offer with a $1 million advance, but they want future receipts, book club sales, and paperback to be credited against the advance.

MARCH 7   Bantam's more penurious if the book is a flop, but if the book is a success, then Bantam is much more generous. We decided to go with Bantam if the oral agreements can be confirmed in a legal contract.

MARCH 8   I taught Sunday school for the first time. It was from First Corinthians 12 and 13. I enjoyed it very much. And the class responded well.

A few years later I began teaching Sunday school each Sunday, or about thirty-five to forty times a year when I am home in Plains. All my Bible lessons (more than five hundred) have been recorded, and I have written two books about my religious faith, Living Faith *and* Sources of Strength.

MARCH 9   I've established a daily routine of getting up about 5:00 a.m., working for a couple of hours on my book, which I enjoy, seeing Amy off to school, having a cup of coffee with Rosalynn, and going back to work in the den until I get tired of writing. I then spend the rest of the day between the typewriter, the woodshop, the yard, the woods, and the farms. In the afternoons I have meetings that are inevitable, with people wanting to visit me in Plains.

MARCH 16   I met with representatives of the Park Service. We're trying to promote the entire Plains area as a national park site. This would increase the number of tourists coming into the town and at the same time preserve its inherent character. We may or may not deed our home to the Park Service before Rosalynn and I both die.

The promotion of our small community of about 635 people has become one of our major commitments. The Park Service plans to create a national park have materialized, a loaded excursion train makes several trips through Plains each week, and we have refurbished the schoolhouse, railroad depot, my boyhood home, and several other tourist sites. We also transferred ownership of our home to the Park Service, much as the Lyndon Johnson family did in Texas.

Lloyd Cutler described a good offer to visit Japan later this year, perhaps combined with a trip to China. They want me to visit Osaka, make a speech and have a ninety-minute panel appearance and some TV interviews. They made an embarrassingly generous offer, plus travel expenses for a party of eight.

Accompanied by a small group of our family friends, Rosalynn and I accepted this offer and made the trip that August, my first visit to China after normalizing diplomatic relations. We traveled widely, and I was greeted very warmly by Deng Xiaoping and other leaders. This was to be the first of many such visits to the region.

MARCH 17–18   Rosalynn and I flew up to Princeton. We met with Doug Cater, director of the Aspen Institute, and afterward with [historians] Henry Graff, Arthur Link, Fred Greenstein, Edmund Morris, Robert Donovan, Dan Boorstin, John McPhee, Teddy White, and C. Vann Woodward.

Rosalynn and I both agreed to write memoirs after leaving the White House, and we were determined to make them both interesting and commercially successful. The historians we consulted warned us not to be defensive or attempt to rewrite history. They also told us that it was generally agreed that the best autobiographical work ever written by a president was the memoirs of Ulysses Grant, although he covered his experiences as an army general, not his time as president. (Personal Memoirs of Ulysses S. Grant *was written in Grant's final days, primarily to keep his family out of the poorhouse.*) *I knew it would be hard to meet Grant's high standard, but I took the advice from the historians to heart.*

MARCH 20   [Emory University president] Jim Laney spent the morning with me. He's really impressive, and he wants very much for me to associate with Emory and to build my library and museum on property available to Emory University. This would mean a substantial financial contribution, and I could spell out the role I want to play on the Emory campus itself. I expressed my aversion to being "captured" by any particular institution and my desire to have other Georgia universities feel that they were part of my library and future institute.

This meeting was to shape my future life. I have now spent twenty-nine years as a distinguished professor at Emory, during which I have had total freedom to express my sometimes controversial political views. In 1994 we signed a contract between The Carter Center and Emory University that established a joint board of trustees and a permanent legal relationship. Emory manages The Carter Center's personnel issues and our endowment fund of several hundred million dollars. We decided to locate the presidential library and The Carter Center about halfway between downtown Atlanta and Emory, and our independent status has permitted us to carry out a wide range of international projects in more than seventy nations. Our motto is "Waging Peace. Fighting Disease. Building Hope." (For more information, go to www.cartercenter.org.)

MARCH 21   [Egyptian] ambassador [Ashraf] Ghorbal called and wanted Jehan Sadat to visit Plains. He asked if I could arrange transportation from Robins Air Force Base to my home, and I told him I had a pickup truck. He paused several seconds and said, "I really was thinking more of a helicopter." I told him that former presidents didn't have helicopters, but we would see what we could do.

MARCH 27   I've been putting in sometimes eight or as many as ten hours a day. I'm now writing on the Mideast negotiations, and it's a very pleasant experience for me because my notes are so good. I figure I'm turning out two to three thousand words per day.

APRIL 7   I decided to make Rosalynn a jewelry cabinet out of ash, designed by myself with her advice. It's going to be a big undertaking, but I want to learn how to make drawers, dovetails with mitered corners, doors, and a hinged top using wooden hinges.

Furniture-making has become a favorite hobby of mine, and during my first year back home I made beds, chairs, tables, chifforobes, and other pieces to furnish completely a log cabin we constructed in the North Georgia mountains. Since then I have designed and built about a hundred pieces of furniture, mostly as a pleasant break from writing books during our all-too-rare days at home. I also have an easel in my woodshop, mostly for painting in oils and sometimes in acrylics. Each year I've donated one of my handmade items or paintings to be auctioned at a benefit for The Carter Center.

APRIL 12   The paperwork still piles in and is delivered twice a day. We are really enjoying this life.

Afterword

Almost three decades after leaving the White House, I can look back on my years as president with relative equanimity, and I have tried to reexamine these years objectively. It is not easy for me to accept criticism, admit my mistakes, or revise my way of doing things, but the words in these diary entries have almost seemed to come from an unrestrained and unbiased third party, and by rereading them I have gained a better understanding of myself and my administration.

This may be my last chance to offer an assessment of my time in the White House and to comment on how the United States and the world have changed since then. As I look back, I am proud of what we accomplished, and I hope this unadorned personal history—along with the notes I have added while reflecting on the entries in this diary—will provide readers with a better understanding of the achievements, frustrations, and disappointments I experienced during my term as president.

It is natural to relish praise or approval, and although four turbulent years cannot be encapsulated in a brief phrase, I especially like Vice President Walter Mondale's retrospective comment about our administration's tenure: "We obeyed the law, we told the truth, and we kept the peace." Another, more narrowly focused accolade came from Veterans Administration head Max Cleland when he brought me a plaque quoting Thomas

Jefferson: I HAVE THE CONSOLATION TO REFLECT THAT DURING THE PERIOD OF MY ADMINISTRATION NOT THE DROP OF BLOOD OF A SINGLE CITIZEN WAS SHED BY THE SWORD OF WAR. But of course both of these statements express only one side of a complicated story. After all, I was not reelected to a second term, and it's worth exploring some of the reasons for this political failure.

I believe I developed good relationships with almost all members of Congress, but sometimes I was not adequately concerned with how my proposals affected the views of the voters on whom they relied for reelection. In one case, however, I assiduously courted the support of a number of senators' constituents: during my long effort to win approval of the Panama Canal treaties, I often spoke directly to large groups of concerned citizens from their home states. But on a number of occasions, I really played hardball with legislators, especially when prohibiting the building of dams that were unnecessary or when vetoing public works bills that were, in my judgment, too full of pork-barrel projects. A somewhat less rigid approach to these sensitive issues could have paid rich dividends.

In addition, I overburdened Congress with an array of controversial and politically costly requests. Looking back, I am struck by how many unpopular objectives we pursued. Not only did we urge the end of U.S. control of the Panama Canal, we also asked Congress to endorse our view that we should sell F-15s to Saudi Arabia, abandon Taiwan and normalize relations with Communist China, let the price of oil and natural gas rise to market value, and relinquish tight government control over the free enterprise system. Further complicating our cause, we supported "leftist" human rights groups instead of friendly authoritarian regimes, equated Palestinian rights with Israeli demands, and insisted that Israel withdraw from occupied territories. We were able to achieve a remarkable amount of what we set out to do, but ultimately the political cost—for my administration and for members of Congress—was very high.

Even the less contentious part of my legislative agenda was also ambitious and aggressive, which created another problem: advancing so many proposals simultaneously was confusing to the Congress, the news media, and the American people. I am convinced that one reason we accomplished so many of our goals was that I assumed personal responsibility for key proposals to the Congress. Most major bills were drafted either in the White House or by my cabinet officers, who attempted to consult closely with affected congressional leaders. In the end, we usually prevailed, thanks to good partnerships with committee chairmen, interminable meetings with individuals and groups of representatives and senators of both parties, and an effective congressional liaison staff. But it is also true that my public image suffered because excessive personal involvement in many pieces of legislation made any modifications of the original plans seem to be my failures, even when we ultimately achieved success. I was sometimes accused of "micromanaging" the affairs of government and being excessively autocratic, and I must admit that my critics probably had a valid point.

As is evident from my diary, I felt at the time that I had a firm grip on my presidential duties and was presenting a clear picture of what I wanted to accomplish in domestic and foreign affairs. The three large themes of my presidency were peace, human rights, and the environment (which included energy conservation). These were the same commitments I emphasized in my announcement as a candidate, my acceptance speech after winning the Democratic nomination, and my inaugural address, and I consistently pursued all three themes as president. In retrospect, though, my elaboration of these themes and departures from them were not as clear to others as to me and my White House staff. The way I saw it, getting good final results was the only scorecard that counted, but that view was not shared by everyone.

In fact, the website of the Miller Center of Public Affairs says: "Carter gained a reputation for political ineptitude, even though his actual record in dealing with Congress belied that image. His success rate in getting presidential initiatives through Congress was much higher than that of his predecessors Eisenhower, Nixon, Ford, and successors Reagan and Bush . . . Carter was also close to Johnson's success rates, and higher than Kennedy's record." This assessment of my record is pleasing now, but it runs contrary to the impression we created while in office.

As an integral part of my ongoing responsibilities, I should have realized how important it was to consider the political aspects of my job, not just the issues I was addressing each week. For instance, it is now obvious that I paid inadequate attention to my responsibilities as head of the Democratic Party. I always felt constrained and uncomfortable as titular leader of the party, mostly because of the many compromises required to assuage the demands of different interest groups. I made minimal efforts to develop and maintain the party's cohesion and its loyalty to me, and I certainly should have worked much harder to prevent the defection in 1980 of many of my more liberal supporters. Some of those neglected Democrats were disaffected enough to support Senator Ted Kennedy in his aggressive but ultimately fruitless effort to challenge me for the Democratic nomination, and many of them later supported John Anderson and Ronald Reagan. But after much reflection, I have concluded that there is little I could have done to prevent Kennedy's attempt to remove me from the political office that he considered his justifiable family heritage.

I should say that I really liked some aspects of campaigning, including the strategic planning of my presidential campaign in the face of formidable odds. I also enjoyed forming personal relationships with multitudes of people, as well as engaging in the multifaceted and tactical combat that is part of any battle with political opponents. Once in office, both as governor and president, I relished the executive duties involved in choosing and defining legislative proposals, and I took considerable pleasure in successful struggles to obtain the votes necessary for their approval. Even more, I felt confident and at ease when dealing with foreign policy, where many decisions can be made by the president with minimal congressional consultation.

Another of my failures as president—one that I did recognize while in office—was my inability to form a mutually respectful relationship with key news media. Because of the United States' defeat in Vietnam and Nixon's Watergate debacle, I inherited a suspicious, almost cynical attitude among the press toward the presidency. There was a plethora of "investigative reporters" who were convinced that my administration had some kind of nefarious agenda that we were concealing behind a facade of truth and transparency. Our consistent attempts to run an open administration had little beneficial impact. Keep in mind that I was president before the days of twenty-four-hour news coverage on multiple cable channels and hundreds of websites; opinion about me and my administration was for the most part shaped by a few major newspapers, a handful of magazines, and three relatively brief evening TV news programs. Their editorial policies were not so divergent as today. It should have been possible, if not exactly easy, to develop a good relationship with the media, but I was unable to do that.

My frequent mentions of this issue in my diary indicate that I was aware of the problem during my entire term. I made efforts to solve it with regular news conferences and evening sessions in our private White House quarters with influential media owners, editors, and reporters. Rereading my diary all these years later, I have been somewhat surprised by the vehemence of my critical feelings toward specific periodicals as well as individual commentators and members of the White House press corps. I am sure my disapproval was evident to those with whom I was seeking reconciliation—hardly a productive approach. And it also didn't help my relationship with the press when, partly in anger, I violated a long-standing tradition by refusing to provide humorous skits and comments at some of the annual banquets held by the news media.

I cannot ignore a related critical assessment—one that has been put forward by Rosalynn, Jody Powell, and others—which is that neither I nor my key staff members participated in Washington's social life. I am sure this apparently aloof behavior drove something of a wedge between us and numerous influential cocktail party hosts. But I wasn't the first president to object to this obligation; during my first briefing from President Ford in the Oval Office, he said that one of the worst things about being president was having to go out almost every night to some kind of social event hosted by either members of Congress or someone in the Washington establishment. When I was governor of Georgia, Rosalynn and I made a decision to avoid these sorts of events, and for better or worse I never had any intention of changing this approach when we moved into the White House.

At least as controversial was my effort to reduce the exalted trappings of the presidency. Influenced by the more humble attitudes of Jefferson and Truman, I banned the European-style trumpeters that Nixon had favored, and also the playing of "Hail to the Chief" when I arrived at public events. I was surprised at the resulting furor among the general public and news media, which persisted until I reversed my decision and permitted the musical accolade to be played at a limited number of appearances. I learned that American citizens strongly prefer the pomp and ceremony that adds an element of royalty to our nation's chief executive.

I am sure several other factors contributed to the abbreviation of my political career, not the least of which was the global inflation caused by massive increases in oil prices, which in turn were the consequence of OPEC's rapacious behavior and the loss of petroleum supplies when Iran and Iraq went to war. But in the fall of 1980, as the presidential campaign neared its conclusion, one factor overwhelmed all others: the sustained captivity of American hostages. Most unfortunately, Election Day happened to be the exact anniversary of their capture, and in the days leading up to November 4, the media focused on this story to an extraordinary extent, with coverage day and night showing the captives blindfolded and being led around like animals. Over the years, in various classrooms and public forums, I have often been asked if there was one substantive action or decision I made as president that I would have changed. Somewhat facetiously, I have answered, "I would have sent one more helicopter to ensure the success of the hostage rescue effort in April 1980." But I truly believe that if I had done so, I would have been reelected.

I regret very deeply my inability to win a second term, because many of my policies and unfulfilled plans were abandoned or reversed by Ronald Reagan and his successors. No one can know "what would have been," but with a new beginning and the millstone of the captive hostages removed, we would have continued our strong commitment to energy conservation, maintained our nation's determined effort to bring peace to Israel and its neighbors, and kept our national budgets in balance. Our belief that peace and human rights must be the essential basis of American foreign policy might have helped provide the benefits of democracy and global harmony to millions of people beyond our borders. Of course, these are highly subjective presumptions, but I have no doubt that the ideas and beliefs that provided the foundation for everything I tried to accomplish as president would have continued to guide me had I served another four years.

While reviewing my years as president, I've been surprised by how many of the major challenges I faced still confront President Obama, which suggests the continuity of history—or the inability of any one administration to resolve difficult issues. Some of the more important ongoing problems are energy and the environment, comprehensive health care, civil liberties and human rights, nuclear proliferation, the economy, abortion, and narcotics. Looking abroad, we continue to face complex challenges in Russia, China, Afghanistan, Iran, Sudan, Zimbabwe, Cuba, and the Middle East.

It may be difficult for some younger readers to realize how much the Washington political scene—and that of the world—has changed in the last thirty years. In dealing with the Congress, I had one presidential advantage that no longer exists: cross-party support when it counted. There has been a dramatic deterioration in the function of the House and Senate since my tenure, and the bipartisanship I enjoyed has now almost disappeared. The tremendous influx of campaign money and the escalation of negative advertising, which tends to polarize the parties, are partly responsible. In addition, the surge in gerrymandered congressional districts has created relatively safe seats for members who parrot and attempt to implement the most extreme partisan positions, causing many moderates either to resign or to face defeat.

In the Senate, the adverse effects of extreme partisanship have been exacerbated by the constant threat of filibusters, which can only be stopped by a so-called supermajority of sixty votes. As a consequence, final action to pass the most important legislation often requires unanimity within the majority party, which gives individual senators a potential veto and enormous bargaining power.

Too often, independent legislators can no longer make their own decisions; bloc voting now prevails in both houses of Congress. The real choices are usually made in party caucuses, where decisions by a bare majority are forced on other members under threat of some kind of punishment. Lobbyists and their overflowing war chests often carry the day, with committee chairmen or influential members receiving enormous sums if they support or oppose particular proposals.

Unfortunately, this distortion of the legislative process is likely to increase greatly, since, in January 2010, the U.S. Supreme Court removed limits on corporate campaign contributions. But even before this decision, coalitions of special interests have habitually mounted nationwide television crusades—which often spread false and distorted information—aimed at killing proposed legislation that might reduce their profits. An especially disheartening example has been the efforts made by insurance, medical, and pharmaceutical companies to derogate and ridicule comprehensive health reform proposals put forward by me, Bill Clinton, Barack Obama, and other presidents.

But the pernicious effects of partisanship have not been limited to Washington; American citizens have also become more polarized in their beliefs, both within local communities and by region. "Red" and "blue" states are now easily identifiable, and there is hardly a Republican house member left in New England or a Democratic representative in a number of western states and in the South.

A significant cause of this rift is the melding of politics and religion, and the roots of the "Moral Majority" can be traced to the period when I was elected president. Since then, for example, the Southern Baptist Convention, with its huge membership, has been torn apart by struggles for political ascendancy, and Baptists and other religious groups have engaged in increasingly divisive debates about such issues as abortion, gay marriage, the status of women, the authority of priests, and whether believers have direct access to God. The alignment of more conservative Christians with the Republican Party has strengthened both political and religious schisms.

It seems to me that almost all segments of American society—the poor, the middle class, and the wealthy—have become more alienated from our government. Observing the behavior of Washington's political establishment, people too often feel only frustration and mistrust; inevitably, we now see frequent exhibitions of anger and vituperation. The most attractive political promise made by successful new candidates is that they will bring about "change," and even longtime veterans spend much of their energy condemning the very government within which they serve. Incumbency would be a great handicap were it not for the campaign coffers filled by rich and powerful interest groups eager to reward compliant voting records.

Seminal changes in the news media over the past three decades have also helped create a more volatile political arena. During my last year in office, I joined with Ted Turner to celebrate the birth of CNN, and this new network provided global news coverage that was accurate, comprehensive, and objective—standards that were later partially sacrificed to meet intense competition from other channels. To gain viewers, the twenty-four-hour news channels have now come to rely on reporting that often dramatizes or exaggerates each reported rumor or fact. In addition, the more radical presentations of information or commentary have proven to be most popular, so radio and television programs, like political alignments, have tended toward extremes. An unfortunate result of the need for constant reporting—especially on Internet news outlets—has been the demise of hundreds of newspapers that have proved unable to compete, leaving major cities and towns with one merged journal or, in some cases, none at all. The free and vigorous presentation of different opinions has been sacrificed to polarized uniformity.

. . .

While our political culture often seems toxic, our government's financial affairs have also become more troubling. Extravagant spending combined with gross tax bounties to the richest Americans have led us into a downward spiral of fiscal irresponsibility. Adverse trade balances and enormous budget deficits have caused the United States to become the greatest debtor of all time. Our enormous and growing deficit not only is breeding deep concern among our own citizens, but also threatens to make us vulnerable to China and other creditors. At the very least, we will have to continue to rely on our international creditors for the next ten or fifteen years to cover the projected difference between what we spend and what we are willing or able to finance ourselves. Meanwhile, the necessary curtailing of expenditures—except for sacrosanct military, homeland security, and entitlement programs—will endanger the well-being of our poorest citizens and reduce the level of foreign aid as a portion of our national wealth.

As president, I fought hard to encourage conservation and limit our dependence on foreign oil. During my time in office, it became painfully obvious that the United States could no longer rely on an endless supply of natural resources, yet little has been done during the past thirty years to curtail our profligate waste of oil and other nonrenewable resources. Now we face an even greater threat as scientists and responsible world leaders come to understand that the burning of fossil fuels is a major cause of potentially catastrophic global warming. It pains me to say that the United States has been more notable for recalcitrance than leadership in addressing these difficult issues.

Internationally, a most significant development has been the weakening and ultimate demise of the Soviet Union as Western democracy inexorably triumphed in dozens of large and small Third World nations, and Moscow lost its ascendancy, not only over its eastern European empire but over territories it had controlled since the time of the tsars. Unfortunately, the long-standing U.S.-Soviet nuclear confrontation—which, although tense and precarious, remained peaceful—has been superseded by serious conflicts in Sri Lanka, the Congo, Somalia, and Sudan. Terrorist attacks, mostly by Islamic radicals, have resulted in other conflicts, as have military invasions by the United States and its allies into Afghanistan and Iraq. And regional strife between Israel and its neighbors has continued.

With the relative decline of Russia, the United States has become the globe's unchallenged military and economic power. But in the years since I was president, we have gained the reputation of unnecessarily injecting ourselves into the internal affairs of other nations, relying on our overwhelming military strength to achieve our goals. More recently, our international ascendancy has been counterbalanced by the costly involvement of our military forces in the sustained war on terrorism. In the meantime, other large and influential nations—including China, Brazil, and South Africa—have avoided armed conflicts as their national policies have become increasingly influential in shaping world affairs. It seems increasingly obvious that if our status as the world's undisputed superpower is not yet in doubt, it almost certainly will be in future years.

During the post-Vietnam years during which I served, Congress and the general public were less inclined to support a strong defense capability than I was, although my general aversion to military combat met with strong approval. Since my tenure, attitudes have changed profoundly, and American forces have been directly engaged—often gratuitously—in Lebanon, Grenada, Panama, Kuwait, Somalia, Bosnia-Herzegovina, Kosovo, Afghanistan, and Iraq. Some of these excursions have had tragic results; others have been lauded as successful, but even in their initial stages they were politically popular. President George W. Bush encapsulated this more bellicose attitude by announcing an official policy of "preemptive war" to replace our historic practice of attacking other nations only when our own security was directly threatened.

Meanwhile, although we have claimed to deplore the dangers of nuclear proliferation, our country has weakened this resolve by abandoning the Anti-Ballistic Missile Treaty and a previous pledge of "no first use" of our atomic arsenal against nonnuclear states. Instead, we have announced plans to manufacture more advanced nuclear weapons and agreed to furnish nuclear fuel and technology to India despite its refusal to sign the Nonproliferation Treaty or comply with international safeguards.

The United States has also defaulted in carrying out one unchallenged and unique responsibility: mediating a peace agreement between Israel and its neighbors. This failure is one of the most obvious reasons for the deep animosity toward us within the Arab world and is a root cause of many despicable terrorist acts. As a result, Israel is deprived of assured peace and full acceptance within the world community, and Palestinians lack basic human freedoms, including the right of self-government.

Our international reputation suffered badly when our leaders overreacted to the terrorist attack of September 11, 2001, by abandoning historical standards of respect for human rights and civil liberties. The appalling, embarrassing photographs of prisoners in Iraq being tortured and humiliated caused millions of people around the world to wonder whether the United States can still legitimately claim to be the champion of human rights. Understandably, many believe that official government renunciation of international treaty commitments—including the Geneva Conventions and the Universal Declaration of Human Rights—has removed that proud banner from our hands.

Even the most heroic efforts by our chosen leaders to correct the many problems we face will be handicapped by some of the political developments described above. Political polarization and distrust of our government will make it difficult for both Congress and the president to take the kinds of bold action that require legislative approval. "Legal bribery" of officeholders almost guarantees that the public interest will often be sacrificed to those that control the moneybags, and it's worrisome that these include corporations that squander our natural resources, despoil the atmosphere, benefit from inefficient government programs, and profit from high oil consumption and the sale of weapons. Meanwhile, legitimate concerns about protecting our country against terrorist acts will make it increasingly difficult to grant the same legal rights to some suspects or accused criminals as have been historically provided by our civil and military courts.

Despite many concerns about our future, I am encouraged and inspired by our long history of overcoming seemingly insurmountable obstacles. Again and again, Americans have demonstrated their inherent resilience, innovative spirit, and high ethical and moral standards. Our heterogeneous population, blessed with the freedom to shape our nation's future through democratic choices, has always found the combined wisdom and sound judgment to correct any major mistake and solve any serious problem. Our challenges are clear, and I am confident we can meet them.

. . .

Looking back across the past three decades, I can say with no hesitation that living and serving in the White House was a rewarding and often enjoyable experience for me and my family. But since leaving office, I have not missed being in the political arena. Perhaps that is because I am not—at least in my own estimation—a natural politician. After all, I never considered seeking public office until I was almost forty years old; indeed, I have spent three-quarters of my adult life as a naval officer, farmer, businessman, teacher, and executive manager.

These later years have been busy and enjoyable for Rosalynn and me. We have been deeply involved in the work of The Carter Center, the Rosalynn Carter Institute for Caregiving, Habitat for Humanity, and the affairs of our hometown of Plains and our expanding family. We have also found much satisfaction in our work as authors and university professors. Almost every aspect of our lives has been affected beneficially by having served as America's First Family. Our experiences during political campaigns and while serving in public office—not to mention the prestige accorded me as a former president—have offered us many opportunities and provided remarkable access to leaders in all areas of life.

Rosalynn and I are especially proud of our work with The Carter Center, which has conducted active programs in more than seventy nations that promote peace, human rights, democracy, food production, and the alleviation of suffering from tropical diseases. As our center has become intimately and personally involved in the lives of some of the world's poorest and most neglected people, our perspective has been transformed and become truly global. In the effort to eradicate dracunculiasis (guinea worm), we have interceded in 23,600 villages; our initiative to control river blindness involves putting medicine in the mouths of more than 13 million Africans each year. The Carter Center has also helped to put long-lasting, insecticide-treated bed nets in every Ethiopian home where malaria threatens. Thanks to these programs and others, we have learned that materially deprived people, when given advice and a chance to act, are as intelligent, ambitious, and hardworking as we are, and their commitment to family values is equal to ours. Since leaving the White House, I have been fortunate to encounter thousands of fine citizens in the world's poorest nations, and I now wish I had known more about them and their needs when I was president.

I have attempted to ensure that my presidential successors have known about the work of The Carter Center and found it acceptable. In addition, I have on a number of occasions visited troubled places around the world, including North Korea, Haiti, Bosnia-Herzegovina, Ethiopia, Zaire, Sudan, Syria, and Palestine. My trips to these countries have sometimes involved consulting and negotiating with political leaders who were off limits to U.S. diplomats but could play a role in resolving problems related to armed conflict or violation of human rights. When undertaking these independent actions involving foreign affairs, I have always informed the White House and State Department of my plans, addressed their concerns, and made immediate reports to them following my trips.

Rosalynn and I have deep roots here in Plains—it has been and always will be our only real home. Just as my father did, I still rise about an hour before daylight, and Rosalynn and I continue to enjoy taking walks in the woods, hunting for arrowheads, and fishing in the nearby creeks and ponds. But we never forget our profound connection to the millions of others with whom we share this earth. In our hearts, we have made a promise to do all we can to help those who have been less fortunate, and in this way, like so many other private citizens, we are striving to do our part to help the United States fulfill its destiny as a democracy worthy of its founders.

Acknowledgments

Reviewing my diaries has been an interesting and enlightening process, but it would not have been possible without the hard work of my White House secretary, Susan Clough, who typed my spoken words into the voluminous documents from which this text was drawn. When I initially decided to write this book, I enlisted my White House press secretary, Jody Powell, my White House communications director, Jerry Rafshoon, and my longtime advisor/researcher, Steve Hochman, all of whom gave me helpful input. As always, my wife, Rosalynn, reviewed the text and shared her thoughts. My editor, John Sterling, provided invaluable assistance, and I am grateful for his help. Sarah Saunders at the Jimmy Carter Library and Museum was instrumental in finding the photographs. I also am grateful to my friend and agent, Lynn Nesbit, and to my assistant, Lauren Gilstrap, for helping to coordinate the process.

This book is dedicated to Hamilton Jordan and Jody Powell, two young men who guided me as a candidate, governor, and president, and served our nation superbly.

Index

Page numbers in *italics* refer to commentary.

Aaron, David, 152, 275, 424, 471
ABC TV, 212, 383, *383*, 415, 476
Abdullah, King of Saudi Arabia, 376
abortion, 70, *71*, 72, 127, 394, 459, 530, 532
Abourezk, James, 184, 188–89, *189*
Abramowitz, Morton, 369
Abzug, Bella, 277
Achebe, Chinua, 116
Adams, Brock, 66, 265, 317, 344, 346
Adams, John, *281*
Advisory Committee for Women, 494–95
affirmative action, 88, *88*, 203, 296, *296*
Afghanistan, 73, 200, 232, 273; address to
  nation on Soviet invasion of (Jan. 4,
  1980), 389; and China, *284*; and CIA,
  311; and current challenges, 530; death
  of Dubs in, 291; and heroin, 367; and
  India, 200, *200*; and Iran, 200, *200*; and
  Pakistan, 200, *200*, 273, 470; Soviet
  invasion of, 282, 291, 297, 305, 306, 356,
  357, 380, 382, *382*, 383, 387–93, 388–89,
  394–95, 396–97, 399–403, 406, 407, 409,
  410, 427, 429, 433, 440–41, 442, 447,
  468, 471, 480, 481, 491, 496; Soviet
  withdrawal from, 388–89; U.S. invasion
  of, *200*, 279, 382, 534
Afghan rebels (freedom fighters), *312*, 388,
  389, 391, 401, 402, 447, 486

Africa, *20*, 30, 77, 112, *144*, 190, 191,
  273, 290, 397, 480; Ali trips to, 400;
  and Carter Center, 536; and Cuba, 27,
  62 *168–69*, 176, 292, 393; Lillian Carter
  trip to, 204; southern, 34, 36, 39, 72, 83,
  87, 105, 322; trip to, of 1978, *180–82*,
  182; and Young, *13*; *see also specific
  countries*
African American Baptists, *455*
African Americans, 79, 82–83, 92, 147,
  148, 187, 287, 322, 445, 465, 480, 485,
  494–95; and federal judgeships, 291, 296,
  296, 350, 352
Agee, James, *363*, 363
agricultural policy, *80*, 110, 111, *144*, 204,
  377; and Soviet grain embargo, 390, 391,
  391, 393, 482
Agriculture, Department of, 35
aircraft carriers, *179*, 180
airplane hijackings, 206, *206*
Akihito, Crown Prince of Japan, 336
Alaska-Canadian natural gas pipeline,
  93, 132
Alaska National Interest Lands Conservation
  Act (1980), 173, 185, 207, 208, 253, *253*,
  264, 334, 399, 448, *449*, 450, 451, 452,
  458, 460, 463, *481*, 483, 490, *490*
Aldrin, Buzz, 347

Algeria, 289, 368, 464, 479; and Iranian hostage crisis, 483, 488–90, 492, 497, 499–500, 504–506, 509–12, *511*, 514
Ali, Muhammad, 238, 379, 389, 397, 400, *400*
Allbritton, Joe, 191
Allen, Jimmy, *14*, *35*, *455*
Allen, Richard, 487, 504
Allman, Cher, 33–34
Allman, Gregg, 33
Al Qaeda, *200*, 389
alternative renewable energy, *121*, 308, 337, *490*; hydroelectric, *121*; solar, *121*, 332, 364; wind, *121*
Always a Reckoning (1995), 138, *514*
American Bar Association (ABA), 260–61, 291, 350, *350*
American Film Institute, 137–38
American Israel Public Affairs Committee (AIPAC), *194–95*
American Jewish Committee, *64*
American Legion, 402, 459
American Medical Association (AMA), 208, *371*
American Motors, 320, 428
American Trucking Association, 280
Amin, Idi, 28–29, *29*, 313
Anderson, Jack, 99, 207
Anderson, John, 389, 446, 453, 459, 460, *460*, *463*, 466, 468, *480*, 528
Anderson, Wendell, 98
Andreotti, Giulio, 47, 209, 336–37
Andrus, Cecil, 56, 98, 177, 187, 203, 207, 253, 319, 399, *449*, 452
Angola, 134, *199–200*, 282, 362, 393, 443
Annenberg, Walter, 272, 278
Anti-Ballistic Missile Treaty, abandonment of, 534
Antiquities Act (1906), *449*
anti-Semitism, 322
apartheid, *20*, 36, *45*, 56
Apollo moon landing, 347
appointments, *15*, 16, *17*, 26; confirmations of, 451; diplomatic, *15*, 26, 318, *350*; of federal judges, 26, 183, 248, 250, 257, 260–62, 276–77, 291, 296, *296*, 348, 350, *350*, 352, 397, 470; of U.S. attorney in Philadelphia, 75
Arab American leaders, 149
Arab-Israeli war of 1967, 150
Arab League, 87, 466
Arabs, 31, 44, 50, 56–57, 64, 67–68, 71, 78, 83, 99, 101, 106, 111, 115, 161–62, 165, 247; and arms sales, 195, 294, 202–203; and Camp David summit, 220, 225, 227–29, 233, 234, 237, 239, 245; and Egyptian-Israeli talks, 257; and Israel, 167, 169, *210*, 279, 294; and Mideast offer of 2002, 376; and terrorism, *121*;

U.S. relations with, 535; and USSR, 305; *see also specific countries and individuals*
Arafat, Yasir, 39, 264, 276, 377
Archer Daniels Midland (ADM), *498*, 521
Arctic National Wildlife Refuge, *490*
Argentina, *17*, 90–92, 94–95, 273, 308–309; trips to, 322
Arms Control and Disarmament Agency (ACDA), 23, 186
arms sales, 45, 51, 74–75, *107–108*, 106, 122, *122*, 172, 190, 192, 194; *see also specific countries and items*
Armstrong, Neil, 249, 347
Arns, Paulo Cardinal, 181
Askew, Reubin, 15
Assad, Hafez al-, 46, *46*, 50, 87, 109, 124, 141, 142, 148, 220, 224, 245, 262
Associated Press (AP), 200, 373, 377
Association of Southeast Asian Nations (ASEAN), 463, *463*
Atlanta Constitution, 25
Atlanta Journal, 25, *471*
Auchincloss, Kenneth, 211
Austin, Paul, 62, 145, *145*, 168
Australia, 274, *463*
Austria, 331, 365
automobiles, 41, 42, 66, 258, 317, 320, *320–21*, 351–52, 428, 445, *490*, 506, *507*
AWACS (airborne warning and control system), 74–75, 110, 376, *376*, 377, 469, 484
Ayers, Brandt, 343
Ayres, Drummond, 278

Bacon, Joe, 80
Bahamas, 96, 309, 380
Baker, Howard: and Camp David Accords, 212, 244; and energy, 63, 127; and F-15s for Saudis, 195; and Iran, 305; and Panama Canal Treaty, 80, 84, 103, 129, 143, 163, 164, 171, *171*; relationship with, 76, *76*, 150, *171*, 324, 484; and Republican presidential nomination contest of 1980, 379, 389; and Superfund, 488
Baker, James, 82
Baker, Rev. James, 31
Bakhtiar, Shapour, 271–73, *273*, 276–78, 280, 286, 288, 290; assassination of, 273
Bakke decision, 88, *88*, 203
Balaguer, Joachín, 94
balance of trade, *see* trade balance
Baldwin, Roger, 509
Ball, George, 390
Baltimore News-American, 425
Bandar, Prince of Saudi Arabia, 376
Bani Sadr, Abolhassan, 397–98, 400, 402, 405, 409, 412, *412–13*, 415
Bank of America, 509

Bank of England, 508–10, 512
Bank Markazi (Iran), 510, 511
Banzer, Hugo, 94
Baptist Church, 35, 41, 167, 182, 189, 284–85, 313, 339, 361, 504; and USSR, 316, 317, 317, 331
Barak, Gen. Aharon, 232, 235, 235, 238, 240–43, 246, 259
Barre, Raymond, 96, 98–99
Bartlett, Dewey, 176, 259
Baryshnikov, Mikhail, 174, 295
Baudouin, King of Belgium, 162
Bayh, Birch, 3, 194
Baz, Osama El-, 235–36, 235, 239
Bazargan, Mehdi, 290–91, 364, 367, 368
Beame, Abraham, 113, 264
Beard, Robin, 208
Beauregard, Gen. P.G.T., 461
Beckwith, Col. Charles, 418, 419, 421, 423, 424
Begin, Aliza, 244, 245
Begin, Menachem, 55–57, 57, 63, 64, 101, 101, 132, 365; and arms sales, 195; and Camp David Accords, 244, 246–48, 247, 255, 255, 297, 360, 417–18, 418; and Camp David summit, 168, 168, 210, 210, 211–47, 213–14, 216, 222, 228, 229–30, 242, 243, 272; Carter meetings with, 150–51, 180, 193, 297–304, 484; and East Jerusalem, 449; and Egyptian-Israeli treaty, 256, 257, 259, 261, 295–304, 299, 303, 307; and Israeli cabinet resignations, 505; and Lebanon, 107; and Nobel Peace Prize, 256; and post-treaty talks, 315, 318, 333, 333, 339–41, 379, 400, 405, 408, 409, 411, 413, 420, 424, 431, 432, 435, 437, 438, 444, 450, 453, 461, 462, 484, 486, 487, 494, 508; and pre–Camp David talks, 147, 161–62, 167, 168, 173, 174, 176, 180; and Sadat, 145–46, 164, 169–70, 170, 174, 311, 311, 315, 341, 387, 391; and Sadat and Carter meetings, 150–51, 151, 153–54, 410, 416–18; and Sadat trip to Jerusalem and Knesset, 135, 137, 139–40, 307; and Soviet Jewish emigration, 308; visit of July 1977, 65, 70, 71; visit of March 1978, 175–76
Beheshti, Ayatollah, 389, 405
Belaúnde, Fernando, 451
Belgium, travels of 1978 to, 162
Belize, 93
Bell, David, 323
Bell, Griffin, 14, 14, 69, 88, 126, 130, 183, 191, 213, 257, 262, 263, 263, 276–77, 291, 350, 352, 354
Bellmon, Henry, 175, 177, 178, 281
Bellow, Saul, 126
Benjamin, Judah, 461
Benson, Ezra Taft, 189

Bentsen, Lloyd, 3, 403
Benyahia, Mohammed, 504, 510, 514
Bergland, Robert, 35, 111
Berlin, 50, 102, 205–207, 205–206; Wall, fall of, 496
Bernardin, Archbishop Joseph, 97
Bernstein, Leonard, 118, 119, 174, 293
Betancourt, Rómulo, 181
Beyond the White House, 280
Bhutto, Zulfikar Ali, execution of, 309
Biddle, Livingston, 111, 116
Biden, Joe, 167, 167, 362, 453
bipartisan cooperation, 171, 531
Bishop, Jimmy, 43
Black Caucus, 92
Blumberg, David, 171
Blumenthal, W. Michael, 36, 38, 53–54, 104, 117, 130, 142, 168, 175, 183–84, 184, 187, 285, 341, 344, 346
B'nai B'rith, 462–63
Bolivia, 90, 91, 94, 94, 346, 447
Bolling, Landrum, 177
bombers: B-1, 61, 63, 66, 67, 67, 78, 118, 122, 201, 459, 486; B-2 "stealth," 67; B-52, 61, 67
Bond, Julian, 3
Bongo, Omar, 120
Bookbinder, Hyman, 177
book contracts, 505, 519, 521, 523, 524
Boorstin, Dan, 523
Bosnia-Herzegovina, 534, 537
Boston Globe, 401
Boston Herald, 401
Botha, P. W., 34, 36, 82, 83
Bourguet, Christian, 402, 412
Bourne, Peter, 74, 74, 131, 176
Bowie, Robert R., 97
Brademas, John, 45, 62
Bradlee, Benjamin, 21–22, 211, 401
Brazil, 37, 42, 43, 59, 61, 90, 273, 274, 283, 534; nuclear program of 17, 17, 47, 160; trip to (1978), 181–82
Brewster, Kingman, 54
Brezhnev, Leonid, 20, 107, 111, 131, 138–39, 152, 184; and Afghanistan, 382, 390, 406, 468; and Jewish emigration from USSR, 308; and Middle East, 82, 305; and Poland, 491; and SALT, 17, 40, 102, 111, 155, 309; and trade, 133; and Vienna summit and SALT II signing, 319, 321–22, 324, 326–31, 331
Brinkley, David, 208
British Conservative Party, 97
British Labour Party, 46, 46
Brock, Lou, 357
Broder, David, 343, 363
Brooke, Edward, 175, 178
Brooks, D. W., 419
Brooks, Herb, 404

Brown, Gen. George, 116, 141
Brown, Harold, 16, *16*, 23, 38, 40, *45*, 56, 66, 66, 67, 75, 116, 121, 123, 130, 133, 135, 137, 141, 143, *185*, 260, 395; and China, 392; and defense spending and weapons systems, 180, 263, 415, 450, *450*, 459; and Greece, 454, 474; and Iran, 276; and Iranian hostage crisis, 372, 371, 375, 377, 419, 420, 422; and Iran-Iraq war, 474; and Korea, 455; and Medal of Freedom, 509; and Mideast peace process, 237, 294, 299, 304; and military draft, 326, 394; and Panama, 177; and post–election of 1980 transition, 488, 494; and Saudi Arabia, 469, 486; and Senate, 287; and South Korea, 279, 365, 491; and USSR, 198; and Vance, 423, 424, *425*; and Vienna summit, 330
Brown, Jerry, 3, 381, 402, 405, 414, 425, 488
Brown, John Y., 449
Bruckner, General, 337
Brzezinski, Zbigniew "Zbig," 11, 12, *13*, 19, 33, 34, 37, 64, 66, 69, 86, 102, 109–10, 120, *430*; accused of anti-Semitism, 194; and Afghanistan, 356; and arms sales, 143; assessment of first year by, 186; and Billy Carter, 448; and Brazil, 181; and Camp David Accords, 222, 227, 228, 244, 247; and China, 174, 178, 197, 266, 286; and covert operations, 380; and Cuba, 176, 199; and defense policy, 143; and draft, 394; and Egyptian-Israeli peace talks, 257, 266, 299, 302; and G7, 440; and Germany, 173, 507; and human rights, 52; and international goals, *45*; and Iran, 276, 364; and Iranian hostage crisis, 371–73, 375, 419, 422, 464; and Israel, 409; and Korea, 318; and Medal of Freedom, 509; and Mideast peace process, 83, 113, 140, 147, 154, 168, 169, 176, 212, 350; and Muskie, 436; and Panama, 124, 155, 460, 462, 495; and papal investiture ceremony, 252; and post-presidency, 520; and presidential campaign of 1980, 456; and Reagan, 520; relationship with Carter, 23–24, *24*; and SALT II, 40, 149, 152, 471; and Saudi Arabia, 486, 488; and Schmidt, 486; and Senate, 287; and shah of Iran, 312; and Shiite-Sunni split, 268; and Soviet invasion of Afghanistan, 389, 392, 406; and terrorism, 121; and transition, 488; and Trilateral Commission, 139; on trip to China, 192, 193, 196, *196*; on trip to Egypt, 299; and Uganda, 28–29; and USSR, 152, 197, 198, 392, 434; and Vance, 198, 267, 289, 363, 364, *425*; and Vance resignation, 423, 424; and Vienna summit, 321–22, 330; and Vietnam War, 379

Buffett, Jimmy, 521
Bumpers, Dale, 98
Bunker, Ellsworth, 29, *30*, 73, 82
Burdick, Quentin, 176
Burg, Josef, 418
Burger, Warren, 103, 111, 172
Burns, Arthur, 110, 135, 154
Burris, Roland, 370
Bush, George H. W., 37, *65*, *107*, *110*, *211*, *333*; and presidential campaign of 1980, 379, 389, 405, 447
Bush, George W., 27, *32*, *41*, *160*, *211*, 290, *333*, *355*, 376, 534
Business Council, 149
Business Roundtable, *120*
Byrd, Bob, 150; and B-1 bomber, 67; and budget, 432, 489; and Camp David Accords, 244; and China, 265; and Chrysler bailout, 375; and elections of 1980, 364; and energy, 88, 110, 116, 119, 127, 246, 252; and Iranian hostages, 419; and Lance, 88, 100, 101; and legislative priorities, 15, 65; and Long, 128; and Middle East, 128, 244, 265, 304, 352; and oil import veto, 434; and Panama Canal Treaty, 85, *85*, 88, 129–30, 135, 141, 163, 172, 176; and presidential nomination contest of 1980, 404, 427, *427*, 451–53, 486; relationship with, 85, *85*, 202, 250, 427, 460; and SALT, 163, 354, 383; and Superfund, 488; and taxes, 379, 449
Byrd, Harry, 352
Byrd Amendment repeal, 34
Byrne, Brendan, 96
Byrne, Jane, 362, 365, *365*, 409
Byron, George Gordon, Lord, 49

cabinet, 120, 125, 126, 139, 147–48, 198, 202, *216*, 259, 326, *350*; assessment of first year by, 185–88, *185*, *188*; meetings of, 26, 33, 64, 66, 108, 120, 130–31, 172, 175, 248, 314, 321, 364; replacements of 1979 in, 341, 344–45, *345*; transition and final meeting of, 491
Caddell, Pat, 81, 118, 316, *316–17*, 323, 340, 341, 357, 401, 414, 420, 426, 446, 462–63, 466, 471, 477, 479, *479*
Califano, Joe, 70, 75, 132, 145, *145*, 175, 183, 187, 203, 208, 262, 295, 306, 308, 308, 320, 325, 341, 345, 346
Callaghan, James C., 46–47, *46*, *49*, 109, 180, 206, 272–75, 344, 420
Cambodia (Kampuchea), 27, 190, *190*, 277, 369, 463, *463*; refugees from, 288, 334, 369, *369*, 370; Vietnamese invasion of, 277, 297

campaign financing, 122, 256, 376–77, 449, 531, 535

Camp David: assessments of administration of July 5–13 at, 340–44; Begin visit to (1977), 70; cabinet use of, 148; energy crisis and discussions of July 1979 at, 340–42, *341*; Khalil-Dayan talks of 1979 at, 295; proposal for second Sadat-Begin meeting in February 1979 at, 296, 297; Sadat-Carter session of February 1978 at, 169–70; visits to, 28, 38, 53, 57, 58, 65, *65*, 70, 84, 99, 111, 116, 125, 146, 164, 171–72, 204, 252, 256, 268, 290, 294, 340, 372, 381, 382, 395, 406, 410, 411, 415, 437, 451, 458, 461, 463, 481–82, 488, 494, 499, 505

Camp David Accords, *244*, 247–48, *247*, 258, 260, 263, 264, 275–77, 276, 279, 297, 360, 365, 376, 417–18, *418*, 431, 435, 438, 452, 462–63, 480, 484, 494; and ancillary letters, *243*, *244*; Begin-Sadat summit leading to, 168, *168*, 210, *210*, 212–46, *213–14*, *216*, *245*, 272, 300, *311*, 322; as framework for regional peace, 307; press conference and address on, 244–48; and Reagan, 487

Camp Hoover, 255, 319

Canada, 26, *46*, 47, 48, 49, 93, 108, 132, 160, 165, 274, 337, 396, 441

Cannon, Bishop William, 353, 419

Cannon, Howard, 176, 178, 188–89, 435

Cardozo, Mike, 510, 515

Caribbean, 115, 363, 496

Carson, Johnny, *19*

Carson, Rachel, 335

Carswell, Bob, 510, 511

Carter, Alton "Buddy" (uncle), 164–65, *164*

Carter, Amy (daughter), *19*, 130, 144, 196, 238; and ceremonies and entertainment, 15, 26, 73, 285, 378, 426; education of, *13*, 22, 22–23, 25, 73, 140, 141, 202, 321, 335, 363, 397, 428, 448, 481, 494, 522; and John Paul II, 321; and Mary Fitzpatrick, 25, *25*; and media, 191, *191*; and political discussions, 476; and presidential election loss of 1980, *481*, 514; relationship and recreation with, *13*, 22, 28, 32–33, 38, 59, 99–100, 116, 125, 203–204, 268, 319, 352, 382, 446, 470, 499; and religion, 13; trips with, 182, 207, 272, 276; trip to Kennedy Space Center of, 249

Carter, Annette (daughter-in-law), 116

Carter, Billy (brother) , 80, 214, 390, 470, 499, 514; alcoholism of, 279, 315, *315–16*, 445; celebrity of, *54*, 279; and family business, 54, *54*, 111; and Libya, 279, *279*, *301*, 373, 438, *438–39*, 443, 445, 446, 448, 450, 453–55, 459, 485, 497; personality of, *315–16*

Carter, Carolyn (wife of Don Carter), 214

Carter, Caron (daughter-in-law), 13, 28

Carter, Chip (son), 4, 9, 13, 16, 38, 215, 252, 402–403, 405, *405*, 406, 437, 481, 504, 520

Carter, Don (cousin), 214, 447

Carter, Hugh "Sonny" (cousin), 70, 104, 164

Carter, Jack (son), 4, 402–403, 437, 472

Carter, James (grandson), 406

Carter, Jeffrey (son), 4, *13*, 116, 134, *134*, 135, 137, 138, 194, *194*, 215, 404, *405*, 456, 481

Carter, Lillian (mother), 59, 79, 108, 144, 153, 215, 313, 470, 471, 480, 498–99, 516; and Ali, *400*; and Billy, *315*; campaigning by, 5, *19*, 262, 379; and Camp David summit, 244; Cronkite interview, 457; and King Hassan of Morocco, 260; and Meir funeral, 264; and Peace Corps, *18*; presidential campaign of 1980, 399, 458; speeches of, 204–205; and Tito funeral, 425; trip to India of, 18, 22; trip to Ireland of, 133; trip to Italy of, 204, *205*, 208

Carter, Rosalynn Smith (First Lady), xiii, *16*, 22, 24, 32, 45, 51, 52, 53, *55*, 58, 59, 68, 73, 79, 91, 101, 103, 114, 119, 123, 139, 141, 144, 176, 214, 268, 295, 312, 339, 351, 383, 470, 506; and antidrug program, 121; assessment of administration by, 529; and astronauts, 249; and Baptist Church, *445*; birthdays of, 458, 459, *459*; and book contracts, 504; and Cambodia, 378; campaigning for Democrats by, 193, 251, 264; and Camp David summit, 228, 229, 244, *245*, 246; and Camp Hoover, 255, 319; and Carter family, 164, 165, *521*; CBS special on, 251; and lunch with Churches, 290; and civil rights, 144; and Commission on Mental Health, 25, 192, 289; and Deng visit, 285; and disasters, 130; duties of, as First Lady, 251, 278; early married life of, *212*; Egyptian-Israeli peace talks and travels to Israel by, *303*; and energy speech, 340, *341*, 342, 343; and ERA, 254; foreign travels of, 121; and Gromyko, 249; and Habitat for Humanity, *431*; and human rights, 295; during inauguration and first days in White House, 9, 10, 11, 15; during inauguration of Reagan, 513–14; and Iranian hostage crisis, 369, 517; and Kissinger, 165; and Latin America, *13*; and mental health issues, 86, *86*, 98, 121, 251, 320, 436, 450, 471; and military draft, 394; mother of, *19*; and Muskie, 429; National Press Club speech by, 202; official duties of, 25; and Panama Canal

Carter, Rosalynn Smith (*continued*)
Treaty, 177; papal visit of, 318–19;
and Plains, *19*, 153, 214–15, 354; and
post-presidency, 522–24, *523*, 536, 537;
and presidential campaign of 1976, 4–5,
89; and presidential campaign of 1980,
456, *458*, 466, 468, 469, 471, 476, 479,
481; and presidential primaries of 1980,
326, 356, 357, 365, 381, 405, 410, 411,
414, 415, 422, 434; and press, 278; and
public opinion polls, 316; recreation of,
177, 203, 282; and Secret Service, 307;
Taiwan and, *191*; and transition, 482,
487, 492, 494, 495, 499, 505, 512; trip to
Belgium of, 159; trip to China of, *522–23*;
trip to Costa Rica of, 193; trip to El
Salvador of, 346; trip to Germany of,
206, 207; trip to Guadeloupe summit of,
272, 276; trip to Guatemala of, 193; trip
to Hungary of, 159; trip to Italy for
pope's funeral of, 213, 214; trip to
Pakistan of, *311*; trip to Peru of, 451,
452; trip to Poland of, 155; trip to Puerto
Rico of, 117; trip to South America of,
42–43,59–62, 64, 91; trip to Thai refugee
camps of, 367–68, 369, *369*; and UN,
112; and vacations, 215, 350, 352, 353,
446; and Vance resignation, 423; and
White House entertaining, 26, 73, 125,
152, 174, *174*, 251
Carter, Sarah Rosemary (granddaughter),
267
Carter, Sybil (sister-in-law), *315*
Carter Center, *144*, *311*, *377*, *417*, *455*,
523–24, 536–37
Carter Doctrine, 395
Carter family: business of, 54, *54*, 111,
111, *498*, *498*, 519, 521, *521*; genealogy
of, 61, *61*
Carter Presidential Library and Museum,
xiii–xiv, *216*, 523
Case, Clifford, 180
Cash, Johnny, 358, 399
Castro, Fidel, 27, 62, *169*, 176, 199–200,
292, 393, *393*; and Iranian hostage crisis,
371; and Mariel refugees, 424, 428, 432,
465, 468; and Soviet invasion of
Afghanistan, 391
Cater, Doug, 523
Catholic Church, *254*, 332, 359–61; and
murder of El Salvadoran nuns, 491; and
liberation theology, *346*
CBS TV, 213, 304, 388, 476
Ceauşescu, Nicolae, 169, 184, *184*,273
Central Intelligence Agency (CIA), 16, 32,
33, 69, 79, 87, 97, 126, 214, 491; and
Afghanistan, 311; and Amin, 313; and
China, 281; and Church Committee,
290; "Intelligence Report to the

President" by, 11; and Iran, 255; and
Iranian hostage crisis, 396, 397, 453;
and Jordan, 313; and Mideast, 173, 213,
213–14, 215; and North and South
Korea, 280; and Panama, 189; and
parapsychology, 313, *313*, 426; and
USSR, 175, 250, 324; and Zambia, 313
Chagall, Marc, 162
Ch'ai Tse-min, 246
Chamber of Commerce, *120*, 208, 369
Chancellor, John, 208, 343
Chappell, Frank, 152–53
Chernenko, Konstantin, 328
Chiang Ching-kuo, 268
Chiang Kai-shek, 266
Chicago Sun-Times, 388
Chile, 90, 91, *91–92*, 94, *94*, 273, 451
Chiles, Lawton, 259
China, Nationalist, *see* Taiwan
China, People's Republic of (P.R.C.), 77,
87, 130, 135, 292, 309, 463; aftermath of
normalization in, 286; Ali trip to, 400;
and Brzezinski, *13*; Brzezinski trip to
(1978), 178, 192; and Cambodia, *190*,
463; and claims-and-assets question, 285;
and Deng visit, 281, *281*, 283–86, *284–
85*; economy of, 265, 286; and G20, 274;
and human rights, 286; and Israel, 284;
and Mirage 2000, 274; Mondale trip of
1979 to, 354; and most-favored-nation
status, 282, 285, 286; National People's
Conference of 1982 in, 285; and
normalization, xiv, 27, 38, *38*, 45, 53, *53*,
68, 78, 84, 85, *147*, *171*, *191*, 193–95,
246, 260, 263–68, *263*, *265*, 266–67, 273,
285, 286, 320, 330, 392, 456, 480, 483,
526; and North Korea, 279; official
diplomatic relations shifted to, *281*; and
press, 319; and religion, 284–85, 360; and
Republicans, 55; rising power of, 534;
and South Korea, 365; and Taiwan
agreement, 265–68, *265–67*, 299, *300*,
375, 379; trip to, of 1981, 285; trip to,
post-presidency, 322, 522, *522–23*;
U.S. intelligence on, *374*, 486, 487, 489;
U.S. policy on, 170, *171*, 174; USSR and,
105, 249, 274, 282, 283, 329–31, *331*,
374, *374*, *381*; and Vance, 128, *128*; and
Vietnam, 260, 284, 285, 296
Chirac, Jacques, 99
Chisholm, Shirley, 45
Choi Kyu Hah, 339
Chona, Mark, 146, 209
Chou En-lai, 283
Christian evangelicals, 394, *468–69*
Christian fellowship ("The Family"), 259
Christian fundamentalists, 473, 532
Christianity, *254*; and Muslims, 279; *see
also specific churches and sects*

Christian missionaries, 35, 35, 41, 284–85
Christopher, Warren, 520; and China, 268; and Iranian hostage crisis, 419, 464, 465, 470, 471, 478–80, 482, 488–90, 492, 504, 505, 506, 509–12, 511, 514, 515; and Liberia, 417; and Mideast peace process, 351, 416; and Panama Canal Treaty, 177–78; and Vance resignation, 423, 423, 424, 425
Chrysler Motors, 320; 1979 bankruptcy of and loan guarantees to, 349, 349–50, 366, 367, 370, 375, 380, 390, 427, 428, 497, 497, 507, 507; 2009 bankruptcy of, 507
Chun Doo Hwan, 455, 455, 464, 488, 489, 491
Church, Frank, 3, 4, 5, 194, 202, 288, 290, 290, 422, 424
church and state, separation of, 14
Churchill, Winston, 246
Civiletti, Benjamin, 191, 352, 374, 403, 438, 439
civil liberties, 530, 535
civil rights, 4, 144, 147, 164, 465
Civil Service Reform Act (1978), 190, 192, 207, 216, 246, 251, 483
Civil War, 204
Clark, Dick, 204, 258, 290
Clark, Joe, 335, 337
Clark, Ramsay, 368
Clausen, A. W. "Tom," 474
Cleland, Max, 525–26
Clemens, Samuel (Mark Twain), 353
Clifford, Clark, 20, 20–21, 50, 97, 100, 102, 103, 128, 153, 203, 268, 378, 378
Clinton, Bill, 97, 107, 211, 333, 414, 423, 433; DNC chairmanship and, 492, 493
Clough, Susan, xiii, 12, 24, 241, 243, 482, 515
CNN, 373, 433, 532
coal, 75, 98, 196, 369, 453, 464; coal miners' strike of 1978, 172, 177
Coca-Cola, 62, 145
Coe, Doug, 259
Cohen, Geula, 452
Cold War, 273; see also Soviet Union
Collins, Mike, 347
Colombia, 43, 59, 62, 91, 452
Commerce, Department of, 17, 18, 113, 185, 364, 413
Commission on Mental Health, 25, 98, 192
Commission on the Holocaust, 291
Committee on Present Danger, 76, 76–77
Common Cause, 121–22, 323
communism, 49, 57, 77, 137, 137, 155, 264, 346
Congo, 533
congressional leaders: and Mideast peace process, 165, 212, 246, 304, 342; meetings with, 14, 15, 31, 36, 40, 42, 45, 45–46,

62–65, 73, 118, 123, 127, 166, 190, 199, 208, 249, 278, 286, 332, 332, 356, 398, 432, 435, 451, 460, 463, 466, 484, 489
Congressional Quarterly, 42
Connally, John, 129, 129, 389
conservatism, 186–87, 211
Constable, Peter, 515
Cooke, Terence Cardinal, 343
Coptic Church, 42
Corman, Jim, 325, 492
Costanza, Midge, 127, 188
Costa Rica, 59, 96, 333, 346, 452; Rosalynn Carter trip to, 193
Council on Drug Abuse, 131
Council on Environmental Quality, 406
Country Music Association, 185, 320
Crane, Philip, 389
Cranston, Alan, 163, 286
criminal justice, 74, 191–92
Crockford, Jack, 447, 447
Cronkite, Walter, 30, 213, 343, 456, 475–76, 493, 509
Crystal, Les, 208
Cuba, 27, 27, 39, 61, 62, 77, 91, 94, 134, 168, 168–69, 273, 393, 393, 463, 483, 530; and Africa, 176, 199, 199–200, 292, 417; and Cambodia, 277; and Central America, 292, 332; and Mariel refugees, 424, 424, 468; and Mexico, 292; MiG-23s in, 260, 260, 262, 262; and missile crisis, 196; prisoners from, 351, 393; relations with, 393; and Soviet invasion of Afghanistan, 391; Soviet troops in, 354–59; and USSR, 282, 329, 383, 427
Cuban Americans, 176
Cuban refugees, 27, 265, 424–25, 427–28, 432–34, 433, 465, 480
Culver, John, 287
Curran, Paul, 354, 362
Curtis, Carl, 79
Curtis, Ken, 98
Cutler, Lloyd, 375, 392, 394, 422, 446, 448, 450, 454, 483, 483, 497, 505, 508–10, 515, 517, 522
Cyprus, 20, 20–21, 34, 50, 51, 114, 115, 128, 143, 273
Czechoslovakia, 382, 442, 493

Daniels, Charlie, 185, 521
Daughenbaugh, Don, 321
Day, Anthony, 343
Dayan, Moshe, 99, 101, 101, 112–13, 162, 168, 171–72, 178, 180, 192, 213, 359; and Camp David Accords, 220, 222, 226, 231–32, 231, 236–38, 240, 241, 246; and Egyptian-Israeli peace talks, 256, 257, 259, 295, 297, 302, 405, 413
Dean, Dizzy, 207

DeBakey, Michael, 411
Deconcini, Dennis, 175–77
Dees, Morris, 69
Defense, Department of, 12, 40, 77, 89,
    150, 167, 187, 200–201, 214, 280, 289,
    424, 492, 495–96, 504; and Reagan, 504;
    security leaks in, 186, 211, 260
defense spending, 26, 26, 67, 67, 134, 148,
    150, 179, 180, 199, 250, 263, 348, 381,
    397, 439, 492, 495–96, 534; and veto,
    179, 214, 216
de Havilland, Olivia, 137–38
Demirel, Süleyman, 51
Democratic National Committee (DNC),
    98, 116, 148, 154, 397, 482, 488, 492,
    493, 495, 504, 520
Democratic National Convention: (1964)
    18–19; (1976) 5, 10; (1980) 322, 412,
    435, 435, 439, 450–53, 456–59
Democratic nomination contest (1980):
    debates, 381, 381–82, 383, 460, 466–68,
    476–77, 476–77; voting and caucuses, 76,
    167, 283, 324, 326, 355, 357, 359, 362,
    363, 365–67, 365–66, 373, 375–78,
    380–81, 387–88, 390, 392, 394–95,
    398–405, 409–12, 412, 414, 415, 417,
    420, 425–28, 432, 434–35
Democratic Party, 64, 127–28, 110, 164,
    258, 258, 288, 368, 404, 431–32, 480,
    486; annual fund-raising dinner, 57;
    failures as leader of, 483, 527–28;
    see also liberal Democrats
democratization, 90, 94, 124, 124, 201, 346,
    486, 486
Deng Xiaoping (Teng Hsiao-ping), 85, 170,
    265, 265, 275, 360, 523; visit of (1979),
    281, 281, 283–86, 284–85
Denktash, Rauf, 114
Denmark, 426
Dennis, Francis, 82
Denton, Harold, 310, 311, 310
Denver, John, 29
deregulation, 202, 456, 472, 472–73, 526;
    air cargo, 132; airline, 65, 132, 190,
    192, 202, 207, 246, 247, 254, 472–73;
    communications, 472, 473; oil and gas,
    62, 100, 104, 305, 306; rail, 265, 429,
    451, 460, 463, 472; truck, 132, 265, 280,
    408, 429, 431, 443, 444
Desai, Morarji, 159–60, 200
Dickey, James, 167, 168
Diego Garcia, 78, 106, 371
Dingell, John, 42
Dinitz, Simcha, 140
Diplomatic Selection Commission, 15
Dirksen, Everett, 164
Distant Mirror, A (Tuchman), 280
Dobrynin, Anatoly, 15, 40, 109, 138,
    296–97, 312, 376, 390

Doe, Samuel, 417
Dole, Robert, 176, 287, 389
dollar, 256, 257, 265, 378, 497
Domenici, Pete, 177, 259
Dominican Republic, 94
Donaldson, Sam, 81
Donilon, Thomas, 457
Donovan, Hedley, 347, 363, 432
Donovan, Robert, 186, 523
Douglas, Anne, 448
Douglas, Kirk, 448, 509
dracunculiasis (guinea worm disease), 536
drugs, illegal, 74, 74, 81, 91, 121, 131, 224,
    367, 531; Hamilton Jordan accused of
    using, 207, 353
Dubs, Adolph, 291
Durkin, John, 362

Eagleton, Tom, 211, 366
Eanes, António Remalho, 443
eastern Europe, 47, 68, 175, 360; see also
    specific countries
Eastland, James, 76, 98
Eban, Abba, 302
Ebenezer Baptist Church, 465
Eckstine, Billy, 152
economic advisors, 321
economy and economic policy, 163, 305,
    340, 342–43, 354, 364, 366, 389, 446–47,
    473, 473–74, 483, 496–97, 505;
    continuing problems of, 530; crisis of
    2007–2010, 350, 414; stimulus package
    (1977), 39, 39, 52, 78, 78; see also inflation;
    interest rates; trade; unemployment
Ecuador, 43, 59, 61, 90, 93–94, 346;
    Rosalynn Carter trip to, 346
education, 22–23, 72, 75, 145, 170, 174,
    163, 199
Education, Department of: established, 45,
    145, 174, 308, 332, 343, 358, 362, 364,
    366, 426, 426, 454; and Reagan, 482, 484
Egypt, 31, 38–39, 42, 69, 101, 112; aid
    package to, 238, 416; ambassador
    exchange with Israel, 405; arms sales to,
    143, 194, 376; Byrd trip to, 265;
    cabinet of, 229–30; fighter planes to, 170;
    Geneva talks of 1977 proposed, 109, 113;
    Iranian hostage crisis and, 371, 375, 377;
    and Iran-Iraq war, 472; and Israel, 136,
    140, 164, 174, 176; and Israeli
    settlements, 123, 323; and Jordan, 438;
    and Mideast peace process (see Camp
    David Accords; Egyptian-Israeli peace
    treaty; Gaza Strip; Sinai; and individual
    issues, leaders, negotiators, and territories);
    and Palestinian refugees, 101; and PLO,
    297–98; and post-presidency, 524; and
    Saudi Arabia, 299; and shah of Iran, 305,

411; and Soviet invasion of Afghanistan, 388; strike forces of, 219–20; and Tito, 175; trips to, 161, 272, 298–300, 303–304; and USSR, 282; Vance trip to, 21

Egyptian-Israeli peace treaty (1979), 272, 309, 484, *485*, *508*; and Begin visit with Carter of March 1979, 297–99; final agreement on, of March 1979, 303–305, *304*, 307; and March 1979 trips to Egypt and Israel, 299–304, *303*, *304*; military and economic aid and, 304, *304*, 307–308; Neiman painting of signing of, 397; signing of, 306–308, *307*; success of, *308*; talks leading to, 220, 251–61, 263, 264, 266–68, 295, 296; and Vienna summit with Brezhnev, 329; and West Germany, 335–36

Eidenberg, Gene, 437

Eilts, Hermann, 215

Eisenhower, Dwight D. "Ike," *30*, 181, 186, *449*, 492, 527

Eizenstat, Stuart 4, 125, 187, 326, 456; and assessment of first year, 188; and budget, 381; and Chrysler Motors bankruptcy, 349; and Congress, *128*, 177, *198*; and draft registration, 394; and early days in White House, 35, *36*, 151–52; and energy, 341; and health care, 208, 312, 325; and Israel, 44, 140; and speeches, 193; and tax reform, 117; and water policy, 140

elections (congressional and state): (1978) *84*, 147, 185, 246, 248, 254, 256, 258, *258*; of 1979, 368; (1980) 404, *404*, 431–32, 480, 486, *486*, 492; *see also* Democratic nomination contest (1980); presidential elections; Republican nomination contest (1980)

electronic surveillance, 41, *41*, 172, 374, *374*, *381*

Elizabeth II, Queen of England, 49

El Salvador, 94, 346, 412, 491, 493

Emory University, *264*, 353, 523, *523–24*

Endangered American Wilderness Act (1978), 173

Endowment for the Arts, 62, 111, *111*, 116

Endowment for the Humanities, 62

energy, xiv, 25, 29, 37, 40, *41–42*, 62, 72, 72, 77, 88, 97, *100–101*, 102, 104, 110, 116–24, *121*, 126–27, 132, 139, 144, 146, *147*, 149, 152, 163, 165, 171, *171*, 185, 190, 192, 202, 207, 212, 246, 252, 258, *258–59*, 287, 306, 308, *316–17*, *319–21*, 321, 332, 335–37, 340–43, 347, 353–54, 364, 368–69, 408, 409, 437, 439, 456, 480, *490*, 527, 530, 533; crisis, 320–21, *320–21*, 332, 336–37, *336*, 339, *341*; and price deregulation, *100–101*, 104; speech of April 1977 about, 41–42, *41–42*;

speech of November 1977 about, 126, 131, *131*, 132; speech of April 1979 about, 309; speech of July 1979 on national goals and energy, 340–41, *341*, 343–44, *344*, *345*, 394; *see also* alternative renewable energy; nuclear energy; oil; oil and gas industry; Organization of Petroleum Exporting Countries; windfall profits tax

Energy, Department of, 25, 29, 72, 76, 77–78, 146, 482, 484

Energy Mobilization Board, proposed, 364, 380, 460

Energy Research and Development Administration (ERDA), 75

Energy Security Corporation, 364, 368–69, 408, 443

environment, 18, 29, 41, 75, 125, 140, 406, 507, 527, 530

environmentalists, 342

Environmental Protection Agency (EPA), 491

Equal Rights Amendment (ERA), 253, *253– 54*, 378, 394, 427–28, 454, 513

Equatorial Guinea, 362

Ethics in Government Act (1978), 256

Ethiopia, 134, 151, 175, 196, 393, 536; trips to, post-presidency, 537

European Community, 97, *404*, 419

European Union (EU), 97, 336, *413*

Evans, Rowland, 120

Evans, Thomas B., Jr., 252

Evron, Ephraim "Eppie," 351, 359, 405, 474, *508*

executive orders, 148, *258*, 332, 399, 400, *400–401*, 510

executive salaries, 190, *191*

Fahd, Crown Prince of Saudi Arabia, 56–57, 161, 245, 276, 304, 307, 371, 376

Fahmy, Ismail, 112

Fallows, Jim, 193

Falwell, Jerry, 455, *469*

Family Liaison Action Group (FLAG), 492

Farah, Empress of Iran, 136, 156

Fatah, *508*

Fabiola, Queen of Belgium, 159, 162

federal budget, 26, 37–38, 40, *40*, 56, 60, 63, 125, 126, 134, *134*, 145, 149–50, 152, 154, 196, 267, 268, 282, 305, 320, 321, 325, 373, 381, 404, 412, 432, 447, 483, 494, 497; attempt to balance, 46, 56, 125, 154, 324, 497, 530; and debt-to-GDP ratio of, 27; and deficits, *110*, *134*, 134, *190–91*, 196, 249–50, 268, 276, 286, 342, 348, 364, 366, 483, 497, 533; and health legislation, *198*, 203; and Reagan, 487, 493; supplementary requests in, 97; and zero-base budgeting, 40, *40*, 263

Federal Bureau of Investigation (FBI), *14*, 26, 163, 263, *263–64*, *290*, 505
Federal Elections Commission, 520
Federal Emergency Management Agency (FEMA), *355*, *355*, 430
federal mining leases, 98
Federal Reserve, 110, 135, 153–54, 348, *347–48*, *414*
Feinstein, Dianne, 444
Ferraro, Geraldine, 247, 461
Few, William, 287
fighter planes: F-5A, 39; F-5, sales to Egypt of, 143; F-15, 179; F-15, sales to Saudis of, 143, *194–95*, 272, 447, 484–87, *487*, 500, 504, 526; F-16, sales to Israel of, 143; F-16, sales to Pakistan of, 470
Filatov, Anatoly, 315
financial reform legislation, 414, *414*
First Baptist Church (Washington, D.C.), 13, *14*, 83, 108
Fisher, Bill and Betty, 343
Fisher, Bishop, 49
Fitzpatrick, Mary, 25, *25*
Fitzsimmons, Frank, 248
Fleming, Peggy, 497, 498
Fonda, Henry, 138
Foote, Shelby, 204
Ford, Betty, *55*
Ford, Gerald, 5, *17*, 29, *30*, 36–37, *37*, *55*, *55*, 80, 82, 83–84, 87, 93, 104, *139*, *143*, 152, 212, 265, 312–13, 324, 409, 453, *480*, 521, 527, 529; and Camp David summit, 244; and China, *266*; friendship with, *409–10*; funeral of, *410*; and Panama Canal Treaty, 177, 178; and presidential campaign of 1980, 378, 447, 448, 475; and Rockefeller, 287, *287*; and SALT, 265, 379; in presidential debates (1976), *476*
Ford, Wendell, 175, 178, 194
Ford Motor Company, 320, 428
foreign affairs breakfasts, 66, *66*, 194, 198, *198*, 210, 374–75, 419, 431, 447, 459, 464, 474, 475, 494, 508–509
foreign aid, 144, *144*
Foreign Intelligence Surveillance Act (FISA), *41*, *290*
France, 46–50, *46*, 98, 433; and Guadeloupe summit, 273; and Iran, 275, *275*, 276, 277, 278; and Iranian hostage crisis, 372, 393; and Mideast peace process, 141, 161–62, 298, 323; and nuclear energy, 136; and nuclear weapons, 486; and Poland, 493, 503; and Soviet invasion of Afghanistan, 392, 399, 410, 441; trip to (1978), 161–62; and USSR, 249, 274, 330
François-Poncet, Jean, 323
Frankel, Max, 212, 343
Fraser, Donald M., 254

Fraser, Douglas, 171, 183, 305, 428
Fraser, Malcolm, 399, 463
Frosch, Robert, 108
Fukuda, Yasuo, 46, 262

G7, *121*, *274*; 1977 summit (London), 46–50, *46*; 1978 summit (Bonn), 206–207; 1979 summit (Tokyo), 321, 334–37, *336*; 1980 summit (Venice), 439–42
G20, *274*
Gabon, 120
Gadhafi, Mu'ammar, *206*, *438*
Gairy, Eric, 95, *95*
Gamasy, Muhammad Al-, 225, 232
Gambrell, David, *129*
Gandhi, Indira, 22, 390
Gandhi, Mohandas K., 159
Gannon, Jim, 383
Gardner, John, 121–22, 323
Gardner, Richard, 208
Garn, Edwin Jacob "Jake," 397
Gas Rationing Act (1979), 368
Gast, Lt. Gen. Philip, 288, 291, 418, *419*
gay rights, 127; marriage, 532
Gaza Strip, 113, 151, 170, 171, 173, 175, 180, 218, 219, 223, 224, 226, 231, 235–37, *235*, 239, 240, 242, 302, 303, 407, 420; autonomy of, 301; in Egyptian-Israeli peace talks, 256–59, 261, 263, 298, 301; elections proposed for, 298; and Hamas, *508*; Israeli assault of 2009 in, *108*; and Israeli settlements in, 255–59, 261, 263; Israel's desire to keep, 275; and PLO, 255
Geisel, Ernesto, 61, 181, 182
General Electric, 345
General Motors, 320, 351–52, 428, *507*
General Services Administration (GSA), 95, 209, *209*, 491
Geneva Conventions, *444*, 535
Geneva Mideast peace conference, proposed, 71, 82, 87, 97, 106, 109, 111–13, 124, 126, 140, *210*
Genscher, Hans-Dietrich, 440, 486
Georgia Institute of Technology, 55, 295, 353
Germany, reunification of, 274
Germany, West (Federal Republic of Germany), 17, 102, 173, 453, 486; Califano trip to, 132; and G7 summits, 46–50, *46*, 205–207, 337, 439–41; and Guadeloupe summit, 272–75; and Iran, 275; and Iranian hostage crisis, 372, 464, 514–17; and Mideast, 335–36; and nuclear energy, 136, 160; and Poland, *461*; and Reagan, 487; and Somalia, 121; and Soviet invasion of Afghanistan, 441; trip to (1978), 205–207, *205–206*; and USSR, 274, *290*, 493, 507

Germond, Jack, 118, 208, 343
Gettysburg, Battle of, 204, 204, 229–30
Geyelin, Phil, 211
Ghorbal, Ashraf, 375, 524
Ghotbzadeh, Sadegh, 373–74, 380, 398, 402, 412
Giamo, Robert, 282
Gierek, Edward, 155, 360
Gillespie, Dizzy, 136, 136
Ginsburg, Ruth Bader, 397, 397
Ginzberg, Alexander, 315
Giscard D'Estaing, Valéry, 109, 207; and G7, 46–47, 50, 336, 337, 441; and Guadeloupe summit, 272–75; and Iran, 276–78, 278, 320, 393; and Middle East, 161–62; Normandy visit with, 162; OPEC and, 441; and Soviet invasion of Afghanistan, 399, 441
Gish, Lillian, 137
Gleason, Ted, 393
Glenn, John, 3, 5, 249
global warming, 533
Goatley, David, 455
Goheen, Robert, 52
Golan Heights, 101, 113, 219, 223, 229, 232, 474, 484, 508
Goldberg, Arthur, 36, 63, 63–64, 68, 82, 179, 241, 259, 390
Gold Kist agricultural cooperative, 111, 111
Goldschmidt, Neil, 348, 454, 488, 506
Goldwater, Barry, 81, 84, 84, 163, 177, 446
González, Felipe, 442
Gorbachev, Mikhail, 282, 388, 496
Graff, Henry, 523
Graham, Billy, 14, 367, 491
Graham, Donald, 401
Graham, Katherine "Kay," 211
Grant, Ulysses S., 523
Grasso, Ella, 415
Gravel, Mike, 253, 334
Great Britain, 54, 97, 441; and Afghanistan, 382; and G7, 46, 46–50; and Guadeloupe summit, 272–75; health program in, 132; and inflation, 348; and Iran, 275; and Middle East, 57; and nuclear weapons, 180, 486; and Pinochet, 91; and Rhodesia, 30, 122, 166, 407; and SALT, 326; and southern Africa, 20, 36, 72; and USSR, 249, 330; visit to (May 1977), 46, 46, 49
Greece, 20, 20–21, 50, 51, 97, 114, 128, 273, 393, 397, 407, 454, 459, 474
Greek Americans, 202, 203
Greenberg, Max, 171
Greenfield, Meg, 343
Greenstein, Fred, 523
Gregg, Fred, 41, 43, 130
Grenada, 95, 333, 534
Grier, Rosie, 381

Griffin, Robert, 177, 209, 209, 210
Grissom, Virgil, 249
Gromyko, Andrei, 53, 96, 103–106, 109, 196–97, 197, 248–49, 249, 267, 274, 327, 328, 330, 397, 406, 427, 429, 429, 433
Guadeloupe summit (1979), 272–76, 273–75
Guantánamo prison, 126
Guatemala, 92–93, 333, 346; Rosalynn Carter trip to, 193
Gunter, Bill, 70, 70
Guyana, 261, 261

Habib, Phil, 320
Habitat for Humanity, 431, 536
Haig, Alexander, 320, 495, 495, 500, 504
Haiti, 537; refugees from, 425
Hall, David, 494
Hall, Tom T., 185, 358, 399, 514
Halloran, Richard, 335
Hamas, 508
Hammond, Jay, 334, 452
Hansen, Clifford, 177
Harman, Jane, 36
Harman, Sidney, 36
Harpster, Wayne, 322, 322, 436, 437, 470, 481
Harriman, Averell, 324, 390, 396
Harris, Fred, 3
Harris, Patricia, 73, 113, 186–87, 345
Hart, Gary, 194, 449
Harvey, George, 466, 481
Haskell, Floyd, 194
Hassan, King of Morocco, 260, 305, 364
Hassidic rabbis, 380
Hatch Act, 251
Hatfield, Mark, 176, 178, 452
Hathaway, William, 194
Hay, Jess, 449
Hayakawa, S. I., 184, 188–89, 189
Health, Education, and Welfare, Department of (HEW), 70, 75, 145, 149, 203, 426
health industry lobby, 312, 332, 370, 370–71, 531
health reform, xiv, 46, 108, 108, 132, 133, 147, 171, 175, 183, 185, 196, 198–99, 198, 203, 203, 208–10, 295, 305, 306, 311, 312, 324, 325, 325, 332, 356, 366, 370, 370, 463, 531; hospital cost containment, 192, 197, 311, 312, 324, 332, 367, 370, 370–71
Heckler, Bill, 203
Heinz, John, 175, 178
Helms, Jesse, 80; amendment on Rhodesia, 207
Helms, Richard, 69, 126, 128
Helsinki Accords, 27, 452

Hertzberg, Hendrik "Rick," 500, 515
Herzog (Bellow), 126
Hesburgh, Father Theodore, 369
Hicks, Carlton, *43*
Hines, Earl "Fatha," 136
Hirohito, Emperor of Japan, 334, *334*, 335
Hispanics, 186, 296, 480, 485, 494–95
Hitler, Adolf, 184, 194, 272, 397
Hodges, Kaneaster, 148
Hodges, Luther, 364
Holocaust, 314
Holocaust Memorial Museum, *193*
Honduras, 94, 346
honorary degrees, 55, *55*
Hoover, Herbert, *56*
Hope, Bob, 196, 381
Hormuz, Strait of, 467, 474
Horne, Billy, 191
Horne, Irene, 191
Horowitz, Vladimir, 173, 174, *174*, 248
housing: community development bill, 118;
    fair, 408, 451
Housing and Urban Development,
    Department of (HUD), 18, 73, 113, 345,
    348, 491
Hua Guofeng, 85, 360, 446, 463
Huang Chen, 128
Huang Hua, 285
Hufstedler, Shirley, 364, 366, 426
Hughes, Harold, 259
human rights, *13*, 17–18, 27, 37, 52, *64*,
    115, 122, *147*, 185, *190*, 486, 496, 507,
    526; and Amin, 29; and antiterrorist
    actions, 535; and Arab Americans, 149;
    and Argentina, 308–309; and Brazil, 61,
    181–82; and Chile, 91, *91–92*, 451; and
    China, 286; continuing problem of, 530;
    and G7, 47–49; and Iran, 136, 137; and
    Latin America, 90–92, *90–92*, 94–96, *94*,
    347; New Delhi speech on, 159; and
    South Korea, 339, 455, *455*; support for,
    181, *181*; as theme of presidency, 527,
    530; and USSR, 20, 105, 282, 295, 317,
    317, 324, 330, 331, *331*
Human Rights, American Convention on,
    61, 91, 94
Human Rights, Inter-American
    Commission on, 90
Human Rights Covenants (UN), 114–15,
    114
Humphrey, Hubert H., 3, 4, 35, 63, 64, *64*,
    89, 122–23, 127, 143–44, 146–47, 153,
    254, *429*; death of, 164, *164*
Humphrey, Muriel, 122, 144, 195
Humphrey Fellows program, 264, *264*
Humphrey-Hawkins Full Employment Act
    (1978), 92, *92*, 256
Hungary, 132, 273, 282; and Crown of Saint
    Stephen, *132*, 133, 143, 148, 159

hurricanes: Frederic, 355; Katrina, 355
Hussein, King of Jordan, 21, 22, 43, *43–44*,
    156, 159, 245, 262, 276, 313, 341, 420;
    meeting with (June 1980), 438
Hussein, Saddam, *416*, *467*, 472, *472*
Hutcheson, Rick, 24
Huyser, Gen. Robert "Dutch," 273, 277,
    277, 278, 287, 288

Iacocca, Lee, *350*, 497, *497*
inauguration: (1977) 9–11, 435, 507, 527;
    (1981) and departure from White House,
    512–14
India, 18, 22, 52, 283, *284*, 390; Ali trip to,
    400; and G20, 274; and Iran and
    Afghanistan, 200, *200*; and nuclear
    energy, 160, *160*, 200, 314; and nuclear
    weapons, *200*, 314; and Pakistan, 200,
    200, 314; trip to (1978), 159–60; and
    USSR, 282
Indians (Native Americans): Alaskan, *253*;
    in Maine, 70, *70*, 213, 471
Indonesia, 274, 282, 283
Infant Formula Act (1980), 468
inflation (anti-inflation), xiv, 39, 135,
    183–84, 190, *190*, 203, 246, *249–50*, 254,
    265, 278, 305, 306, 314, 321, 336, 340,
    348–49, 354, 357, 363, 366, 396, 403,
    408–10, 414, 441, *468*, *473*, *473*, 475,
    497, 505, 529
Ingersoll, Robert, 334
Inouye, Daniel, 486
In Search of Identity (Sadat), 245
inspectors general, 251
intelligence, *374*, *381*; and China, 489;
    executive order on, 165
intelligence agencies, 77, 144;
    reorganization of, 32, *45*, 153; *see also
    specific agencies*
interest rates, *348*, 364, 378, *473*, *473*, 496
Intergovernmental Advisory Commission,
    113
Interior, Department of, 23, 56, 113, 185,
    208, 213
Internal Revenue Service (IRS), 198, *438*
International Atomic Energy Agency, *160*
International Chamber of Commerce, 489
International Fuel Cycle Study, 120
International Sugar Agreement, 94
international treaties, 535
International Women's Year Conference,
    149
Internet, 532
Inuits, *253*, *449*
Iran, Islamic Republic of: and American
    citizens, 295, 296, 304–305, 312–13; and
    American embassy protection, 291, 296;
    American journalists expelled by, 392;

and assassinations, 320; and China, 284, 284; and drug trade, 367; embargo of, 275; feelers to new potential leaders in, 268; and Kissinger, 289; and Mideast peace process, 376; recognition by U.S. of, 296; revolution of 1979 in, 156, 271–78, 271–73, 275, 277, 278, 280, 286–91, 288, 297, 309; and USSR, 427, 464, 467, 495; see also Iranian hostage crisis

Iran, pre-revolutionary, 74–75, 83, 135–36; and Afghanistan, 200, 200, 306; briefings on, 210; and human rights, 137; and India, 200, 200; and Israel, 254–55; and nuclear energy, 136, 136; and Pakistan, 200, 200; military coup threat in, 288–89; protests against shah in, 137, 252, 252, 255, 257–58, 261, 261, 263, 263, 267–68; trip to (1977–78), 156, 156, 159; Vance trip to, 21

Iran, shah of, see Pahlavi, Mohammad Reza, Shah of Iran

Iran Crisis, The (TV show), 476

Iranian hostage crisis, 275, 321; admission of shah to U.S. triggers, 364, 364; and American embassy takeover, 296, 367–69, 367; and Canadian embassy asylum, 374–75, 395, 396, 397; diplomatic relations broken, 415; early attempts to negotiate, 370, 371–82, 381, 372, 373, 388, 389–92, 392, 395, 395, 397–405, 400, 408, 407–409, 438, 440, 442, 446, 452, 453, 464, 464, 465, 466; early release of hostages, 371, 373, 448; and elections of 1980, 479–80, 480, 529–30; and Esfahan oil refinery, 371; and families of hostages, 369, 492, 494, 500, 510, 516; hostages released, 425, 511–17; hostage transfer arranged, 509–10; impounded Iranian assets transferred to Iran, 505–12, 506, 511, 516; Iranian assets impounded during, 370, 409, 411; and Iran-Iraq War, 467, 469; and post-election negotiations, 487–90, 492, 494, 497, 499–500, 503–10, 511; and pre-election negotiations, 466, 470, 472, 474–79, 475–76, 481, 482–85; and Reagan, 487, 487, 512; rescue attempt, 402, 411–12, 411–12, 414–14, 414, 415, 418–24, 418–19, 420, 426, 427, 428, 515, 516, 530; and sanctions, 383, 392, 393, 411, 412–13; and secret communications with hostages, 392, 392, 419, 492; and Waldheim and UN, 383, 389, 400, 401; war as last resort during, 503

Iranian Majlis, 452, 469, 475, 477, 478, 505–507

Iranian Revolutionary Council, 389, 398, 407–409, 415

Iran-Iraq War, 279, 336, 416, 416, 467, 467, 469, 472–73, 473, 474, 479, 529

Iraq, 32, 101, 135, 137, 232, 275, 405; torture of prisoners in, 535; U.S. invasion of, 279, 440, 534

Ireland, 133

Irgun, 57, 151

Islam, 368

Islamic nations, 391–92

Islamic radicals, 371, 534

Islamic sects, 210, 279

Israel, 69, 187, 357, 485; aid to, 304, 313; ambassador exchanged with Egypt, 405; Arab boycott of, 44, 44, 65, 217, 223, 235; arms sales to, 143, 194; Begin condemnation in, 175; Begin elected to head, 57, 57, 64; borders of, 50, 64–65, 220, 225, 233; and Brzezinski, 199; Byrd trip to, 265; and China, 266, 284; current problems of, 534–35; desire for Arab recognition by, 223; and direct negotiations with Egypt, 112, 140; elections of 1977 in, 55–56; and France, 50, 323; and G7, 50; Geneva talks proposed to, 109, 112–13; and Iran, 135, 254–55; isolation of, 298; and Kissinger, 255; and Lebanon, 107, 107–108, 133, 178, 178, 179, 184, 184, 210, 279, 279, 329, 351, 416, 418, 429, 459, 495, 508; and Leeds meeting with Egyptians and Vance, 207; and *Liberty* sinking, 491; and Meir meeting, 131–32; and Mideast arms sales, 194–95, 194–195; and Mideast peace process (see Camp David Accords; Egyptian-Israeli peace treaty; *and individual issues, leaders, negotiators, and territories*); Mondale speech on, 203; nuclear tests in, 405; nuclear weapons in, 75; occupied territories (see Israeli settlements; occupied territories; *and individual territories*); and Palestinians, 97, 99, 101, 105, 112, 147, 161, 279, 284, 508; peace coalition government proposed for (1978), 180; and PLO, 255, 312, 349, 350; and Pope John Paul II, 360; recognition of (1948), 378; and Republicans, 194; and Sadat, 150, 169, 171; Sadat visit to, 136–40, 141; and Saudis, 57; security of, 217–18, 223, 228, 230, 298, 408; and security leaks, 211, 211; security treaty proposal for, 176; and shah of Iran, 163; and South Africa, 101; and Syria, 279; and terrorism, 121; and thoughts on leaving office, 508; trips to, 272; trip to (1973), 21; trip to (January 1978), 161; trip to (March 1979), 298–304, 301; and UN, 469; and U.S. Congress, 130; and USSR, 297, 298; Vance trip to, 21; and Young, 351

Israel Defense Forces, *107*, 224
Israeli cabinet, 229–30, 232, 255, 261, 295,
    296, 299–303, *303*, 355, 416, 505
Israeli Knesset, 232, 240–43, *243*, 248,
    300–302, 405, 413, 452; Egyptian-Israeli
    peace treaty approved by, 306; Sadat visit
    to, 134, 307
Israeli Labor Party, 226, 302, 420
Israeli Likud Party, 55, 57
Israeli lobby, 194–95, *194–95*, 313
Israeli-occupied territories, 57, 64, *64–65*,
    68, 71, 101, *101*, 113, 139, 146, 150,
    179, 180, 204, *508*; and Camp
    David Accords, 218–19, 222, 225, *230*,
    247, 275; Israeli settlements in, *107*,
    113, 123, 151, 161, 162, 165, 167–74,
    176, 214, 214, 218–19, 222, 301, 355,
    376; Israeli withdrawal from, *485*, 526;
    refugee right of return and, 225, *230*; *see
    also* Gaza Strip; Golan Heights; Sinai;
    West Bank
Israeli settlements, 162, 168, 170, 171, 173,
    174, 176, 214, 416; in Gaza, 255–59, 261,
    263; in Sinai, 161, 169, 170, 173, 180,
    218, 223–28, 231–32, 234, 235–36,
    238–43, 248, 253; in West Bank, 161,
    167, 173, 175, 179, 214, 224, 226, 233,
    238–40, 242, 247, 255–59, 261, 263, 323,
    331, 333, 333, 400, 407, 413
Issues and Answers (TV program), 55–56
Italy, *46*, 47–49, 337, 433, 441; Lillian
    Carter trip to, 204, *205*; Rosalynn Carter
    trip to (1979), 318–19; trip to (1980),
    439–42

Jabotinsky, Ze'ev, 151, 234
Jackson, Henry "Scoop," 3, 5, 64, *64*, 77,
    110, 123–24, *123–24*, 129, 130, 149, 200,
    212, *260*, 282, 286, 422, 424, 449, 450,
    451, 472
Jackson, Rev. Jesse, 323, 463, 468
Jamaica, 42, 59, 333, 383
Japan, *13*, *46*, 46–49, 127, 160, *171*, 207,
    329, 403, 428, 441, 453; and Iranian
    hostage crisis, 372; Mondale trip to, 12;
    and trade, 317, *318*, 334, 335; trips to,
    322; trip to, for G7 1979 summit, 332,
    334–37, 335; trip to, for Ohira funeral,
    445–46; trip to, post-presidency, 522
Japanese Diet, *334*
Jarman, Dabney, 146
Javits, Jacob, 170, 180, 281
Jefferson, Thomas, *281*, 525–26, 529
Jenkins, Roy, 336, 337
Jerusalem, 438; and Camp David summit,
    218, 224, 230, 231, 233, 234, 236,
    241–42; East, 241, 258, 399, 406, 407,
    409, 413, 416, 418, 449, 452, *452*, 508;

and Mideast peace process, 151, 394,
    399, 418, 431, 437; and Pope John Paul
    II, 360; Sadat on holy places in, 170;
    Sadat visit to, 169, 224, 237, 239; UN
    Security Council Resolution on, 443–44,
    443–44, 459
Jewish American community, 35–36, *36*, 44,
    46, 63, 64, *64–65*, 67–68, 87, 98, 111,
    115, 122, 124, 126, 167, 169, 171, 172,
    177, 186, 192, 194, *201*, 202–203, 241,
    262, 266, 288, 315, 333, 349, 359–61,
    406, 408, *412*, 443, 447, 454, 459,
    461–63, 472–74, *473*, 480, 485, *485*
Jews: emigration from USSR by, 105, *123*,
    130, 133, 308, 310, 316, 331, *331*, 339,
    340, 452; Iranian assassinations of, 320
John Paul II, Pope, 252, 279, 368, 369;
    Rosalynn Carter visit to, 318, 359; visit to
    U.S. by, 359–61
Johnson, Haynes, 323
Johnson, Lady Bird, 93
Johnson, Lyndon B., *18*, *30*, *42*, *46*, *63*, 146,
    147, 521, *522*, 527
Johnston, J. Bennett, 176
Joint Chiefs of Staff, 38, 78, 82, 83, 89, 116,
    143, 148, 177, 260, 309, 326, 373, 496
Jones, Gen. David C., 78, 259, 309, 372,
    455, 485
Jones, Rev. Jim, 261, *261*
Jones, Reginald, 153, 345, 346
Jonestown murders and suicides, *261*, 279
Jordan: Byrd trip to, 265; and Camp David
    summit, 218, 221, 224, 225, 227, 235,
    239–41; intelligence payments to, 21–22;
    and Mideast peace process, 34, 43, 64,
    68, 69, 71, 101, 109, 112, 113, 115, 258,
    438; and Palestinian refugees, 101, 109;
    and Palestinian territories, *508*; Vance's
    trip to, 21; and West Bank, 101, 113, 150
Jordan, Hamilton, 4, *66*, 109, 116, 120, 125,
    127, 130, 140, 144, 148, 162, 167, 209,
    215, 276, 290, 299, 346, 351, 364, 394,
    423; and assessment of first year, 187–88;
    as chief of staff, 326; and cocaine
    allegations, 207, 353, *353*, 374, *374*, 433,
    439; during early days in White House,
    11, 12, *12*, 15–16, 17; and energy speech,
    341; and Iranian hostage crisis, 372, 378,
    395, *395*, 398–400, 402, 405, 408, 412,
    466, 478, 515; and last year of term,
    407–408; and Mideast peace process,
    168, 212, 244, 301, 304, 314, 350; and
    Panama Canal Treaty, 178; press attacks
    on, 151–52; and Reagan inauguration,
    514; and reelection campaign of 1980,
    390, 414, 437, *437*, 456, 474, 475; during
    transition period, 482, 492; and USSR
    speech, 198
Jordan, Vernon, 432

Josephson, Marvin, 504, 521
J Street, *195*
Juan Carlos, King of Spain, 85, 442
Justice, Department of, 14, *14*, 352, 438, 446

Kahane, Karl, 219–20
Kahn, Fred, 483
Kamal, Muhammad, 164, 207
Kampuchea, *see* Cambodia
Karamanlis, Konstantinos, 51
Kaunda, Kenneth, 36, 146, 209
Keeping Faith, 81, *497*
Kemeny, John G., 366, 377
Kemp, Jack, 448
Kennedy, Edward "Ted," 60, 76, 102, *102*, 287, 288; and Chappaquiddick, 3; and Democratic convention of 1980, 439, 450, 453, 456–58, *458*; and energy speech, *344*; and health reform, 175, 183, 203, 208–10, 295, 305–306, 311, 325, *325*; and Iranian hostage crisis, 375; and post–1980 election transition, 482, 484; in presidential campaign of 1974, 3; in presidential campaign of 1980, 76, *85*, 167, *167*, *183*, 283, *283*, 305, 324, 325, 326, 332, 355–57, *356*, 362–63, 365–67, *365–66*, 373, 375, 378, 380–81, 387, 390, 394–96, 398–402, 404, 405, 409–12, *412*, 414, 415, 417, *417*, 420, 425, 427, 431–32, 434–36, 447, 450, 457, 460, *460*, 474, 480, *480*, 484, 486, 528; Rosalynn Carter and, 289
Kennedy, John F., 42, 146, *183*, 196, *200*, 527; assassination of, 4, *316*; JFK Library dedication speech, 363
Kennedy, Robert F., 381; assassination of, 4, *316*
Kennedy, Rose, 196
Kennedy Space Center, 249
Khaddam, Abd al-Halim, 109, 148
Khalid, King of Saudi Arabia, 160–61, 224, 402
Khalil, Mustafa, 295, 297
Khmer Rouge, *463*
Khomeini, Ayatollah Ruholla, 263, 271, 273, 275–78, 280, 286–88, 291, 296, 320, 367–69, 370, 371–74, *372*, 377, 380, 389, *395*, *400*, 402, 404, 405, 408–409, *413*, 415, 464, *466*, 477–79, 513
Khrushchev, Nikita, 131
Kilpatrick, James, 343
Kim, Pastor Billy, 339
Kim Dae Jung, *340*, 455, *455*, 464, 485, 487, 491, 504
Kim Il Sung, 184, *280*
King, Clennon, 82, *82–83*
King, Coretta, 278

King, Martin Luther, Jr.: assassination of, 4, 264, *316*; and call for national holiday commemorating, 278; national historic site, 471
King, Martin Luther, Sr., 108, 153, 465
Kirbo, Charles, 15–16, *16*, *54*, 59, 89, 111, 127, 145, 213, 250, 423, 451, 498, *498*, 520
Kirkland, Lane, 450, 462
Kissinger, Henry, 23–24, 34–35, 66, *66–67*, 80, 83, 104, 112, 117, 139, 165–66, *166*, 311; advice of, 289–90; and Cambodia, 277; and Camp David Accords, 247; and Iran, 305, 312; and Iranian hostage crisis, 372, *372–73*, 379, 422; and Mideast peace process, 170, *255*, 300, 305, 352; and Nigeria, 181; and Panama Canal Treaty, 177; and SALT, 348–49, 379
Klein, Larry, 473
Klutznick, Philip, 36, 171, 177, 262, 454
Koch, Ed, 108, 112, 119, 168, 322, 378, 408, 409, 454, 474
Kohl, Helmut, 410
Kollek, Teddy, 300–301
Koppel, Ted, 476
Korcak, Dr. Jerome, 515
Korea, 105, 175; South-North meetings, 320, 340, *340*; *see also* North Korea; South Korea
Korean War, *280*
Kornienko, Georgi, 109
Kosovo, 534
Kraft, Joseph, 343
Kraft, Tim, 24, 70, 144
Kreisky, Bruno, 331, 339–40, 365, 375
Kreps, Juanita M., 17, 149, 184, 187
Kriangsak Chomanon, 288, 369
Kucinich, Dennis, 165
Ku Klux Klan, 368, 454, 461, 462, 465
Kuwait, 101, 534
Kyprianou, Spyros, 114

labor, 89, 175, 186, 199, 306, 354, 392, 480
Labor, Department of, 18, 113
labor law reform, 171, 202
Laboulaye, André de, 141
Laden, Osama bin, 389
Laingren, Bruce, 392, *392*, 419, 505, 515, 517
Lake, Tony, 424
Lance, Bert, 28, 51, 87–89, *87–88*, 119, 131, 153, 165; resignation of, 88, 97–104, *108*
Lance, LaBelle, 100, 102–103
Landau, Barry, 439
Landrieu, Maurice E. "Moon," 348, 488, 492
Laney, Jim, 523
Language in Thought and Action (Hayakawa), 189

Laos, 27, 33, 288
Lasch, Christopher, 323
Laster, R. D., 153
Latin America, 88, 90, 92–96, 115, *115*,
  202, 247–48, 292, 333, 349, 486;
  democratization of, 90, 94, 346, *346–47*;
  Rosalynn Carter focus on, *13*; *see also
  specific countries*
Laugerud García, Gen. Kjell, 92–93
Lautenberg, Frank, 171
Laxalt, Paul, 285
League of Arab States, *44*
League of Women Voters, 468
Lebanese refugees, 265
Lebanon, 78, 99, 101, 109, 149, 210, *210*;
  attacks on Israel from, *178*, 179; and
  Camp David summit, 217, 220, 224;
  cedar from, at White House, 192; Israeli
  attacks on, 107, *107–108*, 133, 184, *184*,
  279, 329, 351, 416, *418*, 429, 459, *495*;
  U.S. intervention in, 534
le Carré, John, 134
Lee, Dan, 520
Lee, Gen. Robert E., 204, *204*
Lefkowitz, Louis, 172
legislative veto, 497–98, *498*
Lehman, Bill, 211
Lehrer, Jim, 214, 343
Lenin, V. I., 131
Lennon, John, *174*
less-developed countries (LDCs, Third
  World), *45*, 60, *181*, 190, 283, 441, 483,
  496, 533
Let Us Now Praise Famous Men (Agee), 363
Lewis, Capt. Harold, 510
Lewis, John, 375
Lewis, Samuel, 215
liberal Democrats, 45–46, 76, *134*, 165,
  183, 199, 211, 254, 295, 324, *332*, *365*,
  432, 450, 460, 527–28
Liberia, 82, 417, *417*; trip to (1978), 182
Liberty, USS, Israeli sinking of, 491
Libya, *121*, 137, *206*, 232, 275, 289; Billy
  Carter and, 279, *279*, 438, *438–39*, 443,
  445, 446, 448, 450, 451, 453, 454–55,
  459, 485, 497; and Iranian hostage crisis,
  368, 373
Life on the Mississippi (Twain), 353
Limited Test Ban Treaty, 106, 328
Lincoln, Abraham, *230*, 456
Link, Arthur, 523
Linowitz, Sol, *425*, 505; and Mideast
  negotiations, 36, 203, 366, 377, 379, 394,
  399, 411, 413, 424, 426, 427, 444, 461,
  462, 484, 494; and Panama Canal Treaty,
  29, *30*, 73, 82
Lipshutz, Robert, 35, 36, 65, 125, 131, 140,
  194, 257

Living Faith, 522
lobbyists, *20*, 38, 62–63, 67, *104*, 110, 119,
  119, 169, 194, *194–95*, 195, 212, 258,
  266, 332, *449*, *507*, 531
logging industry, 127
Long, Carolyn, 97, 207
Long, Russell, 43, *43*, 75, 77, 97–98, 102,
  110, 117, 119, 123, 124, 127, 129, 130,
  141–42, 164–65, 175, 196, 202, 207–208,
  251, 311, 312, 324, 325, 449
Longstreet, Gen. James, 204, *204*
López Michelsen, Alfonso, 91
López Portillo, José, 291–94, *292*, 358, 375
Loren, Sophia, 396
Los Angeles Times, 109, 247
Lovins, Amory, 121, *121*
Lugar, Richard, 177
Lukash, Dr. William, 45, 84, 153, 174,
  213, 244, 267, 294, 348, 355, 363, 442,
  506
Luns, Joseph, 426
Lynn, Loretta, 185

Maas, Richard, 171
MacBean, Madeline, 482
Machel, Samora, 36
MacLaury, Bruce, 153
MacNeil, Robert, 214
Macy, John, 355
Maine, Indian claims in, 70, *70*, 213,
  471
malaria, 536
Malek, Redha, 489
Manatt, Chuck, 488, 492, 504
Mancini, Henry, 138
Mandela, Nelson, *20*
Mann, Ted, 171
Mansfield, Mike, 445
Mao Tse-tung, 283
Maranatha Baptist Church (Plains, Ga.),
  78–79, *445*
Marcos, Ferdinand, 114, *115*
Marcos, Imelda, 114, *115*
Marei, Sayed, 202
Marinaro, Vince, 488
Marshall, Ray, 177, 184, 187, 361
Mashek, John, 214
Matesky, Elisabeth, 99
Mathias, Charles, 62
Maxwell, Tom, 488
Mays, Benjamin, 456
MBFR (mutual and balanced force
  reductions), 47, 330, 427
McCarthy, Eugene, 146, 254
McClellan, John, 143
McCloy, John J., 173, 390
McCormack, Mike, 67

McCullough, David, 86, 201
McGee, Thomas W., 398
McGovern, George, 147, 175, *175*, 446
McGrory, Mary, 363
McHenry, Donald, 353, 408, 409, 429, 497
McIntyre, James T., 97, 117, 125, 154, 177, 188, 208, 276, 304, 349, 364, 381
McIntyre, Thomas J., 194
McKinley, William, 140
McNamara, Margaret, 509
McPhee, John, *173*, *173*, 523
Meany, George, 148, 153, 183, 248
Medal of Freedom, 509
Meese, Ed, 488
Meet the Press (TV show), 197, 266, 393, 436
Meir, Golda, *21*, 131–32, 139; funeral of, 264
Melcher, John, 176
Melgar Castro, Gen. Juan, 94
Méndez, Aparicio, 95
mental health, 25, 98, 121, 192
Mental Health Systems Act (1980), 320, 450, 460, 471
Metzenbaum, Howard, 37
Mexico, 26, 283, 380, 309, 333, 375; trip to (1979), 290–94, *292*, *294*
Michel, Bob, 324
Michiko, Crown Princess of Japan, 334–35
Mideast peace process, xiv, 31, 55, 62, 69, 83, 108, 109, 185, 187, 203, 442, 530; and ambassadors at large, 68, *68*; and arms sales, 122, *122*, 143, 194, 309, 195; and Assad, 50, 142; and Begin-Sadat meeting (April 1980), 410, 416–18; and Begin visit to Camp David (March 1978), 176, 180; book on, 505; and Brown's trip (1979), 294; and Byrd's trip (1978), 265; and Camp David Accords, (*see* Camp David Accords); and China, 284, *284*; and Congress, 128, 165; decision to focus on, *13*, *20*, *21*, *31*, *44*, *45*; decision to initiate Camp David meetings, 168, *168*; early meetings and proposals for, 21, 34, *34*, 71, *147*, 150–51, *151*, 153, 154, 193, *193*; and Egyptian-Israeli peace treaty, (*see* Egyptian-Israeli peace treaty); after Egyptian-Israeli treaty, 315, 341, 350–52, 356, 361, 365, 376, 377, *377*, 379, 381; foreign policy team debate on, 168, *168*; and France, 98–99, 141; and G7, 50; and Goldberg, 63, *63–64*, 82; and Humphrey, 63; impact on polls of, 208; and Iran, 156; and Israeli elections of 1977, 44; and Israeli resistance, 99, 101, 164; and Israeli settlements (*see* Israeli settlements); and Jerusalem (*see*

Jerusalem); and Jewish Americans, (*see* Jewish American community); and Jordan, 43, *44*, 420; and Kissinger, 289; lack of progress on (1980), 431, 435, 438, 450, 453, 461, 462; and Leeds meeting (1978), 207; Linowitz takes over from Strauss, 366, 377, 394, 399, 426; Linowitz trip to Mideast, 411, 413; Mideast trip (1978), 159–62; Muskie speech on, 432, 436; and news media, 133, 149, 151, *319*; Palestinian participation in, 97, 99, 109; and Palestinians (*see* Palestinians; Palestinian homeland); and Pope John Paul II, 360; post-1980 elections, *481*, 485, 494, 508; and presidential campaign of 1980, 322; and Reagan, 487; reassessment of (May 1980), 427; and Sadat visit to Israel, 136, 138, 139–40, 141; and Saudi Arabia, 376, *376*; and Saudis, 56–57; and Shiites and Sunnis, 268; and UN meetings (1977), 112–13, 115; and USSR, 105–106, 112, 133, 282, 324; and Vance, 21–22, 78; and Vienna summit (1979), 329; *see also specific countries, individuals, issues, and territories*
Mijatovic, Cvijetin, 442
military draft registration, 326, 394, 395, 396, 408, 437, 444, 448, 462, 487
military-industrial complex, 492, *492*; *see also* defense spending
military intervention, 534
Miller, William, 153–54, 345, 346, 347, 349, *350*, 362, 368, 370, 427, 497, *497*, 507, 510–12, 515
Miller Center of Public Affairs, 42, 527
Milsap, Ronnie, 358
minimum wage, 127, 163
missiles: ALCM (air-launched cruise missile), 106; cruise, 61, *67*, 78, *106*, 107; MIRVed, 106, *106*; MLBM, 106; MX, 323, 487; and SALT, 309; and USSR, 107, 109
Mitchell, George, 429, *429*
Mitterrand, François, 99
Mohammed, Crown Prince of Morocco, 260
Mondale, Joan, 89, 151, 513
Mondale, Walter "Fritz," 3, 33, 35, 51, 54, 64, 70, 87, 89, *89–90*, 101, 109, 116, 120, 151, 162, 172, 197, 267, 411, 422; and Africa, 36, 39, 44; and 1978 agenda, 131; and arms sales, 143; assessment of administration by, 525; and 1980 campaign, 332, 356, 370, 392, 410, 415, 425, 431–32, 434, 435, 444, 447, 454, 459, 464, 479; and Camp David summit, 216, 227, 236, 238, 243, 244, 246, 277; and canceling of energy speech, 341;

Mondale, Walter "Fritz," (*continued*)
and China, 128, 178; and death of
Humphrey, 164, *164*; and Democratic
attacks, 288; and domestic policy, 46,
118, 125, 135; and draft, 394; and foreign
policy, 66, 133; and Guadeloupe summit,
272; and inauguration of Reagan, 513;
and Iran, 272, 276; and Iranian hostage
crisis, 370, 372, 375, 419, 514–15, 517;
and Israel, 131, 203; and Mideast peace
process, 140, 168, 169, 178, 204, 299,
304, 311, 314, 444, 459; and news media,
130, 142; and Panama Canal Treaty, 177,
188; responsibilities of, 146; and security
leaks, 186; and SIOP, 141; and Soviet
invasion of Afghanistan, 388, 389, 392,
406; and Tito funeral, 425; and transition,
482, 484, 488, 506; trip to China by, 354;
trip to Europe and Japan by, 12–13; trip
to Portugal by, 44, 56; trip to South Africa
by, 44, 56; trip to Spain by, 44, 56; and
USSR, 198; and Vance resignation, 423;
as vice presidential choice, 5, 9, *16*, *123*,
429; and Vietnam, 379
Moore, Arch, 103, 459
Moore, Elizabeth, 99
Moore, Frank, 11, 99, 102, 104, 124, 125,
131, 143, 166, 175, 176, 209, *209*, 324,
358, 367, 450, 481, 482, 514
Morales, Rod, 170–71, 485
Morales Bermúdez, Francisco, 90, 93
Moral Majority, 468, 477, 532
Mormon Church, 35, 41, 61, 189
Morocco, 305, 364
Moroz, Valentyn, 316
Morris, Edmund, 523
Morris, Gary and Terry, 185
Morris, Gen. John W., 31
Moscow Philharmonic, 295
Moses, Al, 36, 454, 484–86, 497
Moyers, Bill, 247, 323, 468
Moynihan, Daniel Patrick, 194
Mozambique, 36, 134
Mubarak, Hosni, 260, 263, 307, 311, 472
Mugabe, Robert, 20, 166, 407, *407*, 461
Murdoch, Rupert, 359, 402
Murphy, Tom, 351
Muskie, Edmund, 5, 64, *64*, 252, 282,
287, 315, 320, 432, 433, 436, 437, 443,
444, 470, 473, 479, 494; earns Medal of
Freedom, 509; and G7, 440; and Iran
hostage crisis, 452, 515; Mideast speech
of (1980), 436; and papal investiture
ceremony, 252; and Poland, 462; replaces
Vance as secretary of state, 423–25, *423*,
427, 429, *429–30*; and sinking of USS
Liberty by Israel, 491; and South Korea,
489; and transition, 484, 488–89; and
UN, 459

Muslim leaders, *254*
Myerson, Bess, 108

Nagy, Imre, 132
Namibia, 30, 36, 56, 77, 83
National Advisory Committee for Women,
277
National Aeronautics and Space
Administration (NASA), 63, 108, 370, 483
National Alliance of Businessmen, 196
National Association for the Advancement
of Colored People (NAACP), 148, 445
National Association of Manufacturers
(NAM), *120*, 208, 369
National Association of Women Judges, 470
National Catholic Reporter, 285
National Conference of Catholic Bishops,
97
National Conference of Christians and
Jews, 322
National Council of Churches, 173
National Crime Index, 131
national debt, 27
National Education Association (NEA), 45,
186, 444
National Farmers Organization, 376–77
National Institutes of Health, 430
National Mental Health Association, 436
National Organization for Women (NOW),
378, 379, 469
National Park Service, 522, *522*
National Prayer Breakfasts, 14, *259*,
279, 398
National Rifle Association (NAR),
402–403, *403*
National Security Council (NSC), 12, 24,
45, 59, 60, 79, 89, 123, 130, 167, 186,
215, 376, 403, 424, 427, 436, 469, *480*;
and Cuba, *263*; and Iranian hostage
crisis, 411, 415; and Iran-Iraq War,
467; and Reagan, 509, 520; Special
Coordination Committee, 17; problems
between State Department and NSC
staff, 267, 289, 363; and USSR, 464, 495
National Urban league, 148
natural gas, 144, 207, 215, 216; pipeline, 93,
132; *see also* oil and gas industry
Navon, Yitzhak, 300, 301, 302
Nazism, 47
NBC, 123, 142, 208, 413
Nehru, Jawaharlal, 159
Neiman, LeRoy, 397
Nelson, Gaylord, 325
Nelson, Jack, 109, *109*
Nelson, Willie, *174*, 320, 464–65
Nesbit, Lynn, 504, 521
neutron bomb, 108, 110, *110*, 179, 180, 487
New Baptist Covenant, *455*

Newhouse, Richard, 370
New Republic, The, 488
news media, 24–25, 30–31, 74, 75, 81, 86,
  102, 109, *109*, 126, 130–34, 142, *142*,
  147, 152, *152*, *155*, 192, 195, 196, 199,
  201, 215, 266, 276, 283, 292, *310*, *318*,
  345, 347, 356, 417, 481, 493, 526;
  assessment of coverage by, *319*, 342,
  528–29; changes in, 532; and energy
  speech, *344*; and Iranian hostage crisis,
  373, *476*; and Mideast peace process,
  151, 170, 304, 343; at press conferences,
  17–18, 26, 52, *52*, 103, 125, 133, *142*,
  149, 214, 283, 319, 322, 337, 374, 453,
  454, 528–29; and SALT, 354; suppers for
  news media leaders, 208, 211–14; *see also
  specific individuals, organizations, and
  publications*
Newsom, David D., 424
Newsweek, 25, 211, 214, 479
New York Board of Rabbis, 475
New York City, financial package for, 168,
  199, *201*, 213, 349–50, 408, 412, 464, 469
New York Post, 359, 402
New York Times, 25, 87, 96, 109, *136*, 183,
  196, 200, 211, 212, 214, 278, 321, 335,
  437, 456, 466, 520
Nicaragua, 256, *256–57*, 259, 262, *262*, 263,
  264, 273, 292, 332, 333, 334, 340, 345,
  346, 357, 466, 485
Nigeria, 36, 117, *117*, 283, 383; trip to
  (1978), 182
Nightline (TV show), 476
Nimitz, USS (aircraft carrier), 179, *412*,
  423, 431
Ninth Circuit Court of Appeals, 497–98
Nitze, Paul, 76, 77, 133, 152, *201*, 260
Nixon, Richard M., 5, 9, 12, 29, *30*, 37, *38*,
  55, 104, *139*, 166, 181, 187, *200*, 453,
  521, 527, 529; and Cambodia, 277;
  impeachment of, *316*, 528; and Mideast,
  352; at White House China ceremonies,
  266, *266–67*, 284
Nkomo, Joshua, 166
Nobel Peace Prize: awarded to Begin and
  Sadat, 256; awarded to Carter, 322;
  awarded to Kim Dae Jung, 340, *455*
nonaligned movement during Cold War,
  273, 371, 393
Noriega, Manuel, *124*
North Atlantic Treaty Organization
  (NATO), 45, 51, 105, *121*, 128, 143, 264,
  275, 309, 329, 356, 397, 407, 426, 454,
  459, *461*, 474; conference (1978),
  197–98; keynote address (1977), 51
North Korea, 27, 77, 184, 279, 282, 318,
  338–40, *340*, 365; trip to, post-presidency,
  280, 537
North Yemen, 297

Norway, 274
Novak, Robert, 120, 495
nuclear carriers, 179, 180
nuclear energy, 28, 48, 52, 58, 67, 99, 121,
  136, *136*, 138, 156, 310, *311*, 377;
  breeder reactor, 67, 99, 138, 143; fuel, 48,
  52, 98, 160, *160*, 181, 200, 274, 314;
  waste storage, 48, 400, *400–401*; *see also*
  Three Mile Island accident
nuclear nonproliferation, *45*, 47, 48, 67, 68,
  92, 93, 106, 185, 274, 324, 487, 530
Nuclear Nonproliferation Treaty, *136*, 534
nuclear submarines, 28, 58
Nuclear Test Ban Treaty, *164*
nuclear weapons, xiv, 58, 123, 146, 160,
  201, 456, 486, 507; and arms control, *45*,
  77, 130, 262; comprehensive test ban,
  50, 67, 69, 105, 133, 138, 143, 197,
  200; and Europe, 275; India and, 200,
  200; Iran and, *136*, 200; Israel and,
  220; and Latin America, 17, *17*, 57, *90*,
  115; "no first use" pledge, 534; and
  North Korea, 280; and Pakistan, *200*,
  362; and South Africa, 82, 84, 102; and
  South Korea and Taiwan, 75; spending
  on, 323; and USSR, 20, 23, 34–35, 106,
  106, 107; warhead inventory, 154; *see
  also* SALT
Nunn, Sam, 27, 129, *129*, 149, 175, 191,
  326, 348, 451
Nyerere, Julius, 76, 77, 83, 87

Obama, Barack, 74, 97, *211*, 333, 350, 371,
  401, 530–31
Obasanjo, Olusegun, 36, 182
Ocampo, Octavio, 358
Occupational Safety and Health
  Administration (OSHA), 491
October Surprise (Sick), *480*
Oduber, Daniel, 96
Office of Management and Budget (OMB),
  28, 60, 87, 89, 97, 114, 134
Ohira, Masayoshi, 262, 336, 337; funeral of,
  443–46; meeting with, 317, 334
oil, 287, 392, 441, 464, 533; Egyptian-Israeli
  treaty and, 336; embargo, 72; gasoline
  shortages and price increases, 321, 336,
  341, 343, 396; import fee or tax, 117,
  143, 258, 305; imports, 332, 404, 429,
  434, 459, 490; and Iran, 163, 255, *275*;
  and Iran-Iraq War, 467; and Israel,
  302–303; and Mexico, 291; offshore
  drilling, 72, 139; price increases, 332,
  336, *336*, 337, *341*, 348, 357, 378, 389,
  442, *473*, 526, 529; reserves, 72, *72*; and
  Saudi Arabia, 161, 299; *see also* energy;
  Organization of Petroleum Exporting
  Countries

oil and gas industry, *43*, 77, 83, *100*, *101*, 110, 119, *119*, 122, 127, 142, *142–43*, 144, *258*, 369, 472, *490*; deregulation of, 305, 308
Okinawa, 143
Okita, Saburo, 441
Olympics of 1980; summer (Moscow), 387, 389, 391–94, *395*, 403, 404, 406, 413, 415, 417, 449; winter (Lake Placid), 404
Oman, 418, *419*, 456
O'Neill, Tip, 15, 45, 60, 65, 67, 119, *134*, 183, *183*, 209, *209*, 210, 244, 246, 250, 304, 317, 332, 342, 343, 357, 380, 417, 489, 492
Opinion, La, 95
Organization of African Unity (OAU), 120
Organization of American States (OAS), 85, 90, 93, *93*, 292, 428; and Nicaragua, 257, 259, 332, 333, *334*, 340; speech to (June 1978), 202, *202*; speech to (November 1980), 486
Organization of Petroleum Exporting Countries (OPEC), 48, 93, 332, 336, *336*, 337, *341*, 357, 378, 389, 441, 442, 529; oil embargo by, *316*
Oslo Accords (1993), 377
Oval Office, 11
Owen, David, 72, 83, 143
Owen, Henry, 424

Pakistan, 98, 273, 367, 371, 468; and Afghanistan, 200, *200*, 273, 306; and Bhutto execution, 309, *309*; and India, 200, *200*, 314; and Iran, 200, *200*, 311; and Iranian hostage crisis, 368; and nuclear weapons, *200*, 314, 362; and Soviet invasion of Afghanistan, 311, *311–12*, 388, *388*, 391, 401, 486
Palestinian homeland, state, or entity, 33, 64, 68, 71, 113, 149, 161, 218, 224, 413, *413*, 508
Palestinian Liberation Organization (PLO), 39, 44, 57, 71, 87, 101, 109, 124, 365; attacks on Israel by, 133, *178*; and Camp David Accords, *276*; and Egyptian-Israeli peace talks, 297–98; feelers for negotiation put out by, 312; and Iranian hostage crisis, 368; and Israel's right to exist, 350; and Jordan, 438; and McHenry, 497; opposition to negotiations by, 305; and Palestinian state, 413, *413*; recognition issue, 149; sovereignty issue, 219, 223, 224, 226–27, 229; and UN Security Council Resolution 242, 255, *255*, 349, 350; and West Bank and Gaza, 255; Young meeting with, 351, 352, *352*
Palestinian(s), 78, 99, 101, *121*, 109, 147, 322, 351, 392, 399, 400, 413, 429;
autonomy of, 218, *247*, *255*, *508*; and Camp David Accords, 218, 229, 233, 234, 239–40, *247*, 275, 276, *276*, 277, 365, *418*; communications with, 268; definition of, 225, *230*, *244*; and Egyptian-Israeli peace talks, 258; elections of (1996), 377; and Hamas vs. Fatah, *508*; Israel opposes compromise with, *105*; militants, 297; and negotiations, *255*, 239, 240; post-election thoughts on, 508; refugees, 33, 50, 57, 71, 101, 112–13, 124, 132, 139, 146, 225, 240; rights of, 264, 302, 307, 329, 526, 535; and Sadat, 170; and Saudis, 376; and self-determination, 161, 180, 224, *230*, 234, 236; and self-rule, 169; trips to visit, 537; and UN, 271, 349; and USSR, 106
Panama, 92, 124, 143, 309, *319*, 370; and democratization, 201; election of 1989 in, *124*; and Iranian hostage crisis, 378, 380; and Nicaragua, 333; U.S. interventions in, 534
Panama Canal Treaties, 29, *30*, *45*, *55*, 73, 78–88, *81*, *84*, 87, 90, 92, 93, 96, 98, *98*, 103, 110, 115, 117, 119, 121–22, 126, 129, 130, 135, 139, 141–43, 152, 189–90, 191, 292, 480, 486, 526; impact of, *181*, 208; implementation legislation, 324–25, 333, 357, 358; pre-2000 vs. post-2000 treaties, *30*, *178–79*, 184, 185; Senate ratification of, *163*, 164, 166, *166*, 171, *171*, 172, 175–79, *178–79*, 184, 185, 188–90; speech on, *163*; trip to Panama to exchange treaties, 201
Pan-American Convention on Human Rights, 94
Parade magazine, 99
Paraguay, 90, 92, 257, 333
Park Chung Hee: assassination of, 365; visit with, 318, 338–39
Parton, Dolly, *174*, 358
Passamaquoddy Indians, 70
Pastor, Bob, 124, 263, 391
Path Between the Seas, The (McCullough), 86, 201
Patolichev, Nikolai, 133
Paul VI, Pope, 213
peace, as theme of presidency, *13*, 527
Peace Corps, *18*, *164*, *204*
Pell, Claiborne, 62, 75
Pennington, John, 471, *471*
Penobscot Indians, 70
Percy, Charles "Chuck," 89, 389
Peres, Shimon, 139–40, 233, 302, 420
Peretz, Marty, 488
Pérez, Carlos, 93, 201
Perlman, Itzhak, 308
Persian Gulf, 273, 279, *279*, 329, 394, *394–95*, 469; *see also specific countries*

Personal Memoirs of Ulysses S. Grant, 523
Pertini, Sandro, 205
Peru, 42, 59, 61, 90, 91, 93–94, 94;
    Rosalynn Carter trip to, 451, 452
Peters, Charlie, 323
Peters, Roberta, 68
Peterson, Esther, 509
Petrov, Gen. V. I., 196
Philippines, 309, 329, 371, 403
Picker, Arnold, 171
Pickett, Gen. George, 204
Pindling, Lynden, 96
Pinochet, Gen. Augusto, 91, 91–92
Pius VII, Pope, 442
Plains, Georgia: national park site proposal
    for, 522, 522; post-presidency in, 499,
    505, 522, 522; return to, on inauguration
    of Reagan, 514, 517, 519–20; visits to, 19,
    19, 25, 59, 78–80, 79, 80, 152–53, 165,
    209, 214–15, 268, 313, 354, 445, 498, 499
Plains Baptist Church, 78–79, 82–83, 445
Poe, Edgar Allan, 49, 49
Poland, 361, 485; strikes of 1980 in, 459–62,
    461, 467, 491, 493, 495; trip to (1977),
    155, 155, 156, 360; and USSR, 503
political partisanship, 531–33, 535
Pol Pot, 190, 277, 463
Porterfield, Mr. and Mrs. Marvin, 343
Portugal, 44, 47, 56, 97; trip to, of 1980, 443
Poston, Gretchen, 493, 497
post-presidency, 483, 483, 519–20, 520–24,
    523–24, 536–37
Poveda, Adm. Alfredo, 93
poverty, 114, 361, 480
Powell, Jody, 4, 9, 125, 198, 290, 411, 423,
    450, 481; and assessment of first year,
    188; and Cambodia, 190; and draft
    registration, 394; and drug allegations,
    207, 353, 353; and elections of 1980, 212,
    316, 467; and energy speech, 341; and
    Iranian hostage crisis, 372, 373, 478, 515,
    517; and media relations, 65, 109, 128,
    130, 142, 151–52, 401, 456; and Mexico,
    294; and Mideast peace process, 112,
    113, 213, 299, 304; relationship with, 21,
    21, 87, 195, 195, 520, 529; and transition,
    482, 486, 500, 514; and White House
    press corps correspondents' banquet,
    192–93; and Young resignation, 351, 352
Power and Principle (Brzezinski), 45
Precht, Henry, 416, 515
preemptive war, 534
Prem Tinsulanonda, 369
presidency, assessment of, 525–30;
    economy, 529; failure to win second
    term, 526, 530; foreign policy, 528;
    foreign policy goals, 13, 45, 45; Iranian
    hostage crisis, 529–30; legislation,
    526–28; micromanagement, 527; and

news media, 528–29; political aspects of
    job, as leader of party, 527–28; themes
    and commitment, 527; trappings of
    presidency and, 529; and Washington
    social world, 529
presidency, future challenges of, 530–35;
    alienation from government, 532;
    Arab-Israeli conflict, 534–35;
    Congressional polarization and
    partisanship, 530–31; demise of USSR
    and rise of terrorism, 533–34; economy
    and debt, 533; energy and environment,
    533; human rights and torture, 535;
    military interventions and wars, 534;
    news media, 532; nuclear weapons, 534;
    Obama and, 530–31; religion and
    politics, 532
presidential directives, 456, 496
presidential election of 1968, 144, 147, 254,
    429
presidential election of 1972, 147
presidential election of 1976, 3–5, 19, 30,
    32, 40, 82, 89, 123, 287, 445; primaries
    and caucuses, 3, 10
presidential election of 1980, 19, 40, 76,
    129, 129, 147, 207, 272, 300, 321, 321,
    322, 322, 353–54, 356, 356, 382, 416,
    436, 444, 446–49, 451–54, 456, 459–80,
    468–69, 475–76; campaign debt of, 520,
    521; and Iranian hostage crisis, 369, 382;
    loss to Reagan in, 480–81, 481, 485,
    495, 506, 513, 529–30; and split in
    Democratic party, 527–28; see also
    Democratic nomination contest (1980);
    Republican nomination contest (1980)
presidential election of 1984, 40, 84
Presidential Review Memoranda, 45
Press, Frank, 18, 135, 430, 431
Price, Leontyne, 250, 308, 323, 361
Pride, Charlie, 320
Proxmire, William, 9, 464
*Public Papers of the Presidents: Jimmy
    Carter, 1977*, 76; *1979*, 325
public works, 52, 78, 199; vetoes of bills for,
    249–50, 249–50, 526
Puerto Rico, 117
Pursch, Joseph A., 315, 315

Queen, Richard, 448
Quinn, Archbishop John R., 459

Rabin, Yitzhak, 21, 71, 71, 302; meetings
    with, 31, 31
Rafsanjani, Ali Akbar Hashemi, 470
Rafshoon, Jerry, 36, 118, 142, 195, 195, 207,
    321, 341, 394, 456
Raines, Howell, 125

Randolph, A. Philip, 323
Randolph, Jennings, 103, *104*, 175, 178
Rangel, Charles B., 325
Ra-Shalom asteroid, 257
Rather, Dan, 456
Read, Benjamin H., 424
Reagan, Nancy, 487, 494
Reagan, Ronald: and Afghan rebels, 388;
   and arms control talks with USSR, 77;
   briefing of (November 20, 1980), 486–87,
   487; briefings by, 37; and China, 266;
   and Congress, 527; and defense spending,
   67; and deregulation, 473; and drug
   policy, 74; and economy, 348, 496–97;
   elected president, 480, *480*; and energy,
   27, *258*, 320–21, 344, 490; first term of,
   520; and Haig, 495, *495*, 500;
   inauguration of, *481*, 488, 512–14; and
   intelligence, 32; and Iranian hostage
   crisis, 467, 480, 504, 510, 512, 517; and
   Iraq, 467; and Israel, 333; letter to, on
   inauguration, 517; and Mideast peace
   process, *418*; and nuclear weapons, *110*;
   and Olympic boycott, 415; and Panama
   Canal, 82, 85; and presidential campaign
   of 1980, *84*, 322, 446, 452–53, 454, 456,
   458, 459, 460, *460*, 462–69, *465*, *469*,
   471, 474, *476*, 477–80, 528; and
   presidential debates, 466, 468, 476, *476*,
   477; and Republican presidential
   nomination contest of 1976, 5; and
   Republican presidential nomination
   contest of 1980, *171*, 378, 389, 405, 447,
   448; reversals by, 530; and Rickover, 492,
   492–93; and Saudi F-15 sale, 488, 500,
   504; shooting of *495*; and solar panels,
   332; and South Korea, 487, 488; and
   START, 357; and transition, 482, 484,
   486–88, *487–88*, 491, 504, 509
Reagan-Kemp-Roth tax proposal, 475, 482,
   484
Reasoner, Harry, 81
recession of 1979–80, 332, 340, 348, 431,
   473
Redford, Robert, 29
Reed, Col. Cecil, 65
Refugee Assistance Act (1980), 471
refugees 290, 310, 337
religion, 173, 399, 522; global politics and,
   279; and missionary work in China,
   284–85; *see also specific religions and
   organizations*
religious fundamentalists, 35
religious right, 454, 455, 468, *468–69*, 532
religious leaders, 254, 343
Republican leaders, 249, 266, 324, 370
Republican National Convention of 1980,
   447, 448, 454

Republican nomination contest (1980), 129,
   129, *171*, 379, 405; debates, 389
Republican Party, 14, 38, 76, *76*, 110, 195,
   252, 368, 445, *490*; bipartisan
   cooperation by, *171*; congressional
   leaders of, *42*, *55*, 127, 397; moderates,
   171; and Panama Canal, 103, 129, 152;
   and religious right, *455*, 468, *468–69*,
   532; right wing of, *171*, 287; and SALT,
   152, 203
Reston, James "Scotty," 211, 212, 251, 276
Reynolds, Burt, 434
Reynolds, Frank, 343, 383, *383*
Reza Shah Pahlavi, Shah of Iran: abdication
   and exile of, *156*, 268, 271–78, *272–73*,
   275, 278, 280, 288, 289, 304–305, 309,
   312, *312*; admitted to U.S., for medical
   care, 364, *367*, 368, 370, 372, *373*,
   375–77, 516; assets of, 465, *466*, 478, 492,
   494; asylum in Panama, 378, 380;
   AWACS and, 74–75; death of, 451, 452;
   in Egypt for medical care, 411; Iranian
   claims against, 391; protests against, 252,
   252, 255, 257–58, 261, *261*, 267; and
   Sadat, 163; visit to U.S. (1977), 135–37,
   136, *137*; visit with, in Tehran (1977–78),
   156, *156*, 159
Rhodes, John, 149–50
Rhodesia (*later* Zimbabwe), 19–20, *20*, 30,
   34, 36, *45*, 72, 76, 77, 83, 87, 108, 122,
   143, 166, 167, 207, 208, 407
Ribicoff, Abe, 64, *64*, 89, 170, 177, 195,
   196, 264, 271, 281, 282, 325
Rickover, Adm. Hyman G., 28, *28*, 40, 58,
   72, 134, 138, 143, 309, 430, 492, 492–93
Riley, Richard W., 400, 477
Riss, Lloyd, 481
"River of No Return" Wilderness Act
   (1980), 449
"Road Map of the International Quartet,"
   376
Robb, Lynda, 494
Rockefeller, David, 312, 345–46, 375
Rockefeller, Happy, 287, *287*
Rockefeller, Nelson, 37, 89, 172, 181; death
   of, 287, *287*
Rodgers, Richard, 70
Rodino, Peter, 76
Roe v. Wade, 71
Rogers, Bernie, 326
Rohatyn, Felix, 463–64
Roldós, Jaime, 346
Romania, 27, 169, 282
Romero, Archbishop Oscar, assassination of,
   412
Romero, Carlos, 94
Romney, Marion G., 41
Roosevelt, Franklin D., 127, 185, 361

Rosalynn Carter Institute for Caregiving, 536
Rosenthal, Abe, 214
Rostenkowski, Dan, 125, 193
Rostow, Gene, 76
Rostropovich, Mstislav "Slava," 118, 119, 174, 244, 295, 347, 506
Roth, William, 176
Rowan, Carl, 213, 343
Russell, Richard, 16
Russia, post-Soviet, 274, 282, 440, 530, 534; travels to, 322; see also Soviet Union
Rustin, Bayard, 323
Ryan, Leo, 261, 261

Sá Carneiro, Francisco, 443
Sadat, Anwar, 31, 38–39, 71, 112, 126, 128, 134, 142; and ambassador exchange with Israel, 405; and Arabs, 245–47; assassination of, 311; and Begin, 145–46, 164 169–70, 170, 174, 311, 311, 315, 341; and Begin and Carter meetings, 150–51, 151, 153–54, 410, 416–18; and Camp David Accords, 247, 248; and Camp David summit, 168, 168, 210–47, 210, 213–14, 216, 222, 229, 230, 234, 237, 243, 272, 360, 365; and Egyptian-Israeli treaty, 257, 259, 262, 263, 265, 295–99, 299, 302–304, 307; and Iranian hostage crisis, 371, 375; and Iran-Iraq War, 472; Jerusalem trip of, and Knesset, 135–41, 224, 307; meetings with, in Egypt, 154, 161, 233, 236, 237, 300, 303–304; Mount Sinai shrine and, 311, 311; at National Press Club, 169–70, 170; and Nobel Peace Prize, 256; and post-treaty peace talks, 315, 341, 361, 379, 387, 410, 411, 416–18, 432, 453, 462; and shah of Iran, 163, 411; visits of, in early 1978, 159, 161, 169–71
Sadat, Jehan, 38, visit to Plains, 524
Safire, William, 186
Sagan, Carl, 151
Saint Helens, Mount, 430–31, 431, 436
Sakharov, Andrei, 452
SALT (Strategic Arms Limitation Talks) II, 17–18, 17, 34–35, 37, 40, 50, 53, 61, 78, 89, 99, 102, 104–109, 111, 116, 133, 137, 139, 143, 149, 152, 172, 175, 190, 191, 197, 200, 211, 249, 251, 260, 263–65, 267, 275, 297, 309, 312, 394, 404, 427, 431, 439, 471, 489; and Backfire bomber, 200, 329, 329; background and process of, and SALT I, 17, 328, 456; and China, 284; and Kissinger, 289–90; and Nitze, 133; and Reagan, 484, 486, 487; and Senate ratification, 203, 281–82, 282, 348, 357, 357, 358, 358, 359, 362, 369,

379, 381, 387; and Soviet invasion of Afghanistan, 382, 383, 383, 387, 393, 471; Vienna summit of June 1979 and signing of, 318–19, 321–22, 324, 326–31, 331
SALT III, 17, 17, 107, 326–30, 357, 376, 431
Sanders, Ed, 36, 171, 266
Sandinistas, 257, 333, 466
Sanford, Terry, 3
Saud, Prince of Saudi Arabia, 56–57, 124
Saudi Arabia, 21, 29, 48, 121; arms and F-15 sales to, 143, 194–95, 447, 484–88, 487, 500, 504, 526; Byrd trip to, 265; and Camp David Accords, 276, 276; and China, 284; and Egyptian-Israeli peace treaty, 297, 299, 304, 307; and G20, 274; and Iran, 320; and Iranian revolution, 272; and Iran-Iraq War, 469, 472; and Mecca attacks, 371; and Mideast peace process, 34, 56–57, 124, 150, 151, 154, 159, 376, 376, 379, 420; military bases in, 294; and Panama Canal Treaty, 189, 189; and Persian Gulf, 398; and Soviet invasion of Afghanistan, 388; trip to (1978), 160–61; and Yemen, 297
Saunders, Hal, 400, 409
SAVAK, 137
Scandinavia, 282
Schaefer, Anita, 514
Schindler, Alexander, 171
Schlesinger, James R., 29, 38, 40, 72, 76, 77, 93, 104, 119, 121, 127, 129, 139, 139, 143, 144, 177, 186, 260, 341, 344, 390; resignation of, 342, 345
Schmidt, Helmut, 17, 68–70, 69, 99, 109, 172, 173, 440, 379; and elections of 1980, 485, 486; and G7 summits, 46–48, 50, 205, 206, 335–37, 439–41; and Guadeloupe summit, 272–75; and Iranian hostage transfer, 510, 515; and neutron bomb, 487; and Soviet invasion of Afghanistan, 407
Schmidt, Loki, 70
Schmitt, Harrison, 126
Schorr, Daniel, 433
Schram, Marty, 40
Schultze, Charles L., 37–38, 67, 117, 125, 184, 186, 208, 354, 363, 364, 408, 414, 431
Scouten, Rex, 95, 498
Scranton, William, 34, 241, 390
Sea Around Us, The (Carson), 335
Second Amendment, 403
secrecy, 381
Secret Service, 13–14, 19, 153, 191, 215, 276, 306, 307, 374, 513
Securities and Exchange Commission (SEC), 100

security leaks, *26,* 186, 187, 211, *211,* 260, 266, 288–89, 308, 219, 332, 419
Segovia, Andrés, 174, 404
Selective Service Act, 408, 462
September 11, 2001, attacks, *279, 290,* 535
Sequoia, USS (presidential yacht), 56, *56*
Shakespeare, William, 49
Shamir, Yitzhak, *107*
Shanklin, John, 32
Shapiro, Irving, 153, 203
Shapp, Milton, 3
Sharansky, Natan, 105, *105,* 331
Sharon, Ariel, 173, 301, 302, 355
Shaw, Robert, 174
Shaw, William, *455*
Sheen, Bishop Fulton, 279
Shenouda, Pope, 42
Shepard, Alan, 249
Shiites, *472*
Shippingport Light Water Breeder Reactor, 138, 143
Shriver, Sargent, 3
Shulman, Marshall, 68, 406
Shultz, George, *495*
Sick, Gary, *480,* 515
Sidey, Hugh, 343
Sihanouk, Prince of Cambodia, 277
Silent Spring (Carson), 335
Sills, Beverly, *174*
Silveira, Antonio, 61, 181
Silverman, Fred, 208
Simons, Howard, 211
Sinai, 101, 137, 150, 161, 169, 170, 173, 174, 180, *210,* 253; and Camp David Accords, 218–19, 221, 223–29, 231–32, 234, 235–42, *235,* 248, 249; Egyptian-Israeli peace talks and, 259; Etzion Air Base, 232, 236; Israeli withdrawal from, 305, *307,* 508
Sinai, Mount, shrine, 225, 311, *311*
Sinatra, Frank, 144
Singh, Manmohan, *160*
Singlaub, Maj. Gen. John K., 55
Single Integrated Operational Plan (SIOP), 141, 450, 486
Sirleaf, Ellen Johnson, *417*
60 Minutes (TV show), 456
Small Business Administration (SBA), 491
Smeal, Ellie, 469
Smith, Allie (mother-in-law), 153, 499
Smith, Bailey, 455, *473*
Smith, Gerard, 67, 202, 509
Smith, Hedrick, 109, 212
Smith, Ian, 19–20, 30, 72, 87, 167, *407*
Smith, Wayne, 43
Soares, Mario, 443
social programs, *26,* 45–46
Social Security legislation (1977), 97, 128, 144, 149, 152, *152,* 163

Sofia, Queen of Spain, 442
Soft Energy Paths (Lovins), 121
Solana, Javier, *413*
Solarz, Steve, 46
Solomon, Anthony, 511–12
Solomon, Jay, 209, *209*
Solzhenitsyn, Aleksandr, 202
Somalia, 134, 175, 279, 282, 362, 533, 534; German hostages in, 121
Somoza Debayle, Anastasio, 248, 256, *256–57,* 262, 333, 340, 345; assassination of, *257,* 259, 466
Sources of Strength, 522
South Africa, 19–20, *20,* 30, 34, 36, 39, 44, *45,* 56, 72, 77, 83, 87, 120, 123, 124, 126, 264, 534; arms embargo on, 124, 126; and G20, *274;* and Iranian hostage crisis, 378; and Israel, 101; and nonproliferation policy, 202; and nuclear weapons, 82, 84, 102, 252–53, 357, 365, 405; and Rhodesia, 407; sanctions against, 83, 124; Vance trip to, 251
South Bronx, 113, *114,* 115
Southeast Asian refugees, 310, 333, 334, 337
Southern Baptist Convention (SBC), *14,* 35, 41, 401, 445, 455, *455,* 473, 485, 532; Brotherhood Commission 52–53
Southern Christian Leadership Conference (SCLC), 148, 278
Southern Poverty Law Center, 69
South Korea, 55, 75, 184, 191, 279, *280,* 318, 320, 329, 360, 365, 403, 455, *455,* 464, 489, 491, 504; and Reagan, 487, 488, 489; trip to (1979), 320, 337–40
South Yemen, 232
Soviet Union (USSR), 175, 191, 273; accidental response to false missile attack by, 434; and Afghanistan, 291, 305, 306, 311, 356; Afghanistan invaded by, 273, 282, *312,* 357, 379, 380, 382, *382,* 383, 387–93, 388–89, 394–95, 396, 397, 399–403, 406, 407, 409, 410, 433, 440–42, 452, 468, 471, 480, 481, 491, *496;* and Africa, 77, 206; ambassadorial visit by Dobrynin, 15; American embassy fire in, 86; and Arab terrorism, 136; and arms control, 496; and Berlin, 102; Brezhnev's leadership of, 274; Brezhnev summit planned, 254; and Brzezinski, 131, 197, 199; and Cambodia, 277, *463;* and Camp David Accords, 248; and Ceauşescu, *184;* Central Committee, 15; and China, 38, 274, 283–84, 329–31, *331,* 374, *374;* and Cold War, *13,* 273; and comprehensive test ban, 67, 69; confidential messages to, 20; and Cuba, *169,* 354, 355, 357–59, 393; demise of, 282, *496,* 533; dissidents in, 105, *105,* 331; and Egyptian-Israeli treaty, 329; and espionage, 166; and Ethiopia,

196; and Europe, 110; and G7, 50; and Germany, 47, 379, *440*; grain embargo of, 387–91, 393, 482; and Guadeloupe summit, 273–74; and human rights, 37, 49, 105, *331*; and Hungary, *132*; and India, 390; and Iran, 311, *464*, 467, 495; and Israel, 297, 298; Jewish emigration from, 308, 310, 452; and Kissinger; 290; and Latin America, 91, 292; leadership of, 68; security leaks and antagonism toward, *211*; and Liberia, 417; meetings with, *380*; and Mideast peace process, *34*, 106, 111, 112, 115, 138, 152, 168, *210*, 220, 232, 324; military strength of, 426; and Moscow Olympics, 387, 389, 391–94, *395*, 403, 404, 406, 413, 415, 417, 449; and most-favored-nation status, 282, *282*, 286; Muskie briefed about meeting with Gromyko, 427, 429; and nuclear fuel, 160; and Pakistan, 311; and Poland, 461, 462, 491, 493, 495, 503; Politburo, 15; and press coverage of, *319*; prisoner exchange with, 315–*17*, *317*; and SALT II, 23, 34–35, *45*, 53, 75–78, 77, 89, 102, 104–106, *106*, 108, 109, 137, 149, 175, 249, 281–82, *282*, 312, 317, 354, 382, 383, 394, 439, 489; and SALT III, 254, *260*, 268; satellite falls in Canada, 165; and Somalia, 134; and southern Africa, 39; and South Korea, 365; speech on, at Naval Academy, 198–99; trade with, 104–105, 133; and U.S. Congress, *123–24*, 130, 281–82; and Vance, *13*; and Vienna summit, 312, 324, 326–31; weaknesses of, *496*; and West Germany, 493, 507

space shuttle, 63, 108, 370
Spain, 44, 56, 85, 97, 391–92, 452; Pinochet arrest warrant issued by, *91–92*; trip to (1980), 442–43
Spanish Socialist Party, 442
Spann, Gloria Carter (sister), 144, 470, 499
Sparkman, John, 81, 143
special interest groups, 62–63, 188, 507
speeches and addresses: to American Legion (1980), 459; to B'nai B'rith (1980), 462–63; Camp David Accords (September 18, 1978), 244, 246; in Chicago (1979), 362; concession after loss to Reagan (1980), 480; to Democratic mayors (1980), 436; Democratic nomination acceptance (1976), 10, 507, 527; Democratic nomination acceptance (1980), 448, 451, 452–53, 456, 457; in Detroit, to CWA (1979), 344; at Emory, on ethics (1979), 353; on energy (April 1977), 41, *41–42*; on energy (November 1977), 131–32; on energy (April 1979), 309; farewell address (1981), 500, 505, 507; at Georgia Tech, on foreign affairs

(1979) 295; in Germany (1978), 205; inaugural (1977), 10, 507, 527; on India trip (1978), 159; on Iranian hostages' release (1980), 515–16, 517; to Israeli Knesset (March 12, 1979), 302; in Kansas City, to county commissioners (1979), 344; at Kennedy Library (1979), 363; on Law Day (1978), 193; to Mexican Congress (1979), 290, 293; at National Conference of Christians and Jews (1979), 322; on national goals and energy (July 1979), 340, *341*, 343, 344, *344*; at National Prayer Breakfast (1980), 398; NATO keynote (1977), 51; at Naval Academy, on USSR (1978), 198–99; on *Nimitz* (1980), 431; to OAS (1978), 202, 202; to OAS (1980), *486*; on Panama Canal treaties (January 1978), 163; at Panama Canal treaties exchange (June 1978), 201; during presidential campaign (1980), 461–63, 465, 466, 469, 480; on SALT II (June 1979), 330; on SALT II and Soviet troops in Cuba (September 1979), 358, *358*, 359; at Senate-House Democratic fund-raising dinner (1977), 57; on Soviet invasion of Afghanistan (1980), 388; speechwriting procedure, 131, *131*, 193, 195, *520*; State of the Union (1978), 164, 165; State of the Union (1979), 281, *281*; State of the Union (1980), 391, 394; at UN (March 1977), 33; at UN (October 1977), 111–12, 115; in Venezuela (1978), in Spanish, 181; in West Germany (1978), 205; to World Jewish Conference (1977), 128
Sperling, Godfrey, 32
Speth, Gus, 406
Sri Lanka, 533
Staggers, Harley, 325
Stalin, Joseph, 131
Stapleton, Ruth Carter (sister), 96, 167, *167–68*, 335, 456, 457, 470
Stargell, Willie, 362
START (Strategic Arms Reduction Treaty), 357
State, Department of, 12, 22, 53, 59, 60, 79, 89, 130, 144, 166, 167, 186, 187, 199, 213–15, *213–14*, 314, 408, 452, *463*, 478, 537; and conflicts with NSC, 267, 289, 363; and Reagan, 509; and security leaks and, *211*, *266*, 288–89, *289*; Vance resigns and Muskie replaces as secretary of state, 422–25, *423*, *425*
stealth aircraft, 459, 486; *see also* bombers; fighter planes
Stennis, John, 177, 439
Stern, Isaac, 174
Stevens, Ted, 176, 208, 253, 334, 450, 452
Stevenson, Adlai, III, 3–4, 251

Stone, Marvin, 214, 343
Stone, Richard, 180
Strategic Air Command, 122
Strauss, Robert S., 36, 85, 120, *120*, 130, 170, 183, 184, 186, 187, 202, 207, 311, 313, *313–14, 425*, 492, 495; and Mideast peace process, 314, 315, 333, 339–41, 349, 350, 359, 366; and post-presidency, 520; in presidential primaries of 1980, 383, 396
Strauss, Franz Josef, 410
Strauss, Helen, 130
Stroessner, Gen. Alfredo, 90, *91*
Suárez González, Adolfo, 391–92, 442
Sudan, 232, 279, 530, 533; trips to, post-presidency, 537
Suez Canal, 223, 233, 235, 416
Sullivan, William, 268, 272, 273, 276, 277, 277, 288, 289
Sultan, Prince of Saudi Arabia, 189
Sulzberger, Arthur, 214
Sunni Arabs, 472
Superfund, 451, 463, 481, 487, 488, 490, 493
Switzerland, *17*, 99, 160, 369, 464, 505
synthetic fuels, 368, 380, 444
Syria, 34, 50, 78, 101, 107, 135, 140, 365; Byrd's trip to, 265; and Camp David summit, 224, 227; and invasion of Lebanon, 224; and Iranian hostage crisis, 368, 369; and Mideast peace process, 109, 112, 113, 136, 141, 148, 232; and Palestinian refugees, 101; trips to, post-presidency, 537; Vance trip to, 21
Syrian Jews, 46, *46*

Tabatabai, Sadegh, 465, *466*, 470, 471, 478
Taiwan (Nationalist China), *26*, 34, 38, 68, 75, 78, 191, *191*, *281*, 211, *211*, 309, 403; agreement over, with People's Republic of China, 194, 265–66, *265–66*, 268, 286, 299, *300*, 363, 375, 379, 526; arms sales to, 194, 246
Taliban, *200*, 389
Talmadge, Herman, *164*, 166, *166*, 175, 176, 196
Tamir, Gen. Nadav, 232
Tamir, Shmuel, 301, 302
Tanenbaum, Rabbi Marc, 343
Tanzania, 76
Tarnoff, Peter, 263, 391, 424, 465
Tate, Dan, 448
taxes, 37, 39, *43*, 53–54, 78, 97, 102, 110, 111, 116–18, 125, 142, *142–43*, 152, 154, 175, 185, 190, 192, 207, 246, 251, 324, 343, 381, 446, 447, 449, 482, 533
Taylor, Ken, *396*
terrorism, 99, 121, *121*, 126, 136, *206*, 279, 306, 533–34, 535

Thailand, 288, 368–69; Rosalynn Carter trip to, 368, 369
Thatcher, Margaret, 97, 320, 335–37, 393, 441, 510; visit of, 380, *380*
Things Fall Apart (Achebe), 116
Third World, *see* less-developed countries; *specific countries and regions*
Thomas, Dylan, *46*, 49, *49*
Three Mile Island accident, 309–11, *309–11*, 315; Kemeny commission on, 315, 366, 377
Thurmond, Strom, 80
Time, 25, 74, 193, 208, 347, 456, 479
Timerman, Jacobo, 95
Tiran Straits, 223, 225, *230*, 235, 240
Tito, Josip, 175, *175*, 402; death of, 425, 442
Tlatelolco, Treaty of, *17*, 57, 90, 91, 95, 115, *115*, 292, 486
TNF (theater nuclear force), 427, 431, 439–40
Today (TV show), 378
Tolbert, William, 182, 417
Torrijos, Omar, *30*, 73, 85, 90, 117, 119, 124, 141, 142, 163, 177–78, 189, 201, 340, 378
town halls, 33, 306, *306*, 353, 444–45; in Berlin, Germany, 205, *205–206*; in Shimoda, Japan, 335
trade: bribery issue, 403, *403–404*; with China, 265, 282, *282* 286, *300*; with Japan, *318*; and most-favored-nation status, 282, *282*, 285, 286; multilateral negotiations on, 313, *313–14*; multinational bill of 1979, 347; with USSR, 282, *282*
trade balance, 67, *67*, 286, 366, 497, 533
transition period (November 5, 1980, to January 20, 1981), 480–500, *487–88*, 503–507
transportation, 199, 308; *see also* automobiles; deregulation
Transportation, Department of, 66, 287, 348
Travolta, John, 251
Treasury, Department of, 18, 187, 345
Trentham, Rev. Charles, 139
Trilateral Commission, 139
truckers' strike, 336, 339, *341*
Trudeau, Pierre, 47, 48, 93, 165, 441
Truman, Bess, 401, 462
Truman, Harry S., 23, 186, 378, 477, 521, 529
Tuchman, Barbara, 280
Turkey, 20–21, 273, *284*, 309, 454, 474; and arms embargo, 190, 192, 202, 207, 208, 211; Byrd's trip to, 265; and Cyprus, 114, 128; and Greece, 50, 51; and Iranian hostage crisis, 368; and military assistance treaty, 51
Turner, Adm. Stansfield "Stan," 16–17, *16*, 32, 33, 69, 87, 102, 148, 165, 172, 198, 210, 252–53, 372, 422, 426, 489, 532

Turner, Ted, 433
Turning Point, 471
Tuttle, Elbert, 509
Twain, Mark, *see* Clemens, Samuel

Udall, Morris, 3
Uganda, 28–29, 29, 362
Ullman, Al, 75, 117–18, 165, 251
Underwood, Bill, 455
unemployment, 39, 78, 78, 92, 92, 162, 163, 163, 172, 190, 340, 342, 363, 364, 366, 473, 497, 505
United Auto Workers (UAW), 41, 53, 53, 171, 428
United Jewish Appeal, 108, 404, 428
United Methodist Conference, 419, 420
United Nations, 91, 428; and Cambodia, 277, 463, 463; and Cambodian refugees, 369, 369; charter of, 420, 421; Covenant on Economic, Social, and Cultural Rights, 114; and Cyprus, 21; and Egyptian-Israeli peace talks, 299; Human Rights Commission, 95; Iran commission of, 400, 402, 403, 405, 408–409; and Iranian hostage crisis, 381, 383, 391, 393, 400; and Israel, 125, 184; and Lebanon, 279; McHenry as ambassador to, after Young resignation, 353; and Mideast peace process, 64, 429; and Namibia, 30; and Palestinians, 271; and Sinai, 180, 238; speech and meetings of 1977 at, 33, 111–15; and Taiwan and China, 34; *see also* UN General Assembly, UN Security Council
UN General Assembly, 112, 114; Israel expulsion issue discussed at, 466, 469
UN Security Council, 351, 373, 497, 503; and Israel, 107, 429, 458, 459; and Israeli invasions of Lebanon, 178, 179, 416; and PLO Palestinian state proposal, 413, 413; and Resolution 242, 57, 63, 64, 71, 109, 112, 170, 171, 173, 175, 176, 179, 180, 218, 223, 230, 230, 234–35, 238–40, 255, 255, 275, 349, 350, 432, 484; and Resolution 338, 34, 63, 71, 112, 223; and resolution on Jerusalem (Resolution 478), 406, 412, 443, 443–44
U.S. Air Force, 61, 66, 78
U.S. armed forces, 279, 280, 290
U.S. Army Corps of Engineers, 23, 23, 31
U.S. Army Rangers, 412, 419, 422; Delta Force, 419, 421, 422
U.S. Conference of Mayors, 436
U.S. Congress, xiv, 14, 395, 468, 60, 75, 77, 108, 110, 160, 186, 196, 202–203, 278, 295–96, 377, 503; and Alaska lands, 207, 458, 399, 448–50, 449, 452, 481, 483; and budget, 26, 56, 60, 67, 145, 199, 315,

321, 357, 410, 432, 437, 438, 494; and cabinet, 185; changes, and partisanship in, 530–31, 535; and Chrysler, 367, 375, 380; and civil service reform, 207; conservatives vs. liberals in, 165; and criminal justice, 192; and defense, 77, 179, 180, 214, 348, 492, 534; and deregulation, 207, 431, 443; and draft, 437; and Egyptian-Israeli treaty, 307–308; and energy, 25, 29, 41, 62, 63, 76, 77, 88, 102, 104, 110, 116–20, 119, 123, 124, 126, 127, 132, 142, 143, 146, 207, 212, 246, 252, 258, 258–59, 305, 316, 321, 341, 342, 368, 375, 380, 437, 439, 443; and environment, 173; and F-15s for Saudis, 194–95, 194–95, 486, 488; and final legislation of 1980, 499; and foreign aid, 144; and health reform, 86, 133, 175, 197, 203, 208–209, 295, 312, 370, 371, 324, 325, 325, 367, 370; and human rights, 37; and intelligence, 32, 381; and Iranian hostage crisis, 376, 419, 420, 422; and Israel, 107; Kennedy's influence in, 102; legislative achievements in, 42, 46, 127–28, 252, 254, 526–28; and legislative veto, 497–98, 498; and mental health, 320; and Mideast, 44, 115, 170, 173, 241, 244, 246; Moscow and Olympics, 395; and Muskie as secretary of state, 423–24; and New York City loans, 199, 201, 469; and Panama Canal treaties, 81, 81; and presidential primaries of 1980, 357; relations with, 36, 42, 42, 147, 167, 187–88, 209, 390; Republicans in, 76, 76, 110; and Rhodesia, 207; and SALT, 149, 200, 354; and Social Security, 128, 149–50; and Soviet invasion of Afghanistan, 395; and steel industry, 125; and Superfund, 481, 488; and Taiwan legislation, 299, 300; and tax reform, 54, 142–43, 207, 251; and trade, 286, 314, 347; and Turkey arms embargo, 207, 211; and USSR, 123–24, 133; and vetoes, 102, 249–50, 250–52; and voter registration, 54; and water projects, 23, 23, 31, 199; and windfall profits tax, 379, 380, 409, 413; *see also* U.S. House of Representatives, U.S. Senate
U.S. Constitution, 266, 281, 403
U.S. House of Representatives, 149–50, 199, 211, 246, 247, 357, 367, 370, 431, 437, 453, 458; and elections of 1978, 258; intelligence committee of, 374; International Relations Committee, 192; Jewish Caucus, 115; Panama treaty implementation and, 324–25, 333, 357, 358; Republicans in, 110; Rules Committee, 246
U.S. Naval Academy, 43

U.S. Navy, *216*

U.S. News & World Report, 25, 214, 479

U.S. Senate, 27, 37, 63, 76, 88, 102, 104, 110, 116, 117, 119, 124, 127, 199, 207, 368, 315, 347, *371*, 379, 380, 399, 447–50, *449*, 452, 458, 469, 488; Armed Services Committee, 23; and Billy Carter, 459; Church Committee Hearings on Intelligence, 4; confirmations, 296; and defense and foreign affairs, *129*, *129*, 130; and elections of 1978, 258; and elections of 1979, 364; and elections of 1980, 480, 486; Finance Committee, *43*, 117, 119; foreign affairs discussions in, 287; Foreign Relations Committee, 143, 180, 290, 369; Health Committee, 289; and judicial appointments, 350; and Lance hearings, 100, 103; and Mideast arms sales, 195; nuclear arms issues in, 106; and Panama Canal Treaty, *30*, 73, 84–85, *84*, 87, 88, 117, 129, 130, 135, 141, 143, 163, 172, 175–79, 184, 188–89; partisanship and filibusters in, 116, 531; and SALT II, 203, 281–82, 282, 289–90, 348–49, 362, 369, 379, 381, 383, *383*, 387, 404; and UN, *114*

U.S. Supreme Court, 26, 69, *69*, 88, 102, 111, 203, 379, 397, 448, 531

United Press International (UPI), 200

Universal Declaration of Human Rights, 535

uranium, 48, 75, 274; reprocessed, *136*; *see also* nuclear fuel

Urban, Lt. Matt, 448

Urban League, 454

Urcuyo, Francisco, 345

Uruguay, 92, 95

Ushiba, Nobuhiko, 334

Ustinov, Dmetri, 328, 330

Vajpayee, Atal, 314

Vallalon, Hector, 402

Vance, Cyrus R., 19, 23, 34, 35, *45*, 64, 66, *185*, *198*, 290, 320, 362, 395, 399, 411, 412, 437, 440, 486; and Africa, 72, 82, 124, 126; and arms sales, 122, 143, 376; and Brzezinski, 198, 267, 363, 364; and Cambodia, *463*; and Camp David Accords, 222, 227, 231, 232, 237, 240, 244, 245, 246; and China, *53*, 84, 85, 128, *128*, 174, 178, 192; and draft, 394; and Egyptian-Israeli peace talks, 251, 256, 257, 259, 265, 266, 295, 299, 302, 304; and Guadeloupe summit, 272; and Iran, 272, 276, 277, 289, 291, 304, 305; and Iranian hostage crisis, 370, 372, 373, *373*, 375–77, 401, 402, *419*, 419–20, 474, 475, 515; and Israeli invasion of Lebanon,

178; and Israeli settlements, 406, 409; and Mideast peace process, 44, 68, *68*, 78, 81, 83, 99, 113, 122, 124, 131, 140, 145, 146, 148, 150, 164, 168, 169, 171–72, 176, 177, 192, 204, 207, 210–13, 314, 315, 323, 339, 349, 350, 352; and Panama Canal Treaty, 177; resignation of, 419, 420, 422, 423, 425, *425*, 515; and SALT, 40, 53, 137, 203, 267, 312, 317, 318; and Senate, 287; and Shiite-Sunni conflict, 268; and Soviet invasion of Afghanistan, 390, 397, 400, 401, 406; and State Department discipline, 288, 289; and Taiwan, 299; travel by, *13*; trips to Europe by, 60; trips to Middle East by, 21, 22, 210; trips to USSR by, 35, 254; trip to South Africa by, 251; and USSR, 196, 249; and Vienna summit, 327; and Young resignation, 351

Vance, Gay, 34, 64, 290, 399, 411, 486

Vatican, 439; Second Vatican Council, 360

Vaughan, Sarah, 136

Vaught, Lt. Gen. James, 418, *418–19*, 422

Veil, Simone, 396

Venezuela, 43, 59, 62, 93, 201, 283, 452; trip to, 181, 322

Venus radar probe, 483

Vessey, Gen. John W., 337

Veterans Administration, *434*, 525

vetoes, 251, 434, *434*, 438, 449, 526

Videla, Jorge, 94–95

Vienna summit with Brezhnev (June 1979), 318–19, 321–22, 324, 326–31, *331*

Vietnam, 27, 33, 215, 260; and China, *284*, 284, 285, 296; invasion of Cambodia by, 277, 297, *463*; trip to Hanoi (2009), *190*

Vietnamese refugees, 265, 288, 334

Vietnam War, 4, 33, 146–47, *201*, 273, 290, *316*, 379, 528; bill for veterans' memorial signed, 444

Village Beyond, The (Biddle), 116

Vins, Georgi, 315, 317, *317*, 331

Vladivostok Agreement, 35, 328

Volcker, Paul, 347–48, *347–48*, 378, 403, 404, 448, 468, *468*

Volkswagen, 428

Voorde, Fran, 70

Vorster, John, 19–20, 30, 34, 44, 56, 72, 83, 87

Voyager space mission, 299, 483

Waldheim, Kurt, 114, 369, 383, 389, 395, 400, 401, 403

Walesa, Lech, *461*, 462, 467

Walesa, Stanley, 467

Walker, Herschel, 503

Wallace, George, 3

Wall Street Journal, 25

Walters, Barbara, 212, 224
Warner, William, 256
Warnke, Paul, 23, 27, 40, 69, 137, 152, 200, 200–201
War Powers Act (1973), 419
Warren, Earl, 509
Warsaw Pact, 105, 329
Washington, D.C.: changes in political scene of, 530–31; social life in, 529
Washington, George, 163, 281
Washington Monthly, 323
Washington Post, 21–22, 25, 87, 192, 200, 211, 308, 310, 401, 458
Washington Star, 25, 191, 456, 470
Wasserman, Lew, 122
Watergate affair, 4, 12, 316, 528
water resources projects, 23, 23, 26, 29, 31, 115, 119, 140, 177, 185, 199, 526
Watership Down (Adams), 172–73
Watson, Jack, 125, 130, 188, 365, 424, 433, 434, 437, 437, 480, 494, 497
Watts, André, 347
Waxman, Henry, 367
Wayne, John, 163, 183, 318
Weathermen, 263
Webster, William, 163, 263
Weddington, Sarah, 277
Weicker, Lowell, 194
Weinberger, Caspar "Cap," 504
Weizman, Ezer, 176, 180, 220, 222, 226, 231, 232, 236, 238, 241, 246, 259, 302
welfare reform, 37, 46, 75, 79, 97, 163, 190
West Bank, 62, 65, 71, 101, 113, 150, 151, 180, 170, 171, 207, 210, 230, 231, 235, 275, 318, 350, 394, 399, 405, 407, 431, 508; borders of, 224, 234; and Camp David summit, 218–20, 221, 223, 224, 226, 228, 230, 231, 233–40, 235, 242, 247, 248; and Egyptian-Israeli peace talks, 255–59, 261, 263, 298, 301; and elections, 298, 413; Israeli control over, 508; Israeli settlements in, 161, 167, 173, 175, 179, 214, 224, 226, 233, 238, 239, 240, 242, 247, 255–59, 261, 263, 323, 331, 333, 333, 400, 407, 413; Jordan and, 420; Palestinian "full autonomy" in, 239, 301; and partition proposal, 113; and PLO, 255; sovereignty in, 218, 219, 224
Whiskey Man (Raines), 125
White, John, 154, 417
White, Theodore "Teddy," 523
Whitehead, James, 514
White House: entertainment and state visits in, 26, 136, 136, 137–38, 152, 185, 193, 202, 284, 308, 380, 497, 498 (see also specific entertainers and foreign leaders); inner private office in, 11, 12; Reagan desire for Carters to leave early, 494; solar panels for, 332, 332

White House Conference on Families, 394
White House staff, 15–16, 25–26, 148, 186, 188, 188, 211, 344, 489, 497, 505
White House press corps, 86, 86, 152, 496, 529; correspondents' banquet, 192–93
White House Years, The (Kissinger), 166
Why Not the Best?, 520
Wicker, Tom, 212, 343
Wiesel, Elie, 193, 291, 314
Wiesenthal, Simon, 454
Williams, Miller, 514
Wilson, Lt. Gen. Samuel V., 32
Wilson, Lou, 326
Wilson, Woodrow, 281
windfall profits tax, 142, 258, 305, 308, 356, 364, 375, 379, 380, 408, 409, 413, 414, 482
Wise, Phil, 363, 482
Witcover, Jules, 208
Wolf, Milton A., 331
women: and draft, 448; judicial appointments of, 276–77, 291, 296, 296, 350, 350, 470; rights of, 254, 532
Women and Infant Children (WIC) support program, 71
Women's Advisory Committee, see National Advisory Committee for Women
Wood, Evelyn, 24
Woodcock, Leonard, 53, 53, 68, 170, 266, 296
Woodward, Bob, 21–22
Woodward, C. Vann, 523
Woodworth, Larry, 117
World Bank, 404, 474
World Baptist Alliance, 182
World Court, 489
World Health Organization (WHO), 86
World Jewish Congress, 126, 128, 262, 407
World War I, 162
World War II, 175, 186, 246, 329
Wright, Jim, 449
Wyszinski, Stefan Cardinal, 155

Yadin, Yigael, 301, 302, 355
Yastrzemski, Carl, 359
Yates, Sid, 173
Yazdi, Ebrahim, 367, 368
Yemen, 297
Yoder, Ed, 343
Yost, Charles, 241
Young, Andrew, 4, 13, 19–20, 39, 45, 87, 94, 112, 117, 124, 130, 181, 198, 271, 273, 278, 465, 485, 509; resignation of, 351–52, 352
Young, Don, 264
Young, Milton, 177
Young Presidents Organization, 119

youth employment, 77–78, 381, 451, 460, 463
Yucca Mountain spent nuclear fuel site
    proposed, *401*
Yugoslavia, 175, 282, 427, 442; trip to (1980),
    442

Zaire, 199, *199–200*; trips to, post-
    presidential, 537
Zambia, 36, 73, 146, *146*, 209, 313, 383

Zhuo Lin, Madame, 285
Zia-ul-Haq, Muhammad, 309, *311–12*, 371,
    468; meeting with, 470
Zimbabwe (*formerly* Rhodesia), 20, 56, 72,
    166, 407, 456, 530
Zion Baptist Church (Washington, D.C.),
    108
Zorinsky, Edward, 176, 178
Zorinsky, Cece, 177
Zuckerman, Pinchas, 308

A Note About the Author

JIMMY CARTER, our thirty-ninth president, received the Nobel Peace Prize for 2002. The author of numerous bestsellers—including *An Hour Before Daylight* and *Our Endangered Values*—he and his wife, Rosalynn, live in Plains, Georgia, but continue to travel around the world in support of The Carter Center, a nonprofit organization advancing peace and health, and other humanitarian causes.